Street by Street

C000292321

CHESH

Enlarged areas CHESTER, CREWE, ELLESMERE PORT, MACCLESFIELD, NANTWICH, NORTHWICH, RUNCORN, STOCKPORT, WARRINGTON, WIDNES

Plus Altrincham, Bramhall, Congleton, Hazel Grove, Knutsford, Middlewich, Sale, Sandbach, Whitchurch, Wilmslow, Winsford

2nd edition November 2004
© Automobile Association Developments
Limited 2004

Original edition printed May 2001

Ordnance Survey® This product includes map data licensed from Ordnance Survey ® with the permission of the Controller of Her Majesty's Stationery Office. © Crown copyright 2004. All rights reserved. Licence number 399221.

Published by AA Publishing (a trading name of Automobile Association Developments Limited, whose registered office is Southwood East, Apollo Rise, Farnborough, Hampshire, GU14 0JW. Registered number 1878835).

Mapping produced by the Cartography Department of The Automobile Association. (A02238)

A CIP Catalogue record for this book is available from the British Library.

Printed by GRAFIASA S.A., Porto, Portugal

Ref: ML083z

Key to map pages	ii-iii
Key to map symbols	iv–1
Enlarged map pages	2-21
Main map pages	22-219
Index – towns & villages	220-221
Index – streets	222-269
Index – featured places	269-276
Acknowledgements	276

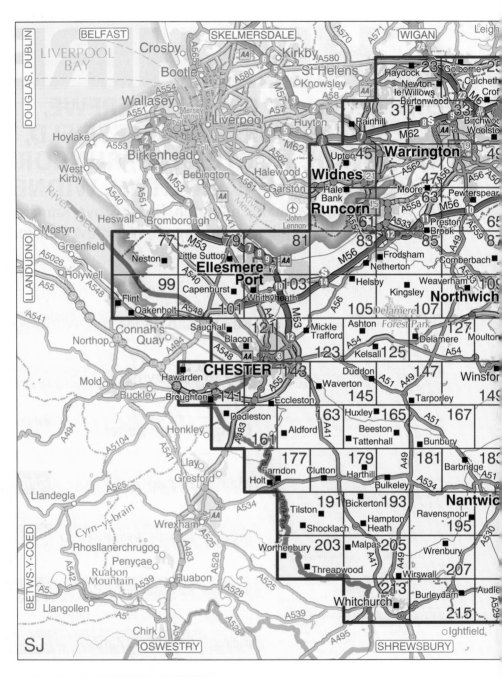

Scale of enlarged map pages 1:10,000   6.3 inches to 1 mile

| 0 | 1/4 | miles | 1/2 |
| 0 | 1/4 | 1/2 kilometres | 3/4 | 1 |

National Grid references are shown on the map frame of each page.
Red figures denote the 100 km square and blue figures the 1 km square.
Example: page 141: Broughton Shopping Park 335 364

The reference can also be written using the National Grid two-letter prefix shown on this page, where 3 and 3 are replaced by SJ to give SJ3564.

2.5 inches to 1 mile   **Scale of main map pages**   1:25,000

miles
kilometres

iv

Junction 9	Motorway & junction	⊖	Underground station
Services	Motorway service area	⊖	Light railway & station
	Primary road single/dual carriageway	+++++++++	Preserved private railway
Services	Primary road service area	LC	Level crossing
	A road single/dual carriageway	•—•—•—•	Tramway
	B road single/dual carriageway	----------	Ferry route
	Other road single/dual carriageway	....	Airport runway
	Minor/private road, access may be restricted	—·—·—·—	County, administrative boundary
← ←	One-way street	▼▼▼▼▼▼▼▼	Mounds
	Pedestrian area	17	Page continuation 1:25,000
===========	Track or footpath	3	Page continuation to enlarged scale 1:10,000
	Road under construction		River/canal, lake
⌐ - - - - ⌐	Road tunnel		Aqueduct, lock, weir
AA	AA Service Centre	465 ▲ Winter Hill	Peak (with height in metres)
P	Parking		Beach
P+	Park & Ride		Woodland
	Bus/coach station		Park
	Railway & main railway station		Cemetery
	Railway & minor railway station		Built-up area

	Featured building			Abbey, cathedral or priory
	City wall			Castle
A&E	Hospital with 24-hour A&E department			Historic house or building
PO	Post Office		Wakehurst Place NT	National Trust property
	Public library		M	Museum or art gallery
i	Tourist Information Centre			Roman antiquity
i	Seasonal Tourist Information Centre			Ancient site, battlefield or monument
	Petrol station, 24-hour Major suppliers only			Industrial interest
†	Church/chapel			Garden
	Public toilets			Garden Centre Garden Centre Association Member
	Toilet with disabled facilities			Garden Centre Wyevale Garden Centre
PH	Public house AA recommended			Farm or animal centre
	Restaurant AA inspected			Zoological or wildlife collection
Madeira Hotel	Hotel AA inspected			Bird collection
	Theatre or performing arts centre			Nature reserve
	Cinema			Aquarium
	Golf course		V	Visitor or heritage centre
▲	Camping AA inspected			Country park
	Caravan site AA inspected			Cave
	Camping & caravan site AA inspected			Windmill
	Theme park			Distillery, brewery or vineyard

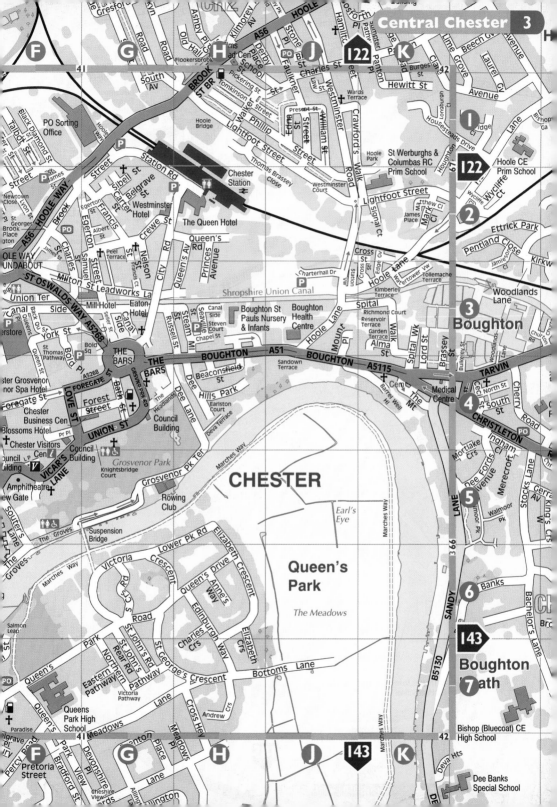

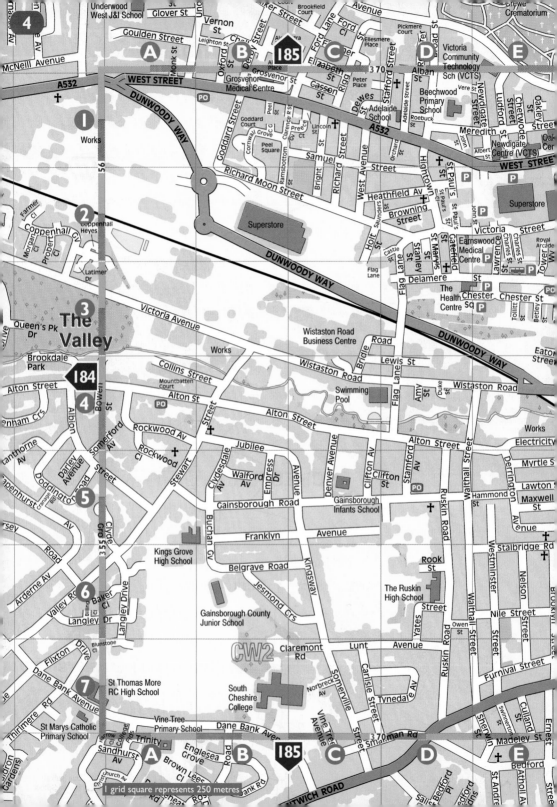

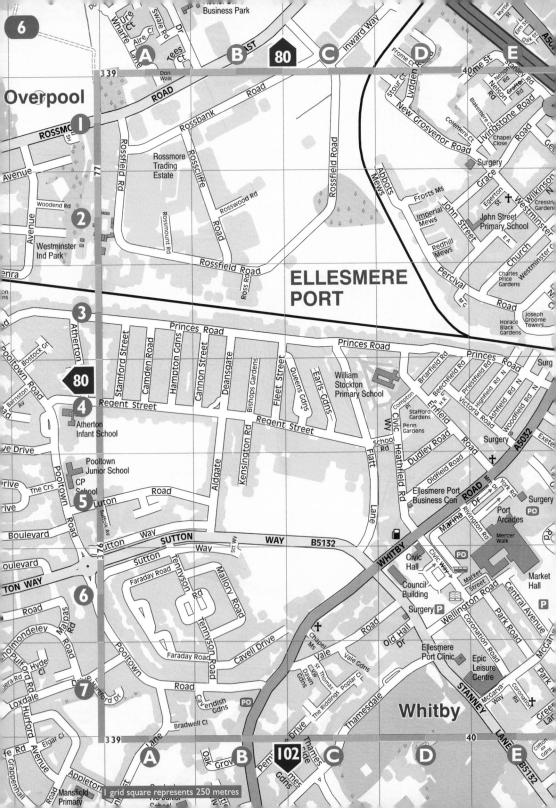

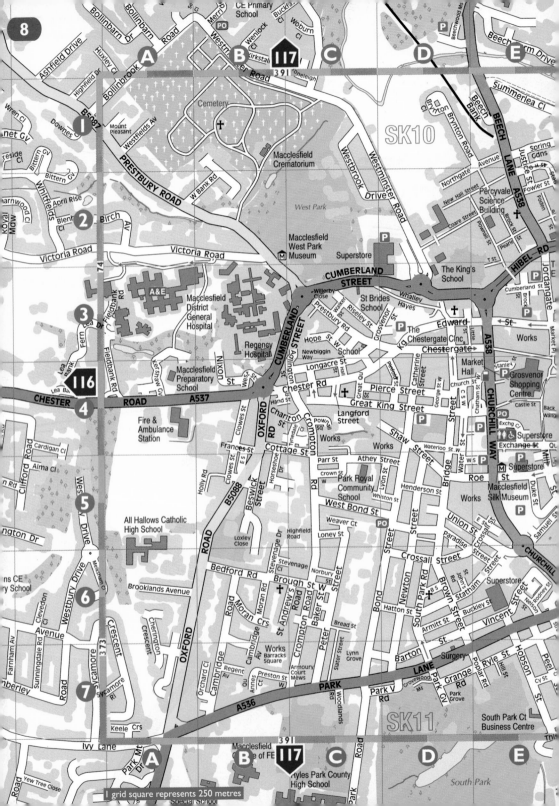

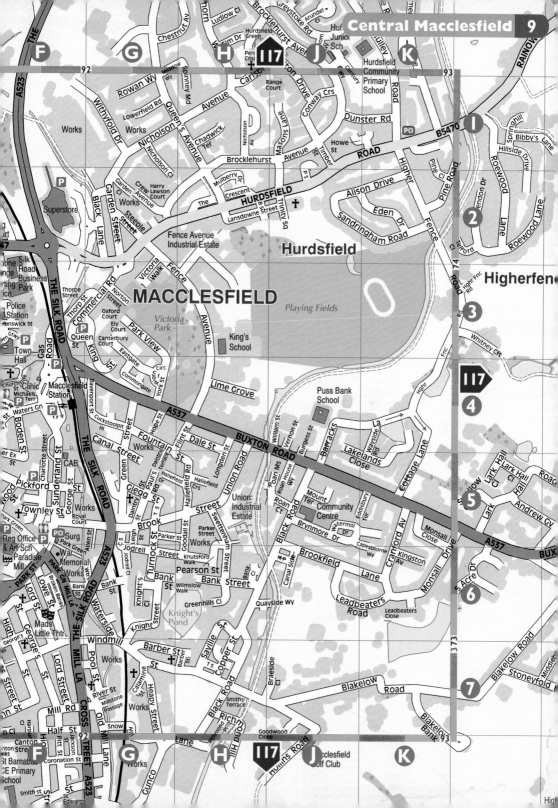

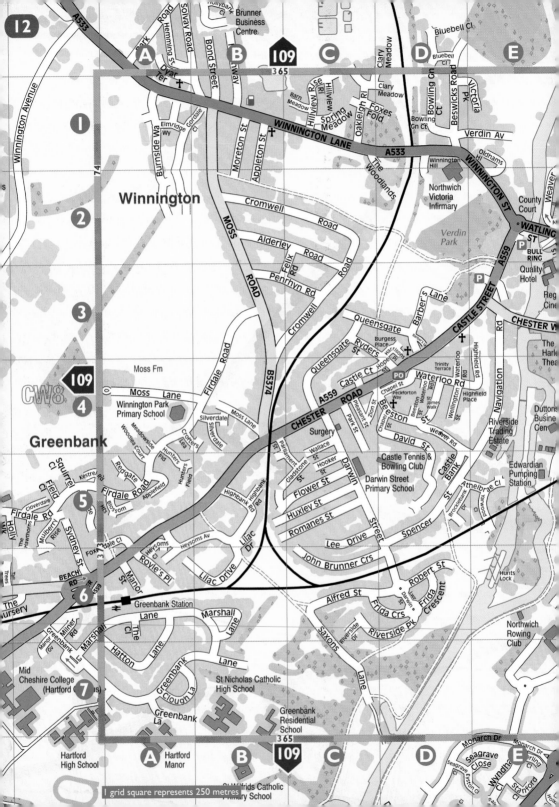

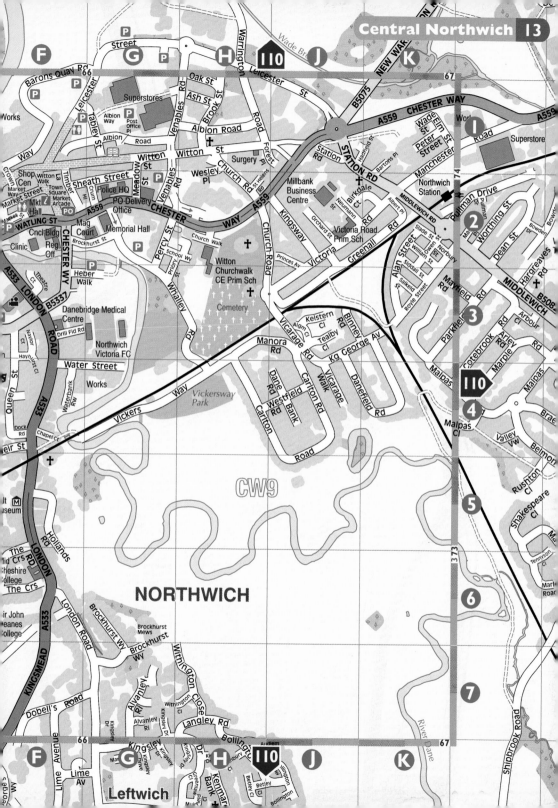

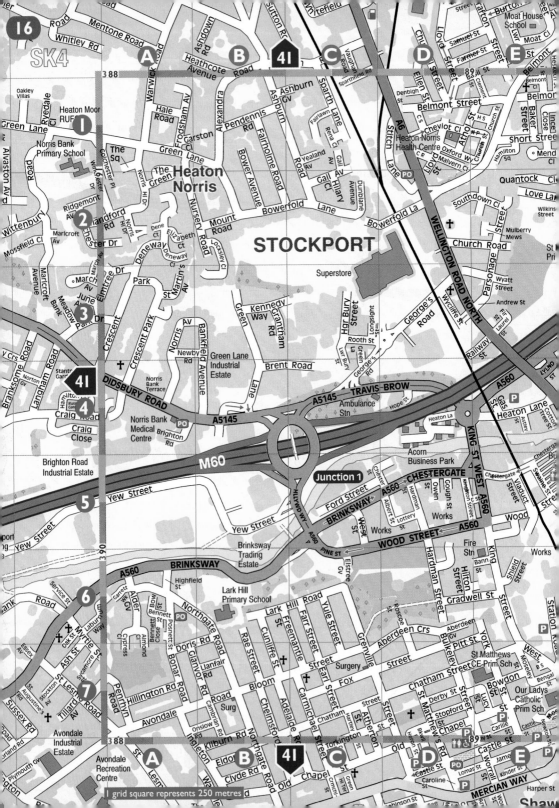

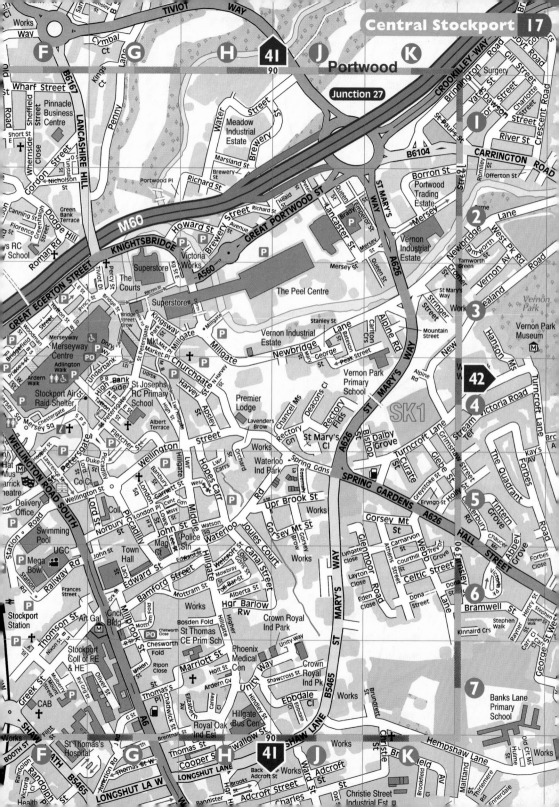

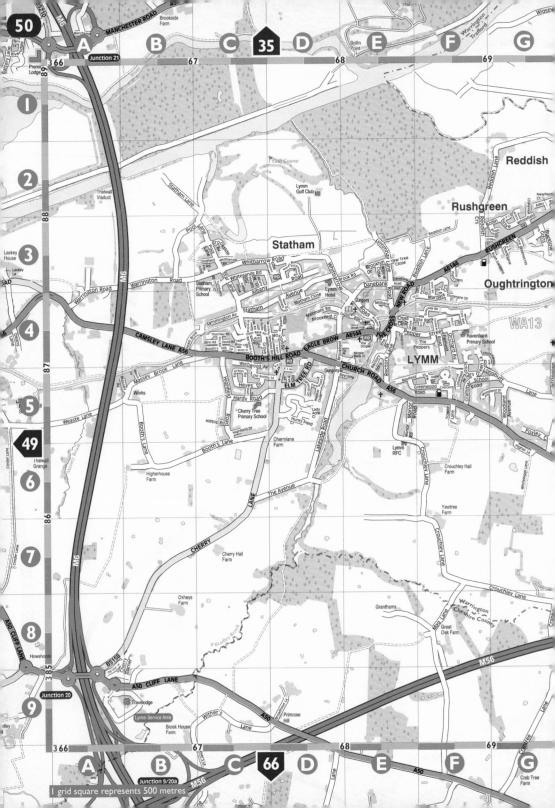

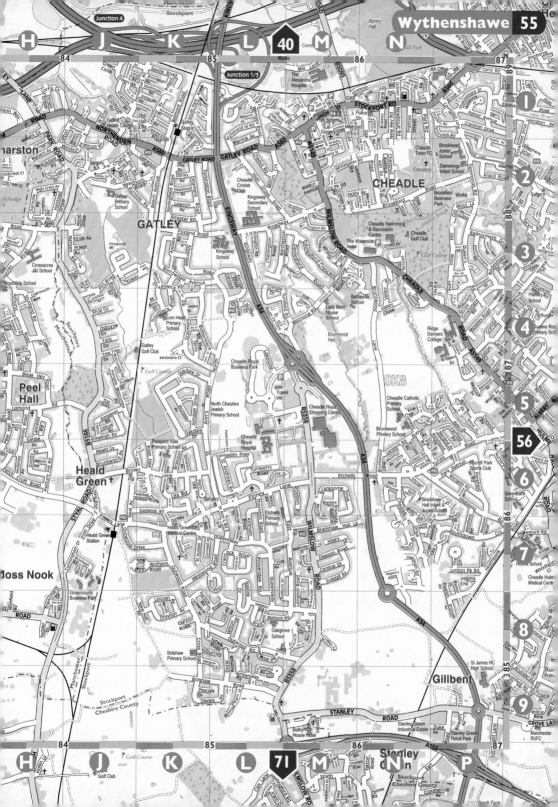

I grid square represents 500 metres

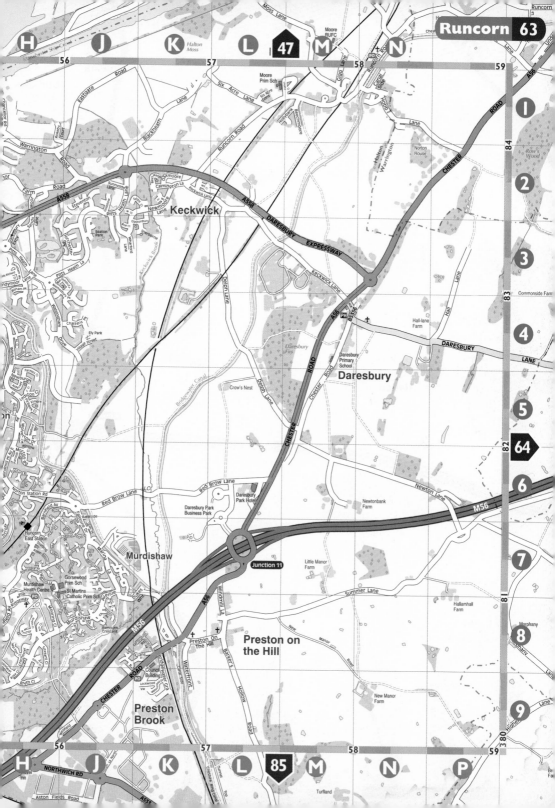

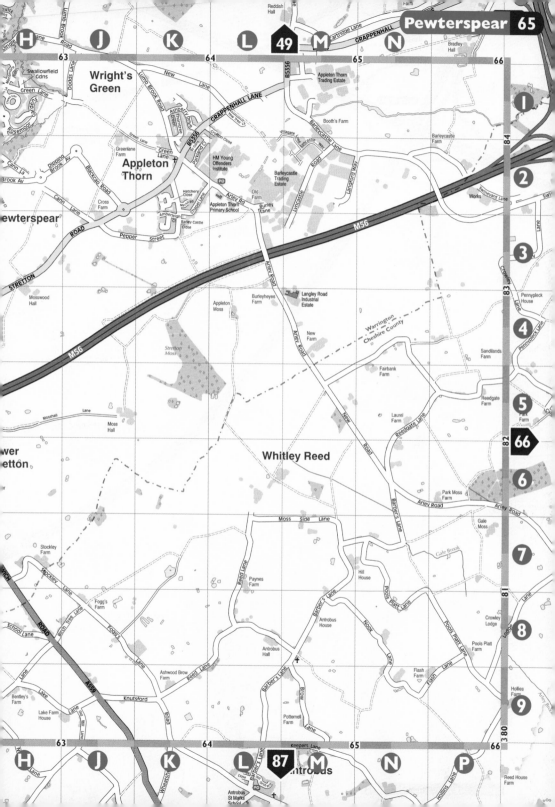

A B C D E F G

3 24 25 26 27

80

1

79

2

3

Wirral
Flint

4

78

5

Wirral
Cheshire County

6

77

7

8

3 76

9

River Dee

3 24 25 98 26 27

A B C D E F G

Heswall
Golf Club

Golf Cou

Gayton
Cott

1 grid square represents 500 metres

H   J   K   L   M

42   43   44   45

80
I
79
2
3
78
4
5
82
6
77
7
Ince

ce
anks

Stanlow
Point

Manchester Ship Canal

Marsh Lane

King's Lane

CH65

Indigo Road

Corridor Road

Oil Sites Road

Stanlow

Bridges Road

Stanlow & Thornton
Station

Pool Lane

Stanney Lane

8

376

9

Elf

South Road

New Bridge Road

Deans Lane

Shellway Lane

Mill Lane
Industrial
Estate

Shropshire
Road

Moorbridge Road

Oil Refinery

H   J   K   L   103 ▽   M   N   P

42   43   44   45

The Paddock

Road

42

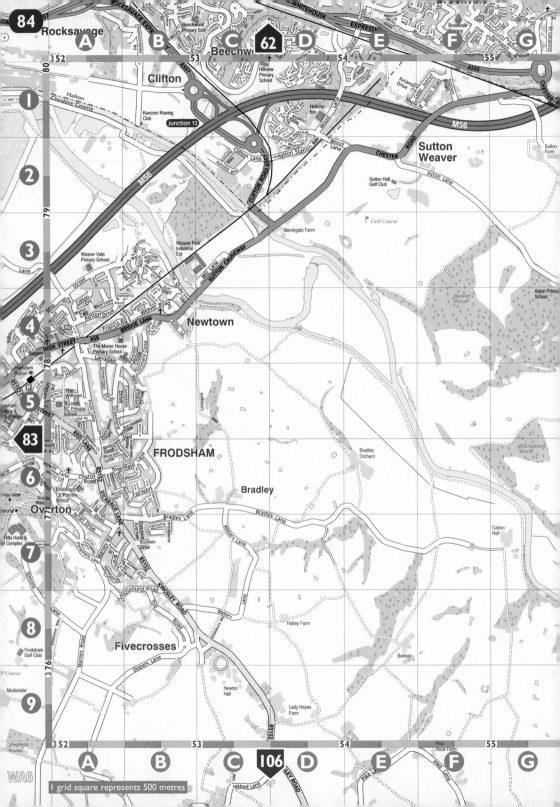

Rocksavage

A   B   C   **62**   D   E   F   G

Beechwood

WHITEHOUSE

EXPRESSI

CHESTER

Clifton

Halton
Cheshire County

I

Runcorn Rowing
Club

Junction 12

Holiday
Inn

Sutton
Weaver

M56

2

Sutton Hall
Golf Club

Golf Course

3

Weaver Vale
Primary School

Weaver Park
Industrial
Est

Marshgate Farm

Beckett's
Wood

Aston Prima
School

Newtown

Weaver Road

Weaver Navigation

4

The Manor House
Primary School

HIGH STREET

Surgery

Langdale

Frodsham
Station

5

The
Willows
St Luke's
RC Primary
School

STREET

83

FRODSHAM

Bradley
Orchard

Blackamoor
Wood

6

Frodsham
CE Primary
School

Church
Road

Bradley

Overton

VICARAGE LANE

Bradley Lane

Catton
Hall

Hills Hotel &
Complex

7

KINGSLEY ROAD

Watery Lane

Lane

8

Frodsham
Golf Club

Hatley Farm

Belleair

Fivecrosses

Dobers Lane

Mickledale

9

Newton
Hall

Lady Heyes
Farm

Shepherds
Houses

3 52   53   **106**   54   55

A   B   C   D   E   F   G

Hillfoot Lane

Pike
Nook Farm

Pike Lane

I grid square represents 500 metres

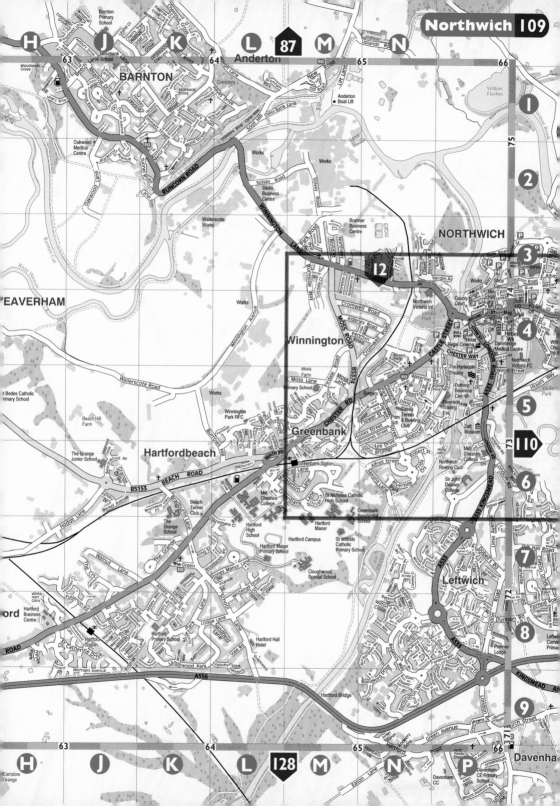

H J K L 89 M N

Plumley

I
2
3
4
5
112
6
7
8
9

Lostock
alam

Peover Eye

Plumley Station

PH

South Dr

Moss Lane

Mollford Moss

Moss Farm

Trouthall Lane

Trouthall Lane

Beech House Farm

Plumley Moor Road

Plumley Moor

Golf Course

Peover Club

The Fields Farm

Cheadle Lane

Back Lane

75

74

Fieldhouse Farm

Langford Farm

Works

Cheadle Farm

Lostock Green

Ridge Farm

Mosslane Farm

Cape of Good Hope Farm

Crow Brook

Patmos Lane

Millgate Farm

M6

73

Hanoman's Lane

Hulse Farm

Hulse Lane

Portford Farm

Hulme Lane

Birches Lane

Birches Hall

Birches Lane

Hulse House Farm

Common Lane

Lach Dennis

PO

Hulme Hall Lane

72

PENNYS LANE B5082

Crowder's Lane

HOLMES CHAPEL ROAD

Highfield Farm

Allostock Hall

Marsh Farm

B5082

Shakerley Mere

3711

H J K L 130 M N P

70 71 72 73

Boundary Farm
New Hall Farm
Beech Lane
Chestnut House Farm

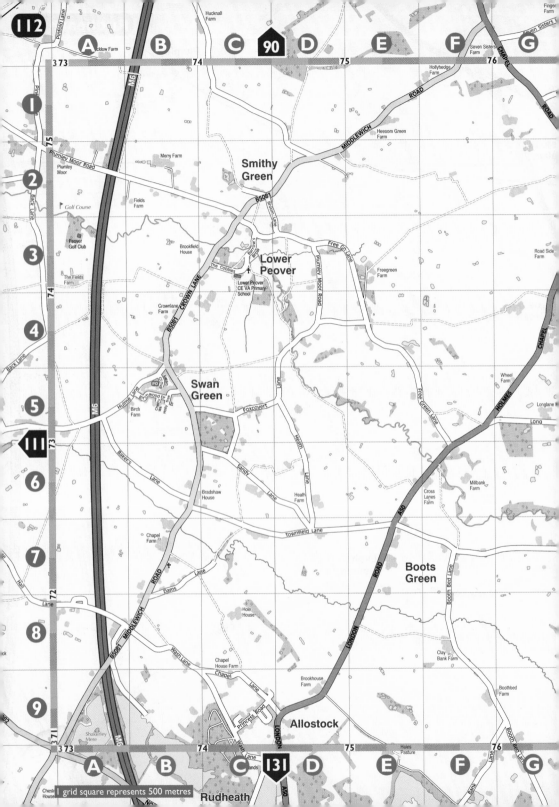

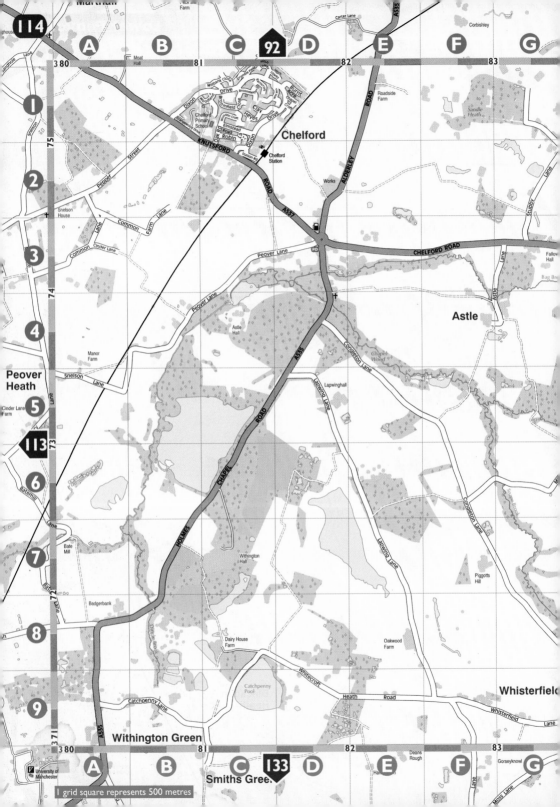

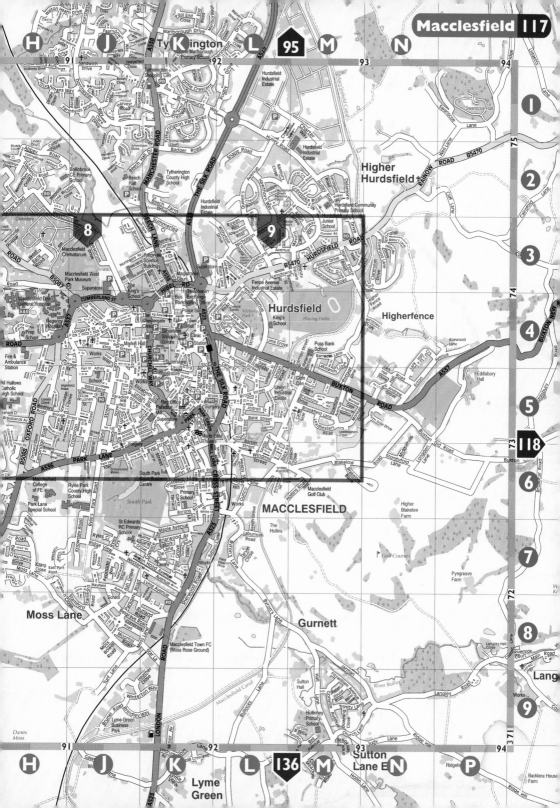

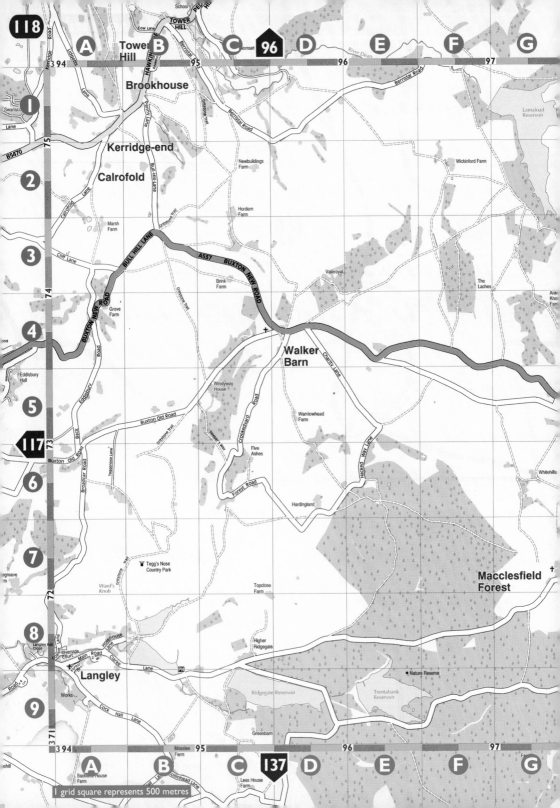

120

A B C D E F G

335 36 37

Saughall

Council
Building

Castle
Farm

Green
Farm

Parkgate
House

Lodge

Long Lane

Fiddlers

Park Lane

Newcroft

Meadowcroft

Green
Way

Astbury
House

Kingswood
Avenue

CH1

Thomas Wedge
Junior School

Shotwick
House

Church Road

Park Way

Darracott Ct

Saughall

The Ridings Infant School

Surgery

Fox Lea

Surgery

Seahill
Road

Seahill
Farm

Hermitage Road

The Ridings

Thornberry
Close

Haymakers Wy

Oulton's
Farm

Aspen Gv

Green
Lane

Cheshire County

Flintshire

Hermitage Road

Blacon

Willow
Farm

Green Lane East

St
Bartholomew's Ct

Waterloo
Farm

Sealand

Deeside
Lane

A548

SEALAND ROAD

Church
Farm

Yew Tree
Farm

Birchenfields
Farm

Wash
Hall

Saughall
Willow

Mayfield
Road

Highfield

JH Godwin
Primary School

Melbourne

Blacon County
High School

Western Avenue
Medical Centre

Western Av

Blacon
Point Road

Deeside
House

Sealand
Nursery

Deeside Lane

Thornleigh
Park

Bank
Farm

Dee Point
County
School

Point
House
Farm

Ferry Lane
Farm

Ferry Lane

River Dee

71

70

69

68

367

I

2

3

4

5

6

7

8

9

A B C D E F G

335 36 37

141

Beeches
Farm

River Dee

1 grid square represents 500 metres

Bridge Trafford

H J K L 104 M

B5132

Morley Hall

I

2

Barnhouse Farm

Swinford House

Norton's Lane

46 47 48

71

Wildmoor Lane

Long Green

B5132

Plemstall

Lane

Plemstall

LC

Holme Farm

Little Barrow

PH

Broomhill Lane

Barnhouse Lane

Swinlordmill Farm

3

Broomhill

70

B5132

Ardmore

Longster Trail

The Avenue

Irons Lane

Barrowhouse Lane

4

Barrowmore Estate

Sellers Brook

5

69

Great Barrow

Hawkins View

Longster Trail

Barrow CE Primary School

Ferma Lane

Mill Street

New Farm Court

Mill Lane

Heath Lane

Manor Park

Hollowmoor Heath

Irons Lane

124

6

BARROW LANE

Longster Trail

Wicker Lane

River Gowy

B5132

Park Hall

68

7

Stamford Bridge

Lansdowne Road

Golf Course

Vicars Cross Golf Club

A51

TARVIN ROAD

A51

The Limes

HOLME STREET

Holme Bank

8

67

Stamford Lane

Cotton Lane

Stamford Heath

Stamford Mill Lane

Mill

Abbeyfield

HOLME STREET

A54

Grosvenor

Townfield La

Field Lane

Crossfields

Dans La

9

H J K L 144 M N P

Birch Bank Farm

Cotton Hall

46 47 48

Tarvi Prim Sch

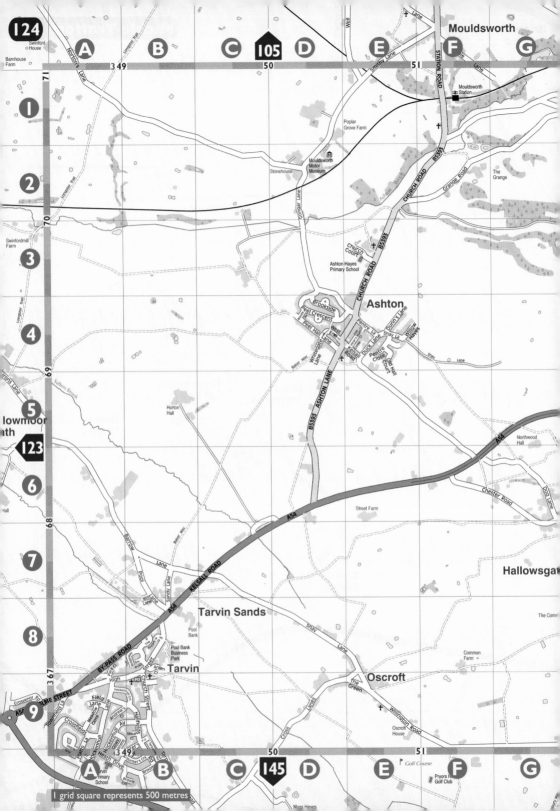

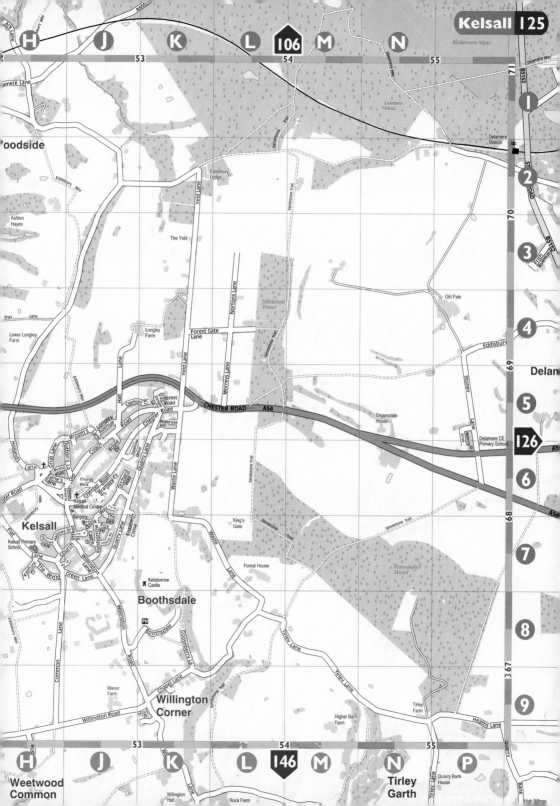

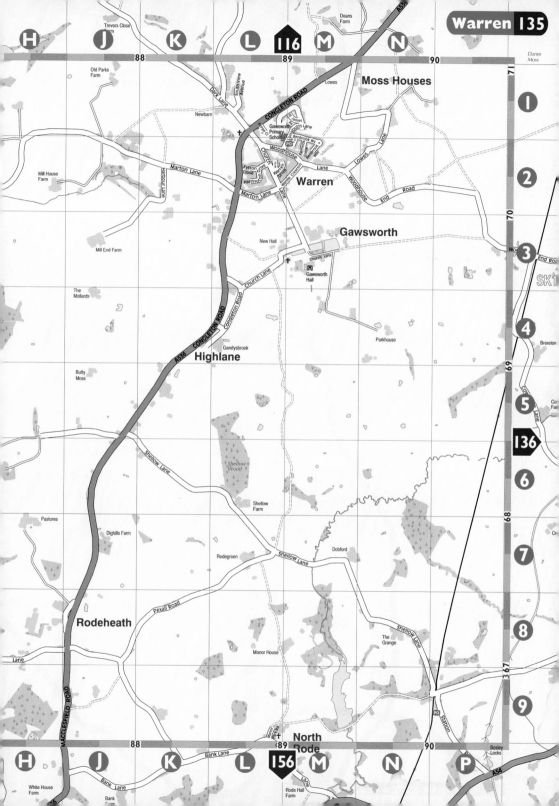

138

A B C **119** D E F G

398 99 400

71 Ferriser

1

Dryknowle Farm
High Ash Farm

70

3 506 gsloe

Higher Barn

Lower Barn

Clough House

Cumberland Cottage

Danebower Hollow

Whetstone Ridge

Dane Bower

Shutlingsloe Farm

Banktop

69

Wood Moss

Sparbent

Holt

4

5 **Wildboarclough**

137

Crag Hall

68

Clough Brook

Berry Bank Farm

A54

Cut-thorn

Three Shire Heads

6

7 Blaze

A54

Heild End Farm

Knar

Far Hole-edge

8

67

Allgreave

Parks

River Dane

9 Midgley Farm

Pearls

A B **C** **159** **D** Burntcliff Top E F G

398 99 400

Helmesley Greens

1 grid square represents 500 metres

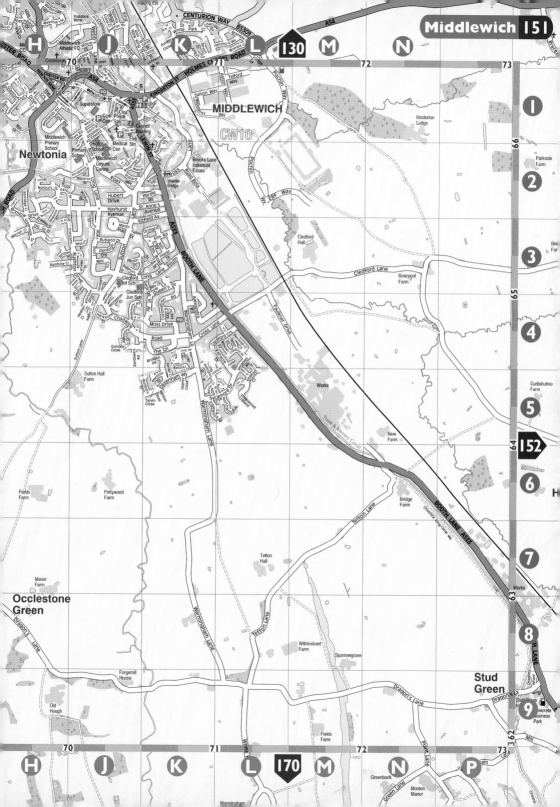

H   J   K   L   **132**   M

77   78   79   80

Stockery Park Farm

Sandlow Green

Davenport Hall Farm

1

66

ON ROAD
Work

Mill Lane
Marsh Lane
Farm

Parkmill Farm

Mill Lane

A54

HOLMES

CHAPEL

ROAD

Grange Farm

A54

Dave

2

Park House Lodge

Park House Lodge

Allum Brook Farm

3

65

Pewit Covert

Brereton Heath Park

Brereton Heath Lane

4

Bagmere Bank Farm

Bagmere Lane

Fox Covert

Back Lane

Bagmere Farm

NEWCASTLE ROAD NORTH

A50

DOG LANE

A50

xcovert rm

Brereton Green

Newcastle Road South

Innkeeper's Lodge Hotel

Brereton CE Primary School

School

Hazelshaw Farm

Hazelshaw Lane

Lightfoot Green Farm

Big Mere

5

64   **154**

6

Duke's Oak Farm

Brownedge

A5022

Illidge Green

Moorhead Lane

7

NEWCASTLE

ROAD

A50

Davenport Lane

Moorhead Farm

Brindley Green

Taxmere Farm

SPARK

LANE

A534

Sparklane Farm

8

63

ssend

A5022

HOLMES CHAPEL ROAD

Brickhouses

Arclid

9

362

80

PO

77   78   79

H   J   K   L   **172**   M   N   P

Junction

The C House Hotel

CONGLETON

A534

Y Farm

ial Estate

Arclid Green

Hall

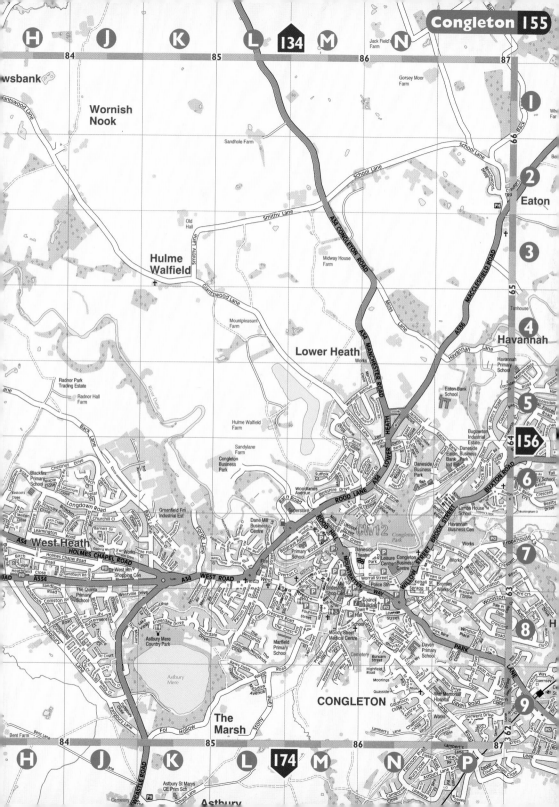

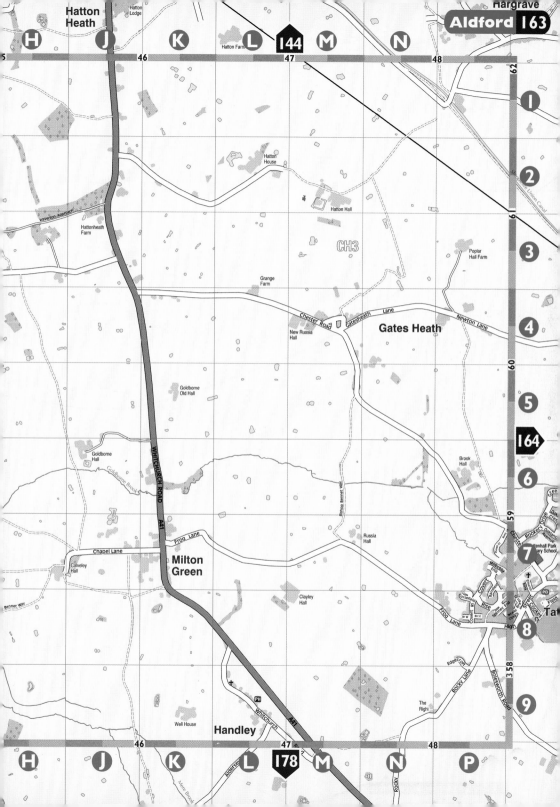

H **J** **K** **L** 148 **M** **N**

9 60 61 62

I

Philps Gorse

Woodgate Farm

Page's Wood

Towns Green

Holme Farm

Manor Farm

Long Lane

Wetter

2

Wettenhall Brook

Eaton Road

Long Lane Farm

Wettenhall Green

3

South View

Long Lane

Long Lane New Farm

4

Calveley Green Farm

Fox Covert

Cholmondeston

5

Calveley green Lane

Calveley Farm

The Elms Farm

Long Lane

Calveley Hall Lane

The Woodlands

168

Barrets Green

Calveley Hall Farm

6

Calveley

The Cherry Orchard

Cow Ct

Calveley CP School

7

Calveley Mill Industrial Estate

A51

Highbank Farm

Calveley Green Lane

Parkfield House Farm

Greenbank Farm

8

Top Farm

Calveley Hall Lane

Wardle Bank

9

NANTWICH

Wardle Bridge Farm

Wardle Industrial Estate

Green Lane

Cross Farm

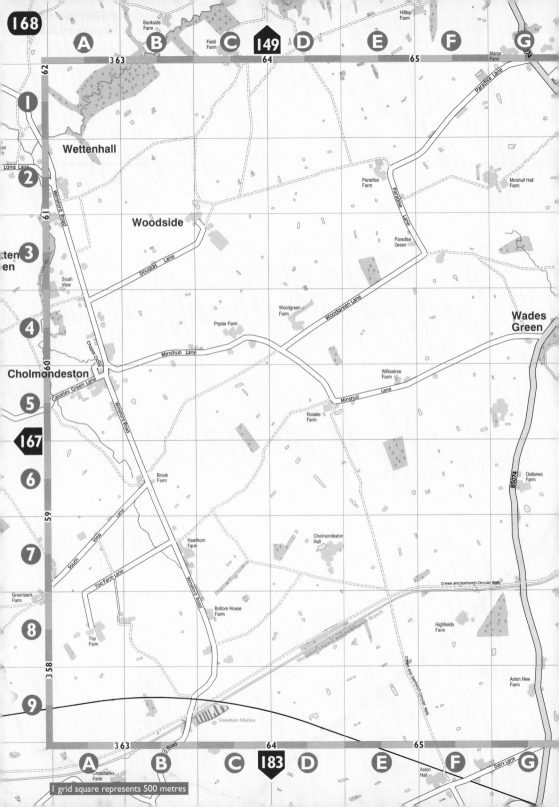

A   B   Field Farm   C   **149**   D   E   F   G

Bankside Farm

Hilltop Farm

Manor Farm

363   64   65

1

62

Paradise Lane

Wettenhall

Long Lane

2

61

Paradise Farm

Paradise Lane

Minshull Hall Farm

Winsford Road

Back Brook

Woodside

3

ten en

South View

Paradise Green

Douglas Lane

Woodgreen Farm

Woodgreen Lane

Wades Green

Poplar Farm

4

60

Chapel Close

Minshull Lane

Willowtree Farm

Cholmondeston

Calveley Green Lane

Minshull Lane

5

Winsford Road

Rosalie Farm

◄167

6

Brook Farm

Outlanes Farm

B5074

59

South View Lane

7

Hawthorn Farm

Cholmondeston Hall

Crewe and Nantwich Circular Walk

Greenbank Farm

Top Farm Lane

8

Top Farm

Winsford Road

Bottom House Farm

Highfields Farm

Shropshire Union Canal Middlewich Branch

Crewe and Nantwich Circular Walk

58

Aston New Farm

9

Venetian Marina

363   64   65

A   Crossbanks Farm   B   d Road   C   **183**   D   E   F   Aston Hall   G

Dairy Lane

1 grid square represents 500 metres

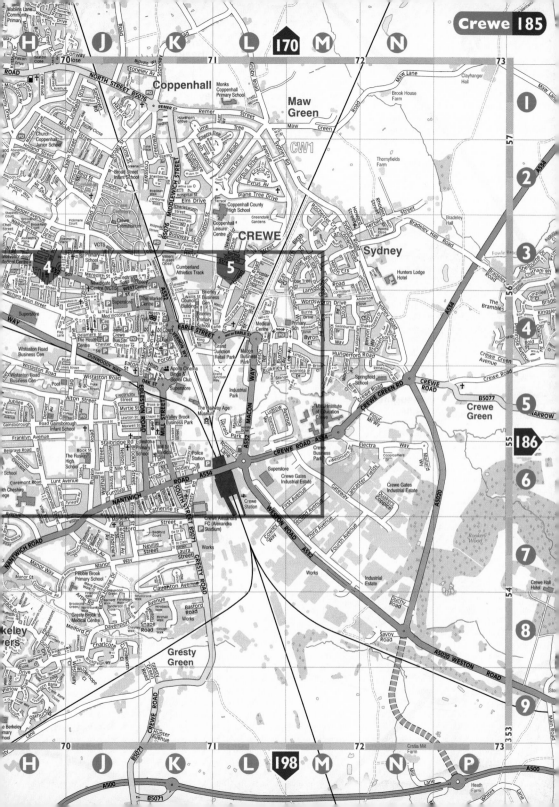

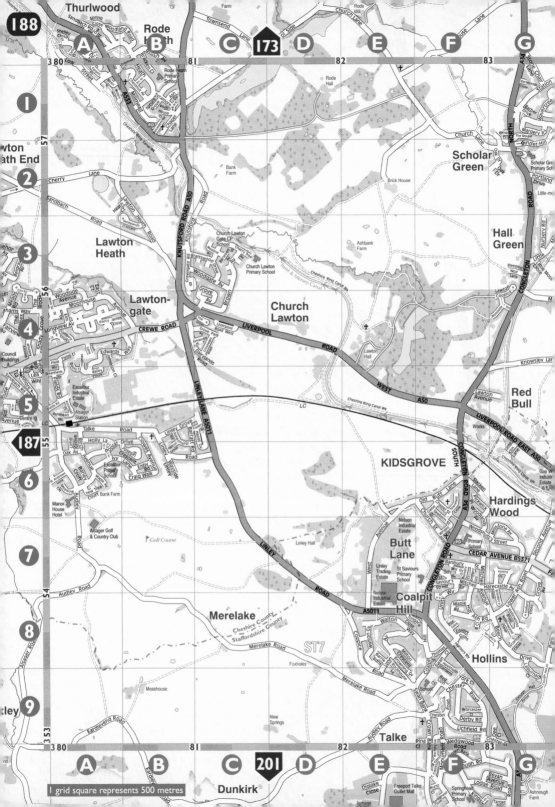

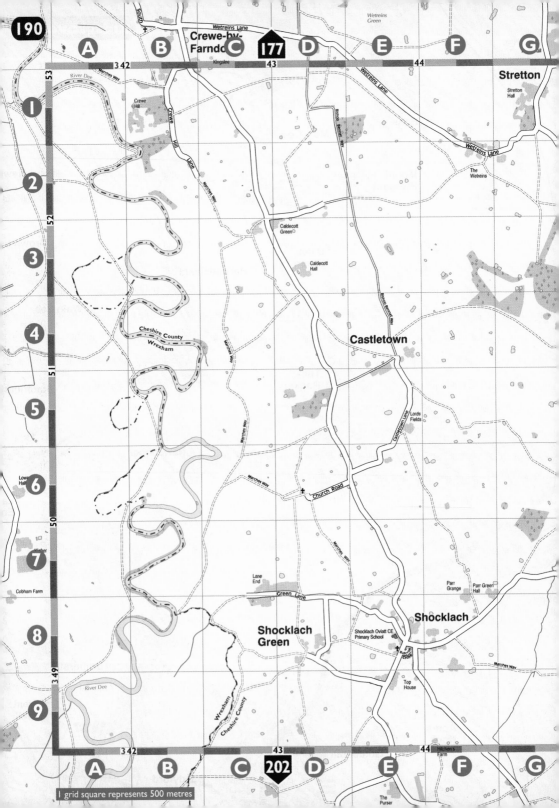

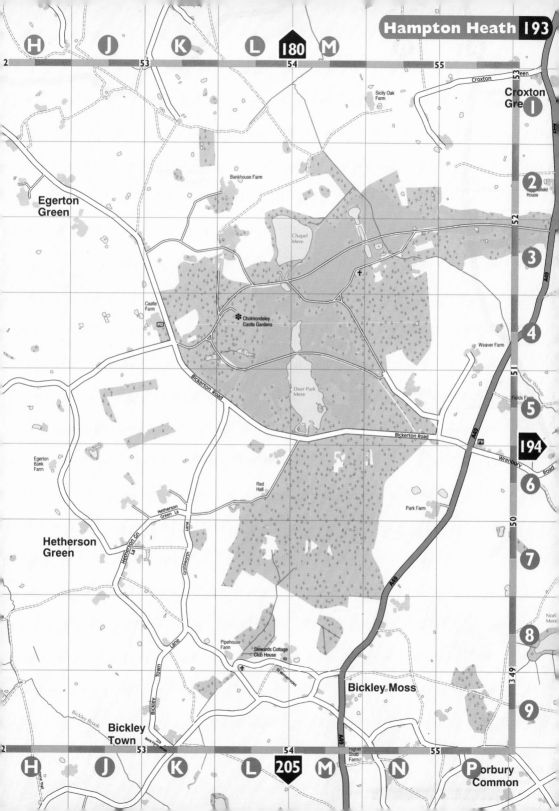

H J K L 180 M

2 53 54 55

Croxton
Croxton Gre I

Sicily Oak Farm

2
sfield House

Bankhouse Farm

Egerton Green

Chapel Mere

3

4
Weaver Farm

Castle Farm

PO

✿ Cholmondeley Castle Gardens

Bickerton Road

Deer Park Mere

51
River Weaver

Fields Farm

5

Bickerton Road

PH

194
Wrenbury Road

6

Egerton Bank Farm

Red Hall

Park Farm

50

Hetherson Green La
Hetherson Grn La
Lane
Grassworth

Hetherson Green

7

A49

Norl Mere

8

Pipehouse Farm

Town Lane

Stewards Cottage Club House

St Wenefredes

49

Bickley Moss

9

Bickley Brook

Bickley Town

Higher Snab Farm

H J K L 205 M N P orbury Common

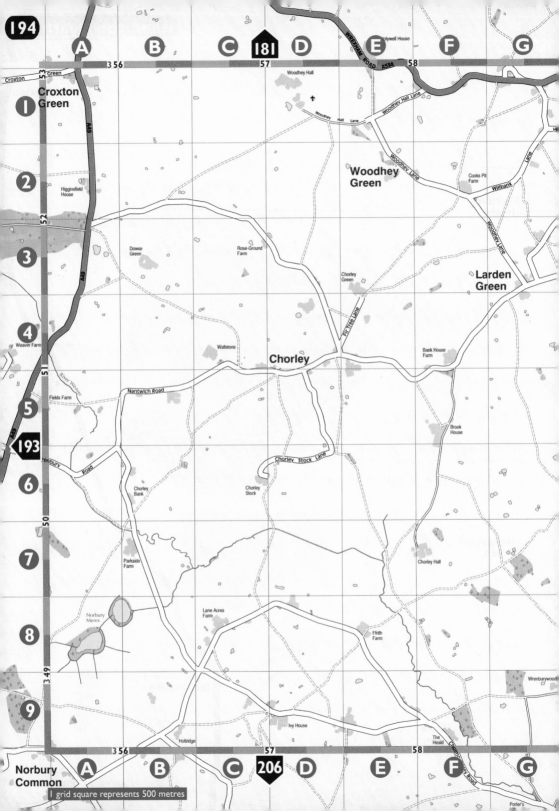

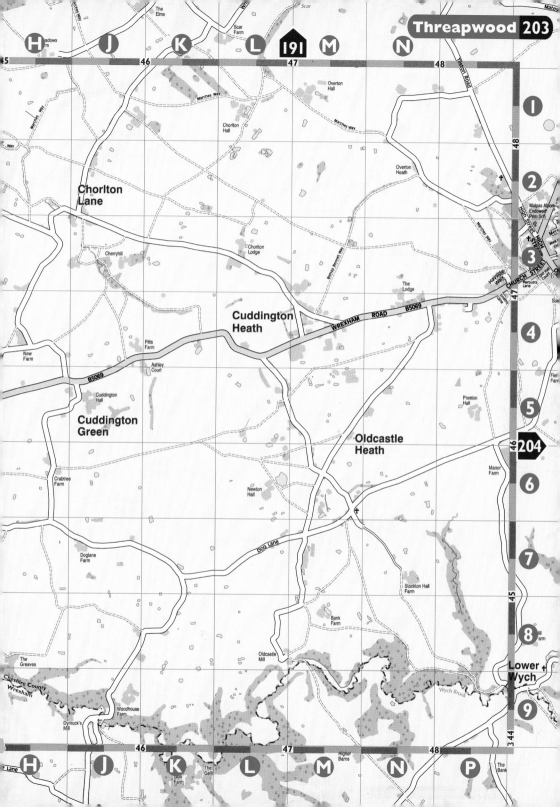

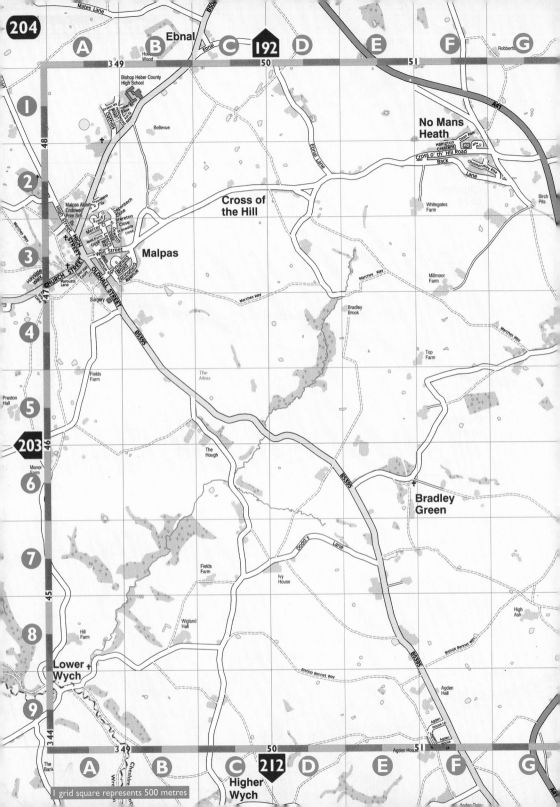

204

A   B   C   D   E   F   G

3 49   50   5 I

Agden
Hall

Agden
House La

Agden House

Agden House La

Agden Dairy
Farm

B5395

Gr
Br

The
Bank

Cheshire County

Wrexham

44

Higher
Wych

Sandholes

Wolvesacre
Mill

Wych
Mill

Maelor Way

I

Highfields

Higher Lanes
Bank

43

Maes-y-groes
Farm

Maelor Way

2

Higher Lane
Farm

Foxholes
Farm

Kiln
Green

Bubney

3

Maelor Way

Wolvesacre
Hall

Bubney
Moor

4

Parkley
Farm

Hall
Green

42

Eastwick

Waenreef

Smoaky Lane

Maelor Way

Hadley

5

Shropshire County

Wrexham

6

Bank
Farm

The
Moor

Whitewell Road

Whitewell

WREXHAM

Redbrook

A525

A495

41

Broad Oak
Farm

The
Chequer

A525

Painters
Green

Blackhoe
Cottages

ELLESMERE ROAD

7

Maelor
Way

Bowxer's Lane

Pear Tree
House

8

40

The Pinfold

LONG LANE

A495

Fenn's
Old Hall

Shropshire Union Canal

Maeshwyn
Close

Mill

Bronington

Bronington
Primary
School

New Hall
Farm

Corbett Lane

Shropshire
Wrexham

9

School Lane

3 49   A495

Fenn's Bank

A   B   C   D   E   F   G

50   5 I

I grid square represents 500 metres

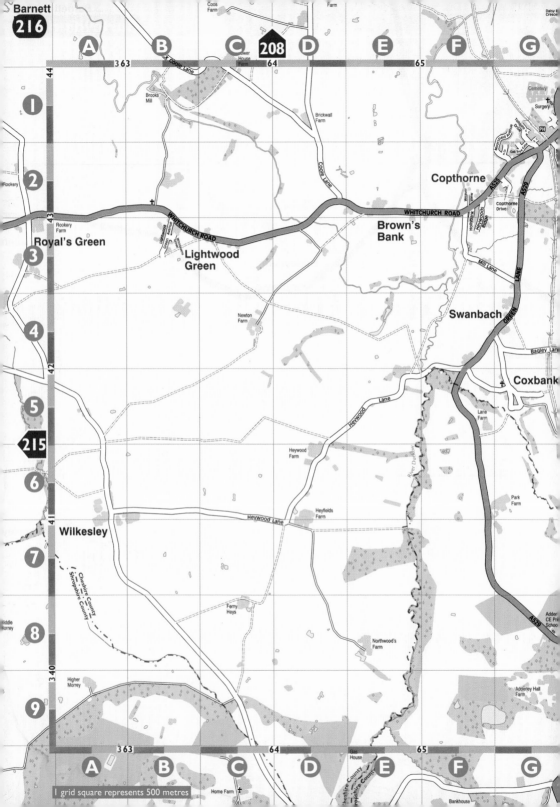

Abbey Hey ... 28 F4
Abbot's Meads ... 121 L7
Acres Nook ... 189 J9
Acton ... 183 J9
Acton Bridge ... 108 A1
Adderley ... 217 H9
Adlington ... 73 H9
Adswood ... 56 D2
Alderley Edge ... 93 L3
Aldersey Green ... 178 C2
Aldford ... 162 A6
Allgreave ... 137 P9
Allostock ... 112 D9
Alpraham ... 166 G5
Alsager ... 187 M5
Altrincham ... 53 K2
Alvanley ... 105 J4
Anderton ... 87 L9
Antrobus ... 87 M1
Apedale ... 201 K8
Appleton ... 45 P5
Appleton Park ... 64 E1
Appleton Thorn ... 65 J2
Arclid ... 153 M9
Arclid Green ... 172 E1
Arden Park ... 42 C4
Arley ... 66 B7
Arley Green ... 66 E8
Arthill ... 51 P7
Ashley ... 69 J1
Ashley Heath ... 53 H7
Ash Magna ... 214 D9
Ashton ... 94 A5
Ashton Upon Mersey ... 38 C2
Astbury ... 174 C1
Astle ... 114 F4
Astmoor ... 62 C3
Aston ... 85 H4
Aston ... 209 M6
Aston ... 85 H5
Aston Heath ... 85 H5
Aston juxta Mondrum ... 183 M2
Audenshaw ... 29 L2
Audlem ... 217 H2
Audley ... 201 H5
Backford ... 102 D8
Backford Cross ... 102 B5
Balderton ... 141 P9
Ball o' Ditton ... 45 L6
Balterley ... 199 P6
Balterley Green ... 199 N5
Balterley Heath ... 199 M6
The Banks ... 59 H5
The Bank ... 189 K1
Barbridge ... 182 E2
Barnett Brook ... 207 P9
Barnhill ... 179 H6
Barnton ... 109 J1
The Barony ... 10 D3
Barrets Green ... 167 H6
Barrowmore Estate ... 123 M5
Barrow's Green ... 46 B3
Barrows Green ... 169 N8
Barthomley ... 200 A2
Barton ... 177 P7
Bate Heath ... 88 F2
Bearstone ... 218 E9
Beechwood ... 62 C9
Beeston ... 165 M7
Belgrave ... 161 H5
Belle Vue ... 28 B4
Bell o' th' Hill ... 205 L7
Benchill ... 54 E5
Berkeley Towers ... 184 G8
Betchton Heath ... 172 B4
Betley ... 199 M9
Betley Common ... 199 K9
Bewsey ... 33 H8
Bickerton ... 192 E1
Bickley Moss ... 193 M9
Bickley Town ... 193 J9
Bickleywood ... 205 H2
Biddulph ... 175 J9
Bignall End ... 201 J4
Birchall Moss ... 209 M5
Birch Heath ... 165 N1
Birchwood ... 34 F4
Blackbrook ... 22 E4
Blackbrook ... 33 P6
Blackden Heath ... 113 M9
Blacon ... 121 J5
Blakelow ... 197 M3
Blakenhall ... 210 F5
Bold Heath ... 31 K9
Bollington ... 95 P6
Bollington Cross ... 95 K6
Boon Hill ... 201 J5
Booth Bank ... 51 P8
Booth Green ... 73 L7
Boothsdale ... 125 J8
Boots Green ... 112 E7
Bosley ... 157 K2
Bostock Green ... 129 K4
Boughton ... 122 B9
Boughton Heath ... 143 H2
Bowdon ... 52 E6
Bowgreen ... 52 E6
Braddocks Hay ... 175 N9
Bradeley ... 205 L8
Bradeley Green ... 169 M6
Bradley ... 84 C6
Bradley Green ... 204 E6
Bradley Mount ... 73 P7
Bradwall Green ... 152 F6
Bramhall ... 72 D1
Bramhall Moor ... 57 H5
Bramhall Park ... 56 C6
Brassey Green ... 165 J3
Bredbury ... 42 D5
Bredbury Green ... 43 K5
Brereton Green ... 153 K5
Brereton Heath ... 154 A4
Bretton ... 141 J6

Brickhouses ... 172 B1
Bridgemere ... 210 D7
Bridge Trafford ... 104 A9
Brindley ... 182 A8
Brinnington ... 42 A3
Broadheath ... 37 P9
Broad Meadow ... 201 P9
Broad Oak ... 22 D5
Broadoak ... 160 D7
Broken Cross ... 110 F5
Broken Cross ... 116 D4
Bronington ... 212 A9
Brook Bottom ... 59 J6
Brookhouse ... 118 B1
Brookhouse Green ... 173 K2
Brooklands ... 38 E6
Brooklands ... 213 K4
Brookvale ... 62 F9
Broomedge ... 51 K6
Broomhall Green ... 207 P3
Broomhill ... 123 N5
Broughall ... 214 C6
Broughton ... 140 G7
Brown Edge ... 30 B1
Brownedge ... 153 K6
Brown Heath ... 144 B4
Brown Knowl ... 179 J8
Brownlow ... 173 P2
Brownlow Heath ... 173 N4
Brown's Bank ... 216 E3
Broxton ... 178 G6
Bruche ... 34 A9
Bruera ... 162 E3
Bryn ... 108 D6
Bucklow Hill ... 67 P3
Buckoak ... 105 M7
Buddileigh ... 199 L8
Budworth Heath ... 88 B4
Burford ... 183 J8
Burland ... 182 E9
Burleydam ... 215 L3
Burnage ... 40 F3
Burton ... 100 B2
Burton ... 145 M6
Burton ... 160 C9
Burtonwood ... 32 C2
Burwardsley ... 179 N2
Butley Town ... 95 J5
Butters Green ... 201 K5
Butt Green ... 197 J4
Butt Lane ... 188 E7
Byley ... 130 F4
Cadishead ... 36 E5
Cale Green ... 56 F1
Callands ... 32 G6
Calrofold ... 118 A2
Calveley ... 167 H7
Capenhurst ... 101 M4
Carr Green ... 51 M1
Carrington ... 37 K2
Carrington Moss ... 37 L5
Castlefields ... 62 D4
Castle Hill ... 62 B7
Castletown ... 190 E4
Catterslaisane ... 214 B7
Chadkirk ... 42 D4
Chapel End ... 217 K2
Cheadle ... 55 N2
Cheadle Heath ... 41 H9
Cheadle Hulme ... 56 A7
Checkley ... 211 J5
Checkley Green ... 210 G6
Chelford ... 114 D1
Chemistry ... 213 J6
The Chequer ... 212 A7
Cherry Tree ... 43 L6
Chester ... 3 H5
Chesterton ... 201 N8
Childer Thornton ... 79 M5
Cholmondeston ... 167 P5
Chorley ... 194 D4
Choriton ... 198 B7
Choriton-cum-Hardy ... 39 N1
Choriton Lane ... 203 J2
Chowley ... 178 E3
Christleton ... 143 N2
Church Hill ... 149 N3
Church Lawton ... 188 E3
Church Minshull ... 169 L4
Churton ... 176 G2
Cinnamon Brow ... 34 B4
Clark Green ... 95 N2
Clifton ... 84 B1
Clive ... 150 E1
Clive Green ... 150 E4
Clock Face ... 31 J5
Clotton ... 146 B6
Clotton Common ... 146 B4
Cloud Side ... 157 H7
Clough Hall ... 189 H8
Clutton ... 178 B6
Coalpit Hill ... 188 E8
Cobbs ... 48 F7
Coddington ... 177 P5
Cold Moss Heath ... 171 P4
Collins Green ... 23 H8
Colshaw ... 139 P7
Comberbach ... 87 M6
Commonside ... 106 A2
Common Side ... 126 G8
Compstall ... 43 M5
Congleton ... 175 N8
Congleton Edge ... 175 K4
Cookson Green ... 107 K3
Coppenhall ... 185 K1
Coppenhall Moss ... 170 C8
Copthorne ... 216 F2
Cotebrook ... 147 K3

Coxbank ... 216 G5
Crackley ... 201 N6
Cracow Moss ... 211 N2
Cranage ... 131 M5
Crewe ... 5 G1
Crewe-by-Farndon ... 177 J9
Crewe Green ... 185 P5
Croft ... 25 K9
Cronton ... 45 H2
Cross Lane ... 169 L3
Cross o' th' Hill ... 204 C2
Cross Town ... 90 F3
Crowton ... 107 M3
Crow Wood ... 46 B5
Croxton Green ... 193 P1
Cuddington ... 108 A8
Cuddington Green ... 203 J5
Cuddington Heath ... 203 L4
Cuerdley Cross ... 46 E4
Culcheth ... 26 A6
Dale Brow ... 94 C8
Dales Green ... 189 L3
Dallam ... 33 J7
Dane Bank ... 29 H7
Danebank ... 75 J1
Danebridge ... 158 F3
Dane in Shaw ... 156 C9
Daresbury ... 65 M5
Darland ... 160 C9
Davenham ... 129 H1
Davenport ... 56 E3
Davenport ... 154 A3
Davenport Green ... 54 B2
Davenport Green ... 93 H2
Day Green ... 172 C9
Dean Row ... 71 P6
Deansgreen ... 51 H7
Debdale ... 28 F5
Delamere ... 126 A5
Delamere Park ... 107 N7
Denton ... 29 M6
Derbyshire Hill ... 22 D7
Didsbury ... 40 C5
Disley ... 58 F9
Ditton ... 45 H8
Doddleston ... 160 D2
Doe Green ... 46 C4
Dones Green ... 86 D6
Dorrington ... 218 G6
Duckington ... 192 B3
Duddon ... 145 N4
Duddon Common ... 146 A3
Dudlows Green ... 64 C1
Dunham-On-The-Hill ... 104 E6
Dunham Town ... 52 B3
Dunham Woodhouses ... 51 P5
Dunkirk ... 102 A5
Dunkirk ... 201 K1
Dutton ... 85 L1
Earlestown ... 23 K6
East Didsbury ... 40 E7
Eaton ... 156 A6
Eaton ... 156 A2
Ebnal ... 192 B9
Eccleston ... 142 C9
Edge Green ... 192 A4
Edgeley ... 41 K9
Egerton Green ... 193 H2
Ellesmere Port ... 8 B2
Elton ... 82 A9
Elton Green ... 104 A2
Elworth ... 171 J4
Englesea brook ... 199 M3
Ettiley Heath ... 153 J4
Faddiley ... 182 A9
Fairfield ... 28 G2
Fanshowe ... 115 L8
Farndon ... 177 H6
Farnworth ... 45 N4
Farnhead ... 34 B6
Feidy ... 88 C1
Fiddler's Ferry ... 46 G6
Finney Green ... 71 L4
Fivecrosses ... 84 A8
Flash ... 139 L8
Foggbrook ... 42 E9
Fourlanes End ... 173 H5
Fowley Common ... 26 B2
Foxley ... 187 P9
Foxwist Green ... 127 P5
Frandley ... 87 J2
Frodsham ... 83 B6
Fullers Moor ... 179 K7
Fulshaw Park ... 71 J5
Furness Vale ... 75 N3
Gallantry Bank ... 179 P8
Gates Heath ... 163 N4
Gatley ... 55 J5
Gauntons Bank ... 206 C2
Gawsworth ... 145 J5
Gee Cross ... 43 K1
Gemini ... 32 G5
Gibb Hill ... 87 M4
Gillbent ... 55 P9
Gillow Heath ... 175 J7
Ginclough ... 73 P5
Glazebrook ... 35 P2
Glazebury ... 25 B3
Golborne ... 24 D2
Goostrey ... 132 A2
Gorse Covert ... 34 E1
Gorstage ... 108 D6
Gorstella ... 141 L9
Gorstyhill ... 199 K5
Gorton ... 28 C5
Gosland Green ... 166 G8
Gradeley Green ... 195 H2
Grange ... 62 A7
Grappenhall ... 64 D2
Gravel ... 150 B2
Gravenhunger Moss ... 219 J3
Great Barrow ... 123 L5
Great Budworth ... 88 B6
Great Moor ... 57 J1

Great Sankey ... 47 M1
Great Sutton ... 79 P8
Great Warford ... 92 D6
Greave ... 43 J4
Greendale ... 94 C6
Greenlooms ... 144 F6
Gresty Green ... 185 K8
Grindley Brook ... 212 G2
Grosvenor Park ... 184 F1
Guilden Sutton ... 122 G6
Gurnett ... 117 M8
Hack Green ... 208 F1
Hague Bar ... 59 K7
Hale ... 53 K5
Hale ... 64 D4
Hale Bank ... 61 L2
Halebarns ... 53 P7
Hall Green ... 188 C3
Hall Green ... 212 D4
Hallowsgate ... 124 C7
Halmer End ... 200 F8
Halton ... 62 D6
Halton Brook ... 62 B5
Halton View ... 46 A6
Hampton Green ... 192 G8
Hampton Heath ... 192 D8
Handbridge ... 142 C5
Handforth ... 71 L2
Hand Green ... 165 N3
Handley ... 163 L9
Hankelow ... 209 K7
Hapsford ... 104 E3
Harden Park ... 93 K2
Hardings Wood ... 188 G6
Hargrave ... 144 C9
Harriseahead ... 189 M3
Hartford ... 108 G8
Hartfordbeach ... 109 H8
Hatherton ... 209 P2
Hatton ... 64 B5
Hatton Heath ... 144 A9
Haughton Green ... 29 N9
Haughton Moss ... 181 L2
Havannah ... 155 P4
Hawarden ... 140 B2
Hawk Green ... 58 C4
Haydock ... 23 H5
Haymoor Green ... 197 M5
Hazel Grove ... 57 N6
Heald Green ... 55 J6
Heath ... 61 K2
Heatley ... 51 K2
Heaton ... 158 B8
Heaton Chapel ... 41 J4
Heaton Mersey ... 40 F5
Heaton Norris ... 16 A2
Hebden Green ... 149 H5
Helsby ... 105 J1
Henbury ... 116 B4
Hermitage Green ... 24 D9
Hetherson Green ... 193 H7
Higher Burwardsley ... 179 P9
Higher Disley ... 59 H1
Higherfence ... 117 M8
Higher Hurdsfield ... 117 M2
Higher Marston ... 88 C8
Higher Poynton ... 73 P4
Higher Runcorn ... 14 E5
Higher Shurlach ... 110 E7
Higher Walton ... 48 A8
Higher Whitley ... 64 C9
Higher Wincham ... 88 F8
Higher Wych ... 212 C1
High Lane ... 58 C3
Highlane ... 135 K4
High Legh ... 67 H3
Hightown ... 156 A8
Hillcliffe ... 48 E8
Hinderton ... 77 N4
Hob Hill ... 191 K5
Hockley ... 73 N3
Hodgehill ... 133 P3
Hollinfare ... 35 M4
Hollin Green ... 195 H1
Hollins ... 188 F8
Hollins Green ... 43 K6
Hollinsgreen ... 152 A6
Hollowmoor Heath ... 123 P5
Hollyhurst ... 206 D8
Holmes Chapel ... 131 L9
Holt ... 176 F8
Honley Green ... 44 D9
Hoofield ... 145 N6
Hoo Green ... 67 L4
Hoole ... 122 D4
Hoole Bank ... 122 D4
Hooley Hill ... 29 L2
Hooton ... 79 K5
Hope Green ... 83 M5
Horton Green ... 191 J7
Hough ... 93 M4
Hough ... 198 G5
Hough Green ... 44 G6
Houghton Green ... 33 P5
Howbeck Bank ... 208 A7
Howley ... 19 J6
Hulme ... 33 J4
Hulme Walfield ... 155 K5
Huntington ... 143 H4
Hurdsfield ... 9 J1
Huxley ... 164 F2
Illidge Green ... 153 M7
Ince ... 81 H8
Ireland's Cross ... 218 B5
Irlam ... 27 M8
Jodrell Bank ... 132 C2
Keckwick ... 63 K2

Kelsall ... 125 H7
Kenyon ... 25 J5
Kerridge ... 95 N1
Kerridge-end ... 118 A2
Kettleshulme ... 97 J1
Key Green ... 156 E6
Kidnal ... 191 M8
Kingsgrove ... 188 E6
Kingsley ... 107 H2
Kingston ... 29 P6
Kingsway ... 21 G2
Kingswood ... 32 D5
Kinsey Heath ... 217 J3
Kitt's Moss ... 56 C5
Knighton ... 219 H8
Knolls Green ... 92 A1
Knotbury ... 139 J6
Knowl Bank ... 200 B8
Knutsford ... 90 G4
Lacey Green ... 71 K5
Lach Dennis ... 111 K7
Lache ... 142 A5
Laffak ... 22 C2
Lane Ends ... 75 J2
Lane Ends ... 170 D6
Lane Head ... 25 H9
Langley ... 138 A3
Larden Green ... 194 F3
Latchford ... 48 C4
Latchford ... 160 E8
Lawton-gate ... 188 B4
Lawton Heath ... 188 A3
Lawton Heath End ... 187 P2
Lea by Backford ... 102 C3
Lea Forge ... 198 D9
Lea Green ... 30 E3
Lea Green ... 169 H1
Ledsham ... 101 K2
Leftwich ... 129 P7
Levenshulme ... 28 C9
Ley Hey Park ... 43 K9
Lightwood Green ... 216 B3
Lindow End ... 92 C5
Lingley Green ... 31 P9
Lingley Mere ... 32 A8
Little Barrow ... 123 M4
Little Bollington ... 52 A5
Little Budworth ... 148 B3
Little Heath ... 143 N2
Little Heath ... 209 H9
Little Leigh ... 86 E8
Little Moor ... 57 K2
Little Neston ... 77 K7
Littler ... 128 A9
Little Stanney ... 102 G3
Little Sutton ... 79 L7
Littleton ... 143 M1
Little Town ... 145 K7
Locking Stumps ... 34 C4
Longbarn ... 34 D7
Longford ... 33 L7
Long Green ... 123 N2
Longmoss ... 116 C4
Lostock Gralam ... 110 G2
Lostock Green ... 111 H4
Lowcross Hill ... 191 L4
Lower Bredbury ... 42 B8
Lower Bunbury ... 166 C9
Lower Carden ... 191 K1
Lower Heath ... 155 M4
Lower House ... 20 D3
Lowerhouse ... 95 L5
Lower Kinnerton ... 140 G9
Lower Peover ... 112 C3
Lower Pexhill ... 116 A8
Lower Stretton ... 64 E6
Lower Threapwood ... 202 G8
Lower Walton ... 48 C7
Lower Whitley ... 86 F2
Lower Withington ... 133 J3
Lower Wych ... 203 M4
Low Leighton ... 59 P7
Lowton ... 24 F5
Lowton Common ... 25 J1
Lowton Heath ... 24 E3
Lowton St Mary's ... 24 ...
Lugsdale ... 46 A8
Lunts Heath ... 45 N4
Thelwall ... 49 N4
Lyme Green ... 136 C1
Lymm ... 50 E4
Macclesfield ... 9 J1
Macclesfield Forest ... 118 G3
Makin's Bank ... 172 A6
Malpas ... 204 B3
Manley ... 105 N8
Manley Common ... 106 A7
Manor Park ... 150 G2
Marbury ... 206 A6
Marley Green ... 206 C6
Marple ... 58 C1
Marple Bridge ... 43 N6
Marpleridge ... 58 A2
Marshall's Cross ... 30 G3
Marshfield Bank ... 184 C4
Marsh Green ... 83 K5
Marsh Green ... 175 L7
The Marsh ... 155 L9
Marston ... 110 C1
Marthall ... 92 A9
Martinscroft ... 35 H4
Martin's Moss ... 173 J3
Marton ... 134 D7
Marton Green ... 127 N7
Maw Green ... 185 N1
Meadowbank ... 128 E6
Mellor ... 59 J1
Mere ... 67 H7
Mere Heath ... 128 G2
Merelake ... 188 C9
Mickle Trafford ... 122 F3
Middlewich ... 151 N1
Middlewood ... 75 P3
Midway ... 73 K9

Miles Green	201	H7
Milners Heath	144	C8
Milton Green	163	K7
Mobberley	91	M2
Mollington	120	G2
Monk's Heath	115	K3
Moore	47	L9
Moorend	59	L1
Moorside	77	J6
The Moor	140	C1
Morley	77	P8
Morley Green	70	D5
Moss Bank	46	B7
Mossbrow	36	C9
Moss End	88	C3
Moss Houses	135	N1
Moss Lane	117	H8
Mossley	75	J2
Moss Nook	22	D8
Moss Nook	55	H7
Moston	121	N2
Moston Green	170	G2
Mottram St Andrew	94	A4
Mouldsworth	105	N9
Moulton	128	G4
Mount Pleasant	189	K2
Mow Cop	189	L1
Murdishaw	63	J7
Nantwich	10	E5
Ness	77	P8
Nessholt	77	L9
Neston	77	K6
Nether Alderley	93	J7
Netherton	83	M7
Newall Green	23	K5
New Boston	54	C3
Newchapel	189	N6
Newchurch Common	127	M4
Newhall	207	L7
New Lane End	25	J7
New Mills	59	M7
New Pale	106	A6
Newsbank	154	C1
Newton	106	C2
Newton	121	P6
Newton	164	D5
Newton	164	D8
Newtonia	151	H2
Newton-Le-Willows	75	P1
Newton Park	24	B7
Newton Wood	29	N3
Newtown	75	M1
Newtown	84	B4
Newtown	207	P2
New Woodhouses	215	H4
Nick i'th' Hill	175	H5
No Mans Heath	204	F1
Noonsun	92	A4
Norbury	206	A3
Norbury Common	205	P1
Norbury Moor	57	L6
Norcott Brook	64	E8
Norley	107	K6
Northenden	39	N8
Northern Moor	39	J7
North Reddish	28	E8
North Rode	135	M9
Northwich	13	G6
Norton	62	G5
Nova Scotia	127	M6
Nut Grove	30	B2
Oakenholt	98	E9
Oakgrove	136	B4
Oakhanger	187	H7
Oakmere	126	E4
Oakwood	34	F5
Occlestone Green	151	H8
Offerton	42	D9
Offerton Green	57	N1

Old Boston	23	M2
Oldcastle Heath	203	M5
Oldfield Brow	52	F2
Old Warren	140	C6
Old Woodhouses	214	G3
Ollerton	91	J7
Onneley	219	L3
Openshaw	28	C1
Orford	33	N7
Oscroft	124	E9
Oughtrington	50	F3
Over Knutsford	50	G5
Over Peover	113	L4
Overpool	80	B6
Over Tabley	67	N9
Overton	83	P6
Paddington	34	C8
Paddockhill	92	C1
Padgate	34	A7
Painters Green	212	D7
Palacefields	62	D9
Park End	200	D3
Parkgate	77	J4
Parkgate	113	M4
Parr	22	C7
Partington	36	E6
Peasley Cross	22	A8
Peckforton	180	D3
Peel Hall	55	H5
Penketh	47	N5
Peover Heath	113	P5
Pewterspear	65	H3
Pickmere	88	F6
Picton	103	L9
Pinsley Green	206	G4
Pipe Gate	219	J7
Piper's Ash	122	D7
Plemstall	123	J2
Plumley	89	M9
Pocket Nook	25	L1
Polfold	175	N5
Portwood	41	P5
Pott Shrigley	96	B2
Poulton	161	K7
Pownall Park	71	H6
Poynton	73	M2
Prestbury	94	C7
Preston Brook	63	K9
Preston on the Hill	63	L8
Puddinglake	130	F3
Puddington	100	C5
Pulford	160	F7
Quarrybank	146	G3
Queen's Park	3	B6
Quoisley	205	N6
Raby	78	A1
Radmore Green	182	A4
Radway Green	187	K2
Rainhill	30	C5
Rainhill Stoops	30	D6
Rainow	96	B8
Rainowlow	96	B6
Ravenshall	211	M2
Ravensmoor	195	N5
Rease Heath	183	L6
Redbrook	212	E6
Red Bull	188	D5
Reddish	50	G2
Reddish	28	D8
Red Street	201	P4
Rhuddall Heath	147	J9
Risley	34	F2
Rixton	35	N6
Robin Hill	175	P9
Roche Grange	159	K7
Rocksavage	61	P9
Rodeheath	135	J8
Rode Heath	173	J9
Romiley	43	J6

The Rookery	189	L5
Rosehill	52	G6
Rostherne	68	C3
Roundthorn	54	A2
Row-of-Trees	92	E2
Rowton	143	P5
Rowton Moor	143	P4
Royal's Green	215	P3
Rudheath	110	D6
Rudheath Woods	131	J1
Ruloe	107	N5
Runcorn	15	H5
Rushgreen	50	D7
Rushton	147	P5
Rushton Spencer	157	N9
Saighton	143	P9
Sale	38	B5
Salterswall	128	B8
Saltney	141	N5
Sandbach	171	M3
Sandbach Heath	172	A3
Sandiway	108	D9
Sandlow Green	153	L1
Sankey Bridges	47	N3
Saughall	120	E2
Scholar Green	188	F2
School Green	149	K5
Sealand	120	B5
Sharston	55	H2
Shavington	198	B5
Shaw Heath	41	M9
Shaw Heath	91	H2
Shell Green	46	C5
Shocklach	190	E8
Shocklach Green	190	C8
Shotwick	100	E8
Shraleybrook	200	D7
Siddington	115	J9
Siddington Heath	134	A2
Sidway	219	P9
Simm's Cross	21	K3
Sinderland Green	37	J7
Skelhorn Green	73	K6
Slaughter Hill	186	B5
Smallwood	173	J4
Smethwick Green	154	B7
Smiths Green	133	K1
Smith's Green	186	G9
Smithy Green	56	B7
Smithy Green	112	C2
Snow Hill	10	A4
Somerford	154	B3
Sound	207	P1
Sound Heath	207	N2
Southgate	62	C7
South Reddish	41	M3
Spen Green	173	L3
Sproston Green	131	J9
Spurstow	181	H2
Stamford Bridge	123	K7
Stanley Green	71	N1
Stanlow	81	K8
Stapeley	197	L7
Statham	50	D3
Stepping Hill	57	K3
Stoak	103	H5
Stockport	42	B3
Stockton Heath	48	E6
Stoneley Green	195	N5
Stretton	64	G4
Stretton	190	G1
Strines	58	G6
Stud Green	151	H2
Styal	71	H2
Sutton	31	K1
Sutton Green	101	M1
Sutton Heath	30	D2
Sutton Lane Ends	136	E1
Sutton Leach	31	K3

Sutton Manor	30	F6
Sutton Weaver	84	F2
Swanbach	216	F4
Swan Green	112	B5
Swanwick Green	205	P2
Swettenham	133	H8
Sworton Heath	66	F1
Sydney	185	N3
Tabley Hill	90	B2
Talke	188	E9
Talke Pits	201	P2
Tallarn Green	202	C9
Tarbock Green	44	C3
Tarporley	147	H8
Tarvin	124	B8
Tarvin Sands	124	B8
Tattenhall	164	A8
Tatton Dale	68	B5
Taxal	97	N1
Thorns Green	69	N1
Thornton-le-Moors	103	M3
Threapwood	202	F7
Thurlwood	173	H9
Tilston	191	J4
Tilstone Bank	166	B5
Tilstone Fearnall	166	B3
Timbersbrook	156	D8
Timperley	38	D9
Tirley Garth	146	F1
Tiverton	165	P4
Torkington	57	P5
Tower Hill	96	A3
Town End	45	J1
Town Fields	149	M3
Town of Lowton	24	C4
Town Park	62	F5
Turnhurst	189	P8
Twemlow Green	132	E6
Twiss Green	25	N4
Two Mills	101	J5
Tytherington	95	K9
Upper Threapwood	202	D6
Upton	45	H5
Upton	121	N5
Upton Heath	122	A3
Upton Rocks	45	L4
Utkinton	146	E3
The Valley	184	G4
Vicarscross	122	F8
Vulcan Village	23	N9
Wades Green	168	G4
Wain Lee	189	P4
Walgherton	197	P9
Walker Barn	118	D4
Walley's Green	169	N2
Warburton	35	P8
Warburton Green	53	N9
Wardle	182	D1
Wardle Bank	167	L8
Wardsend	73	N5
Wargrave	23	N8
Warmingham	170	D2
Warren	135	M2
Warren Mountain	140	B7
Warrington	18	B3
Waverton	144	B6
Wavertree	213	P7
Way's Green	150	N2
Weaverham	109	H4
Weetwood Common	146	A1
Well Green	53	P4
Wells Green	184	F9
Werneth	42	C4
Werneth Low	43	L3
Wervin	103	J8
West Bank	61	M1
Westbrook	32	D7
West Didsbury	39	P3
West Heath	155	H7

Weston	61	M7
Weston	116	F5
Weston	199	N2
Weston Point	61	K6
Westy	49	H2
Wettenhall	168	A2
Wettenhall Green	167	P3
Whaley Bridge	75	N7
Wharton	128	G8
Wharton Green	129	J7
Wheelock	171	L7
Wheelock Heath	171	N9
Whirley Grove	116	E1
Whisterfield	114	G9
Whitby	6	D7
Whitbyheath	102	B5
Whitchurch	213	L6
Whitegate	128	B4
Whitehill	189	L6
Whitley Green	95	L3
Whitemore	175	L3
Whitewell	212	B6
Whitley Reed	65	L6
Widnes	20	L4
Wildboarclough	138	A5
Widerspool	48	E5
Wilkesley	216	A7
Willaston	78	F5
Willington Corner	125	K9
Willow Green	86	D8
Wilmslow	71	K8
Wimbolds Park	1	M7
Wimboldsley	150	G6
Wimbolds Trafford	103	P6
Wincham	110	D1
Wincle	158	D2
Windle	30	A1
Windle Hill	77	P8
Windlehurst	58	C6
Windmill Hill	62	G4
Windyharbour	133	M2
Winnington	12	A2
Winsford	128	E9
Winterley	186	D1
Winwick	33	L1
Winwick Quay	33	L4
Wirswall	205	M9
Wistaston	184	D7
Wistaston Green	184	D6
Withington	40	D2
Withington Green	114	A9
Wolverham	7	F7
Woodbank	101	J6
Woodend	58	G7
Woodford	72	D4
Woodhey Green	194	E2
Woodhouse Green	157	J8
Woodhouse Park	54	E6
Woodhouses	37	N6
Woodhouses	83	L9
Woodlane	201	K6
Wood Lanes	73	N6
Woodley	43	H5
Woodside	125	H2
Woodside	168	B3
Woods Moor	57	H4
Woodworth Green	166	E9
Woolstanwood	184	E4
Woolston	34	D9
Woore	219	H4
Worleston	183	P2
Wornish Nook	155	J1
Worthenbury	202	A5
Wrenbury	207	J2
Wright's Green	65	J1
Wrinehill	211	M3
Wybunbury	197	P7
Wythenshawe	54	D4

USING THE STREET INDEX

Street names are listed alphabetically. Each street name is followed by its postal town or area locality, the Postcode District, the page number, and the reference to the square in which the name is found.

Standard index entries are shown as follows:

Aarons Dr ALS/KID ST7 ....201 J5

Street names and selected addresses not shown on the map due to scale restrictions are shown in the index with an asterisk:

Abbeyfield Sq OP/CLY M11 * 28 B1

GENERAL ABBREVIATIONS

ACC	ACCESS	CHYD	CHURCHYARD	CTS	COURTS	FK	FORK	HGR	HIGHER
ALY	ALLEY	CIR	CIRCLE	CTYD	COURTYARD	FLD	FIELD	HL	HILL
AP	APPROACH	CIRC	CIRCUS	CUTT	CUTTINGS	FLDS	FIELDS	HLS	HILLS
AR	ARCADE	CL	CLOSE	CV	COVE	FLS	FALLS	HO	HOUSE
ASS	ASSOCIATION	CLFS	CLIFFS	CYN	CANYON	FLS	FLATS	HOL	HOLLOW
AV	AVENUE	CMP	CAMP	DEPT	DEPARTMENT	FM	FARM	HOSP	HOSPITAL
BCH	BEACH	CNR	CORNER	DL	DALE	FT	FORT	HRB	HARBOUR
BLDS	BUILDINGS	CO	COUNTY	DM	DAM	FWY	FREEWAY	HTH	HEATH
BND	BEND	COLL	COLLEGE	DR	DRIVE	FY	FERRY	HTS	HEIGHTS
BNK	BANK	COM	COMMON	DRO	DROVE	GA	GATE	HVN	HAVEN
BR	BRIDGE	COMM	COMMISSION	DRY	DRIVEWAY	GAL	GALLERY	HWY	HIGHWAY
BRK	BROOK	CON	CONVENT	DWGS	DWELLINGS	GDN	GARDEN	IMP	IMPERIAL
BTM	BOTTOM	COT	COTTAGE	E	EAST	GDNS	GARDENS	IN	INLET
BUS	BUSINESS	COTS	COTTAGES	EMB	EMBANKMENT	GLD	GLADE	IND EST	INDUSTRIAL ESTATE
BVD	BOULEVARD	CP	CAPE	EMBY	EMBASSY	GLN	GLEN	INF	INFIRMARY
BY	BYPASS	CPS	COPSE	ESP	ESPLANADE	GN	GREEN	INFO	INFORMATION
CATH	CATHEDRAL	CR	CREEK	EST	ESTATE	GND	GROUND	INT	INTERCHANGE
CEM	CEMETERY	CREM	CREMATORIUM	EX	EXCHANGE	GRA	GRANGE	IS	ISLAND
CEN	CENTRE	CRS	CRESCENT	EXPY	EXPRESSWAY	GRG	GARAGE	JCT	JUNCTION
CFT	CROFT	CSWY	CAUSEWAY	EXT	EXTENSION	GT	GREAT	JTY	JETTY
CH	CHURCH	CT	COURT	F/O	FLYOVER	GTWY	GATEWAY	KG	KING
CHA	CHASE	CTRL	CENTRAL	FC	FOOTBALL CLUB	GV	GROVE	KNL	KNOLL

L....LAKE	MTS....MOUNTAINS	PREC....PRECINCT	SCH....SCHOOL	TRL....TRAIL
LA....LANE	MUS....MUSEUM	PREP....PREPARATORY	SE....SOUTH EAST	TWR....TOWER
LDG....LODGE	MWY....MOTORWAY	PRIM....PRIMARY	SER....SERVICE AREA	U/P....UNDERPASS
LGT....LIGHT	N....NORTH	PROM....PROMENADE	SH....SHORE	UNI....UNIVERSITY
LK....LOCK	NE....NORTH EAST	PRS....PRINCESS	SHOP....SHOPPING	UPR....UPPER
LKS....LAKES	NW....NORTH WEST	PT....PORT	SKWY....SKYWAY	V....VALE
LNDG....LANDING	O/P....OVERPASS	PTH....PATH	SMT....SUMMIT	VA....VALLEY
LTL....LITTLE	OFF....OFFICE	PZ....PIAZZA	SOC....SOCIETY	VIAD....VIADUCT
LWR....LOWER	ORCH....ORCHARD	QD....QUADRANT	SP....SPUR	VIL....VILLA
MAG....MAGISTRATE	OV....OVAL	QU....QUEEN	SPR....SPRING	VIS....VISTA
MAN....MANSIONS	PAL....PALACE	QY....QUAY	SQ....SQUARE	VLG....VILLAGE
MD....MEAD	PAS....PASSAGE	R....RIVER	ST....STREET	VLS....VILLAS
MDW....MEADOWS	PAV....PAVILION	RBT....ROUNDABOUT	STN....STATION	VW....VIEW
MEM....MEMORIAL	PDE....PARADE	REP....REPUBLIC	STR....STREAM	W....WEST
MKT....MARKET	PH....PUBLIC HOUSE	RES....RESERVOIR	STRD....STRAND	WD....WOOD
MKTS....MARKETS	PK....PARK	RFC....RUGBY FOOTBALL CLUB	SW....SOUTH WEST	WHF....WHARF
ML....MALL	PKWY....PARKWAY	RI....RISE	TDG....TRADING	WK....WALK
MLL....MILL	PL....PLACE	RMP....RAMP	TER....TERRACE	WKS....WALKS
MNR....MANOR	PLN....PLAIN	RW....ROW	THWY....THROUGHWAY	WLS....WELLS
MS....MEWS	PLNS....PLAINS	S....SOUTH	TNL....TUNNEL	WY....WAY
MSN....MISSION	PLZ....PLAZA		TOLL....TOLLWAY	YD....YARD
MT....MOUNT	POL....POLICE STATION		TPK....TURNPIKE	YHA....YOUTH HOSTEL
MTN....MOUNTAIN	PR....PRINCE		TR....TRACK	

POSTCODE TOWNS AND AREA ABBREVIATIONS

AIMK....Ashton-in-Makerfield
ALS/KID....Alsager/Kidsgrove
ALT....Altrincham
AUD/MAD/W....Audlem/Madeley/Woore
AULW....Ashton-under-Lyne west
BEB....Bebington
BIDD....Biddulph
BNG/LEV....Burnage/Levenshulme
BRAM/HZG....Bramhall/Hazel Grove
BRUN/LGST....Brunswick/Longsight
BURS/TUN....Burslem/Tunstall
BUX....Buxton
CCHDY....Chorlton-cum-Hardy
CH/BCN....Chester/Blacon
CHD/CHDH....Cheadle (Gtr. Man)/Cheadle Hulme
CHF/WBR....Chapel-en-le-Frith/Whaley Bridge
CHNE....Chester northeast
CHSE....Chester southeast
CHSW/BR....Chester southwest/Broughton
CONG....Congleton

CQ....Connah's Quay
CW/HAS....Crewe/Haslington
CW/SHV....Crewe/Shavington
DID/WITH....Didsbury/Withington
DROY....Droylsden
DTN/ASHW....Denton/Audenshaw
DUK....Dukinfield
ECC....Eccles
ECCL....Eccleston
EDGY/DAV....Edgeley/Davenport
EP....Ellesmere Port
FLINT....Flint
FROD/HEL....Frodsham/Helsby
GLSP....Glossop
GOL/RIS/CUL....Golborne/Risley/Culcheth
GTN....Gorton
GTS/LS....Great Sutton/Little Sutton
HALE/TIMP....Hale/Timperley
HES....Heswall
HLWD....Halewood
HOLMCH....Holmes Chapel
HTNM....Heaton Moor
HYDE....Hyde

IRL....Irlam
KNUT....Knutsford
LEEK....Leek
LEIGH....Leigh
LYMM....Lymm
MALPAS....Malpas
MANAIR....Manchester Airport
MCFLDN....Macclesfield north
MCFLDS....Macclesfield south
MKTDR....Market Drayton
MPL/ROM....Marple/Romiley
MWCH....Middlewich
NANT....Nantwich
NEWLW....Newton-le-Willows
NEWUL....Newcastle-under-Lyme
NM/HAY....New Mills/Hayfield
NSTN....Neston
NTHLY....Netherley
NTHM/RTH....Northern Moor/Roundthorn
NWCHE....Northwich east
NWCHW....Northwich west
OFTN....Offerton
OP/CLY....Openshaw/Clayton

PART....Partington
POY/DIS....Poynton/Disley
PR/KW....Prescot/Knowsley
PS/BROM....Port Sunlight/Bromborough
RAIN/WH....Rainhill/Whiston
RDSH....Reddish
RNFD/HAY....Rainford/Haydock
RUNC....Runcorn
RUSH/FAL....Rusholme/Fallowfield
SALE....Sale
SBCH....Sandbach
SPK/HALE....Speke/Hale
STHEL....St Helens
STKP....Stockport
STRET....Stretford
TPLY/KEL....Tarporley/Kelsall
TYLD....Tyldesley
URM....Urmston
WALK....Walkden
WARR....Warrington
WARRN/WOL....Warrington north/Woolston
WARRS....Warrington south

WARRW/BUR....Warrington west/Burtonwood
WDN....Widnes
WGTN/LGST....West Gorton/Longsight
WHTCH....Whitchurch
WILM/AE....Wilmslow/Alderley Edge
WRX/GR/LL....Wrexham/Gresford/Llay
WRXS/E....Wrexham south & east
WSFD....Winsford
WYTH/NTH....Wythenshawe/Northenden

Index - streets

3rd - Alb

3rd Av CONG CW12....155 K6

A

Aarons Dr ALS/KID ST7....201 J5
Abberton Rd DID/WITH M20....40 B2
Abbey CI ALT WA14....52 E6
 GOL/RIS/CU WA3....25 J9
 NWCHW CW8....128 B4
 WDN WA8....45 J7
 WSFD CW7....149 M4
Abbeydale CI CW/SHV CW2....199 H5
Abbey Flds CW/SHV CW2....184 D8
Abbeyfield Sq OP/CLY M11 *....28 B1
Abbey Gn CH/BCN CH1....2 D3
Abbey Gv STKP SK1....42 A8
Abbey Hey RUNC WA7....62 G6
Abbey Hey La GTN M18....28 E5
 NWCHW CW8....109 K7
Abbey La NWCHW CW8....126 B6
Abbey PI CW/HAS CW1....185 K2
Abbey Rd CHD/CHDH SK8....56 A2
 GOL/RIS/CU WA3....117 H2
 MCFLDN SK10....117 H2
 RNFD/HAY WA11....23 J2
 SALE M33....38 D2
 WDN WA8....171 K3
Abbey Sq CH/BCN CH1....2 E3
Abbey St CH/BCN CH1....2 E3
Abbey Wy NWCHW CW8....109 K8
 RNFD/HAY WA11 *....22 F1
Abbeyway North
 RNFD/HAY WA11....23 L2
Abbeyway South
 RNFD/HAY WA11....23 L3
Abbeywood Av GTN M18 *....28 E5
Abbotsbury CI CW/SHV CW2....185 H8
 POY/DIS SK12....73 K1
Abbots CI MCFLDN SK10....117 H2
 SALE M33....38 B8
Abbot's Dr CW/HAS CW1....121 M7
Abbotsfield CI WARRS WA4....48 C9
Abbotsfield Rd WARR WA5....31 K3
Abbotsford Gv ALT WA14....38 B8
Ackers La BRAM/HZG SK7....121 M8
Abbots Hall Av STHEL WA9....31 J5
Abbots Knoll CH/BCN CH1....121 M7
Abbotsleigh Dr BRAM/HZG SK7....56 B8
Abbots Mere CI NWCHW CW8 *....127 J1
Abbots Ms EP CH65....6 D2
Abbot's Nook CHNE CH2....121 L0
Abbots Pk CH/BCN CH1....121 M7
Abbots Wy NSTN CH64....77 K4
 NWCHW CW8....109 K8

Abbotts CI CHSE CH3....144 B5
 CONG CW12....175 J1
 RUNC WA7....15 F7
Abbotts Rd CHSE CH3....144 B5
Abbotts Wy WSFD CW7....128 B9
Aber Av OFTN SK2....57 J3
Abercrombie Ct SALE M33....38 G3
Aberdare Ct
 WARRW/BUR WA5....33 H7
Aberdaron Dr CH/BCN CH1....121 H8
Aberdeen Crs EDGY/DAV SK3....16 C7
Aberdeen Gv EDGY/DAV SK3....16 D6
Aberdeen Wk MCFLDN SK10....116 F2
Aberfeldy CI HOLMCH CW4....131 N9
Aberford Rd NTHM/RTH M23....54 C2
Abergele St OFTN SK2....57 F1
Aber Las FLINT CH6....98 B8
Abingdon Av WARR WA1....34 F9
Abingdon St MCFLDN SK10....116 C4
Abingdon Crs CHSW/BR CH4....142 B4
Abingdon Gv HLWD L26....44 A6
Abingdon Rd BRAM/HZG SK7....56 E5
 RDSH SK5....41 N1
Abington CI CW/HAS CW1....185 H2
Abington Rd SALE M33....38 F5
Abstone CI WARR WA1....34 C9
Acacia Av CHD/CHDH SK8....56 A5
 DTN/ASHW M34....29 N6
 HALE/TIMP WA15....53 K4
 KNUT WA16....90 C4
 WARR WA1....34 E8
 WDN WA8....45 P4
 WILM/AE SK9....71 H9
Acacia CI CHNE CH2....104 C1
Acacia Crs CW/HAS CW1....185 L2
Acacia Dr GTS/LS CH66....102 B5
 HALE/TIMP WA15....53 K4
 KNUT WA16....90 C4
 WDN WA8....54 B8
 SBCH CW11 *....171 K2
Acacia Gdns ALS/KID ST7....189 L5
Acacia Gv RDSH SK5....41 N4
 RUNC WA7....15 K7
Acacia St NEWLW WA12....23 K5
Academy St WARR WA1....18 E6
Academy Wy WARR WA1....18 D7
Acer Av CW/HAS CW1....185 L1
Acheson St GTN M18....28 D4
Achilles Av WARRN/WOL WA2....33 L6
Ackerley CI WARRN/WOL WA2....34 A5
Ackers La WARRS WA4....48 C6
Ackers Rd WARRS WA4....48 C6
Ack La East BRAM/HZG SK7....56 D9
Ack La West CHD/CHDH SK8....56 B8
Ackroyd Av GTN M18....28 G3
Ackroyd St OP/CLY M11....28 G3
Ackworth Dr NTHM/RTH M23....54 C1
Acorn Av CHD/CHDH SK8....55 N1
Acorn Bank CI CW/SHV CW2....185 H9

Acorn CI NWCHW CW8....127 J1
 STHEL WA9 *....31 H4
 WSFD CW7....150 A2
Acorn Dr EP CH65....102 D3
Acorn St NEWLW WA12....23 N6
The Acreage HOLMCH CW4....132 B2
 TPLY/KEL CW6....166 B9
Acrefield SALE M33....38 D5
Acrefield Av HTNM SK4....41 H4
Acrefield Rd WDN WA8....45 H6
Acre Gn HLWD L26....44 A9
Acre La CHD/CHDH SK8....56 B9
Acre Rd GTS/LS CH66....79 P8
Acres Ct WYTH/NTH M22....54 F3
Acres Crs FROD/HEL WA6....106 F2
Acresfield Rd HALE/TIMP WA15....38 D8
Acres La CHNE CH2....122 B3
Acres Nook Rd BURS/TUN ST6....189 J9
Acres Rd CHD/CHDH SK8 *....55 J2
Acre St DTN/ASHW M34....29 L6
 MPL/ROM SK6....61 L8
Acreville Gv GOL/RIS/CU WA3....26 C2
Acton Av WARRS WA4....64 F3
Acton CI NWCHW CW8....108 B1
Acton La NWCHW CW8....108 B1
 WARRW/BUR WA5....32 G2
Acton Wy ALS/KID ST7....187 P2
 GTS/LS CH66....79 N9
Adam CI CHD/CHDH SK8....56 B3
 GTS/LS CH66....79 P9
Adams CI WARRS WA4....49 K5
Adams CI NEWLW WA12....23 F7
 POY/DIS SK12....73 L4
Adams HI KNUT WA16....90 E4
Adamson Ct WARRS WA4....49 K5
Adamson Gdns DID/WITH M20....40 A5
Adamson St WARRS WA4....49 K5
 St WARRN/WOL WA2....19 F1
Adaston Av PS/BROM CH62....79 F1
Ada St STHEL WA9....22 A8
Adcroft St STKP SK1....41 N9
Adder HI CHSE CH5....143 K5
Adderley CI RUNC WA7....15 J5
Addingham Av WDN WA8....45 J8
Addison CI CW/HAS CW1....184 F8
Addison Rd HALE/TIMP WA15....53 J5
 PART M31....37 J2
Addison Sq WDN WA8....45 N6
Adelaide Rd BRAM/HZG SK7....56 C6
Adelaide Rd BRAM/HZG SK7....120 C7
 CH/BCN CH1....16 B7
 EDGY/DAV SK3....16 B7
Adelaide St CW/HAS CW1 *....4 E7
 MCFLDN SK10 *....9 G2
 GTS/LS CH66....101 P1
Adela Rd RUNC WA7....14 C3
Adey Rd LYMM WA13....50 C2
Adfalent La NSTN CH64....76 E6
Adlington CI HALE/TIMP WA15....53 P1
 POY/DIS SK12....73 M4

Adlington Ct GOL/RIS/CU WA3....34 G3
Adlington Dr NWCHE CW9....110 A7
 SBCH CW11....171 P2
Adlington Pk MCFLDN SK10....73 J5
Adlington Rd CW/SHV CW2....184 F5
 RUNC WA7....63 H4
 WILM/AE SK9....71 N7
Adlington St MCFLDS SK11....3 J3
Adlington Wk STKP SK1....17 F4
Admirals Rd GOL/RIS/CU WA3....34 G5
Admiral St DID/WITH M20....40 D5
Adria Rd DID/WITH M20....40 D5
Adshall Rd CHD/CHDH SK8....56 A2
Adshead CI WYTH/NTH M22....54 D4
Adshead Ct MCFLDN SK10....95 P5
Adswood Gv EDGY/DAV SK3....56 D1
Adswood La East OFTN SK2....56 F1
Adswood La West
 EDGY/DAV SK3....56 E1
Adswood Old Hall Rd....56 D3
Adswood Rd CHD/CHDH SK8....56 D3
Adswood Ter EDGY/DAV SK3....56 E1
Adwell CI GOL/RIS/CU WA3....25 J1
Adwy Wynt FLINT CH6....98 B8
Aegean Rd ALT WA14....52 E1
Afton WDN WA8....54 B8
Agden Brow LYMM WA13....51 K7
 WHITCH SY13....204 F9
Agden Brow Pk LYMM WA13....51 K6
Agden La LYMM WA13....51 L6
Agden La LYMM WA13....51 L8
Agecroft Rd MPL/ROM SK6....42 L7
 NWCHE CW9....110 C5
Agnes St BNG/LEV M19....28 A7
 STHEL WA9....31 H5
Agnew Rd GTN M18....28 C4
Aigburth Gv RDSH SK5....28 E7
Aimson Rd HALE/TIMP WA15....53 P1
Aimson Rd West....53 N1
Ainley CI RUNC WA7....62 E9
Ainley Rd WYTH/NTH M22....54 D4
Ainscough Rd GOL/RIS/CU WA3....34 F5
Ainsdale CI BRAM/HZG SK7....56 C8
 WARRW/BUR WA5....47 K3
Ainsdale Dr CHD/CHDH SK8....55 K6
 SALE M33....38 B6
Ainsdale Gv RDSH SK5....28 F9
Ainsford Rd DID/WITH M20....40 D6
Ainsworth Dr DTN/ASHW M34....29 H6
Ainsworth La NWCHW CW8....108 G5
Ainsworth Sq WALK....21 N2
Aintree Av SALE M33....37 P5
Aintree Rd BRAM/HZG SK7....57 M5
Aintree Gv EDGY/DAV SK3....56 E1
Aire WDN WA8....45 H5
Aire CI EP CH65....80 C6
Airedale CI CHD/CHDH SK8....55 L1

 WARRW/BUR WA5....32 C9
Airedale Ct ALT WA14....53 J2
Aire PI WSFD CW7....150 B1
Airfield Vw CHSW/BR CH4....140 F4
Aitchison Rd NWCHE CW9....110 G2
Aitken St BNG/LEV M19 *....28 C8
Ajax Av WARRN/WOL WA2....33 L6
Akesmoor Dr OFTN SK2....57 J1
Akesmoor La BIDD ST8....189 P7
Alamein Crs WARRN/WOL WA2....18 E1
Alamein Dr MPL/ROM SK6....43 K6
 WSFD CW7....149 M2
Alamein Rd NWCHW CW8....87 H9
Alandale Av DTN/ASHW M34....29 L2
Alandale Rd EDGY/DAV SK3....41 K9
Alan Dr HALE/TIMP WA15....53 L7
 MPL/ROM SK6....58 C7
Alan Rd DID/WITH M20....40 D2
 HTNM SK4....41 H9
Alan St NWCHW CW9....13 K5
Alban St CW/HAS CW1 *....4 D1
Albany Av OP/CLY M11....28 F2
Albany Crs LYMM WA13 *....50 D5
Albany Gdns GTS/LS CH66....79 N6
Albany Gv LYMM WA13....50 C4
Albany Rd BRAM/HZG SK7....72 E2
 LYMM WA13....50 C4
 WILM/AE SK9....71 H9
Albany St BURS/TUN ST6....189 L1
Albany Ter RUNC WA7....14 E3
Albemarle Av DID/WITH M20....40 B2
Albemarle Rd WGTN/LGST M12....33 G9
Alberta St STKP SK1....17 H6
Albert Av FLINT CH6....98 B7
 GTN M18....28 E5
Albert CI CHD/CHDH SK8....56 A5
Albert Ct ALT WA14....53 H5
Albert Dr NSTN CH64....77 K5
 WARRW/BUR WA5....47 H1
Albert Gv WGTN/LGST M12....28 A5
Albert Hill St DID/WITH M20 *....40 C5
Albert PI ALT WA14....52 E6
 NWCHE CW9....13 K2
Albert Rd CHD/CHDH SK8....56 A5
 HALE/TIMP WA15....53 J4
 HTNM SK4....41 J5
 MCFLDN SK10....95 L5
 SALE M33....38 B6
 WARRS WA4....49 M8
 WDN WA8....21 K1
 WILM/AE SK9....71 H9
Albert Rd East
 HALE/TIMP WA15....53 J4
Albert Sq ALT WA14....53 H4
 WDN WA8....21 J2
Albert St ALS/KID ST7....201 H4
 BIDD ST8....175 K9
 BRAM/HZG SK7....72 C2
 CH/BCN CH1....2 C3
 CW/HAS CW1....4 E5

DTN/ASHW M34 * 29 M6
EDGY/DAV SK3 .....16 D5
IRL M44 .....36 D2
KNUT WA16 .....90 D1
MCFLDS SK11 * 8 C4
NANT CW5 .....10 C3
NEWUL ST5 .....201 P8
RUNC WA7 .....14 E5
Albert Ter STKP SK1 .....17 C4
Albion Cl HTNM SK4 .....41 M5
Albion Gv SALE M33 .....38 D4
Albion Pk GOL/RIS/CU WA3 * 26 E5
Albion Pl BRAM/HZG SK7 * 57 K4
 CH/BCN CH1 .....2 E6
Albion Rd NM/HAY SK22 .....59 N8
 NWCHE CW9 .....13 H1
Albion St CH/BCN CH1 .....2 E5
 CW/SHV CW2 .....184 G5
 SALE M33 .....38 E4
Albion Wy NWCHE CW9 .....13 G1
Albury Cl RNFD/HAY WA11 .....22 G2
Albury Dr BNG/LEV M19 .....40 E6
Alcester Av EDGY/DAV SK3 .....40 G9
Alcester Rd CHD/CHDH SK8 .....55 K5
 SALE M33 .....38 E6
Alcock St RUNC WA7 .....15 F1
Alcott Pl WARR WA2 .....33 K2
Aldborough Cl DID/WITH M20 .....40 C2
Aldcliffe GOL/RIS/CU WA3 .....25 H2
Aldcroft St GTN M18 * 2 E3
Aldelyme Rd AUD/MAD/W CW5 .....216 G1
Alder Av POY/DIS SK12 .....73 M5
 WDN WA8 .....45 N4
Alderbank Rd
 WARRW/BUR WA5 .....47 L1
Alder Cl ALS/KID ST7 .....189 J8
Alder Ct MCLFDN SK10 .....95 K8
Alder Crs WARRN/WOL WA2 .....33 M8
Aldercroft Av WYTH/NTH M22 .....54 E5
 MPL/ROM SK6 .....58 C8
Alderdale Dr HTNM SK4 .....41 H5
Alderdale Gv WILM/AE SK9 .....70 C3
Alderdale Rd CHD/CHDH SK8 .....76 C3
Alder Dr GTS/LS CH66 .....102 E5
 HALE/TIMP WA15 .....53 P2
Alderfield Dr SPK/HALE L24 .....60 A4
Alder Gv CHNE CH2 .....122 C7
 DTN/ASHW M34 .....29 L5
 EDGY/DAV SK3 .....16 A6
 NEWUL ST5 .....201 N7
 WDN WA8 .....45 N4
Alderley La ALS/KID ST7 .....189 L4
Alder Rd FROD/HEL WA6 .....83 L2
 WARRN/WOL WA2 .....33 L1
 WARRW/BUR WA5 .....32 D1
 WDN WA8 .....44 F3
Alderley Av GOL/RIS/CU WA3 .....24 F2
 POY/DIS SK12 .....73 M4
 SBCH CW11 .....172 A2
Alderley Dr MPL/ROM SK6 .....42 D4
Alderley Ldg WILM/AE SK9 .....71 J9
Alderley Pl CH/BCN CH1 .....121 H5
 MCFLDN SK10 .....93 P3
Alderley Rd MCFLDN SK10 .....116 D1
 MCFLDS SK11 .....114 D2
 NWCHW CW8 .....12 B2
 RDSH SK5 .....33 H6
 SALE M33 .....39 H6
 WARRS WA4 .....49 M3
 WILM/AE SK9 .....71 J8
Alderley Wk MCFLDS SK11 * 9 H6
Aldermary Rd CCHDY M21 .....39 N5
Aldermoor Cl OP/CLY M11 .....28 F2
Alderney Cl EP CH65 .....102 E5
 MCFLDN SK10 .....116 F4
Alder Ri CHF/WBR SK23 .....75 P6
Alder Rd CHD/CHDH SK8 .....55 M2
 GOL/RIS/CU WA3 .....25 H1
 NWCHW CW8 * 108 F4
 WARR WA1 .....34 E9
Alder Root La
 WARRN/WOL WA2 .....32 G1
Aldersey Av WYTH/NTH M22 .....54 E2
Aldersey La CHSE CH3 .....178 A5
Aldersey Rd CW/SHV CW2 .....184 G5
Aldersgate NM/HAY SK22 .....59 H7
Aldersgate Av RUNC WA7 .....63 H7
Aldersgate Dr HLWD L26 .....44 A9
Aldersgate Rd CHD/CHDH SK8 .....72 C1
 OFTN SK2 .....57 H1
Aldersgreen Av MPL/ROM SK6 .....58 D8
Alders Rd POY/DIS SK12 .....58 E8
 WYTH/NTH M22 .....54 D2
Alder St NEWLW WA12 .....23 N6
Alders Wy MCFLDN SK10 .....94 G7
Alderue Av WYTH/NTH M22 .....54 E1
Aldewood Cl GOL/RIS/CU WA3 .....35 H2
Aldfield Rd NTHM/RTH M23 .....39 H7
Aldford Cl CW/SHV CW2 .....198 D5
 DID/WITH M20 * 40 D5
Aldford Pl WILM/AE SK9 .....93 H3
Aldford Rd CHNE CH2 .....122 A5
Aldgate EP CH65 .....6 B5
Aldington Dr MWCH CW10 .....151 K5
Aldridge Dr WARRW/BUR WA5 .....52 C1
Aldwick Av DID/WITH M20 .....40 D5
Aldwinians Cl DTN/ASHW M34 .....29 L4
Aldworth Gv SALE M33 .....38 A4
Aldwyn Cl DTN/ASHW M34 .....29 L4
Aldwyn Crs BRAM/HZG SK7 .....57 J5
Aldwyn Park Rd
 DTN/ASHW M34 .....29 J2
Aled Wy RUNC WA7 .....141 P5
Alexander Dr HALE/TIMP WA15 .....53 L1
 WDN WA8 .....45 J3
Alexandra Av RUNC WA7 .....15 J4
Alexandra Cl EDGY/DAV SK3 .....56 C1
Alexandra Dr BNG/LEV M19 .....40 G1
Alexandra Gv IRL M44 .....27 M9
Alexandra Rd DTN/ASHW M34 .....29 N5
 HTNM SK4 .....16 B1

MWCH CW10 .....151 K4
SALE M33 .....38 G5
WARRS WA4 .....48 F6
WARRS WA4 .....49 H5
Alexandra St EP CH65 * 6 E1
WARR WA1 .....19 K2
WDN WA8 .....21 G5
WSFD CW7 .....149 L1
Alexandra Ter BNG/LEV M19 .....28 A8
Alford Av STHEL WA9 .....30 G4
Alforde St WDN WA8 .....21 H5
Alford Rd WILM/AE SK9 .....93 H4
Alfred Cl WDN WA8 .....21 G5
Alfred St GOL/RIS/CU WA3 .....25 J1
 RNFD/HAY WA11 .....23 J2
Alfreton Av IRL M44 .....36 D2
 NEWLW WA12 .....24 A6
 NWCHW CW8 .....13 H3
 WDN WA8 .....21 J3
Alfreton Rd OFTN SK2 .....57 K1
Alfriston Dr NTHM/RTH M23 .....39 K6
Algernon St RUNC WA7 .....14 C1
 WARR WA1 .....16 E3
 WARRS WA4 .....16 B5
Algreave Rd EDGY/DAV SK3 .....41 H8
Alice Ct WDN WA8 .....21 J5
Alice St HYDE SK14 .....43 K1
 SALE M33 .....38 G4
 STHEL WA9 .....22 C9
Alison Dr HOLMCH CW4 .....132 A3
Alkington Gdns WHITCH SY13 .....213 L7
Alkington Rd WHITCH SY13 .....213 L7
Allandale ALT WA14 .....52 F3
Allan Rd RNFD/HAY WA11 .....22 A2
Allans Cl NSTN CH64 .....77 L7
Allansford Av CHSE CH3 .....144 A6
Allans Meadow NSTN CH64 .....77 L6
Allanson Rd WYTH/NTH M22 .....39 P7
Allanson St STHEL WA9 .....30 C9
Allcard St WARRW/BUR WA5 .....18 A1
Alldis St OFTN SK2 .....57 H2
Allen Av GOL/RIS/CU WA3 .....26 C5
Allenby Rd IRL M44 .....36 C4
Allendale HUNT * 62 F8
Allendale Av RAIN/WH L35 .....30 A5
Allen Dr NWCHE CW9 .....128 C1
Allen Pl CW/HAS CW1 .....185 K5
Allen Rd WDN WA8 .....61 K7
Allen St MCFLDS SK11 * 9 J2
 WARRN/WOL WA2 .....18 C4
Allerby Wy GOL/RIS/CU WA3 .....24 C1
Allerdean Wk HTNM SK4 .....40 G5
Allerton Rd WDN WA8 .....45 P6
Allgreave Cl MWCH CW10 .....151 J4
 SALE M33 .....38 G7
Allington Cl WARRN/WOL WA2 .....39 N7
Allington Pl CHSW/BR CH4 .....142 G3
Allman Cl CW/HAS CW1 .....184 F1
Allotment Rd IRL M44 .....36 C3
All Saints Dr WARRS WA4 .....49 N4
All Saints' Rd HTNM SK4 .....41 L5
Allt Goch FLINT CH6 .....98 A6
Alma Av CW/HAS CW1 .....185 J2
Alma Cl ALS/KID ST7 .....188 G1
 MCFLDS SK11 .....116 C5
Alma La WILM/AE SK9 .....71 J8
Alma Pl STHEL WA9 .....22 A7
Alma Rd BNG/LEV M19 .....28 A9
 BRAM/HZG SK7 .....57 N7
 HTNM SK4 .....41 J3
 SALE M33 .....38 B6
Alma St CHSE CH3 .....3 K3
 NEWLW WA12 * 23 M6
 STHEL WA9 .....22 A7
Almeda Rd SPK/HALE L24 .....60 A7
Almer Dr WARRW/BUR WA5 .....47 N2
Almere Ferry Rd
 WRX/GR/L L12 * 176 E3
Almond Av CW/HAS CW1 .....185 K2
 RUNC WA7 .....15 J7
Almond Cl EDGY/DAV SK3 .....16 A6
 RNFD/HAY WA11 .....22 D4
Almond Dr SALE M33 .....38 C2
 WARRW/BUR WA5 .....32 C2
Almond Gv NWCHW CW8 .....108 G5
 WARR WA1 .....34 C9
 WDN WA8 .....30 D1
Almond Pl NEWUL ST5 .....201 N6
Almond Tree Rd
 CHSE CH3 .....56 A6
Alnwick Dr EP CH65 .....102 F2
Alpha Ct DTN/ASHW M34 .....29 J6
Alphagate Dr DTN/ASHW M34 .....29 J6
Alpha Sq OP/CLY M11 .....28 E2
Alpine Cl NEWLW WA12 .....23 L6
Alport Rd WHITCH SY13 .....213 M4
Alpraham Crs CHNE CH2 .....121 P5
Alsager Cl CCHDY M21 .....39 L2
Alsager Rd ALS/KID ST7 .....200 C4
 SBCH CW11 .....171 M9
Alsfeld Wy NM/HAY SK22 .....59 L7
Alstead Av HALE/TIMP WA15 .....53 L4
Alston Av SALE M33 .....38 C5
Alston Cl BRAM/HZG SK7 * 57 M8
Alstone Dr ALT WA14 .....52 E1
Alstone Rd HTNM SK4 .....41 K2
Alston Gdns BNG/LEV M19 .....40 G3
Alston Rd GTN M18 .....28 D1
 WDN WA8 .....45 H5
Altair Av WYTH/NTH M22 .....54 F1
Altcar Gv RDSH SK5 .....28 E2
Altcar Wk WYTH/NTH M22 * 54 F1
Alton Cl MCFLDN SK10 .....117 M2
Alton Rd WILM/AE SK9 .....71 H6
Alton Sq OP/CLY M11 .....28 E2
 EDGY/DAV SK3 .....184 G5
Altrincham Rd NTHM/RTH M23 .....39 K9
 WILM/AE SK9 .....70 G2
 WILM/AE SK9 .....70 G6
 WYTH/NTH M22 .....54 G2

Alt Wk WSFD CW7 * 129 H9
Alumbrook Av HOLMCH CW4 .....131 P8
Alum Ct HOLMCH CW4 .....152 G1
Alun Crs CHSW/BR CH4 .....142 C4
Alundale Rd WSFD CW7 .....128 D8
Alvanley Cl SALE M33 .....38 E7
Alvanley Ct GOL/RIS/CU WA3 .....56 C1
Alvanley Dr FROD/HEL WA6 .....105 J2
Alvanley Ri NWCHE CW9 .....13 C7
Alvanley Rd FROD/HEL WA6 .....105 J2
 GTS/LS CH66 .....80 A9
Alvanley Vw CHNE CH2 .....104 B1
Alvan Sp OP/CLY M11 * 28 E2
Alvaston Av HTNM SK4 .....41 J5
Alvaston Dr GTN M18 .....28 E5
 NANT CW5 .....10 C5
Alvaston Rd CW/SHV CW2 .....184 G6
Alveley Av DID/WITH M20 .....40 D3
Alverstone Cl
 WARRW/BUR WA5 .....31 P9
Alverstone Rd DID/WITH M20 .....40 D2
Alverton Cl WDN WA8 .....20 B3
Alveston Cl MCFLDN SK10 .....116 F3
Alveston Dr WILM/AE SK9 .....71 L6
Alvingham Cl NWCHE CW9 .....13 J5
Alvington Gv BRAM/HZG SK7 .....56 G6
Alwinton Av HTNM SK4 .....40 F5
Alwyn Gdns CHNE CH2 .....121 P3
Alyndale Rd CHSW/BR CH4 .....141 P4
Alyn Rd CHNE CH2 .....122 C2
Amanda Rd RAIN/WH L35 .....30 A3
Ambassador Dr HLWD L26 .....44 A6
Ambassador Pl
 HALE/TIMP WA15 * 53 J2
Amber Gdns DUK SK16 * 29 P1
Ambergate Cl WARRS WA4 .....31 J1
Amberleigh Cl WARRS WA4 .....65 J3
Amberley Dr HALE/TIMP WA15 .....53 M7
 IRL M44 .....27 N8
 NTHM/RTH M23 .....54 C2
Amberley Rd MCFLDS SK11 .....116 C6
 SALE M33 .....38 B3
Amberwood NTHM/RTH M23 .....53 P1
Ambleside CHNE CH2 * 121 J5
Ambleside Av HALE/TIMP WA15 .....53 N2
Ambleside Cl CW/SHV CW2 .....184 E6
 MCFLDS SK11 .....116 F6
 WSFD CW7 .....128 D8
Ambleside Crs
 WARRN/WOL WA2 .....33 M5
Ambleside Rd EP CH65 .....102 E2
 RDSH SK5 .....41 N2
Ambrose Ct WYTH/NTH M22 * 39 N7
Ambrose Dr DID/WITH M20 .....39 N4
Ambrose Rd BURS/TUN ST6 .....189 P9
Ambrose St CW/HAS CW1 .....184 G1
Ambuscade Cl CW/HAS CW1 * 5 H1
Ambush St OP/CLY M11 .....28 F2
Amelia Cl WDN WA8 .....45 P3
Amelia St DTN/ASHW M34 .....29 M5
Amersfoot Dr NTHM/RTH M23 .....53 P1
Amersham Cl MCFLDN SK10 .....117 J2
Amersham St BNG/LEV M19 .....41 H2
Amesbury Gv RDSH SK5 .....41 N3
Amherst Rd DID/WITH M20 .....40 D1
Amis Gv GOL/RIS/CU WA3 .....24 C1
Amlwch Av OFTN SK2 .....57 K1
Amy St CW/SHV CW2 .....204 B1
Ancaster St BURS/TUN ST6 .....189 M9
The Anchorage CHSE CH3 * 144 A5
Anchorside Cl CCHDY M21 .....39 L1
Ancoats Rd KNUT WA16 .....92 A5
Anderson Cl CW/HAS CW1 .....185 M4
 RAIN/WH L35 .....30 C7
 WARRN/WOL WA2 .....33 M9
Andersons La MCFLDS SK11 * 8 C4
Anderton Wy WILM/AE SK9 .....71 M3
Andover Cl WARRN/WOL WA2 .....33 P7
Andover Rd RNFD/HAY WA11 .....23 J1
Andrew Cl WDN WA8 .....45 J7
Andrew Crs CHSW/BR CH4 .....142 C2
Andrew Gv GOL/RIS/CU WA3 .....117 N5
Andrew La MPL/ROM SK6 .....58 C6
Andrew's Cl CHSE CH3 .....124 A9
Andrew St BURS/TUN ST6 .....189 L9
 HTNM SK4 .....41 M1
Andromeda Wy STHEL WA9 .....31 M1
Anemone Wy STHEL WA9 .....31 M1
Anerley Rd DID/WITH M20 .....40 C4
Anfield Rd CHD/CHDH SK8 .....55 P5
 SALE M33 .....38 F3
Angel Cl DUK SK16 .....29 P1
Angelina Cl SBCH CW11 .....171 J2
Angel St BRAM/HZG SK7 .....57 N7
 DTN/ASHW M34 .....29 N5
Anglers Rest IRL M44 .....36 D3
Anglesey Cl EP CH65 .....102 F2
Anglesey Dr POY/DIS SK12 .....57 L9
Anglesey Gv CHD/CHDH SK8 .....55 P1
Anglesey Water POY/DIS SK12 .....57 L9
Angleside Av BNG/LEV M19 .....40 F4
Angus Gv MWCH CW10 .....130 C9
Angus Wk MCFLDN SK10 * 116 F2
Ankers Knowl La
 MCFLDN SK11 .....119 H4
Ankers La MCFLDS SK11 .....119 H5
Annable Rd GTN M18 .....28 E3
 IRL M44 .....27 M9
 MPL/ROM SK6 .....58 C6
Annald Sq DROY M43 .....28 G1
Annan Ct CONG CW12 .....156 A9
Ann Cl GTS/LS CH66 .....79 P6
Anne Ct ALS/KID ST7 .....201 N2
Anne Gv STHEL WA9 .....31 H1
Anne St BURS/TUN ST6 .....189 L9

STHEL WA9 .....31 J1
Anne's Wy CHSW/BR CH4 .....3 H6
Annette Av NEWLW WA12 .....23 L4
Annie St WARRN/WOL WA2 .....19 F3
Annions La NANT CW5 .....197 N6
Annis Cl WILM/AE SK9 .....93 K3
Annis Rd WILM/AE SK9 .....93 K5
Ann St AULW OL7 .....28 A1
 DTN/ASHW M34 .....29 L6
 NWCHE CW9 .....110 D3
 RDSH SK5 .....41 M4
Ann St West WDN WA8 .....21 J5
Ansdell Av CCHDY M21 .....39 L1
Ansdell Rd RDSH SK5 .....28 G8
 WDN WA8 .....45 P5
Ansdell Villas' Rd RAIN/WH L35 .....30 B4
Ansell Cl GTN M18 .....28 D3
Anson Cl BRAM/HZG SK7 .....72 F1
 WARRN/WOL WA2 .....33 P6
Anson Pl POY/DIS SK12 .....73 P3
Ansty Gv HTNM SK4 .....41 N5
Anthony Dr NWCHE CW9 .....128 C4
Antilles Cl WGTN/LOST M12 .....28 A5
Antony Rd CW/HAS CW1 .....5 J7
Antrim Cl BNG/LEV M19 .....40 E6
 RNFD/HAY WA11 .....22 G2
Antrim Rd WARRN/WOL WA2 .....33 N6
Antrobus St CONG CW12 .....155 M7
Anvil Cl CH/BCN CH1 .....120 D2
 CHNE CH2 .....82 B9
 SBCH CW11 .....171 J3
Apedale Rd NEWUL ST5 .....201 M9
Appleby Av HALE/TIMP WA15 .....53 N2
Appleby Cl EDGY/DAV SK3 .....56 D2
 MCFLDS SK11 .....116 F7
 SALE M33 .....38 B3
Appleby Wk WDN WA8 .....21 J6
Applecorn Cl STHEL WA9 .....31 H4
Applecross Cl NTHM/RTH M23 .....54 D1
Appledale Dr CHNE CH2 .....121 P6
Appledore Dr NTHM/RTH M23 .....53 P1
Appledore Gv ALS/KID ST7 .....189 N8
 STHEL WA9 .....31 H4
Applefield NWCHW CW8 .....12 A5
Appleford Cl WARRS WA4 .....48 G8
Apple Market St NWCHE CW9 .....12 E2
Appleton Cl NANT CW5 .....197 J2
Appleton Dr EP CH65 .....102 E1
Appleton Gv SALE M33 .....38 B6
Appleton St CHNE CH2 .....121 P6
 HALE/TIMP WA15 .....53 J2
 HTNM SK4 .....41 L2
 WDN WA8 .....22 A7
Appleton Vlg WDN WA8 .....21 J6
Appleton Wy WILM/AE SK9 .....71 N3
Apple Tree Gv GTS/LS CH66 .....102 B4
Apple Tree Rd NM/HAY SK22 .....59 N5
Appleyards La CHSW/BR CH4 .....142 F3
April Ri MCFLDN SK10 .....116 G3
Apsley Cl ALT WA14 .....52 F6
Apsley Gv ALT WA14 .....52 F6
Apsley Rd DTN/ASHW M34 .....29 M5
Apsley St STKP SK1 .....17 J3
Aragon Wy MPL/ROM SK6 .....58 C1
Aran Cl HALE/TIMP WA15 .....53 N6
Aran Gv SPK/HALE L24 .....60 A4
Arbor Av BNG/LEV M19 .....41 H1
Arbor Dr BNG/LEV M19 .....41 H1
Arbour Cl MCFLDN SK10 .....117 K1
 NWCHE CW9 .....110 C4
Arbour Crs MCFLDN SK10 .....117 K1
Arbour Ms MCFLDN SK10 .....117 K1
Arbour St ALS/KID ST7 .....201 N2
Arbury Av EDGY/DAV SK3 .....40 G9
Arcadia Av SALE M33 .....38 A5
Archer Av WARRS WA4 .....48 G5
Archer Cl MCFLDN SK10 .....95 L6
Archer Gv STHEL WA9 .....30 G4
Archers Gn PS/BROM CH62 .....79 J1
Archers Wy CH/BCN CH1 .....121 K8
 GTS/LS CH66 .....102 A3
Arclid Cl WILM/AE SK9 .....71 M3
Arcon Pl ALT WA14 .....52 E1
Arden Wk WA8 .....45 J7
Ardenbrook Ri MCFLDN SK10 .....117 J3
Arden Cl CHSE CH3 .....124 B8
 GOL/RIS/CU WA3 .....25 J1
Arden Dr BRAM/HZG SK7 .....56 D2
 CONG CW12 .....177 J2
Arden Dr NSTN CH64 .....77 J5
Ardenfield DTN/ASHW M34 .....42 F1
Ardenfield Dr WYTH/NTH M22 .....42 F1
Arden Lodge Rd
 NTHM/RTH M23 .....39 J6
Arden Rd MPL/ROM SK6 .....42 D7
Ardens Meadow
 TPL/BDN SK 165 P1

Argyll Av CHSW/BR CH4 .....142 C3
 PS/BROM CH62 .....79 H1
Argyll Cl MCFLDN SK10 .....116 G3
Argyll Rd CHD/CHDH SK8 .....55 P2
Arkenshaw Rd GOL/RIS/CU WA3 .....34 B5
Arkenstone Cl WDN WA8 .....45 J5
Arkle Av CHD/CHDH SK8 .....71 N2
Arklow Dr SPK/HALE L24 .....60 D4
Ark St BNG/LEV M19 .....28 A7
Arkwright Cl RUNC WA7 .....149 J2
 RUNC WA7 .....62 D3
Arkwright Dr MPL/ROM SK6 .....58 E1
Arkwright Rd MPL/ROM SK6 .....58 E1
 RUNC WA7 .....62 D3
Arley Av DID/WITH M20 .....40 A3
 WARRS WA4 .....48 F6
Arley Cl ALS/KID ST7 .....187 N5
 ALT WA14 .....52 A8
 CHNE CH2 .....122 A5
 MCFLDS SK11 .....116 C6
Arley Dr SALE M33 .....38 D6
 WDN WA8 .....45 H5
Arley Gv EDGY/DAV SK3 .....56 D3
Arley End KNUT WA16 .....90 E5
Arley Mere Cl CHD/CHDH SK8 .....55 P4
Arley Mossend La NWCHE CW9 .....88 D3
Arley Pl CW/SHV CW2 .....184 G8
 NWCHE CW9 .....13 J7
Arley Rd WARRS WA4 .....65 H6
Arley Wk SBCH CW11 .....171 J4
Arlington Av DTN/ASHW M34 .....29 N7
Arlington Cl CW/SHV CW2 .....185 J8
Arlington Crs WILM/AE SK9 .....70 G9
Arlington Dr GOL/RIS/CU WA3 .....25 J1
 MCFLDS SK11 .....116 C5
 OFTN SK2 .....73 J1
 POY/DIS SK12 .....73 K3
 WARRW/BUR WA5 .....116 C5
Arlington Rd CHD/CHDH SK8 .....55 L3
Armadale Cl EDGY/DAV SK3 .....56 E3
Armistead Wy HOLMCH CW4 .....131 M6
Armitage Pl ALT WA14 .....53 H4
Armitstead Rd SBCH CW11 .....171 L6
Armitt St MCFLDS SK11 .....8 D6
Armour Av WARRN/WOL WA2 .....33 L8
Armoury Court Ms MCFLDS SK11 .....8 C7
Armoury St EDGY/DAV SK3 .....17 F7
Armstrong
 AUD/MAD/W CW3 .....216 G2
 GOL/RIS/CU WA3 .....34 E4
Armthorpe Dr GTS/LS CH66 .....79 M8
Arncliffe Dr NTHM/RTH M23 .....79 M8
Arndale RUNC WA7 .....62 C9
Arne Cl OFTN SK2 .....57 N2
Arnesby Av SALE M33 .....39 H2
Arnfield Rd DID/WITH M20 .....40 D2
 EDGY/DAV SK3 .....40 C2
Arnhem Crs WARRN/WOL WA2 .....18 E1
Arnhem Wy CHSE CH3 .....143 K5
Arnold Av HYDE SK14 .....43 L1
Arnold Cl STHEL WA9 .....22 A8
Arnold Dr HYDE SK14 .....43 L1
Arnold Rd HYDE SK14 .....43 L1
Arnold's Crs CHSW/BR CH4 .....140 E7
Arnold St EDGY/DAV SK3 .....41 M9
 NANT CW5 .....10 C3
 WARR WA1 .....19 J3
Arnside Av BRAM/HZG SK7 .....57 J5
 CONG CW12 .....155 J8
 HTNM SK4 .....41 L2
Arnside Cl CW/SHV CW2 .....128 E9
 SALE M33 .....38 D8
Arnside Gv SALE M33 .....38 D8
 MPL/ROM SK6 .....58 C7
Arpley Rd WARR WA1 .....18 D5
Arpley St WARR WA1 .....16 C5
Arradon Ct CHNE CH2 .....121 P6
Arran Av EP CH65 .....102 E3
 SALE M33 .....38 A3
Arran Cl HOLMCH CW4 .....152 G1
 RNFD/HAY WA11 .....22 C3
 WARRN/WOL WA2 .....34 B6
Arran Dr ALS/KID ST7 .....189 P8
 FROD/HEL WA6 .....84 A6
Arras Gv RDSH SK5 .....41 P1
Arron Pl CW/SHV CW2 .....184 D5
Arrowcroft Rd CHSE CH3 .....122 G6
Arrowfield Rd CCHDY M21 .....39 N2
Arrowsmith Dr
 RNFD/HAY WA11 .....23 K2
Arthill La ALT WA14 .....51 P6
Arthog Dr HALE/TIMP WA15 .....53 K7
Arthog Rd DID/WITH M20 .....53 K7
 HALE/TIMP WA15 .....53 K7
Arthur Av EP CH65 .....7 C5
Arthur St CH/BCN CH1 .....121 K9
 CW/SHV CW2 .....5 C5
 NWCHE CW9 .....110 C2
 RDSH SK5 .....41 M1
Artillery Pl WYTH/NTH M22 * 55 H5
Artists La MCFLDN SK10 .....93 K7
Arundel Av CW/SHV CW2 .....184 E8
 HALE/TIMP WA15 .....53 L6
 KNUT WA16 .....90 E5
 MCFLDN SK10 .....117 M2
Arundel Cl EP CH65 .....102 G1
Arundel Rd CHD/CHDH SK8 .....55 K4
Arundel St NM/HAY SK22 .....59 P8
Ascar Av RUNC WA7 .....11 P9
Ascol Dr MCFLDN SK10 .....117 J1
 SALE M33 .....37 P5
Ascot Cl CONG CW12 .....155 M6
 MCFLDN SK10 .....117 J1
 WARR WA1 .....34 F9
 WARRS WA4 .....49 L5

Ascot Dr BRAM/HZG SK7 ......57 N5
GTS/LS CH66 ......101 P1
Ascot Pde BNG/LEV M19 ......40 C2
Ash Av ALT WA14 ......52 E2
CHD/CHDH SK8 ......55 M3
IRL M44 ......36 C3
NWCHW WA12 ......3 G7
Ash Bnk CHE CH3 * 122 D7
Ashbank NWCHE CW9 ......110 D5
Ashberry CI WILM/AE SK9 ......71 M6
Ashberry Dr WARRS WA4 ......65 K1
Ashbourne Av CHD/CHDH SK8 ......81 P6
RUNC WA7 ......61 P6
Ashbourne CI GTS/LS CH66 ......102 A4
Ashbourne Crs SALE M33 ......38 C6
Ashbourne Dr MPL/ROM SK6 ......58 C9
Ashbourne Ms MCFLDN SK10 * ..116 F4
Ashbourne Rd BRAM/HZG SK7 ......57 M7
DTN/ASHW M34 ......29 L7
WARRW/BUR WA5 ......47 J2
Ashbrook Av WYTH/NTH M22 ......29 H6
RUNC WA7 ......84 D2
Ashbrook CI CHD/CHDH SK8 ......55 K6
DTN/ASHW M34 ......29 H6
Ashbrook Crs WARRN/WOL WA2 ..33 N8
Ashbrook Dr MCFLDN SK10 ......96 G2
Ashbrook Farm CI RDSH SK5 ......28 F7
Ashbrook La RDSH SK5 ......28 F7
MCFLDN SK10 ......93 P7
Ashbrook Rd MCFLDN SK10 ......95 M6
Ashbrook St OP/CLY M11 ......28 C2
Ashburn Av BNG/LEV M19 ......40 C5
Ashburn Rd HTNM SK4 ......16 B1
Ashburton Rd EDGY/DAV SK3 ......56 E5
Ashbury CI HLWD L26 ......63 H4
Ashbury Dr RNFD/HAY WA11 ......23 H2
Ashby Av BNG/LEV M19 ......40 F4
Ashby Dr SBCH CW11 ......171 H4
Ashby PI CHNE CH2 ......121 P7
Ash CI GTS/LS CH66 ......102 B3
HOLMCH CW4 ......132 A7
MALPAS SY14 ......204 B1
OFTN SK2 ......57 G2
TPLY/KEL CW6 ......147 H8
Ashcott Av WYTH/NTH M22 ......54 F3
Ashcroft Av CW/SHV CW2 ......198 A4
Ashcroft Gv HTNM SK4 ......71 H9
Ashcroft Rd LYMM WA13 ......51 H5
Ashcroft St STHEL WA9 ......22 A6
Ashdale CI ALS/KID ST7 ......187 N5
RDSH SK5 ......41 N3
Ashdale Dr CHD/CHDH SK8 ......55 K5
DID/WITH M20 ......40 E3
Ashdene Rd DID/WITH M20 ......40 E2
HTNM SK4 ......40 F9
WILM/AE SK9 ......71 H9
Ashdown Av MPL/ROM SK6 ......43 H3
Ashdown Crs STHEL WA9 ......31 H4
Ashdown Gv HLWD L26 ......44 A6
Ashdown La GOL/RIS/CU WA3 ......35 H3
Ashdown Rd HTNM SK4 ......41 K5
KNUT WA16 ......94 G7
Ashenhurst Rd ALS/KID ST7 ......188 B5
Ashenough Rd ALS/KID ST7 ......201 N1
Ashfield CI LYMM WA13 ......29 N4
RAIN/WH L35 ......30 C5
Ashfield Crs CH/BCN CH1 ......120 C6
CHD/CHDH SK8 ......55 M1
Ashfield Dr MCFLDN SK10 ......116 G2
Ashfield Gv EDGY/DAV SK3 * 56 F3
GTN M18 ......28 F5
IRL M44 ......36 D2
MPL/ROM SK6 ......43 N7
Ashfield Rd CHD/CHDH SK8 ......55 M1
EDGY/DAV SK3 ......56 F3
HALE/TIMP WA15 ......53 J4
SALE M33 ......38 E3

Ashley CI CW/HAS CW1 ......186 B3
RAIN/WH L35 ......30 C6
WARRS WA4 ......49 L4
Ashley Ct WRXS/E LL13 ......176 FB
Ashley Dr BRAM/HZG SK7 ......56 C9
NWCHW CW8 ......109 J6
SALE M33 ......38 B6
Ashley Gdns MALPAS SY14 ......178 C7
MPL/ROM SK6 ......58 B7
Ashley Gra NWCHE CW9 ......109 N9
Ashley Gn WDN WA8 ......20 B2
Ashley Meadow CW/HAS CW1 ..186 B3
Ashleymill La ALT WA14 ......53 H7
Ashley Mill La North ALT WA14 ..53 H7
Ashley Rd ALT WA14 ......53 J7
ALT WA14 ......53 J7
KNUT WA16 ......68 B6
OFTN SK2 ......42 B8
WALM SK2 ......71 K5
Ashley Wy WDN WA8 ......21 H6
Ashley Wy West WDN WA8 ......21 F5
Ashmead CI ALS/KID ST7 ......188 A5
Ashmeade HALE/TIMP WA15 ......53 M6
Ashmead Ms ALS/KID ST7 ......188 A5
Ashmoor Rd WYTH/NTH M22 ......54 F6
Ashmore Av EDGY/DAV SK3 ......40 C9
Ashmore CI GOL/RIS/CU WA3 ......35 H5
MWCH CW10 ......151 J4
Ashmore's La ALS/KID ST7 ......187 P5
Ashness CI BRAM/HZG SK7 ......56 F7
Ashover Gv BURS/TUN ST6 ......189 H8
Ash Priors WDN WA8 ......45 K4
Ashridge Dr DUK SK16 ......29 P2
Ashridge St RUNC WA7 ......14 D1
Ash Rd CHNE CH2 ......104 C1
CW/HAS CW1 ......185 K2
DTN/ASHW M34 ......28 G5
GOL/RIS/CU WA3 ......35 P6
LYMM WA13 ......50 C4
NWCHW CW8 ......127 J1
PART M31 ......36 C5
POY/DIS SK12 ......73 M3
RNFD/HAY WA11 ......23 L2
WARRN/WOL WA2 ......33 L2
WARRW/BUR WA5 ......47 K3
WHITCH SY13 ......214 A7
Ashstead Rd SALE M33 ......38 F7
Ash St BRAM/HZG SK7 ......57 K4
DTN/ASHW M34 ......29 K2
EDGY/DAV SK3 ......41 J8
NWCHE CW9 ......13 H1
Ash Ter MCFLDS SK11 ......117 J8
Ashton Av ALT WA14 ......53 J1
MCFLDN SK10 ......116 D3
RAIN/WH L35 ......30 B6
Ashton CI CONG CW12 ......156 B9
FROD/HEL WA6 ......84 A4
MWCH CW10 ......151 K5
NWCHW CW8 ......109 N8
PS/BROM CH62 ......79 J2
RUNC WA7 ......61 M8
Ashton Dr FROD/HEL WA6 ......84 A4
Ashton Hill La DROY M43 ......28 G1
Ashton La CHSE CH3 ......124 D5
SALE M33 ......38 A8
Ashton Old Rd OP/CLY M11 ......28 C2
Ashton PI BRAM/HZG SK7 ......57 M6
Ashton Rd DTN/ASHW M34 ......29 L4
FROD/HEL WA6 ......106 D9
MPL/ROM SK6 ......42 D4
PART M31 ......37 H5
Ashtons Green Dr STHEL WA9 ....22 D7
Ashton St DUK SK16 ......29 K6
MPL/ROM SK6 ......43 H2
WARRN/WOL WA2 ......18 D4
Ashtree CI MCFLDN SK10 ......95 J5
NSTN CH64 ......77 H6
Ashtree Cft NSTN CH64 ......78 E6
Ashtree Farm Ct NSTN CH64 ......78 E5
Ashurst CI RNFD/HAY WA11 ......22 C5
Ashurst Dr EDGY/DAV SK3 ......56 D6
RNFD/HAY WA11 ......22 C5
Ashurst Rd WYTH/NTH M22 ......55 H4
Ashville Ct CW/SHV CW2 ......185 H9
Ashville Rd RUNC WA7 ......189 K6
Ash View ALS/KID ST7 ......189 K6
Ashway Clough North
OFTN SK2 * 57 K2
Ashway Clough South
OFTN SK2 * 57 K2
Ashwell Rd NTHM/RTH M23 ......55 M6
Ashwood ALT WA14 ......52 F7
Ashwood Av DID/WITH M20 ......39 P4
DTN/ASHW M34 ......28 G6
GOL/RIS/CU WA3 ......24 F1
SALE M33 ......38 B5
WARR WA1 ......19 K1
Ashwood CI GTS/LS CH66 * 101 P5
NWCHW CW8 ......109 K1
Ashwood Crs MPL/ROM SK6 ......49 K1
NWCHW CW8 ......109 K1
Ashwood La CHNE CH2 ......103 J7
WHITCH SY13 ......214 E9
Ashwood Rd POY/DIS SK12 ......59 H9
Ashworth Av DTN/ASHW M34 ......29 L2
Ashworth CI ALT WA14 ......52 F6
Ashworth Pk WYTH/NTH M22 ......90 D5
Ashworth St DTN/ASHW M34 ......29 L5
Askerbank La MCFLDS SK11 ......157 N9
Askern Av WYTH/NTH M22 ......54 F4
Askett CI RNFD/HAY WA11 ......22 B5
Askrigg Av GTS/LS CH66 ......102 A3
Aspen CI ALS/KID ST7 ......189 N5
GTS/LS CH66 ......102 A3
HALE/TIMP WA15 ......54 A2
WARRS WA4 ......48 C7
WARR WA1 ......44 G2
Aspen Gn DTN/ASHW M34 ......29 H7
Aspen Gv CW/HAS CW1 ......186 G2
Aspen Qy CH/BCN CH1 ......120 E4

The Aspens CHD/CHDH SK8 * 55 J1
NWCHW CW8 ......107 P7
Aspen Wy CHNE CH2 ......122 C7
MPL/ROM SK6 ......58 E8
Aspenwood CI MPL/ROM SK6 ......43 K9
Aspenwood Dr SALE M33 ......37 H4
Aspinall CI WARRN/WOL WA2 ......34 B5
Aspland Rd HYDE SK14 ......43 L1
Aspull CI GOL/RIS/CU WA3 ......34 D4
CW/HAS CW1 ......186 A3
Asquith St RDSH SK5 ......28 F8
Assheton Av DTN/ASHW M34 ......29 K1
Assheton Wk SPK/HALE L24 ......60 E4
Astbury CI CW/HAS CW1 ......189 L5
CW/HAS CW1 ......184 C1
GOL/RIS/CU WA3 ......25 K1
HALE/TIMP WA15 ......53 J1
Astbury Crs EDGY/DAV SK3 ......56 D1
Astbury Dr NWCHW CW8 ......87 J9
Astbury Lane Ends
CONG 174 F1
Astbury St CONG CW12 ......155 L8
Aster Crs RUNC WA7 ......84 D1
Aster Rd RNFD/HAY WA11 ......23 K9
Astle CI WARRS WA4 ......16 C7
Astle Ct MCFLDS SK11 ......114 C1
Astle La MCFLDN SK10 ......114 A8
Astley CI KNUT WA16 ......90 C6
WARRS WA4 ......48 D4
Astle Rd IRL M44 ......27 L9
Astley Gdns DUK SK16 ......29 P1
Astley Rd IRL M44 ......27 J4
Astley St DUK SK16 ......29 P1
Astmoor Bridge La RUNC WA7 ....62 D4
RUNC WA7 ......62 E3
Astmoor Rd RUNC WA7 ......62 C3
Aston Av GOL/RIS/CU WA3 ......34 C4
WSFD CW7 ......128 C9
Aston CI EDGY/DAV SK3 ......56 C1
Aston Ct WARR WA1 ......34 D7
Aston Fields Rd RUNC WA7 ......85 H1
Aston Grange La RUNC WA7 ......85 M7
Aston La North RUNC WA7 ......85 J1
Aston La South RUNC WA7 ......85 J4
Aston Wy NWCHW CW10 ......151 L1
Astor Dr WARRS WA4 ......49 H1
Astor Rd BNG/LEV M19 ......40 F1
Atcherley St NANT CW5 ......196 F7
Athelbrae CI NWCHW CW8 ......12 D5
Athens St STKP SK1 ......17 K5
Atherton La IRL M44 ......36 D3
Atherton Rd EP CH65 ......80 B7
Atherton St WARR WA1 ......16 C7
Athey St MCFLDS SK11 ......112 G7
Athlone Av CHD/CHDH SK8 ......56 C2
Athlone Rd WARRN/WOL WA2 ....18 C1
Atholl CI NEWLW WA12 ......23 K5
Atholl Av CW/SHV CW2 ......185 J7
Atholl CI MCFLDN SK10 ......116 G3
Atholl Rd BRAM/HZG SK7 ......72 D1
Atis CI FLINT CH6 ......08 C7
Atkin CI CONG CW12 ......155 J7
Atkinson Rd SALE M33 ......38 D2
Atkinson St STKP SK1 ......41 P9
Atlanta Av MANAIR M90 ......54 A4
Atlantic St ALT WA14 ......52 E1
Atlas Pk WYTH/NTH M22 * 55 H6
Atlow Dr NTHM/RTH M23 ......54 D2
Attenbury's La ALT WA14 ......38 B1
Attenburys Park Est
ALT WA14 * 38 B8
Atterbury CI WDN WA8 ......45 J5
Attercliffe Rd CCHDY M21 ......39 K1
Attlee Av GOL/RIS/CU WA3 ......26 B5
Attwell St OP/CLY M11 ......28 C1
Attwood Av HALE/TIMP WA15 ....53 M2
Attwood Rd HALE/TIMP WA15 ..53 M2
Attwood St ALS/KID ST7 ......189 J6
WGTN/LGST M12 ......28 A3
Atwood Rd DID/WITH M20 ......40 D5
Aubourn CI WDN WA8 ......45 J7
Aubrey Dr DID/WITH M20 ......40 F2
Aubrey St BURS/TUN ST6 ......189 K9
Auburn Av MPL/ROM SK6 ......42 D4
Auburn Rd DTN/ASHW M34 ......29 K7
Auckery Av GTS/LS CH66 ......101 P1
Auckland Rd CH/BCN CH1 ......120 F7
Audenshaw Hall Gv
DTN/ASHW M54 ......29 J2
Audenshaw Rd DTN/ASHW M34 ..29 J2
Audie Murphy Rd
WARRW/BUR WA5 ......47 M1
Audlem CI RUNC WA7 ......84 D1
Audlem Dr NWCHE CW9 ......110 A7
AUD/MAD/W CW5 ......209 K7
Audlem Rd AUD/MAD/W CW5 ..218 G4
NANT CW5 ......196 F4
Audley Crs CHSW/BK CH4 ......142 F4
Audley Rd ALS/KID ST7 ......188 B3
ALS/KID ST7 ......201 N5
BNG/LEV M19 * 39 P2
CW/SHV CW2 ......200 A2
Audley St CW/HAS CW1 ......185 K3
Audre CI WARRW/BUR WA5 ......47 N5
Audrey Av GTN M18 ......28 E4
Aughton Wy CHSW/BK CH4 ......141 H6
Augusta Dr MCFLDN SK10 ......93 L9
Augusta St ALS/KID ST7 ......30 C1
Austell CI RNFD/HAY WA11 ......22 D4
Austell Rd WYTH/NTH M22 ......54 F6
Austen Av BURS/TUN ST6 ......189 J6
Austen Dr WARRN/WOL WA2 ......33 K2
Austin CI WSFD CW7 ......127 P4
Austin Dr DID/WITH M20 ......40 D4
Austin St NWCHW CW8 ......87 J9
Austins Hi CHSE CH3 ......145 J2

Austin St NWCHE CW9 ......110 D2
Austral Av WARR WA1 ......34 C9
Australia La WARRS WA4 ......48 C9
Autumn Av KNUT WA16 ......90 G3
Avalon Dr DID/WITH M20 ......40 D8
Avebury CI RIS/CU WA3 ......46 C4
WDN WA8 ......45 G4
Aveley Rd HYDE SK14 ......43 L1
Aveley CI WARR WA1 ......34 C9
Avens Rd PART M31 ......36 E5
Avenue St STKP SK1 ......17 H2
ALS/KID ST7 ......187 N4
The Avenue ALS/KID ST7 ......189 H7
CHD/CHDH SK8 ......55 J6
CHSE CH3 ......123 N4
CQ CH5 ......140 A2
HALE/TIMP WA15 ......54 A2
KNUT WA16 ......67 J1
LYMM WA13 ......50 C6
MPL/ROM SK6 ......42 C5
NEWLW WA12 ......23 N5
NWCHE CW9 ......110 B1
SALE M33 * 38 A5
SBCH CW11 ......171 K1
TPLY/KEL CW6 ......145 N4
TPLY/KEL CW6 ......166 F2
WARRS WA4 ......48 C5
WARRW/BUR WA5 ......46 G5
Back Lanes TPLY/KEL CW6 ......146 F8
Back Legh St NEWLW WA12 ......23 L6
Back Market St NEWLW WA12 ....23 L5
Back Massie St CHD/CHDH SK8 *..55 M1
Back Paradise St MCFLDS SK11 * ..8 D5
Back Queen St CH/BCN CH1 ......3 F3
Back Union Rd NM/HAY SK22 ....59 M8
Back Wallgate MCFLDS SK11 ......8 E4
Back Water St STKP SK1 * 17 H2
Bacon Av DTN/ASHW M34 ......42 H7
Badbury CI RNFD/HAY WA11 ......23 H2
Baddiley CI NANT CW5 ......195 L5
Baddiley Hall La NANT CW5 ......195 K7
Baddington La NANT CW5 ......196 E6
Badger Av CW/HAS CW1 ......184 F2
Badger Bait NSTN CH64 ......77 M7
Badger CI RUNC WA7 ......62 E8
MCFLDN SK10 ......94 C6
Badger Rd MCFLDN SK10 ......117 K2
Badgers CI CHSE CH3 ......143 N5
GTS/LS CH66 ......102 B4
WSFD CW7 ......149 J4
Badgers Pk NSTN CH64 ......77 M7
Badgers La GTS/LS CH66 ......79 H9
Badgers Set NWCHW CW8 ......107 P7
Badgers Wk CHNE CH2 ......121 P1
WYTH/NTH M22 ......54 C6
Badgers Wd CW/HAS CW1 ......184 E8
Bagley La NWCHW CW8 ......107 H5
Bagley La AUD/MAD/W CW5 ......216 C4
SBCH CW11 ......153 K5
Bagmere CI SBCH CW11 ......171 L2
Bagmere La SBCH CW11 ......153 M5
Bagnall CI WARRW/BUR WA5 ......47 N2
Bagot Av WARRW/BUR WA5 ......33 J8
Bagstock Av POY/DIS SK12 ......73 L4
Baguley Av WDN WA8 ......56 D1
Baguley Crs EDGY/DAV SK3 ......56 D1
Baguley La SALE M33 ......39 H4
Baguley Rd SALE M33 ......39 H4
Bahama CI RNFD/HAY WA11 ......23 H1
Bahama Rd RNFD/HAY WA11 ......23 H1
Bailey Av GTN M18 ......80 B7
Bailey Bridge CI CHNE CH2 ......121 N7
Bailey CI ALS/KID ST7 ......185 J1
Bailey Ct GTS/LS CH66 ......188 A5
Bailey Crs CONG CW12 ......156 A6
SBCH CW11 ......172 A3
Bailey La MANAIR M90 ......54 C3
PART M31 ......36 E4
Bailey's Bnk BIDD ST8 ......180 A3

Aynsley Ct STHEL WA9 ......45 N2
Aynsley Ct STHEL WA9 ......30 D1
Aysgarth Av CT BRAM/HZG SK7 ..57 N5
Ayres Ct STHEL WA9 ......30 D1
Ayrshire CI MWCH CW10 ......130 C9
Ayrshire Wy CONG CW12 ......156 A9
Aysgarth Av CW/SHV CW2 ......185 J7
CW/HAS CW1 ......184 G6
GTN M18 ......28 E3
Aysgarth CI SALE M33 ......38 A5
Ayshford CI ALT WA14 ......52 F1
Azalea Av GTN M18 ......28 E3
Azalea Gv RUNC WA7 ......84 D1

B

Babbacombe Rd OFTN SK2 ......57 J1
WARRW/BUR WA5 ......47 J3
Bache Av CHNE CH2 ......121 N6
Bache Dr CHNE CH2 ......121 N6
Bachefield Av CHSE CH3 ......121 N6
Bache Hall Ct CHNE CH2 ......121 N6
Bachelor's La CHSE CH3 ......143 J2
Back Adcroft St STKP SK1 * 41 N9
Back Bridge St NEWLW WA12 ....23 M6
NM/HAY SK22 ......59 N6
Back Brook PI WARRS WA4 ......48 C4
Back Chapel St BNG/LEV M19 ....28 A8
BRAM/HZG SK7 * 57 L4
Back Coole La NANT CW5 ......207 P8
Back Cross La NEWLW WA12 ......23 M5
Back Eastford Rd
WARRS WA4 ......48 C6
Back Eddisbury Rd
MCFLDN SK10 ......118 A5
Backford CI RUNC WA7 ......62 G9
Backford Gdns GTS/LS CH66 ....102 B5
Back Forshaw St
WARRN/WOL WA2 ......19 F2

Back Heathcote St
ALS/KID ST7 * 189 J6
Back High St RUNC WA7 ......14 C2
Back La ALT WA14 ......51 P7
AUD/MAD/W CW5 ......199 N7
CHSE CH3 ......165 H7
CONG CW12 ......154 G9
CONG CW12 ......154 G5
CW/SHV CW2 ......198 D5
FROD/HEL WA6 ......105 J2
HALE/TIMP WA15 ......69 K1
KNUT WA16 ......68 A9
KNUT WA16 ......111 P5
MALPAS SY14 ......202 F7
MALPAS SY14 ......204 F2
NANT CW5 ......198 B8
NWCHE CW9 ......66 E8
SBCH CW11 ......172 G2
TPLY/KEL CW6 ......145 N4
TPLY/KEL CW6 ......166 F2
WARRS WA4 ......48 C5
WARRW/BUR WA5 ......46 G5

Balmain Av *GTN* M18 .....28 C6
Balmer Rd *NTHM/RTH* M23 ....54 C2
Balmer St *STHEL* WA9 ....30 C1
Balmoral Av *CHD/CHDH* SK8 ....56 A5
  CW/SHV CW2 ....185 H7
  DTN/ASHW M34 ....29 K2
  NWCHE CW9 ....110 A7
  STHEL WA9 ....31 H1
Balmoral Cl *KNUT* WA16 ....90 F4
  WSFD CW7 ....128 D8
Balmoral Cl *MCFLDN* SK10 ....117 M2
Balmoral Dr *ALT* WA14 ....38 C8
  DTN/ASHW M34 ....28 C5
  FROD/HEL WA6 ....83 H9
  HOLMCH CW4 ....131 N9
  MPL/ROM SK6 ....25 K3
  POY/DIS SK12 ....73 K3
Balmoral Gdns *CONG* CW12 ....155 P6
  EP CH65 ....102 F2
Balmoral Gv *BRAM/HZG* SK7 ....57 M4
Balmoral Pk *CH/BCN* CH1 ....121 C7
Balmoral Pl *NANT* CW5 ....197 L5
Balmoral Rd *HALE/TIMP* WA15 ....53 P2
  HTNM SK4 ....41 H5
  WARRS WA4 ....49 H5
  WDN WA8 ....45 N3
Balmoral St *GTN* M18 ....28 C5
Balmoral Wy *WILM/AE* SK9 ....71 J8
Balmore Wy WA4 ....31 J5
Balshaw Av *IRL* M44 ....27 N7
Balshaw St *IRL* M44 ....27 N7
Baltic Rd *ALT* WA14 ....52 E1
Bamber Av *SALE* M33 ....39 H5
Bamburgh Cl *EP* CH65 ....102 C1
Bamford Av *DTN/ASHW* M34 ....29 M9
Bamford Cl *CHD/CHDH* SK8 ....55 M7
  MCFLDN SK10 ....95 N6
  RUNC WA7 ....62 A8
Bamford Gdns
  HALE/TIMP WA15 ....53 P2
Bamford Rd *DID/WITH* M20 ....40 B5
Bamford St *DID/WITH* M20 ....40 B5
Bamford St *MCFLDN* SK10 ....9 H2
  STKP SK1 ....17 G6
Bampton Cl *OFTN* SK2 ....42 A9
Bampton Rd *WYTH/NTH* M22 ....54 E4
Banastre Dr *NEWLW* WA12 ....24 B6
Banbury Cl *MCFLDN* SK10 ....117 L2
Banbury Dr *ALT* WA14 ....38 B8
  WARRW/BUR WA5 ....47 N3
Banbury Rd *NTHM/RTH* M23 ....54 B2
Banbury St *ALS/KID* ST7 ....188 F7
  STKP SK1 ....17 G5
Bancroft Av *CHD/CHDH* SK8 ....56 A6
Bancroft Cl *MPL/ROM* SK6 ....42 D5
Bancroft Rd *HALE/TIMP* WA15 ....53 L4
  WDN WA8 ....46 B5
Bandon Cl *SPK/HALE* L24 ....60 D4
Bangor Cl *GTS/LS* CH66 ....102 A6
Bangor Rd *CHD/CHDH* SK8 ....55 P1
Bangor St *RDSH* SK5 ....41 N4
Bank Cl *CHNE* CH2 ....121 P6
  MCFLDS SK11 ....9 H6
Bankes' La *RUNC* WA7 ....77 N7
Bankfield Av *CW/SHV* CW2 ....184 D9
  HTNM SK4 ....16 B3
  IRL M44 ....36 C3
Bankfield Rd *CHD/CHDH* SK8 ....55 P6
  NM/ROM SK6 ....42 C6
  SALE M33 ....38 B2
  WDN WA8 ....45 H6
Bankfields Dr *PS/BROM* CH62 ....79 N1
Bankfield St *RDSH* SK5 ....41 M4
Bank Gdns *WARRW/BUR* WA5 ....47 J3
Bankhall La *HALE/TIMP* WA15 ....53 J7
Bankhall Rd *HTNM* SK4 ....41 H6
Bankhey *NSTN* CH64 ....77 M8
Bankhouse Dr *CONG* CW12 ....156 A6
Bank House La *FROD/HEL* WA6 ....83 J2
  SBCH CW11 ....173 J2
Banklands Cl *IRL* M44 ....36 C5
Bank La CON *CONG* CW12 ....156 D1
  MCFLDN SK10 ....96 C7
  NANT CW5 ....182 F8
Bankley St *BNG/LEV* M19 ....28 A8
Bank Mellor Rd *NM/HAY* SK22 ....59 N6
Bank Ms *FROD/HEL* WA6 ....83 J9
Bank Rd *NM/ROM* SK6 ....42 C6
Banks Cl *CONG* CW12 ....155 L7
Bankside Ct *HTNM* SK4 ....41 H6
Bankside Rd *DID/WITH* M20 ....40 C9
Banks La *STKP* SK1 ....42 A8
Bank St KD CH5 ....140 B1
Bank St *ALS/KID* ST7 ....188 L4
  CHD/CHDH SK8 ....55 N1
  DROY M43 ....28 F1
  DTN/ASHW M34 ....29 M3
  DTN/ASHW M34 ....29 P9
  GOL/RIS/CU WA3 ....35 P5
  MCFLDS SK11 ....9 H6
  MPL/ROM SK6 ....42 C3
  NEWLW WA12 ....23 K6
  SALE M33 ....38 F3
  WARR WA1 ....18 E6
  WILM/AE SK9 ....71 M5
Bank for *CHF/WBR* SK23 * 97 K1
The Bank *ALS/KID* ST7 ....189 K1
Bank Vw *HOLMCH* CW4 ....132 B3
Banky Flds *CONG* CW12 ....155 L8
Bannacle Cl *NANT* CW5 ....197 L1
Bannister Dr *CHD/CHDH* SK8 ....55 P5
Bannister St *STKP* SK1 ....41 N9

Bann St *EDGY/DAV* SK3 ....16 E6
Banstead Av *WYTH/NTH* M22 ....39 N9
Barbara St *STHEL* WA9 ....31 K5
Barbauld St *WARR* WA1 ....18 D7
Barber La *ALS/KID* ST7 ....188 C1
Barberry Cl *ALT* WA14 ....38 B1
Barber's La *NWCHE* CW9 ....87 L1
  NWCHW CW8 ....128 C3
Barber St *WILM/AE* SK9 ....11 J7
  OP/CLY M11 * 28 E2
Barbican St *DID/WITH* M20 ....40 C1
Barbondale Cl
  WARRW/BUR WA5 ....32 C9
Barbridge Rd *NEWUL* ST5 ....201 N5
Barcheston Rd *CHD/CHDH* SK8 ....55 L3
Barcicroft Rd *BNG/LEV* M19 ....40 F4
Barclay Pk *KNUT* WA16 ....91 P1
Barclay Rd *POY/DIS* SK12 ....73 L4
Bardell Cl *POY/DIS* SK12 * 73 K4
Bardon Rd *NTHM/RTH* M23 ....54 B1
Bardsea Av *WYTH/NTH* M22 ....54 F6
Bardsey Cl *EP* CH65 ....102 E3
Bardsley Av *WARRW/BUR* WA5 ....35 J6
Bardsley St *HTNM* SK4 ....41 L5
Barfold Cl *OFTN* SK2 ....42 F1
Barfoot Br *SALE* M33 ....38 F1
Barford Cl *WARRW/BUR* WA5 ....34 C3
Barford Dr *ALS/KID* ST7 ....25 J1
  WILM/AE SK9 ....71 L5
Barford Gra *NSTN* CH64 ....78 F5
Bargates *WHITCH* SY15 ....213 L5
Bar HI *AUD/MAD/W* CW3 ....219 P1
Barington Dr *RUNC* WA7 ....63 J7
Baristow Cl *CHNE* CH2 ....121 N8
Barke Rd *MPL/ROM* SK6 ....42 E5
Barker's Hollow Rd
  WARRS WA4 ....63 L8
Barker's La *SALE* M33 ....38 C3
Barker St *CW/SHV* CW2 ....185 K7
  NANT CW5 ....10 B6
Bark HI *WHITCH* SY13 ....213 M6
Barkhill Rd *CHSE* CH3 ....122 C8
Barley Castle La *WARRS* WA4 ....65 K3
Barleycastle Cl *WARRS* WA4 ....65 M1
Barleycorn Cl *SALE* M33 ....39 J5
Barley Cft *ALS/KID* ST7 ....188 A6
  CHD/CHDH SK8 ....55 P7
  CHSE CH3 ....143 J3
Barleycroft Ter *ALS/KID* ST7 ....189 H1
Barley Dr *BRAM/HZG* SK7 ....56 E8
Barleyfields *ALS/KID* ST7 ....200 C5
Barley Mow Cl *CH/BCN* CH1 ....101 N2
Barley Rd *WARRS* WA4 ....65 J1
Barleywood Cl *CW/SHV* CW2 ....185 H8
Barlow Crs *MPL/ROM* SK6 ....38 C7
Barlow Dr *WSFD* CW7 ....149 H2
Barlow Fold Rd *MPL/ROM* SK6 ....43 J5
  RDSH SK5 ....28 F9
Barlow Hall Rd *CCHDY* M21 ....39 N5
Barlow HI *MCFLDS* SK11 ....158 D1
Barlow La North *RDSH* SK5 ....28 F8
Barlow Moor Cl *DID/WITH* M20 ....40 A4
Barlow Moor Rd *CCHDY* M21 ....39 L1
Barlow Rd *ALT* WA14 ....37 N8
  BNG/LEV M19 ....28 C8
  NWCHE CW9 ....128 C4
  WILM/AE SK9 ....71 K5
Barlow's La South
  BRAM/HZG SK7 ....57 J4
Barlow Wy *SBCH* CW11 ....171 M1
Barlow Wood Dr *MPL/ROM* SK6 ....58 A6
Barmouth Cl *WARRW/BUR* WA5 ....33 H6
Barnabas Av *CW/HAS* CW1 ....184 F3
Barnaby Cl *POY/DIS* SK12 ....73 J4
Barnaby Rd *POY/DIS* SK12 ....73 J4
Barnack Cl *WARR* WA1 ....34 B8
Barnacre Av *NTHM/RTH* M23 ....54 B1
Barnacre Dr *NSTN* CH64 ....77 P6
Barnard Av *HTNM* SK4 ....41 J6
Barnard Cl *MCFLDS* SK11 ....116 F6
Barnard Rd *GTN* M18 ....28 B6
Barnbridge Cl *ALS/KID* ST7 ....188 G1
Barnbrook Cl *WSFD* CW7 ....149 J1
Barnby St *WGTN/LGST* M12 ....28 A6
Barnclose Rd *WYTH/NTH* M22 ....54 F6
Barn Cft *FROD/HEL* WA6 ....63 H7
Barncroft *RUNC* WA7 ....63 H7
Barncroft Gdns
  WYTH/NTH M22 * 54 E2
Barn Croft Rd *HLWD* L26 ....44 H1
Barncroft Av *HTNM* SK4 ....41 H6
Barnes Cl *CH/BCN* CH1 ....121 J5
  CW/HAS CW1 ....186 A4
  WARRW/BUR WA5 ....46 B1
  WDN WA8 ....46 B5
Barneston Rd *WDN* WA8 ....46 C4
Barnett Av *DID/WITH* M20 ....40 C2
  NEWLW WA12 ....23 L1
Barnett St *MCFLDS* SK11 * 9 K5
Barnett Wv *CW/SHV* CW2 ....185 J8
Barnfield *CHSE* CH3 ....143 P6
Barnfield Av *MPL/ROM* SK6 ....43 P8
  RUNC WA7 ....77 J7
Barnfield Cl *ALS/KID* ST7 ....188 B7
  WHITCH SY13 ....213 K5
Barnfield Crs *SALE* M33 ....38 B3
Barnfield Rd *BNG/LEV* M19 ....40 F4
  MCFLDN SK10 ....95 M6
  WARR WA1 ....34 D9
Barnfield Rd East
  EDGY/DAV SK3 ....56 D3
Barnfield Rd West
  EDGY/DAV SK3 ....56 D3
Barnfield St *DTN/ASHW* M34 ....29 P8
Barngate Rd *CHD/CHDH* SK8 ....55 J1
Barn Gv *DTN/ASHW* M34 ....29 K2
Barnham Cl *GOL/RIS/CU* WA3 ....24 C1

Barnhill Gra *CHSE* CH3 ....179 H5
Barnhill Rd *CHSE* CH3 ....178 G7
Barnhouse La *CHSE* CH3 ....123 N3
Barn La *GOL/RIS/CU* WA3 ....24 B2
Barnley Cl *IRL* M44 ....27 P6
Barnsfold Rd *MPL/ROM* SK6 ....58 D4
Barnside Wy *MCFLDN* SK10 ....117 J1
  NWCHE CW9 ....128 C3
Barns La *LYMM* WA13 ....51 N2
Barnsley St *STKP* SK1 ....17 K6
Barnstaple Wy
  WARRW/BUR WA5 ....47 J3
Barnstead Av *DID/WITH* M20 ....40 B5
Barnston Av *EP* CH65 ....80 D8
Barnston Cl *CHSE* CH3 ....176 G6
Barn St *WDN* WA8 ....21 G7
Barnswood Cl *WARRS* WA4 ....49 L6
Barnton Cl *GOL/RIS/CU* WA3 ....24 F2
Barnview Dr *IRL* M44 ....27 N8
Barnwell Av *GOL/RIS/CU* WA3 ....23 M6
Barnwell Cl *CW/SHV* CW2 ....185 H8
  DTN/ASHW M34 ....29 L4
Barnwood Rd *NTHM/RTH* M23 ....54 C2
Baron Cl *WARR* WA1 ....34 E9
Barons Cl *CH/BCN* CH1 ....121 M7
Barons Quay Rd *NWCHE* CW9 ....13 F1
Barons Rd *CW/SHV* CW2 ....184 E4
  NANT CW5 ....183 N2
Barony Blds *NANT* CW5 ....10 C3
Barony Ct *NANT* CW5 ....10 C1
Barony Rd *NANT* CW5 ....10 C1
Barony Wy *CHSW/BR* CH4 ....142 A6
Barrack HI *MPL/ROM* SK6 ....42 F6
Barrack Hill Cl *MPL/ROM* SK6 ....42 F5
Barracks La *CHSE* CH3 ....180 A5
  MCFLDN SK10 ....- --
  NANT CW5 ....195 P5
Barrass Sq *MCFLDS* SK11 ....8 F7
Barrass St *OP/CLY* M11 ....28 D2
Barrastitch La *NWCHW* CW8 ....108 A6
Barratt Rd *ALS/KID* ST7 ....188 B5
Barrel Well Hl *CHSE* CH3 ....3 K4
Barrie Gdns *ALS/KID* ST7 ....188 E8
Barrington Av *CHD/CHDH* SK8 ....55 J2
Barrington Dr *MWCH* CW10 ....151 J3
Barrington Rd *ALT* WA14 ....53 H1
Barrow Av *WARRN/WOL* WA2 ....33 N6
Barrow Cl *WARRN/WOL* WA2 ....33 N6
Barrowdale Rd
  WYTH/NTH M22 ....54 C5
Barrow Hall La
  WARRW/BUR WA5 ....32 B9
  CHSE CH3 ....123 L6
Barrow La *CHSE* CH3 ....124 A7
  GOL/RIS/CU WA3 ....24 D1
  HALE/TIMP WA15 ....53 M8
  NWCHE CW9 ....87 H3
Barrow Meadow
  CHD/CHDH SK8 ....55 N7
Barrows Cl *CW/HAS* CW1 ....169 P9
Barrow's Green *WDN* WA8 ....46 C5
Barrow's Rw *WDN* WA8 ....45 P3
Barry Cl *EP* CH65 ....102 E4
Barrymore Av *WARRS* WA4 ....49 H5
Barrymore Crs *NWCHE* CW9 ....87 L5
Barrymore Rd *NWCHW* CW8 ....108 C3
  RUNC WA7 ....61 P7
Barry Ri *ALT* WA14 ....52 G4
Barry Rd *NTHM/RTH* M23 ....39 L6
  RDSH SK5 ....41 N3
Barsbank Cl *LYMM* WA13 ....50 C4
Barsbank La *LYMM* WA13 ....50 C4
Barshaw Gdns *WARRS* WA4 ....64 G3
The Bars *CH/BCN* CH1 ....3 K5
Bartholomew Cl *RAIN/WH* L35 ....30 D7
Bartholomew Wy
  CHSW/BR CH4 ....142 G4
Barthomley Crs *CW/SHV* CW2 ....184 D4
Barthomley Rd *ALS/KID* ST7 ....200 C5
  CW/HAS CW1 ....199 P1
  CW/SHV CW2 ....199 P1
  CW/SHV CW2 ....200 A2
Bartlegate *RUNC* WA7 ....62 F9
Bartlett St *OP/CLY* M11 ....28 B2
Bartley Rd *WYTH/NTH* M22 ....39 M8
Barton Av *WARRS* WA4 ....49 H5
Barton Cl *ALS/KID* ST7 ....188 F1
Barton Cl *RUNC* WA7 ....63 H7
  WILM/AE SK9 ....71 M4
Barton Ct *WSFD* CW7 ....149 P1
  CONG CW12 ....155 P8
  MALPAS SY14 ....177 L7
Bartons Pl *NWCHE* CW9 ....13 K1
Barton St *GOL/RIS/CU* WA3 ....24 C1
  MCFLDS SK11 ....8 D4
Barwell Av *RNFD/HAY* WA11 ....22 A3
Barwick Pl *SALE* M33 ....38 C4
Barwood Av *ALS/KID* ST7 ....188 C3
Barwood Rd *SALE* M33 ....38 E5
Basford Av *ALS/KID* ST7 ....185 M8
Basford Wy *WSFD* CW7 ....149 K1
Basildon Cl *CHNE* CH2 ....30 D2
Basil St *HTNM* SK4 ....41 H5
Basle Cl *BRAM/HZG* SK7 ....58 E4
Baslow Av *BNG/LEV* M19 ....28 B7

Baslow Dr *BRAM/HZG* SK7 ....57 M7
  CHD/CHDH SK8 ....55 L7
Baslow Gv *RDSH* SK5 ....41 N3
Baslow Rd *DTN/ASHW* M34 ....29 M9
Bassett Cl *NANT* CW5 ....197 L1
Bass St *DUK* SK16 ....29 P1
Batchelor Cl *CCHDY* M21 ....39 P1
Batemans St *CW/SHV* CW2 ....185 H8
Batemill Cl *MCFLDN* SK10 ....116 F3
Batemill La *MCFLDS* SK11 ....113 P7
Batemill Rd *NM/HAY* SK22 ....59 P5
  FROD/HEL WA6 ....83 K9
Batemill La *MCFLDS* SK11 ....113 P7
Bateson St *STKP* SK1 ....17 J3
Batey Av *RAIN/WH* L35 ....30 A4
Bath Cl *BRAM/HZG* SK7 ....57 N5
Bath Crs *CHD/CHDH* SK8 ....56 B9
Batherton Cl *WDN* WA8 ....21 J5
Atherton La *NANT* CW5 ....196 C5
Bath La *AUD/MAD/W* CW3 ....217 H2
Bath St *ALT* WA14 ....53 H5
  CHNE CH2 ....2 D2
  SBCH CW11 ....171 J3
  WARR WA1 ....18 C5
  WHITCH SY13 ....213 N5
Bathwood Dr *NSTN* CH64 ....77 L8
Batterbee Ct *CW/HAS* CW1 ....186 B5
Battersby La *WARRN/WOL* WA2 ....18 C5
Battersby St *OFTN* SK2 * 57 L1
Battersby La *WARRN/WOL* WA2 ....19 F3
Battersea Ct *WDN* WA8 * 45 M4
Battersea Rd *HTNM* SK4 ....40 F7
Battery La *WARR* WA1 ....48 A9
Bawtry Ct *WARRN/WOL* WA2 ....33 P7
Baxter Cl *RUNC* WA7 ....63 H7
Baxter Gdns *NTHM/RTH* M23 ....39 K9
Baxter Rd *SALE* M33 ....22 B9
Baxter St *WARRW/BUR* WA5 ....48 A2
Baycliffe Cl *RUNC* WA7 ....62 B9
Baycliffe Cl *RUNC* WA7 ....62 B9
Baycroft Gv *NTHM/RTH* M23 ....39 K7
Bayley Rd *NANT* CW5 ....197 L2
Bayswater Cl *RUNC* WA7 ....69 K2
Baytree Av *DTN/ASHW* M34 ....29 K2
Baytree Cl *MPL/ROM* SK6 ....102 B5
Baytree Dr *MPL/ROM* SK6 ....42 E4
Bayvil Cl *RUNC* WA7 ....69 K2
Bazley Rd *NTHM/RTH* M23 ....39 L9
Beach Gv *NWCHW* CW8 ....109 L6
Beachin La *CHSE* CH3 ....177 P5
  MALPAS SY14 ....178 A5
Beach Rd *NWCHW* CW8 ....109 L6
Beacomfold *MPL/ROM* SK6 ....43 N5
Beacon Dr *NTHM/RTH* M23 ....54 C5
Beacon Gv *RNFD/HAY* WA11 ....22 C1
Beacon Hill Vw *RUNC* WA7 ....61 K7
Beaconsfield *RUSH/FAL* M14 * 40 D1
Beaconsfield Crs *WDN* WA8 ....45 N3
Beaconsfield Rd *ALT* WA14 ....38 A9
  RUNC WA7 ....14 B6
Beaconsfield St *CHSE* CH3 ....3 H4
Beacon Vw *MPL/ROM* SK6 ....43 L8
Beadnell Dr *WARRW/BUR* WA5 ....47 J4
Beadnall Gv *RNFD/HAY* WA11 ....12 C4
Beagle Pt *WSFD* CW7 ....149 J1
Beal Cl *HTNM* SK4 ....41 J5
Bealey Cl *GTN* M18 ....28 B5
Beam Heath Wy *NANT* CW5 ....10 D1
Beaminster Rd *HTNM* SK4 ....40 F4
Beamish Cl *WARRS* WA4 ....64 F3
Beamont St *WDN* WA8 ....61 N2
Beamsley Dr *WYTH/NTH* M22 ....54 C5
Beam St *NANT* CW5 ....10 D5
Bean Leach Av *OFTN* SK2 ....57 M1
Bean Leach Dr *OFTN* SK2 ....57 M1
Bean Leach Rd *BRAM/HZG* SK7 ....57 L1
Beard Crs *NM/HAY* SK22 ....59 P7
Beard Rd *GTN* M18 * 28 C5
Beardsmore Dr
  GOL/RIS/CU WA3 ....24 C1
Bearhurst La *MCFLDS* SK11 ....115 P7
Bearstone Rd *MKTDR* TF9 ....219 H8
Beasley Cl *GTS/LS* CH66 ....101 P1
Beatrice Av *BRAM/HZG* SK7 ....57 L1
Beatrice Av *CHD/CHDH* SK8 ....56 B5
Beatrice Gdns *WHITCH* SY13 ....213 N5
Beatrice St *ALS/KID* ST7 ....29 L6
  WARRS WA4 ....48 F4
Beatrice Wignall St *DROY* M43 ....33 M7
Beatty Av *WARRN/WOL* WA2 ....33 M7
Beatty Dr *CONG* CW12 ....156 A6
Beatty Rd *NANT* CW5 ....196 E3
Beaufort Av *DID/WITH* M20 ....40 B3
  SALE M33 ....38 F5
Beaufort Cha *WILM/AE* SK9 ....71 P5
Beaufort Cl *RUNC* WA7 ....61 P7
  WARRW/BUR WA5 ....47 J2
  WDN WA8 ....44 G7
  WILM/AE SK9 ....71 J8
Beaufort Rd *OFTN* SK2 ....57 K3
Beaufort St *STHEL* WA9 ....48 E3
  WARRW/BUR WA5 ....48 A3
Beaulieu Av *WSFD* CW7 ....128 G3
Beaumaris Cl *BRAM/HZG* SK7 ....57 J7
Beaumaris Dr *EP* CH65 ....102 F2
Beaumont Cl *BIDD* ST8 ....175 L7
  CHSW/BR CH4 ....142 A6
Beaumont Rd *CCHDY* M21 ....39 L1
Beauty Bnk *NWCHW* CW8 ....127 P6
  WSFD CW7 ....127 P6
Beauvale Av *OFTN* SK2 ....57 J3
Beaverbrook Av
  GOL/RIS/CU WA3 ....26 B5
Bebington Rd *DID/WITH* M20 ....40 C5
  EDGY/DAV SK3 ....56 F1
  HALE/TIMP WA15 ....53 J4

Bebington Rd *GTS/LS* CH66 ....79 P9
Becconsall Cl *CW/HAS* CW1 ....169 P9
Becconsall Dr *CW/HAS* CW1 ....169 P9
Beccles Rd *SALE* M33 ....38 E7
Bechers *WDN* WA8 ....45 H4
Beckenham Gv *WSFD* CW7 ....149 J1
Beckett Av *WSFD* CW7 ....150 D2
Beckett Dr *WARRN/WOL* WA2 ....33 K3
Beckett's La *CHSE* CH3 ....143 J2
Beckett St *GTN* M18 ....28 C5
Beckfield Rd *NTHM/RTH* M23 ....54 B2
Beckford Cl *CW/HAS* CW1 ....169 N9
Beckside *RDSH* SK5 ....28 E8
Becks La *MCFLDN* SK10 ....116 E2
Beck St *OP/CLY* M11 * 28 E2
Beckton Gdns *WYTH/NTH* M22 ....54 E4
Becontree Dr *NTHM/RTH* M23 ....54 B1
Bedells La *WILM/AE* SK9 ....71 J8
Bedford Av *EP* CH65 ....102 C2
  SALE M33 ....38 G6
Bedford Av East *EP* CH65 ....102 D2
Bedford Cl *CW/SHV* CW2 ....185 K7
Bedford Dr *HALE/TIMP* WA15 ....53 J4
Bedford Gn *CW/SHV* CW2 ....185 K7
Bedford Gn *IRL* M44 ....36 B2
Bedford Gv *ALS/KID* ST7 ....187 M3
Bedford Pl *CW/SHV* CW2 ....185 J7
Bedford Rl *WSFD* CW7 ....187 L2
Bedford Rd *WILM/AE* SK9 ....189 J5
  MCFLDS SK11 ....8 B6
Bedford St *RDSH* SK5 ....41 M1
  STHEL WA9 ....22 B7
  WARRS WA4 ....48 F7
Bedwards Rw *CH/BCN* CH1 ....2 C4
Beech *ALS/KID* ST7 ....173 J9
  BRAM/HZG SK7 ....57 L5
  CHD/CHDH SK8 ....29 K5
  DTN/ASHW M34 ....29 K5
  EDGY/DAV SK3 ....56 F1
  FROD/HEL WA6 ....84 A5
  GOL/RIS/CU WA3 ....26 A6
  KNUT WA16 ....69 J8
  NM/HAY SK22 ....59 P6
  RNFD/HAY WA11 ....23 K2
  STHEL WA9 ....31 J3
  WARRS WA4 ....49 M4
  WHITCH SY13 ....213 L7
  WYTH/NTH M22 ....39 N8
Beech Bnk *MCFLDN* SK10 ....8 E1
Beech Cl *BIDD* ST8 ....175 P8
  CONG CW12 ....155 J6
  HOLMCH CW4 ....132 K7
  KNUT WA16 ....91 K7
  NEWLW WA12 ....23 N7
  WILM/AE SK9 ....93 J5
Beech Cots *WARRS* WA4 * 64 C4
  WILM/AE SK9 ....93 J5
Beech Ct *WILM/AE* SK9 * 71 M8
Beech Crs *POY/DIS* SK12 ....73 L2
Beech Dr *CW/SHV* CW2 ....185 H9
Beechcroft Dr *EP* CH65 ....102 D1
Beech Dr *ALS/KID* ST7 ....188 C3
  CW/SHV CW2 ....184 E6
  KNUT WA16 ....90 F3
Beeches Ms *DID/WITH* M20 ....40 A4
The Beeches *CHNE* CH2 ....122 A5
  CHSW/BR CH4 ....141 H2
  DID/WITH M20 ....83 J9
  FROD/HEL WA6 ....83 J9
  GTS/LS CH66 ....79 P9
  NANT CW5 ....3 J1
  STHEL WA9 ....31 J3
  WHITCH SY13 ....213 L5
Beech Farm Dr *MCFLDN* SK10 ....117 K2
  NWCHE CW9 ....128 C3
  SALE M33 ....38 C6
Beechfield *ALT* WA14 ....52 C4
  NWCHE CW9 ....128 F3
  SALE M33 ....38 C6
Beechfield Cl *WILM/AE* SK9 ....70 C9
Beechfield Dr *MWCH* CW10 ....130 A9
Beechfield Gdns *NWCHW* CW8 ....130 A9
Beechfield Rd *CHD/CHDH* SK8 ....56 B7
  EDGY/DAV SK3 ....56 D3
  EP CH65 ....102 D3
  WARRS WA4 ....65 K5
  WILM/AE SK9 ....93 K5
Beech Gv *CW/SHV* CW2 ....150 B2
Beech Gv *CHNE* CH2 ....122 B8
  CW/HAS CW1 ....93 J5
  GTS/LS CH66 ....102 C4
  LYMM WA13 ....50 B5
  MCFLDS SK11 ....117 L7
  NWCHW CW8 ....109 L6
  SALE M33 ....172 A3
  SBCH CW11 ....172 A3
  WARR WA1 ....34 B9
  WILM/AE SK9 ....71 J8
Beech Hall Dr *MCFLDN* SK10 ....117 J2
Beech Heyes Cl *NWCHW* CW8 ....108 G4
Beech Heyes Dr *NWCHW* CW8 ....108 F4
Beech Hey La *NSTN* CH64 ....78 F4
Beech HI *KNUT* WA16 * 91 H1
Beech La *FROD/HEL* WA6 ....84 A5
  MCFLDN SK10 ....83 H6
  MPL/ROM SK6 ....43 H6
  NWCHW CW8 ....109 J1
  TPLY/KEL CW6 ....147 M4
Beech Lawn *ALT* WA14 ....53 J4

MPL/ROM SK6 58 D8
RUNC WA7 15 K7
RUNC WA7 84 F1
SALE M33 38 G4
TPLY/KEL CW6 147 P1
WARRS WA4 48 E7
WILM/AE SK9 93 K2
Beech St MWCH CW10 151 J1
Beech St West CW/HAS CW1 * 4 D2
Beech Tree Cl NANT CW5 197 L2
Beechtree Farm Cl KNUT WA16 51 J8
Beechtree La KNUT WA16 51 J8
Beechurst Rd CHD/CHDH SK8 56 B2
Beech View Rd
FROD/HEL WA6 106 G3
Beechway CHNE CH2 121 M5
MCFLDN SK10 95 N6
MPL/ROM SK6 58 D8
WILM/AE SK9 71 H9
Beechways WARRS WA4 64 F1
Beechways Dr NSTN CH64 77 K5
Beechwood ALT WA14 52 F6
KNUT WA16 90 G3
Beechwood Av CCHDY M21 39 M1
MPL/ROM SK6 43 H6
NEWLW WA12 23 P5
NWCHW CW8 109 J6
RUNC WA7 62 D9
WARR WA1 33 P8
WARRW/BUR WA5 47 K2
Beechwood Dr ALS/KID ST7 187 M4
CONG CW12 155 P2
GTS/LS CH66 101 P3
MPL/ROM SK6 58 E1
NWCHE CW9 88 F7
SALE M33 37 P4
WILM/AE SK9 * 71 N6
Beechwood Gv CHD/CHDH SK8 56 A7
Beechwood La
GOL/RIS/CU WA3 25 M5
Beechwood Ms MCFLDN SK10 117 J2
Beechwood Rd CHSW/BR CH4 141 P5
Beecroft Cl WARRW/BUR WA5 32 G7
Beede St OP/CLY M11 28 B1
Beenham Cl SALE M33 37 P5
Beeston Av HALE/TIMP WA15 53 K1
Beeston Brow MCFLDN SK10 95 P4
Beeston Cl GOL/RIS/CU WA3 34 E4
HOLMCH CW4 131 M8
MCFLDN SK10 95 P4
MWCH CW10 151 K5
Beeston Ct RUNC WA7 * 62 G2
Beeston Dr ALS/KID ST7 187 N5
KNUT WA16 90 E5
WSFD CW7 149 L3
Beeston Gn GTS/LS CH66 80 A8
Beeston Gv EDGY/DAV SK3 56 E2
Beeston Mt MCFLDN SK10 95 P4
Beeston Pathway
CHSW/BR CH4 142 G3
Beeston Rd CHSW/BR CH4 140 F7
SALE M33 38 B4
WILM/AE SK9 71 M1
Beeston St NWCHW CW8 12 D4
Beeston Ter MCFLDS SK11 116 E6
Beeston Vw ALS/KID ST7 189 J9
CHSW/BR CH4 142 G3
Beeth St OP/CLY M11 28 D3
Beggarman's La KNUT WA16 90 E6
Begley Cl MPL/ROM SK6 42 E7
Begonia Gdns STHEL WA9 31 M1
Beilby Rd RNFD/HAY WA11 23 K2
Belcroft Cl WYTH/NTH M22 39 P8
Belfield Rd DID/WITH M20 40 C5
Belford Av DTN/ASHW M34 28 G6
Belfry Cl WILM/AE SK9 71 M6
Belfry Dr MCFLDN SK10 95 J9
Belgate Cl WGTN/LGST M12 28 A5
Belgrave Av ALS/KID ST7 187 P3
CHSW/BR CH4 142 A4
CHSW/BR CH4 161 J2
CHSW/BR CH4 161 M3
CONG CW12 155 L7
MPL/ROM SK6 58 D1
WARR WA1 34 A9
Belgrave Cl CHSW/BR CH4 160 D3
LEIGH WN7 25 L1
WDN WA8 46 C4
Belgrave Crs OFTN SK2 56 G3
Belgrave Dr EP CH65 80 B8
Belgrave Pl CHSW/BR CH4 142 F3
Belgrave Rd ALT WA14 52 G4
CHSE CH3 143 K2
CW/SHV CW2 4 B6
IRL M44 36 C3
MCFLDS SK11 117 J8
NWCHE CW9 110 A8
SALE M33 38 D4
Belgrave St CH/BCN CH1 3 G2
Belgravia Ct WDN WA8 45 M4
Belgravia Gdns
HALE/TIMP WA15 53 J7
Bellaport Rd MKTDR TF9 217 P9
Bellard Dr CHNE CH2 122 B7
Bell Av MCFLDS SK11 117 M9
Bellcast Cl WARRS WA4 48 E9
Belldale Cl HTNM SK4 41 H6
Bellemonte Rd FROD/HEL WA6 83 P7
Belleville Av WYTH/NTH M22 54 G7
Bellevue La CHSE CH3 122 E7
Belle Vue St WGTN/LGST M12 28 A3
Belle Vue Ter SBCH CW11 171 N3
Bellfield Av CHD/CHDH SK8 56 B6
WARRS WA4 47 P8
Bellhouse La WARRS WA4 49 L6
Bell House Rd WDN WA8 46 A6
Bellingham Dr RUNC WA7 15 F6
Bell La RAIN/WH L35 30 F6
WARRS WA4 49 N4
Bell Meadow Ct
TPLY/KEL CW6 146 G8
Bell's Hollow NEWUL ST5 201 P4
Belmont Av DTN/ASHW M34 29 K5
MCFLDN SK10 116 C3
SBCH CW11 171 M2
WARRS WA4 49 H4
Belmont Cl HTNM SK4 16 E1
Belmont Crs WARRW/BUR WA5 47 L1
Belmont Dr CHSW/BR CH4 141 M4
MPL/ROM SK6 43 N7
Belmont Rd BRAM/HZG SK7 72 E1
CHD/CHDH SK8 55 K1
HALE/TIMP WA15 53 J5
NWCHE CW9 87 P4
NWCHE CW9 110 C5
SALE M33 38 D2
WDN WA8 46 B5
Belmont St HTNM SK4 16 E1
Belmont Ter PART M31 * 37 J2
Belmont Wy HTNM SK4 16 E1
Belper Rd HTNM SK4 40 G7
Belsay Dr NTHM/RTH M23 54 C3
Belstone Av NTHM/RTH M23 54 C4
Belstone Cl BRAM/HZG SK7 56 F5
Belton Cl WHITCH SY13 213 K6
Belton Rd WHITCH SY13 213 K7
Beltony Dr CW/HAS CW1 169 P8
Belvedere Av RDSH SK5 28 F7
STHEL WA9 31 J2
Belvedere Cl FROD/HEL WA6 84 A4
Belvedere Dr CH/BCN CH1 121 H7
MPL/ROM SK6 42 B5
Belvedere Rd NEWLW WA12 23 M5
Belvedere Ter ALS/KID ST7 188 B1
Belvoir Av BNG/LEV M19 * 28 A7
BRAM/HZG SK7 57 L7
Belvoir Rd WARRS WA4 48 D7
WDN WA8 45 P6
Belvor Av DTN/ASHW M34 29 L2
Belwood Rd CCHDY M21 39 K1
Bembridge Cl
WARRW/BUR WA5 31 P9
WDN WA8 45 M3
Bembridge Dr MWCH CW10 151 J2
Bembridge Rd DTN/ASHW M34 29 P9
Bempton Cl OFTN SK2 57 N2
Bemrose Av ALT WA14 52 G1
Benbow St SALE M33 38 E3
Benbrook Wy MCFLDS SK11 135 M2
Benchill Court Rd
WYTH/NTH M22 54 G3
Benchill Dr WYTH/NTH M22 54 F2
Benchill Rd WYTH/NTH M22 54 E1
Bendall St OP/CLY M11 28 E1
Ben Davies Ct MPL/ROM SK6 * 43 H6
Bendee Av NSTN CH64 77 N6
Bendee Rd NSTN CH64 77 M6
Benfleet Cl WGTN/LGST M12 * 28 A3
Bengal St EDGY/DAV SK3 16 E7
Benjamins Wy ALS/KID ST7 201 J5
Bennet Cl NSTN CH64 78 E5
Bennet Rd NWCHE CW9 110 D6
Bennett Av WARR WA1 49 H1
Bennett Cl CW/HAS CW1 5 J2
EDGY/DAV SK3 16 A6
Bennett Randle Cl SBCH CW11 171 K2
Bennetts La MCFLDS SK11 157 L4
WDN WA8 46 C6
Bennett St EDGY/DAV SK3 16 A6
WARR WA1 18 E6
Ben Nevis Dr GTS/LS CH66 79 K7
Benson Rd GOL/RIS/CU WA3 34 E6
Bentham Av WARRN/WOL WA2 33 M5
Bentham Rd GOL/RIS/CU WA3 26 A7
Bentinck Cl ALT WA14 * 52 G3
Bentinck Rd ALT WA14 52 G3
Bentinck St RUNC WA7 14 C1
STHEL WA9 22 B8
Bent La CONG CW12 155 H9
GOL/RIS/CU WA3 26 A7
LYMM WA13 51 J1
NWCHW CW8 107 M3
Bentley Dr CW/HAS CW1 185 N3
Bentley Gv WSFD CW7 149 L4
Bentley Rd DTN/ASHW M34 29 M6
Bentley's Farm La WARRS WA4 64 G9
Bentley St STHEL WA9 31 H4
Benton Dr CHNE CH2 121 M7
MPL/ROM SK6 43 P8
Bents Av MPL/ROM SK6 42 E5
Bentside Rd POY/DIS SK12 75 H1
Benty Heath La NSTN CH64 78 E2
Beresford Crs RDSH SK5 28 E6
Beresford St STHEL WA9 30 D1
WARR WA1 19 K2
Berisford Cl HALE/TIMP WA15 38 B9
Berkeley Av ALS/KID ST7 187 P3
Berkeley Cl LEIGH WN7 25 L1
OFTN SK2 42 B8
Berkeley Crs CW/SHV CW2 184 G8
Berkeley Ri WSFD CW7 149 J2
Berkeley Rd BRAM/HZG SK7 57 M4
Berkley Av BNG/LEV M19 28 A7
Berkley Dr CHSW/BR CH4 142 G4
Berkshire Cl MCFLDN SK10 116 E2
Berkshire Dr CONG CW12 155 M6
IRL M44 36 B3
WARR WA1 34 E9
Berlin Rd EDGY/DAV SK3 56 D1
Bernard Av WARRS WA4 48 F7
Berne Cl BRAM/HZG SK7 56 E3
Bernisdale Rd KNUT WA16 91 K1
Berrie Gv BNG/LEV M19 28 A9
Berristal Rd MCFLDN SK10 96 B9
Berry Cl GTS/LS CH66 101 N1
WILM/AE SK9 71 J9
Berrycroft La MPL/ROM SK6 42 F5
Berry Dr GTS/LS CH66 79 N9
Berry Rd WDN WA8 20 A1
Berrys La STHEL WA9 22 D8
Berrystead NWCHW CW8 109 K8
Bertha St OP/CLY M11 28 B2
Bertram St NEWLW WA12 23 K6
SALE M33 39 H4
WGTN/LGST M12 * 28 A3
Berwick Av HTNM SK4 40 E6
PS/BROM CH62 79 J1
Berwick Cl MCFLDN SK10 116 F2
WARR WA1 49 N1
Berwick Ct HOLMCH CW4 131 N9
Berwick Gdns GTS/LS CH66 79 M7
Berwick Gv GTS/LS CH66 79 M7
Berwick Rd GTS/LS CH66 79 L7
Berwyn Av CHD/CHDH SK8 56 B2
Berwyn Cl GTS/LS CH66 79 L7
Berwyn Gv STHEL WA9 22 D6
Bessancourt HOLMCH CW4 131 P8
Bessemer Rd IRL M44 36 E2
Bessemer St OP/CLY M11 28 C2
Beswicks La WILM/AE SK9 92 E2
Beswicks Rd NWCHW CW8 12 D1
Beswick St MCFLDS SK11 8 B5
Betchton Cl SBCH CW11 171 P2
Betchton Rd SBCH CW11 171 P6
Betchworth Crs RUNC WA7 62 B8
Betchworth Wy MCFLDN SK10 95 J9
Bethany Cl RNFD/HAY WA11 22 E2
Betjeman Cl WARRS WA4 49 H3
Betjeman Wy CW/HAS CW1 185 M3
Betley Cl NWCHE CW9 110 A7
Betley Hall Gdns
AUD/MAD/W CW3 199 M9
Betleymere Rd CHD/CHDH SK8 55 P3
Betley Rd RDSH SK5 28 F8
Betley St CW/HAS CW1 4 E3
Betnor Av STKP SK1 42 A7
Betsyfield Dr GOL/RIS/CU WA3 34 B1
Betty's La TPLY/KEL CW6 166 A8
Bevan Av ALS/KID ST7 201 N1
Bevan Cl STHEL WA9 30 C2
WARRW/BUR WA5 47 P1
Beverley Av DTN/ASHW M34 29 N7
WARRS WA4 48 F7
Beverley Rd OFTN SK2 42 B8
WARRW/BUR WA5 47 N1
Beverley Wy GTS/LS CH66 79 M6
MCFLDN SK10 95 J9
Beverly Rd RUSH/FAL M14 40 E1
Bevin Av GOL/RIS/CU WA3 26 B5
Bevyl Rd NSTN CH64 77 H3
Bewley Ct CHSE CH3 143 J3
WARRW/BUR WA5 32 G8
Bewsey Park Cl
WARRW/BUR WA5 33 J9
Bewsey Rd WARRW/BUR WA5 33 J9
Bewsey St WARR WA1 18 D5
Bexhill Av HALE/TIMP WA15 53 K1
WARRN/WOL WA2 33 L4
Bexhill Rd EDGY/DAV SK3 56 E3
Bexington Dr CW/HAS CW1 170 A9
Bexton Av WSFD CW7 149 J1
Bexton La KNUT WA16 90 D6
Bexton Rd KNUT WA16 90 D5
Beyer Cl GTN M18 28 C4
Bibby Av WARR WA1 48 G1
Bibby La BNG/LEV M19 40 G2
Bibby's La MCFLDN SK10 117 N3
Bibby St ALS/KID ST7 188 A1
Bibury Av WYTH/NTH M22 54 D4
Bickerdike Av WGTN/LGST M12 28 B6
Bickerton Av FROD/HEL WA6 84 B6
Bickerton Cl GOL/RIS/CU WA3 34 E4
Bickerton Dr BRAM/HZG SK7 56 G6
Bickerton Rd ALT WA14 52 F2
MALPAS SY14 193 K5
Bickerton Wy NWCHE CW9 109 N8
Bickley Cl CW/SHV CW2 198 D5
RUNC WA7 15 J5
WARRN/WOL WA2 34 A5
Bickley Town La MALPAS SY14 193 K9
Bicknell Cl WARRW/BUR WA5 32 E8
Bida La CONG CW12 175 J1
Biddall Dr NTHM/RTH M23 54 D1
Biddulph Av OFTN SK2 57 J2
Biddulph Common Rd
BIDD ST8 175 P2
Biddulph Park Rd BIDD ST8 175 P4
Biddulph Rd ALS/KID ST7 189 N2
CONG CW12 156 B9
Biddulph St CONG CW12 175 K2
Bideford Av STHEL WA9 31 H3
Bideford Dr NTHM/RTH M23 39 J9
Bideford Rd OFTN SK2 42 B7
WARRW/BUR WA5 47 J3
Bidston Av RNFD/HAY WA11 22 B4
Bidston Cl CHNE CH2 121 N6
Bidston Dr WILM/AE SK9 71 N4
Bidston Gn GTS/LS CH66 79 P9
Bidston Wy RNFD/HAY WA11 22 B4
Bidvale Wy CW/HAS CW1 170 B9
Big Field La TPLY/KEL CW6 146 F3
Biggin Ct WARRN/WOL WA2 33 P7
Bignall End Rd ALS/KID ST7 201 K3
Billinge Crs RNFD/HAY WA11 22 B3
Billingham Rd STHEL WA9 30 C1
Billington Av NEWLW WA12 23 N4
Billington Cl CW/SHV CW2 184 G6
WARRW/BUR WA5 32 B8
Billington Rd WDN WA8 45 H3
Bill Williams Cl OP/CLY M11 28 C1
Bilson Dr EDGY/DAV SK3 41 J9
Bilston Cl WDN WA8 46 C5
Bilton Wy CW/SHV CW2 184 E3
Bingham Dr NTHM/RTH M23 54 B1
Binney Rd NWCHE CW9 13 J3
Binsley Cl IRL M44 27 N8
Binyon Wy CW/HAS CW1 185 N4
Birchacre Gv RUSH/FAL M14 40 E1
Birchall Av GOL/RIS/CU WA3 25 M5
Birchall Gn MPL/ROM SK6 42 E3
Birchall Moss La NANT CW5 209 M4
Birchall St GOL/RIS/CU WA3 34 B1
Birchall Wk CW/SHV CW2 185 K8
Birch Av ALS/KID ST7 188 A5
CW/HAS CW1 5 K1
HTNM SK4 41 J4
IRL M44 36 C3
MCFLDN SK10 116 G3
MPL/ROM SK6 43 J6
SALE M33 38 E5
WARRN/WOL WA2 33 K4
WILM/AE SK9 71 H8
WSFD CW7 150 A1
Birch Brook Rd LYMM WA13 51 J2
Birch Cl CW/HAS CW1 185 M3
HOLMCH CW4 132 A8
Birch Ct CONG CW12 155 H7
Birch Crs NEWLW WA12 23 K5
Birchdale ALT WA14 52 G5
Birchdale Av CHD/CHDH SK8 55 K5
Birchdale Crs WARRS WA4 48 E7
Birchdale Rd WARR WA1 34 B9
WARRS WA4 48 E8
Birch Dr BRAM/HZG SK7 57 J5
Birchen Rd HLWD L26 44 A8
Birchenwood Rd
BURS/TUN ST6 189 N8
Birchenwood Wy ALS/KID ST7 189 K7
Birches Croft Dr MCFLDN SK10 116 F3
Birches La NWCHE CW9 111 J6
The Birches CHSW/BR CH4 140 F7
CW/SHV CW2 185 J8
SALE M33 38 B3
Birchfield Av ALS/KID ST7 188 B1
WDN WA8 45 N5
Birchfield Rd EDGY/DAV SK3 41 H9
LYMM WA13 51 H3
WARRW/BUR WA5 47 M2
WDN WA8 45 N5
Birchfields HALE/TIMP WA15 53 K6
Birchfield St STHEL WA9 30 C1
Birch Fold HOLMCH CW4 131 N2
Birchgate Cl MCFLDN SK10 116 E3
Birch Gv DTN/ASHW M34 29 L6
DTN/ASHW M34 29 M3
GTS/LS CH66 102 C3
HALE/TIMP WA15 54 A2
KNUT WA16 91 H3
NWCHE CW9 88 F8
NWCHE CW9 111 H5
WARR WA1 34 A9
WARRS WA4 48 F4
Birch Heath La CHSE CH3 143 N2
Birch Heath Rd TPLY/KEL CW6 165 N1
Birch Hl FROD/HEL WA6 106 A4
Birch House Rd NEWUL ST5 201 N7
Birchinall Cl MCFLDS SK11 116 G6
Birchin Cl NANT CW5 11 F3
Birchin La NANT CW5 10 E3
Birch La CW/SHV CW2 198 E5
MWCH CW10 129 N9
Birchlea HALE/TIMP WA15 53 K3
Birchmuir Cl CW/HAS CW1 185 H2
Birch Ri CHNE CH2 121 N5
Birch Rd ALS/KID ST7 201 J6
CHD/CHDH SK8 55 J2
CHSW/BR CH4 142 B5
CONG CW12 155 H7
GOL/RIS/CU WA3 36 A6
PART M31 36 C5
PART M31 37 L5
POY/DIS SK12 73 M4
RNFD/HAY WA11 23 J2
RUNC WA7 15 H6
WDN WA8 45 N4
Birch St DROY M43 * 29 H1
WGTN/LGST M12 28 A3
Birch Tree Av BRAM/HZG SK7 57 N6
Birch Tree Cl ALT WA14 52 G6
Birch Tree Dr WYTH/NTH M22 54 F4
Birch Tree La ALS/KID ST7 189 K1
HOLMCH CW4 131 P3
WARRS WA4 65 H8
Birch Tree Rd GOL/RIS/CU WA3 25 H1
Birchvale Av MPL/ROM SK6 43 J5
Birch Valley Rd ALS/KID ST7 189 L7
Birchway BRAM/HZG SK7 56 D8
MPL/ROM SK6 58 D8
Birch Wy MCFLDN SK10 94 E7
MCFLDN SK10 95 N5
Birchways WARRS WA4 64 G1
Birchwood Bvd
GOL/RIS/CU WA3 34 E6
Birchwood Cl CHNE CH2 82 C9
GTS/LS CH66 101 P3
Birchwood Dr KNUT WA16 112 B5
NANT CW5 10 E4
WILM/AE SK9 71 M6
Birchwood Park Av
GOL/RIS/CU WA3 34 E3
Birchwood Wy
GOL/RIS/CU WA3 34 G4
WARRN/WOL WA2 33 P8
Bird Hall Av CHD/CHDH SK8 56 C3
Birdhall Gv BNG/LEV M19 28 A9
Bird Hall La EDGY/DAV SK3 41 J9
Bird Hall Rd CHD/CHDH SK8 56 B2
Birdlip Dr NTHM/RTH M23 54 C4
Birds La CHSE CH3 164 D8
TPLY/KEL CW6 147 H9
TPLY/KEL CW6 166 E9
Birdwell Dr WARRW/BUR WA5 47 L2
Birkdale Cl BRAM/HZG SK7 56 F8
MCFLDN SK10 95 J9
Birkdale Ct NWCHE CW9 13 J2
Birkdale Dr ALS/KID ST7 189 L5
SALE M33 38 B6
Birkdale Gdns WSFD CW7 128 B9
Birkdale Gv RDSH SK5 41 N3
Birkdale Pl SALE M33 * 38 C2
Birkdale Rd RDSH SK5 41 N3
WARRW/BUR WA5 47 K3
WDN WA8 45 P2
Birkenhead Rd NSTN CH64 78 C4
Birkenhead St NWCHE CW9 110 C4
Birkett Av EP CH65 102 E2
Birkinheath La ALT WA14 68 F2
Birkworth Ct OFTN SK2 57 K1
Birley Cl HALE/TIMP WA15 38 C9
Birley Pk DID/WITH M20 40 A5
Birley St NEWLW WA12 23 P5
Birling Dr NTHM/RTH M23 54 D3
Birnam Dr RAIN/WH L35 30 C6
Birstall Av RNFD/HAY WA11 22 A4
Birstall Ct RUNC WA7 62 B7
Birtles Av RDSH SK5 28 F6
Birtles Cl CHD/CHDH SK8 55 P2
SBCH CW11 171 P2
Birtles La MCFLDN SK10 115 M3
Birtlespool Rd CHD/CHDH SK8 55 P3
Birtles Rd MCFLDN SK10 116 D3
WARRN/WOL WA2 33 M7
Birtwistle Rd NWCHE CW9 110 D6
Bisham Pk RUNC WA7 63 H4
CHSE CH3 164 D5
Bishop Bennet Wy CHSE CH3 177 L8
MALPAS SY14 202 G2
MALPAS SY14 203 M3
WHITCH SY13 205 K6
WHITCH SY13 213 K2
Bishopdale Cl
WARRW/BUR WA5 32 C9
Bishopdale Dr RAIN/WH L35 30 C6
Bishopgates Dr NWCHE CW9 109 N8
Bishop Reeves Rd
RNFD/HAY WA11 23 J2
Bishop Rd MCFLDN SK10 95 N6
Bishop's Cl ALS/KID ST7 188 F8
ALT WA14 52 F6
CHD/CHDH SK8 56 A2
Bishops Ct CHSW/BR CH4 140 G6
WARRN/WOL WA2 33 J4
Bishops Gdns EP CH65 6 B4
Bishops Ga CHNE CH2 122 B8
Bishops Ms SALE M33 38 B2
Bishop St CHNE CH2 122 A8
STKP SK1 17 J4
Bishops Wy WDN WA8 46 B4
Bishops Wd NANT CW5 196 G4
Bishopton Cl BNG/LEV M19 28 C8
Bishopton Dr MCFLDS SK11 116 G4
Bisley Av NTHM/RTH M23 54 B1
Bispham Av RDSH SK5 28 F7
Bispham Rd WARRW/BUR WA5 47 M3
Bittern Cl POY/DIS SK12 72 G3
RUNC WA7 63 H6
WARRN/WOL WA2 33 N5
Bittern Gv MCFLDN SK10 116 G3
Blackacres Cl SBCH CW11 171 L3
Blackberry Cl ALT WA14 37 N8
Blackberry La RDSH SK5 42 A1
Blackbird Wy ALS/KID ST7 189 P7
BIDD ST8 175 M9
Blackboards La GTS/LS CH66 79 L6
Blackbrook Av NEWUL ST5 201 M7
WARRN/WOL WA2 34 A7
Blackbrook Cl WDN WA8 45 J4
Black Brook Rd HTNM SK4 41 L1
Blackbrook Rd RNFD/HAY WA11 22 C4
Blackburn Cl GOL/RIS/CU WA3 25 H1
Blackburne Av WDN WA8 61 H1
Blackburne Cl
WARRN/WOL WA2 34 D6
Blackburn Gdns DID/WITH M20 40 B4
Blackcap Rd WARRS WA4 65 J2
Blackcarr Rd NTHM/RTH M23 54 D2
Blackcroft Av NWCHW CW8 109 J2
Blackden La HOLMCH CW4 132 C2
KNUT WA16 113 L5
MCFLDS SK11 134 A3
Black Denton's Pl WDN WA8 46 A6
Black Diamond St CH/BCN CH1 3 F1
Blackdown Cl GTS/LS CH66 79 L8
Blackdown Gv STHEL WA9 22 D7
Blackeys La NSTN CH64 77 L5
Black Firs La CONG CW12 154 G5
Blackford Rd BNG/LEV M19 41 J1
Black Friars CH/BCN CH1 2 D6
Blackheath La RUNC WA7 63 K2
Blackhill La KNUT WA16 90 D5
Blackhorse St STHEL WA9 22 B4
Blackhurst Brow MCFLDN SK10 94 B2
Blackhurst Farm Rd NANT CW5 195 H3
Blackhurst St WARR WA1 18 E6
Black La MCFLDN SK10 9 G2
Blackledge Cl WARRN/WOL WA2 34 B5
Blackley Cl MCFLDN SK10 95 H9
WARRS WA4 48 F4
Black Lion La GTS/LS CH66 79 M7
Blackmore Gv WHITCH SY13 213 M5
Black Moss Rd ALT WA14 37 K9
Black Park Rd WHITCH SY13 213 P5
Black Rd MCFLDS SK11 9 H7
Blackshaw Cl CONG CW12 156 B9
Blackshaw Dr
WARRW/BUR WA5 32 E7
Blackshaw La WILM/AE SK9 93 H4
Blackshaw St EDGY/DAV SK3 17 F6
MCFLDS SK11 8 D6
Blackstone Av RNFD/HAY WA11 22 B4
Blackstone Rd OFTN SK2 57 K2
Blackthorn Av BNG/LEV M19 41 H1
Blackthorn Cl CHSE CH3 143 J5
CHSW/BR CH4 140 F7
CW/SHV CW2 185 H8
Blackthorne Av GTS/LS CH66 102 C4
Blackthorne Dr SALE M33 38 A6
Blackthorne Rd HYDE SK14 43 K2
Blackthorn Pl NEWUL ST5 201 P7
Blackwell Cl MWCH CW10 151 K4
Blackwin St WGTN/LGST M12 28 A3
Blackwood Dr NTHM/RTH M23 38 G8
Blacon Av CH/BCN CH1 121 J6
Blacon Hall Rd CH/BCN CH1 121 J6
Blacon Point Rd CH/BCN CH1 120 G8
Bladen Cl CHD/CHDH SK8 56 A3
Bladon Cl NWCHE CW9 109 N8
Bladon Crs ALS/KID ST7 187 N3
Blagg Av NANT CW5 196 D3
Blair Cl BRAM/HZG SK7 57 J7
SALE M33 37 P7
Blair Dr WDN WA8 45 H4
Blairgowrie Dr MCFLDN SK10 95 H9
Blaizefield Cl
AUD/MAD/W CW3 219 H3
Blake Cl CH/BCN CH1 121 J5
CW/SHV CW2 184 F7
Blakeden La NWCHE CW9 148 F1
Blake Dr OFTN SK2 42 D9
Blake La NWCHW CW8 127 K1

Blakeley La KNUT WA16 70 A7
Blakelow Bnk MCFLDS SK11 9 K7
Blakelow Cl MWCH CW10 151 H3
Blakelow Crs NANT CW5 197 N4
Blakelow Rd MCFLDS SK11 9 J7
Blakemere Av SALE M33 39 H5
Blakemere Cl WHITCH SY13 213 N5
Blakemere Ct EP CH65 6 E1
Blakemere Dr NWCHE CW9 109 N7
Blakemere La FROD/HEL WA6 107 H8
Blakemere Wy SBCH CW11 171 L1
Blake St CONG CW12 155 L8
Blakey St WGTN/LGST M12 28 A5
Blandford Dr MCFLDN SK10 116 F4
NWCHE CW9 109 N9
Blandford Rd HTNM SK4 41 J6
WARRW/BUR WA5 47 M2
Blanefield Cl CCHDY M21 39 P1
The Blankney NANT CW5 10 B6
Blantyre St RUNC WA7 61 M3
Blaven Cl EDGY/DAV SK3 56 F2
Blaydon Gv STHEL WA9 30 C1
Blaze Hl MCFLDN SK10 96 B5
Blazemoss Bnk OFTN SK2 57 K2
Bleak Hey Rd WYTH/NTH M22 55 H5
Bleasdale Rd CW/HAS CW1 170 A8
NEWLW WA12 23 M5
WYTH/NTH M22 54 C5
Bleatarn Rd STKP SK1 42 A9
Bleeding Wolf La ALS/KID ST7 188 G3
Blenheim Cl ALT WA14 53 H5
CW/SHV CW2 * 184 E8
MCFLDN SK10 116 G3
NWCHE CW9 109 P8
POY/DIS SK12 73 M2
WARRN/WOL WA2 33 P6
WILM/AE SK9 71 M7
Blenheim Ct ALS/KID ST7 187 N3
Blenheim Gdns WSFD CW7 149 L3
Blenheim Rd CHD/CHDH SK8 56 B5
Bletchley Rd HTNM SK4 40 F7
Bloomsbury Gv
HALE/TIMP WA15 53 L1
Bloomsbury La
HALE/TIMP WA15 53 L1
Bloomsbury Wy WDN WA8 45 K4
Bloom St EDGY/DAV SK3 16 B7
Blossom Hts NWCHW CW8 12 A5
Blossom Rd PART M31 36 D6
Blossoms Hey CHD/CHDH SK8 55 N6
Blossoms La BRAM/HZG SK7 72 A4
Blossoms St OFTN SK2 41 N9
Bluebell Av RNFD/HAY WA11 23 J2
Bluebell Cl CHSE CH3 143 K4
MCFLDN SK10 117 K1
NWCHW CW8 109 N3
Bluebell Ct RUNC WA7 84 D1
Bluebell Gv CHD/CHDH SK8 55 M3
Bluebell La MCFLDN SK10 117 J1
Bluebell Ms MCFLDN SK10 * 117 K1
Bluebell Wy ALS/KID ST7 187 M5
WILM/AE SK9 71 L5
Blueberry Rd ALT WA14 52 E5
Blue Bridge La FROD/HEL WA6 83 J8
Blue Cap La MALPAS SY14 192 C8
Bluecoat St WARRN/WOL WA2 18 D2
Blue Hatch FROD/HEL WA6 84 A5
Blue Ridge Cl WARRW/BUR WA5 32 B9
Bluestone Dr HTNM SK4 40 F5
Bluestone Rd DTN/ASHW M34 28 G7
Blunstone Cl CW/SHV CW2 184 G6
Blyth Cl HALE/TIMP WA15 53 P1
MCFLDN SK10 116 E3
RUNC WA7 63 H9
Blythe Av BRAM/HZG SK7 56 C9
CONG CW12 155 J8
WDN WA8 45 P3
Blythe Pl WSFD CW7 150 B1
The Blythings TPLY/KEL CW6 146 G7
Boardmans La STHEL WA9 22 C5
Boathorse Rd ALS/KID ST7 189 H8
Boathouse La NSTN CH64 77 H3
Boat La IRL M44 27 P7
WYTH/NTH M22 39 P7
Boat Stage LYMM WA13 50 E4
Bob Massey Cl OP/CLY M11 28 C1
Bob's La IRL M44 36 C4
Boddens Hill Rd HTNM SK4 41 H7
Bodden St STHEL WA9 31 J4
Boden Dr NANT CW5 197 L3
Boden St MCFLDS SK11 9 F4
Bodiam Ct EP CH65 102 G2
Bodlondeb FLINT CH6 98 B8
Bodmin Av MCFLDN SK10 116 E3
Bodmin Cl RUNC WA7 62 F8
Bodmin Crs RDSH SK5 42 A3
Bodmin Dr BRAM/HZG SK7 56 E8
Bodmin Gv RNFD/HAY WA11 22 B2
Bodmin Rd SALE M33 38 A3
Bodnant Cl CW/HAS CW1 169 P9
Bogguard Rd MPL/ROM SK6 59 L3
Bognor Rd EDGY/DAV SK3 56 E3
Bohars TPLY/KEL CW6 166 A1
Bolam Cl NTHM/RTH M23 39 J7
Bolderstone Pl OFTN SK2 57 L3
Bold La WARRW/BUR WA5 31 P1
Bold Pl CH/BCN CH1 3 F3
Bold Rd STHEL WA9 31 L1
Bold Sq CH/BCN CH1 3 G3
Bold St ALT WA14 53 H4
CW/HAS CW1 186 A4
RUNC WA7 15 G1
SBCH CW11 171 N3
WARR WA1 18 C7
WDN WA8 21 G5
Bolesworth Hill Rd CHSE CH3 179 J6
Bolesworth Rd CHNE CH2 122 A5
CHSE CH3 163 P9
Boleyn Cl CH/BCN CH1 121 H5
Boleyn Ct RUNC WA7 62 G3
Bollands Rw NANT CW5 10 C6
Bollin Av ALT WA14 52 F7
WSFD CW7 129 J9
Bollinbarn MCFLDN SK10 117 H2
Bollinbarn Dr MCFLDN SK10 116 G2
Bollinbrook Rd MCFLDN SK10 8 A1
Bollin Cl ALS/KID ST7 187 K5
GOL/RIS/CU WA3 26 A7
LYMM WA13 50 G3
SBCH CW11 171 K2
WSFD CW7 129 J9
Bollin Dr ALT WA14 38 B8
CONG CW12 155 P9
LYMM WA13 50 F3
SALE M33 38 E6
Bollin Gv BIDD ST8 175 M8
MCFLDN SK10 94 F6
Bollington La MCFLDN SK10 115 H2
Bollington Rd HTNM SK4 41 L3
MCFLDN SK10 95 K7
Bollinhead La MCFLDS SK11 137 J1
Bollin Hl WILM/AE SK9 71 K6
Bollin Ms MCFLDN SK10 94 G6
Bollin Sq ALT WA14 52 F6
Bollin Wk WILM/AE SK9 71 K7
Bollinway HALE/TIMP WA15 53 L7
Bollin Wy MCFLDN SK10 94 G8
Bollinwood Cha WILM/AE SK9 71 M7
Bolshaw Cl CW/HAS CW1 184 G1
Bolshaw Farm La
CHD/CHDH SK8 55 L9
Bolshaw Rd CHD/CHDH SK8 55 K9
Bolton Av BNG/LEV M19 40 E6
CHD/CHDH SK8 56 B9
WARRS WA4 49 H3
Bolton Cl GOL/RIS/CU WA3 25 K1
POY/DIS SK12 73 K2
Bolton St RDSH SK5 41 M1
STHEL WA9 22 A5
Bombay Rd EDGY/DAV SK3 41 K9
Bomish La MCFLDS SK11 113 P8
Bonar Cl EDGY/DAV SK3 * 16 A6
Bonar Rd EDGY/DAV SK3 16 A7
Boncarn Dr NTHM/RTH M23 54 C3
Bonchurch Wk WGTN/LGST M12 28 B3
Bond Cl WARRW/BUR WA5 47 P3
Bondmark Rd GTN M18 28 C3
Bond St DTN/ASHW M34 29 M6
MCFLDS SK11 8 C6
NWCHW CW8 109 M3
Bongs Rd OFTN SK2 42 E9
Bonington Ri MPL/ROM SK6 43 N8
Bonis Crs OFTN SK2 57 J3
Bonis Hall La MCFLDN SK10 94 G3
Bonville Cha ALT WA14 52 E3
Bonville Rd ALT WA14 52 E2
Boon Hill Rd ALS/KID ST7 201 J6
Booth Av CHSE CH3 124 D4
RUSH/FAL M14 40 E1
SBCH CW11 172 A3
TPLY/KEL CW6 148 B3
Boothbank La ALT WA14 51 N9
Booth Bed La HOLMCH CW4 131 P2
KNUT WA16 112 G9
Boothby St MCFLDN SK10 * 8 C3
OFTN SK2 57 J3
Boothcote DTN/ASHW M34 29 K3
Boothfield Rd WYTH/NTH M22 54 E1
Boothfields KNUT WA16 90 G3
Booth La MWCH CW10 151 K3
Booth Rd ALT WA14 52 G3
DTN/ASHW M34 28 G2
NWCHW CW8 109 J8
SALE M33 38 E2
WILM/AE SK9 71 J5
Booths Cl CHNE CH2 * 104 A2
Boothsdale TPLY/KEL CW6 125 K8
Booths Hill Cl LYMM WA13 50 D5
Booth's Hill La LYMM WA13 50 C4
Booth's Hill Rd LYMM WA13 50 C4
Booth's La LYMM WA13 50 B5
WARRS WA4 64 G8
Boothsmere Cl SBCH CW11 171 L1
Booth St ALS/KID ST7 200 G5
CONG CW12 155 L8
DTN/ASHW M34 29 M4
EDGY/DAV SK3 41 M9
STHEL WA9 30 C1
WARRW/BUR WA5 48 A3
Border Wy CHSE CH3 143 L1
Bordley Wk NTHM/RTH M23 39 H7
Bordon Rd EDGY/DAV SK3 41 J9
Borough Gv FLINT CH6 98 B6
Borough Rd CONG CW12 155 P7
HALE/TIMP WA15 53 J3
Borras Rd WRXS/E LL13 176 B8
Borron Rd NEWLW WA12 23 M4
Borron St STKP SK1 17 K2
Borrowdale Av CHD/CHDH SK8 55 K3
WARRN/WOL WA2 33 L5
Borrowdale Cl CW/SHV CW2 184 E5
FROD/HEL WA6 84 B5
Borrowdale Crs DID/WITH M20 39 P4
Borrowdale Rd OFTN SK2 42 A9
WDN WA8 45 J7
Borth Av OFTN SK2 42 B9
Borwell St GTN M18 28 D3
Boscombe Dr BRAM/HZG SK7 57 J5
Boscombe St RDSH SK5 28 F7
Boscow Crs STHEL WA9 31 J1
Bosden Av BRAM/HZG SK7 57 L4
Bosden Cl WILM/AE SK9 71 M1
Bosden Fold STKP SK1 17 G6
Bosdenfold Rd BRAM/HZG SK7 57 L4
Bosden Hall Rd BRAM/HZG SK7 57 L4
Bosley Brk BIDD ST8 175 L4
Bosley Cl MWCH CW10 151 J4
WILM/AE SK9 71 M4
Bosley Dr POY/DIS SK12 73 N3
Bosley Gv BURS/TUN ST6 189 L9
Bosley Rd EDGY/DAV SK3 41 H8
Bosley Vw CONG CW12 156 B9
Bossington Cl OFTN SK2 42 B8
Bostock Gn EP CH65 80 B8
Bostock Rd MCFLDS SK11 116 E5
MWCH CW10 129 L7
Bostock Rd WSFD CW7 129 H7
Bostock St WARRW/BUR WA5 48 A1
Boston Av RUNC WA7 15 H6
Boston Bvd WARRW/BUR WA5 32 F9
Boston Cl BRAM/HZG SK7 56 D8
GOL/RIS/CU WA3 25 P5
Boswell Av WARRS WA4 48 D5
Bosworth Rd RNFD/HAY WA11 22 A3
Bosworth St OP/CLY M11 28 A1
Botany Rd MPL/ROM SK6 42 F2
Boteler Av WARRW/BUR WA5 33 J9
Bottesford Av DID/WITH M20 40 A3
Bottoms La CHSW/BR CH4 3 H7
Boughey Rd ALS/KID ST7 201 J5
Boughton CHSE CH3 3 J4
Boughton Hall Av CHSE CH3 143 J1
Boughton Hall Dr CHSE CH3 143 K1
Boulder Dr NTHM/RTH M23 54 C5
The Boulevard BRAM/HZG SK7 57 L5
CHSW/BR CH4 140 G7
EP CH65 80 B9
Boulting Av WARRW/BUR WA5 33 J6
Boulton Cl SBCH CW11 171 P6
Boundary Cl MPL/ROM SK6 43 H3
Boundary Gv SALE M33 39 J6
Boundary La CHSW/BR CH4 141 P5
CONG CW12 175 H1
KNUT WA16 113 P5
MALPAS SY14 202 F6
MCFLDS SK11 133 N4
Boundary La North
NWCHW CW8 127 J1
Boundary La South
NWCHW CW8 127 J1
Boundary Pk NSTN CH64 77 K5
Boundary Rd CHD/CHDH SK8 55 P1
Boundary St NWCHE CW9 110 D2
WARR WA1 * 33 P9
WGTN/LGST M12 28 A4
Boundary Ter WYTH/NTH M22 * 55 H9
Boundry Gn DTN/ASHW M34 29 L4
Bourchier Wy WARRS WA4 49 J7
Bourne Av GOL/RIS/CU WA3 24 F1
Bourne Cl NWCHW CW8 108 G5
Bournelea Av BNG/LEV M19 40 G2
Bournemouth Cl RUNC WA7 63 H8
Bourne Rd ALS/KID ST7 189 H6
Bourne St ALS/KID ST7 189 L1
HTNM SK4 41 M4
WILM/AE SK9 71 H8
Bournville Av HTNM SK4 41 M4
Bournville Gv BNG/LEV M19 28 B8
Bourton Dr GTN M18 28 B5
Bouverie St CH/BCN CH1 2 C1
Bowden Cl CONG CW12 155 H6
GOL/RIS/CU WA3 25 P5
Bowden Crs NM/HAY SK22 59 P7
Bowden Dr NWCHE CW9 110 C4
Bowden La MPL/ROM SK6 43 K9
Bowden St BRAM/HZG SK7 57 L4
DTN/ASHW M34 29 L6
Bowden View La KNUT WA16 67 M4
Bowdon Cl WARR WA1 * 34 A8
Bowdon Ri ALT WA14 53 H5
Bowdon Rd ALT WA14 52 G4
Bowdon St EDGY/DAV SK3 16 E7
Bowen Cl BRAM/HZG SK7 72 F1
WDN WA8 45 K3
Bowen Cooke Av
CW/HAS CW1 184 G2
Bowen St CW/SHV CW2 184 G5
Bower Av BRAM/HZG SK7 57 K6
HTNM SK4 16 B1
Bower Crs WARRS WA4 64 F4
Bower End La
AUD/MAD/W CW3 211 N8
Bowerfield Av BRAM/HZG SK7 57 K7
Bowerfield Crs BRAM/HZG SK7 57 L7
Bowerfold La HTNM SK4 16 C2
Bower Rd HALE/TIMP WA15 53 J6
Bowers Rw NANT CW5 10 B5
Bowers St RUSH/FAL M14 40 E1
Bower St RDSH SK5 28 F7
WDN WA8 46 A6
Bowery Av CHD/CHDH SK8 55 P9
Bowe's Gate Rd TPLY/KEL CW6 166 E7
Bowfell Cl BEB CH63 79 H2
Bowfell Dr MPL/ROM SK6 58 C7
Bow Green Rd ALT WA14 52 E6
Bowhill La AUD/MAD/W CW3 199 P9
Bowker Av DTN/ASHW M34 29 N9
Bowkers Cft SBCH CW11 171 L9
Bowkers La WHITCH SY13 212 C7
Bowlacre Rd HYDE SK14 43 J2
Bowland Av GTN M18 28 G5
STHEL WA9 30 F5
Bowland Cl GOL/RIS/CU WA3 35 J3
OFTN SK2 57 L2
RUNC WA7 62 C9
Bowland Cft CW/HAS CW1 170 A8
Bowland Ri WSFD CW7 149 K3
Bowland Rd DTN/ASHW M34 29 H6
MPL/ROM SK6 42 G3
NTHM/RTH M23 54 B1
Bow La ALT WA14 52 E7
Bowler St BNG/LEV M19 28 B9
Bowles Cl SBCH CW11 171 M3
Bowley Av WYTH/NTH M22 54 C5
Bowling Green Ct NANT CW5 * 10 C5
NWCHW CW8 12 D1
Bowling Rd GTN M18 28 E6
Bowman Av WARRS WA4 49 J2
Bowmere Cl TPLY/KEL CW6 147 H9
Bowmere Dr WSFD CW7 149 L2
Bowmere Rd TPLY/KEL CW6 147 H9
Bowmont Cl CHD/CHDH SK8 56 A3
Bowness Av CHD/CHDH SK8 56 B6
HTNM SK4 41 M2
IRL M44 36 C4
WARRN/WOL WA2 33 M6
WSFD CW7 128 E9
Bowness Cl HOLMCH CW4 131 M8
Bowness Ct CONG CW12 155 J9
Bowness Dr SALE M33 38 C3
Bowness Rd CW/SHV CW2 184 D5
Bowness St OP/CLY M11 28 F2
Bowood Ct WARRN/WOL WA2 33 K4
Bowring Dr NSTN CH64 77 H4
Bow St EDGY/DAV SK3 16 A6
Bowyer Av NANT CW5 10 C4
Boxgrove Cl WDN WA8 45 P4
Boxgrove Rd SALE M33 38 B3
Boxhill Dr NTHM/RTH M23 * 39 K7
Box La CONG CW12 155 H7
Boxmoor Cl CHSW/BR CH4 142 C5
Boxtree Av GTN M18 28 D6
Box Tree Ms MCFLDS SK11 116 G5
Boydell Av WARRS WA4 49 H3
Boydell Av WARRS WA4 49 K5
Boydell Wy CHSW/BR CH4 160 D2
Boyd St WGTN/LGST M12 28 A2
Boyle Av WARRN/WOL WA2 33 P7
Boyles Hall Rd ALS/KID ST7 201 H5
Brabant Rd CHD/CHDH SK8 56 B5
Brabyns Av MPL/ROM SK6 43 J5
Brabyns Brow MPL/ROM SK6 43 M9
Brabyns Rd HYDE SK14 43 K1
Bracadale Dr EDGY/DAV SK3 56 E3
Bracewell Cl STHEL WA9 31 H2
WGTN/LGST M12 28 A4
Bracken Cl ALS/KID ST7 173 J9
CHSW/BR CH4 140 G7
GOL/RIS/CU WA3 34 D3
MCFLDN SK10 116 F3
MPL/ROM SK6 43 P9
SALE M33 37 P3
Bracken Ct STHEL WA9 31 H4
Brackendale CHNE CH2 104 B1
RUNC WA7 62 B6
Bracken Dr NTHM/RTH M23 54 D2
Brackenfield Wy WSFD CW7 149 J2
Brackenlea Pl EDGY/DAV SK3 56 D2
Bracken Rd GTS/LS CH66 80 A9
Brackenside RDSH SK5 28 G9
Bracken Wy FROD/HEL WA6 84 A7
KNUT WA16 90 E5
NWCHE CW9 87 L6
NWCHE CW9 110 C1
NWCHW CW8 109 K1
Brackenwood Cl
CW/SHV CW2 185 H8
Brackenwood Dr
CHD/CHDH SK8 55 M3
WDN WA8 44 G8
Brackenwood Ms WILM/AE SK9 71 N5
Brackley Av IRL M44 36 C2
Brackley Rd HTNM SK4 41 L3
Brackley St RUNC WA7 14 C1
WARRS WA4 48 E6
Bradburn Rd IRL M44 36 D1
Bradburns La NWCHW CW8 109 K6
Bradbury Av ALT WA14 52 E2
Bradbury Gdns CONG CW12 174 G1
Bradbury Rd WSFD CW7 129 H8
Bradda Mt BRAM/HZG SK7 56 F5
Braddan Av SALE M33 38 F5
Braddon Cl NWCHE CW9 109 P8
Braddon Rd MPL/ROM SK6 42 F3
Brade Cl OP/CLY M11 28 C1
Bradeley Green La
WHITCH SY13 205 L8
Bradeley Hall Rd CW/HAS CW1 185 P3
Bradeley Rd CW/HAS CW1 186 A4
Bradfield Cl RDSH SK5 28 E7
CW/HAS CW1 169 P9
Bradford La MCFLDN SK10 93 J7
Bradford Rd WSFD CW7 128 F5
Bradford St CHSW/BR CH4 142 F3
Bradgate Av CHD/CHDH SK8 55 M6
Bradgate Cl WYTH/NTH M22 39 P8
Bradgate Rd ALT WA14 52 E2
SALE M33 38 E6
Bradlegh Rd NEWLW WA12 23 N7
Bradley Byd WARRW/BUR WA5 47 M1
Bradley Cl HALE/TIMP WA15 38 B9
MWCH CW10 151 H3
Bradley Farm La WHITCH SY13 205 H7
Bradley La FROD/HEL WA6 84 B7
STRET M32 38 E1
WARRW/BUR WA5 23 L8
Bradley St MCFLDS SK11 * 9 H7
Bradnor Rd WYTH/NTH M22 39 N9
Bradshaw Av CHSW/BR CH4 141 M3
DID/WITH M20 40 C1
Bradshaw Crs MPL/ROM SK6 43 M9
Bradshaw Hall La
CHD/CHDH SK8 55 M7
Bradshaw La LYMM WA13 51 K4
WARRS WA4 49 K4
Bradshaw Rd MPL/ROM SK6 43 L9
Bradshaw St WDN WA8 45 N5
Bradwall Cl EP CH65 102 C1
Bradwall Rd SBCH CW11 152 F9
Bradwall St SBCH CW11 171 N2
Bradwell Av DID/WITH M20 40 A2
Bradwell Cl EP CH65 6 A7
Bradwell Dr CHD/CHDH SK8 55 L8
Bradwell Gv CONG CW12 155 P8
Bradwell Rd BRAM/HZG SK7 57 L7
GOL/RIS/CU WA3 24 G2
Bradwen Cl DTN/ASHW M34 29 N8
Brady St STKP SK1 17 J2
Braemar Av NWCHE CW9 110 C5
Braemar Cl CHSE CH3 122 D8
CW/SHV CW2 * 184 E8
HOLMCH CW4 131 P9
WARRN/WOL WA2 34 B5
Braemar Ct EP CH65 102 G1
Braemar Dr SALE M33 37 P6
Braemar Rd BRAM/HZG SK7 57 M4
Braeside Cl GTS/LS CH66 79 N8
MCFLDS SK11 9 J7
OFTN SK2 57 M2
Bragenham St GTN M18 28 C4
Brains La TPLY/KEL CW6 166 D4
Braintree Rd WYTH/NTH M22 54 G7
Braithwaite Cl RAIN/WH L35 30 B5
RUNC WA7 62 B9
Brakeley La NWCHW CW8 86 F9
Brakenwood Ms WARRS WA4 * 49 L6
Brakespeare St BURS/TUN ST6 189 L9
The Brake ALS/KID ST7 189 K1
Brake Village ALS/KID ST7 189 K1
Bramall Cl SBCH CW11 171 P2
Bramble Cl CHSE CH3 143 J3
MCFLDN SK10 117 H2
MWCH CW10 130 D9
WARRW/BUR WA5 47 J4
WSFD CW7 128 D8
The Brambles CW/HAS CW1 185 P4
NWCHE CW9 110 C1
Bramble Wy RUNC WA7 84 C1
Brambling Cl OFTN SK2 57 N3
RUNC WA7 62 C9
Brambling Wy GOL/RIS/CU WA3 24 G2
Bramcote Av NTHM/RTH M23 54 D1
RNFD/HAY WA11 22 B3
Bramhall Cl HALE/TIMP WA15 53 P1
SALE M33 39 H5
WSFD CW7 149 K1
Bramhall Dr HOLMCH CW4 131 M8
PS/BROM CH62 79 K2
Bramhall La EDGY/DAV SK3 56 F2
Bramhall La South
BRAM/HZG SK7 56 E9
Bramhall Moor La
BRAM/HZG SK7 57 H6
Bramhall Park Rd
BRAM/HZG SK7 56 C6
Bramhall Rd CW/SHV CW2 184 E6
Bramhalls Pk NWCHE CW9 109 L1
Bramhall St GTN M18 * 28 E4
WARRW/BUR WA5 48 A3
Bramhall Wy MCFLDN SK10 116 G4
Bramham Rd MPL/ROM SK6 58 D3
Bramley Av BNG/LEV M19 28 A9
Bramley Cl BRAM/HZG SK7 56 E9
GTS/LS CH66 102 B4
WILM/AE SK9 92 F1
Bramley Ct TPLY/KEL CW6 125 J6
Bramley Crs HTNM SK4 41 J7
Bramley Dr BRAM/HZG SK7 56 E9
Bramley Ms WARRS WA4 48 E7
Bramley Rd BRAM/HZG SK7 56 E9
Brampton Av MCFLDN SK10 116 G2
Brampton Ct STHEL WA9 22 F6
Brampton Rd BRAM/HZG SK7 56 F5
Bramshill Cl GOL/RIS/CU WA3 35 H2
Bramway BRAM/HZG SK7 56 C8
MPL/ROM SK6 58 D8
Bramwell St STHEL WA9 22 C5
STKP SK1 42 A8
Brancaster Dr GOL/RIS/CU WA3 25 J2
Brancepeth Ct EP CH65 102 F1
Branch Wy RNFD/HAY WA11 23 H3
Brancker Av RAIN/WH L35 30 A4
Branden Dr KNUT WA16 90 F4
Brandon WDN WA8 44 G5
Brandon Av CHD/CHDH SK8 55 K6
DTN/ASHW M34 28 F6
WYTH/NTH M22 39 M8
Brandon Cl WILM/AE SK9 71 M4
Brandreth Cl RAIN/WH L35 30 B5
Brandwood Av CCHDY M21 39 N4
WARRN/WOL WA2 33 L6
Branfield Av CHD/CHDH SK8 55 M6
Branksome Dr CHD/CHDH SK8 55 M6
Branksome Rd HTNM SK4 41 J7
Branscombe Dr SALE M33 37 P3
Bransdale Cl WARRW/BUR WA5 32 B9
Bransdale Wy MCFLDS SK11 116 F5
Bransford Rd OP/CLY M11 28 D1
Branson Wk HALE/TIMP WA15 53 N1
Brantfield Ct WARRN/WOL WA2 33 P6
Brantwood Rd CHD/CHDH SK8 55 P6
HTNM SK4 41 K4
Brassey's Contract Rd
MALPAS SY14 191 P5
Brassey St CHSE CH3 3 K4
Brassey Wy NANT CW5 197 L2
Brassington Rd HTNM SK4 40 F4
Brassington St
AUD/MAD/W CW3 199 M9
Brathay Cl WARRN/WOL WA2 33 M5
Brattswood Dr ALS/KID ST7 188 B3
Bray Cl CHD/CHDH SK8 55 N5
CW/HAS CW1 5 J1
RUNC WA7 62 B8
Brayford Rd WYTH/NTH M22 54 F6
Bray Rd CHSW/BR CH4 142 B4
Brayside Rd DID/WITH M20 40 E4
Braystan Gdns CHD/CHDH SK8 55 K1
Braystones Cl ALS/KID ST7 189 N8
Brayton Av DID/WITH M20 40 D6
SALE M33 38 A3
Breach House La KNUT WA16 69 K4
Bread St GTN M18 28 E3
MCFLDS SK11 8 C6
Breck Rd WDN WA8 45 P6
The Breck GTS/LS CH66 80 A6
Brecon Av BNG/LEV M19 40 G1
CHD/CHDH SK8 55 N6
DTN/ASHW M34 29 M8
Brecon Cl POY/DIS SK12 73 M2
Brecon Dr GTS/LS CH66 102 A3
Brecon Wy CW/SHV CW2 184 G9
WSFD CW7 149 L3
Bredbury Gn MPL/ROM SK6 42 F7
Bredbury Park Wy
MPL/ROM SK6 42 D3
Bredon Cl GTS/LS CH66 79 L7
Breen Cl CHSE CH3 164 A8
Breezehill Cl NSTN CH64 77 L5
Breezehill Pk NSTN CH64 77 M5
Breezehill Rd NSTN CH64 77 M5
Brenchley Dr NTHM/RTH M23 39 K6
Brencon Av SALE M33 38 F7
Brendall Cl OFTN SK2 57 N2
Brendon Av RDSH SK5 41 N2
WARRN/WOL WA2 33 K5
Brendon Gv STHEL WA9 * 22 E5
Brennus Pl CH/BCN CH1 2 C3
Brent Cl POY/DIS SK12 73 H2
Brentfield WDN WA8 45 L5

Brentford Rd RDSH SK5 41 N2
Brent Moor Rd BRAM/HZG SK7 56 G4
Brentnall Cl
WARRW/BUR WA5 * 47 N2
Brentnall St STKP SK1 17 G7
Brenton Av SALE M33 38 D4
Brent Rd HTNM SK4 16 B4
NTHM/RTH M23 39 K6
Brentwood SALE M33 38 D4
Brentwood Av ALT WA14 38 B9
IRL M44 36 C2
Brentwood Cl RDSH SK5 42 C3
Brentwood Crs ALT WA14 53 J1
Brentwood Dr CHD/CHDH SK8 55 K2
Brentwood Rd CH/BCN CH1 121 H6
Brereton Cl ALT WA14 52 G6
CW/SHV CW2 184 E6
MALPAS SY14 204 A3
RUNC WA7 62 E6
SBCH CW11 171 P2
Brereton Ct CONG CW12 154 B4
Brereton Dr NANT CW5 10 E2
Brereton Gv IRL M44 36 D2
Brereton Heath La
CONG CW12 154 B4
Brereton La HOLMCH CW4 131 H9
Brereton Rd NWCHW CW8 109 J8
WILM/AE SK9 71 N3
Bretherton Pl RAIN/WH L35 30 B4
Brethren's Ct DROY M43 28 G1
Breton Cl CHNE CH2 121 P6
Bretton Dr CHSW/BR CH4 140 F7
Bretton La CHSW/BR CH4 141 K5
Bretton Rd CHSW/BR CH4 141 J6
Brett St WYTH/NTH M22 39 P7
Brewer's Gn BRAM/HZG SK7 57 K4
Brewery La CHSE CH3 176 G5
Brewery St ALT WA14 53 H3
STKP SK1 17 H2
Brian Av WARRN/WOL WA2 33 N8
WARRS WA4 48 G6
Briar Av BRAM/HZG SK7 57 M5
GOL/RIS/CU WA3 36 A6
Briar Cl KNUT WA16 90 E2
SALE M33 37 P4
Briar Crs WYTH/NTH M22 54 G2
Briardale Cl CW/SHV CW2 184 F8
Briardale Gdns GTS/LS CH66 79 N7
Briardale Rd GTS/LS CH66 79 N7
NSTN CH64 78 E5
Briardene DTN/ASHW M34 * 29 N5
Briardene Gdns WYTH/NTH M22 54 G3
Briarfield Av WDN WA8 44 G6
Briarfield Rd CHD/CHDH SK8 56 B4
DID/WITH M20 40 E2
EP CH65 6 D4
HALE/TIMP WA15 53 N1
HTNM SK4 41 M2
Briar Gv MPL/ROM SK6 42 F3
Briargrove Rd NM/HAY SK22 59 P3
Briar Hollow HTNM SK4 41 J7
Briarlands Av SALE M33 38 C6
Briarlands Cl BRAM/HZG SK7 56 D9
Briar La NWCHW CW8 108 G5
Briarlea Gdns BNG/LEV M19 40 F3
Briarley Gdns MPL/ROM SK6 43 H2
Briar Rd GOL/RIS/CU WA3 24 D1
Briars Cl RAIN/WH L35 30 C7
Briars Mt HTNM SK4 41 H6
Briars Pk CHD/CHDH SK8 56 C6
Briarstead Cl BRAM/HZG SK7 56 D8
Briarswood ALS/KID ST7 189 K7
Briarwood RUNC WA7 62 F5
WILM/AE SK9 71 L7
Briarwood Av MCFLDS SK11 117 K7
NTHM/RTH M23 38 G8
WARR WA1 19 K1
Briarwood Cha CHD/CHDH SK8 56 B6
Briarwood Crs MPL/ROM SK6 58 D3
Brice St DUK SK16 29 P1
Brick Bank La HOLMCH CW4 131 N2
Brickbridge Rd MPL/ROM SK6 58 E2
Brickhill La HALE/TIMP WA15 69 M2
Brickhurst Wy WARR WA1 34 C8
Brickkiln La ALT WA14 52 A4
Brick Kiln La MWCH CW10 129 J4
Brick-kiln La NEWUL ST5 201 P8
Brickkiln Rw ALT WA14 52 G6
Brick St NEWLW WA12 23 K6
WARR WA1 19 F5
Bridge Av MPL/ROM SK6 42 F3
WARRS WA4 49 H3
Bridge Cl ALS/KID ST7 201 J5
CW/SHV CW2 184 G9
LYMM WA13 51 H4
PART M31 36 F5
Bridge Ct NSTN CH64 77 L6
WRXS/E LL13 176 G8
Bridgecrest Ct CHD/CHDH SK8 * 56 A5
Bridgedown TPLY/KEL CW6 146 G9
Bridge Dr CHD/CHDH SK8 55 M3
CHSE CH3 143 M3
WILM/AE SK9 71 M3
Bridge End Dr MCFLDN SK10 94 G6
Bridge End La MCFLDN SK10 94 G6
Bridgefield Av WILM/AE SK9 71 L5
Bridgefield St STKP SK1 17 F4
Bridge Gn MCFLDN SK10 94 G6
Bridge Gv HALE/TIMP WA15 38 C9
Bridge La BRAM/HZG SK7 56 G6
FROD/HEL WA6 84 A4
HOLMCH CW4 132 D1
NWCHW CW8 108 B9
WARR WA1 49 L1
WARRS WA4 48 G8
Bridgelea Ms DID/WITH M20 40 C2
Bridgelea Rd DID/WITH M20 40 C2
Bridgeman Rd CH/BCN CH1 121 H8
Bridgeman St
WARRW/BUR WA5 47 P3
Bridge Meadow GTS/LS CH66 102 B2
Bridgemere Cl SBCH CW11 171 L1
Bridgemere La NANT CW5 209 M5
Bridgemere Ms NANT CW5 210 E6
Bridgemere Wy NWCHE CW9 109 N8
Bridgend Cl CHD/CHDH SK8 56 B3
WDN WA8 45 K4
WGTN/LGST M12 28 A3
Bridge Pl CH/BCN CH1 2 E6
Bridge Rd HALE/TIMP WA15 38 F9
STHEL WA9 31 J6
WARR WA1 34 D9
Bridge Rw CONG CW12 155 N6
Bridges Rd EP CH65 81 H8
Bridge St CH/BCN CH1 2 E5
CHSW/BR CH4 141 P3
CONG CW12 155 M8
DROY M43 28 E1
DTN/ASHW M34 29 M2
GOL/RIS/CU WA3 24 C2
MCFLDS SK11 8 D5
NANT CW5 198 B7
NEWLW WA12 23 M6
NEWLW WA12 24 C2
NM/HAY SK22 59 N6
NSTN CH64 77 L6
NWCHE CW9 110 E2
RUNC WA7 15 G2
STKP SK1 17 G3
WARR WA1 18 E7
WRXS/E LL13 176 G8
Bridge Street Brw STKP SK1 17 G3
Bridge Street Rw East
CH/BCN CH1 2 E5
Bridge Street Rw West
CH/BCN CH1 2 D5
Bridge View Cl WDN WA8 61 N2
Bridge Wk RUNC WA7 * 62 D7
Bridgewater Av WARRS WA4 49 H3
Bridgewater Cl CONG CW12 156 B9
Bridgewater Dr CHSE CH3 122 D9
Bridgewater Gra RUNC WA7 63 K8
Bridgewater Ms WARRS WA4 48 E7
Bridgewater Pl WSFD CW7 149 J2
Bridgewater Rd ALT WA14 38 A9
Bridgewater St LYMM WA13 50 E4
RUNC WA7 14 E1
SALE M33 38 E3
WHITCH SY13 213 M6
Bridgeway East RUNC WA7 62 G4
Bridgeway West RUNC WA7 62 F4
Bridgewood Dr GTS/LS CH66 101 N2
Bridgfield Cl MPL/ROM SK6 58 C8
Bridgnorth Gv NEWUL ST5 201 P5
Bridle Ct STHEL WA9 22 A9
Bridle Hey NANT CW5 196 G5
Bridlemere Ct WARR WA1 33 P8
Bridle Rd BRAM/HZG SK7 72 F3
CW/SHV CW2 4 C4
Bridle Wy BRAM/HZG SK7 72 F4
GTS/LS CH66 101 P1
Bridleway NM/HAY SK22 59 P6
Brien Av ALT WA14 53 H1
Briercliffe Cl GTN M18 28 C3
Brierley Cl DTN/ASHW M34 29 L7
Brierley Rd CONG CW12 156 B9
Brierley St CW/HAS CW1 5 G2
WARRW/BUR WA5 18 A4
Briers Cl WARRN/WOL WA2 34 A5
Brierton Dr WYTH/NTH M22 54 D6
Brieryhurst Rd ALS/KID ST7 189 K5
Brigadier Cl DID/WITH M20 40 C2
Briggs Av CW/SHV CW2 185 K7
Briggs Cl SALE M33 37 P7
Brigham St OP/CLY M11 28 C1
Brightman St GTN M18 28 D3
Brighton Av BNG/LEV M19 40 G1
RDSH SK5 28 F7
Brighton Crs MCFLDS SK11 117 P9
Brighton Gv SALE M33 38 D3
Brighton Range GTN M18 * 28 F5
Brighton Rd HTNM SK4 16 A4
Brighton St WARRW/BUR WA5 48 A1
Brights Av ALS/KID ST7 189 K6
Bright St CW/HAS CW1 4 C2
Brightwell Cl WARRW/BUR WA5 47 J2
Brigstock Av GTN M18 28 C4
Brimelow Crs
WARRW/BUR WA5 47 J4
Brimelow St MPL/ROM SK6 42 B5
Brimscombe Av
WYTH/NTH M22 54 E5
Brindale Rd RDSH SK5 42 B4
Brindley Av MPL/ROM SK6 58 D2
SALE M33 38 G2
WARRS WA4 49 H3
WSFD CW7 149 K1
Brindley Cl ALS/KID ST7 188 G7
Brindley Hall Rd NANT CW5 182 A7
Brindley La SBCH CW11 152 G6
Brindley Lea La NANT CW5 181 P8
Brindley Pk SBCH CW11 171 L6
Brindley Rd RUNC WA7 62 D3
STHEL WA9 31 K2
Brindley St RUNC WA7 14 D1
Brindleys Wy ALS/KID ST7 201 J5
Brindley Wy CONG CW12 156 B9
MCFLDS SK11 117 J9
Brinell Dr IRL M44 36 E3
Brine Pits La NANT CW5 208 F4
Brine Rd NANT CW5 196 F4
Brinkburn Rd BRAM/HZG SK7 57 N4
Brinklow Cl OP/CLY M11 28 E2
Brinkshaw Av WYTH/NTH M22 54 G5
Brinksway EDGY/DAV SK3 16 C5
Brinnington Crs RDSH SK5 42 A4
Brinnington Rd RDSH SK5 42 B4
Brinsop Sq GTN M18 28 B3
Brinton Cl WDN WA8 20 B3
Briony Av HALE/TIMP WA15 53 N5
Brisbane Cl BRAM/HZG SK7 72 F1
Brisbane Rd CH/BCN CH1 120 F7
Brisbane St STHEL WA9 30 C1
Bristol Av BNG/LEV M19 28 B9
RUNC WA7 63 J8
Bristol Cl CH/BCN CH1 120 F7
Bristol Dr GTS/LS CH66 102 A3
Bristow Cl WARRW/BUR WA5 32 E8
Britannia Rd SALE M33 38 E3
Britannia St AULW OL7 29 M1
Brittain Av NEWUL ST5 201 P8
Brittania Dr NWCHE CW9 110 E5
Brittania Gdns FROD/HEL WA6 105 H3
Brittania Rd FROD/HEL WA6 105 H2
Brixham Av CHD/CHDH SK8 55 P8
Brixham Dr SALE M33 38 A2
Brixham Wk BRAM/HZG SK7 56 E8
Brixton Av DID/WITH M20 40 B2
Broadacre NWCHE CW9 87 M6
Broadacres NANT CW5 208 A2
Broadbent Av WARRS WA4 49 H4
Broadcar Rd MCFLDS SK11 118 A6
Broadfield Cl DTN/ASHW M34 29 N7
Broadfield Gv RDSH SK5 28 E6
Broadfield Rd GTN M18 28 E6
Broadfields RUNC WA7 62 G6
Broadheath Ter WDN WA8 45 K6
Broad Hey MPL/ROM SK6 43 J5
Broadheys La KNUT WA16 50 D9
Broadhey Vw NM/HAY SK22 59 M6
Broad Hill Cl BRAM/HZG SK7 56 G5
Broadhill Rd BNG/LEV M19 40 F2
Broadhurst DTN/ASHW M34 29 N4
Broadhurst Av GOL/RIS/CU WA3 25 P7
WARRW/BUR WA5 47 P3
Broadhurst La CONG CW12 155 L7
Broadhurst St EDGY/DAV SK3 41 M9
Broadlake NSTN CH64 78 D5
Broadland Gdns GTS/LS CH66 102 B2
Broadland Rd GTS/LS CH66 102 B2
Broad La HALE/TIMP WA15 53 M7
HOLMCH CW4 152 B2
NANT CW5 197 H5
WARRS WA4 49 K7
WARRW/BUR WA5 23 H9
WRX/GR/LL LL12 * 176 A2
Broadlea Rd BNG/LEV M19 40 F3
Broadleigh Wy CW/SHV CW2 185 J8
Broadley Av GOL/RIS/CU WA3 24 E2
WYTH/NTH M22 54 F3
Broadmead CHSE CH3 122 D9
Broad Meadow Ct NEWUL ST5 201 P9
Broad Oak Av CHSW/BR CH4 140 E7
RNFD/HAY WA11 22 E3
WARRW/BUR WA5 47 J3
Broadoak Av WYTH/NTH M22 54 E2
Broadoak Dr WYTH/NTH M22 54 F2
Broad Oak La DID/WITH M20 40 D8
KNUT WA16 67 K1
Broadoak La KNUT WA16 69 J8
Broadoak Rd BRAM/HZG SK7 56 F5
Broad Oak Rd STHEL WA9 22 C6
Broadoak Rd WYTH/NTH M22 54 E3
Broadoaks WRX/GR/LL LL12 160 F9
Broadoaks Rd SALE M33 38 D4
SALE M33 38 F3
Broadstone Hall Rd North
HTNM SK4 41 L2
Broadstone Hall Rd South
HTNM SK4 41 M2
Broadstone Rd HTNM SK4 41 L2
Broad St CW/HAS CW1 185 J3
Broadwalk MCFLDN SK10 94 G8
Broad Wk WILM/AE SK9 71 H6
Broadway BRAM/HZG SK7 56 F5
CHD/CHDH SK8 55 L3
DROY M43 28 G1
HALE/TIMP WA15 53 L6
HYDE SK14 29 P4
IRL M44 27 N8
NWCHW CW8 109 K1
OFTN SK2 42 B9
PART M31 36 F4
SALE M33 38 D3
WDN WA8 44 G6
WILM/AE SK9 71 K8
Broadway Av CHD/CHDH SK8 55 M2
Broadway East CHNE CH2 121 P6
Broadway North DROY M43 28 G1
Broadways AUD/MAD/W CW3 216 G1
The Broadway MPL/ROM SK6 42 D4
NANT CW5 10 E5
Broadway West CHNE CH2 121 N6
Broadwood Cl MPL/ROM SK6 58 D8
Broady Ct CW/SHV CW2 4 E6
Brock Cl OP/CLY M11 28 D2
Brock Dr CHD/CHDH SK8 56 A7
Brock Hall Cl STHEL WA9 * 31 H4
Brock Hollow SBCH CW11 171 L5
Brockhurst Ms NWCHE CW9 13 G6
Brockhurst St NWCHE CW9 13 F2
Brockhurst Wy NWCHE CW9 13 G7
Brocklebank Dr NWCHW CW8 12 D5
Brocklehurst Av MCFLDN SK10 9 H1
Brocklehurst Dr MCFLDN SK10 94 G6
Brocklehurst Wy
MCFLDN SK10 117 K1
Brock Rd GOL/RIS/CU WA3 34 E5
Brock St MCFLDN SK10 8 E3
Brockway East CHSE CH3 163 P8
Brockway West CHSE CH3 163 P8
Brodie Cl CHNE CH2 121 M2
Brogan St GTN M18 28 D4
Brogden Av GOL/RIS/CU WA3 25 N5
Brogden Dr CHD/CHDH SK8 55 K2
Brogden Gv SALE M33 38 D5
Broken Banks MCFLDS SK11 9 F6
Broken Cross MCFLDS SK11 116 E4
Bromilow Rd STHEL WA9 22 D7
Bromleigh Av CHD/CHDH SK8 55 K1
Bromley Av GOL/RIS/CU WA3 24 F2
Bromley Cl CW/HAS CW1 169 N9
WARRN/WOL WA2 34 A5
Bromley Dr HOLMCH CW4 131 P9
Bromley Rd CONG CW12 155 N8
MCFLDN SK10 116 E4
SALE M33 38 F6
Bromley St DTN/ASHW M34 * 29 M6
Brompton Gdns
WARRW/BUR WA5 33 H9
Brompton Rd HTNM SK4 41 H6
Brompton Wy GTS/LS CH66 102 A3
Bronington Cl WYTH/NTH M22 39 P9
Bron Llwyn FLINT CH6 98 A8
Bronte Cl WARRN/WOL WA2 33 K2
Brookash Rd WYTH/NTH M22 55 J7
Brook Av BNG/LEV M19 28 B7
CW/SHV CW2 198 B2
HALE/TIMP WA15 53 J1
HTNM SK4 41 L3
WARRS WA4 48 G6
WARRS WA4 49 H2
WILM/AE SK9 71 M3
Brook Bottom Rd
NM/HAY SK22 59 K6
Brookburn Rd CCHDY M21 39 K1
Brook Cl CW/HAS CW1 5 K4
HALE/TIMP WA15 53 J1
WDN WA8 45 J1
Brookcot Rd NTHM/RTH M23 39 J9
Brook Ct SBCH CW11 171 N3
Brookcroft Av WYTH/NTH M22 54 F2
Brookcroft Rd WYTH/NTH M22 54 F2
Brookdale RAIN/WH L35 44 G4
Brookdale Av DTN/ASHW M34 29 L2
MPL/ROM SK6 58 E3
Brookdale Cl MPL/ROM SK6 42 E5
Brookdale Pk CW/SHV CW2 184 G5
Brookdale Pl CH/BCN CH1 3 F3
Brookdale Ri BRAM/HZG SK7 56 F5
Brookdale Rd BRAM/HZG SK7 56 F6
CHD/CHDH SK8 55 H2
Brookdale Wy CHSE CH3 144 B5
Brookdene Rd BNG/LEV M19 40 F2
Brook Dr MPL/ROM SK6 58 D3
TPLY/KEL CW6 125 J7
WARRW/BUR WA5 47 L2
Brooke Av CHNE CH2 122 A3
Brooke Dr WILM/AE SK9 71 M2
Brook End STHEL WA9 22 E8
Brookes Av CHSW/BR CH4 140 F7
Brooke Wy WILM/AE SK9 * 71 M2
Brook Farm Cl PART M31 36 D7
Brookfield CW/HAS CW1 186 B3
WHITCH SY13 213 K5
Brookfield Av CCHDY M21 39 M1
HALE/TIMP WA15 38 C9
MPL/ROM SK6 42 F4
POY/DIS SK12 73 J3
RAIN/WH L35 30 B3
RUNC WA7 62 C4
STKP SK1 41 P9
Brookfield Cl LYMM WA13 50 D4
OFTN SK2 41 P9
TPLY/KEL CW6 166 A1
Brookfield Ct CW/HAS CW1 185 H3
Brookfield Crs CHD/CHDH SK8 55 M2
HOLMCH CW4 132 C2
Brookfield Dr ALS/KID ST7 187 N3
HALE/TIMP WA15 38 D9
HOLMCH CW4 131 N8
Brookfield Gdns
WYTH/NTH M22 54 F1
Brookfield La MCFLDS SK11 9 J6
Brookfield Pk WARRS WA4 49 J5
Brookfield Rd CHD/CHDH SK8 55 N2
GOL/RIS/CU WA3 25 L5
LYMM WA13 50 D4
NWCHE CW9 87 M5
Brookfield St NEWLW WA12 23 M6
Brookfold Rd HTNM SK4 41 L2
Brook Furlong FROD/HEL WA6 83 N4
Brook Gdns BIDD ST8 175 L7
Brook Green La GTN M18 28 F6
Brook Gv IRL M44 27 N7
Brookhead Av DID/WITH M20 * 40 A1
Brookhead Dr CHD/CHDH SK8 56 A2
Brook Hey NSTN CH64 77 H3
Brookheys Rd PART M31 37 K4
Brookhouse Cl MCFLDN SK10 116 F3
Brook House Ct LYMM WA13 * 50 E4
Brook House Dr CW/SHV CW2 185 J8
Brook House La CHSE CH3 * 145 K5
CONG CW12 155 P7
Brookhouse La CONG CW12 156 C8
CW/HAS CW1 169 L3
TPLY/KEL CW6 145 K4
WARRS WA4 86 D3
Brookhouse Rd ALS/KID ST7 187 P5
SBCH CW11 171 N3
Brookhurst Av BEB CH63 79 H1
Brookhurst Rd GTN M18 28 D5
Brookland Av CW/SHV CW2 184 F8
DTN/ASHW M34 29 K7
Brookland Dr SBCH CW11 172 A3
Brookland La STHEL WA9 22 E7
Brooklands Av DID/WITH M20 40 B2
MCFLDS SK11 8 A6
Brooklands Cl HTNM SK4 41 L3
IRL M44 27 M7
Brooklands Crs SALE M33 38 E5
Brooklands Dr HOLMCH CW4 132 B2
NWCHE CW9 110 A8
Brooklands Fls CW/HAS CW1 * 185 J2
Brooklands Gdns NSTN CH64 77 J4
Brooklands Gv CW/HAS CW1 184 G2
Brooklands Rd BRAM/HZG SK7 57 L6
CONG CW12 155 H7
NSTN CH64 77 J4
NTHM/RTH M23 38 F8
RDSH SK5 28 E7
Brooklands Station Ap SALE M33 38 D5
The Brooklands CW/SHV CW2 198 D4
Brookland St WARR WA1 33 P9
Brook La CHNE CH2 121 N8
CHSW/BR CH4 140 G2
CONG CW12 173 P4
GOL/RIS/CU WA3 35 H8
HALE/TIMP WA15 53 J1
KNUT WA16 90 F4
NANT CW5 182 B8
NANT CW5 182 F8
NSTN CH64 77 J3
NWCHE CW9 110 D5
WILM/AE SK9 93 H2
Brooklawn Dr DID/WITH M20 40 C4
Brookledge La MCFLDN SK10 73 J9
Brookleigh Rd DID/WITH M20 40 E2
Brooklyn Crs CHD/CHDH SK8 55 M2
Brooklyn Dr EP CH65 80 B8
LYMM WA13 50 E3
Brooklyn Rd CHD/CHDH SK8 55 M2
OFTN SK2 57 J1
Brooklyn St CW/SHV CW2 4 E6
Brookmere Cl SBCH CW11 171 K1
Brookmoore Ct CHNE CH2 121 M8
Brook Pl CH/BCN CH1 3 F2
WARRS WA4 * 48 G4
Brook Rd CHD/CHDH SK8 55 M1
GTS/LS CH66 79 P8
HTNM SK4 41 K3
LYMM WA13 50 D3
RUSH/FAL M14 40 D1
TPLY/KEL CW6 166 A1
WHITCH SY13 213 N6
Brooks Av BRAM/HZG SK7 57 K4
Brooks Dr HALE/TIMP WA15 53 P1
HALE/TIMP WA15 53 P7
CHSE CH3 124 D4
Brookside CHSE CH3 143 J2
FROD/HEL WA6 106 G2
NWCHW CW8 108 B9
Brook Side NWCHW CW8 108 E3
Brookside Av LYMM WA13 50 C3
MCFLDS SK11 117 M9
OFTN SK2 57 L1
POY/DIS SK12 73 L3
WARRS WA4 48 F6
WARRW/BUR WA5 47 L2
Brookside Cl CHD/CHDH SK8 55 M3
RNFD/HAY WA11 22 F2
Brookside Gn CW/SHV CW2 185 J8
Brookside La MPL/ROM SK6 58 C8
Brookside Rd CHD/CHDH SK8 55 J1
CONG CW12 155 M7
FROD/HEL WA6 83 N5
SALE M33 38 D6
Brookside Ter CHNE CH2 121 N7
Brookside Vw RNFD/HAY WA11 22 F2
Brookside Wy RNFD/HAY WA11 22 F2
Brook Slack TPLY/KEL CW6 147 P1
Brooks La MCFLDS SK11 136 C9
MWCH CW10 151 K2
Brooks St STKP SK1 41 N9
Brookstone Cl CCHDY M21 39 N2
Brook St BRAM/HZG SK7 57 L5
CH/BCN CH1 3 F2
CHD/CHDH SK8 55 P1
CONG CW12 155 P7
CW/SHV CW2 5 F5
GOL/RIS/CU WA3 24 C2
KNUT WA16 90 E4
MCFLDS SK11 9 G5
NSTN CH64 77 L5
NWCHE CW9 13 H1
RUNC WA7 14 E2
SALE M33 38 F3
CHNE CH2 3 H1
Brookthorn Cl OFTN SK2 57 M2
Brookthorpe Av BNG/LEV M19 40 F2
Brookvale Av North RUNC WA7 62 F9
Brookvale Av South RUNC WA7 62 F8
Brookvale Cl WARRW/BUR WA5 32 C2
Brookview Cl CW/SHV CW2 185 H8
Brook Vls ALS/KID ST7 * 188 A5
Brookway HALE/TIMP WA15 53 K1
Brook Wy NANT CW5 196 F4
WARRW/BUR WA5 47 L2
Brookway Cl BNG/LEV M19 40 F4
Brookway La STHEL WA9 22 D8
Brook Well NSTN CH64 77 L8
Brookwood Av SALE M33 38 B5
Brookwood Cl DTN/ASHW M34 42 F1
WARRS WA4 48 D7
Broom Av BNG/LEV M19 28 B9
RDSH SK5 41 N2
WARRS WA4 48 G9
Broom Crs CHSE CH3 145 H1
Broome Ct RUNC WA7 62 F9
Broomehouse Av IRL M44 27 L9
Broomfield Cl MCFLDS SK11 114 C1
RDSH SK5 41 N2
WILM/AE SK9 * 71 N6
WSFD CW7 149 J2
Broomfield Crs EDGY/DAV SK3 56 G3
Broomfield Dr RDSH SK5 41 N2
Broomfield La HALE/TIMP WA15 53 J5
NWCHW CW8 87 H9
Broomfield Rd HTNM SK4 41 K4
Broomfields DTN/ASHW M34 29 N4
Broomfields Rd WARRS WA4 48 F8
Broomgrove La DTN/ASHW M34 29 N5
Broomheath La CHSE CH3 145 J1
CHSE CH3 145 J3
Broomhill Dr BRAM/HZG SK7 56 D6
CHSE CH3 123 M3
Broomhill La CHSE CH3 179 J8
Broom La BNG/LEV M19 28 B9
KNUT WA16 112 C2
Broom Rd HALE/TIMP WA15 53 J4
PART M31 36 E6
Broom's La TPLY/KEL CW6 125 J6
Broomstair Rd DTN/ASHW M34 29 M3
Broom St CW/HAS CW1 184 G3
Broomville Av SALE M33 38 E4
Broomwood Rd
HALE/TIMP WA15 53 N2
Broseley Av DID/WITH M20 40 E5
GOL/RIS/CU WA3 25 M5
Broseley La GOL/RIS/CU WA3 25 M4
Brotherhood Dr STHEL WA9 31 J1
Brotherton Wy NEWLW WA12 23 M5
Brough St West MCFLDS SK11 8 B6
Broughton Av
GOL/RIS/CU WA3 24 F2
Broughton Cl WARRS WA4 49 H7
Broughton Crs WRXS/E LL13 202 B5
Broughton Hall Rd
CHSW/BR CH4 140 G7
Broughton La CW/SHV CW2 184 F7

Broughton Mills Rd
CHSW/BR CH4 ....141 K4
Broughton Rd CW/HAS CW1 ..170 D8
MCFLDN SK10 ....73 J9
RDSH SK5 ....41 N4
Broughville Dr DID/WITH M20 ..40 A4
Brow La NWCHE CW9 ....65 M9
Browmere Dr DID/WITH M20 ..40 A4
GOL/RIS/CU WA3 ....34 E7
Brownacre St DID/WITH M20 ..40 C2
Brown Av ALS/KID ST7 ......188 C4
NANT CW5
Brown Heath Rd CHSE CH3 ..144 A3
Brownhill Dr WARR WA1 ......34 A8
Brownhills Rd TPLY/KEL CW6 ..147 M4
Brownhill St OP/CLY M11 * ...28 A1
Browning Av WDN WA8 ....20 E5
Browning Cl CH/BCN CH1 ....121 J5
SBCH CW11 ....171 J4
Browning Gn EP CH65 ....80 B9
Browning Gv ALS/KID ST7 ...188 E8
Browning Rd RDSH SK5 ......28 G2
Browning St CW/HAS CW1 .....4 D2
Browning Wy WSFD CW7 ....149 H5
Brown Knowl La CHSE CH3 ...179 J8
Brown Lees Cl CW/SHV CW2 ..184 G7
Brown Lees Rd ALS/KID ST7 ..189 P4
Brownley Court Rd
WYTH/NTH M22 ....54 F2
Brownley Rd WYTH/NTH M22 ..54 G2
Brownlow Cl POY/DIS SK12 ...73 L4
Brownlow St WHITCH SY13 ...213 M5
Brown's La CHSW/BR CH4 ...142 E3
WILM/AE SK9 ....71 N6
Brown St ALT WA14 ....53 H4
CONG CW12 ....155 N7
MCFLDN SK11 ....8 D6
STKP SK1 ....17 K3
WDN WA8 ....45 J8
WILM/AE SK9 ....93 J4
Brownsville Rd HTNM SK4 ....41 J3
Brownwood Av STKP SK1 .....42 A7
Brownwood Cl SALE M33 .....38 F7
Burnsall Av GOL/RIS/CU WA3 ..21 H1
The Brow FROD/HEL WA6 ...106 G2
Broxton Av MWCH CW10 ....151 K4
Broxton Cl WDN WA8 ....45 J4
Broxton Rd GTS/LS CH66 ....80 A8
MALPAS SY14 ....178 D7
Broxwood Cl GTN M18 * 28 B7
Bruce Av WARRN/WOL WA2 ..33 N7
Bruce Dr GTS/LS CH66 ....79 N9
Bruche Av WARR WA4 ....34 A9
Bruche Dr WARR WA4 ....34 A9
The Bruen CHSE CH3 ....124 B8
Brundage Rd WYTH/NTH M22 ..54 F1
Brundrett Pl SALE M33 ....38 C4
Brundrett St STKP SK1 ....17 K7
Brunel Rd MCFLDS SK11 ......117 J9
Brunner Gv NANT CW5 ....11 H6
Brunner Pl WSFD CW7 ....149 J2
Brunner Rd WDN WA8 ....21 G2
Brunstead Cl NTHM/RTH M23 ..53 P1
Brunswick Cl ALT WA14 ......38 A9
DID/WITH M20 ....40 D2
NEWLW WA12 ....43 K5
Brunswick St CONG CW12 ...155 P7
MCFLDN SK10 ....9 F3
STHEL WA9 ....22 E6
Bruntleigh Av WARRS WA4 ...49 J4
Brunton Rd RDSH SK5 ....41 N2
Bruntwood Av CHD/CHDH SK8 ..55 N5
Bruntwood La CHD/CHDH SK8 ..55 N5
Brussels St EDGY/DAV SK3 ...56 D1
Bryant Av WARRS WA4 ......49 H3
Brydges Rd MPL/ROM SK6 ...58 C2
Bryndale Gv SALE M33 ....38 C7
Brynden Av DID/WITH M20 ...40 D5
Bryn Derw FLINT CH6 ....98 B8
Bryn Dr RDSH SK5 ....41 N3
Bryn Estyn Av WHITCH SY13 ..213 L5
Bryn Gwyn FLINT CH6 ....98 B8
Bryn Helig FLINT CH6 ....98 B8
Brynlow Dr MWCH CW10 ....151 L4
Brynmore Dr MCFLDN SK11 ...9 J5
Brynn St WDN WA8 ....21 J3
Bryn Onnen FLINT CH6 ......98 B8
Bryn Siriol FLINT CH6 ....98 B7
Brynton Rd MCFLDN SK10 ...10 D1
Bryone Dr OFTN SK2 ....57 H2
Bryony Cl WYTH/NTH M22 ...54 E6
Buchan Cl WARRW/BUR WA5 ..32 E8
Buchan Gv CW/SHV CW2 ......4 B5
Buckden Av HOLMCK CW4 ...132 B2
Buckden Rd HTNM SK4 ....41 J1
Buckden Wy MCFLDS SK11 * ..8 C3
Buckfast Av RNFD/HAY WA11 ..23 K2
Buckfast Cl CHD/CHDH SK8 ..56 B8
HALE/TIMP WA15 ....53 M1
MCFLDN SK10 ....117 H2
POY/DIS SK12 ....73 K5
WARRW/BUR WA5 ....47 J4
Buckfast Cl RUNC WA7 ....63 J5
Buckfast Rd SALE M33 ....38 L2
Buckhurst Rd BNG/LEV M19 ..28 A8
Buckingham Av CHSE CH3 ...143 N3
WDN WA8 ....45 H3
Buckingham Cl CONG CW12 ..156 A4
CW/SHV CW2 ....184 E8
Buckingham Dr KNUT WA16 ..90 F4
NWCHE CW9 ....109 N8
WARRW/BUR WA5 ....31 J9
WSFD CW7 ....149 L3
Buckingham Gdns EP CH65 ..102 F2

Buckingham Rd ALT WA14 ....38 C7
CHD/CHDH SK8 ....55 P5
HTNM SK4 ....55 K1
IRL M44 ....36 B2
POY/DIS SK12 ....73 K2
WILM/AE SK9 ....71 H8
Buckingham Rd West
HTNM SK4 ....41 H4
Buckingham St OFTN SK2 * ..56 G1
Buckingham Wy
HALE/TIMP WA15 ....53 L1
Buckland Cl WDN WA8 ......20 A4
Buck La CW/SHV CW2 ......198 D4
SALE M33 ....38 B2
Buckley Av GTN M18 ....28 C5
MWCH CW10 ....130 E4
Buckley Cl HYDE SK14 ....43 K1
MWCH CW10 * 151 H2
Buckley Dr MPL/ROM SK6 ...42 F7
Buckley Rd GTN M18 ....28 B5
DTN/ASHW M34 ....29 K2
MCFLDS SK11 ....8 D6
OP/CLY M11 ....28 E2
RDSH SK5 ....28 G1
WARRN/WOL WA2 ....18 C3
Bucklow Av KNUT WA16 ......91 L1
PART M31 ....36 E4
Bucklow Dr WYTH/NTH M22 ..39 P8
Bucklow Gdns LYMM WA13 ..50 G5
Bucklowhill La KNUT WA16 ...67 N4
Bucklow Vw ALT WA14 ....52 F4
Buckthorn Cl CCHDY M21 ....39 N2
HALE/TIMP WA15 ....54 A5
Buckthorn Gdns STHEL WA9 ..30 B2
Buckwood Cl BRAM/HZG SK7 ..57 N4
Bude Av RDSH SK5 ....42 A3
Bude Cl ALS/KID ST7 ....187 M5
BRAM/HZG SK7 ....56 F8
CW/HAS CW1 ....170 A9
Bude Rd WDN WA8 ....45 L5
Budsworth Av DID/WITH M20 ..40 C1
Budworth Av STHEL WA9 ....30 C5
WARRS WA4 ....49 H3
WDN WA8 ....45 K5
Budworth Cl RUNC WA7 .....62 B7
SBCH CW11 ....171 L2
Budworth Heath La
NWCHE CW9 ....88 B4
Budworth La RNFD/HAY WA6 ..105 M4
Budworth Rd GTS/LS CH66 ..102 A2
KNUT WA16 ....89 K3
SALE M33 ....39 H5
Buerton Ap CHSE CH3 ......162 C5
Buggen La NSTN CH64 ....77 K5
Buildwas Rd NSTN CH64 .....77 L3
Bulford Av WYTH/NTH M22 ..54 D5
Bulkeley Hall La MALPAS SY14 ..179 P8
Bulkeley Rd CHD/CHDH SK8 ..55 P7
POY/DIS SK12 ....73 L3
WILM/AE SK9 ....71 J9
Bulkeley St CHSE CH3 ......143 J1
CW/HAS CW1 ....5 J4
EDGY/DAV SK3 ....16 D6
Bullcroft Cl MALPAS SY14 ...190 E8
Buller St DROY M43 ....29 H1
TPLY/KEL CW6 ....146 C7
Bull Hi NSTN CH64 ....77 M7
Bull Hill La MCFLDN SK10 ...118 B2
MCFLDN SK10 ....118 B3
Bullocks House Rd
ALS/KID ST7 ....189 N5
Bullocks La MCFLDS SK11 ...117 L9
Bullock St OFTN SK2 ....41 N9
NWCHW CW8 ....12 E2
Bumpers La CH/BCN CH1 ...142 B1
Bunbury Cl CHNE CW21 ....105 J5
Bunbury Com
TPLY/KEL CW6 ....166 A7
Bunbury Dr RUNC WA7 .....62 A8
Bunbury Gn EP CH65 ....102 F2
Bunbury La TPLY/KEL CW6 ..181 J1
Bunbury Rd TPLY/KEL CW6 ..166 E6
Bunce La MCFLDS SK11 .....134 B8
Bunce St CH/BCN CH1 ....2 D6
Bungalow Rd NEWLW WA12 ..43 N3
The Bungalows Red Bnk
NEWLW WA12 * 24 A8
The Bungalows
BRAM/HZG SK7 * 57 M3
Bunkershill Rd MPL/ROM SK6 ..57 M5
Bunting Cl GOL/RIS/CU WA3 ..24 C1
Buntingford Rd WARRS WA4 ..49 L4
Bunts La CONG CW12 ......155 N9
Burbage Rd NTHM/RTH M23 ..54 C5
Burdett Rd GTS/LS CH66 ...102 A2
Burdon Av WYTH/NTH M22 ..54 C5
Burfield Dr WARRS WA4 .....49 J4
Burford Dr BRAM/HZG SK7 ..72 C1
NEWLU ST5 ....201 N6
Burford Crs WILM/AE SK9 ...70 F6
Burford Gv SALE M33 ....38 B7
Burford La LYMM WA13 .....51 J5
Burgamot La NWCHE CW9 ...87 L5
Burgess Av WARRS WA4 .....48 D4
Burgess Cl NANT CW5 ....11 H7
Burgess La FROD/HEL WA6 ..107 M7
Burgess Pl NWCHW CW8 ....12 C3
Burgess St MCFLDN SK10 .....9 J5
Burges St CHNE CW2 ....122 A8
Burjen Wy CW/HAS CW1 ....185 H2
Burland Cl NEWLW WA12 ....24 A6
Burland Ct RUNC WA7 ......14 C8
Burland Rd HLWD L26 ....44 A9
NEWLU ST5 ....201 M5
Burlea Cl CW/SHV CW2 ....184 E3
Burlea Dr CW/SHV CW2 ....198 A2
Burleigh Cl BRAM/HZG SK7 ..56 G6
Burleigh Ms CCHDY M21 ....39 L2
Burlescombe Cl ALT WA14 ...52 F1

Burley Ct HTNM SK4 * 16 A2
Burleyhurst La KNUT WA16 ..70 A8
Burley La WARRS WA4 ......65 L2
Burlington Cl HTNM SK4 .....40 F6
Burlington Dr EDGY/DAV SK3 ..56 C6
Burlington Gdns EDGY/DAV SK3 ..56 F5
Burlington Ms EDGY/DAV SK3 ..56 F5
Burlington Rd ALT WA14 ...211 M1
DID/WITH M20 ....40 D1
Burman St OP/CLY M11 .....28 E2
Burnage Av STHEL WA9 .....31 H4
Burnage Hall Rd BNG/LEV M19 ..40 F1
Burnage La BNG/LEV M19 ...40 E5
HTNM SK4 ....40 E5
Burnage Range BNG/LEV M19 ..28 A8
Burnbray Av BNG/LEV M19 ..40 E6
Burnell Cl NANT CW5 ......196 C4
Burnell Rd EP CH65 ....7 J7
Burnet Cl WARRN/WOL WA2 ..34 D6
Burnfell GOL/RIS/CU WA3 ...25 N5
Burnfield Rd GTN M18 ......28 D6
Burnham Av RDSH SK5 .....28 B8
Burnham Cl CHD/CHDH SK8 ..55 P5
GOL/RIS/CU WA3 ....25 N5
HALE/TIMP WA15 ....53 P8
WARRW/BUR WA5 ....47 K2
WDN WA8 ....20 A4
Burnham Dr BNG/LEV M19 ..40 F1
Burnham Rd CHSW/BR CH4 ..142 B4
DTN/ASHW M34 ....29 J8
Burnsall Av WARRN/WOL WA2 ..33 M6
Burns Av CHD/CHDH SK8 ....55 P5
ALS/KID ST7 ....173 H9
Burns Cl ALS/KID ST7 ......189 J8
GTS/LS CH66 ....80 A9
Burns Dr CHNE CW2 ....42 D9
WDN WA8 ....21 F2
Burns Gn ALS/KID ST7 * 189 J8
CH/BCN CH1 ....121 H5
CW/HAS CW1 ....5 K3
MWCH CW10 ....151 M5
SBCH CW11 ....171 J5
Burnside Cl MPL/ROM SK6 ..56 K2
WILM/AE SK9 ....92 E5
Burnside Dr BNG/LEV M19 ..40 F1
Burnside Rd CHD/CHDH SK8 ..55 J2
Burnside Wy NWCHW CW8 ..12 A2
Burns Rd CONG CW12 .....156 A8
DTN/ASHW M34 ....42 F1
STHEL WA9 ....30 F5
Burns St BK/BCN CH1 ......121 H5
Burnt Acre MCFLDS SK11 ...114 D1
Burnwood Gv ALS/KID ST7 ..189 K6
Burran Rd WYTH/NTH M22 ..54 F7
Burrough Cl GOL/RIS/CU WA3 ..34 G5
Burrows Av CCHDY M21 .....39 L2
RNFD/HAY WA11 ....22 C2
Burrows Hi NWCHW CW8 ...109 K5
Burrows St RNFD/HAY WA11 ..22 E3
The Burrows NWCHW CW8 ..107 P7
Bursar Cl NEWLW WA12 ....22 A8
Burslam St CONG CW12 ....155 N8
Burstead St GTN M18 ....28 E3
Burston St GTN M18 ....28 C3
Burton Av DID/WITH M20 ...40 C2
TPLY/KEL CW6 ....146 C7
Burton Cl GOL/RIS/CU WA3 ..75 P6
WDN WA8 ....45 M4
Burton Dr POY/DIS SK12 ....73 K2
Burton Gn GTS/LS CH66 ....79 P9
Burton Gv CW/HAS CW1 * ..170 A8
Burton Hall Rd
WRX/GR/LL LL12 ....160 B8
Burton La TPLY/KEL CW6 ...145 M4
Burton Rd CH/BCN CH1 ....121 H6
DID/WITH M20 ....40 A4
NSTN CH64 ....77 L7
WARRN/WOL WA2 ....33 N7
Burton St HTNM SK4 ....41 M5
HTNM SK4 ....41 M4
Burtonwood Rd
WARRW/BUR WA5 ....32 D6
Burtree Cl WARRN/WOL WA12 * ..28 A3
Burwardsley Rd CHSE CH3 ..164 A7
Burwardsley Wy NWCHE CW9 ..109 N8
Burwell Gv NTHM/RTH M23 ..39 J9
Bury St RDSH SK5 ....41 N5
Busheli Rd NSTN CH64 ......77 M5
Bushell's Dr STHEL WA9 ....31 J5
Bushey Dr NTHM/RTH M23 ..54 C2
Bush Rd CHSE CH3 ....143 N3
WDN WA8 ....61 H1
Butcher La NTHM/RTH M23 ..38 G9
Butler Wy NANT CW5 ......196 F4
Butley Cl MCFLDN SK10 ...117 H2
MWCH CW10 ....151 J4
Butley Lanes MCFLDN SK10 ..94 C5
Butley St BRAM/HZG SK7 ...57 L3
Butman St GTN M18 ....28 F3
Butterbache Rd CHSE CH3 ..143 J4
Butterbur Cl CHSE CH3 ....143 J1
Buttercup Dr EDGY/DAV SK3 ..56 D3
Buttercup Cl CHD/CHDH SK8 ..56 B6
WARR WA1 ....18 E6
Buttermere Av EP CH65 ....102 E1
Buttermere Cl ALS/KID ST7 ..187 M5
WYTH/NTH M22 ....33 M5
Buttermere Crs FROD/HEL WA6 ..84 B5
Buttermere Dr CONG CW12 ..155 J8
Buttermere Gv RUNC WA7 ...10 C3
Buttermere Rd CW/HAS CW1 ..170 A8
HALE/TIMP WA15 ....53 N9
WILM/AE SK9 ....92 G6
Buttermere Rd CHD/CHDH SK8 ..55 K4
PART M31 ....36 D5
WSFD CW7 ....149 K1
Butterly Cl IRL M44 ....27 P6
Butterton La CW/HAS CW1 ..186 D7
Butterton La CW/HAS CW1 ..186 F6

Butterwick Cl WGTN/LGST M12 ..28 B6
Butterworth St OP/CLY M11 ..28 A1
Butteryhouse La
HALE/TIMP WA15 ....54 A5
Button La WYTH/RTH M23 ...39 J6
Buttress La GTN M18 ......28 C3
The Butts ALS/KID ST7 .....187 P4
AUD/MAD/W CW3 ....211M1
Buxton Av CW/HAS CW1 .....5 J4
DID/WITH M20 ....40 A2
Buxton Cl WARRW/BUR WA5 ..32 D8
Buxton Crs SALE M33 ......38 G7
Buxton La DROY M43 ....28 E1
MPL/ROM SK6 ....56 G2
Buxton New Rd MCFLDN SK10 ..118 A4
Buxton Old Rd CONG CW12 ..155 P6
MCFLDN SK11 ....117 N5
POY/DIS SK12 ....59 H9
Buxton Rd BRAM/HZG SK7 ..57 N7
CONG CW12 ....155 P6
MCFLDN SK10 ....9 F4
NM/HAY SK22 ....59 M9
POY/DIS SK12 ....57 J5
Buxton St BRAM/HZG SK7 ...57 K4
CHD/CHDH SK8 ....55 P5
Byfield Rd WYTH/NTH M22 ..54 E3
Byland Av CHD/CHDH SK8 ...56 B9
Byland Cl WDN WA8 ....46 A2
Bylands Cl POY/DIS SK12 * ..73 K2
Bylands Fld CW/HAS CW1 ..130 D9
Byley La MWCH CW10 ......30 F5
Byng Av IRL M44 ....36 B4
By-Pass Rd CHSE CH3 .....124 A8
Byre Cl SALE M33 ....39 K5
Byrom La BNG/LEV M19 ....28 C8
Byron Cl ALS/KID ST7 * 57 K4
WARRN/WOL WA2 ....33 M6
Byron Cl CH/CHDH SK8 .....56 B9
CW/SHV CW2 ....4 B9
Byron Crs DTN/ASHW M34 ..28 E1
Byron Rd DTN/ASHW M34 ..29 M9
Byron's Dr HALE/TIMP WA15 ..53 L1
Byron's La MCFLDS SK11 ...117 L7
Byron Rd MCFLDS SK11 ....117 L6
Byron St RUNC WA7 ....14 C8
Byron Wy CW/SHV CW2 ...184 F7
Bythom Cl CHSE CH3 ......143 N3

C

Cabot Cl WARRW/BUR WA5 ...32 F7
Cabot Pl RDSH SK5 ....41 N4
Cabul Cl WARRN/WOL WA2 ..19 H1
Cadishead Wy IRL M44 ......36 F1
Cadnam Dr WYTH/NTH M22 ..55 H4
Cadnant Cl CHSW/BR CH4 ..141 H5
Cadnant Cl CH/BCN CH1 ...120 C8
Cadshaw Cl GOL/RIS/CU WA3 ..25 N5
Cae Bychan FLINT CH6 ......98 B8
Cae Derw FLINT CH6 ....98 B7
Cae Hir FLINT CH6 ....98 B8
Caerleon Cl WSFD CW7 ....149 J2
Caernarvon Av WSFD CW7 ..149 J2
Caernarvon Cl EP CH65 ....102 F2
Caernarvon Dr BRAM/HZG SK7 ..57 J6
Caernarvon Rd CW/SHV CW2 ..184 E8
Caesar Av WSFD CW7 .....149 H2
Cairn Ct STHEL WA9 ....30 C1
Cairns Crs CH/BCN CH1 ...120 C7
Cairo St WARR WA1 ....16 E6
Caister Wy WSFD CW7 ....149 L5
Caistor St STKP SK1 ....42 A5
Caithness Cl NTHM/RTH M23 ..54 C3
Caithness Rd RUNC WA7 ....15 F7
Calamine St MCFLDS SK11 ...9 G7
Calbourne Crs WGTN/LGST M12 ..28 B6
Calcutta Rd EDGY/DAV SK3 ..56 C6
Calday Gv RNFD/HAY WA11 ..22 L1
Caldbeck Av WARRN/WOL WA2 ..33 J6
Calder Av CW/HAS CW1 ....185 N3
IRL M44 ....27 M8
WYTH/NTH M22 ....39 N8
Calderbrook Dr CHD/CHDH SK8 ..56 A3
Calder Cl MCFLDN SK10 ....95 M5
POY/DIS SK12 ....73 K4
RDSH SK5 ....41 P3
WDN WA8 ....61 J1
Calder Dr RAIN/WH L35 ....30 G5
Calderfield Cl WARRS WA4 ..49 J7
Caldervale Av CCHDY M21 ..39 M6
Calder Wy GTS/LS CH66 ....79 N8
Caldicott Cl WSFD CW7 ...149 L3
Caldwell Av WARRW/BUR WA5 ..33 J6
Caldwell Cl NANT CW5 * ...197 J5
Caldwell's Gate La NWCHE CW9 ..66 A5
Caldwell St STHEL WA9 .....32 B6
Caldy Cl CHS3 * 56 A3
Caldy Dr GTS/LS CH66 .....79 P9
Caldy Gv RNFD/HAY WA11 ..22 C2
Caldy Rd ALS/KID ST7 .....71 M5
WILM/AE SK9 ....71 M5
Caldy Valley Rd CHSE CH3 ..143 J8
Caldy Wy WSFD CW7 .....149 K5
Cale Gn EDGY/DAV SK3 ....56 F1
Cale St OFTN SK2 ....41 N9
Calgary St GTN M18 ....28 C6
Calico Cl CHF/WBR SK23 ....75 P2
California Cl WARRW/BUR WA5 ..32 F8

Callands Rd WARRW/BUR WA5 ..32 G6
Callingdon Rd CCHDY M21 ..39 N5
Callon Av RNFD/HAY WA11 ..22 C4
Calluna Ms DID/WITH M20 ..40 D4
Calmington La RUNC WA7 ...62 E2
Calrofold Dr NEWLU ST5 ...201 N6
Calrofold La MCFLDN SK10 ..118 A3
Calstock Cl WARRW/BUR WA5 ..47 J4
Calve Croft Rd WYTH/NTH M22 ..54 F6
Calveley Av PS/BROM CH62 ..79 K1
Calveley Cl NWCHE CW9 ...109 N7
Calveley Green La
TPLY/KEL CW6 ....167 L7
Calveley Hall La TPLY/KEL CW6 ..167 H5
Calveley Rd HLWD L26 .....44 B9
MCFLDN SK10 ....116 F3
Calverley Av RDSH SK5 ....56 A2
Calverley Cl RUNC WA7 ....62 G9
Calverly Cl RUNC WA7 .....62 G9
Calver Rd WARRN/WOL WA2 ..33 K5
Camberley Cl BRAM/HZG SK7 ..56 G8
Cambert La GTN M18 ......28 D4
Camberwell Park Rd WDN WA8 ..46 B3
Camborne Av MCFLDN SK10 ..116 E4
Camborne Cl CONG CW12 ..174 F1
RUNC WA7 ....62 G8
Camborne Av
RNFD/HAY WA11 ....22 B2
Cambourne Rd
WARRW/BUR WA5 ....32 C2
Cambo Wk HTNM SK4 ......40 G5
Cambrai Av WARR WA4 ....48 E5
Cambrian Av CHSE CH3 ....122 C9
Cambrian Cl GTS/LS CH66 ..79 L7
EDGY/DAV SK3 ....16 B7
Cambrian Wy WSFD CW7 ..149 E2
Cambridge Av MCFLDS SK11 ..91 H7
WILM/AE SK9 ....71 H7
WSFD CW7 ....149 J2
Cambridge Cl BIDD ST8 ...175 K8
SALE M33 ....38 A5
WARRS WA4 ....48 D7
Cambridge Gdns
FROD/HEL WA6 ....83 K9
WARRS WA4 ....48 E9
Cambridge Rd CHD/CHDH SK8 ..55 K1
CHEH 122 A6
EP CH65 ....3 J6
HALE/TIMP WA15 ....53 J5
HTNM SK4 ....41 K3
Cambridge St OFTN SK2 ....56 G1
RUNC WA7 ....15 J2
WDN WA8 ....21 J4
Camden Ct RUNC WA7 .....63 H5
Camden Rd EP CH65 ....5 G4
Camden St CW/HAS CW1 * ..5 G2
Camellia Gdns STHEL WA9 ..31 N1
Camelot Cl MCFLDS SK11 ...23 K5
Cameron Gv CW/SHV CW2 ..198 A4
Cameron Av CH/BCN CH1 ...14 B7
RUNC WA7 ....14 B7
Cameron Ct WARRN/WOL WA2 ..33 M4
Cameron St WDN WA8 ......21 G3
Camm St CW/SHV CW2 ......5 F6
Campbell Av RUNC WA7 ....14 C7
Campbell Cl CONG CW12 ...156 A6
CW/HAS CW1 ....186 A4
NWCHE CW9 ....109 P8
Campbell Crs WARRW/BUR WA5 ..47 K4
Campbell Rd SALE M33 ....38 C5
Campbell St RDSH SK5 ....28 H8
Campden Wy WILM/AE SK9 ..71 M2
Campion Cl CHSE CH3 ....143 J4
GOL/RIS/CU WA3 ....34 D3
Campsey Ash WDN WA8 ...45 M4
Camrose Cl RUNC WA7 ....62 A8
Camsley La LYMM WA13 ...50 D4
Canaan GOL/RIS/CU WA3 ..34 B6
Canada Cl WARRN/WOL WA2 ..34 B6
Canada St OFTN SK2 ......56 G1
Canadian Av CHNE CW2 ...122 B7
Canal Reach RUNC WA7 ....62 G4
CONG CW12 ....155 P9
Canal Side CH/BCN CH1 .....3 G3
MCFLDS SK11 ....9 J6
NWCHW CW8 ....109 K2
RUNC WA7 ....61 K7
WARRS WA4 ....49 L6
Canalside EP CH65 ....7 H2
Canal St CH/BCN CH1 ....2 C3
CONG CW12 ....155 N8
MCFLDN SK10 ....9 G4
NEWLW WA12 ....58 E1
NEWLW WA12 * 43 K2
RUNC WA7 ....15 H2
STKP SK1 ....17 H6
Canal Ter MWCH CW10 ...151 L2
Canal Vw LYMM WA13 * ...50 C4
Canal Wk MCFLDN SK10 ...95 M2
Canberra Av WARRS WA4 ...30 D1
Canberra Rd BRAM/HZG SK7 ..79 E1
WARRN/WOL WA2 ....120 C7
Canberra Sq WARRN/WOL WA2 ..33 N7
Candelan Wy KNUT WA16 ...67 J2
Candleford Pl OFTN SK2 ....57 J3
Candleford Rd DID/WITH M20 ..40 C2
Candover Cl AUD/MAD/W CW3 ..218 G3
Candleston Cl
WARRW/BUR WA5 ....33 H7
Candy La MCFLDN SK10 ....73 J6
Canford Cl CW/HAS CW1 ...170 A9
Canley Cl WARR WA1 ......47 N1
Canley Cl STKP SK1 ....17 K3
Cannell Ct RUNC WA7 .....62 E8
Cannell St WARRN/WOL WA2 ..18 F5
Canning St CH/BCN CH1 .....2 D3
HTNM SK4 ....17 F2

Canniswood Rd RNFD/HAY WA11 ....22 E4
Cann La NWCHE CW9 ....88 F2
  WARRS WA4 ....65 H2
Cann La North WARRS WA4 .....48 G3
Cannock Cl GTS/LS CH66 ....102 A4
Cannon St EP CH65 ....6 D1
  STHEL WA9 ....31 K5
Canon Dr ALT WA14 ....52 F6
Canons Cl WARRW/BUR WA5 ...47 P1
Canon St RUNC WA7 ....14 D1
Canon Wilson Cl RNFD/HAY WA11 ....23 H3
Canterbury Cl GTS/LS CH66 ...102 A4
Canterbury Ct MCFLDN SK10 ....9 G3
Canterbury Pk DID/WITH M20 ..40 A5
Canterbury Rd CH/BCN CH1 ...121 J6
  HALE/TIMP WA15 ....53 N4
  STKP SK1 ....42 A7
Canterbury St WARRS WA4 ....48 E5
Cantley Cl KID ST7 ....62 B8
Canton St MCFLDS SK11 .....117 K6
Canton Wks MCFLDS SK11 ....117 K6
Canute Pl KNUT WA16 ....90 E5
Capeland Cl CHSW/BR CH4 ...142 A5
Capenhurst Av CW/SHV CW2 ..184 F5
  WARRN/WOL WA2 ....34 B6
Capenhurst Cl NTHM/RTH M23 ..54 B3
Capenhurst La CH/BCN CH1 ...101 L5
  EP CH65 ....102 C1
Capesthorne Rd ALS/KID ST7 ..187 N5
  BRAM/HZG SK7 ....57 M7
  HOLMCH WA4 ....131 N6
  NWCHE CW9 ....109 P8
  SBCH CW11 ....171 P2
  WDN WA8 ....20 D2
• Capesthorne Rd CHSE CH3 ....57 M7
  CHSE CH3 ....144 B5
  CW/SHV CW2 ....184 G6
  HALE/TIMP WA15 ....53 P1
  MPL/ROM SK6 ....58 C8
  WARRN/WOL WA2 ....33 P6
  WILM/AE SK9 ....70 G9
Capesthorne Wy MCFLDS SK11 ...9 J5
Cape St DID/WITH M20 ....40 D1
Capital Rd OP/CLY M11 ....28 F2
Capitol Wk CONG CW12 * 155 M8
Capper Cl ALS/KID ST7 ....189 J6
Cappers La SBCH CW11 ....172 E7
  TPLY/KEL CW6 ....181 M4
Capstone Rd MPL/ROM SK6 ....58 C1
Captain Clarke Rd HYDE SK14 ..29 P4
Capton Cl BRAM/HZG SK7 .....56 G5
Carberry Rd GTN M18 ....28 E4
Carden Av WSFD CW7 ....149 K1
Carden Cl GOL/RIS/CU WA3 ....34 D4
Cardeston Cl RUNC WA7 ....84 D2
Cardew Av WYTH/NTH M22 .....54 G3
Cardiff Cl GTS/LS CH66 ......102 A4
Cardigan Cl MCFLDS SK11 ....116 G6
  WARRW/BUR WA5 ....32 C6
Cardus St BNG/LEV M19 ....28 A8
Carey St WDN WA8 ....21 J1
Carfax St GTN M18 ....28 D4
Carisbrook Av MCFLDN SK10 ....9 H1
Carisbrook Av WSFD CW7 ....149 L3
Carisbrooke Av BRAM/HZG SK7 .57 K6
Carisbrooke Cl CW/SHV CW2 ..184 E8
Carleton Rd POY/DIS SK12 ....74 A2
Carlile St EDGY/DAV SK3 .....16 E7
Carlin Ga HALE/TIMP WA15 ....53 L1
Carling Dr WYTH/NTH M22 ....54 G5
Carlingford Cl EDGY/DAV SK3 ..56 E2
Carlingford Rd WARRS WA4 ....48 D7
Carlisle Cl KNUT WA16 ....91 L1
  MCFLDS SK11 ....116 F7
  MPL/ROM SK6 ....42 F7
  WSFD CW7 ....149 J1
  IRL M44 ....33 P8
Carlisle Rd CH/BCN CH1 .....121 H6
Carlisle St CW/SHV CW2 ....4 C7
  WARRS WA4 ....48 C7
  WILM/AE SK9 ....95 J5
Carlow Rd NTHM/RTH M23 ....39 L1
Carlow Cl SPK/HALE L24 ....60 C4
Carlow Dr WYTH/NTH M22 ....54 G5
Carlton Av BRAM/HZG SK7 ....72 D1
  CHD/CHDH SK8 ....57 J6
  CHSW/BR CH4 ....141 P4
  MPL/ROM SK6 ....58 J5
  RUNC WA7 ....62 B4
  WILM/AE SK9 ....71 L4
Carlton Cl CHNE CH2 ....122 F5
  NSTN CH64 ....77 J3
Carlton Ct HALE/TIMP WA15 ...53 M6
Carlton Crs GTS/LS CH66 .....17 K3
  STKP SK1 ....17 K3
Carlton Dr CHD/CHDH SK8 .....55 J1
Carlton Pl BRAM/HZG SK7 * ..57 M6
  CHNE CH2 ....122 B7
Carlton Range GTN M18 * 28 F5
Carlton Rd HALE/TIMP WA15 ...53 M5
  HTNM SK4 ....41 H6
  LYMM WA13 ....51 H2
  NWCHE CW9 ....13 H4
  SALE M33 ....38 D2
Carlton St WARRS WA4 ....48 E7
  WDN WA8 ....20 B5
Carlyle Gv GOL/RIS/CU WA3 ....36 B3
Carlyle Cl ALS/KID ST7 .....173 H9
Carlyn Av SALE M33 ....38 C5
Carmarthen Cl WARRW/BUR WA5 ....32 C6
  WSFD CW7 ....149 L5
Carmel Cl CH/BCN CH1 ......120 C8
Carmel Ct WDN WA8 ....45 P3
Carmel Ms WILM/AE SK9 ......71 K4
Carmenna Dr BRAM/HZG SK7 ..56 F8
Carmichael Cl PART M31 ....36 D5
Carmichael St EDGY/DAV SK3 ..16 C7

Carna Rd RDSH SK5 ....28 E7
Carnarvon St STHEL WA9 .....30 C1
  STKP SK1 ....17 K6
Carnegie Av BNG/LEV M19 ....28 B8
Carnegie Cl SALE M33 ....38 A5
Carnegie Crs STHEL WA9 .....22 C9
Carnforth Dr SALE M33 ....38 D5
Carnforth Gv ALS/KID ST7 ...189 N8
Carnforth Rd CHD/CHDH SK8 ..56 B5
  WARRS WA4 ....41 L2
Carnoustie Cl WILM/AE SK9 ...71 M6
  WSFD CW7 ....128 C9
Carnoustie Dr CHD/CHDH SK8 ..55 J4
  MCFLDN SK10 ....95 J8
Carole Cl STHEL WA9 ....31 K2
Caroline St EDGY/DAV SK3 ....41 L9
  IRL M44 ....27 J9
Carol St WARRS WA4 ....48 F4
Carpenter Gv WARRN/WOL WA2 ..34 B7
Carpenters Wk DROY M43 .....28 F1
Carradale Dr SALE M33 ....37 P5
Carr Brow MPL/ROM SK6 .....58 E8
Carr Cl STKP SK1 ....42 A5
Carrfield Av EDGY/DAV SK3 ...56 C5
  HALE/TIMP WA15 ....53 L1
Carrgate Rd DTN/ASHW M34 ...29 P8
Carrgreen Cl BNG/LEV M19 ....40 C3
Carrgreen La LYMM WA13 .....51 M1
Carrhill Rd DTN/ASHW M34 ....29 P3
Carr La NM/HAY SK22 ....75 P1
  NWCHE CW9 ....12 D3
  WRXS/E LL13 ....176 F8
Carr Mill Ms WILM/AE SK9 * ..71 K5
Carr Mill Rd RNFD/HAY WA11 ..22 A2
Carroll Dr CW/SHV CW2 ....184 B8
Carrill Gv East BNG/LEV M19 ..28 A8
Carrington Cl GOL/RIS/CU WA3 ..34 D4
Carrington Field St OFTN SK2 ..41 N9
Carrington La SALE M33 ......38 B3
Carrington Rd STKP SK1 ......42 A5
Carrington Wy CW/SHV CW2 ..170 A9
Carr La KID ST7 ....200 D6
  GOL/RIS/CU WA3 ....25 J2
Car La LEIGH WN7 ....25 N1
  SPK/HALE L24 ....60 C4
  SALE M33 ....92 F3
Carr Mdw ALT WA14 * 52 C3
Carrick Dr EP CH65 ....102 D2
Carrick Rd CHSW/BR CH4 ....142 C5
Carrs La CHSE CH3 ....164 E8
Carrs Rd CHD/CHDH SK8 ......55 P1
Carr St ALS/KID ST7 ....189 F7
Carrswood Rd NTHM/RTH M23 ..38 F8
Carr Vw NM/HAY SK22 * 75 P1
Carrwood Rd HALE/TIMP WA15 ...53 M8
  KNUT WA16 ....90 G5
Carrwood Av BRAM/HZG SK7 ...57 J4
Carrwood Cl RNFD/HAY WA11 ..22 E7
Carr Wood Rd BRAM/HZG SK7 ..56 D6
Carrwood Rd WILM/AE SK9 ....71 H8
Carsdale Rd WYTH/NTH M22 ...54 G8
Carson Rd BNG/LEV M19 ......28 A9
Carstairs Av EDGY/DAV SK3 ...56 C3
Carter Av TPLY/KEL CW6 .....125 J7
Carter Cl DTN/ASHW M34 * ...29 M7
Carter La MCFLDS SK11 ....92 C9
Carter St CH/BCN CH1 ....2 B3
Cartier Cl WARRW/BUR WA5 ...32 F8
Cartlake Cl NANT CW5 ....196 D2
Cartledge Cl NWCHW CW8 ...108 C9
Cartmel Av HTNM SK4 ....41 L2
  WARRN/WOL WA2 ....33 M5
Cartmel Cl BRAM/HZG SK7 ....57 J4
  CHD/CHDH SK8 ....55 L4
  HOLMCH WA4 ....131 M8
  MCFLDN SK10 ....117 H2
  WARRW/BUR WA5 ....48 C6
  WSFD CW7 ....128 E9
Cartmel Dr GTS/LS CH66 .....102 B2
  HALE/TIMP WA15 ....53 P1
Cartmell Cl RUNC WA7 ....77 K8
Cartridge La WYTH/NTH M22 ...55 H4
Cartridge La WARRS WA4 .....49 M9
Cartwright Rd CW/HAS CW1 ..186 B2
Cartwright St DTN/ASHW M34 ..29 M3
  RUNC WA7 ....15 J3
  WARRW/BUR WA5 ....48 A1
Carver Av HOLMCH WA4 ......131 M5
Carver Cl WSFD CW7 ....129 H8
Carver Dr MPL/ROM SK6 .....58 C2
Carver Rd HALE/TIMP WA15 ...53 L1
  MPL/ROM SK6 ....58 C2
Case Rd RNFD/HAY WA11 ......23 H5
Casey La CW/SHV CW2 ....198 E4
Cashmere Rd EDGY/DAV SK3 ...43 J9
Caspian Rd ALT WA14 ....52 C3
Cassia Green La WSFD CW7 ..127 N6
Cassley Rd SPK/HALE L24 .....60 A5
Casson St CW/HAS CW1 ....4 C1
Castillon Dr WHITCH SY13 ...213 N5
Castle Av DTN/ASHW M34 .....29 M3
  STHEL WA9 ....22 C6
Castle Bnk NWCHW CW8 ......12 D5
  CHSW/BR CH4 ....140 F4
Castle Cl CHSW/BR CH4 .....160 G7
  TPLY/KEL CW6 ....125 J7
Castle Cl NWCHW CW8 ....12 D5
Castle Croft Rd CHSW/BR CH4 .142 D5
Castle Dr CH/BCN CH1 ....102 C1
  EP CH65 ....102 C1
Castle Dyke St FLINT CH6 .....98 B5
Castle Edge Rd NM/HAY SK22 ..59 L5
Castle Farm La OFTN SK2 .....57 J2
Castlefields CHSE CH3 ....164 D7
Castlefields Av East RUNC WA7 .62 E5
Castlefields Av North RUNC WA7 ....62 E6
Castlefields Av South RUNC WA7 ....62 E6
Castleford Dr MCFLDN SK10 ...94 E7
Castlegate MCFLDN SK10 .....94 E7

Castlegate Ms MCFLDN SK10 ...94 F7
Castle Gn WARRW/BUR WA5 ...32 E6
Castlehill CHSW/BR CH4 .....160 F7
Castle HI CHSW/BR CH4 .....160 E7
  NEWLW WA12 ....6 D3
  WHITCH SY13 ....213 M6
Castle Hill Pk MPL/ROM SK6 * ..42 E2
Castle Inn Rd CONG CW12 ....175 K2
Castlemead Wk NWCHE CW9 ..109 N8
Castlemere Dr CW/HAS CW1 ..175 J1
  HALE/TIMP WA15 ....53 K9
Castle Mill La HALE/TIMP WA15 180 L1
Castle Mt NEWLW ST5 ....201 P9
Castle Pl CH/BCN CH1 ....2 E6
Castle Ri CO CH5 ....140 B2
  MCFLDN SK10 ....94 F7
  RUNC WA7 ....62 B4
Castle Rd ALS/KID ST7 ......189 M1
  FLINT CH6 ....98 B5
  RUNC WA7 ....62 D6
Castle Shaw Rd OFTN SK2 ....57 K2
Castle St CH/BCN CH1 ....2 D6
  CW/HAS CW1 ....4 D2
  CW/SHV CW2 ....5 H2
  MCFLDS SK11 ....98 B5
  NANT CW5 ....8 E4
  NEWLW ST5 ....201 P8
  NWCHW CW8 ....12 D3
  WDN WA8 ....176 F8
Castle St MI MCFLDS SK11 * ...8 E4
Castleton Dr MPL/ROM SK6 ...58 D9
Castleton Rd BRAM/HZG SK7 ..57 L6
Castleton St ALT WA14 ....37 P9
Castletown La CHSE CH3 ....165 J9
Castletown St CHSE CH3 ....190 E5
Castleview Gv BURS/TUN ST6 ..189 P9
Castleview Rd ALS/KID ST7 ...189 K5
Castle Wy CHSW/BR CH4 .....160 D3
Castleway HALE/TIMP WA15 ...53 N8
Castlewood Gdns OFTN SK2 ...57 J2
Castle Yd STKP SK1 ....17 G3
Castner Av RUNC WA7 ....61 L7
Catalan Cl WSFD CW7 ....150 A1
Catchpenny La MCFLDS SK11 ..114 A9
Catford Cl WDN WA8 ....45 J5
Catford Rd NTHM/RTH M23 ...54 B2
Catfoss Cl WARRN/WOL WA2 ..33 P7
Catherine Rd ALT WA14 ......52 C4
  MPL/ROM SK6 ....42 E7
Catherine St BRAM/HZG SK7 ..57 L3
  CH/BCN CH1 ....2 B3
  CW/SHV CW2 ....5 J3
  DID/WITH M20 ....28 D4
  FLINT CH6 ....98 B5
  MCFLDS SK11 ....8 E4
  NANT CW5 ....8 D3
  OP/CLY M11 ....28 E2
  WARRW/BUR WA5 ....18 B2
  WDN WA8 ....21 H6
Catherine Wy NEWLW WA12 ..23 M7
  RNFD/HAY WA11 * 22 D3
Catherine St East DTN/ASHW M34 ....29 K6
Catherine St West DTN/ASHW M34 ....29 K6
Catteral Av STHEL WA9 ......31 J2
  WARRN/WOL WA2 ....33 N6
Catterall La WHITCH SY13 ...214 B7
Catterick Rd DID/WITH M20 ...40 D5
  SALE M33 ....37 P6
Catterwood Dr MPL/ROM SK6 ..43 N6
Caughall Rd CHNE CH2 ....121 P5
Caunce Av GOL/RIS/CU WA3 ..24 C2
  RNFD/HAY WA11 * 22 D3
Causeway Av WARRS WA4 ....48 E4
The Causeway ALT WA14 .....53 H3
Cavalier Dr CH/BCN CH1 .....121 H5
Cavan Cl EDGY/DAV SK3 .....40 G9
Cavell Dr EP CH65 ....40 G6
Cavendish Av MCFLDN SK10 ...40 A2
  GOL/RIS/CU WA3 ....34 F3
Cavendish Cl MCFLDN SK10 ...117 K1
  WARRN/BUR WA5 ....32 C9
Cavendish Crs ALS/KID ST7 ..187 N5
Cavendish Farm Rd RUNC WA7 .77 H9
Cavendish Gdns EP CH65 * 6 B7
Cavendish Ms WILM/AE SK9 ...71 J9
Cavendish Pl GOL/RIS/CU WA3 ..34 C3
Cavendish Rd ALT WA14 .....52 C4
  BRAM/HZG SK7 ....57 K6
  CHD/CHDH SK8 ....55 L4
  CW/SHV CW2 ....184 E5
  DID/WITH M20 ....40 A2
  EDGY/DAV SK3 ....40 G6
Cavendish Wy HOLMCH WA4 ..131 L9
Caversham Ct WARRS WA4 ....41 K9
Cawdor Dr CHSE CH3 ....122 B9
Cawdor Pl HALE/TIMP WA15 ...53 N1
  WARRS WA4 ....48 E7
Cawfield Av WDN WA8 ....20 B1
Cawley Av GOL/RIS/CU WA3 ..35 H8
Cawley La MCFLDS SK11 ....75 L7
  RUNC WA7 ....14 E5
Cawood St MPL/ROM SK6 ....58 D2
  STKP SK1 * 17 G7
Caxton Rd HALE/TIMP WA15 ...30 D7
Cayton St WGTN/LGST M12 ...28 A6
The Ceal MPL/ROM SK6 ......43 N6
Cecil Av SALE M33 ....38 D5
Cecil Cv GTN M18 ....28 D5
Cecil Rigby Cl SBCH CW11 ...171 N5
Cecil St CHSE CH3 ....143 J1
  DUK SK16 ....29 H1
  EDGY/DAV SK3 * 41 M9
  STHEL WA9 ....31 L1

Cedab Rd EP CH65 ....7 F3
  ALS/KID ST7 ....187 P5
Cedar Av ALS/KID ST7 ....188 F7
  ALT WA14 ....52 C3
  BRAM/HZG SK7 ....57 L5
  GOL/RIS/CU WA3 ....35 J2
  GTS/LS CH66 ....79 N7
  RUNC WA7 ....62 A7
  WARR WA1 ....84 E1
  WDN WA8 ....45 P4
Cedar Ct HOLMCH WA4 ......131 L4
  MWCH CW10 ....151 L4
  NWCHE CW9 ....110 C1
  POY/DIS SK12 ....73 L3
  SBCH CW11 ....171 P4
Cedar Ct CONG CW12 ....174 C1
  GOL/RIS/CU WA3 ....25 P7
  HALE/TIMP WA15 * 53 P1
  NANT CW5 ....197 L1
Cedar Crs ALS/KID ST7 ......201 J6
  NEWLW WA12 ....23 P7
Cedardale Dr GTS/LS CH66 ..102 B5
Cedardale Pk WDN WA8 ....45 N8
Cedar Dr CHNE CH2 ....122 C7
  NWCHW CW8 ....12 D3
Cedarfield Rd LYMM WA13 ....51 H2
Cedar Gv BIDD ST8 ....175 P8
  CHNE CH2 ....122 C7
  DTN/ASHW M34 ....29 L6
  HTNM SK4 ....41 L5
  MCFLDS SK11 ....117 K7
  NANT CW5 ....197 L1
  NSTN CH64 ....77 M5
  RNFD/HAY WA11 ....22 D3
  WARR WA1 ....48 F6
  WARRW/BUR WA5 ....47 K1
  WSFD CW7 ....149 K5
Cedar Lawn CHD/CHDH SK8 * ..56 A5
Cedar Ms CH/BCN CH1 ......121 H7
Cedar Pk CHSE CH3 ....122 D9
Cedar Rd CHD/CHDH SK8 * 56 A5
  HALE/TIMP WA15 ....53 J4
  MPL/ROM SK6 ....58 C3
  NEWLW ST5 ....201 N6
  NWCHW CW8 ....108 E4
  OFTN SK2 ....57 H3
  PART M31 ....36 C5
  SALE M33 ....38 B3
  WARRW/BUR WA5 ....47 K1
Cedars The WYTH/NTH M22 ...54 E5
Cedar Wy CW/SHV CW2 ......185 H9
Cedarway WILM/AE SK9 ......71 M8
Cedarways WARRS WA4 ......41 L4
Cedarwood NWCHW CW8 ....107 P7
Cedarwood Ct TPLY/KEL CW6 ..146 J5
Celandine Cl CHSE CH3 ......143 J5
Celandine Wy NEWLW WA12 ...31 N1
Celestria Cl SBCH CW11 ....171 J2
Celtic Av ALS/KID ST7 ....189 D5
Celtic St STKP SK1 ....17 K6
Celyn Crs CHSW/BR CH4 .....141 P5
Cement Pl CH/BCN CH1 * 3 F2
  CW/SHV CW2 * 5 J3
Cemetery Rd DTN/ASHW M34 ..29 M3
  DTN/ASHW M34 ....29 M8
Cemlyn Cl CH/BCN CH1 ......121 H8
Centenary Pl BNG/LEV M19 ...28 A7
Central Dr BRAM/HZG SK7 ....56 D5
  CHD/CHDH SK8 ....55 P1
  MPL/ROM SK6 ....43 N5
  NWCHW CW8 ....109 J1
  RDSH SK5 ....41 P3
  RNFD/HAY WA11 ....22 F3
Central Expy RUNC WA7 ......62 C7
Central Gv NWCHE CW9 ......110 D5
Central Rd DID/WITH M20 ....40 A2
  MANAIR M90 ....54 E9
  NWCHE CW9 ....110 D5
  PART M31 ....36 E5
  WARRS WA4 ....48 D5
Central St ALS/KID ST7 ......189 K2
  NEWLW WA12 ....23 H3
  WARRN/WOL WA2 ....18 C4
Centre Pk WARR WA1 ....48 C3
Centre Park Sq WARR WA1 ...48 C3
Centurion Ct GOL/RIS/CU WA3 ..34 E4
Centurion Wy MWCH CW10 ...130 D9
Century Wy MCFLDN SK10 ...117 J2
Chaddesley Wk OP/CLY M11 * ..28 A1
Chadkirk Rd MPL/ROM SK6 ...42 G7
Chads Gn NANT CW5 ....197 N6
Chadvil Rd CHD/CHDH SK8 ...55 L2
Chadwell Rd OFTN SK2 ......57 K2
Chadwick Av GOL/RIS/CU WA3 ..34 E6
  WARRS WA4 ....48 C6
Chadwick Cl WILM/AE SK9 ....71 L5
Chadwick Rd MWCH CW10 ...151 J4
  RNFD/HAY WA11 ....22 A2
  RUNC WA7 ....84 B2
Chadwick St MPL/ROM SK6 ...58 D2
  STKP SK1 ....17 G7
Chaffinch Cl CONG CW12 ....155 N9
  GOL/RIS/CU WA3 ....24 E8
  WYTH/NTH M22 ....54 F5
Chaffinch Wy WSFD CW7 ....149 M4
Chain La RNFD/HAY WA11 .....22 C3
Chain Maker's Rw CHSW/BR CH4 ....142 A3
Chalfield Av GTS/LS CH66 ....79 M9
Chalfield Ct CW/SHV CW2 ...185 H9
  GTS/LS CH66 ....79 N8
Chalfont Cl WARRS WA4 .....48 G9

Chalfont Crs CW/SHV CW2 ...198 D5
Chalford Rd NTHM/RTH M23 ...54 C4
Chalgrave Cl WDN WA8 ......46 C4
Challenor Sq WGTN/LGST M12 * ..28 A3
Challinor St CHSE CH3 ....143 J1
Chamber Brook La FROD/HEL WA6 ....106 G2
Chamberlain Ct CW/HAS CW1 ..186 A5
Chamberlain Dr WILM/AE SK9 ..71 M5
Chamberlain Wy BIDD ST8 ...175 M9
Chambers St CW/SHV CW2 * 5 F7
Chance Hall La ALS/KID ST7 ..173 L8
Chancel La WILM/AE SK9 .....71 K6
Chancellor Rd RUNC WA7 .....63 H1
Chancel Ms STKP SK1 ....17 J4
Chancery La ALS/KID ST7 ....187 M5
  MCFLDN SK10 ....95 P6
  STHEL WA9 ....22 C6
Chanders Ct RUNC WA7 ....14 B4
Chandler Wy GOL/RIS/CU WA3 ..34 F3
Chandley Cl CHD/CHDH SK8 * ..55 M1
Chandos Cl CHNE CH2 ....142 C4
Chandos Rd HTNM SK4 ....41 J2
Change La NSTN CH64 ....79 P5
Chantler Av WARRS WA4 ......48 C3
Chantry Av NWCHW CW8 ....109 K8
Chantry Cl POY/DIS SK12 .....75 J1
  RDSH SK5 ....41 M1
Chantry Ct CW/HAS CW1 * 5 J3
  MCFLDS SK11 ....117 K7
Chantry Fold POY/DIS SK12 ...59 J3
Chantry Rd POY/DIS SK12 ....59 H9
The Chantry TPLY/KEL CW6 ..167 H7
Chapel Av FROD/HEL WA6 ...106 C2
Chapel Bnk ALS/KID ST7 ....189 M1
Chapel Cl ALS/KID ST7 ......189 K2
  AUD/MAD/W CW5 ....216 C2
  CH/BCN CH1 ....120 D2
  CHSE CH3 ....144 A5
  EP CH65 ....6 E1
  NWCHE CW9 ....87 M6
  WSFD CW7 ....168 A4
Chapel Ct ALT WA14 ....53 H3
  NWCHE CW9 ....13 H4
Chapel Cft MCFLDS SK11 ....114 D1
Chapel Cross Rd WARRN/WOL WA2 ....34 B6
Chapel Dr HALE/TIMP WA15 ...53 N8
Chapel Field Rd DTN/ASHW M34 ....29 M6
Chapelfields FROD/HEL WA6 ..83 N5
Chapel Gn DTN/ASHW M34 ....29 M6
Chapel House La WSTN CH64 ..100 G5
Chapel La ALS/KID ST7 ......189 N4
  BIDD ST8 ....175 P8
  CH/BCN CH1 ....101 J4
  CHSE CH3 ....143 J1
  CHSE CH3 ....162 B5
  CHSE CH3 ....170 C8
  CW/HAS CW1 ....170 C8
  FROD/HEL WA6 ....105 M8
  FROD/HEL WA6 ....106 G2
  GOL/RIS/CU WA3 ....35 N7
  HALE/TIMP WA15 ....53 N8
  KNUT WA16 ....112 C9
  MALPAS SY14 ....202 F6
  MCFLDN SK10 ....96 C8
  MCFLDS SK11 ....133 N2
  MKTDR TF9 ....219 H8
  NANT CW5 ....195 N5
  NWCHE CW9 ....38 B5
  NWCHW CW8 ....128 F5
  PART M31 ....36 E5
  RAIN/WH L35 ....30 C6
  SALE M33 ....38 B2
  TPLY/KEL CW6 ....125 K9
  WARRS WA4 ....65 K3
  WARRW/BUR WA5 ....86 C6
  WDN WA8 ....45 J2
  WILM/AE SK9 ....93 J4
  WRXS/E LL13 ....176 F8
Chapelmere Cl SBCH CW11 ...171 K2
Chapelmere Ct CW/HAS CW1 ..185 G1
Chapel Ms EP CH65 ....18 D5
  KNUT WA16 ....91 K7
  SALE M33 ....47 J4
  WARRW/BUR WA5 ....47 J4
  WILM/AE SK9 ....93 J4
  WSFD CW7 ....128 C9
  WYTH/NTH M22 ....39 N8
Chapel Rw NANT CW5 ....196 E2
Chapel Side EP CH65 ....18 C4
  ALS/KID ST7 ....189 K2
Chapel St ALS/KID ST7 ......189 N4
  BNG/LEV M19 ....28 B8
  BRAM/HZG SK7 ....57 L4
  CHSE CH3 ....55 M2
  CHSE CH3 ....143 J1
  CONG CW12 * 155 M8
  CW/SHV CW2 ....5 F5
  DUK SK16 ....29 P1
  FLINT CH6 ....98 A6
  HTNM SK4 ....41 J2
  MCFLDN SK10 ....95 P5
  MCFLDS SK11 ....8 C4
  MPL/ROM SK6 ....58 D2
  NEWLW WA12 ....23 M6
  NM/HAY SK22 ....59 M9
  NWCHE CW9 ....110 C1
  NWCHW CW8 ....12 D4
  RNFD/HAY WA11 ....23 J5
  RUNC WA7 ....14 D1
  SBCH CW11 ....171 M5
  SBCH CW11 ....171 N5
  STHEL WA9 ....31 L1
  WILM/AE SK9 ....93 J4
  WRXS/E LL13 ....176 F8
Chapel Wks CHD/CHDH SK8 * ..56 A4

Chapman Cl WDN WA8 ....45 K3
Chapman Ms GTN M18 * 28 D4
Chapman St GTN M18 ....28 D3
Chapterhouse Cl EP CH65 ....7 K4
Charcoal Rd ALT WA14 ....52 C4
Charcoal Woods ALT WA14 ....52 E4
Chard Dr WYTH/NTH M22 ....54 F6
Chardin Av MPL/ROM SK6 ....45 P8
Chariot St OP/CLY M11 ....28 D1
Charity La MCFLDS SK11 ....118 D4
Charlbury Av RDSH SK5 ....43 J6
Charlcote Crs CW/SHV CW2 ....185 J8
Charlecote Rd POY/DIS SK12 ....73 M2
Charles Av DTN/ASHW M34 ....28 C2
　MPL/ROM SK6 ....43 H9
　NWCHE CW9 ....128 C3
　WARRW/BUR WA5 ....47 K1
Charles Crs CHSW/BR CH4 ....3 H7
Charles Dr FLINT CH6 ....98 B7
Charles Price Gdns EP CH65 ....6 E3
Charles Rd CHNE CH2 ....121 M2
Charles Sq SBCH CW11 ....172 C7
Charles St BRAM/HZG SK7 ....5 K4
　CH/BCN CH1 ....121 L8
　CHNE CH2 ....3 J1
　CW/HAS CW1 ....4 E2
　DTN/ASHW M34 ....29 M4
　IRL M44 ....36 D2
　STKP SK1 ....13 G4
Charleston Cl GTS/LS CH66 ....101 P1
　SALE M33 ....38 A6
Charlestown Rd East OFTN SK2 ....56 G4
Charlestown Rd West
　EDGY/DAV SK3 ....56 F4
Charlesworth Av
　DTN/ASHW M34 ....29 M9
Charlesworth Crs
Charlesworth Rd 75 P3
　CHF/WBR SK23 ....75 P3
Charlesworth St CW/HAS CW1 ....185 K2
　STKP SK1 ....41 N9
Charlock Sq ALT WA14 ....37 N8
Charlotte St BURS/TUN ST6 ....189 L9
　CH/BCN CH1 ....2 B3
　CHD/CHDH SK8 ....55 M2
　MCFLDS SK11 ....9 F5
　STKP SK1 ....42 A5
Charlotte Wk WDN WA8 ....21 J5
Charlton Cl RUNC WA7 ....62 E7
Charlton Dr SALE M33 ....38 B7
Charlton Rd HALE/TIMP WA15 ....53 J3
Charlton St MCFLDS SK10 ....95 N6
　WARRS WA4 ....49 H4
Charminster Cl
　WARRW/BUR WA5 ....47 M2
Charnock Wk
　WYTH/NTH M22 ....55 H4
Charnock Av NEWLW WA12 ....23 K6
Charnock Rd GOL/RIS/CU WA3 ....25 P6
Charnville Rd CHD/CHDH SK8 ....55 H3
Charnwood ALS/KID ST7 * 189 K7
Charnwood Av
　DTN/ASHW M34 ....29 H6
Charnwood Cl
　GOL/RIS/CU WA3 ....35 J3
　MCFLDS SK10 ....95 J9
Charnwood Crs BRAM/HZG SK7 ....57 K7
Charnwood Rd MPL/ROM SK6 ....43 H5
Charnwood St STHEL WA9 ....22 C5
Charter Av WARRW/BUR WA5 ....33 K8
Charter Cl SALE M33 ....38 A5
Charter Crs GTS/LS CH66 ....102 A1
Charterhall Dr CHNE CH2 ....3 J3
Charter Rd HALE/TIMP WA15 ....53 J3
Charton St MCFLDS SK10 ....117 N1
Chartley Gv MWCH CW10 ....130 C9
Chartwell Dr NTHM/RTH M23 ....38 D9
Chartwell Gv HLWD L26 ....44 A6
　WSFD CW7 ....149 L5
Chartwell Pk SBCH CW11 ....171 M5
Chase Briar Wd
　CHD/CHDH SK8 * 56 B6
Chase Dr GTS/LS CH66 ....102 A2
Chasefield ALT WA14 ....52 E5
Chaser Ct CH/BCN CH1 ....121 J8
Chase Wy GTS/LS CH66 ....101 P1
Chasewood BNG/LEV M19 * 28 A8
Chatburn Ct GOL/RIS/CU WA3 ....25 N7
Chatcombe Rd WYTH/NTH M22 ....54 F3
Chater Dr NANT CW5 ....196 F4
Chatfield Dr GOL/RIS/CU WA3 ....35 J3
Chatham Av DID/WITH M20 * 40 B2
Chatham Ct DID/WITH M20 ....40 B2
Chatham Rd OFTN SK2 ....56 G7
Chatham St CHNE CH1 * 6 A4
　HYDE SK14 ....43 J1
　MCFLDS SK11 ....9 J3
Chatham St EDGY/DAV SK3 ....16 C7
Chatsworth Av
　GOL/RIS/CU WA3 ....25 P5
　MCFLDS SK11 ....116 E6
Chatsworth Cl CW/SHV CW2 ....184 C9
　CONG CW12 ....79 N8
　HALE/TIMP WA15 ....53 N2
Chatsworth Dr CHNE CH2 ....122 B6
　WDN WA8 ....19 K8
Chatsworth Ms BRAM/HZG SK7 ....56 D5
Chatsworth Rd BRAM/HZG SK7 ....57 M6
　GTN M18 ....28 C5
　MPL/ROM SK6 ....58 D9
　RAIN/WH L35 ....30 A9
　WILM/AE SK9 ....92 C1
Chatteris Pk RUNC WA7 ....63 P3
Chatterley Dr ALS/KID ST7 ....189 J9
Chatterton Cl DID/WITH M20 ....40 D2
Chatterton Dr RUNC WA7 ....63 J6
Chatwell Gdns WARRS WA4 ....65 H1

Chaucer Av DTN/ASHW M34 ....42 F1
　RDSH SK5 ....28 D9
Chaucer Cl CH/BCN CH1 ....121 H5
Chaucer Gv SBCH CW11 ....171 H4
Chaucer Ms STKP SK1 ....42 A7
Chaucer Pl WARRS WA4 ....49 K8
Chaucer St RUNC WA7 ....14 C4
Cheadle La MCFLDS SK11 ....111 N3
Cheadle Old Rd EDGY/DAV SK3 ....41 L9
Cheadle Pl CHD/CHDH SK8 * 56 B2
Cheadle Rd CHD/CHDH SK8 ....55 N5
Cheadle St OP/CLY M11 ....28 D1
Cheadle Wd CHD/CHDH SK8 ....55 N7
Cheam Rd HALE/TIMP WA15 ....38 C8
Checkley Dr BIDD ST8 ....175 L8
Checkley La AUD/MAD/W SK9 ....211 J5
Checkley Rd NEWUL ST5 ....201 M6
Cheddar Gv WARRW/BUR WA5 ....32 C1
Cheddar St GTN M18 ....28 D4
Chedlee Dr CHD/CHDH SK8 ....55 N6
Chedworth Dr NTHM/RTH M23 ....54 C3
　WDN WA8 ....45 J3
Cheerbrook Rd NANT CW5 ....197 K5
Cheervble St DROY SK3 ....28 F1
Cheese Hill La NWCHW CW8 ....107 M8
Cheetham Pl MPL/ROM SK6 ....58 A3
Cheethams Fld KNUT WA16 * 88 F6
Chelford Av GOL/RIS/CU WA3 ....24 F2
　CH/BCN CH1 ....121 J9
　HALE/TIMP WA15 ....53 J1
　WARRS WA4 ....48 E7
Chelford Dr NWCHE CW9 ....109 P7
Chelford Gv EDGY/DAV SK3 ....56 C2
Chelford La KNUT WA16 ....113 N5
Chelford Rd CONG CW12 ....154 G6
　HOLMCH CW4 ....132 E4
　KNUT WA16 ....92 F9
　MCFLDS SK10 ....92 E8
　MCFLDS SK10 ....94 B8
　MCFLDS SK11 ....114 E3
　SALE M33 ....39 H6
Chell St CW/HAS CW1 ....185 H5
Chelmsford Rd EDGY/DAV SK3 ....16 B7
Chelsea Cl BIDD ST8 ....175 K8
Chelsea Gdns
　WARRW/BUR WA5 ....47 N3
Chelsfield Gv CHDY M21 ....39 N1
Chelston Dr CHD/CHDH SK8 ....55 L9
Cheltenham Cl MCFLDS SK10 ....95 J9
　WARRW/BUR WA5 ....32 D8
Cheltenham Crs CW/HAS CW1 ....185 H1
　RUNC WA7 ....61 P8
Cheltenham Dr NEWLW WA12 ....23 N4
　SALE M33 ....38 F4
Cheltenham Rd EDGY/DAV SK3 ....49 H9
　EP CH65 ....102 F1
Chemical St NEWLW WA12 ....23 M6
Chemistry WHITCH SY13 ....213 J6
Chemys Cl OP/CLY M11 * 28 D2
Chepstow Av SALE M33 ....37 P5
Chepstow Cl BIDD ST8 ....175 K8
　MCFLDS SK10 ....95 J9
　WARRW/BUR WA5 ....33 H5
　WSFD CW7 ....149 L3
Chepstow Dr BRAM/HZG SK7 ....57 N5
Cherington Cl NTHM/RTH M23 ....39 L6
　WILM/AE SK9 ....92 E4
Cherington Crs MCFLDS SK11 ....4 A6
Cherington Rd CHD/CHDH SK8 ....55 L3
Cheriton Av SALE M33 ....38 F5
Cheriton Rl OFTN SK2 ....57 N1
Cheriton Wy CW/SHV CW2 ....184 G8
Cherrington Rd NANT CW5 ....196 F4
　RUNC WA7 ....62 D9
Cherry Cl NEWLW WA12 ....23 K5
　NEWUL ST5 ....201 N6
　WARRS WA4 ....48 D9
Cherry Cnr LYMM WA15 ....50 A9
Cherry Crs WSFD CW7 ....149 L2
Cherrycroft MPL/ROM SK6 ....43 K7
Cherry Dale Rd CHSW/BR CH4 ....140 E7
Cherryfields Rd MCFLDS SK11 ....116 F5
Cherry Gv GTS/LS CH66 ....102 C3
　NANT CW5 ....196 E2
Cherry Grove Rd CHSE CH3 ....143 J1
Cherry Holt Av HTNM SK4 ....40 G4
Cherry La ALS/KID ST7 ....188 G3
　LYMM WA13 ....50 D5
　NWCHW CW8 ....108 F4
　NWCHW CW8 ....127 J1
　SALE M33 ....37 P6
Cherry Orchard Cl
　BRAM/HZG SK7 ....56 D6
Cherry Rd CO CH5 ....140 B5
Cherry Rd CHSE CH3 ....143 J1
Cherrysutton WDN WA8 ....45 H4
Cherry Tree Av ALS/KID ST7 ....188 C3
　LYMM WA13 ....50 D5
　NWCHW CW8 ....108 G3
　POY/DIS SK12 ....73 M3
　RUNC WA7 ....15 J6
　WARRW/BUR WA5 ....47 K3
Cherry Tree Cl CHNE CH2 ....82 B9
　HALE/TIMP WA15 ....53 M2
　MPL/ROM SK6 ....43 K6
　RNFD/HAY WA11 * 41 J7
　WILM/AE SK9 ....71 N6
Cherry Tree Ct OFTN SK2 ....57 J3
Cherry Tree Dr BRAM/HZG SK7 ....57 N7
　WARRS WA4 ....22 E7
Cherry Tree La ALT WA14 ....52 G9
　AUD/MAD/W CW3 ....218 G3
　MPL/ROM SK6 ....43 K6
　OFTN SK2 ....57 J2
Cherry Tree Rd ALS/KID ST7 ....201 J6
　CHD/CHDH SK8 ....55 P6
　CW/HAS CW1 ....185 K2
　GOL/RIS/CU WA3 ....25 H1
　NEWUL ST5 ....201 P6

NTHM/RTH M23 ....39 J7
　SALE M33 ....38 A7
Cherry Tree Wy CONG CW12 ....155 N8
Cherry Wk CHD/CHDH SK8 ....56 C7
　KNUT WA16 ....112 B5
Cherrywood Crs NWCHW CW8 ....109 K1
Chertsey Cl DTN/ASHW M34 ....28 E4
Cherwell Cl CHD/CHDH SK8 ....56 A8
　WARRN/WOL WA2 ....33 N6
Cheryl Ct NWCHW CW8 ....108 C8
Cheryl Dr WDN WA8 ....46 B6
Chesford Gra WARR WA1 ....34 F9
Chesham Av WYTH/NTH M22 ....54 E3
Chesham Cl WARRN/WOL WA2 ....33 K5
Chesham Ct EP CH65 ....7 G7
Chesham Pl ALT WA14 ....52 C5
Chesham St CH/BCN CH1 * 3 C2
Cheshire Oaks Wy EP CH65 ....102 C3
Cheshire Ring Canal Wk
　ALS/KID ST7 ....172 C9
　ALS/KID ST7 ....172 G9
　ALT WA14 ....188 E5
　MCFLDS SK10 ....94 G6
　MPL/ROM SK6 ....42 G2
　MWCH CW10 ....129 L3
　NWCHW CW8 ....109 L2
　WARRS WA4 ....171 J6
　WARRS WA4 ....85 L1
Cheshire Rd PART M31 ....36 C6
Cheshire St AUD/MAD/W SK9 ....216 C1
Cheshire Vw CHSW/BR CH4 ....142 G5
Cheshyre Dr RUNC WA7 ....62 D5
Cheshyre's La RUNC WA7 ....61 L8
Chester Av GOL/RIS/CU WA3 ....24 F7
　HALE/TIMP WA15 ....53 K5
　SALE M33 ....37 N7
　WHITCH SY13 ....213 K5
Chester Cl ALS/KID ST7 ....188 F9
　IRL M44 ....36 C3
　RUNC WA7 ....62 D5
　WILM/AE SK9 ....71 H4
Chesterfield Cl WSFD CW7 ....149 H1
Chesterfield Rd
　PS/BROM CH62 ....79 H1
Chestergate EDGY/DAV SK3 ....16 C5
　MCFLDS SK10 ....8 D5
　STKP SK1 ....17 F4
Chestergate MI MCFLDS SK11 * 8 C4
Chester High Rd NSTN CH64 ....77 L1
Chester La STHEL WA9 ....30 C4
　WSFD CW7 ....127 N9
Chester New Rd WARRS WA4 ....48 G8
Chester Rd ALS/KID ST7 ....200 C5
　ALT WA14 ....52 B9
　BRAM/HZG SK7 ....57 K8
　BRAM/HZG SK7 ....72 D4
　CHSE CH3 ....143 J4
　CHSE CH3 ....164 A7
　CHSE CH3 ....177 H4
　CHSW/BR CH4 ....141 K5
　FLINT CH6 ....98 C1
　FROD/HEL WA6 ....83 M7
　GTS/LS CH66 ....79 M5
　GTS/LS CH66 ....102 C3
　HOLMCH CW4 ....131 N9
　KNUT WA16 ....67 P5
　KNUT WA16 ....89 N5
　MCFLDS SK11 ....96 G3
　MWCH CW10 ....151 H1
　NANT CW5 ....182 E2
　NWCHW CW8 ....108 G8
　NWCHW CW8 ....127 M1
　POY/DIS SK12 ....73 H2
　RUNC WA7 ....84 E2
　TPLY/KEL CW6 ....125 L5
　WARRS WA4 ....49 H6
　WARRS WA4 ....63 H5
　WHITCH SY13 ....213 K4
　WSFD CW7 ....128 A9
Chester Sq CW/HAS CW1 ....4 D5
Chester St CHSW/BR CH4 ....142 B5
　DTN/ASHW M34 ....29 J7
　EDGY/DAV SK3 ....16 C5
　FLINT CH6 ....98 A6
　WDN WA8 ....21 J1
Chesterton Cl MWCH CW10 ....151 L5
Chesterton Ct CHNE CH2 ....121 N7
Chesterton Dr CW/SHV CW2 ....184 F7
　WARRN/WOL WA2 ....33 K5
Chesterton Gv SBCH CW11 ....171 J4
Chesterton Rd WYTH/NTH M22 ....38 G8
Chester Wy NWCHE CW9 ....12 E3
Chestnut Av ALS/KID ST7 ....188 B1
　CHD/CHDH SK8 ....55 N2
　CW/SHV CW2 ....198 B2
　GTS/LS CH66 ....102 B3
　IRL M44 ....36 H6
　MCFLDS SK10 ....117 L2
　RNFD/HAY WA11 ....22 D4
　WARRW/BUR WA5 ....47 K1
Chestnut Cl CHNE CH2 ....122 B8
　MWCH CW10 ....151 K8
　NWCHW CW8 ....108 F3
　TPLY/KEL CW6 ....147 H8
　WHITCH SY13 ....213 J6
Chestnut Ct ALS/KID ST7 ....201 J6
　CHD/CHDH SK8 ....55 P6
　CW/HAS CW1 ....185 K2
　CONG CW12 ....155 H6
　HOLMCH CW4 ....132 A8

POY/DIS SK12 ....73 M3
　SALE M33 ....38 A7
Chestnut Gdns DTN/ASHW M34 ....29 L7
　GOL/RIS/CU WA3 ....5 H1
　NEWUL ST5 ....201 P6
　NWCHW CW8 ....87 K9
　RNFD/HAY WA11 ....22 B2
　WSFD CW7 ....149 L2
Chesworth Cl GTS/LS CH66 ....17 G6
Chesworth Fold STKP SK1 ....17 G7
Chetham Ct WARRN/WOL WA2 ....33 K5
Chetton Dr RUNC WA7 ....79 H8
Chetwode Cl MKTDR TF9 ....219 H8
Chetwode St CW/HAS CW1 ....4 E1
Chetwood Dr WDN WA8 ....45 M3
Chetwynd Cl SALE M33 ....38 B2
Cheveley Cl MCFLDS SK10 ....117 J2
Chevington Dr HTNM SK4 ....40 E5
Cheviot Av CHD/CHDH SK8 ....55 P5
　STHEL WA9 ....22 C6
　WARRN/WOL WA2 ....33 J5
Cheviot Cl HTNM SK4 ....16 D1
Cheviot Ct WSFD CW7 ....149 K3
Cheviot Rd BRAM/HZG SK7 ....57 H6
Chevithorne Cl ALT WA14 ....52 C7
Chevrot Cl GTS/LS CH66 ....79 M8
Chevron Hey CH/BCN CH1 ....120 C7
Chevron Pl ALT WA14 ....38 A9
Cheyne Wk NANT CW5 ....196 F4
Cheyney Rd CH/BCN CH1 ....2 B1
Cheyney Wk CW/SHV CW2 ....185 J8
Chicago Av MANAIR M90 ....54 D8
Chichester Cl RUNC WA7 ....63 H8
　SALE M33 ....39 H4
　WARRS WA4 ....49 J8
Chichester Rd MPL/ROM SK6 ....43 H6
Chichester St CH/BCN CH1 ....2 B1
Chidlow Av DID/WITH M20 ....40 F1
Chidlow Cl CW/SHV CW2 ....198 D4
　WDN WA8 ....61 M3
Chidwall Rd WYTH/NTH M22 ....54 D5
Chigwell Cl WYTH/NTH M22 ....54 E3
Chilcote Av SALE M33 ....38 A4
Childer Crs GTS/LS CH66 ....79 M6
Childer Gdns GTS/LS CH66 ....79 M6
Child's La CONG CW12 ....173 P3
Childwall Gdns GTS/LS CH66 ....79 M6
Childwall St STHEL WA9 ....22 C5
Chilham Cl WSFD CW7 ....149 L3
Chilham Pl MCFLDS SK11 ....116 F6
Chillington Av WDN WA8 ....20 D8
Chillingham Cl MWCH CW10 ....130 C9
Chilmark Dr NTHM/RTH M23 ....54 C1
Chiltern Av GTS/LS CH66 ....118 D3
　HALE/TIMP WA15 ....53 N2
Chiltern Cl WARRN/WOL WA2 ....33 K5
　CHSW/BR CH4 ....142 D5
　NWCHW CW8 ....127 K1
Chiltern Crs WARRN/WOL WA2 ....33 J5
Chiltern Dr HALE/TIMP WA15 ....53 C3
　OFTN SK2 ....56 C3
Chiltern Gdns SALE M33 ....38 C8
Chiltern Rd GOL/RIS/CU WA3 ....24 N5
　STHEL WA9 ....22 B4
　WARRN/WOL WA2 ....33 J5
Chilton Cl WSFD CW7 ....149 K3
Chilton Dr GTS/LS CH66 ....102 A2
Chilwell Cl WDN WA8 ....45 K3
Chilworth Cl CW/SHV CW2 ....185 J8
China La WARRS WA4 ....48 G7
The Chines NWCHW CW8 ....107 P7
Chinley Cl BRAM/HZG SK7 ....57 M4
　NTHM/RTH M23 ....41 J5
　SALE M33 ....38 G5
Chinnor Cl STHEL WA9 ....53 G5
Chinwell Vw BNG/LEV M19 * 28 A8
Chippenham Av OFTN SK2 ....42 B9
Chippingdall Cl
　WARRW/BUR WA5 ....47 N2
Chipstead Cl WDN WA8 ....109 J8
Chirk Cl CHNE CH2 ....122 A5
Chirk Gdns EP CH65 ....102 F1
Chirk Pl WSFD CW7 ....149 K3
Chirton Cl RNFD/HAY WA11 ....23 H7
Chiseldon Av WYTH/NTH M22 ....54 C5
Chisholm St OP/CLY M11 ....28 D2
Chisledon Cl RNFD/HAY WA11 ....23 H7
Chiswick Cl RUNC WA7 * 62 A5
Chiswick Gdns WARRS WA4 ....49 H9
Chiswick Rd DID/WITH M20 ....40 A3
Chisworth Cl BRAM/HZG SK7 ....56 E4
Chokeberry Cl ALT WA14 ....38 E8
Cholerton Cl KNUT WA16 ....67 J2
Cholmley Dr NEWLW WA12 ....24 A7
Cholmondeley La
　MALPAS SY14 ....180 C7
Cholmondeley Rd EP CH65 ....192 D8
　MALPAS SY14 ....192 D8
　NANT CW5 ....194 P9
　RUNC WA7 ....62 B9
Cholmondeston St MCFLDS SK11 * 8 E7
　WDN WA8 ....61 N2
Chorley Hall Cl WILM/AE SK9 ....93 K4
Chorley Hall La WILM/AE SK9 ....93 H4
Chorley Rd SALE M33 ....39 H6
Chorley's La WDN WA8 ....46 B4
Chorley Stock La NANT CW5 ....194 D6
Chorley St WARRN/WOL WA2 ....16 C2
Chorlton Wood Av
　BNG/LEV M19 * 40 G2
Chorleywood Cl MCFLDS SK10 ....95 H9
Choriton Cl RUNC WA7 ....55 N1
Choriton Cv CHD/CHDH SK8 ....55 H1
Choriton La CW/SHV CW2 ....42 A9
Choriton La CW/SHV CW2 ....198 F6
Chowley Oak La CHSE CH3 ....178 F5
Chretien Rd WYTH/NTH M22 ....126 C5
Chrimes Dr NWCHW CW8 ....108 B5
Christchurch Av WSFD CW7 ....183 M2
Christchurch Rd SALE M33 ....37 P3
Christie Cl GTS/LS CH66 ....79 L3

Christie Cl STKP SK1 ....17 K7
　WDN WA8 ....46 B6
Christleton Av CW/SHV CW2 ....184 D3
　HTNM SK4 ....41 L3
　NWCHE CW9 ....110 A8
Christleton Ct RUNC WA7 ....62 C2
Christleton Dr GTS/LS CH66 ....80 A7
Christleton Rd CHSE CH3 ....143 J1
Christopher Cl RAIN/WH L35 ....30 A6
Chudleigh Cl ALT WA14 ....52 F1
　BRAM/HZG SK7 ....56 G4
Church Av NWCHW CW9 ....29 N9
Church Bnk CL/KID ST7 ....200 C5
　CHF/WBR SK23 ....75 P6
　CHSE CH3 ....164 A7
　HOLMCH CW4 ....132 C2
　TPLY/KEL CW6 ....125 J6
Church Brow ALT WA14 ....52 F5
Church Cl NWCHW CW8 ....108 F3
Church College Cl
　CH/BCN CH1 ....121 L8
Church Cft CHSW/BR CH4 ....160 D3
Church Dr NEWLW WA12 ....23 N8
　WARRN/WOL WA2 ....34 B7
Church Farm NANT CW5 ....207 H2
Churchfield Rd FROD/HEL WA6 ....84 A6
Churchfields ALT WA14 ....52 F6
　AUD/MAD/W SK9 ....217 H1
　DTN/ASHW M34 ....29 L2
　FROD/HEL WA6 ....83 M4
　GOL/RIS/CU WA3 ....34 C1
　KNUT WA16 ....90 G3
　NANT CW5 ....198 A7
　NWCHW CW8 ....109 K1
　NWCHW CW8 ....127 L1
　SALE M33 ....38 H4
　STHEL WA9 ....30 E3
Churchfield Wk OP/CLY M11 * 28 A1
Churchgate STKP SK1 ....17 G4
Church Gn LYMM WA13 ....36 A8
Church Hall BRAM/HZG SK7 ....57 J5
Church Hall Cl CH/BCN CH1 ....121 J7
Church HI KNUT WA16 ....90 E3
Churchill Av GOL/RIS/CU WA3 ....26 B5
Churchill Cr CONG CW12 ....155 J7
Churchill Crs MPL/ROM SK6 ....43 J9
　RDSH SK5 ....28 E8
Church Hill Dr TPLY/KEL CW6 ....147 H9
Churchill Gdns STHEL WA9 ....30 B2
Churchill Pkwy WSFD CW7 ....149 M2
Churchill St HTNM SK4 ....41 L5
Churchill Wy MCFLDS SK11 ....8 D4
　NSTN CH64 ....77 L5
　ALS/KID ST7 ....173 L9
Church La ALS/KID ST7 ....189 N1
　BNG/LEV M19 ....40 G2
　BRAM/HZG SK7 ....72 C4
　CHNE CH2 ....102 E8
　CHNE CH2 ....105 J5
　CHNE CH2 ....121 N4
　CHSE CH3 ....122 C7
　CHSE CH3 ....162 A6
　CHSE CH3 ....164 F2
　CHSW/BR CH4 ....159 J9
　CONG CW12 ....156 D1
　CONG CW12 ....140 B2
　CONG CW12 ....184 G9
　GOL/RIS/CU WA3 ....24 F2
　GOL/RIS/CU WA3 ....25 P6
　GTS/LS CH66 ....79 P9
　KNUT WA16 ....69 M9
　MCFLDS SK10 ....96 C9
　MCFLDS SK11 ....116 B4
　MCFLDS SK11 ....117 M9
　MCFLDS SK11 ....135 M3
　MPL/ROM SK6 ....43 H6
　MPL/ROM SK6 ....58 E2
　NANT CW5 ....10 B6
　NM/HAY SK22 ....59 N7
　NSTN CH64 ....77 L4
　NWCHE CW9 ....108 E3
　PS/BROM CH62 ....79 J1
　SALE M33 ....38 B2
　SBCH CW11 ....172 B3
　SBCH CW11 ....173 J4
　WARRS WA4 ....49 K6
　WILM/AE SK9 ....91 H7
Churchley Cl EDGY/DAV SK3 ....56 A1
Churchley Rd EDGY/DAV SK3 ....41 H9
Church Md CHSE CH3 ....177 J3
Church Mdw NWCHW CW8 ....86 F9
　WHITCH SY13 ....213 M4
Church Meadow Wk WDN WA8 ....41 L1
Churchmere Cl CW/HAS CW1 ....185 J1
Church Ms DTN/ASHW M34 ....29 L6
　MCFLDS SK10 ....95 N5
　NWCHE CW9 ....88 E8
Church Pde EP CH65 * 7 J2
Church Rd NWCHW CW8 ....127 L1
　MCFLDS SK11 ....187 H4
　CH/BCN CH1 ....120 D2
　CHD/CHDH SK8 ....56 B8
　CHSE CH3 ....124 C2
　CHSE CH3 ....179 N5
　CHSW/BR CH4 ....190 D6
　CHSW/BR CH4 ....142 G8
　FROD/HEL WA6 ....84 A6
　HTNM SK4 ....41 J5
　LYMM WA13 ....50 D5
　MALPAS SY14 ....191 J5
　MPL/ROM SK6 ....59 J1
　NANT CW5 ....183 M2
　NM/HAY SK22 ....59 N8
　NWCHE CW9 ....13 H2

NWCHW CW8 .....86 F9
WARRN/HAY WA11 .....109 K2
RNFD/HAY WA11 .....23 J3
SALE M33 .....38 G4
SPK/HALE L24 .....60 E6
WILM/AE SK9 .....71 M3
WILM/AE SK9 .....92 G1
WRXS/EL L13 .....202 A5
WYTH/NTH M22 .....39 N7
Church Rd East SALE M33 .....38 G4
Churchside MCFLDS SK11 .....9 F4
Churchston Av BRAM/HZG SK7 .....56 G5
ALS/KID ST7 .....188 F7
Church St ALS/KID ST7 .....189 K4
ALS/KID ST7 .....189 L2
ALS/KID ST7 .....200 C5
ALS/KID ST7 .....201 K6
ALT WA14 .....53 H2
CH/BCN CH1 .....55 J5
CH/CHDH SK8 .....55 M1
CHSE CH3 .....124 B9
CHSE CH3 .....176 G6
DTN/ASHW M34 * 29 M2
DUK SK16 .....29 P1
EP CH65 .....6 F5
FLINT CH6 .....98 A6
FROD/HEL WA6 .....83 P5
HTNM SK4 .....16 E1
MALPAS SY14 .....203 P5
MCFLDN SK10 .....95 P5
MCFLDS SK11 .....42 F3
MPL/ROM SK6 .....58 D2
NEWLW ST5 .....24 A6
NEWUL ST5 .....201 P8
NWCHE CW9 .....88 A5
NWCHE CW9 .....88 E8
NWCHE CW9 .....110 A9
NWCHE CW9 .....128 G3
NWCHW CW8 .....108 L5
RUNC WA7 .....14 E1
SBCH CW11 .....171 K8
TPLY/KEL CW6 .....125 H7
WARR WA1 .....19 F5
WDN WA8 .....61 N1
WHITCH SY13 .....213 M5
WILM/AE SK9 .....71 K7
WSFD CW7 .....149 N1
Church St North
TPLY/KEL CW6 .....125 J6
Church St West MCFLDS SK11 .....8 D4
Church Ter SALE M33 * 38 D2
WILM/AE SK9 .....71 M2
Church Vw ALS/KID ST7 .....189 P7
AUD/MAD/W CW3 .....217 H1
CW/HAS CW1 .....186 H3
FROD/HEL WA6 .....106 F2
IRL M44 .....27 N7
KNUT WA16 .....90 E3
LYMM WA16 .....51 H5
Church Wk ALT WA14 .....53 H2
EP CH65 .....6 F5
KNUT WA16 .....90 E3
NEWUL ST5 .....201 P8
NWCHE CW9 .....13 H2
NWCHW CW8 .....107 M2
Church Wks CHSE CH3 .....143 N2
Church Wy CW/SHV CW2 .....198 D4
NWCHE CW9 .....109 N8
Churton Dr WHITCH SY13 .....216 N1
Churton Rd CHSE CH3 .....176 G6
GTN M18 .....28 C6
Churton St CHSE CH3 .....122 B9
Churwell Av HTNM SK4 .....40 C4
Cicely Mill La KNUT WA16 .....68 A3
Cinder Hl NWCHW CW8 .....127 P5
Cinder-hill La ALS/KID ST7 .....188 G2
Cinder La CHSE CH3 .....122 G7
KNUT WA16 .....113 N5
MCFLDS SK11 .....114 A3
NANT CW5 .....188 L6
NWCHE CW9 .....110 G4
WARRS WA4 .....49 P7
Cinder Rock Wy ALS/KID ST7 .....189 L7
Cinnamon La
WARRN/WOL WA4 .....34 A5
Cinnamon La North
WARRN/WOL WA4 .....34 A4
Cinnamon Pk
WARRN/WOL WA4 * 34 D6
Circle Av NANT CW5 .....197 M2
The Circle CW/SHV CW2 .....185 K7
Circuit La
The Circuit CHD/CHDH SK8 .....56 A8
DID/WITH M20 .....40 C3
EDGY/DAV SK3 .....56 C1
WILM/AE SK9 .....70 F9
WILM/AE SK9 .....93 K2
Circular Dr CHSW/BR CH4 .....142 N6
Circular Rd DID/WITH M20 .....40 C2
DTN/ASHW M34 .....29 L8
City Av DTN/ASHW M54 * 29 L7
City Gdns DTN/ASHW M54 * 29 L7
City Rd CH/BCN CH1 .....3 G5
City Walls CH/BCN CH1 .....2 C5
City Walls Rd CH/BCN CH1 .....2 C4
Civic Cn WHITCH SY15 .....213 P6
Civic Wy EP CH65 .....6 D4
Civic Wy EP CH65 .....6 D6
MWCH CW10 .....151 J1
Clamhunger La KNUT WA16 .....88 A7

Clanfield Av WDN WA8 .....45 J4
Clapgate MPL/ROM SK6 .....42 F7
Clap Gate Crs WDN WA8 .....61 H1
Clap Gates Rd
WARRW/BUR WA5 .....33 H9
Clare Av CHNE CH2 .....122 A8
WILM/AE SK9 .....71 L5
Clare Ct STHEL WA9 .....30 D1
Clare Dr CW/SHV CW2 .....184 F7
EP CH65 .....102 D5
MCFLDN SK10 .....117 J1
Claremont Av WA14 .....38 A8
DID/WITH M20 .....40 B3
HTNM SK4 .....41 K3
MPL/ROM SK6 .....58 A1
WDN WA8 .....45 P3
Claremont Cl NWCHE CW9 .....109 P9
Claremont Dr ALT WA14 .....38 A8
WDN WA8 .....45 P3
Claremont Gv DID/WITH M20 .....40 B5
HALE/TIMP WA15 .....53 J2
CW/SHV CW2 .....4 C5
GOL/RIS/CU WA3 .....25 M5
OFTN SK2 .....56 A7
RUNC WA7 .....14 D4
SALE M33 .....38 E3
Clarence Av CHSE CH3 .....122 C9
WARRW/BUR WA5 .....47 H1
WDN WA8 .....45 N3
Clarence Ct STHEL WA9 * 22 A7
Clarence Ct WILM/AE SK9 .....71 J8
Clarence Gv CW/HAS CW1 .....4 C1
Clarence Rd HALE/TIMP WA15 .....53 K4
HTNM SK4 .....41 J3
MCFLDN SK10 .....95 N5
WARRS WA4 .....49 K5
Clarence St NEWLW WA12 .....23 K5
RUNC WA7 .....14 C1
WARR WA1 .....19 K2
Clarence Ter RUNC WA7 .....14 E1
Clarendon Av HALE/TIMP WA15 .....53 J2
HTNM SK4 .....41 J3
Clarendon Cl CHSW/BR CH4 .....142 C4
RUNC WA7 .....63 H7
Clarendon Ct WARRN/WOL WA3 .....33 J4
Clarendon Crs SALE M33 .....38 C3
Clarendon Dr MCFLDN SK10 .....117 N3
Clarendon Rd BRAM/HZG SK7 .....57 M4
DTN/ASHW M34 .....28 G2
HYDE SK14 .....29 P7
M6 .....36 D1
SALE M33 .....38 A8
Clarendon St DUK SK16 .....29 N1
DUK SK16 .....29 P1
RDSH SK5 * 41 N4
Clare Pl WSFD CW7 .....149 L3
Clare Rd BNG/LEV M19 .....28 A3
RDSH SK5 * 41 N4
Clares Farm Cl WARR WA1 .....34 C9
Clare St ALS/KID ST7 .....189 L2
ALS/KID ST7 .....189 L3
DTN/ASHW M34 .....29 L5
Clark Av GTN M18 .....28 E4
Clarke Av GOL/RIS/CU WA3 .....25 P5
WARRS WA4 .....48 F5
Clarke Crs HALE/TIMP WA15 .....53 M4
Clarke Gdns WDN WA8 .....21 J5
Clarke La MCFLDN SK10 .....95 M8
MCFLDS SK11 .....118 A8
Clarkes Ter RUNC WA7 .....61 K7
Clarke St AULW OL7 * 29 M1
Clarkson Cl DTN/ASHW M34 .....29 K7
NWCHW CW8 .....12 G3
Claude Rd CCHDY M21 .....39 K1
Claude St WARR WA1 .....19 G3
Claughton Av CW/SHV CW2 .....185 K7
Claverton Cl RUNC WA7 .....61 P8
Claverton Rd NTHM/RTH M23 .....54 A3
Clayton Cl KLWD L26 .....60 A8
Claydon Gdns GOL/RIS/CU WA3 .....35 N7
Clay Heyes MCFLDS SK11 .....114 C1
Clayhill MCFLDS SK11 .....77 M3
Clayhill Gn GTS/LS CH66 .....79 N6
Clayhill Gv GOL/RIS/CU WA3 .....25 K1
Clay La CW/HAS CW1 .....186 B2
HALE/TIMP WA15 .....53 N3
KNUT WA16 .....113 L4
MALPAS SY14 .....179 N8
NTHM/RTH M23 .....54 B3
SBCH CW11 .....170 F5
WARRW/BUR WA5 .....32 B8
WARRW/BUR WA5 .....71 L1
WILM/AE SK9 .....92 E1
WILM/AE SK9 .....127 L7
Claymore St GTN M18 .....28 E3
Claypit Rd CHSW/BR CH4 .....142 D5
Claypits La CHSE CH3 .....143 N8
Claypit St WHITCH SY13 .....213 M5
Clayton Av CONG CW12 .....155 P5
DID/WITH M20 .....40 C5
GOL/RIS/CU WA3 .....24 G1
Clayton Crs RUNC WA7 .....14 C4
WDN WA8 .....21 H1
Clayton Dr WHITCH SY13 .....213 M4
Clayton La OP/CLY M11 .....28 B1
Clayton La South OP/CLY M11 .....28 A2
Clayton Rd GOL/RIS/CU WA3 .....34 G2
Claytons Rw NANT CW5 .....188 F5
Clayton St DTN/ASHW M34 .....29 M7
Cleadon Av GTN M18 .....28 L5
Cleadon Wy WDN WA8 .....45 L3
Cleaver Ms MCFLDS SK11 .....117 J1
Cleaver Rd CH/BCN CH1 .....121 H7
Cledford Crs NWCH SK10 * 151 M3
Cledford La MWCH CW10 .....151 M3
Cledwen Rd CHSW/BR CH4 .....140 G5
Cleethorpes Rd RUNC WA7 .....62 G7
Cleeve Rd NTHM/RTH M23 .....39 K6
Cleeve Wy CHD/CHDH SK8 .....56 B9
Clegge St WARRN/WOL WA5 .....18 E2

Clegg St MPL/ROM SK6 .....42 E5
Clelland St WARRS WA4 .....48 E4
Clement Rd MPL/ROM SK6 .....43 N9
Clement St HTNM SK4 .....16 E1
Clemley Cl TPLY/KEL CW6 .....125 J5
Clerewood Av CHD/CHDH SK8 .....55 K8
Clevedon Cl MCFLDS SK11 .....116 G5
Cleveland Av BNG/LEV M19 .....28 B7
Cleveland Dr GOL/RIS/CU WA3 .....24 F1
GTS/LS CH66 .....79 L7
Cleveland Rd HALE/TIMP WA15 .....53 K4
HTNM SK4 .....41 H4
Cleveland St STHEL WA9 .....22 A8
Cleveland Wy WSFD CW7 .....149 K5
Cleveleys Av CCHDY M21 .....39 M1
CHD/CHDH SK8 .....55 K6
WDN WA8 .....46 B4
Cleveleys Rd
WARRW/BUR WA5 .....47 M5
Cleves Cl CH/BCN CH1 .....120 C5
Clifden Dr WYTH/NTH M22 .....54 C5
Cliffe Rd CW/HAS CW1 .....185 H1
NSTN CH64 .....77 M8
WARRS WA4 .....18 A5
Cliffe St WARR WA1 .....18 A6
Cliff Gv HTNM SK4 .....41 J4
Cliff La LYMM WA13 .....50 B9
Cliffmere Cl CHD/CHDH SK8 .....55 P4
HALE/TIMP WA15 .....53 L1
Clifford Av DTN/ASHW M34 .....29 L4
HALE/TIMP WA15 .....53 L1
Clifford Dr CHSW/BR CH4 .....142 B5
Clifford Pl CHSW/BR CH4 .....142 B5
Clifford Pl WSFD CW7 * 149 L5
Clifford Rd MCFLDS SK11 .....116 C5
POY/DIS SK12 .....73 J2
WARRW/BUR WA5 .....47 L3
Clifford St WARR WA1 .....18 A6
CW/SHV CW2 .....4 C5
GOL/RIS/CU WA3 .....25 M6
CHD/CHDH SK8 .....55 J5
MPL/ROM SK6 .....43 L3
PS/BROM CH62 .....13 J2
Clifton Cl WARR WA1 .....34 D9
RUNC WA7 .....14 B4
Clifton Crs FROD/HEL WA6 .....84 A4
Clifton Dr CH/BCN CH1 .....121 H8
CHD/CHDH SK8 .....55 J8
CHD/CHDH SK8 .....55 J5
MPL/ROM SK6 .....43 L3
NWCHE CW9 .....110 A7
WILM/AE SK9 .....92 G1
Clifton Gdns EP CH65 .....102 C4
Clifton La RUNC WA7 .....84 C2
Cliftonmill Mdw
GOL/RIS/CU WA3 .....24 B1
Clifton Park Rd OFTN SK2 .....56 C2
Clifton Rd HTNM SK4 .....41 H4
RUNC WA7 .....62 A8
SALE M33 .....38 E5
SBCH CW11 .....171 J2
Clifton St CW/SHV CW2 .....4 C5
WARRS WA4 .....48 F5
WILM/AE SK9 .....93 J4
Clifton Vls EP CH65 * 102 C4
Cliftonville Rd WARR WA1 .....34 D9
Clincton Cl WDN WA8 .....44 G7
Clincton Vw WDN WA8 .....44 G7
Clipsley Brook Vw
RNFD/HAY WA11 .....22 D5
Clipsley Crs RNFD/HAY WA11 .....22 F3
Clipsley La RNFD/HAY WA11 .....22 F3
Cliston Wk BRAM/HZG SK7 .....56 G5
Clitheroe Rd NWCHW CW8 .....108 F3
Clive Av WARRN/WOL WA2 .....33 M7
Clive Back La WSFD CW7 .....150 C3
Cliveden Rd CHSW/BR CH4 .....142 B5
Clivegreen La MWCH CW10 .....150 C3
Clive La WSFD CW7 .....150 C2
Clock Face Rd WDN WA8 .....31 K9
Clock Face Shop Pde
SALE M33 * 31 H4
Cloister Rd HTNM SK4 .....41 J5
The Cloisters CHD/CHDH SK8 .....56 A2
SALE M33 .....38 E8
Cloister Wy EP CH65 .....7 K5
NANT CW5 .....11 G7
NANT CW5 .....11 G7
ALS/KID ST7 .....187 L6
Close La ALS/KID ST7 .....189 H1
The Close, Red Bank School
NEWLW WA12 * 24 A8
Close St STHEL WA9 .....30 D1
The Close ALS/KID ST7 .....187 L5
ALT WA14 .....52 G2
CH/BCN CH1 .....120 C6
MPL/ROM SK6 .....43 M7
NWCHW CW8 .....12 A6
RNFD/HAY WA11 .....44 A4
Clothorn Rd DID/WITH M20 .....40 C4
Cloud Vw CONG CW12 .....156 A8
Clough Av MPL/ROM SK6 .....58 C1
SALE M33 .....38 A7
WARRN/WOL WA3 .....45 J4
WILM/AE SK9 .....71 K4
Clough Bnk MCFLDN SK10 .....95 M6
Clough Hall Dr ALS/KID ST7 .....188 G9
Clough Hall Rd ALS/KID ST7 .....188 G9
Clough La NWCHW CW8 .....12 B4
Clough Meadow MPL/ROM SK6 .....43 H5
Clough Rd WSFD CW7 .....149 N1
Clough Side MPL/ROM SK6 .....43 P9
Cloughside POY/DIS SK12 .....59 J8
The Clough MPL/ROM SK6 .....43 A2
RUNC WA7 .....62 D5

Clough Wk CW/SHV CW2 .....185 K8
Clovelly Av STHEL WA9 .....31 J2
WARRW/BUR WA5 .....32 B9
Clovelly Gv RUNC WA7 .....62 F9
Clovelly Rd OFTN SK2 .....42 B8
Clover Av EDGY/DAV SK3 .....56 C1
FROD/HEL WA6 .....84 B6
Cloverbank Av EDGY/LEV M19 .....40 E4
Clover Ct RUNC WA7 .....61 G7
Clover Cft SALE M33 .....38 E7
Cloverdale NWCHW CW8 .....109 L5
Cloverdale Rd MCFLDS SK11 .....116 L2
Clover Dr KNUT WA16 .....88 F7
WSFD CW7 .....128 E8
Cloverfield RUNC WA7 * 62 G7
Cloverfield Gdns GTS/LS CH66 .....79 P6
Cloverfields CW/HAS CW1 .....185 P4
Cloverley Dr HALE/TIMP WA15 .....53 L5
Clover La CHSW/BR CH4 .....142 B5
Clover Pl CHSW/BR CH4 .....142 B5
Clover La HALE/TIMP WA15 .....53 L2
MPL/ROM SK6 .....43 K5
Clowes Av ALS/KID ST7 .....188 B5
Clowes St MCFLDS SK11 .....79 M8
WSFD CW7 * 128 E8
Club St OP/CLY M11 .....28 F2
Clumber Cl POY/DIS SK12 .....73 L3
Clumber Rd GTN M18 .....28 F5
POY/DIS SK12 .....73 L3
Clutha Rd EDGY/DAV SK3 .....56 F5
Clwyd Av EDGY/DAV SK3 .....41 L9
Clwyd Cl CHSW/BR CH4 .....140 F4
Clwyd Wy GTS/LS CH66 .....79 L7
Clyde Av BIDD ST8 .....175 M8
Clyde Rd DID/WITH M20 .....40 A4
EDGY/DAV SK3 .....41 K9
Clydesdale EP CH65 .....102 D1
Clydesdale Av CW/SHV CW2 .....4 B5
Clydesdale Rd WARRS WA4 .....48 F5
CHSE CH3 .....178 G5
MALPAS SY14 .....179 M8
TPLY/KEL CW6 .....126 E9
Coalbrookdale Rd NSTN CH64 .....77 M5
Coalburn St WGTN/LGST M12 .....28 A4
Coalpit HI ALS/KID ST7 .....188 F9
CH/BCN CH1 .....101 N9
Coalpit La CH/BCN CH1 .....101 N9
Coalpit La CH/BCN CH1 .....117 P8
MWCH CW10 .....150 F5
Coalport Dr WSFD CW7 .....128 G8
Coalport Wk STHEL WA9 .....30 B2
Coalville Rd RNFD/HAY WA11 .....22 B3
Coare St MCFLDN SK10 .....77 H4
Cobbett's Wy WILM/AE SK9 .....93 H1
Cobblers Cross La
TPLY/KEL CW6 .....147 J7
The Cobbles CHSW/BR CH4 .....142 F5
KNUT WA16 .....90 F7
NWCHW CW8 .....107 P7
Cobbs La CW/SHV CW2 .....198 D6
NANT CW5 .....10 D1
WARRN/WOL WA2 .....48 G7
Cobden St NEWLW WA12 .....23 J6
WARRN/WOL WA4 .....18 E2
Cob Hall La FROD/HEL WA6 .....105 K7
Cob Moor Rd ALS/KID ST7 .....189 J4
Cock Brow HYDE SK14 .....43 P1
Cockfield La MCFLDS SK11 .....118 A9
Cockington Cl NWCHE CW9 .....110 G6
Cocklade La SPK/HALE L24 .....60 D5
Cock La NANT CW5 .....208 A2
Cock Lane Ends WDN WA8 * 61 H1
Cockpit La NWCHW CW8 .....127 L1
Cocksheadhey Rd
MCFLDN SK10 .....96 A4
Cocksmoss Rd MCFLDS SK11 .....134 D8
Cocoa Yd NANT CW5 .....10 B6
Coddington Av OP/CLY M11 .....28 E1
Coed Onn Rd FLINT CH6 .....98 A7
Coe La ALT WA14 .....38 A8
Cogshall La NWCHE CW9 .....87 J6
Colborne Av MPL/ROM SK6 .....42 G6
RDSH SK5 * 28 G2
Colchester Cl NTHM/RTH M23 .....39 H7
Colchester Rd DTN/ASHW M34 .....29 K4
Colchester Sq CHSW/BR CH4 .....142 B5
Colclough La BURS/TUN ST6 .....189 M9
Coldfield Dr NTHM/RTH M23 .....54 B1
Coldmoss Dr SBCH CW11 .....171 P5
Coldstream Cl
WARRN/WOL WA2 .....33 P4
Coldstream Dr GTS/LS CH66 .....79 L7
Cole Av NEWLW WA12 .....23 N5
Colebrook Ct GOL/RIS/CU WA3 .....35 H4
Colebrook Rd HALE/TIMP WA15 .....53 L1
Coleby Av WYTH/NTH M22 .....55 H6
Coleclough Pl GOL/RIS/CU WA3 .....25 P5
Colehill Bnk CONG CW12 .....155 N8
Colemere Cl WARRW/BUR WA4 .....49 H4
Colemere Dr GTS/LS CH66 .....79 N7
Colemore Av DID/WITH M20 .....40 E5
Colenso Gv HTNM SK4 .....41 J5
Coleport Cl CHD/CHDH SK8 .....56 A6
Coleridge Cl CH/BCN CH1 .....121 K6
RDSH SK5 .....28 G2
SBCH CW11 .....171 H4
Coleridge Gv WDN WA8 .....20 D1
Coleridge Rd RDSH SK5 .....28 E8
Coley La CW/HAS CW1 .....5 K1
Coleshill St FLINT CH6 .....
Coliers Moss La
ALS/KID ST7 .....41 H4
Colinwood Av CHSW/BR CH4 .....140 F7
Coliseum Wy EP CH65 .....102 F5
Collar House Dr MCFLDN SK10 .....94 E7
College Cl OFTN SK2 .....57 H1
WARR WA1 .....19 H5
WARRN/WOL WA4 .....34 B6
WILM/AE SK9 .....70 G6

College Flds CW/SHV CW2 .....184 G7
College Gn CHSW/BR CH4 .....142 F5
College La TPLY/KEL CW6 .....166 C8
College Rd ALS/KID ST7 .....187 M3
FROD/HEL WA6 .....84 B6
Colley La SWCH CW9 * 172 A5
Colley Ls NANT CW5 .....184 B8
Colliers La NWCHE CW9 .....
Collier's Rw RUNC WA7 .....61 L7
Collier St RUNC WA7 .....61 M5
Colliery Green Cl NSTN CH64 .....77 L8
Colliery Green Ct NSTN CH64 .....77 L8
Colliery Green Dr NSTN CH64 .....77 L8
Collin Av GTN M18 .....28 C5
Collin Cl CW/SHV CW2 .....185 H7
Collingham St CW/SHV CW2 .....
Collingham Wy WSFD CW7 .....149 K5
Collington Cl WGTN/LGST M12 .....28 A4
Collingtree Av WSFD CW7 .....129 F7
Collingwood Cl MCFLDS SK10 .....117 H2
POY/DIS SK12 .....73 J2
Collingwood Rd NEWLW WA12 .....23 M6
Collins Green La
WARRW/BUR WA5 .....
Collinson Rd BURS/TUN ST6 .....189 M9
Collins St CW/SHV CW2 .....4 A4
Colne Dr STHEL WA9 .....48 A2
Colne St WARRW/BUR WA5 .....31 J1
Colonial Bd OFTN SK2 .....56 C1
Colorado Cl WARRW/BUR WA5 .....32 F9
Colshaw Dr WILM/AE SK9 .....71 M5
Colshaw La MCFLDS SK11 .....133 P2
Coltsfoot Cl CHSE CH3 .....143 J5
Coltsfoot Dr ALT WA14 .....37 N8
Columbia Av STN M18 .....28 C6
Columbine Cl CHSE CH3 .....143 J4
WDN WA8 .....45 H3
Columbine St STHEL WA9 .....
Columbine Wy STHEL WA9 .....33 K5
Colville Gv HALE/TIMP WA15 .....53 L1
SALE M33 .....38 B7
Colville Rd MCFLDS SK11 .....116 F4
Colwick Av ALT WA14 .....53 J1
Colwyn Cl EP CH65 .....102 F1
Colwyn Crs RDSH SK5 .....41 N5
Colwyn Rd BRAM/HZG SK7 .....57 M5
CHD/CHDH SK8 .....55 N6
Colyton Av STHEL WA9 .....
Comberbach Dr NANT CW5 .....197 H3
Combermere Av DID/WITH M20 .....40 B1
Combermere Ct CHD/CHDH SK8 .....55 P5
Comber Wy KNUT WA16 .....90 E5
Comboy Dr NWCHE CW9 .....110 G6
Combs Cl NM/HAY SK22 .....59 L7
Comer Ter SALE M33 .....38 E8
Commercial Av CHD/CHDH SK8 .....71 N1
Commercial Rd BRAM/HZG SK7 .....57 K4
MCFLDN SK10 .....9 G3
Common Farm La
MCFLDS SK11 .....114 A3
Commongate MCFLDN SK10 .....9 G2
Commonhall St CH/BCN CH1 .....2 C5
Common La AUD/MAD/W CW3 .....199 L9
CHSE CH3 .....144 A6
FROD/HEL WA6 .....105 N3
MCFLDS SK11 .....9 F4
NWCHE CW9 .....111 L7
PART M31 .....36 C3
TPLY/KEL CW6 .....125 H9
TPLY/KEL CW6 .....146 A3
WARRS WA4 .....48 G5
WARRS WA4 .....64 G6
Common Rd NEWLW WA12 .....23 J6
Commonside FROD/HEL WA6 .....105 N3
Commons MI SBCH CW11 .....171 N5
The Commons SBCH CW11 .....171 N5
Common St NEWLW WA12 .....
STHEL WA9 * 30 C1
Commonwealth Cl
WSFD CW7 * 149 L4
Commonwealth Cl
WRXS/EL L13 .....176 B3
Como Wk GTN M18 .....28 B5
Company's Cl RUNC WA7 .....61 M8
Compass Cl RUNC WA7 .....63 H9
Compass St OP/CLY M11 .....28 E3
Compstall Gv GTN M18 * 28 E3
Compstall Mills Est
MPL/ROM SK6 .....43 N6
Compstall Rd MPL/ROM SK6 .....43 L2
Compton Ct RNFD/HAY WA11 .....22 G2
Compton Dr NTHM/RTH M23 * 54 B1
Compton Pl CHSW/BR CH4 .....142 C4
EP CH65 .....6 F5
Concorde Pl WARRN/WOL WA2 .....33 D7
Concourse Wy STHEL WA9 .....
Condliffe Cl SBCH CW11 .....171 H4
Conery Cl FROD/HEL WA6 .....
Conery La WHITCH SY13 .....212 C9
Coney Gv NTHM/RTH M23 .....39 K6
RUNC WA7 .....62 F9
Congleton Cl WILM/AE SK9 .....93 J5
Congleton Edge Rd
CONG CW12 .....175 J4
Congleton La MCFLDS SK11 .....114 P7
ALS/KID ST7 .....174 F9
Congleton Rd ALS/KID ST7 .....188 F7
BIDD ST8 .....
CHSW/BR CH4 .....140 G4
CONG CW12 .....133 J6
CONG CW12 .....155 M8
CONG CW12 .....173 P4
MCFLDN SK10 .....93 J7
MCFLDS SK11 .....116 G8
MCFLDS SK11 .....154 D7
SBCH CW11 .....

SBCH CW11 ...172 C1
SBCH CW11 ...173 J4
Congleton Rd North
ALS/KID ST7 ...188 G4
Congleton Rd South
ALS/KID ST7 ...188 F6
Conifer Cl GTS/LS CH66 ...102 C4
Conifer Gv WARRW/BUR WA5 ...32 C9
The Conifers ALS/KID ST7 ...187 M5
Coniston Av CONG CW12 ...155 H8
SALE M33 ...9 K6
WARRW/BUR WA5 ...47 H5
WSFD CW7 ...128 D9
Coniston Cl DTN/ASHW M34 ...29 H7
GTS/LS CH66 ...79 L4
NANT CW5 ...11 F5
RUNC WA7 ...8 A3
WILM/AE SK9 ...92 C6
Coniston Dr FROD/HEL WA6 ...84 B5
HOLMCH CW4 ...131 L8
WILM/AE SK9 ...71 L2
Coniston Rd CHD/CHDH SK8 ...55 K1
CHME CH2 ...122 A6
MPL/ROM SK6 ...58 B7
NSTN CH64 ...77 L7
PART M31 ...36 D4
RDSH SK5 ...41 N2
Coniston Wk HALE/TIMP WA15 ...53 P2
Coniston Wy MCFLDS SK10 ...116 F7
Connaught Av WARRW/BUR WA5 ...33 P9
Connaught Cl WILM/AE SK9 ...71 L6
Connaught Dr NEWLW WA12 ...23 N7
Connell Rd NTHM/RTH M23 ...54 C1
Connie St OP/CLY M11 ...28 C1
Conrad Cl CW/HAS CW1 ...5 J2
Conroy Wy NEWLW WA12 ...23 N8
Consett Av NTHM/RTH M23 ...54 C1
Consett Rd STHEL WA9 ...30 C3
Consort Cl MCFLDS SK10 ...95 L7
Consort Pl ALT WA14 ...52 E5
Constable Av NEWLW ST5 ...201 P9
Constable Dr MPL/ROM SK6 ...43 N8
WILM/AE SK9 ...71 N6
Constables Cl RUNC WA7 ...62 E5
Constable Rd PART M31 ...36 E3
Constance Wy WARR WA4 ...61 N1
Consul St WYTH/NTH M22 ...39 P7
Convamore Rd BRAM/HZG SK7 ...56 D9
Conway Av IRL M44 ...27 M9
WARRW/BUR WA5 ...33 N3
WSFD CW7 ...149 L3
Conway Cl CHSW/BR CH4 ...141 P5
CW/HAS CW1 ...170 B9
KNUT WA16 ...90 E5
WARRW/BUR WA5 ...47 K1
Conway Crs MCFLDS SK10 ...9 J1
Conway Dr BRAM/HZG SK7 ...57 J8
HALE/TIMP WA15 ...53 N1
NEWLW WA12 ...24 A6
SALE M33 ...55 N5
Conway St RDSH SK5 ...41 M4
Coogee Av WARRW/BUR WA5 ...32 B9
Cook Av RNFD/HAY WA11 ...23 J2
Cookes Ct CHSE CH5 ...164 A8
Cooke's La NWCHE CW9 ...110 F5
Cooke St BRAM/HZG SK7 ...57 K4
DTN/ASHW M34 ...29 M6
Cook's Br WRX/CR/LL LL12 ...176 A3
Cooks La WHITCH SY13 ...205 J8
Cooksmere La SBCH CW11 ...152 D9
Cook St DTN/ASHW M34 ...29 M5
EDGY/DAV SK3 ...16 E5
EP CH65 ...7 F3
Coole La ALS/MAD/W CW3 ...216 D2
NANT CW5 ...196 E5
Coombe Dr RUNC WA7 ...14 D7
Coombes Av MPL/ROM SK6 ...58 D2
Coombes St OFTN SK2 ...57 H2
Co-operative La ALCDY M17 ...200 G8
Co-operative St BRAM/HZG SK7 ...52 L4
Cooper Av NEWLW WA12 ...23 K6
WARRW/WOL WA3 ...33 L6
Cooper La RNFD/HAY WA11 ...22 G3
Coope Rd MCFLDN SK10 ...95 L7
Coopers Cft CHSE CH3 ...143 J3
Coopers Pl WARRS WA4 ...48 E6
Cooper St BRAM/HZG SK7 ...57 M4
CONG CW12 ...155 N7
NEWLW ST5 ...201 P9
RUNC WA7 ...14 E1
STKP SK1 ...41 N9
WDN WA8 ...45 P6
Coopers Wy BIDD ST8 ...175 J9
Copage Dr MPL/ROM SK6 ...42 F4
Cope Av NANT CW5 ...196 E5
Cope Cl OP/CLY M11 * ...28 E2
Copeland Gv RUNC WA7 ...62 C9
Copeland Rd WARRS WA4 ...48 D5
Copes La NANT CW5 ...196 F2
Copeswood Cl CHSW/BR CH4 ...140 C7
Copgrove Rd CCHDY M21 ...39 L1
Coppenhall Gv CW/SHV CW2 ...136 N1
Coppenhall Heyes
CW/SHV CW2 ...184 G4
Coppenhall La NANT CW5 ...184 E4
Copperas La DROY M43 ...28 E1
Copper Beach Cl
CHSW/BR CH4 ...140 G7
Copperbeech Cl
WYTH/NTH M22 ...39 P7
Copperfield Cl GOL/RIS/CU WA3 ...34 D5
Copperfield Rd CHD/CHDH SK8 ...72 B3
POY/DIS SK12 ...73 K4
Copperfields TPLY/KEL CW6 ...147 H8
WILM/AE SK9 ...71 L6
Copperfield Rd CONG CW12 ...175 J2
Coppermine La MALPAS SY14 ...179 P7
Copper St MCFLDS SK11 ...9 H7

Copper Wd NWCHW CW8 ...108 A7
Copperwood RUNC WA7 ...62 C5
Coppice Av POY/DIS SK12 ...58 E9
SALE M33 ...38 A6
Coppice Cl MPL/ROM SK6 ...42 G4
NANT CW5 ...197 L1
Coppice Dr MWCHW CW10 ...151 L4
WYTH/NTH M22 ...39 N7
Coppice La POY/DIS SK12 ...58 E9
WARRW/BUR WA5 ...32 D7
Coppicemere Dr CW/HAS CW1 ...185 N6
Coppice Rd MCFLDS SK11 ...117 K7
Coppice Rd ALS/KID ST7 ...188 E8
NANT CW5 ...197 L1
POY/DIS SK12 ...73 P5
The Coppice HALE/TIMP WA15 ...53 M7
NANT CW5 ...196 G4
NWCHE CW9 ...110 C1
NWCHW CW8 ...107 N7
SBCH CW11 ...171 L9
Coppice Wk DTN/ASHW M34 ...29 K7
Coppice Wy WILM/AE SK9 ...71 L6
Coppins Cl CHSE CH5 ...122 B9
FROD/HEL WA6 ...105 H1
The Coppins WARRN/WOL WA2 ...33 M6
WILM/AE SK9 ...71 L6
Copplestone Dr SALE M33 ...37 P5
Copse Av WYTH/NTH M22 ...54 C2
The Copse HALE/TIMP WA15 ...53 P8
MPL/ROM SK6 ...42 A9
NEWLW WA12 ...23 L5
NANT CW5 ...62 E8
Copson St DID/WITH M20 ...40 C1
Copthorne Cl CONG CW12 ...155 P8
Copthorne Dr
AUD/MAD/W CW3 ...216 G2
Copyhold NWCHW CW8 * ...108 F4
Coral Av CHD/CHDH SK8 ...56 A6
STHEL WA9 ...30 E1
Coral Dr RNFD/HAY WA11 ...23 K8
Coram St GTN M18 ...28 F5
Corbar Rd OFTN SK2 ...56 G2
Corbet Av WARRN/WOL WA2 ...33 L8
Corbet Dr MKTDR TF9 ...217 H4
Corbet St WARRN/WOL WA2 * ...33 L8
Corby St WCTN/LGST M12 ...28 C5
Corcoran Dr MPL/ROM SK6 ...43 L6
Corda Av WYTH/NTH M22 ...39 N8
Cordingley Av DROY M43 ...28 F1
Cordova Av DTN/ASHW M34 ...29 M7
Corfe Crs BRAM/HZG SK7 ...57 K6
Corfe Wy WSFD CW7 ...149 L3
Coriander Cl MWCH CW10 ...130 B8
Corks La POY/DIS SK12 ...75 J1
Corley St EDGY/DAV SK3 ...40 C9
Cormorant Cl CW/HAS CW1 ...185 M4
Cormorant Dr RUNC WA7 ...14 B3
Cornbrook Rd MCFLDS SK11 ...117 J8
Corner Cft WILM/AE SK9 ...95 J1
Cornerhouse La WDN WA8 ...45 J5
The Corners NWCHW CW8 ...108 G5
Cornfield Cl GTS/LS CH66 ...102 B3
MCFLDN SK10 ...117 J1
SALE M33 * ...39 J5
Cornfield Dr WYTH/NTH M22 ...54 D4
Cornfield Rd MCFLDS SK10 ...43 K5
Cornford Av GTN M18 ...28 B6
Cornhill Cl NEWLL ST5 ...201 N6
Cornmill Ct GOL/RIS/CU WA3 * ...25 P3
Cornubia Rd WDN WA8 ...46 A8
Cornwall Av BNG/LEV M19 ...28 B9
RUNC WA7 ...14 E3
Cornwall Cl CONG CW12 ...175 H1
MCFLDN SK10 ...116 E3
MPL/ROM SK6 ...58 C8
Cornwall Crs RDSH SK5 ...42 B2
Cornwall Gv CW/HAS CW1 ...4 B1
Cornwall Rd CHD/CHDH SK8 ...55 J2
CW/HAS CW1 ...4 C1
IRL M44 ...36 C3
WDN WA8 ...45 J5
Cornwall St CH/BCN CH1 ...2 E1
OP/CLY M11 ...28 D2
STHEL WA9 ...22 B7
WDN WA8 ...45 J5
Cornwell Ct WILM/AE SK9 ...71 M6
Corona Pk NEWLW ST5 * ...201 P7
Coronation Av ALS/KID ST7 ...187 L5
GOL/RIS/CU WA3 ...26 C2
WARRS WA4 ...49 K5
WYTH/NTH M22 * ...149 N1
Coronation Crs CW/HAS CW1 ...185 L2
SBCH CW11 ...171 M4
Coronation Dr FROD/HEL WA6 ...84 B4
NEWLW WA12 ...24 A8
RNFD/HAY WA11 ...23 L2
WARRW/BUR WA5 ...47 K3
WDN WA8 ...45 H7
Coronation Gv NWCHW CW8 ...108 A3
Coronation Rd CHSW/BR CH4 ...140 F7
CONG CW12 ...155 P8
EP CH65 ...7 F3
MWCH CW10 ...151 K4
RUNC WA7 ...14 C4
Coronation St CHSW/BR CH4 ...142 B5
CW/HAS CW1 ...185 K3
DTN/ASHW M34 ...29 M5
MCFLDS SK11 ...117 K6
OP/CLY M11 * ...28 E3
RDSH SK5 ...41 M4
Coroner's La WDN WA8 ...45 N2
Coronet Av NWCHE CW9 ...109 P8
Coronet Wy WDN WA8 ...44 G7
Corporation Rd DTN/ASHW M34 ...29 K4
Corporation St FLINT CH6 ...98 A5
STKP SK1 ...17 H3
Correction Brow POY/DIS SK12 ...58 A9

Corridor Rd EP CH65 ...81 K8
Corrie Cl DTN/ASHW M34 ...29 M8
Corrie Wy MPL/ROM SK6 ...42 D5
Corrigan St GTN M18 ...28 E3
Corringham Rd BNG/LEV M19 ...41 K1
Corsican Gdns STHEL WA9 ...30 E2
Corwen Cl WARRW/BUR WA5 ...33 H7
Cosham Rd WYTH/NTH M22 ...55 H4
Cossack Av WARRN/WOL WA2 ...33 L7
Cotebrook Dr CHME CH2 ...121 P4
Cotebrook Rd NWCHE CW9 ...110 C5
Cotefield Cl MPL/ROM SK6 * ...58 D2
Cotefield Rd WYTH/NTH M22 ...54 D5
Cote Green La MPL/ROM SK6 ...43 N7
Cote Green Rd MPL/ROM SK6 ...43 N7
Cote Lea Ct RUNC WA7 ...62 D8
Cotes Pl CH/BCN CH1 ...121 H8
Cotgreaves Ct CHSW/BR CH4 ...142 C5
Cotman Dr MPL/ROM SK6 ...43 P8
Cotswold Av BRAM/HZG SK7 ...57 H6
GOL/RIS/CU WA3 ...24 F3
Cotswold Cl CHME CH2 ...122 A5
NWCHW CW8 ...107 L1
Cotswold Gv STHEL WA9 ...22 E6
Cotswold Rd HTNM SK4 ...16 D1
WARRN/WOL WA2 ...33 L5
Cotswold Wy WSFD CW7 ...149 K3
Cottage Cl NSTN CH64 ...77 L6
Cottage Dr East HES CH60 ...76 F1
Cottage Gdns MPL/ROM SK6 ...58 D2
Cottage La WILM/AE SK9 ...70 C9
Cottage La BIDD ST8 ...175 P8
MCFLDN SK10 ...9 K5
Cottage Pl STHEL WA9 * ...31 H4
Cottage Rd CW/BR CH4 ...142 D5
Cottage St WCFLDS SK11 ...9 K4
Cottam Crs MPL/ROM SK6 ...43 N9
Cottam Dr WARRN/WOL WA2 ...34 B5
Cotterdale Cl WYTH/NTH M22 ...31 H2
Cotterill Cl SALE M33 ...38 F7
Cotterill RUNC WA7 ...62 A6
Cotterill St WARRS WA4 ...34 D9
Cotton Cl CW/SHV CW2 ...5 F7
Cottesmore Gdns
HALE/TIMP WA15 ...53 N7
Cotton Hl DID/WITH M20 ...40 D2
Cotton La CHSE CH5 ...125 K9
DID/WITH M20 ...40 D2
RUNC WA7 ...62 B6
Cotton Tree St HTNM SK4 ...16 C4
Cottonwood Dr SALE M33 ...37 P9
Cottonwood Gv ALS/KID ST7 ...189 N5
Cottrell Rd HALE/TIMP WA15 ...53 P8
Coulton Rd WDN WA8 ...46 C4
CHD/CHDH SK8 ...55 P2
Councillor La CHD/CHDH SK8 ...56 B3
Countess Av CHD/CHDH SK8 ...56 B5
Countess Cl MCFLDS SK11 ...116 F5
Countess Rd DID/WITH M20 ...40 C5
MCFLDS SK11 ...116 G5
Countess St OFTN SK2 ...57 H1
Country Ter KNUT WA16 ...90 E4
Courier St GTN M18 ...28 E5
Court Av HLWD L26 ...44 A6
Courthill St STKP SK1 ...17 K6
Courtney Pl ALT WA14 ...52 E6
Courtney Rd CHSW/BR CH4 ...142 A6
Courts Vw SALE M33 ...38 F3
The Court NSTN CH64 ...77 M7
The Courtyard SBCH CW11 ...173 K1
Cousens Wy CH/BCN CH1 ...121 L7
Covell Rd POY/DIS SK12 ...73 K1
Covent Gdn STKP SK1 ...17 G5
Coventry Av CHD/CHDH SK8 ...56 A4
GTS/LS CH66 ...102 A4
Coverdale Av WDN WA8 ...30 C6
Coverdale Cl WARRW/BUR WA5 ...32 D9
Coverdale Fold SBCH CW11 ...171 J4
Covert Cl WSFD CW7 ...149 K2
Covert Gdns ALS/KID ST7 ...188 F8
Covert Ri CHSE CH5 ...163 P8
Covert Rd WYTH/NTH M22 ...54 C2
The Cove HALE/TIMP WA15 ...53 P8
Covington Pl WILM/AE SK9 ...71 K8
Cowanway WDN WA8 ...45 M3
Cowbrook La MCFLDS SK11 ...136 A5
Cowburn Dr NM/HAY SK22 ...59 N6
Cowdell St WARRN/WOL WA2 ...18 E1
Cowfields NANT CW5 ...10 C4
Cowhey Cl CHSW/BR CH4 ...141 N8
Cow Hey La RUNC WA7 ...61 N9
Cow La BRAM/HZG SK7 ...57 K3
CHSE CH5 ...144 G8
FROD/HEL WA6 ...69 K1
HALE/TIMP WA15 ...53 N1
MCFLDN SK10 ...96 B9
MCFLDS SK11 ...117 K6
SALE M33 ...39 H2
WSFD CW7 ...149 N2
Cowley Wy CW/HAS CW1 ...185 L7
Cowlishaw Rd HYDE SK14 ...43 J2
Cown Edge Wy MPL/ROM SK6 ...58 C3
OFTN SK2 ...57 N3
Cowper Cl CW/SHV CW2 ...184 G9
Cowper St STHEL WA9 * ...22 A8
Cowthorne Dr CHSE CH3 ...144 A1
Coxton Rd WYTH/NTH M22 ...54 C6
Coylton Av RAIN/WH SK5 ...30 C6
Crab La WARRN/WOL WA2 ...34 C5
Crabmill Dr SBCH CW11 ...171 J2
Crabmill La WARRN/WOL WA2 ...34 D6
Crabtree Av HALE/TIMP WA15 ...53 P8
POY/DIS SK12 ...75 J1

Crabtree Cl NEWLW WA12 ...24 A6
Crabtree Fold RUNC WA7 ...62 C6
Crabtree Gv CW/HAS CW1 ...185 L2
Crabtree La KNUT WA16 ...66 G1
Crabwall Pl CH/BCN CH1 ...121 J6
Crackley Bnk NEWLL ST5 ...201 P5
Cracow Moss
AUD/MAD/W CW3 ...211 M3
Craddock Rd SALE M33 ...38 F6
Cradley WDN WA8 ...45 J5
Cradock Av CHF/WBR WA6 * ...9 L2
Cragside Wy WILM/AE SK9 ...71 L8
Craig Cl HTNM SK4 ...41 J7
MCFLDS SK11 ...117 H7
Craig Gdns GTS/LS CH66 ...80 A6
Craigleigh Gv PS/BROM CH62 ...79 K1
Craigs Av DID/WITH M20 ...40 D5
Craig Rd CONG CW12 ...155 P6
GTN M18 ...28 B7
HTNM SK4 ...41 J7
MCFLDS SK11 ...117 H7
Craigside BIDD ST8 ...175 K9
Craig Wk ALS/KID ST7 ...188 B6
Craigwell Av DID/WITH M20 ...40 D5
Craithie Rd CHSE CH3 ...122 D9
Crampton Dr HALE/TIMP WA15 ...53 N7
Crampton La PART M31 ...37 J2
Cranage Cl RUNC WA7 ...62 B7
Cranage La NWCHE CW9 ...110 B3
Cranage Rd BNG/LEV M19 ...28 B9
CW/SHV CW2 ...184 G5
Cranage Vls NWCHE CW9 * ...99 J9
Cranberry Cl WARRW/BUR WA5 ...32 D8
Cranberry Dr NEWLL ST5 ...201 N6
Cranberry La ALS/KID ST7 ...187 N8
Cranberry Moss La
ALS/KID ST7 ...187 L5
Cranborne Av WARRS WA4 ...48 D6
Cranborne Rd CW/HAS CW1 ...185 L2
Cranbourne Av CHD/CHDH SK8 ...56 B5
Cranbourne Cl
HALE/TIMP WA15 ...53 L1
Cranbourne Rd HTNM SK4 ...41 J4
Cranbrook Rd GTN M18 ...28 E6
Crandon Dr DID/WITH M20 ...40 D8
Crane Av STHEL WA9 ...31 J2
Cranebrook Cl CW/HAS CW1 ...169 P7
Cranesbill Cl WYTH/NTH M22 ...54 E6
Cranfield Dr ALS/KID ST7 ...187 L5
Cranford Av DID/WITH M20 ...40 E4
KNUT WA16 ...90 D4
MCFLDS SK11 ...9 K6
Cranford Cl PS/BROM CH62 ...79 K1
Cranford Ct CHSW/BR CH4 ...142 C5
WARR WA1 * ...34 F2
Cranford Dr IRL M44 ...27 M6
Cranford Gdns MPL/ROM SK6 ...43 L9
Cranford Ms ALS/KID ST7 ...187 L5
Cranford Rd WILM/AE SK9 ...71 J5
Cranford Sq KNUT WA16 ...90 D4
Cranham Av GOL/RIS/CU WA3 ...24 G2
Cranham Rd WYTH/NTH M22 ...54 D4
Cranleigh Av HTNM SK4 ...40 G4
Cranleigh Cl BRAM/HZG SK7 ...57 N7
CHD/CHDH SK8 ...55 L7
Cranleigh Dr SALE M33 ...38 D3
SALE M33 ...38 E5
Cranmere Av BNG/LEV M19 ...23 C9
Cranmere Cl NWCHE CW9 ...110 A9
Cranmere Dr SALE M33 ...38 A6
Cranmer Rd DID/WITH M20 ...40 E4
Cranshaw Av STHEL WA9 ...31 J5
Cranshaw La WDN WA8 ...45 P2
Cranston Dr DID/WITH M20 ...40 C8
SALE M33 ...39 H5
Cranston Gv CHD/CHDH SK8 ...55 L2
Cranswick Gn GTS/LS CH66 ...79 N8
Crantock Dr CHD/CHDH SK8 ...55 L7
Crantock St WGTN/LGST M12 ...28 B6
Cranwell Dr BNG/LEV M19 ...42 A9
Cranford Rd CONG CW12 ...155 P2
Craven Av GOL/RIS/CU WA3 ...24 G2
Craven Ct ALT WA14 * ...37 P9
WARRW/BUR WA5 ...32 B9
Craven Dr ALT WA14 ...37 P9
RAIN/WH SK5 ...30 E5
RDSH SK5 ...41 N2
Craven Ter SALE M33 ...38 F4
Crawford Av WDN WA8 ...45 P9
WYTH/NTH M22 ...54 F4
Crawford Cl STHEL WA9 ...31 J4
Crawford Dr STHEL WA9 ...31 J4
Crawford St STHEL WA9 ...22 B7
Crawford's Wk CHNE CH2 ...3 J1
Crawley Av
WARRN/WOL WA2 * ...33 N5
WYTH/NTH M22 ...54 F4
Crawley Gv OP/CLY M11 ...28 C1
Crayford Av CONG CW12 ...156 A5
Craydon St OP/CLY M11 ...28 C1
Crayfield Rd BNG/LEV M19 ...28 B9
Crayford Av CONG CW12 ...156 A5
Creden Av WYTH/NTH M22 ...54 F1
Crediton Cl ALT WA14 ...52 F1
Crescent Cl GTS/LS CH66 ...101 L6
Crescent Ct EDGY/DAV SK3 ...55 L4
Crescent Gv BNG/LEV M19 * ...28 A8
HTNM SK4 ...15 J9
Crescent Rd ALT WA14 ...52 E2
CHD/CHDH SK8 ...55 M1
CONG CW12 ...155 L8
EP CH65 ...7 F3
HALE/TIMP WA15 ...38 C9

The Crescent ALT WA14 ...52 E2
BNG/LEV M19 ...28 A8
CHD/CHDH SK8 ...55 M1
CHNE CH2 ...121 N7
CONG CW12 ...155 L8
EDGY/DAV SK3 ...56 C3
EP CH65 ...80 B8
HALE/TIMP WA15 ...38 C9
IRL M44 ...27 P6
KNUT WA16 ...68 A3
LYMM WA13 ...50 F5
MCFLDN SK10 ...9 J2
MCFLDN SK10 ...94 A3
MPL/ROM SK6 ...42 C4
MWCH CW10 ...151 H1
NANT CW5 ...10 D4
NM/HAY SK22 ...59 M7
NWCHE CW9 ...13 F6
NWCHW CW8 ...108 F3
NWCHW CW8 ...109 J7
TPLY/KEL CW6 ...146 F3
Cressbrook Rd WARRS WA4 ...48 E7
Cressfield Wy CCHDY M21 ...39 N1
Cressington Gdns EP CH65 ...6 E2
Cresswell Av NEWLL ST5 ...201 N6
NM/HAY SK22 ...59 N7
Cresswell Cl HLWD L26 ...44 A6
WARRW/BUR WA5 ...32 C6
Cresswell Gv DID/WITH M20 ...40 B3
Cresswellshawe Rd
ALS/KID ST7 ...187 P3
Cresswell St NM/HAY SK22 ...59 N7
Cresta Dr RUNC WA7 ...61 M8
The Crest DROY M43 ...28 G2
Crew Av MCFLDN SK10 ...9 G2
Crewe Green Av CW/HAS CW1 ...185 H4
Crewe Green Rd CW/HAS CW1 ...185 N5
Crewe Hill La CHSE CH3 ...190 B1
Crewe La CHSE CH3 ...177 H7
Crewe La South CHSE CH3 ...177 H7
Crewe & Nantwich Cicular Wk
ALS/KID ST7 ...187 L5
CW/HAS CW1 ...5 J6
CW/HAS CW1 ...170 D7
CW/HAS CW1 ...186 D2
CW/SHV CW2 ...198 B3
CW/SHV CW2 ...198 C5
NANT CW5 ...196 F6
NANT CW5 ...197 G4
SBCH CW11 ...170 G7
SBCH CW11 ...171 H5
Crewe Rd NANT CW5 ...11 H5
CW/HAS CW1 ...197 L1
CW/HAS CW1 ...209 N8
NTHM/RTH M23 ...5 M7
SBCH CW11 ...171 N3
Crewe St CH/BCN CH1 ...3 G2
CW/HAS CW1 ...5 F3
Crewood Common Rd
FROD/HEL WA6 ...107 L1

Crib La TPLY/KEL CW6 ...165 L2
Criccieth Ct EP CH65 ...102 F2
Criccieth Wy EDGY/DAV SK3 ...41 H9
Cricket St DTN/ASHW M34 ...29 N5
Cricklewood Rd
WYTH/NTH M22 ...54 E6
Crimea St GOL/RIS/CU WA3 ...101 N2
Crimes La CHSE CH3 ...165 H5
Cringle Dr CHD/CHDH SK8 ...55 L3
Cringle Rd BNG/LEV M19 ...41 J1
Crisham Av NANT CW5 ...196 F7
Crispin Rd WYTH/NTH M22 ...54 C7
Critchley Rd SPK/HALE L24 ...60 A4
Critenton St RDSH SK5 ...42 B1
Croasdale Dr RUNC WA7 ...62 C9
Crocus Gdns STHEL WA9 ...31 M1
Croesmere Dr GTS/LS CH66 ...79 N8
Croes Atti La FLINT CH6 ...98 C7
Croft Cl CHSE CH5 ...144 A5
CONG CW12 ...155 P6
HALE/TIMP WA15 ...53 N9
TPLY/KEL CW6 ...146 F3
Croft Dr NSTN CH64 ...77 L8
Crofter Cl BIDD ST8 ...175 J9
Crofters Cl CW/SHV CW2 ...185 H6
CHSE CH5 ...102 A3
Crofters Ct HOLMCH CW4 ...131 P7
NEWLL ST5 ...201 N4
Crofters Gn WILM/AE SK9 ...71 H8
Crofters Heath GTS/LS CH66 ...102 A3
Crofters Lea NWCHW CW8 ...12 A4
The Crofters SALE M33 ...39 H5
Crofters La CHSE CH5 ...120 C5
Croft Gdns WARRS WA4 ...49 J8
Croft Heath Gdns
GOL/RIS/CU WA3 ...25 J3
Croftlands Rd WYTH/NTH M22 ...54 G5
Croft La CHSW/BR CH4 ...160 C2
KNUT WA16 ...66 D3
Crofton Av HALE/TIMP WA15 ...38 D8
WARRS WA4 ...65 L1
Crofton Gdns GOL/RIS/CU WA3 ...25 N6
Crofton Rd RUNC WA7 ...14 A5
Croft Rd CHD/CHDH SK8 ...56 B4
SALE M33 ...92 C1
WILM/AE SK9 ...71 L8
Croftside Wy WILM/AE SK9 ...71 L8

Cromdale Wy
WARRW/BUR WA5 ....47 J1
Cromer La *DID/WITH* M20 ....40 C2
DTN/ASHW M34 ....28 C6
Cromer Dr *CW/HAS* CW1.......170 A9
Cromer Rd *CHD/CHDH* SK8.....53 H3
SALE M33 ....38 F5
Cromer St *STKP* SK1 ....17 K3
Cromley Rd *MPL/ROM* SK6 ......58 C8
OFTN SK2 ....56 G4
Crompton Cl *MPL/ROM* SK6....43 L9
Crompton Dr *WARRN/WOL* WA2.33 K2
Crompton Rd *BNG/LEV* M19 .....41 H1
MCFLDS SK11...............................8 C7
Cromwell Av *CHD/CHDH* SK8....55 J1
MPL/ROM SK6 ....43 H9
WARRW/BUR WA5........................32 F8
Cromwell Av South
WARRW/BUR WA5 ....47 N3
Cromwell Cl *NEWLW* WA12......23 L5
Cromwell Ct *WARR* WA1 ....18 B6
Cromwell Dr *CW/BNG* CW2.....198 B4
Cromwell Rd *BRAM/HZG* SK7...56 D9
EP CH65......................................2 E6
IRL M44......................................36 D1
MPL/ROM SK6 ....46 C2
NWCHW CW8 ....12 C3
Cromwell St *BIDD* ST8...........175 K8
HTNM SK4...................................16 C1
Cronkinson Av *NANT* CW5.....196 G3
NANT CW5....................................10 D7
Cronshaw St *BNG/LEV* M19.....28 B9
Cronton La *RAIN/WH* L35.........30 A7
WDN WA8....................................30 A8
WDN WA8....................................45 M2
Cronton Park Cl *WDN* WA8 .....45 J1
Cronulla Dr *WARRW/BUR* WA5.32 A9
Crooked La *CHSE* CH3............145 P7
Crookedyard Rd *MCFLDS* SK11..118 C5
Crookenden Cl *CHNE* CH2......121 M2
Crookenden Rd *CHNE* CH2.....121 M2
Crookilley Wy *MPL/ROM* SK6...17 K1
STKP SK1......................................17 K1
Crook La *WSFD* CW7...............129 H9
Crook St *CHNE* CH2 ....2 D4
Croppers Rd *WARRN/WOL* WA2.34 A5
Crosby Av *WARRW/BUR* WA5...33 K8
Crosby Gv *NSTN* CH64.............77 M7
Crosby St *OFTN* SK2................41 N9
Crosfield Gv *GTN* M18..............28 D5
Crosfield St *WARR* WA1..........16 C3
Crossacres Rd *WYTH/NTH* M22..55 H3
Crossall St *MCFLDS* SK11.........8 B5
Cross Bank *CHD/CHDH* SK8......56 A4
Cross Farm Rd *STHEL* WA9.......22 A0
Crossfield Av *GOL/RIS/CU* WA3.25 P7
LYMM WA13..................................50 F4
WSFD CW7 ....149 M3
Crossfield Cl *DTN/ASHW* M34...29 N7
Crossfield Gv *MPL/ROM* SK6....57 H3
OFTN SK2 ....57 H3
Crossfield Rd *HALE/TIMP* WA15.53 M5
MCFLDS SK10...............................95 L7
WILM/AE SK9 ....71 M2
Crossfields *CHSE* CH5............124 A9
Crossford Br *SALE* M33 ....37 L3
Crossford Ct *SALE* M33 * 38 E2
Crossgate Av *WYTH/NTH* M22...54 F1
Crossgates *WDN* WA8 ....46 D4
Cross Gn *CHNE* CH2...............121 P5
Cross Gv *HALE/TIMP* WA15.....38 C8
Cross Hey *CHSW/BR* CH4.........57 N4
Cross Hillocks La *RAIN/WH* L35.44 E4
The Crossings *NEWLW* WA12...23 N6
Crosslands *CONG* CW12.........156 A9
CW/HAS CW1...............................186 B4
Cross La *ALS/KID* ST7.............201 H5
CONG CW12 ....133 H7
CONG CW12 ....175 H1
CW/HAS CW1..............................169 K3
FROD/HEL WA6...........................83 H5
GOL/RIS/CU WA3.........................34 E1
GTN M18......................................28 D5
HOLMCH CW8 ....132 F6
MPL/ROM SK6 ....58 C2
MWCH CW10 ....151 K4
NANT CW5..................................169 H4
NEWLW WA12 ....23 M6
NSTN CH64..................................77 M5
SBCH CW11................................171 P4
SBCH CW11................................173 J4
WARRS WA4 ....49 J5
WILM/AE SK9 ....71 P6
Cross La East *PART* M31.........36 E6
CONG CW12 ....124 D9
Cross Lanes *CHSE* CH5..........145 J2
Cross La South
GOL/RIS/CU WA3.........................34 E2
Cross La West *PART* M31.........36 D6
Crossley Av *GTS/LS* CH66 ....80 A7
Crossley Crs *CHNE* CH2.........122 C6
Crossley Rd *BNG/LEV* M19......41 H1
SALE M33 ....38 D2
Crossley St *GTN* M18..............28 B3
WARR WA1 ....18 C5
Crossmoor Crs *MPL/ROM* SK6..43 H6
Crossmoor Gv *MPL/ROM* SK6..43 H6
Cross o' th' Hill Rd
MALPAS SY14.............................204 F2
Cross Rd *CCHDY* M21...............39 L1
CHD/CHDH SK8............................55 K8
CW/HAS CW1..............................186 B4
Cross St *ALS/KID* ST7.............187 N5
ALT WA14....................................13 G5
BIDD ST8....................................175 K9
CHNE CH2...................................3 K3
CW/HAS CW1..............................186 B4
DTN/ASHW M34...........................29 L4
GOL/RIS/CU WA3.........................24 C2
MCFLDS SK11...............................9 F7

NEWUL ST5 ....201 N7
NM/HAY SK22 * 59 N7
NSTN CH64.................................77 L5
NWCHE CW9 ....110 C1
NWCHW CW8 ....109 K1
RUNC WA7 * 14 E1
SALE M33 ....38 A6
WARRN/WOL WA2......................18 E1
WDN WA8...................................21 K1
WRXS/E LL15.............................176 C7
The Cross *LYMM* WA13.............50 E4
WRXS/E LL13 ....176 F8
Crosstree La *CO* CH5..............140 B7
Cross Tree Ri *CO* CH5..............140 B2
Crosswaite Rd *OFTN* SK2.........57 L1
Crossway *BNG/LEV* M19...........72 E1
CW/HAS CW1...............................185 K2
DID/WITH M20 ....40 C5
OFTN SK2....................................56 C5
WDN WA8....................................20 A2
Crossways *BIDD* ST8..............175 M8
Crossways Rd *ALS/KID* ST7....188 C3
The Crossway *BEB* CH65.........77 P1
Cross Wood St *NANT* CW5......169 L6
Crosthwaite Av *PS/BROM* CH62..79 K1
Croston Av *RAIN/WH* L35.........30 A3
Croston Cl *WDN* WA8 ....45 J3
WILM/AE SK9 ....93 L4
Crotia Av *CW/SHV* CW2..........198 C2
Croton St *HTNM* SK4 ....40 F6
Crouch La *CONG* CW12...........156 D6
Crouchley Hall Ms
LYMM WA13 * 50 F6
Crouchley La *LYMM* WA13 ....50 F6
Crouch St *STHEL* WA9 ....22 B9
Croughton *OP/CLY* M11 * 28 D2
Croughton Rd *CHNE* CH2........103 J5
GTS/LS CH66 ....80 D5
Crowcroft Rd *BRUN/LGST* M13..28 A6
NWCHE CW9 ....110 C8
Crowe Av *WARRN/WOL* WA2.....33 L5
Crowland Gdns *CHD/CHDH* SK8..56 B9
Crowland Rd *NTHM/RTH* M23...54 B4
Crow La East *NEWLW* WA12.....23 M5
Crow La West *NEWLW* WA12....23 M5
Crowley La *NWCHE* CW9 ....65 P3
Crowley Rd *HALE/TIMP* WA15...53 M1
Crown Av *WDN* WA8 ....45 H7
Crown Bnk *ALS/KID* ST7..........188 F9
SBCH CW11................................171 H5
Crown Bank Crs *ALS/KID* ST7..201 N1
Crown Ct *BRAM/HZG* SK7.........57 K4
Crown Ctyd
AUD/MAD/W CW3 * 216 C1
Crowndale H *BURS/TUN* ST6...189 N8
Crown Fields Cl *NEWLW* WA12..23 M4
Crown Gdns *ALS/KID* ST7........201 N1
NEWLW WA12 ....23 M4
Crown Ga *RUNC* WA7 ....62 D7
Crown Gn *LYMM* WA13.............51 H4
Crown La *KNUT* WA16..............112 B4
Crown Ms *NANT* CW5 * 10 B5
Crown Park Dr *NEWLW* WA12...23 M5
Crown Passages
HALE/TIMP WA15 ....53 J5
Crown St *DTN/ASHW* M34.........29 L5
MPL/ROM SK6 * 42 F5
MPL/ROM SK6 ....58 D4
NEWLW WA12 ....23 L6
STHEL WA9 * 30 C1
WARR WA1..................................18 D5
Crown St West *MCFLDS* SK11...8 C5
Crowsdale Pl *OFTN* SK2...........57 L3
Crowther St *GTN* M18...............28 D4
Crowthorn Dr *NTHM/RTH* M23...54 C5
Crowthorn Rd *HTNM* SK4.........41 L1
Crowton Av *SALE* M33...............53 G8
Crow Wood La *WDN* WA8 ....46 B5
Crow Wood Pl *WDN* WA8..........46 B4
Croxton Cl *MPL/ROM* SK6.........58 C2
SALE M33 ....38 A6
Croxton Gn *MALPAS* SY14......193 P3
Croxton La *MWCH* CW10.........129 P6
Croxton Wy *NWCHW* CW8.......100 J8
Croyde Cl *WYTH/NTH* M22........55 H8
Croyde Pl *STHEL* WA9...............31 H4
Croyde Rd *SPK/HALE* L24.........63 G3
Crum Hl *NWCHE* CW9 ....13 G2
Crummock Rd *CHD/CHDH* SK8..55 K4
Cruttenden Rd *OFTN* SK2..........57 J3
Cryers La *CHNE* CH2...............104 A2
Cuckoo La *NANT* CW5.............185 H8
NSTN CH64 ....77 P6
Cuckstoolpit Hl *MCFLDN* SK10..9 G4
Cuddington Crs *EDGY/DAV* SK3..56 D1
Cuddington La *NWCHW* CW8...107 N9
Cuerden Gn *WDN* WA8 ....46 E5
Cuerdley Rd *WARRW/BUR* WA4..44 E9
Cuerdon Dr *WARRS* WA4..........49 M6
Culbert Av *DID/WITH* M20 ....40 D5
Culbin Cl *GOL/RIS/CU* WA3.......35 H2
Culchetch Av *MPL/ROM* SK6....58 D1
Culcheth Hall Dr
GOL/RIS/CU WA3.........................25 P5
Culcheth Rd *ALT* WA14............47 G3
Culford Cl *RUNC* WA7 ....63 H5
Culland St *CW/SHV* CW2 ....4 E7
Cullen Cl *BEB* CH63 ....68 C9
Cullen Rd *RUNC* WA7................61 K7
Cullercoats Wk
WGTN/LGST M12 * 28 B6
Culmere Rd *WYTH/NTH* M22.....54 F6
Culver Rd *EDGY/DAV* SK3.........56 D2
Cumber Cl *WILM/AE* SK9 ....93 G9
Cumber Dr *WILM/AE* SK9...........92 F1
Cumberland Av *IRL* M44............10 E3
NANT CW5....................................10 E3
RDSH SK5...................................42 B4
Cumberland Cl *ALS/KID* ST7...188 G9
CW/HAS CW1..............................185 K3
Cumberland Crs
RNFD/HAY WA11 ....22 E3

Cumberland Dr *ALT* WA14.........52 E7
MCFLDN SK10..............................95 P5
Cumberland Rd *CONG* CW12...155 J7
PART M31....................................38 C6
SALE M33....................................38 F6
Cumberland St *MCFLDN* SK10...8 C2
WARRS WA4................................48 F4
WILM/AE SK9 ....70 F9
Cumbermere Dr *SBCH* CW11..171 K2
Cumbers Dr *NSTN* CH64..........77 N8
Cumbers La *NSTN* CH64..........77 N8
Cumbrae Dr *EP* CH65..............102 E3
Cumbrae Rd *BNG/LEV* M19......28 C8
Cundiff Cl *MCFLDS* SK11 * 9 H7
Cundiff Rd *CCHDY* M21............39 L2
Cunliffe Av *NEWLW* WA12.........23 M4
Cunliffe Ct *RUNC* WA7..............62 E7
Cunliffe Dr *SALE* M33 * 53 J4
Cunliffe St *EDGY/DAV* SK3.......16 B6
Cunningham Cl
WARRW/BUR WA5.......................47 K2
Cunningham Dr *RUNC* WA7......14 B6
Cunningham Rd *WDN* WA8........20 B3
Cuppin St *CH/BCN* CH1.............2 D5
Curate St *STKP* SK1..................1 J2
Curlender Wy *SPK/HALE* L24....60 E4
Curlew Cl *GOL/RIS/CU* WA3......24 F1
MCFLDN SK10..............................9 M8
WSFD CW7..................................149 L5
Curlew Gn *OFTN* SK2 ....34 F5
Curlew Rd *ALS/KID* ST7...........189 N7
Currans Rd *WARRN/WOL* WA2..33 K6
Curtis Rd *BNG/LEV* M19............28 C8
Curzon Av *ALS/KID* ST7...........187 P5
HTNM SK4...................................41 H6
Curzon Cl *BRAM/HZG* CH4......142 C2
Curzon Dr *HALE/TIMP* WA15....53 M1
WARRS WA4................................49 J8
Curzon Gn *OFTN* SK2...............42 C8
Curzon Gv *WSFD* CW7............149 P1
Curzon Ms *WILM/AE* SK9 ....71 J8
CHSW/BR CH4 ....71 J8
Curzon Pk South
CHSW/BR CH4............................142 C3
Curzon Rd *CHD/CHDH* SK8.......55 K8
OFTN SK2....................................42 C8
POY/DIS SK12..............................73 L4
SALE M33....................................38 E3
Curzon St *CHSW/BR* CH4........142 B5
Cutgate Cl *NTHM/RTH* M23.......39 H7
Cuthbert Av *BNG/LEV* M19.......28 C8
Cuthbert Rd *CHD/CHDH* SK8.....55 N1
Cutnook La *IRL* M44..................27 M4
Cwm Edison *FLINT* CH6............98 B8
Cwrt Erwain *CHSW/BR* CH4 * ..142 A3
Cycle St *OP/CLY* M11................28 B1
Cygnet Cl *GTS/LS* CH66............79 P9
Cygnet Ct *WARR* WA1 ....15 J4
Cyman Cl *CH/BCN* CH1............120 C8
Cymbal Ct *RDSH* SK5...............41 M5
Cynthia Av *WARR* WA1..............34 C9
Cynthia Dr *MPL/ROM* SK6.........58 D2
Cypress Av *GTS/LS* CH66........102 E5
WDN WA8....................................45 P4
Cypress Cl *EDGY/DAV* SK3.......16 A6
WARR WA1..................................34 F9
Cypress Gdns *STHEL* WA9........30 B1
Cypress Gv *DTN/ASHW* M34.....29 N0
NEWUL ST5 ....201 M2
RUNC WA7..................................62 A7
Cypress Ms *NWCHW* CW8.......108 C5
Cypress Wy *MPL/ROM* SK6......58 D4
Cyril Bell Cl *LYMM* WA13..........50 F4
Cyril St *WARRN/WOL* WA2........18 E2

D

Daffodil Cl *WDN* WA8 ....46 C3
Dagnall Av *CCHDY* M21.............39 L2
WARRW/BUR WA5........................33 J6
Daine Av *NTHM/RTH* M23..........39 L7
Daintry St *MCFLDS* SK11...........9 G5
Daintry Ter *MCFLDN* SK10..........9 G5
Dairydale Cl *IRL* M44................171 K2
Dairy Farm Cl *LYMM* WA13.......50 F4
Dairyground Rd *BRAM/HZG* SK7..56 B8
Dairyhouse La *ALT* WA14..........37 N9
Dairy House La *BRAM/HZG* SK7..72 B3
Dairy House Rd *CHD/CHDH* SK8..72 B1
Dairy House Wy *CHSW/BR* CW2..184 F6
Dairylands Rd *ALS/KID* ST7.....188 C4
Dairy La *NANT* CW5..................183 K4
Daisy Av *NEWLW* WA12............23 N7
Daisy Bank *NANT* CW5............196 E2
Daisy Bank Crs
AUD/MAD/W CW3........................208 C9
Daisybank Dr *CONG* CW12......155 M5
SBCH CW11................................171 P5
Daisy Bank La *NWCHW* CW8....109 L1
Daisy Bank Mill Cl
GOL/RIS/CU WA3.........................25 N6
Daisy Bank Rd *LYMM* WA13......50 F4
WARRW/BUR WA5 * 47 K3
Daisyfield Cl *WYTH/NTH* M22....54 F6
Daisyhill Cl *SALE* M33 ....39 H4
Daisy La *WRX/GR/LL* LL12.......176 A4
Daisy Ms *EDGY/DAV* SK3..........56 D3
Daisy St *OFTN* SK2 ....41 N9
Daisy Wy *MPL/ROM* SK6............58 D8
Dakley St *OP/CLY* M11 ....28 B1
Dalby Cl *GOL/RIS/CU* WA3.........35 J5
RNFD/HAY WA11 ....22 A4

Dalby Gv *STKP* SK1.................17 K4
Dale Av *BRAM/HZG* SK7............56 F7
GTS/LS CH66 ....79 N7
Dalebrook Cl *HTNM* SK4 * 16 B4
Dalebrook Rd *SALE* M33...........38 F7
Dale Cl *WARRW/BUR* WA5.........47 P3
WDN WA8....................................44 G7
Dale Ct *MWCH* CW10 ....151 K3
Dale Crs *CONG* CW12.............155 P8
STHEL WA9 ....31 J2
Dalecroft *FROD/HEL* WA6........104 E5
SALE M33....................................39 J5
Dale End *EP* CH65...................211 N3
EP CH65......................................80 B8
Dale Farm *RAIN/WH* L35 * 44 B3
Dalefords La *WSFD* CW7.........127 P6
Dale Gv *CONG* CW12...............156 A9
MPL/ROM SK6 ....58 C9
NM/HAY SK22 ....59 N8
Dale Rd *GOL/RIS/CU* WA3.........24 C2
MPL/ROM SK6 ....58 C9
NM/HAY SK22 ....59 M7
Dalesford Cl *LEIGH* WN7..........25 L1
Dalesford Crs *MCFLDN* SK10...116 E4
Dales Green Rd *ALS/KID* ST7...189 L3
Daleside *CHNE* CH2.................121 N3
Dale St *CHSE* CH5....................43 L9
EDGY/DAV SK3 ....9 H4
RUNC WA7..................................14 E5
The Dale *NSTN* CH64................77 K7
TPLY/KEL CW6............................165 P5
Dale Vw *ALS/KID* ST7..............189 L3
DTN/ASHW M34...........................42 F1
WARRW/BUR WA5........................47 L2
Dale Wy *ALS/KID* ST7..............189 L3
DTN/ASHW M34...........................42 F1
Dalewood Av *WDN* WA8............18 B4
Dalewood Crs *CHNE* CH2........104 A1
Dalkeith Rd *RDSH* SK5.............41 N1
Dalkeith St *GTN* M18................28 B3
Dallam Ct *WARRN/WOL* WA2 * ..18 C2
Dallam La *WARRN/WOL* WA2.....18 C4
Dallimore Rd *NTHM/RTH* M23...54 A1
Dalmahoy Cl *WSFD* CW7 * 108 D9
Dalry St *BNG/LEV* M19..............28 B8
Dalston Dr *BRAM/HZG* SK7.......72 C1
DID/WITH M20 ....40 D6
Dalton Av *WARRW/BUR* WA5.....18 A1
Dalton Bnk *WARR* WA1.............19 C4
Dalton Cl *CH/BCN* CH1 * 140 B3
Dalton Ct *RUNC* WA7................62 C3
SBCH CW11................................171 K2
Dalton Dr *GOL/RIS/CU* WA3.......34 F5
RUNC WA7..................................62 B4
Dalton Rd *SALE* M33 * 38 F2
Dalton Wy *MWCH* CW10...........151 K4
Dalveen Dr *HALE/TIMP* WA15...38 C9
Dalwood Cl *RUNC* WA7.............63 J7
Damery Hollow *CHD/CHDH* SK8..55 M8
Damery Ct *BRAM/HZG* SK7 ....56 E7
Damery Rd *BRAM/HZG* SK7.......56 E7
Dam Head La *GOL/RIS/CU* WA3..34 B6
Damhead La *NSTN* CH64...........78 C6
Damian Dr *NEWLW* WA12...........23 L4
Damien St *BNG/LEV* M19...........28 B7
Dam La *BIDD* ST8.....................175 P7
GOL/RIS/CU WA3.........................34 A1
GOL/RIS/CU WA3.........................34 F5
KNUT WA16..................................91 N2
WARR WA1..................................34 E9
Dams La *KNUT* WA16...............112 B7
Damson La *KNUT* WA16............91 M1
Dan Bnk *MPL/ROM* SK6............58 A1
Danby Cl *BNG/LEV* M19............28 B7
WARRW/BUR WA5........................33 H9
Danby Fold *RAIN/WH* L35..........30 A3
Dane Av *EDGY/DAV* SK3 * 41 H8
PART M31....................................36 E4
Dane Bank Av *CONG* CW12.....155 N6
CW/SHV CW2...............................185 P1
Danebank Ms *DTN/ASHW* M34..29 P7
Danebank Rd *LYMM* WA13.........50 E3
Dane Bank Rd *NWCHE* CW9......39 J5
Danebank Rd East *LYMM* WA15..50 E3
Dane Cl *ALS/KID* ST7...............187 L5
BRAM/HZG SK7............................56 C5
CHSW/BR CH4.............................142 B5
MWCH CW10 ....171 K2
Dane Dr *BIDD* ST8...................175 M8
WILM/AE SK9...............................93 J8
Danebridge Rd *CONG* CW12....121 K5
Danefield Ct *CHD/CHDH* SK8.....55 M7
Danefield Rd *HOLMCH* CW4......13 J4
NWCHE CW9 ....13 J4
SALE M33....................................38 F2
Dane Gdns *ALS/KID* ST7..........189 L6
Dane Gv *CHNE* CH2.................122 C5
Dane Hill Cl *POY/DIS* SK12.......75 H1
Daneholme Rd *ALS/KID* ST7....189 L6
Dane Ms *SALE* M33 * 185 K2
WSFD CW7 ....150 B1
Dane Rd *DTN/ASHW* M34..........28 C7
SALE M33....................................38 C9
SALE M33....................................38 D3
Danesbury Ri *CHD/CHDH* SK8..55 M2
Danescroft *WDN* WA8...............45 H4
Danesmoor Rd *DID/WITH* M20...40 B3
Danes Sq *MCFLDS* SK11..........117 K7
Dane St *CONG* CW12...............155 L7
MWCH CW10 ....130 C9
OP/CLY M11................................28 E2
Daneswell Rd *SPK/HALE* L24....60 A4
Danett Cl *WGTN/LGST* M12.......28 A3
Dane Valley Wy *HOLMCH* CW4..131 H7
Danforth Gv *BNG/LEV* M19........28 B9
Daniel Adamson Av *PART* M31...36 C5
Daniel Cl *GOL/RIS/CU* WA3........35 H4
Daniell Wy *CHSE* CH3...............143 J5

Daniel's La *STKP* SK1 * 17 G3
Daniel St *BRAM/HZG* SK7..........57 L5
Dans Rd *WDN* WA8...................46 C5
Danwood Cl *HYDE* SK14............29 P8
Dappleheath Rd *CW/SHV* CW2..184 C7
Darby Cl *NSTN* CH64 ....76 F2
Darby Rd *IRL* M44 ....11 J8
Darden Ct *RNFD/HAY* WA11......22 F5
Darent Rd *RNFD/HAY* WA11......22 F3
Daresbury Cl *EDGY/DAV* SK3....56 D2
HOLMCH CW4.............................131 M8
SALE M33....................................39 J5
WILM/AE SK9 ....71 L6
RUNC WA7..................................15 K2
WARRS WA4................................63 L3
Daresbury La *WARRS* WA4.......63 P4
Dargle Rd *SALE* M33 ....38 E2
Darlan Av *WYTH/NTH* M22.........54 E2
Dario Gradii Dr *CW/SHV* CW2...185 K7
Dark Ark La *CHSE* CH3.............106 B6
Darkie Meadow *TPLY/KEL* CW6..166 B9
Dark La *CHSE* CH3...................179 K1
FROD/HEL WA6...........................106 C3
MCFLDS SK11..............................116 A4
MCFLDS SK11..............................116 D6
NWCHE CW9 ....88 C6
WARRS WA4................................64 F9
WHITCH SY14.............................214 E4
Darland Cl *WRX/GR/LL* LL12....160 F9
WRX/GR/LL LL12........................160 F9
Darley Av *CCHDY* M21..............39 M2
CHD/CHDH SK8 ....84 C3
CW/SHV CW2...............................184 C5
DID/WITH M20 ....39 P4
WARRW/BUR WA5........................33 P5
Darley Gv *BRAM/HZG* SK7 * 57 M8
Darley Rd *BRAM/HZG* SK7.........57 M8
Darley Sh *SALE* M33.................38 E4
Darlington Av *CW/HAS* CW1.....120 D3
Darlington Rd *DID/WITH* M20.....40 C3
Darlington St *MWCH* CW10.......151 J1
Darnaway Cl *GOL/RIS/CU* WA3..35 J2
Darnbrook Dr *WYTH/NTH* M22...54 D6
Darnhall School La *WSFD* CW7..149 L5
Darras Rd *GTN* M18...................28 C6
Dart Cl *ALS/KID* ST7.................187 L4
BIDD ST8 ....175 L8
Dartford Av *RDSH* SK5..............42 A2
Dartington Cl *BRAM/HZG* SK7....56 F4
NTHM/RTH M23............................53 P1
Dartmouth Crs *RDSH* SK5.........42 B3
Dartnall Cl *POY/DIS* SK12.........58 E9
Darwin Gv *BRAM/HZG* SK7 * 58 D3
STHEL WA9..................................30 D1
Darwin Rd *CH/BCN* CH1...........120 F7
Darwin St *NWCHW* CW8............12 C5
Dashwood Cl *WARRS* WA4........49 J3
Daten Av *GOL/RIS/CU* WA3.......24 D2
Dauncey Cl *CHNE* CH2............121 M2
Davehall Av *WILM/AE* SK9..........71 J7
Davenfield Gv *DID/WITH* M20.....40 C5
Davenfield Rd *DID/WITH* M20.....40 C5
Davenham Av *WARR* WA1..........33 P8
Davenham Ct *NWCHE* CW9.......110 E9
Davenham Rd *NWCHE* CW9......110 E9
RDSH SK5...................................38 C5
SALE M33....................................38 B2
WILM/AE SK9 ....93 J2
Davenham Wy *MWCH* CW10....151 K5
Davenhill Rd *BNG/LEV* M19.......28 B8
Davenport Av *CW/SHV* CW2.....185 J8
DID/WITH M20 ....40 C1
NANT CW5....................................49 H1
WARRS WA4................................49 J2
WILM/AE SK9 ....92 G1
Davenport Cl *SBCH* CW11.......172 A1
Davenport Gn *MPL/ROM* SK6....62 A2
Davenport La *KNUT* WA16.........69 N8
MCFLDS SK11..............................153 N8
Daven Rd *CONG* CW12.............155 P9
Davenlands *WILM/AE* SK9.........71 M8
Davey La *WILM/AE* SK9 ....93 J3
David Cl *DTN/ASHW* M34...........29 N8
David Rd *LYMM* WA13...............55 J3
Davids Av *WARRW/BUR* WA5.....47 L2
Davidson Av *CONG* CW12.........156 A5
David St *DTN/ASHW* M34............29 L4
NWCHW CW8 ....12 D4
RDSH SK5...................................42 A3
Davies Av *CHD/CHDH* SK8.........55 K9
NEWLW WA12 ....23 L4
WARRS WA4................................49 H5
Davies Cl *WDN* WA8 ....45 P5
Davies Rd *MPL/ROM* SK6..........46 C5
PART M31....................................36 C5
Davies St *STHEL* WA9...............30 D1
WILM/AE SK9...............................71 K7
Davis Av *WARRW/BUR* WA5......32 E5
Davis Cl *ALS/KID* ST7...............188 A4
Davy Av *GOL/RIS/CU* WA3.........23 N7
Davy Rd *RUNC* WA7..................62 C3
Dawlish Av *CHD/CHDH* SK8.......55 P3
RDSH SK5...................................42 A3
Dawlish Cl *BRAM/HZG* SK7........56 F9
GOL/RIS/CU WA3.........................35 J1
SALE M33....................................38 B2
Dawlish Rd *SALE* M33...............38 E5
Dawnay St *OP/CLY* M11 * 1 M2
Dawn Cl *NSTN* CH64.................77 M8
STHEL WA9..................................30 D1
Dawn Gdns *EP* CH65.................2 C6
Dawpool Cl *CHNE* CH2............121 N6
Dawpool Dr *WARRW/BUR* WA5..33 J1
Dawson Av *STHEL* WA9.............31 J1
Dawson Dr *CH/BCN* CH1..........121 M8

Dawson Rd ALT WA14 ....38 A9
  CHD/CHDH SK8 ....55 M7
  MCFLDN SK10 ....95 N6
  WILM/AE SK9 ....116 F5
Dawson St STKP SK1 ....2 D2
Daylesford Cl CHD/CHDH SK8 ....55 L3
Daylesford Crs CHD/CHDH SK8 ....55 M3
Daylesford Rd CHD/CHDH SK8 ....55 M3
Deacon Cl ALT WA14 ....52 F6
  GOL/RIS/CU WA3 ....25 J9
Deacon Rd WDN WA8 ....17 J1
Deacons Cl STKP SK1 ....17 J4
  WSFD CW7 ....128 G7
Deakin's Rd WSFD CW7 ....129 H7
Deal Av RDSH SK5 ....42 A2
Dean Bnk TPLY/KEL CW6 ....165 P6
Dean Cl MCFLDN SK10 ....95 N6
  PART M31 ....36 E4
  SBCH CW11 ....171 K1
  WDN WA8 ....21 J2
  WILM/AE SK9 ....71 L5
Dean Ct GOL/RIS/CU WA3 ....24 C2
Dean Crs WARRN/WOL WA2 ....33 L8
Dean Dr ALT WA14 ....52 F6
  WILM/AE SK9 ....71 L5
Deane Av CHD/CHDH SK8 ....55 P2
  HALE/TIMP WA15 ....53 J2
Deane Ct NANT CW5 ....197 J3
Deanery Cl DTN/ASHW CH1 ....121 M7
Deanery Wy STKP SK1 ....17 G3
Dean Hollow ALS/KID ST7 ....200 C5
Dean La BRAM/HZG SK7 ....57 L7
Dean Meadow NEWLW WA12 ....23 N5
Dean Moor Rd BRAM/HZG SK7 ....58 G5
Dean Pk MALPAS SY14 ....204 F2
Dean Rd GOL/RIS/CU WA3 ....24 C2
  GTN M18 ....28 E5
  IRL M44 ....36 D2
  WILM/AE SK9 ....71 N3
Dean Row Rd WILM/AE SK9 ....71 P6
Deans Cl CHNE CH2 ....121 N5
  CHSE CH5 ....145 H1
Deansfield Wy CHNE CH2 ....104 A1
Deansgate EP CH65 ....6 B4
Deansgate La
  HALE/TIMP WA15 ....38 B9
Dean's La ALS/KID ST7 ....201 M5
  CW/SHV CW2 ....199 P5
  MALPAS SY14 ....192 E3
  SBCH CW11 ....171 K3
  WARRS WA4 ....49 P4
Deans Wy STHEL WA9 ....30 C5
Dearnley Av RNFD/HAY WA11 ....22 C4
Debdale La GTN M18 ....28 F5
Debra Cl GTS/LS CH66 ....101 N1
Dee Av GTS/LS CH66 ....101 N1
Dee Banks CHSE CH3 ....143 J2
Dee Cl ALS/KID ST7 ....188 C9
  BIDD ST8 ....175 M8
  SBCH CW11 ....171 K1
Dee Crs CHSE CH3 ....176 G6
Dee Fords Av CHSE CH3 ....143 J1
Dee Hills Pk CHSE CH3 ....3 H4
Dee La CHSE CH3 ....3 H4
  WRXS/E LL13 ....176 F9
Dee Pk WRXS/E LL13 ....176 F9
Deepcar St BNG/LEV M19 ....28 A7
Deepdale WDN WA8 ....45 J4
Deepdale Cl RDSH SK5 ....28 F8
Deepdale Dr RAIN/WH L35 ....62 D5
Deeracre Av OFTN SK2 ....57 J1
Deerfold Cl GTN M18 ....28 D4
Deermoss WHITCH SY13 ....213 M5
Dee Rd CHNE CH2 ....122 G2
  RAIN/WH L35 ....30 A5
Deeroak Cl GTN M18 ....28 B8
Deer Park Ct RUNC WA7 ....62 D8
Deerwood Cl GTS/LS CH66 ....79 P6
  MCFLDN SK10 ....116 F3
Deeside EP CH65 ....102 D1
  WRXS/E LL13 ....176 G8
Deeside Cl EP CH65 ....102 D2
Deeside Crs CH/BCN CH1 ....120 B6
Deeside La CH/BCN CH1 ....120 B6
Dee Vw CHSE CH3 ....176 G6
Dee Wy WSFD CW7 ....129 H9
Deganwy Gv RDSH SK5 ....43 H5
Deirdre Av WDN WA8 ....21 H1
De Lacy Rw RUNC WA7 ....62 F4
Delafield Cl WGTN/LGST M12 ....28 A7
Delafield Cl WARRN/WOL WA2 ....34 A5
Delaford Cl EDGY/DAV SK3 ....56 E3
Delahays Dr HALE/TIMP WA15 ....53 L5
Delahays Range GTN M18 ....28 F5
Delahays Rd HALE/TIMP WA15 ....53 M5
Delaine Rd DTN/ASHW M20 ....40 A2
Delaisy Wy WSFD CW7 ....150 A1
Delamere Av
  GOL/RIS/CU WA3 ....24 C3
  GTS/LS CH66 ....80 A8
  PS/BROM CH62 ....99 J1
  SALE M33 ....39 H5
  STHEL WA9 ....30 C5
  WDN WA8 ....45 J6
Delamere Cl BRAM/HZG SK7 ....57 N4
  MPL/ROM SK6 ....43 L8
  NWCHW CW8 ....109 J1
  PS/BROM CH62 ....79 J1
  SBCH CW11 ....171 L1

Delamere Ct ALS/KID ST7 ....187 K4
Delamere Dr GTS/LS CH66 ....80 A9
  MCFLDN SK10 ....117 M2
Delamere La CHSE CH3 ....125 H1
Delamere Park Wy East
  NWCHW CW8 ....107 P7
Delamere Park Wy West
  NWCHW CW8 ....107 P7
Delamere Ri WSFD CW7 ....149 K1
Delamere Rd BNG/LEV M19 ....28 A9
  BRAM/HZG SK7 ....57 N4
  CHD/CHDH SK8 ....55 K2
  CONG CW12 ....155 H7
  DTN/ASHW M34 ....29 H7
  FROD/HEL WA6 ....106 F6
  NANT CW5 ....196 F4
  OFTN SK2 ....57 H3
  WILM/AE SK9 ....71 M2
Delamere St CH/BCN CH1 ....2 D2
  CW/HAS CW1 ....185 H3
  OP/CLY M11 ....28 F2
  WARRW/BUR WA5 ....48 A2
  WSFD CW7 ....149 J1
  FROD/HEL WA6 ....84 A8
Delamere Wy FROD/HEL WA6 ....106 F6
  WARRS WA4 ....64 C7
Delamer Rd ALT WA14 ....52 G4
Delamore's Acre NSTN CH64 ....78 E5
Delaunays Rd SALE M33 ....38 C4
Delenty Dr GOL/RIS/CU WA3 ....24 H4
Delery Dr WARR WA1 ....33 P8
Delfur Rd BRAM/HZG SK7 ....56 F8
Delhi Rd IRL M44 ....27 M9
Dell Dr WARRN/WOL WA2 ....34 B6
Dell Side MPL/ROM SK6 ....42 D5
Dellside Gv STHEL WA9 ....22 A9
The Dell CHSE CH3 ....122 C6
  NWCHW CW8 ....107 N8
  TPLY/KEL CW6 ....125 J7
Delmar Rd KNUT WA16 ....90 C4
Delphfields Rd WARRS WA4 ....48 E8
Delphield RUNC WA7 ....63 H6
Delph La WARRN/WOL WA2 ....33 J4
  WARRN/WOL WA2 ....33 J7
  WARRS WA4 ....63 J3
Delphside ALS/KID ST7 ....201 J5
Delta Cl CHSE CH3 ....141 M4
Delta Crs WARRW/BUR WA5 ....32 F6
Delta Rd DTN/ASHW M34 ....29 J4
  STHEL WA9 ....22 D5
Delves Av WARRW/BUR WA5 ....33 J9
Delves Cl CW/SHV CW2 ....198 A3
Delves St CHSE CH3 ....143 K3
Delvine Dr CHNE CH2 ....121 N5
Delwood Gdns
  WYTH/NTH M22 ....54 F3
Demage Dr GTS/LS CH66 ....101 P1
Demage La CH/BCN CH1 ....120 C1
  CHNE CH2 ....121 N3
De-massey Cl MPL/ROM SK6 * 42 C2
Demmings Rd CHD/CHDH SK8 ....55 N6
Denbigh Av STHEL WA9 ....31 H1
  FROD/HEL WA6 ....104 D3
Denbigh Cl EP CH65 ....102 F1
Denbigh Crs MCC CW10 ....151 J3
Denbigh Dr WSFD CW7 ....149 K3
Denbigh Gdns EP CH65 ....102 F1
Denbigh Rd DTN/ASHW M34 ....29 M8
Denbigh St CH/BCN CH1 ....2 D1
  HTNM SK4 ....16 D1
Denbury Av WARRS WA4 ....49 H5
Denbury Dr ALT WA14 ....53 K8
Denbury Gn BRAM/HZG SK7 ....56 G5
Denby La HTNM SK4 ....16 B4
Dene Av NEWLW WA12 ....23 K5
Dene Brow DTN/ASHW M34 ....29 P9
Dene Dr HTNM SK4 ....16 B2
Dene Dr WSFD CW7 ....149 M2
Denefield Cl MPL/ROM SK6 ....43 N7
Deneford Av DID/WITH M20 ....39 M3
Dene Hollow RDSH SK5 ....28 G8
Denehurst Cl
  WARRW/BUR WA5 ....47 K3
Denehurst Park Wy
  NWCHW CW8 ....107 P7
Dene Pk DID/WITH M20 ....39 M3
Dene Rd DID/WITH M20 ....40 B5
Dene Rd West DID/WITH M20 ....40 A5
Denesgate WSFD CW7 ....149 M2
Deneside Av CW/HAS CW1 ....185 J2
Deneside Crs BRAM/HZG SK7 ....57 N4
Denesway SALE M33 ....38 B5
Deneway BRAM/HZG SK7 ....56 C8
Deneway HTNM SK4 ....16 A2
Deneway Ms HTNM SK4 ....16 A2
Denford Cl CHSW/BR CH4 ....140 C6
Denford Pl ALS/KID ST7 ....187 P2
Denhall Cl CHNE CH2 ....121 N6
Denhall La NSTN CH64 ....99 N2
Denham Av WARRW/BUR WA5 ....47 M2
Denham Dr BRAM/HZG SK7 ....56 J8
  IRL M44 ....27 M8
Denholm Rd DID/WITH M20 ....39 M3
Denise Av WARRW/BUR WA5 ....47 J2
Denman Wy WARR WA1 ....30 D1
Denison Rd BRAM/HZG SK7 ....57 J7
Deniston Rd HTNM SK4 ....41 J3
Den La NANT CW5 ....198 F9
Denmark Rd SALE M33 ....38 C2
Denmark St ALT WA14 ....53 H5
Dennett Cl WARR WA1 ....49 N1
Dennis Av CW/SHV CW2 ....204 G5
Dennis Dr CHSW/BR CH4 ....142 D4
Dennis Rd WDN WA8 ....46 B8
Densham Av WARRN/WOL WA2 ....33 L8
Denshaw Cl DTN/ASHW M34 ....29 H4
Denshaw Dr BNG/LEV M19 ....40 D5
Denson Rd HALE/TIMP WA15 ....38 B8
Denston Cl CW/SHV CW2 ....185 H7

Denstone Av SALE M33 ....38 B5
Denstone Dr CHSW/BR CH4 ....142 C6
Denstone Rd RDSH SK5 ....28 F8
Dentith Dr CH/BCN CH1 ....121 H6
Denton Av DID/WITH M20 ....39 P3
Denton Dr NWCHE CW9 ....110 C3
Denton Hall Farm Rd
  DTN/ASHW M34 ....29 J7
Denton Rd DTN/ASHW M34 ....29 H3
Denton St WDN WA8 ....46 A6
Denver Av CW/SHV CW2 ....189 P3
Denver Dr HALE/TIMP WA15 ....53 L1
Denver Rd WARRS WA4 ....48 D8
Denville Crs WYTH/NTH M22 ....54 G4
Denzell Gdns ALT WA14 * 52 E4
Depenbech Cl MALPAS SY14 ....204 A3
Depleach Rd CHD/CHDH SK8 ....55 M2
Depmore La FROD/HEL WA6 ....106 E2
Deptford Av NTHM/RTH M23 ....54 C4
De Quincey Rd ALT WA14 ....38 A7
Derby Av IRL M44 ....36 B3
Derby Cl SALE M33 ....38 F5
Derby Dr WARR WA1 ....34 A6
Derby Gv BNG/LEV M19 ....28 B8
Derby Pl CHNE CH2 ....121 P8
Derby Range SK4 ....41 J4
Derby Rd ALS/KID ST7 ....188 F9
  DTN/ASHW M34 ....41 K4
  NM/HAY SK22 ....59 P6
  RUSH/FAL M14 ....28 A5
  SALE M33 ....38 B2
  WARRS WA4 ....48 E7
  WDN WA8 ....45 P4
  WDN WA8 ....46 B3
Derby Rw CHD/CHDH SK8 * 55 H4
Derbyshire Hill Rd STHEL WA9 ....22 E6
Derbyshire Rd PART M31 ....36 C6
  POY/DIS SK12 ....74 B1
  SALE M33 ....38 F4
Derbyshire Rd South SALE M33 ....38 G5
Derbyshire St OP/CLY M11 ....28 G3
Derby St ALT WA14 ....53 J2
  CONG CW12 ....155 M7
  CW/HAS CW1 ....185 H3
  EDGY/DAV SK3 ....16 D7
  NEWLW WA12 ....23 M7
  NEWLW WA12 ....23 M6
Dereham Wy RUNC WA7 ....63 H5
Derek Av WARRN/WOL WA2 ....33 N7
Dermot Murphy Cl
  DID/WITH M20 ....40 A2
Dernford Av BNG/LEV M19 ....40 C3
Derrington Av CW/SHV CW2 ....204 C5
Derry Av WYTH/NTH M22 ....54 G3
Derwen Rd EDGY/DAV SK3 ....41 M9
Derwent Av CCHDY M21 ....39 N3
  HALE/TIMP WA15 * 53 P7
Derwent Cl ALS/KID ST7 ....187 L4
  DTN/ASHW M34 ....29 H7
  GOL/RIS/CU WA3 ....26 A7
  HOLMCH CW4 ....131 M8
  MCFLDS SK11 ....116 G6
  NANT CW5 ....197 L1
  PART M31 ....36 B6
  RAIN/WH L35 ....30 A5
Derwent Crs ALS/KID ST7 ....189 L6
Derwent Dr BIDD ST8 ....175 M8
  CHD/CHDH SK8 ....55 P7
  CONG CW12 ....155 P9
  GTS/LS CH66 ....79 P8
  SALE M33 ....38 D6
  WILM/AE SK9 ....71 L1
Derwent Rd CHNE CH2 ....122 A6
  MPL/ROM SK6 ....58 C7
  WARRS WA4 ....48 C5
  WDN WA8 ....20 B8
Derwent Wy NSTN CH64 ....77 M7
  WILM/AE SK9 ....92 B6
Desford Av RNFD/HAY WA11 ....22 B3
Desmond Rd WYTH/NTH M22 ....54 C3
Desoto Rd WDN WA8 ....60 E1
Desoto Rd East WDN WA8 ....20 E7
De Tabley Rd MCFLDN SK10 ....116 B1
De the Traffords IRL M44 ....27 N8
Deva Av CHSW/BR CH4 ....141 P4
Deva Cl BRAM/HZG SK7 ....57 K6
  FLINT CH6 ....98 C7
  POY/DIS SK12 ....73 H2
Deva Gv BIDD ST8 ....175 K8
Deva Link CH/BCN CH1 ....121 K8
Deva Rd CW/SHV CW2 ....184 D4
Deva Ter CHSE CH3 ....3 H4
Deverill Av WGTN M18 ....28 F5
Devisdale Gra ALT WA14 * 52 F4
Devisdale Rd ALT WA14 ....52 F4
Devoke Rd WYTH/NTH M22 ....54 D5
Devon Cl MCFLDN SK10 ....116 F2
Devon Gdns
  DTN/ASHW M34 ....29 L8
Devon Gv BIDD ST8 ....175 K8
Devon Rd PART M31 ....36 D6
Devonshire Dr ALT WA14 ....93 K3
Devonshire Gdns
  NEWLW WA12 ....23 N7
Devonshire Park Rd OFTN SK2 ....56 G2
Devonshire Pl CH/BCN CH1 ....2 D1
  RUNC WA7 ....14 E2
Devonshire Rd ALT WA14 ....52 C1
  CHSW/BR CH4 ....140 C6
  CHNE CH2 ....140 G2
  HTNM SK4 ....41 J6
  NANT CW5 ....204 A4
Dewar Ct RUNC WA7 ....62 C5
De Warenne Cl WHITCH SY13 ....213 N6
Dewar St GOL/RIS/CU WA3 ....34 F5
Dewes Av CW/HAS CW1 ....174 F5
Dewey St OP/CLY M11 ....28 D1
Dewhurst Rd GOL/RIS/CU WA3 ....34 E6

Dewint Av MPL/ROM SK6 ....43 N8
Dexter Wy MWCH CW10 ....130 C9
Dial La CONG CW12 ....156 G9
Dial Park Rd OFTN SK2 ....57 K3
Dial Rd HALE/TIMP WA15 ....53 N7
Dialstone La OFTN SK2 ....57 H3
Dial St WARR WA1 ....18 E5
Diamond Cl ALS/KID ST7 ....189 K6
Diamond Cl BIDD ST8 ....175 K9
Diamond St CONG CW12 ....156 C1
Diamond Ter MPL/ROM SK6 ....58 B4
Dickens Cl CHD/CHDH SK8 ....72 B1
  SBCH CW11 ....171 J3
Dickens La POY/DIS SK12 ....73 L5
Dickenson St WARRN/WOL WA2 ....19 F2
Dickinson Cl RNFD/HAY WA11 ....22 C5
Dickson Cl WDN WA8 ....21 J2
Dicksons Dr CHNE CH2 ....121 N6
Dickson St WARRW/BUR WA5 ....21 H2
Didcot Rd WYTH/NTH M22 ....54 E6
Didley Sq WGTN/LGST M12 * 28 A3
Didsbury Pk DID/WITH M20 ....39 P5
Didsbury Rd HTNM SK4 ....41 J7
Dierdens Ter CW10 ....151 J1
Dierden St WSFD CW7 ....150 B1
Diglake Cl ALS/KID ST7 ....201 M1
Diglake St ALS/KID ST7 ....201 J4
Diglands Av NM/HAY SK22 ....59 N6
Dig La CO OFTN
  FROD/HEL WA6 ....83 N6
  NANT CW5 ....195 N3
  NANT CW5 ....198 A5
  WARRN/WOL WA2 ....34 B4
Diglee Rd CHF/WBR SK23 ....75 N5
Dilhorn CH/HAS CW1 ....169 P8
Dilworth Cl OFTN SK2 ....57 L2
Dinas Cl CHNE CH2 ....120 C8
Dingle Av NEWLW WA12 ....23 K7
  WILM/AE SK9 ....93 F2
Dingle Bank CHSW/BR CH4 ....140 G8
Dingle Bank Cl LYMM WA13 ....50 E4
Dingle Bank Rd BRAM/HZG SK7 ....56 D5
Dingle Cl MCFLDN SK10 ....117 H1
  MPL/ROM SK6 ....43 J6
Dingle Gv CHD/CHDH SK8 ....55 H1
Dingle La NANT CW5 ....210 F9
  SBCH CW11 ....171 P3
  TPLY/KEL CW6 ....125 K5
  WSFD CW7 ....149 M1
The Dingle BRAM/HZG SK7 ....56 C6
  CW/HAS CW1 ....186 B5
  HYDE SK14 ....42 G2
  LYMM WA13 ....51 H6
Dingle Wy NWCHW CW8 ....108 A7
Dingleway WARRS WA4 ....48 F7
Dinmor Rd WYTH/NTH M22 ....54 E7
Dinnington Ct WDN WA8 ....45 M4
Dinting Av DID/WITH M20 ....39 N3
Diploma Dr MWCH CW10 ....130 D9
  WARRS WA4 ....64 G2
Discovery Pk HTNM SK4 * 41 K3
Disley Av DID/WITH M20 ....40 A2
Distaff Rd POY/DIS SK12 ....73 H2
Ditchfield Cl WARR WA1 ....67 J3
Ditchfield Pl WDN WA8 ....45 M6
Ditchfield Rd
  WARRW/BUR WA5 ....45 M4
  WDN WA8 ....45 H7
Ditton Rd WDN WA8 ....21 H6
Dixon Av NEWLW WA12 ....23 L8
Dixon Cl RNFD/HAY WA11 ....23 L1
  SALE M33 ....38 G7
Dixon Dr MCFLDS SK11 ....114 B1
Dixon Rd CONG CW12 ....156 A5
  DTN/ASHW M34 ....29 P8
Dixon's Rw NEWLW ST5 ....201 N8
Dixon St IRL M44 ....27 L9
  WARR WA1 ....17 J7
Dobb Hedge Cl
  HALE/TIMP WA15 ....53 N9
Dobbinetts La HALE/TIMP WA15 ....54 A4
  NTHM/RTH M23 ....54 A3
Dobcross Cl BRUN/LGST M13 ....28 A7
Dobell's Rd NWCHE CW9 ....13 F7
  FROD/HEL WA6 ....84 B9
Dock Rd NWCHE CW9 ....13 F1
  WDN WA8 ....61 N1
Dock St EP CH65 ....6 E1
  WDN WA8 ....61 N1
Dock Yard Rd EP CH65 ....7 H3
Doctors Cl BIDD ST8 ....175 J5
Doddington Dr SBCH CW11 ....171 P1
Doddington Rd CW/SHV CW2 ....189 N3
Doddington Wk
  DTN/ASHW M34 ....29 L8
Dodd's Gates La WHITCH SY13 ....215 L3
Dodd's La CONG CW12 ....174 D2
  MALPAS SY14 ....203 M6
  WARRS WA4 ....65 J1
Dodge Fold OFTN SK2 ....57 L1
Dodge Hill HTNM SK4 ....17 F2
Dodgsley Dr FROD/HEL WA6 ....83 M6
Dodington SY13 ....213 M6
Dodleston La CHSW/BR CH4 ....160 F6
Doeford Cl GOL/RIS/CU WA3 ....25 H4
Dog La CHSE CH3 ....145 J1
  HOLMCH CW4 ....131 P8
  MALPAS SY14 ....203 L7
  NANT CW5 ....10 B4
  TPLY/KEL CW6 ....124 G6
Dogmore La TPLY/KEL CW6 ....147 P3
Dolphin Cl WARRS WA4 ....61 P4
Dolphin Crs GTS/LS CH66 ....102 A2
Dombey Rd POY/DIS SK12 ....73 H4
Domestic Ap MANAIR M90 ....54 E9
The Dome ALT WA14 * 53 H3
Domine Cl NTHM/RTH M23 ....77 H3
Domville Cl LYMM WA13 ....51 H5
Donagh Cl MCFLDN SK10 ....116 F2
Dona St STKP SK1 ....17 K6

Doncaster Av DID/WITH M20 ....40 B1
Donkey La WILM/AE SK9 ....71 J9
Donne Pl CH/BCN CH1 ....121 K5
Donnington Av
  CHD/CHDH SK8 ....55 P2
Donnington Dr DTN/ASHW M18 ....55 F4
Donnington Wy CHSW/BR CH4 ....142 D3
Donnison St WGTN/LGST M12 ....28 A1
Don Wk EP CH65 ....80 C6
Doodson Av IRL M44 ....27 M7
Dooley La MPL/ROM SK6 ....42 G9
Dooley's Grig MCFLDS SK11 ....133 J2
Dooley's La WILM/AE SK9 ....70 C4
Dorac Av CHD/CHDH SK8 ....55 L9
Dorchester Av DTN/ASHW M34 ....29 M8
  HALE/TIMP WA15 ....53 M7
  WILM/AE SK9 ....71 M6
Dorchester Cl CHD/CHDH SK8 ....56 B6
  SALE M33 ....53 P9
Dorchester Dr NTHM/RTH M23 ....39 H7
Dorchester Pk RUNC WA7 ....63 H5
Dorchester Rd BRAM/HZG SK7 ....57 H6
  BIDD ST8 ....175 K8
  WARRW/BUR WA5 ....32 C2
Dorchester Wy MCFLDN SK10 ....117 J1
  WARRW/BUR WA5 ....32 C2
Doreen Av CONG CW12 ....175 J3
Dorfield Cl MPL/ROM SK6 ....42 D5
Dorfold Cl SBCH CW11 ....171 P2
Dorfold Dr CHNE CH2 ....121 P5
Dorfold St CW/HAS CW1 ....169 P8
Dorfold Wy CHNE CH2 ....121 P5
Dorgan Cl RAIN/WH L35 ....30 A1
Doric Av FROD/HEL WA6 ....84 A6
Doris Rd EDGY/DAV SK3 ....42 C5
Dorking Cl STKP SK1 ....17 A7
Dorlan Av GTN M18 ....28 E5
Dorland Gv OFTN SK2 ....42 A9
Dorman St OP/CLY M11 ....28 D3
Dormer Cl CHSE CH3 ....144 A5
Dormer St BOL BL1 ....48 J9
Dorney St GTN M18 ....28 D5
Dornoch Ct HOLMCH CW4 ....131 N9
Dorothea St WARRN/WOL WA2 ....19 F1
Dorothy Rd BRAM/HZG SK7 ....57 M4
Dorric Wy CW/HAS CW1 ....30 D1
Dorrington Cl RUNC WA7 ....185 J1
Dorrington Dr RUNC WA7 ....62 F5
  SALE M33 ....38 A4
Dorris St BRAM/HZG SK7 ....28 B9
Dorrit Cl POY/DIS SK12 ....73 L4
Dorset Av CW/SHV CW2 ....56 D6
Dorset Av CHD/CHDH SK8 ....56 C5
  DTN/ASHW M34 ....29 J5
  RDSH SK5 ....42 B3
Dorset Cl CONG CW12 ....155 N6
Dorset Dr BIDD ST8 ....175 K9
Dorset Pl ALS/KID ST7 ....189 J5
  CHNE CH2 ....122 B6
Dorset Rd ALT WA14 ....52 F5
  BNG/LEV M19 ....28 C9
  CHNE CH2 ....122 A4
  IRL M44 ....36 C2
Dorset St WK MCFLDN SK10 * 116 E2
Dorset Wy WARRW/BUR WA5 ....34 B6
Dougall Wk WGTN/LGST M12 ....31 N2
Douglas Cl NWCHW CW8 ....109 J1
  WDN WA8 ....45 D4
Douglas La WGTN/LGST M12 ....28 A3
Douglas Pl CHSW/BR CH4 ....140 G8
Douglas Rd BRAM/HZG SK7 ....57 L4
  EDGY/DAV SK3 ....56 E3
Doulton Cl WSFD CW7 ....128 G8
Dounte Ct EP CH65 ....102 F1
Dounrey Cl WARRN/WOL WA2 ....34 B6
Douthwaite Dr MPL/ROM SK6 ....43 K7
Dove Cl CHNE CH2 ....80 B6
  EP CH65 ....80 B6
  FROD/HEL WA6 ....83 J8
  GOL/RIS/CU WA3 ....34 G4
Dove Ct IRL M44 ....171 M1
Dovecot Cl CW/SHV CW2 ....189 N3
Dovecote Dr RNFD/HAY WA11 ....22 C5
Dovecote Gn WARRW/BUR WA5 ....32 D5
Dovedale Av DID/WITH M20 ....40 B5
Dovedale Cl BURS/TUN ST6 ....189 K9
  GOL/RIS/CU WA3 ....156 A6
  MPL/ROM SK6 ....58 C7
  WARRW/WOL WA2 ....33 P5
Dovedale Ct EDGY/DAV SK3 ....42 C9
Dove Dr IRL M44 ....27 M9
Dove Gv BIDD ST8 ....175 L8
Dove Rd BNG/LEV M19 ....28 C9
Dover Cl EP CH65 ....102 F2
Dover Ct EP CH65 ....102 F2
Dovercourt Av HTNM SK4 * 40 G5
  WSFD CW7 ....149 K4
Dover Rd CHSW/BR CH4 ....142 C5
  MCFLDN SK10 ....117 M2
  WARRS WA4 ....48 G7
Dover St RDSH SK5 * 41 M1
  RUNC WA7 ....15 G1
Doveston Rd SALE M33 ....38 E2
Doward St WDN WA8 ....46 A5
Dowes La WHITCH SY13 ....213 J4
Downall Cl MCFLDN SK10 * 116 H4
Downes Wy WYTH/NTH M22 ....54 F4
Downfields RDSH SK5 ....28 G8
Downham Av
  GOL/RIS/CU WA3 ....25 P7
Downham Cha
  HALE/TIMP WA15 ....53 M1
Downham Pl CH/BCN CH1 ....121 H7
Downham Rd CHNE CH2 ....141 L3
Downing Cl CHSW/BR CH4 ....142 C4
Downham Wk NTHM/RTH M23 ....38 G8
Downland Wy STHEL WA9 ....22 D9
Downs Dr ALT WA14 ....38 B8

Downs End KNUT WA16 ....90 G4
Downsfield Rd CHSW/BR CH4 ..142 B4
Downside WDN WA8 ....7 K4
Downs Rd RUNC WA7 ....15 F5
The Downs ALT WA14 ....53 H4
  CHD/CHDH SK8 ....55 M4
  NWCHW CW8 ....107 P7
Downway La STHEL WA9 ....22 E8
Doyle La MPL/ROM SK6 ....42 C5
Dragon's La MWCH CW10......151 N8
  SBCH CW11 ....151 P9
Dragon Sq NEWLL ST5 ....201 P7
Dragon Yd MWCH CW10 ......152 A9
Dragon Yd WDN WA8 ....45 P5
Drake Av IRL M44 ....36 D2
Drake Cl WARRW/BUR WA5 ....53 G7
Drake Ct RDSH SK5 ....41 M4
Drake Gdns STHEL WA9 ....30 D2
Drake Rd ALT WA14 ....37 N8
  NSTN CH64 ....5 K1
Drakes Wy MALPAS SY14 .....204 A1
Draycott Dr NEWLL ST5 ......201 N5
Drayford Cl NTHM/RTH M23 ...39 J6
Drayton Av CHD/CHDH SK8 ....55 K8
Drayton Cl RUNC WA7 ....14 C4
  SALE M33 ....38 A6
  WILM/AE SK9 ....71 M5
Drayton Crs CW/HAS CW1 .....5 K1
  RNFD/HAY WA11 ....22 E3
Drayton Gv HALE/TIMP WA15 ..53 L3
Drenfell Rd ALS/KID ST7 ....189 H1
The Dresser Cen OP/CLY M11 *..28 E2
Drill Field Rd NWCHE CW9 ...13 F3
The Drive ALS/KID ST7 ......201 K9
  CHD/CHDH SK8 ....56 C3
  DID/WITH M20 ....40 D5
  HALE/TIMP WA15 ....53 P7
  HOLMCH CW4 ....131 P9
  LYMM WA13 ....51 K6
  MPL/ROM SK6 ....58 C1
  SALE M33 ....38 B7
Dronfield Rd WYTH/NTH M22 ..54 N8
Drovers Wy SBCH CW11 ......171 M4
Drumber La ALS/KID ST7 ....174 C9
The Drumber WSFD CW7 ......149 M1
Drumble Fld MCFLDS SK11 ...114 C1
Drumburn Cl BURS/TUN ST6 ...199 P6
Drummond Av CW/HAS CW1 .....79 N9
Drummond Dr WDN WA8 ....46 B5
Drummond Rd BURS/TUN ST6 ..189 L9
Drummond Wy MCFLDN SK10 ..116 E3
Druridge Dr WARRW/BUR WA5 ..47 K3
Drury Cl CW/HAS CW1 ....5 K9
Drury La CW/HAS CW1 ....170 C5
  KNUT WA16 ....90 E5
Dryden St BNG/LEV M19 ......28 A8
Dryden Cl CHD/CHDH SK8 .....55 N1
Dryden Cl CW/SHV CW2 .....184 C8
  MPL/ROM SK6 ....58 C1
Dr P WARRN/WOL WA2 ....33 M6
Dryebeck Gv STHEL WA9 .....31 J2
Dryhurst La POY/DIS SK12 ...59 H9
Dryhurst La POY/DIS SK12 ...59 H9
Dublin Cft GTS/LS CH66 ....102 A3
Duchy Rd CW/HAS CW1 ......185 N8
Duchy St EDGY/DAV SK3 ......41 L9
Duck La CH64 ....124 E4
Duckworth Gv
  WARRN/WOL WA2 ....34 B7
Duddon Cl TPLY/KEL CW6 ....145 N4
Duddon Hook La
  TPLY/KEL CW6 ....145 M4
  TPLY/KEL CW6 ....145 P5
Dudleston Rd GTS/LS CH66 ...79 M7
Dudley Av RUNC WA7 ....62 B4
Dudley Crs PS/BROM CH62 ....79 M2
Dudley Pl STHEL WA9 ....22 B6
Dudley Rd EP CH65 ....38 E9
  HALE/TIMP WA15 ....38 E9
  IRL M44 ....36 C4
  SALE M33 ....38 F2
Dudley Rd DTN/ASHW M34 .....29 L5
  WARRN/WOL WA2 ....18 E1
Dudley Wk MCFLDS SK11 ....116 F5
Dudlow Green Rd
  WARRS WA4 ....64 F1
Duke Av CHD/CHDH SK8 ......55 P9
  GOL/RIS/CU WA3 ....26 C2
Duke Cl RUNC WA7 ....14 C2
Dukefield St WYTH/NTH M22 ..39 F8
Duke's Av SBCH CW11 ......171 M1
Duke St CH/BCN CH1 ....4 D3
  CW/SHV CW2 ....4 E3
  DTN/ASHW M34 ....29 L6
  FLINT CH6 ....98 A6
  MCFLDS SK11 ....11 H5
  NEWLW WA12 ....23 M6
  STKP SK1 ....17 F5
  WARR WA1 ....93 K3
Dukesway CHNE CH2 ....121 P4
Dukes Wy NWCHE CW9 ....109 N7
Dulas Ct CHNE CH2 ....121 P5
Dulgar St OP/CLY M11 * 28 B1
Dulverton Dr CHSE CW9 .....122 D9
Dulwich Cl SALE M33 ....38 A5
Dumbah La MCFLDN SK10 .....95 J7
Dumbarton Cl RDSH SK5 .....41 N2
Dumbarton Rd RDSH SK5 .....41 N3
Dumber La SALE M33 ....38 C2
Dumbers MCFLDS SK11 ......136 F9
Dunbar Av NTHM/RTH M23 ....54 C4
Dunbar Cl GTS/LS CH66 ......79 N8
  HOLMCH CW4 ....131 H9
Duncansby Crs
  WARRW/BUR WA5 ....47 J1
Duncansby Dr BEB CH63 ......78 C1

Duncan St DUK SK16 ....29 P3
  WARRN/WOL WA2 ....19 G1
Dunchurch Rd SALE M33 .....38 B4
Duncombe Cl BRAM/HZG SK7 ..56 C4
Dundalk La WDN WA8 ....20 B2
Dundalk Rd WDN WA8 ....20 B2
Dundee Cl WARRN/WOL WA2 ...33 P4
Dundee Ct EP CH65 ....12 C1
Dundonald Av WARRS WA4 ....48 E6
Dundonald Rd CHD/CHDH SK8 ..56 A8
  DID/WITH M20 ....40 D5
Dundonald St OFTN SK2 .....56 F1
Dundrennan Gv POY/DIS SK12 ..73 K1
Dunecroft DTN/ASHW M34 * ...29 N5
Dunedin St WDN WA8 ....38 C1
Dunelm Dr NTHM/RTH M23 ....38 D7
Dunham Cl ALS/KID ST7 ....187 N5
  PS/BROM CH62 ....79 K1
Dunham Ct EP CH65 ....38 D8
Dunham Crs CW/SHV CW2 ....185 H8
Dunham Lawn ALT WA14 .....52 F3
Dunham Ms ALT WA14 * 52 E5
Dunham Ri ALT WA14 ....52 C5
Dunham Rd ALT WA14 ....52 F3
  LYMM WA15 ....36 D9
  NWCHE CW9 ....109 P8
  PART M31 ....37 J5
  WILM/AE SK9 ....71 M5
Dunham Wy CHNE CH2 ....122 A5
Dunkeld Rd NTHM/RTH M23 ...54 B1
Dunkery Rd WYTH/NTH M22 ...54 F6
Dunkirk Av WSFD CW7 ......149 M2
Dunkirk Cl DTN/ASHW M34 ...28 F7
Dunkirk La ALS/KID ST7 ...102 C3
Dunkirk La CH/BCN CH1 ....101 N4
  GTS/LS CH66 ....102 C3
  HYDE SK14 ....29 P5
Dunley Cl GOL/RIS/CU WA3 ...5 L6
  WGTN/LGST M12 ....28 A4
Dunlin Cl NEWLW WA12 .....23 N5
Dunlin Cl OFTN SK2 ....57 N2
  POY/DIS SK12 ....72 C2
  RUNC WA7 ....62 D9
  WARRN/WOL WA2 ....33 P5
Dunlop Gv GOL/RIS/CU WA3 ..34 F4
Dunmail Gv RUNC WA7 ....84 C1
Dunmaston Av
  NTHM/RTH M23 ....38 G9
Dunmore Cl ASHW CW10 ....151 J3
Dunmore Crs GTS/LS CH66 ...79 M7
  GTS/LS CH66 ....79 M7
Dunmow Rd CHD/CHDH SK8 ...56 B1
Dunmow Rd DTN/ASHW M34 ...43 J5
Dunnillow Fld NANT CW5 ...197 H3
Dunnisher Rd NTHM/RTH M23 ..54 D3
Dunnock Cl OFTN SK2 ....57 M2
Dunnock Gv GOL/RIS/CU WA3 ..34 F4
Dunnocksfold Rd
  ALS/KID ST7 ....187 K4
Dunnockswood ALS/KID ST7 .187 L4
Dunnock Wy BIDD ST8 ......175 M9
Dunoon Cl HLMCH CW4 .....131 N9
Dunoon Rd RDSH SK5 ....41 N1
Dunraven Rd NSTN CH64 .....74 F6
Dunscar Cl GOL/RIS/CU WA3 ..34 F4
Dunscroft STHEL WA9 ....31 J1
Dunsfold Dr NTHM/RTH M23 ..38 G8
Dunsmore Cl RNFD/HAY WA11 ..22 C2
Dunsop Av STHEL WA9 ....31 J4
Dunstable Rd LYMM WA13 ....28 B8
Dunstall Rd WYTH/NTH M22 ..54 E6
Dunstan La NSTN CH64 .....100 C2
Dunster Av DTN/ASHW M34 ...29 L2
Dunster Av RDSH SK5 ....42 E3
  NWCHE CW9 ....110 A8
Dunster Gv WIRRL WA3 ......31 J4
Dunster Rd MCFLDN SK10 ....9 G1
Dunton Gn RDSH SK5 ....42 A2
Dunvegan Rd BRAM/HZG SK7 ..57 M6
Dunwood Dr ALS/KID ST7 ...187 P2
Durban Av CHSE CW9 ....143 M3
Durber Cl ALS/KID ST7 ....200 C6
Durham Dr MPL/ROM SK6 .....42 F7
  WARR WA1 ....46 F2
Durham Dr WSFD CW7 ....149 L3
Durham Gv IRL M44 ....36 C4
Durham Rd DTN/ASHW M34 ...121 J6
  WDN WA8 ....7 J4
Durham St DROY M43 ....28 C1
  RDSH SK5 ....28 E7
Durley Av HALE/TIMP WA15 ..38 E9
Duriston Cl WDN WA8 ....45 J5
Durrell Wy GOL/RIS/CU WA3 .26 A1
Dutton Gn EP CH65 ....103 H1
Dutton La FROD/HEL WA6 ...107 H6
Dutton's La TPLY/KEL CW6 ..24 A7
Dutton St CW/HAS CW1 * ...185 J10
  NANT CW5 ....196 F4
Duxford Ct WARRN/WOL WA2 ..33 P7
Dyar Ter NWCHW CW8 ....109 M3
Dye House La NM/HAY SK22 ...59 N7
Dye La MPL/ROM SK6 ....42 C6
Dyers Cl MCFLDN SK10 .....50 G3
Dyers Ct MCFLDN SK10 .....95 P5
Dyers La LYMM WA13 ....50 G3
Dyer St GOL/RIS/CU WA3 ....28 D1
  OP/CLY M11 ....28 B1
Dysart St STKP SK1 ....17 J7
Dyserth Gv RDSH SK5 ....41 N3
Dyserth Rd CH/BCN CH1 ....120 G8
Dysteleph Rd POY/DIS SK12 ..59 H9

E

Eadie Gv CW/HAS CW1 ......184 C5
Eagals Wy MCFLDN SK10 ....116 F2
Eagland Pl CONG CW12 .....155 N6
Eagle Brow LYMM WA13 .....50 D4
Eagle La GTS/LS CH66 ....79 P6
Eagle Park Dr
  WARRN/WOL WA2 ....33 K7
Eaglesfield NWCHW CW8 ....109 L8
Eaglesfield Cl STHEL WA9 * ..31 H1
Eagles Wy RUNC WA7 ....62 C8
Ealing Pl BNG/LEV M19 * 41 H2
Ealing Rd WARRW/BUR WA5 ...47 L2
Eanleywood La RUNC WA7 ....62 C7
Eardley Crs CONG CW12 ....155 M6
Eardleyend Rd ALS/KID ST7 ..188 A9
Eardswick Cl CHNE CH2 ....121 N8
Eardswick La MWCH CW10 ..151 J4
Earle Cl NEWLW WA12 ....23 K6
Earle Ct NSTN CH64 ....77 K4
Earle Dr NSTN CH64 ....77 L5
Earle Rd BRAM/HZG SK7 .....56 E5
  WDN WA8 ....21 K5
Earlesfield Cl SALE M33 ....38 A6
Earles La NWCHE CW9 ....88 E7
  TPLY/KEL CW6 ....125 H6
Earle St CW/HAS CW1 ....5 H3
  CW/HAS CW1 ....5 H3
  NEWLW WA12 ....23 K7
Earl Rd CHD/CHDH SK8 ......71 N1
  HTNM SK4 ....41 K4
  WDN WA8 ....71 N2
Earls Gdns EP CH65 ....2 B5
Earls Oak CHNE CH2 ....121 N4
Earls Port CH/BCN CH1 ....2 B3
Earls Cv CW/SHV CW2 ......198 A3
Earlston Av DTN/ASHW M34 ..28 C6
Earlston Ct CHSE CH3 ....3 J4
Earls St DTN/ASHW M34 .....28 C6
  EDGY/DAV SK3 ....16 C7
  FLINT CH6 ....98 A5
  STHEL WA9 ....22 A5
  WARRN/WOL WA2 ....18 E1
Earlsway CW/SHV CW2 ......142 C3
  MCFLDS SK11 ....12 A6
Earls Wy NWCHE CW9 ....109 N8
Earl Wy EP CH65 ....62 C8
Earnley Cl NANT CW5 ......196 E5
Earnshaw Av STKP SK1 ......42 A7
Easby Cl CHD/CHDH SK8 .....55 L6
  RUNC WA7 ....15 J5
Easenhall Cl WDN WA8 ......45 P3
Easington Rd STHEL WA9 ....30 C2
East Av BNG/LEV M19 ....40 C1
  CHD/CHDH SK8 ....55 M7
  CW/SHV CW2 ....199 H2
  MCFLDN SK10 ....9 H5
  NWCHE CW9 ....110 D6
  WARRN/WOL WA2 ....33 M8
  WARRS WA4 ....48 F6
  WARRW/BUR WA5 ....47 L3
Eastbury Cl WDN WA8 ....45 N3
Eastcote Rd RDSH SK5 .....41 N3
Eastcott Cl CONG CW12 ....155 N6
East Cl ALS/KID ST7 ....189 K6
Eastdale Pl ALT WA14 ....38 A9
Eastdale Rd WARR WA1 ......34 B9
East Downs Rd ALT WA14 ....55 P5
  CHD/CHDH SK8 ....55 P5
East Dr BIDD ST8 ....175 L9
  MPL/ROM SK6 ....58 D4
East Dudley St WSFD CW7 ..149 P1
Easter Ct WARRW/BUR WA5 ...32 E6
Eastern By-Pass OP/CLY M11 ..28 D1
Eastern Cir EDGY/DAV SK3 ..41 H7
Eastern Pathway
  CHSE CH4 ....3 G7
Eastern Rd NANT CW5 ......197 M2
Eastfields Gv CH/BCN CH1 ..120 D5
Eastford Rd WARRS WA4 ....48 E6
Eastgate Mcfldn SK10 ....9 H5
Eastgate Rd HOLMCH CW4 ...132 A8
  RUNC WA7 ....63 J1
Eastgate Rw North CH/BCN CH1 .2 E4
Eastgate Rw South CH/BCN CH1 .2 E4
Eastgate St CH/BCN CH1 .....2 E4
Eastern Cl EDGY/DAV SK3 ....17 J6
Eastham Ms PS/BROM CH62 ...79 L1
Eastham Rake GTS/LS CH66 ..78 G3
Eastholme Dr BNG/LEV M19 ..41 J1
Eastleigh Dr NTHM/RTH M23 ..40 C1
East Lancashire Rd
  GOL/RIS/CU WA3 ....24 D3
  RNFD/HAY WA11 ....22 B1
East La NWCHW CW8 ....108 C9
  RUNC WA7 ....62 D7
East Lawns ALD/MAD/W CW3 .199 M9
East Lea DTN/ASHW M34 .....29 K2
Eastleigh Rd CHD/CHDH SK8 ..55 K6
East Mains SPK/HALE L24 ....60 A3
East Meade CHDDY M21 .....54 G2
East Millwood Rd SPK/HALE L24 .60 A2
East Park Rd MCFLDS SK11 ..117 H7
East Rd DTN M18 ....28 D2
  MANAIR M90 ....54 E8
  MWCH CW10 ....151 H1
  SPK/HALE L24 ....60 B1
  WGTN/LGST M12 ....28 D2
Eastry Av RDSH SK5 ....42 E3
East Side STHEL WA9 ....22 A7
East St DTN/ASHW M34 ......46 B6
  WARRS WA4 ....49 K5
East Vw NANT CW5 ....10 C4
  WARRS WA4 ....49 K5

Eastville Gdns BNG/LEV M19 ..40 F3
Eastward Av WILM/AE SK9 ....71 H8
Eastway GTS/LS CH66 ....79 P6
  SALE M33 ....38 C7
Eastwood Rd WARR WA1 .....20 A1
Eastwood Cl STHEL WA9 .....62 G5
Eastwood Dr NEWLW WA12 ...24 B6
Eastwood Rd
  WARRW/BUR WA5 ....32 C1
Eastwood St DTN/ASHW M34 ..29 K2
Eaton Av CHSW/BR CH4 .....142 F3
  GTS/LS CH66 ....155 P5
Eaton Crt CHD/CHDH SK8 ....55 P1
  CHSW/BR CH4 ....140 C6
  POY/DIS SK12 ....73 N3
  SBCH CW11 ....171 P7
Eaton Crs NWCHE CW9 ......128 F1
Eaton Dr HALE/TIMP WA15 ...38 D8
  WILM/AE SK9 ....93 H3
Eaton Gv CHSW/BR CH4 ....142 A5
Eaton La HOLMCH CW4 .....117 K7
  MCFLDN SK11 ....117 K7
  NWCHE CW9 ....128 E1
  TPLY/KEL CW6 ....147 L4
Eaton Ms CHSW/BR CH4 ....142 F3
Eaton Rd ALS/KID ST7 .....187 N4
  ALT WA14 ....52 G6
  CHSW/BR CH4 ....142 F3
  TPLY/KEL CW6 ....147 N9
  WSFD CW7 ....167 M2
Eaton St CW/SHV CW2 ....4 E3
  RUNC WA7 ....14 C3
Eaton Vw NWCHE CW9 ......128 F3
Eaton Wy ALD/MAD/W CW3 ..27 P1
Eaves Brow Rd
  GOL/RIS/CU WA3 ....34 C1
Eaves Knoll Rd NM/HAY SK22 .59 L6
Eaves La STHEL WA9 ....30 G2
Ebbdale Cl STKP SK1 ....17 J7
Ebenezer St RNFD/HAY WA11 .22 D3
  MALPAS SY14 ....192 C9
Ebor Rd WYTH/NTH M22 * 54 C3
Ebury Pl CHSW/BR CH4 ....142 F3
Ecclesbridge Rd MPL/ROM SK6 .58 D2
Eccles Cl WF/WBR SK23 .....75 P6
Eccles Ct NSTN CH64 ....77 K4
Eccles Gv CHSW/BR CH4 ...142 A5
Eccleston Av CHSW/BR CH4 .142 F4
  GTS/LS CH66 ....80 A8
Eccleston Cl GOL/RIS/CU WA3 .34 D4
Eccleston Dr RUNC WA7 .....15 K5
Eccleston Rd EDGY/DAV SK3 ..54 A5
Eccups La WILM/AE SK9 .....70 E6
Echo Cl CHSW/BR CH4 .....142 A5
Eckersley Cl NTHM/RTH M23 ..54 B1
Ecton Av MCFLDN SK10 ....116 D3
Ecton Cl WSFD CW7 ....129 H7
Edale Av DTN/ASHW M34 .....54 C6
Edale Av DTN/ASHW M34 .....29 M9
  RDSH SK5 ....28 C8
Edale Cl ALT WA14 ....52 G6
  BRAM/HZG SK7 ....57 L6
  BURS/TUN ST6 ....189 K9
  CHD/CHDH SK8 ....71 N8
  IRL M44 ....36 A3
Edale Dr TPLY/KEL CW6 ....125 J6
Edale Gv SALE M33 ....38 B6
Eddarbridge Est WDN WA8 * ..61 M7
Eddisbury Dr NEWLL ST5 ...201 N5
Eddisbury Hi NWCHW CW8 ...125 J6
Eddisbury Rd GTS/LS CH66 ..102 B2
Eddisbury Ter MCFLDS SK11 ..9 J5
  CHSE CH3 ....106 A9
  CHSE CH3 ....125 H2
  CHSE CH3 ....164 F3
Eddisbury Wy CHSE CH3 ....180 A1
  NWCHE CW9 ....128 E1
Eden Av GOL/RIS/CU WA3 ....25 M4
Edelsten St WARRW/BUR WA5 .48 B2
Eden Av ALS/KID ST7 ......189 K6
  MPL/ROM SK6 ....58 C8
  WSFD CW7 ....128 G9
Edenbridge Cl CW/SHV CW2 ..19 B6
Edenbridge Gdns WARR WA1 ..64 G5
Edenbridge Rd CHD/CHDH SK8 ..56 B8
Eden Cl ALS/KID ST7 ......189 K6
  BIDD ST8 ....175 M8
  GTS/LS CH66 ....79 N8
  STKP SK1 ....17 J6
  WILM/AE SK9 ....70 G9
Edendale WDN WA8 ....45 H5
Edendale Dr WYTH/NTH M22 ..54 F6
Eden Dr MCFLDN SK10 ....9 K7
Edenfield Cl KNUT WA16 ....91 L2
Edenfield Rd KNUT WA16 ....91 L2
Edenhall Cl HOLMCH CW4 ..131 M8
Edenhurst Dr HALE/TIMP WA15 .53 M2
Eden Pl CHD/CHDH SK8 .....55 M8
Edensor Dr HALE/TIMP WA15 ..53 M3
Edensor St NEWLL ST5 .....201 P8
Edgar Pl CHSW/BR CH4 ....2 E7
Edgars Dr WARRN/WOL WA2 ..34 B6
Edgecroft CHSW/BR CH4 ....163 P8
Edgedale Av BNG/LEV M19 ...40 F3
Edge Gv CHNE CH2 ....3 J1
Edgefield CHSW/BR CH4 ....142 A5
Edge La La MALPAS SY14 ...192 C6
  OP/CLY M11 ....28 E1
Edgeley Fold EDGY/DAV SK3 ..41 K9
Edgeley Gdns WHITCH SY13 .213 N7
Edgeley Rd EDGY/DAV SK3 ...41 K9
  WHITCH SY13 ....213 N7
Edgemoor ALT WA14 ....52 E5
Edgerley La CHSE CW9 .....177 L2
Edgerton Rd GOL/RIS/CU WA3 .24 C1
Edge St STHEL WA9 ....30 B2
Edge View La KNUT WA16 ....92 D3
Edgeview Rd CHSE CW9 ....130 G6
Edgeway MCFLDS SK11 .....116 C4

Edgewell La TPLY/KEL CW6 ..147 L7
Edgeworth Dr CW/SHV CW2 .184 G9
Edgeworth Cl STHEL WA9 ....21 J2
Edgeworth Dr RUSH/FAL M14 ..40 F1
Edgeworth St WARR WA1 ....31 J5
Edgworth St WARR WA1 .....20 A1
Edinburgh Cl CHD/CHDH SK8 ..55 P1
Edinburgh Ct EP CH65 .....102 F1
Edinburgh Dr MCFLDN SK10 .116 G3
  MPL/ROM SK6 ....43 H4
Edinburgh Rd CONG CW12 ..155 P8
  CW/SHV CW2 ....188 E8
  WDN WA8 ....44 G7
Edinburgh Wy CHSW/BR CH4 ..3 H6
Edison Rd RUNC WA7 ....62 B3
Edison St OP/CLY M11 ......28 E2
Edith St RUNC WA7 ....14 D1
  STHEL WA9 ....1 H5
Edleston Hall La NANT CW5 .195 P5
Edleston Rd CW/SHV CW2 .....5 H5
Edlinburgh Cl SALE M33 ....38 G5
Edmondson St STHEL WA9 * ..22 D6
Edmonton Rd EDGY/DAV SK3 ..56 G3
Edmund Cl HTNM SK4 ....41 M5
Edmund St DROY M43 ....28 C1
Edmund Wright Wy
  NANT CW5 ....196 D2
Edna Cl CHNE CH2 ....3 J1
Edward Cl ALT WA14 ....37 N9
Edward Gdns WARR WA1 ....49 H2
Edward German Dr
  WHITCH SY13 ....213 N6
Edwards Av WARRN/WOL WA5 .47 H1
Edwards Av CW/SHV CW2 ....198 B2
Edwards Cl CW/SHV CW2 ....198 A2
  MPL/ROM SK6 ....58 C2
Edwards St ALS/KID ST7 ...201 L4
  CW/SHV CW2 ....5 F7
  DROY M43 ....29 K2
  DTN/ASHW M34 ....5 G6
  EP CH65 ....6 E5
  MCFLDS SK11 ....11 G5
  MPL/ROM SK6 ....43 M7
  OP/CLY M11 ....110 C4
  RNFD/HAY WA11 ....10 C5
  SALE M33 ....39 H4
  STHEL WA9 ....17 G6
  WDN WA8 ....46 B6
Edwards Wy ALS/KID ST7 ...188 A4
  MPL/ROM SK6 ....58 C2
Edwin Dr FLINT CH6 ....98 B7
Edwin St STKP SK1 ....17 J7
  WDN WA8 ....46 A6
Egerton Cl CHD/CHDH SK8 ...46 C5
Egerton KNUT WA16 ....67 J1
Egerton Ct LYMM WA13 .....56 B8
  NWCHW CW8 ....109 J8
  WARR WA1 ....33 P9
Egerton Dr DID/WITH M20 * ..40 C7
Egerton Dr CHNE CH2 .....121 N6
Egerton La SALE M33 ....38 E5
Egerton Ms DROY M43 *......28 C1
Egerton Pl WHITCH SY13 ...213 M5
Egerton Gdns CHSE CH4 ....144 A5
  EDGY/DAV SK3 ....41 K9
  HALE/TIMP WA15 ....50 C5
  LYMM WA13 ....50 C5
  WHITCH SY13 ....213 N5
  WILM/AE SK9 ....71 K6
Egerton Rd North HTNM SK4 ..41 K3
Egerton Rd South HTNM SK4 ..41 K3
Egerton St CH/BCN CH1 .....120 C6
  DTN/ASHW M34 ....29 K4
  EP CH65 ....6 C5
  RUNC WA7 ....14 D2
  STHEL WA9 ....22 B8
  WARR WA1 ....33 P9
  WARRS WA4 ....48 E6
Egerton Ter RUSH/FAL M14 ..40 E1
Egerton Vw CHSW/BR CH4 ..140 E8
Eggbridge La CHSE CH4 ....144 A5
Egremont Av CHD/CHDH SK8 ..71 N1
Egremont Cl NTHM/RTH M23 ..40 B1
  RAIN/WH L35 ....30 A1
Egremont Lawn NTHLY L27 ...24 A3
Egret Cl IRL M44 ....27 N6
Egypt St WARR WA1 ....21 F4
  WDN WA8 ....21 F4
Eisenhower Cl
  WARRW/BUR WA5 ....47 M2
Elaine Cl GTS/LS CH66 .....79 N9
  WDN WA8 ....44 A8
Elaine St WARR WA1 ....19 J2
Elandor Rd SBCH CW11 ....171 J2
Elanor St WARR WA1 ....19 J3
Elcho Rd ALT WA14 ....52 F5
Elcho St ALT WA14 * 18 C5
Elcombe Av GOL/RIS/CU WA3 .25 N6
Elderberry Wy WILM/AE SK9 .71 N6
Elder Cl OFTN SK2 ....57 M2
Eldercroft Rd HALE/TIMP WA15 .53 N2
Elder Dr CHSW/BR CH4 ....142 A5
Elderfield Dr MPL/ROM SK6 ..42 E4
Elderswood Rd RAIN/WH L35 .30 A1
Eldon Cl DTN/ASHW M34 ....41 K9
Eldon Dr EDGY/DAV SK3 ....41 K9
  MCFLDN SK10 ....116 F4
Eldon St WARR WA1 ....19 J3
Eldon Ter NSTN CH64 ......77 K4
Eleanor Cl CW/HAS CW1 ...184 F3
Eleanor St EP CH65 ....7 F2
  WDN WA8 ....21 H5
Electo St OP/CLY M11 ......28 B1
Electra Wy CW/HAS CW1 ...185 M6
Electricity St CW/SHV CW2 ...4 E4

Elephant La STHEL WA9 .....30 D1
Elf Mill Cl EDGY/DAV SK3 .....56 E1
Elford Gv GTN M18 .....28 A6
Elgar La EP CH65 .....102 B1
Elgar St WGTN/LGST M12 .....28 A6
Elgin Av DTN/ASHW M20 * 40 E5
  HOLMCH CW4 .....131 N9
  MCFLDN SK10 .....116 G2
  WARRS WA4 .....48 C5
Elgin Cl CHSE CH3 .....122 B8
Elgin Ct CHSW/BR CH4 * 30 C6
Elgin Dr SALE M33 .....53 H5
Elgol Cl EDGY/DAV SK3 .....56 E6
Elgood La BURS/TUN ST6 .....189 L9
Eliot Cl CW/HAS CW1 .....185 N4
Elizabethan Wy NWCHE CW9 .....109 L4
  POY/DIS SK12 .....75 H1
  STKP SK1 .....17 H7
Elizabeth Av TPLY/KEL CW6 .....125 J7
Elizabeth Ct ALS/KID ST7 .....201 N2
  HTNM SK4 .....16 A2
  RUSH/FAL M14 .....40 E1
  WDN WA8 .....21 J5
Elizabeth Crs CHSW/BR CH4 .....3 H6
  WARR WA4 .....34 B8
Elizabeth Rd PART M31 .....36 E4
  WDN WA8 .....23 J2
Elizabeth Slinger Rd
  DID/WITH M20 .....39 P4
Elizabeth St CONG CW12 .....155 L8
  CW/HAS CW1 .....185 H3
  DTN/ASHW M34 .....29 L6
  MCFLDS SK11 .....8 E5
  STHEL WA9 .....22 C9
  STHEL WA9 .....31 J1
  WHITCH SY13 .....213 N5
Elizabeth Ter WDN WA8 .....20 B1
Eliza St STHEL WA9 .....31 L1
Elkan Cl WDN WA8 .....46 C4
Elkan Rd WDN WA8 .....46 B4
Elk Vw MALPAS SY14 .....202 C9
Ellaby Rd RAIN/WH L35 .....90 F3
Ellamsbridge Rd STHEL WA9 .....31 K1
Elland Dr GTS/LS CH66 .....79 N8
Ellenbrook Cl WGTN/LGST M12 .....28 B5
Ellen Brook Rd WYTH/NTH M22 .....54 F7
Ellen Gdn STHEL WA9 .....31 K1
Ellen St DROY M43 .....29 H1
  HTNM SK4 .....41 L5
  STHEL WA9 .....31 K1
  WARRW/BUR WA5 .....18 A2
Ellen Wilkinson Crs
  WGTN/LGST M12 .....28 A4
Ellerby Cl RUNC WA7 .....63 J7
Ellerslie Av RAIN/WH L35 .....30 B3
Ellerton Av GTS/LS CH66 .....79 N8
Ellerton Cl WDN WA8 .....45 K4
Ellesmere Av CHNE CH2 .....121 N6
  CHSW/BR CH4 .....141 H6
  MPL/ROM SK6 .....58 D1
Ellesmere Cl SBCH CW11 .....171 K1
Ellesmere Dr CHD/CHDH SK8 .....56 A2
Ellesmere Pl CW/HAS CW1 .....185 H3
Ellesmere Rd ALT WA14 .....53 H1
  EDGY/DAV SK3 .....43 J5
  GOL/RIS/CU WA3 .....25 N5
  NWCHE CW9 .....110 A8
  WARRS WA4 .....48 D6
  WHITCH SY13 .....212 D8
Ellesmere Rd North HTNM SK4 .....41 K5
Ellesmere St RUNC WA7 .....15 G2
  WARR WA1 .....19 G3
Ellesmere Ter RUSH/FAL M14 .....40 E1
Ellesworth Cl WARRW/BUR WA5 .....32 F8
Ellingham Wy NWCHE CW9 .....109 N9
Elliott Av WDN WA8 .....21 J2
Elliott Dr SALE M33 .....38 B4
Ellis La FROD/HEL WA6 .....82 E9
Ellison St WARRS WA4 .....48 F6
Ellis St CW/HAS CW1 .....21 F5
Ellon Av RAIN/WH L35 .....30 C6
Elloway Rd SPK/HALE L24 .....60 A3
Ellwood Cl SPK/HALE L24 .....60 A2
Ellwood Cn CW/SHV CW2 .....198 D4
Ellwood Rd STKP SK1 .....A7
Elm Av WDN WA8 .....45 H2
Elmbank Av DID/WITH M20 .....39 P4
Elm Beds Rd POY/DIS SK12 .....14 A4
Elm Cl ALS/KID ST7 .....189 K8
  CW/SHV CW2 .....184 E6
  POY/DIS SK12 .....73M3
  TPLY/KEL CW6 .....147 H8
  WHITCH SY13 .....213 L7
Elm Crs WILM/AE SK9 .....93 K5
Elmdale Av CHD/CHDH SK8 .....56 A1
Elm Dr CW/HAS CW1 .....185 L2
  DTN/ASHW M34 .....29 K4
  HOLMCH CW4 .....132 A7
  MCFLDN SK10 .....117 L2
Elmfield Av WYTH/NTH M22 .....39 H8
Elmfield Dr MPL/ROM SK6 .....58 C1
Elmfield Rd DTN/ASHW M34 .....29 L6
  EDGY/DAV SK3 .....56 F2
  WILM/AE SK9 .....93 K5
Elmgate Gv BNG/LEV M19 .....28 A8
Elm Gv ALS/KID ST7 .....188 A4
  CHSW/BR CH4 .....142 A5
  DID/WITH M20 .....40 C5
  GTS/LS CH66 .....102 C3
  SALE M33 .....38 B5
  WARR WA1 .....34 A9
  WILM/AE SK9 .....93 J3
  WYTH/NTH M22 .....150 A1
Elmhurst Dr BNG/LEV M19 .....40 C3
Elmley Cl OFTN SK2 .....57 N2
Elmore Cl HOLMCH CW4 .....131 N8
  RUNC WA7 .....63 H5

Elmridge Dr HALE/TIMP WA15 .....53 N7
Elmridge Wy NWCHW CW8 .....12 A1
Elm Rl FROD/HEL WA6 .....84 A6
  MCFLDN SK10 .....94 E7
Elms Cl DID/WITH SK8 .....55 J2
  CONG CW12 .....155 K7
Elm St DID/WITH M20 .....40 B4
  GOL/RIS/CU WA3 .....35 P6
  HALE/TIMP WA15 .....53 J4
  MPL/ROM SK6 .....58 D8
  MWCH CW10 .....151 K3
  NSTN CH64 .....77 K5
  NWCHW CW8 .....108 F5
  RNFD/HAY WA11 * 23 J2
  RUNC WA7 .....15 K6
  WARRN/WOL WA2 .....33 L4
  WARRW/BUR WA5 .....45 K4
Elm Rd South EDGY/DAV SK3 .....41 H9
Elmsett Cl WARRW/BUR WA5 .....47 J2
Elmsleigh Rd CHD/CHDH SK8 .....55 J4
Elmsmere Rd DID/WITH M20 .....40 C5
Elm Sq CHSW/BR CH4 .....142 B4
Elm St EP CH65 .....80 E6
Elmstead Av WDN WA8 .....40 B2
Elmstead Crs CW/HAS CW1 .....169 N9
Elmstead Rd MCFLDS SK11 .....114 C1
Elmstead Cl CHD/CHDH SK8 .....56 B4
The Elms GOL/RIS/CU WA3 .....25 H2
  KNUT WA16 * 92 A3
  MALPAS SY14 .....202 C9
  RUNC WA7 .....14 D5
Elm St MPL/ROM SK6 .....42 E4
  NWCHE CW9 .....13 K1
Elmsway BRAM/HZG SK7 .....56 C8
  HALE/TIMP WA15 .....53M7
  MCFLDN SK10 .....95 N6
  MPL/ROM SK6 .....58 C9
Elmsworth Av RAIN/WH L35 .....30 D6
Elmsworth Av BNG/LEV M19 .....28 B8
Elm Tree Av LYMM WA13 .....50 D5
  WARR WA1 .....34 A8
Elm Tree Ct TPLY/KEL CW6 .....147 L7
Elm Tree Dr ALS/KID ST7 .....201 J6
Elmtree Dr HTNM SK4 .....41 J6
Elm Tree Dr WYTH/NTH M22 .....54 F4
Elm Tree La SBCH CW11 .....171 J1
Elm Tree Rd GOL/RIS/CU WA3 .....25 H2
  LYMM WA13 .....50 D5
  MPL/ROM SK6 .....42 B5
Elmwood RUNC WA7 .....62 C5
  SALE M33 .....37 P4
Elmwood Av CHNE CH2 .....122 A7
  WARR WA1 .....19 K2
Elmwood Cl ALS/KID ST7 .....188 B4
Elmwood Gv NWCHW CW8 .....87 K9
Elsa Rd BNG/LEV M19 .....28 C8
Elsbeck Gv STHEL WA9 .....31 J2
Elsdon Dr GTN M18 .....28 B5
Elsham Gdns GTN M18 .....28 B5
Elsinore Av IRL M44 .....27 M8
Elsmere Av NEWLW WA12 .....23 M4
Elstree Av CHSE CH3 .....122 C8
Elstree Gv EDGY/DAV SK3 .....56 E6
Elswick Av BRAM/HZG SK7 .....56 E8
  CCHDY M21 .....39 N4
Eltham Av OFTN SK2 * 57 J2
Eltham Cl WDN WA8 .....46 C4
Eltham St BNG/LEV M19 .....28 A7
Elton Av BNG/LEV M19 .....28 A7
  GOL/RIS/CU WA3 .....24 G2
  PS/BROM L62 .....79 J2
  WILM/AE SK9 .....71 N5
Elton Crossings Rd
  SBCH CW11 .....171 J3
Elton Dr BRAM/HZG SK7 .....57 K7
Elton Head Rd STHEL WA9 .....30 C3
Elton Head Rd STHEL WA9 .....30 G5
Elton La FROD/HEL WA6 .....82 E9
Elton La SBCH CW11 .....171 J8
Elton Lordship La
  FROD/HEL WA6 .....38 A6
Elton Rd SALE M33 .....38 A6
  STHEL WA9 .....171 H4
Elton Ter BURS/TUN ST6 .....189 L9
Elverston St WYTH/NTH M22 .....39 P7
Elvington Cl CONG CW12 .....155 N8
  RUNC WA7 .....84 D2
  WARR WA5 .....11 J7
Elworth Av WDN WA8 .....45 N2
Elworth Rd SBCH CW11 .....171 J3
Elworth St SBCH CW11 .....171 M1
Elwyn Av RAIN/WH L35 * 39 N9
Elwyn Dr HLWD L26 .....A4 A7
Ely Cl GTS/LS CH66 .....102 A4
Ely Ct MCFLDN SK10 .....9 G5
Ely Pk RUNC WA7 .....63 J4
Elysian St OP/CLY M11 .....28 C1
Embassy Cl EP CH65 .....120 F6
Emberton Pl
  AUD/MAB/W CW8 .....209 H9
Emberton St NEWLW WA12 .....23 M4
Embleton Ct RUNC WA7 .....62 B9
Embridge Cswy BUX SK17 .....97 M8
Emerald Dr SBCH CW11 .....171 P1
Emerald Rd WYTH/NTH M22 .....55 H8
Emerald St DTN/ASHW M34 .....29 M2
Emery Av CCHDY M21 .....39 N4
Emery Cl ALT WA14 .....38 A9
Emily St STHEL WA9 .....30 B1
Emley St BNG/LEV M19 .....28 A8
Emlyn Gv CHD/CHDH SK8 .....56 A1
Emlyn St WARRS WA4 .....22 B8
Emmett St NWCHW CW8 .....109 K1
  STHEL WA9 .....30 B1
Emperor St STKP SK1 .....17 J2
Empress Av MPL/ROM SK6 .....58 D2
Empress Dr CW/SHV CW2 .....4 B5
  HTNM SK4 .....41 L4

Emral Ct WRXS/E LL13 .....202 B5
Emslie Ct NSTN CH64 .....77 J5
Emsworth Dr SALE M33 .....38 F7
Endcott Cl GTN M18 .....28 B5
Enderby Av RNFD/HAY WA11 .....22 A3
Enderby Rd CH/BCN CH1 * 2 C1
Endon Av MCFLDN SK10 .....95 N6
Endsleigh Gdns CHNE CH2 .....121 P5
Endsleigh Rd DID/WITH M20 .....40 D2
Enfield Av BNG/LEV M19 .....41 H2
Enfield Cl CW/SHV CW2 .....198 A4
Enfield Park Rd
  WARRN/WOL WA2 .....33 P4
Enfield Rd EP CH65 .....6 C4
  GOL/RIS/CU WA3 .....25 H4
Enfield St HYDE SK14 * 43 K1
Enford Av WYTH/NTH M22 .....54 C5
Enford Dr STHEL WA9 .....31 J1
Engell Cl GTN M18 .....28 C4
Englefield Av CHSW/BR CH4 .....141 P4
Englefield Cl CW/HAS CW1 .....169 P9
Englefield Dr FLINT CH6 .....96 D2
Englesea Brook La
  CW/SHV CW2 .....199 L5
Englesea Gv CW/SHV CW2 .....184 C7
Ennerdale CHNE CH2 .....122 A6
  MCFLDS SK11 .....116 F7
Ennerdale Av CCHDY M21 .....39 N4
  PS/BROM L62 .....79 K1
  WARRN/WOL WA2 .....33 L4
Ennerdale Cl WILM/AE SK9 .....92 B6
  WSFD CW7 .....128 C8
Ennerdale Dr CHD/CHDH SK8 .....55 K4
  CONG CW12 .....155 K8
  FROD/HEL WA6 .....84 A5
Ennerdale Rd CW/SHV CW2 .....184 E5
  MPL/ROM SK6 .....42 C4
  PART M31 .....36 D5
  STKP SK1 .....82 A9
Ennis Cl NTHM/RTH M23 .....54 A2
  SPK/HALE L24 .....60 D6
Ensor Wy NM/HAY SK22 .....58 N8
Enticott Rd IRL M44 .....36 B3
Enville St DTN/ASHW M54 .....29 L2
  WARRS WA4 .....48 E3
Ebourne Rd WYTH/NTH M22 .....54 C6
Epping Cl RAIN/WH L35 .....30 C6
Epping Ct WILM/AE SK9 * 71 K8
Epping Dr SALE M33 .....37 P5
  WARR WA1 .....34 E8
Epping Rd DTN/ASHW M54 .....29 H7
Epsom Av BNG/LEV M19 .....40 G2
  WILM/AE SK9 .....71 N2
Epsom Cl BRAM/HZG SK7 .....57M5
Epsom Gdns WARRS WA4 .....48 C8
Epsom Dr STHEL WA9 .....22 D5
  PS/BROM L62 .....79 J2
Epsom St STHEL WA9 .....31 J1
Era St SALE M33 .....38 E4
Erf Wy MWCH CW10 .....151 L2
Erica Cl RDSH SK5 .....28 F9
Erica Dr BNG/LEV M19 .....40 F4
Eric Av WARR WA1 .....33 P8
Eric Bullows Cl
  WYTH/NTH M22 .....54 E6
Eric Fountain Rd EP CH65 .....79 P2
Eric St WDN WA8 .....46 A6
Erindale Crs FROD/HEL WA6 .....83 N7
Erin St OP/CLY M11 * 28 E2
Erith Cl RDSH SK5 .....42 A2
Erlesmere Av DTN/ASHW M34 .....36 A3
Ermine Rd CHNE CH2 .....121 P7
Ermeley Cl WGTN/LGST M12 .....28 B6
Ernest St CHD/CHDH SK8 .....55 L1
  CW/SHV CW2 .....4 E7
  OFTN SK2 .....56 C1
Ernocroft Gv GTN M18 .....28 E3
Ernocroft Rd MPL/ROM SK6 .....48 A9
Errington Cl OFTN SK2 .....57 L1
Errington Av EP CH65 .....6 E2
Errol Av WYTH/NTH M22 .....54 E5
Errwood Av BNG/LEV M19 .....28 A9
Errwood Rd BNG/LEV M19 .....41 H2
Erskine Cl RNFD/HAY WA11 .....22 A3
Erskine Rd PART M31 .....36 E5
Erskine St MPL/ROM SK6 .....43 N6
Erwood Rd HTNM SK4 .....40 G3
Erwood St WARRN/WOL WA2 .....18 C3
Eryngo St STKP SK1 .....17 K5
Esher Dr SALE M33 .....38 B8
Eskdale CHD/CHDH SK8 .....55 L3
  EP CH65 .....102 D1
Eskdale Av BRAM/HZG SK7 .....72 C1
  DID/WITH M20 .....40 B1
Eskdale Cl RUNC WA7 .....62 B9
  WSFD CW7 .....128 D9
Eskdale Dr HALE/TIMP WA15 .....38 F9
Esk Rd WSFD CW7 .....129 H9
Essex Av DID/WITH M20 .....40 D8
  EDGY/DAV SK3 .....41 J8
Essex Cl CONG CW12 .....155 N5
Essex Dr ALS/KID ST7 .....189 H6
  BIDD ST8 .....175 L7
Essex Gdns IRL M44 .....36 E6
Essex Rd CHNE CH2 .....122 B6
  RDSH SK5 .....28 F6
Essex Wk MCFLDN SK10 .....116 D4
Esthers La NWCHW CW8 .....108 F4
Esthwaite Av RNFD/HAY WA11 .....22 A1
Etchells Rd CHD/CHDH SK8 .....55M6
Etchells St STKP SK1 .....17 J3
Ethelda Dr CHNE CH2 .....122 B6
Ethel St BNG/LEV M19 .....28 A8
Etherley Cl IRL M44 .....36 E6
Etherow Av MPL/ROM SK6 .....43 K6
Etherow Cl SBCH CW11 .....171 K2
Eton Hall Dr STHEL WA9 .....31 J1
Eton Rd EP CH65 .....6 C7
Etterick Pk CHSE CH3 .....122 B9
Ettiley Av SBCH CW11 .....171 H4

Ettrick Cl OP/CLY M11 .....28 D2
Ettrick Pk CHSE CH3 .....122 B9
Euclid Av WARRS WA4 .....48 F5
Eurolink STHEL WA9 .....30 E4
Europa Bvd WARRW/BUR WA5 .....32 C5
Europa Wy CHD/CHDH SK8 .....56 C1
  EP CH65 .....7 F5
Eustace St WARRN/WOL WA2 .....18 B4
Evan Cl DID/WITH M20 .....40 B5
Evans Cl DID/WITH M20 .....40 B5
  RNFD/HAY WA11 .....23 K2
Evelyn Pi WARRS WA4 .....33 P8
Evans St CW/HAS CW1 .....185 J2
  FLINT CH6 .....98 A5
Eva Rd EP CH65 .....6 D4
Eva St SBCH CW11 .....171 J1
Evelyn Av STHEL WA9 .....22 C6
Evelyn Rd WARRW/BUR WA5 .....47 P3
Evelyn Cl GTN M18 * 28 E5
Evenwood STHEL WA9 .....31 H2
Everdon Cl WSFD CW7 .....128 C8
Everest Cl GTS/LS CH66 .....102 B1
Everest Rd ALS/KID ST7 .....189 L5
Everett Rd DID/WITH M20 .....40 C1
Everglade Cl MCFLDS SK11 .....117 H7
Evergreen Wy STHEL WA9 .....31 M1
Everite Rd WDN WA8 .....45 H5
Eversley WDN WA8 .....45 H5
Eversley Cl FROD/HEL WA6 .....84 A7
  WARR WA4 .....65 H1
Eversley Ct CHSW/BR CH4 .....121M7
Eversley Pk CHNE CH2 .....121M7
Eversley Rd DID/WITH M20 .....28 C8
Everton Gv RNFD/HAY WA11 .....22 A2
Everton Rd RDSH SK5 .....28 F7
Evesham Av HALE M33 .....38 E3
  NTHM/RTH M23 .....53 J3
Evesham Cl MCFLDN SK10 .....95 L9
  WARRS WA4 .....48 D8
Evesham Drive WILM/AE SK9 .....71 L4
Evesham Cv SALE M33 .....39 H4
Eveside Cl CHD/CHDH SK8 .....55 J4
Ewan St DTN/ASHW M34 .....29 L2
Ewart St CHSW/BR CH4 .....141M5
Ewloe Ct EP CH65 .....120 F2
Ewrin La MCFLDN SK10 .....96 C8
Exbourne Rd WYTH/NTH M22 .....54 B6
Exbury St RUSH/FAL M14 .....40 E1
Excalibur Wy IRL M44 .....36 E1
Exchange Cl WYTH/NTH M22 .....54 B6
Exchange Pl EDGY/DAV SK3 .....16 E5
  MCFLDS SK11 .....8 E4
Exeter Av DTN/ASHW M34 .....29M8
Exeter Dr IRL M44 .....55 P7
Exeter Dr IRL M44 .....27 P7
Exeter Pl CH/BCN CH1 .....121 J6
Exeter Rd EP CH65 .....6 E2
Exford Cl RDSH SK5 .....41 N2
Exit Rd West MANAIR M90 * 54 D8
Exmouth Av RDSH SK5 .....42 A2
Exmouth Crs RUNC WA7 .....63 J8
Exmouth Rd SALE M33 .....38 A3
Exmouth Wy WARRW/BUR WA5 .....32 C2
Extension Vw STHEL WA9 .....22 D8
Exton Pk CH/BCN CH1 .....2 C3
Eyam Gv OFTN SK2 .....57 K3
Eyam Rd BRAM/HZG SK7 .....57 K3
Eyebrook Rd ALT WA14 .....52 E6
Eynford Av RDSH SK5 .....42 A2
Eyston Cl NWCHE CW9 .....109 N7

F

Factory La POY/DIS SK12 .....59 J9
  WARR WA1 .....18 B7
  WDN WA8 .....45 H2
Factory Dr MWCH CW10 .....151 K4
Fairacres Rd MPL/ROM SK6 .....58 C7
Fairbourne Av WILM/AE SK9 .....93 K2
Fairbourne Cl
  WARRW/BUR WA5 .....33 H5
  WILM/AE SK9 .....93 H1
Fairbourne Dr HALE/TIMP WA15 .....53M8
  WILM/AE SK9 .....93 H1
Fairbourne Rd BNG/LEV M19 .....29 L7
  DTN/ASHW M34 .....29 L7
Fairbrook CW/SHV CW2 .....184 E6
Fairbrother Crs
  WARRN/WOL WA2 .....33 N6
Fairburn Av CW/SHV CW2 .....184 E6
Fairburn Cl WARR WA1 .....46 C4
Fairclough Av WARR WA1 .....19 F7
Fairclough Crs RNFD/HAY WA11 .....30 A5
Fairclough Rd RAIN/WH L35 .....30 C5
Fairclough St NEWLW WA12 .....23 M6
  WARRW/BUR WA5 .....33 H2
Fairfax Av DID/WITH M20 .....40 B1
  HALE/TIMP WA15 .....53 L1
Fairfax Cl MPL/ROM SK6 .....58 D3
Fairfax Dr NANT CW5 .....196 E1
  RUNC WA7 .....63 N9
Fairfield Av CHD/CHDH SK8 .....55 P5
  DROY M43 .....28 C1
  EP CH65 .....102 C2
  MCFLDN SK10 .....95 N6
  SBCH CW11 .....171 H4
Fairfield Gdns WARRS WA4 .....48 C5
Fairfield Rd CHNE CH2 .....122 B7
  CHSW/BR CH4 .....141 N8
  HALE/TIMP WA15 .....53 N2
  IRL M44 .....36 E7
  LYMM WA13 .....50 F4
  NWCHE CW9 .....110 A8
  OP/CLY M11 .....28 E2
  WARRS WA4 .....48 F5
  WDN WA8 .....45 P6
Fairfields ALS/KID ST7 .....201 J5
Fairfield Sq DROY M43 .....28 C1
Fairfield St BIDD ST8 .....175 P8
  WARR WA1 .....19 G3
Fairford Av RDSH SK5 .....41 N5
Fairford Cl CHSW/BR CH4 .....142 B4
Fairford Rd RDSH SK5 .....41 N5
Fairford Wy WILM/AE SK9 .....71 M7
Fairhaven Av CCHDY M21 .....39 L1
Fairhaven Cl BRAM/HZG SK7 .....57M5
  MCFLDN SK10 .....95 H9
  WARRW/BUR WA5 .....47 M3
Fairhaven Rd WDN WA8 .....46 A5
Fairhills Rd IRL M44 .....27 N9
Fairholme Cl CH/BCN CH1 .....120 E2
Fairholme Rd DID/WITH M20 .....40 D2
  HTNM SK4 .....16 B1
Fairhome Wy WDN WA8 .....129 H3
Fair Isle Cl EP CH65 .....102 C4
Fairlands Rd SALE M33 .....38 C6
Fairlawn HTNM SK4 .....16 C1
Fairlea DTN/ASHW M34 .....40 D6
Fairlie Av DID/WITH M20 .....40 D6
Fairlie Dr HALE/TIMP WA15 .....38 F8
Fairman Cl WILM/AE SK9 .....30 C6
Fair Md KNUT WA16 .....16 C6
Fairmeadow CHSW/BR CH4 .....160 C7
Fairmead Rd NTHM/RTH M23 .....39M7
Fairmile Dr DID/WITH M20 .....40 D8
Fairoak Cl RUNC WA7 .....149 K2
Fairoak Ct CW/SHV CW2 .....85 K2
Fairoak La RUNC WA7 .....85 K2
Fair Oak Rd BNG/LEV M19 .....40 G4
  NEWLW WA12 .....201 N6
Fairstead Wk OP/CLY M11 .....28 F2
Fairview WRXS/E LL13 .....176 F3
Fairview Av ALS/KID ST7 .....187 P4
  CW/SHV CW2 .....198 C2
Fairview Cl MPL/ROM SK6 .....28 C8
Fair View Cl NWCHW CW8 .....109 H1
  MPL/ROM SK6 .....43 L9
Fairview Pk NANT CW5 * 207 K3
Fairview Rd DTN/ASHW M34 .....28 C2
  GTS/LS CH66 .....102 C2
  HALE/TIMP WA15 .....53 N2
  MCFLDS SK11 .....116 C6
Fairway BRAM/HZG SK7 .....56 D9
  CHD/CHDH SK8 .....55 K3
  DROY M43 .....28 C1
Fairway Av NTHM/RTH M23 .....38 C9
Fairway Dr SALE M33 .....38 C8
Fairways FROD/HEL WA6 .....84 B6
  WARR WA1 * 64 F1
Fairways Dr GTS/LS CH66 .....79 P6
  WHITCH SY13 .....213 M4
The Fairways WILM/AE SK9 .....128 B9
The Fairway ALS/KID ST7 * 30 E4
  OFTN SK2 .....42 C9
Fairwood Rd NTHM/RTH M23 .....38 C9
Fairy La SALE M33 .....39 J4
Fairywell Cl WILM/AE SK9 .....71M5
Fairywell Dr SALE M33 .....38 D7
Fairywell Rd HALE/TIMP WA15 .....53 N2
Falcon Cl MWCH CW10 .....151 K4
  NM/HAY SK22 .....59 P7
  WSFD CW7 .....149 M4
Falcondale Rd
  WARRN/WOL WA2 .....33 L2
Falcon Dr CW/HAS CW1 .....170 A9
  IRL M44 .....27 P5
Falconers Gn
  WARRW/BUR WA5 .....32 E6
Falcon Rd GTS/LS CH66 .....102 B1
Falcons Wy RUNC WA7 .....62 C8
Fallibroome Cl MCFLDN SK10 .....116 C4
Fallibroome Rd MCFLDN SK10 .....116 E4
Fallon Ct MWCH CW10 .....151 J3
Fallow Cl WDN WA8 .....31 H4
Fallowfield RUNC WA7 .....62 B5
Fallowfield Cl WSFD CW7 .....149 H1
Fallowfield Ct CW/HAS CW1 .....184 G2
Fallowfield Gv
  WARRN/WOL WA2 .....34 C7
Falls Gv CHD/CHDH SK8 .....55 J4
Falmer Dr WYTH/NTH M22 .....54 F6
Falmouth Av SALE M33 .....38 A3
Falmouth Cl MCFLDN SK10 .....116 E4
Falmouth Crs RDSH SK5 .....42 B3
Falmouth Pl RUNC WA7 .....63 J8
Falmouth Rd CONG CW12 .....174 F1
  CW/HAS CW1 .....184 G2
  IRL M44 .....27 P7
Falstaff Ms MPL/ROM SK6 .....42 F5
Falstone Cl GOL/RIS/CU WA3 .....35 J2
Falstone Dr RUNC WA7 .....63 J6
Fancroft Rd WYTH/NTH M22 .....54 E2
Fanner's La KNUT WA16 .....66 C1
Fanshawe La MCFLDS SK11 .....115M8
Fanshawe Wk CW/SHV CW2 .....185 J8
Faraday Rd EP CH65 .....6 A7
Faraday St GOL/RIS/CU WA3 .....34 F3
Farams Rd ALS/KID ST7 .....188 A1
Farbailey Cl CHSW/BR CH4 .....142 D5
Farcroft Cl NTHM/RTH M23 .....39 J8
Far Cromwell Rd MPL/ROM SK6 .....42 C2
Farden Dr NTHM/RTH M23 .....38 G8
Farfields Cl SBCH CW11 .....135M2
Faringdon Rd
  WARRN/WOL WA2 .....33 L2
Farlands Dr DID/WITH M20 .....40 C9
Far La GTN M18 .....28 D5
Farley Av GTN M18 .....28 D5
Farley Cl MWCH CW10 * 151 H2
Farley Ct CHD/CHDH SK8 .....55 P3

Farley Rd SALE M33 38 F6
Farley Wy RDSH SK5 28 E8
Farm Cl HTNM SK4 41 K2
NWCHW CW8 108 F3
Farmdale Dr CHNE CH2 104 A1
Farmer Cl CW/SHV CW2 184 G4
Farmers Cl NTHM/RTH M23 39 K6
Farmers Heath GTS/LS CH66 101 P2
Farmer's La WARRW/BUR WA5 32 D2
Farmer St HTNM SK4 41 L5
Farmfield SALE M33 38 B2
Farmfields Dr MCFLDN SK10 117 H1
Farmfields Ri
AUD/MAD/W CW3 219 H4
Farm La MCFLDS SK11 133 H2
POY/DIS SK12 58 E9
WARRS WA4 48 G7
Farmleigh Dr CW/HAS CW1 169 N9
Farmleigh Gdns
WARRW/BUR WA5 47 N1
Farm Rd NWCHE CW9 110 E5
NWCHW CW8 108 F3
NWCHW CW8 126 C3
STHEL WA9 31 J5
Farmside Av IRL M44 27 N6
Farmside Cl WARRW/BUR WA5 33 H9
Farmstead Wy GTS/LS CH66 102 A3
Farm Wk ALT WA14 52 C5
Farm Wy NEWLW WA12 24 A8
Farm Yd BNG/LEV M19 28 A8
Farn Av RDSH SK5 28 C7
Farndale WDN WA8 45 N2
Farndale Cl CW/SHV CW2 197 P1
WARRW/BUR WA5 32 C9
Farndale Wk MCFLDS SK11 * 117 K6
Farndon Av BRAM/HZG SK7 57 M3
STHEL WA9 30 G4
Farndon Cl CHSW/BR CH4 140 G6
NWCHW CW8 108 C9
SALE M33 39 H5
Farndon Dr HALE/TIMP WA15 53 L1
Farndon Rd GTS/LS CH66 80 A7
RDSH SK5 28 E7
Farne Cl EP CH65 102 E4
Farnham Av MCFLDS SK11 116 G6
Farnham Cl CHD/CHDH SK8 56 A8
WARRS WA4 48 G8
Farnham Dr IRL M44 27 N8
Farnhill Cl RUNC WA7 63 H6
Farnley Cl RUNC WA7 63 H5
Farnley St WGTN/LGST M12 * 28 A3
Farnworth Cl WDN WA8 45 P3
WARRW/BUR WA5 46 G4
Farnworth Rd
WARRW/BUR WA5 47 H3
Farnworth St STHEL WA9 22 A5
WDN WA8 45 P3
Farrant Rd WGTN/LGST M12 28 A6
Farrant St WDN WA8 21 K2
Farrar Rd DROY M43 28 F1
Farrell Rd WARRS WA4 48 E7
Farrell St WARR WA1 19 H5
Far Ridings MPL/ROM SK6 43 J5
Farrier Cl SALE M33 39 J5
Farriers Wy WSFD CW7 149 J1
Farrier Wk STHEL WA9 31 H4
Farringdon Cl STHEL WA9 30 E3
Farr St EDGY/DAV SK3 16 C6
Farwood Cl MCFLDN SK10 116 F3
Fastnet St OP/CLY M11 28 A1
Faulkner Dr HALE/TIMP WA15 53 M3
MWCH CW10 151 L4
Faulkners La CHSE CH3 143 M3
KNUT WA16 92 A2
Faulkner St CHNE CH2 122 A8
Fawborough Rd
NTHM/RTH M23 39 J7
Fawley Gv WYTH/NTH M22 54 F3
Fawley Rd RAIN/WH L35 30 D7
Fawns Keep WILM/AE SK9 71 M7
Fawns Leap NWCHW CW8 108 A7
Faywood Dr MPL/ROM SK6 58 E1
Fearndown Wy MCFLDN SK10 95 J9
Fearnhead Cross
WARRN/WOL WA2 * 33 P7
Fearnhead La
WARRN/WOL WA2 34 B6
Fearnhead La
WARRN/WOL WA2 34 D5
Feathers La CH/BCN CH1 * 2 D5
Feathers St FLINT CH6 98 A5
Feeny St STHEL WA9 * 30 G6
Feilden Ct CH/BCN CH1 121 J2
Feldom Rd NTHM/RTH M23 39 J6
Felix Rd NWCHW CW8 12 C3
Fellbrigg Cl GTN M18 28 C6
Fellpark Rd NTHM/RTH M23 39 K6
Felltop Dr RDSH SK5 28 G9
Felskirk Rd WYTH/NTH M22 54 E7
Felt Ct DTN/ASHW M34 29 J7
Felton Av WYTH/NTH M22 54 E4
Fence Av MCFLDN SK10 9 G3
Fencegate Av HTNM SK4 41 L3
Fence La CONG CW12 174 D6
Fence St OFTN SK2 57 K3
Fencot Dr WGTN/LGST M12 28 A5
Fenham Dr WARRW/BUR WA5 47 J3
Fenmore Av GTN M18 28 B6
Fennel St WARR WA1 19 F5
Fenside Rd WYTH/NTH M22 54 G2
Fenton Av OFTN SK2 57 J3
Fenton Cl CONG CW12 156 A9
WDN WA8 45 J4
Fenwick Dr HTNM SK4 40 F5
Fenwick La RUNC WA7 62 B8
Fenwick Rd GTS/LS CH66 102 A2
Ferguson Av GTS/LS CH66 80 A7
Ferguson Dr WARRN/WOL WA2 33 N7
Ferma La CHSE CH3 123 L5
Fernacre SALE M33 38 F3
Fern Av NEWLW WA12 23 P7
Fernbank Cl CW/HAS CW1 185 M5
GOL/RIS/CU WA3 34 F4
WSFD CW7 * 150 B1
Fern Bank Dr NTHM/RTH M23 39 H9
Fernbank Ri MCFLDN SK10 95 P5
Fernbray Av BNG/LEV M19 40 E4
Fern Cl GOL/RIS/CU WA3 34 E4
MPL/ROM SK6 58 D1
Fern Ct CW/HAS CW1 5 J4
Fern Crs CONG CW12 156 A8
Ferndale Av CHNE CH2 104 A1
OFTN SK2 57 H3
Ferndale Cl CW/SHV CW2 198 G2
SBCH CW11 171 P4
WARR WA1 34 D9
WDN WA8 31 K9
Ferndale Crs MCFLDS SK11 116 E5
Ferndale Gdns ALS/KID ST7 189 N5
BNG/LEV M19 40 F2
Ferndale Rd SALE M33 38 E6
Ferndene Rd DID/WITH M20 40 C3
Ferndown Av BRAM/HZG SK7 57 J6
Ferndown Dr IRL M44 27 N6
Ferndown Rd NTHM/RTH M23 38 G8
Ferngate Dr DID/WITH M20 40 C2
Fernhill MPL/ROM SK6 58 F1
Fernhill Dr GTN M18 28 B5
Fernhill Rd CH/BCN CH1 121 H5
Fernhurst RUNC WA7 62 B6
Fernhurst Rd DID/WITH M20 40 D3
Fernilee Cl NM/HAY SK22 59 N6
Fern Lea CHD/CHDH SK8 55 K6
Fernlea HALE/TIMP WA15 53 K6
Fernlea Av STHEL WA9 30 C1
Fern Lea Dr MCFLDS SK11 116 G4
Fernleaf Cl ALS/KID ST7 173 J9
Fernlea Rd NWCHE CW9 88 B7
Fernleigh NWCHW CW8 109 L5
Fernleigh Av BNG/LEV M19 28 C8
Fernleigh Cl MWCH CW10 151 L4
WSFD CW7 149 J1
Fernley Av DTN/ASHW M34 29 N7
Fernley Rd OFTN SK2 57 H1
Fernone WILM/AE SK9 71 M3
Fern Rd EP CH65 102 C2
Fernside Av DID/WITH M20 40 E3
Fern Vw HALE/TIMP WA15 54 A2
Fern Wy NWCHW CW8 108 E3
Fernwood MPL/ROM SK6 43 P9
RUNC WA7 62 F5
Fernwood Av GTN M18 28 D6
Fernwood Gv WILM/AE SK9 71 L6
Ferris St OP/CLY M11 28 D1
Ferrous Wy IRL M44 36 E2
Ferryhill Rd IRL M44 27 N7
Ferry La CH/BCN CH1 141 N1
WARRS WA4 49 N3
Ferry Rd IRL M44 27 P7
Festival Av AUD/MAD/W CW3 217 M1
WARRN/WOL WA2 33 N6
Festival Crs WARRN/WOL WA2 33 N6
Festival Dr MCFLDN SK10 93 P7
Festival Hl CONG CW12 155 P8
Festival Rd EP CH65 80 B8
Festival Wy RUNC WA7 15 J6
Ffordd Cledwen
CHSW/BR CH4 140 G5
Ffordd Glyndwr FLINT CH6 98 B7
Ffordd Llaneurgain FLINT CH6 98 A9
Ffordd Llewelyn FLINT CH6 98 B7
Ffordd y Fran FLINT CH6 98 B8
Fiddlers Ferry Rd WDN WA8 46 B7
Fiddlers La CH/BCN CH1 120 E1
IRL M44 27 P6
Field Av CW/SHV CW2 184 F7
Field Bank Gv BNG/LEV M19 28 B8
Fieldbank Rd MCFLDN SK10 8 A3
Field Cl BRAM/HZG SK7 72 D2
MCFLDN SK10 95 M6
MPL/ROM SK6 58 B2
NWCHW CW8 109 L5
Fielden Rd DID/WITH M20 40 A3
Fieldfare WSFD CW7 150 A2
GOL/RIS/CU WA3 24 F1
Fieldfare Cl GOL/RIS/CU WA3 34 G4
Fieldgate WDN WA8 45 H9
Fieldhead Ms WILM/AE SK9 71 N6
Fieldhead Rd WILM/AE SK9 71 N6
Field Hey La NSTN CH64 78 F4
Field House La MPL/ROM SK6 58 E1
Fieldhouse Rw RUNC WA7 62 B7
Fielding Av POY/DIS SK12 73 L4
CHSE CH3 124 A9
Field La CHSE CH3 164 A8
CW/SHV CW2 184 D6
WARRS WA4 48 E9
Field Pl DID/WITH M20 * 40 C5
Field Rd SALE M33 38 B2
STHEL WA9 31 J5
Fields Cl ALS/KID ST7 188 A4
Fields Dr SBCH CW11 171 M4
Fieldsend Dr LEIGH WN7 25 L1
Fieldside CQ CH5 140 A1
TPLY/KEL CW6 145 P4
Fieldside Cl HOLMCH CW4 132 B2
Field Side Cl KNUT WA16 91 L1
ALS/KID ST7 187 P5
CONG CW12 174 F1
CW/HAS CW1 186 B4
The Fields NANT CW5 197 L2
Field St DROY M43 28 F1
GTN M18 28 E3
MPL/ROM SK6 42 E5
Fields View Cl NANT CW5 198 A7
Fieldsway RUNC WA7 61 N8
Field Vale Dr RDSH SK5 28 G8
Fieldvale Rd SALE M33 38 B7
Field Vw BIDD ST8 175 L8
Field View Dr MCFLDS SK11 117 L7
Fieldview Dr WARRN/WOL WA2 33 M7
Field Wk HALE/TIMP WA15 * 53 M4
Field Wy ALS/KID ST7 188 A4
Fieldway CH/BCN CH1 120 D1
CHNE CH2 121 P7
FROD/HEL WA6 84 A6
GTS/LS CH66 79 M6
NWCHW CW8 108 E3
Field Wy RAIN/WH L35 30 B3
Fieldway WDN WA8 46 C5
Fife Rd WARR WA1 19 K2
Fifth Av ALS/KID ST7 188 G7
DUK SK16 29 N1
FLINT CH6 98 A7
RUNC WA7 62 D7
Fildes Cl WARRW/BUR WA5 47 N2
Filey Rd OFTN SK2 42 B9
Filkin's La CHSE CH3 143 J1
Finchale Dr HALE/TIMP WA15 53 M6
Finch Cl STHEL WA9 31 J5
Finchdale Gdns
GOL/RIS/CU WA3 25 K1
Finchett Dr CH/BCN CH1 2 A1
Finch La HLWD L26 44 B9
Finchley Dr RNFD/HAY WA11 22 A2
Finchley Rd HALE/TIMP WA15 53 J4
Finchwood Rd WYTH/NTH M22 54 G2
Findlay Cl NEWLW WA12 23 N7
Findon Rd NTHM/RTH M23 54 C1
Finger House La WDN WA8 31 J7
Finger Post La FROD/HEL WA6 107 K7
Finland Rd EDGY/DAV SK3 41 L9
Finlan Rd WDN WA8 21 F5
Finlay Av WARRW/BUR WA5 47 J4
Finlow Hill La MCFLDN SK10 93 M7
Finney Cl WILM/AE SK9 71 L4
Finney Dr CCHDY M21 39 K1
WILM/AE SK9 71 L4
Finney Gv RNFD/HAY WA11 23 J3
Finney La WYTH/NTH M22 55 J7
Finney's La MWCH CW10 130 A9
Finningley Ct WARRW/WOL WA2 33 P7
Finny Bank Rd SALE M33 38 D2
Finsbury Cl WARRW/BUR WA5 47 N3
Finsbury Pk WDN WA8 46 A2
Finsbury Rd RDSH SK5 28 E9
Finsbury Wk WSFD CW7 149 J1
Finsbury Wy WILM/AE SK9 71 N4
Fir Avennue HLWD L26 44 A7
Fir Av BRAM/HZG SK7 56 E7
Firbank CHNE CH2 104 C1
Firbank Cl RUNC WA7 63 H5
Firbank Rd NTHM/RTH M23 54 C4
Firbeck Cl CHSW/BR CH4 140 F7
Firbeck Gdns CW/SHV CW2 184 D4
Fir Cl HLWD L26 44 A7
POY/DIS SK12 73 L3
TPLY/KEL CW6 147 H8
Firdale Rd NWCHW CW8 109 L5
Firemans Sq CH/BCN CH1 * 2 D3
Firethorn Av BNG/LEV M19 40 G2
Fir Gv BNG/LEV M19 28 A8
MCFLDS SK11 117 J7
NWCHW CW8 108 G4
WARR WA1 34 A9
Fir La NWCHW CW8 127 K1
Firman Cl WARRW/BUR WA5 32 E8
Fir Rd BRAM/HZG SK7 56 E7
DTN/ASHW M34 29 N6
MPL/ROM SK6 58 C3
Firsby Av MPL/ROM SK6 42 E4
Firsby St BNG/LEV M19 28 A8
Firs Gv CHD/CHDH SK8 55 J3
Firs La WARRS WA4 48 D9
Firs Rd CHD/CHDH SK8 55 J4
SALE M33 38 B3
First Av ALS/KID ST7 188 G7
CW/HAS CW1 5 J7
FLINT CH6 98 A7
MCFLDN SK10 73 K5
RAIN/WH L35 30 A4
SBCH CW11 171 M4
First Dig La NANT CW5 197 J7
The Firs ALT WA14 52 F5
KNUT WA16 * 92 A3
WHITCH SY13 213 L5
Fir St HTNM SK4 16 E3
IRL M44 36 B2
WDN WA8 46 A5
First Wood St NANT CW5 10 A4
Firs Wy SALE M33 37 P5
Firswood Mt CHD/CHDH SK8 55 J3
Firth Flds NWCHE CW9 128 G1
Firth Fields Cl NWCHE CW9 128 G1
Firthland Wy STHEL WA9 22 D7
Fir Tree Av CHSW/BR CH4 142 D5
GOL/RIS/CU WA3 25 H1
KNUT WA16 90 G5
SALE M33 37 P4
Firtree Av WARR WA1 34 B8
Firtree Cl NWCHW CW8 87 K9
Fir Tree Cl WARRS WA4 64 F5
Firtree Cl WSFD CW7 150 B1
Firtree Gv GTS/LS CH66 102 C4
Fir Tree La CHSE CH3 143 N1
NANT CW5 194 E4
WARRW/BUR WA5 32 D2
Firvale Av CHD/CHDH SK8 55 K6
Firwood Cl OFTN SK2 42 B8
Firwood Rd BIDD ST8 175 M8
Firwood Wk CW/SHV CW2 185 J8
Fisher Av WARRN/WOL WA2 33 L7
Fisherfield Dr GOL/RIS/CU WA3 35 H2
Fishermans Cl CW/HAS CW1 186 D1
Fisher Rd CH/BCN CH1 121 H7
Fishers Gn TPLY/KEL CW6 146 F5
Fishers La NANT CW5 182 E8
Fisher St RUNC WA7 15 H1
STHEL WA9 31 K1
Fishpool Rd NWCHW CW8 126 C8
Fistral Av CHD/CHDH SK8 55 L7
Fitton Av CCHDY M21 39 L2
Fitton's Cl NANT CW5 208 A1
Fitton St NWCHE CW9 110 F2
Fitz Cl MCFLDN SK10 117 K1
Fitz Crs MCFLDN SK10 117 K1
Fitzherbert St
WARRN/WOL WA2 18 E1
Fitzroy St DROY M43 29 H1
Fitzwalter Rd WARR WA1 34 E9
Fitzwilliam Av MCFLDS SK11 117 M9
Five Ashes Rd CHSW/BR CH4 142 D5
Flagcroft Dr NTHM/RTH M23 54 D2
Flagg Wood Av MPL/ROM SK6 43 J9
Flag La CW/HAS CW1 4 C3
NSTN CH64 77 M6
Flag La North CHNE CH2 121 P3
Flamingo Cl CW/HAS CW1 184 F1
WGTN/LGST M12 28 A3
Flamstead Av NTHM/RTH M23 54 A1
Flander Cl WDN WA8 45 J5
Flashes La NSTN CH64 77 P8
Flash La MCFLDN SK10 95 K6
NWCHE CW9 65 P9
Flat La SBCH CW11 171 N3
TPLY/KEL CW6 125 H7
Flatt La EP CH65 6 C4
Flatts La CHF/WBR SK23 97 K1
Flavian Cl MWCH CW10 130 B9
Flavian Wk OP/CLY M11 * 28 B1
Flaxcroft Rd WYTH/NTH M22 54 D5
Flaxley Cl GOL/RIS/CU WA3 35 H3
Flaxmere Dr CHSE CH3 143 K2
Fleet La STHEL WA9 22 C7
Fleet St EP CH65 6 B4
GTN M18 28 F3
Fleetwood Cl WARRW/BUR WA5 47 M3
Fleetwood Dr NEWLW WA12 23 M5
Fleetwood Wk RUNC WA7 62 G7
Fleming Dr WARRN/WOL WA2 33 K2
Fleming Rd WYTH/NTH M22 54 F5
Fleming St EP CH65 7 F2
Flemish Rd HYDE SK14 29 P7
Flers Av WARRS WA4 48 E4
Fletcher Dr ALT WA14 52 G6
POY/DIS SK12 58 D9
Fletcher Gv NWCHE CW9 110 C6
Fletchers La LYMM WA13 50 F3
Fletcher St CW/HAS CW1 185 H3
STKP SK1 17 G4
WARRS WA4 48 D4
Fletsand Rd WILM/AE SK9 71 L8
Flint Cl BRAM/HZG SK7 57 J6
NSTN CH64 77 K7
Flint Ct EP CH65 102 F2
Flint Dr NSTN CH64 77 L6
Flint Gv IRL M44 36 B2
Flint Meadow NSTN CH64 77 L6
Flint St EDGY/DAV SK3 41 M9
MCFLDN SK10 9 H4
Flittogate La KNUT WA16 89 K4
Flixton Dr CW/SHV CW2 184 G6
Floatshall Rd NTHM/RTH M23 54 B1
Floats Rd NTHM/RTH M23 54 A2
Flookersbrook CHNE CH2 121 P8
Florence Ct EDGY/DAV SK3 * 41 J9
Florence Park Ct DID/WITH M20 40 D4
Florence St DROY M43 29 H1
HTNM SK4 17 F2
SALE M33 38 E2
STHEL WA9 30 B1
WARRS WA4 48 F4
Florida Cl WARRW/BUR WA5 32 F9
Florist St EDGY/DAV SK3 41 M9
Flour Mill Wy CW/HAS CW1 185 N5
Flowerscroft NANT CW5 11 F7
Flowers La CW/HAS CW1 169 M8
Flower St NWCHW CW8 12 C5
Flowery Fld OFTN SK2 56 G4
Floyd Av CCHDY M21 39 M2
Fluin La FROD/HEL WA6 84 A5
Flying Fields Dr MCFLDS SK11 116 G7
Foden Av ALS/KID ST7 188 B5
Foden La BRAM/HZG SK7 72 D3
WILM/AE SK9 92 E3
Foden St MCFLDN SK10 8 E2
Fog Cots STHEL WA9 * 30 F3
Fogg's La WARRS WA4 65 J8
Fog La BNG/LEV M19 40 E4
Fold La BIDD ST8 175 M5
MCFLDS SK11 136 C9
Fold Ms BRAM/HZG SK7 57 L4
Folds Rd RNFD/HAY WA11 22 D3
The Fold MCFLDN SK10 94 C5
Fol Hollow CONG CW12 155 K9
Foliage Crs RDSH SK5 42 A3
Foliage Gdns RDSH SK5 42 B3
Foliage Rd RDSH SK5 42 A4
Folkestone Cl MCFLDN SK10 117 H2
Folkstone Wy RUNC WA7 62 G7
Follows St GTN M18 28 D3
WARRW/BUR WA5 18 A1
Fonthill Gv SALE M33 38 C7
Fooley Cl DROY M43 28 E1
Forber Crs GTN M18 28 C6
Forbes Cl GOL/RIS/CU WA3 34 F4
SALE M33 38 G6
STKP SK1 42 A8
Forbes Pk BRAM/HZG SK7 56 D8
Forbes Rd STKP SK1 42 A7
Forbes St MPL/ROM SK6 42 E4
Fordbank Rd DID/WITH M20 40 B6
Ford Cl CW/HAS CW1 185 H3
Fordington Rd
WARRW/BUR WA5 47 M2
Ford La CHSE CH3 164 E5
CW/HAS CW1 185 H3
DID/WITH M20 40 C6
WYTH/NTH M22 39 P7
Ford Ldg DID/WITH M20 40 C6
Fords La ALS/KID ST7 189 M2
BRAM/HZG SK7 56 D9
Ford St EDGY/DAV SK3 16 C5
WARR WA1 19 H3
Foregate St CH/BCN CH1 3 F4
Foreland Cl WARRW/BUR WA5 31 P9
Forest Av HOLMCH CW4 131 P2
Forest Cl MCFLDN SK10 96 C8
NWCHW CW8 108 B9
Forest Dr CHSW/BR CH4 140 F7
HALE/TIMP WA15 53 K1
MCFLDS SK11 118 A9
SALE M33 38 B6
Forester Av KNUT WA16 90 G3
Foresters Cl FROD/HEL WA6 107 L6
Forest Gdns PART M31 36 C5
Forest Gate La TPLY/KEL CW6 125 K4
Forest La FROD/HEL WA6 106 G6
Forest Pl NWCHE CW9 13 H1
Forest Range BNG/LEV M19 28 A8
Forest Rd GTS/LS CH66 80 A6
MCFLDS SK11 118 C6
STHEL WA9 30 F5
TPLY/KEL CW6 147 H7
WSFD CW7 149 K2
Forest St CH/BCN CH1 3 G4
NWCHW CW8 108 E4
Forest Wk RUNC WA7 * 62 D7
Forge Cl MCFLDS SK11 135 L1
WDN WA8 45 J2
Forge Flds SBCH CW11 171 L6
Forge La CONG CW12 155 K7
Forge Rd CHF/WBR SK23 75 P7
GTS/LS CH66 79 N7
WARRW/BUR WA5 47 K2
Forge St CW/HAS CW1 5 F3
Forge Wy CHSW/BR CH4 142 B6
Formby Av CCHDY M21 39 N1
Formby Cl WARRW/BUR WA5 47 K3
Formby Dr CHD/CHDH SK8 55 K7
Forrester Av STHEL WA9 30 B1
Forrester Cl BIDD ST8 175 K9
Forrest Rd DTN/ASHW M34 29 P8
Forrest Wy WARRW/BUR WA5 47 P4
Forshaw Av GTN M18 28 F3
Forshaw's La WARRW/BUR WA5 23 J9
Forshaw St DTN/ASHW M34 29 K5
WARRN/WOL WA2 19 F2
Forster Av NWCHW CW8 108 G4
Forster St WARRN/WOL WA2 18 E2
Fortescue Rd OFTN SK2 42 C9
Fortyacre Dr MPL/ROM SK6 42 D5
Forty Acre La HOLMCH CW4 132 G6
Forty Acres La HOLMCH CW4 * 132 E5
Fosbrook Av DID/WITH M20 40 D4
Foscarn Dr NTHM/RTH M23 54 D2
Fossa Cl MWCH CW10 130 B9
Foster Rd CONG CW12 156 A5
Fosters Gv RNFD/HAY WA11 22 D3
Fosters Rd RNFD/HAY WA11 22 D3
Foster St DTN/ASHW M34 29 M6
WDN WA8 45 P6
Fothergill St WARR WA1 19 J2
Fotheringay Ct EP CH65 102 F2
Foulkes Av CW/HAS CW1 184 F2
Foundry Bnk CONG CW12 155 N7
Foundry La ALS/KID ST7 189 H1
SBCH CW11 171 J2
WDN WA8 61 J1
Foundry St MCFLDN SK10 95 P5
NEWLW WA12 23 M6
WARRN/WOL WA2 18 D4
Fountain Av HALE/TIMP WA15 53 M4
Fountain Ct BIDD ST8 175 L8
Fountain La FROD/HEL WA6 83 N5
NWCHE CW9 128 G1
Fountains Av RNFD/HAY WA11 23 K2
Fountains Cl MWCH CW10 150 G1
RUNC WA7 62 G9
Fountains Rd CHD/CHDH SK8 56 B9
Fountain St CONG CW12 155 M8
MCFLDN SK10 9 G4
STHEL WA9 30 B2
Fountains Wk GOL/RIS/CU WA3 25 K1
Four Acre La STHEL WA9 31 H4
Fouracres Rd NTHM/RTH M23 54 B2
Four Lanes End CW/SHV CW2 199 L5
Fourseasons Cl CW/SHV CW2 185 H8
Fourth Av ALS/KID ST7 189 H7
CW/HAS CW1 185 M7
FLINT CH6 98 A7
RUNC WA7 62 D7
Fourways CW/SHV CW2 198 G2
Fovant Crs RDSH SK5 28 E8
Fowey Cl MCFLDN SK10 116 D3
Fowler Av GTN M18 28 F2
Fowler Rd CH/BCN CH1 120 G7
Fowlers-bench La CHSE CH3 180 A3
Fowler St MCFLDN SK10 8 E2
Fowley Common La
GOL/RIS/CU WA3 26 B4
Fownhope Av SALE M33 38 C5
Fownhope Rd SALE M33 38 C5
Foxall Wy GTS/LS CH66 101 P2
Fox Bench Cl CHD/CHDH SK8 56 C9
Foxbench Wk CCHDY M21 39 N2
Fox Cl HALE/TIMP WA15 53 K1
Foxcote WDN WA8 45 H5
Foxcote Cl CH/BCN CH1 120 G6
Fox Cover CHSE CH3 122 G6
Fox Covert RUNC WA7 62 G7
Fox Covert La CHNE CH2 122 B1
Foxcovert La KNUT WA16 112 C5
Fox Covert Wy CW/HAS CW1 169 P8
Foxendale Cl NWCHW CW8 109 L6
Foxes Fold NWCHW CW8 12 C1
Foxes Hey NWCHW CW8 107 P7
Foxes Hollow CW/HAS CW1 185 L1
Foxes La WHITCH SY13 214 E5
Foxes Wk CHSE CH3 143 J3
Foxfield Cl WARRN/WOL WA2 33 P5
Foxfield La WSFD CW7 149 H1
Foxfield Rd NTHM/RTH M23 54 C4
Fox Gdns ALS/KID ST7 188 F8
LYMM WA13 50 C3
Foxglove Cl CHSE CH3 143 J4
CW/SHV CW2 185 H9
MCFLDN SK10 96 A5
Foxglove Ct FROD/HEL WA6 84 A5
Foxglove Dr ALT WA14 37 P8
Foxglove Wy NSTN CH64 77 L8
Fox Gv KNUT WA16 90 G4
Foxhall Rd DTN/ASHW M34 29 K5
HALE/TIMP WA15 53 J1
Foxhill ALT WA14 52 E2
Fox Hl TPLY/KEL CW6 125 J7
Foxhill Cha OFTN SK2 57 N2
Foxhill Ct TPLY/KEL CW6 147 H9
Foxhill Gv FROD/HEL WA6 83 K9
Foxhills Cl WARRS WA4 64 F3

Fox Hunter Cl CHSE CH3 ....124 E4
Foxland Rd WYTH/NTH M22 ....54 D4
Foxland Rd CHD/CHDH SK8 ....55 K3
Fox La CHSE CH3 ....144 B5
  MALPAS SY14 ....178 D7
Fox Lea CH/BCN CH1 ....120 D5
Foxlea NWCHE CW9 ....87 L6
Foxley Cl LYMM WA13 ....50 G5
Foxley Hall Ms LYMM WA13 * 50 G6
Foxley Heath WDN WA8 ....20 E2
Fox St EDGY/DAV SK3 ....16 C7
  RUNC WA7 ....10 C4
  WARRW/BUR WA5 ....48 A2
Foxton Cl RNFD/HAY WA11 * 22 B4
Foxwist Cl CHNE CH2 ....121 N8
Foxwist Gn NWCHW CW8 ....127 P5
Foxwood STHEL WA9 ....30 B1
Foxwood Dr KNUT WA16 ....113 L4
Foxwood Gdns BNG/LEV M19 ....40 F5
Framingham Rd SALE M33 ....38 E6
Framley Rd CCHDY M21 ....40 A1
Frances Av CHD/CHDH SK8 ....55 J1
Frances St CHD/CHDH SK8 ....120 C5
  CSH/SV CW2 ....5 F7
  DTN/ASHW M34 ....29 P9
  EDGY/DAV SK3 ....17 F6
  IRL M44 ....36 D3
  MCFLDS SK11 ....8 B4
Frances St West HYDE SK14 ....29 P6
Francis Cl RAIN/WH L35 ....30 B4
  WDN WA8 ....45 J7
Francis Ct CH/BCN CH1 ....3 G3
Francis La WRXS/E LL13 ....176 F9
Francis Rd DID/WITH M20 ....40 D5
  FROD/HEL WA6 ....84 A4
  IRL M44 ....27 M9
  WARRS WA4 ....48 D6
Francis St CH/BCN CH1 ....3 G2
  STHEL WA9 ....31 L1
Frank Bott Av CW/HAS CW1 ....184 G1
Franklin Cl DTN/ASHW M34 ....28 D7
  MCFLDS SK11 ....117 H7
  WARRW/BUR WA5 ....32 F8
Franklyn Av CW/SHV CW2 ....4 B5
Franklyn Rd GTN M18 ....28 D6
Frank Perkins Wy IRL M44 ....36 E1
Frank St WDN WA8 ....46 A6
Frank Webb Av CW/HAS CW1 ....184 G2
Fraser Av SALE M33 ....38 F6
Fraser Ct CHSW/BR CH4 ....142 F3
  WHITCH SY13 ....213 M7
Fraser Rd WARRW/BUR WA5 ....47 H1
Frawley Av NEWLW WA12 ....2 C8
Freckleton Av CCHDY M21 ....39 M4
Freckleton Cl
  WARRW/BUR WA5 ....47 M3
Freda Av STHEL WA9 ....31 H2
Frederick St DTN/ASHW M34 ....29 M4
  STHEL WA9 ....31 L1
  WARRS WA4 ....48 F4
  WDN WA8 ....21 J2
Fredric Pl RUNC WA7 ....15 C1
Free Green La KNUT WA16 ....112 D3
Freemantle Av STHEL WA9 ....30 E1
Freemantle St EDGY/DAV SK3 ....16 B6
Freeman Av GTN M18 ....28 D6
French La NANT CW5 ....206 C2
French St WDN WA8 ....46 B6
Freshfield Cl CHD/CHDH SK8 ....55 K6
Freshfield Cl MPL/ROM SK6 ....43 N7
Freshfield Dr MCFLDS SK10 ....117 J1
Freshfield Rd HTNM SK4 ....40 G6
Freshfields CW/SHV CW2 ....184 G9
  KNUT WA16 ....90 C2
  NWCHE CW9 ....87 L6
Freshfields Dr
  WARRN/WOL WA2 ....34 C7
Freshford STHEL WA9 ....31 J3
Freshmeadow La
  FROD/HEL WA6 ....104 G2
Freshpool Wy WYTH/NTH M22 ....54 G1
Freshwater WARRW/BUR WA5 ....32 A9
Freshwater Cl
  WARRW/BUR WA5 ....32 A9
Freshwater Dr CW/SHV CW2 ....198 G6
  DTN/ASHW M34 ....29 P9
Freshwater St GTN M18 ....28 E3
Frewland Av EDGY/DAV SK3 ....56 F3
Friars Av WARRW/BUR WA5 ....47 J2
  MCFLDN SK11 ....96 B8
  WILM/AE SK9 ....70 C6
Friars Cl CQ CHS 140 K2
Friars Ga WARR WA1 ....18 D7
Friars La WARR WA1 ....18 D7
Friar's Rd SALE M33 ....38 E4
Friars Wy MCFLDN SK10 ....116 E2
Frida Crs NWCHW CW8 ....12 D6
Friendship Av GTN M18 ....28 E5
Friends La WARRW/BUR WA5 ....47 H1
Friesian Gdns ALS/KID ST7 ....201 M5
Frieston Rd ALT WA14 ....44 G4
Frilsham Wy WYTH/NTH M22 ....54 F4
Frinton Cl SALE M33 ....38 C7
Frith Av NWCHW CW8 ....126 A5
Frith La NANT CW5 ....206 B2
Frith Rd DID/WITH M20 ....40 D3
Frith Ter MCFLDS SK11 ....117 K8
Frobisher Ct WARRW/BUR WA5 ....32 C8
Frobisher Pl RDSH SK5 ....41 M4
Frobisher Rd NSTN CH64 ....77 L5
Froda Av FROD/HEL WA6 ....84 A4
Frodsham Av HTNM SK4 ....16 A1
Frodsham Dr RNFD/HAY WA11 ....22 B4
Frodsham Rd FROD/HEL WA6 ....83 L6
  SALE M33 ....39 H6
Frodsham Sq CH/BCN CH1 ....2 E3
Frodsham St CH/BCN CH1 ....2 E3
Froghall La KNUT WA16 ....51 L8
  WARR WA1 ....18 A4
  WARRW/BUR WA5 ....48 B2
Frog La CHSE CH5 ....165 K7
  KNUT WA16 ....88 C4
  WRXS/E LL13 ....176 F8

Frogmore Av HYDE SK14 ....43 K1
Frome Av OFTN SK2 ....57 J2
Frome Ct EP CH65 ....6 D2
Front St SBCH CW11 ....171 N5
Frosts Ms EP CH65 ....6 E1
Fryer St GTN M18 ....28 C3
Fryer Rd NWCHE CW9 ....110 C1
Fry St STHEL WA9 ....31 H1
Fuchsia Cl GTS/LS CH66 ....102 B3
Fulbeck WDN WA8 ....45 J5
Fulbeck Av CW/SHV CW2 ....185 H8
Fulbrook Dr CHD/CHDH SK8 ....56 A9
Fuller Dr CW/SHV CW2 ....184 G8
Fullerton Rd HTNM SK4 ....41 J6
  NWCHW CW8 ....109 J8
Fulmar Cl POY/DIS SK12 ....72 C2
Fulmar Ct CW/HAS CW1 ....184 G2
Fulmar Dr OFTN SK2 ....57 M2
  SALE M33 ....37 P6
Fulmards Cl WILM/AE SK9 ....71 L7
Fulneck Sq DROY M43 ....28 C1
Fulshaw Av WILM/AE SK9 ....71 J9
Fulshaw Ct WILM/AE SK9 ....71 J9
Fulshaw Pk WILM/AE SK9 ....93 J1
Fulshaw Pk South
  WILM/AE SK9 ....93 H1
Fulstone Ms OFTN SK2 ....57 H1
Fulton Gv NWCHE CW9 ....109 P9
Fulwood Gdns GTS/LS CH66 ....79 N7
Fulwood Rd GTS/LS CH66 ....79 N7
Fulwood Rd COL/RIS/CU WA3 ....24 C3
  GTS/LS CH66 ....79 N7
Furber St CW/HAS CW1 ....4 E1
Furlong Rd WYTH/NTH M22 ....54 E5
Furne Rd CH/BCN CH1 ....121 H7
Furness Av CW/SHV CW2 ....184 G2
  POY/DIS SK12 ....72 D2
  WSFD CW7 ....149 K2
Furness Gv NSTN SK4 ....41 H7
Furness Lodge Cl
  CHF/WBR SK23 ....75 P2
Furness Rd CHD/CHDH SK8 ....56 C9
Furnival Cl DTN/ASHW M34 ....28 J7
Furnival St SBCH CW11 ....171 N2
Furnival St CW/SHV CW2 ....4 B9
  RDSH SK5 ....28 E7
Furrocks Cl NSTN CH64 ....77 M8
Furrocks La NSTN CH64 ....77 M8
Furrocks Wy NSTN CH64 ....77 M8
The Furrows GTS/LS CH66 ....102 A4
Fylde Av CHD/CHDH SK8 ....55 L7
Fylde Rd HTNM SK4 ....39 L9
Fytton Cl MCFLDS SK11 ....135 L2

G

Gable Av WILM/AE SK9 ....71 J7
Gable Ct NANT CW5 ....10 B4
Gables Cl WARRN/WOL WA2 ....34 A5
The Gables ALS/KID ST7 ....187 N5
  WARR WA1 ....38 E5
Gable St NEWLW WA12 ....23 L6
Gabriel Bnk NWCHW CW8 ....107 L5
Gadbrook Pk NWCHE CW9 ....110 D7
Gadbrook Rd NWCHE CW9 ....110 D6
Gaddum Rd ALT WA14 ....52 E6
  DID/WITH M20 ....40 D5
Gail Av HTNM SK4 ....16 C2
Gail Cl WILM/AE SK9 ....93 M1
Gainford Av CHD/CHDH SK8 ....55 K3
Gainford Cl WDN WA8 ....45 J4
Gainford Rd RDSH SK5 ....28 E8
Gainsborough Av
  DID/WITH M20 ....40 D3
  MPL/ROM SK6 ....43 M9
Gainsborough Dr
  CHD/CHDH SK8 ....55 P1
Gainsborough Rd CW/SHV CW2 ....4 B9
  NEWLW ST5 ....57 J5
  WARRS WA4 ....48 D5
Gairloch Cl WARRN/WOL WA2 ....34 A4
Gair Rd RDSH SK5 ....41 N4
Gaisgill Ct WDN WA8 ....45 J6
Gale Cl CHSW/BR CH4 ....140 G7
Galbraith Cl CHNE CW12 ....155 L8
Galbraith Rd CHD/CHDH M20 ....40 D5
Gale Av WARRW/BUR WA5 ....33 J7
Galion Wy WDN WA8 ....45 M3
Galleys Bnk ALS/KID ST7 ....189 K5
Galloway Cl WARRW/BUR WA5 ....131 P9
Gallowsclough Lt
  FROD/HEL WA6 ....107 K8
Galston Av RAIN/WH L35 ....30 C6
Galston Ct OP/CLY M11 ....28 A1
Galway Gv CW/SHV CW2 ....198 A3
Game St SBCH CW11 ....171 L6
Ganton Cl WDN WA8 ....45 D1
Garden Cl MCFLDN SK10 ....9 G2
Garden Ct CH/BCN CH1 ....2 A3
Gardeners Wy RAIN/WH L35 ....30 B3
Garden La ALT WA14 ....53 H2
  MCFLDN SK10 ....9 G2
Garden Rd KNUT WA16 ....90 D2
Garden St DTN/ASHW M34 ....29 M3
  MCFLDN SK10 ....9 G2
  OFTN SK2 ....57 J5
Garden Ter CHSE CH3 ....143 F2
Gardner Av RNFD/HAY WA11 ....22 G3
Gardner St WGTN/LGST M12 ....28 B5
Garfield Av BNG/LEV M19 ....28 B8
Garfield St STKP SK1 * 17 J2
Garfit St MWCH CW10 ....130 B9
Garland Rd WYTH/NTH M22 ....54 G4
Garlick St GTN M18 ....28 D4
Garner Av HALE/TIMP WA15 ....38 D7

Garner Cl ALT WA14 ....53 H5
Garner's La EDGY/DAV SK3 ....56 F2
Garnet St WARRN/WOL WA2 ....19 G1
Garnet St STHEL WA9 ....31 J1
Garnett Av WA4 ....49 H3
Garnett Cl NANT CW5 ....196 G5
Garnetts La RAIN/WH L35 ....44 D6
  WDN WA8 ....60 C3
Garnett St STKP SK1 ....28 C4
Garratt Wk WGTN M18 ....28 C4
Garratt Fld GOL/RIS/CU WA3 ....34 E3
Garrett Wk EDGY/DAV SK3 ....56 A9
Garriggle Cl GTN M18 ....28 C4
Garriggil Ct WDN WA8 ....45 D6
Garrigill St WYTH/NTH M22 ....54 F3
Garsdale Av RAIN/WH L35 ....30 C6
Garsdale Cl WARRW/BUR WA5 ....32 C9
Garside Av GOL/RIS/CU WA3 ....24 F2
Garside St DTN/ASHW M34 ....29 M7
Garston Ct HTNM SK4 ....16 A1
Garth Av HALE/TIMP WA15 ....53 P1
Garth Dr CHNE CH2 ....121 M6
Garth Ganol FLINT CH6 ....60 A1
Garthland Rd BRAM/HZG SK7 ....57 M4
Garthorp Rd NTHM/RTH M23 ....39 H7
Garth Rd MPL/ROM SK6 ....58 E1
  OFTN SK2 ....57 P3
  WYTH/NTH M22 ....54 F3
Gartons La STHEL WA9 ....31 H5
Garven Pl WARR WA1 ....16 D5
Garwood Cl WARRW/BUR WA5 ....32 E8
Gaskell Av KNUT WA16 ....90 D3
  WARRS WA4 ....48 D6
Gaskell Rd ALT WA14 ....53 H1
Gaskell St STHEL WA9 ....22 B8
  WARRS WA4 ....48 E6
Gas Rd MCFLDN SK10 ....9 F4
Gas St HTNM SK4 ....16 E4
Gateacre Ct GTS/LS CH66 ....80 E5
Gateacre Wk NTHM/RTH M23 ....55 K5
Gatefield St CW/HAS CW1 ....4 D2
Gateley Cl WARRS WA4 ....49 N4
Gatesheath Dr CHNE CH2 ....121 N4
Gatesheath La CHSE CH3 ....163 M4
Gate St DUK SK16 ....29 N3
  OP/CLY M11 ....28 C1
Gate Warth St
  WARRW/BUR WA5 * 47 P4
  CW/HAS CW1 ....5 K6
  NEWLW ST5 ....201 N5
Gateway Rd DTN M18 * 28 C4
Gathill Cl CHD/CHDH SK8 ....55 P6
Gathurst Ct WDN WA8 ....20 A2
Gathurst St GTN M18 ....28 E3
Gatley Gn CHD/CHDH SK8 ....55 L2
Gatley Rd CHD/CHDH SK8 ....55 L2
  SALE M33 ....39 H5
Gatling Av WGTN/LGST M12 ....28 A2
Gatwick Av NTHM/RTH M23 ....54 D1
Gaunts Wy RUNC WA7 ....62 C8
Gawer Pk CH/BCN CH1 ....121 M7
Gawsworth Av CW/SHV CW2 ....184 F5
  DID/WITH M20 ....40 D7
Gawsworth Cl BRAM/HZG SK7 ....72 E1
  EDGY/DAV SK3 ....56 D2
  HALE/TIMP WA15 ....38 D6
  HOLMCH CW4 ....131 N8
  POY/DIS SK12 ....73 M4
Gawsworth Ct
  COL/RIS/CU WA3 * 34 G2
Gawsworth Dr SBCH CW11 ....171 P1
Gawsworth Ms GTS/LS CH66 ....79 K8
Gawsworth Rd GTS/LS CH66 ....80 A9
  MCFLDS SK11 ....116 D8
  SALE M33 ....39 H6
Gawthorne Cl BRAM/HZG SK7 ....57 J5
Gaydon Rd SALE M33 ....38 A4
Gayhurst Av
  WARRN/WOL WA2 * 34 A6
Gaymoore Cl DID/WITH M20 ....2 D1
Gaynor Av RNFD/HAY WA11 ....23 K2
Gayton Cl CHNE CW2 ....121 P6
Gee Cross Fold LYNDE SK14 ....43 K1
Gee St EDGY/DAV SK3 ....16 C7
Gemmull Cl AUD/MAD/W CW3 ....216 G1
General St WARR WA1 ....19 F5
Geneva Av BRAM/HZG SK7 ....56 D4
  GE CW7 ....149 L1
George Bates Cl ALS/KID ST7 ....187 N5
George La MPL/ROM SK6 ....42 F4
George Mann Ct
  WYTH/NTH M22 ....54 E6
George Richards Wy ALT WA14 ....37 N9
Georges Crs WARRS WA4 ....49 K5
George Cl GTN M18 ....28 D4
Georges Cl RAIN/WH L35 ....30 C4
George's La NWCHE CW9 ....88 D4
George's Rd HTNM SK4 ....16 D3
  SALE M33 ....38 E5
George's Rd West
  POY/DIS SK12 ....73 K3
George St ALS/KID ST7 ....200 C6
  CH/BCN CH1 ....2 D4
  DTN/ASHW M34 ....29 N6
  EP CH65 ....6 E1
  IRL M44 ....27 P6
  KNUT WA16 ....90 D3
  MCFLDS SK11 ....9 F5
  MPL/ROM SK6 ....44 B9
  NEWLW WA12 ....23 L5
  NWCHW CW8 ....109 K1
  SBCH CW11 ....171 K1
  STKP SK1 ....17 J4
  WHITCH SY13 ....213 N5
  WILM/AE SK9 ....93 J4
  WSFD CW7 ....149 N1
George St East MCFLDS SK11 ....42 A8
George St West MCFLDS SK11 ....8 D4
Georges Wk SBCH CW11 * 171 N3
Georges Wy ALS/KID ST7 ....201 J5

George VI Av MWCH CW10 ....151 J3
George VI Cl MWCH CW10 * 151 K4
Gerard Dr NANT CW5 ....196 D5
Gerards Av RNFD/HAY WA11 * 21 J2
Gerards La STHEL WA9 ....31 J1
Gerosa Av WARRN/WOL WA2 ....24 D9
Gerrard Av CW/SHV CW2 ....198 D6
  HALE/TIMP WA15 ....53 N9
Gerrard Dr NWCHW CW8 ....38 D6
Gerrard Gv CW/SHV CW2 ....38 B6
Gerrard Rd WILM/AE SK9 ....34 B1
Gerrards Av CHSE CH3 ....143 J1
Gerrards Cl NANT CW5 ....27 M7
Gerrards Gdns HYDE SK14 ....43 K1
Gerrards Hollow HYDE SK14 ....43 J1
Gerrards Wd HYDE SK14 ....43 J1
Gertrude St STHEL WA9 ....30 B2
Giantswood La CONG CW12 ....155 H1
Gibb Hl NWCHE CW9 ....87 M4
Gibbon Av WYTH/NTH M22 ....55 J2
Gibbon Dr NWCHE CW9 ....59 J2
Gibbon Dr NWCHE CW9 ....110 C1
Gib La NTHM/RTH M23 ....39 M8
Gibraltar La DTN/ASHW M34 ....29 P9
Gibsmere Cl HALE/TIMP WA15 ....53 P1
Gibson Cl EP CH65 ....80 D5
Gibson Crs SBCH CW11 ....171 J5
Gibson Gv NEWLW ST5 ....201 N7
Gibson St WARR WA1 ....19 G6
  WARRS WA4 ....48 F6
Gibson Wy ALT WA14 ....37 N9
Gilwood Rd WYTH/NTH M22 ....39 M8
Gidlow St GTN M18 ....28 E3
  WARRS WA4 ....49 H7
Gigg La WARRS WA4 ....63 M1
Gig La WARR WA1 ....19 N3
Gilbertbank MPL/ROM SK6 ....42 E4
Gilbert Cl ALS/KID ST7 ....189 J6
Gilbert Rd HALE/TIMP WA15 ....53 J6
Gilbert St BURS/TUN ST6 ....189 L9
Gilchrist Av GTN M18 ....28 A5
Gilchrist Rd IRL M44 ....36 D2
Gilderdale Cl COL/RIS/CU WA3 ....25 J8
Giles St WGTN/LGST M12 ....28 A5
Gillan Cl RUNC WA7 ....62 G9
Gill Bank Rd ALS/KID ST7 ....189 K8
Gillbrook Rd CHD/CHDH SK8 ....56 A9
Gillow Cl CW/HAS CW1 ....169 P9
Gill St STKP SK1 ....42 A1
Gillwood Dr MPL/ROM SK6 ....42 E7
Gilmore St EDGY/DAV SK3 ....81 M9
Giltbrook Cl WDN WA8 ....45 M3
Gilwell Dr NTHM/RTH M23 ....55 K8
Gilwell Dr NTHM/RTH M23 ....56 B3
Gingerbread La NANT CW5 ....11 L6
Gipsy La CH/BCN CH1 ....121 J1
  OFTN SK2 ....57 J1
Girton Cl EP CH65 ....7 G6
Girton Rd EP CH65 ....7 G6
Girvin Dr NSTN CH64 ....64 C6
Gladeside Rd WYTH/NTH M23 ....54 E3
The Glade HTNM SK4 ....41 H7
Gladewood Cl WILM/AE SK9 ....71 L6
Gladstone Av CH/BCN CH1 ....2 A3
  HTNM SK4 ....41 H7
Gladstone Ms HTNM SK4 * 17 F1
Gladstone Rd ALT WA14 ....53 H1
  CH/BCN CH1 ....2 B1
  CHSW/BR CH4 ....140 F7
  NSTN CH64 ....77 L5
Gladstone St CW/HAS CW1 ....4 E2
  NANT CW5 ....197 L1
  NWCHW CW8 ....12 C5
  OFTN SK2 ....57 J5
  WARRN/WOL WA8 ....21 J2
  WDN WA8 ....21 J2
Gladstone Wy NEWLW WA12 ....23 M5
Gladwyn Av DID/WITH M20 ....39 P4
Glaisdale Cl CW/SHV CW2 ....197 P1
Glamis Cl CHSE CH3 ....122 B9
Glamis Ct CHSE CH3 ....122 B9
Glan Aber Pk CHSW/BR CH4 ....141 J6
Clandon Dr CHD/CHDH SK8 ....56 C8
Glan Gors FLINT CH6 ....60 B8
Clanvor Rd EDGY/DAV SK3 ....16 A7
Glastonbury Av CHD/CHDH SK8 ....55 N1
  CHNE CH2 ....122 A4
  COL/RIS/CU WA3 ....25 K1
  HALE/TIMP WA15 ....53 M5
Glastonbury Cl RUNC WA7 ....11 K8
  POY/DIS SK12 ....73 M4
Glaswen Gv RDSH SK5 ....41 N4
Glazebrook La COL/RIS/CU WA3 ....25 P2
Glazebrook St WARR WA1 ....19 H4
Glazebury Dr NTHM/RTH M23 ....54 D2
Glaziers La GOL/RIS/CU WA3 ....36 A1
Gleadmere WDN WA8 ....45 J5
Gleave Av MCFLDN SK10 ....95 P5
Gleave Rd NWCHW CW8 ....108 F3
  WARRW/BUR WA5 ....32 C2
Gleave St SALE M33 ....38 F3
Glebe Av WARRS WA4 ....49 L6
Glebe Cl NANT CW5 ....197 L1
Glebecroft Av CHNE CH2 ....104 A1
Glebe Green Dr WSFD CW7 ....149 L4
Glebeland COL/RIS/CU WA3 ....25 K1
Glebelands Rd KNUT WA16 ....90 E4
  NTHM/RTH M23 ....38 D2
  SALE M33 ....38 D2
Glebe La WDN WA8 ....21 H8
Glebe Mdw CHNE CW2 ....122 C2
Glebe Rd WARRW/BUR WA5 ....32 B9
Glebe St ALS/KID ST7 ....200 C6
Glebe Green WSFD CW7 ....148 G4
Glebe St CW/HAS CW1 ....4 B2
  STKP SK1 ....17 K5
The Glebe RUNC WA7 ....11 J5
Gledhill St DID/WITH M20 ....40 C1
Gleggs Cl CHSE CH3 ....143 K3

Clegg St MCFLDN SK10 ....9 G5
Glenacre Gdns GTN M18 ....28 E6
Clenathol Rd GTS/LS CH66 ....79 N9
Glen Av SALE M33 ....38 D2
Glenbourne Pk
  BRAM/HZG SK7 ....72 D1
Clenburn Av PS/BROM CH62 ....79 J2
Glenby Av WYTH/NTH M22 ....55 H4
Clencastle Rd GTN M18 ....28 C5
Glen Cl COL/RIS/CU WA3 ....36 A6
Glencoe Rd GTS/LS CH66 ....37 P6
Glencourse Rd WDN WA8 ....45 N2
Clendale Av CW/HAS CW1 ....104 A1
Glendale Cl AUD/MAD/W CW3 ....217 N1
  CW/SHV CW2 ....4 C5
Clendene Av BRAM/HZG SK7 ....72 D1
Glendyke Rd GTS/LS CH66 ....79 N9
Gleneagles Cl BRAM/HZG SK7 ....56 G8
  CHSE CH3 ....122 C8
  WILM/AE SK9 ....71 M6
Gleneagles Dr HOLMCH CW4 ....131 N9
  MCFLDN SK10 ....13 L5
  RNFD/HAY WA11 ....22 E4
  WDN WA8 ....45 N2
  WSFD CW7 ....128 D3
Gleneagles Rd CHD/CHDH SK8 ....55 L8
  GTS/LS CH66 ....79 N9
Glenesk Rd GTS/LS CH66 ....79 N9
Glenfield Cl WA4 ....52 F5
Glenfield Dr POY/DIS SK12 ....73 K3
Glenholme Rd BRAM/HZG SK7 ....56 D8
Glenhurst Rd BNG/LEV M19 * 40 F3
Clenlea Dr DID/WITH M20 ....40 C8
Glenmaye Rd GTS/LS CH66 ....79 N9
Clenmere Rd DID/WITH M20 ....40 D8
Glenmore Rd STKP SK1 ....17 J5
Glenmore Av DID/WITH M20 ....39 P4
Glenn Pl WDN WA8 ....21 J2
Clenorchy Cl HOLMCH CW4 ....131 P9
Glen Rd HALE/TIMP WA15 ....53 L2
Glen Rd GTS/LS CH66 ....79 N9
Glenside Cl CH/BCN CH1 ....120 G6
Glenside Gv WDN WA8 ....20 A6
Glenside Dr MPL/ROM SK6 ....42 G5
  WILM/AE SK9 ....71 L8
The Glen CH/BCN CH1 ....121 H6
  RUNC WA7 ....62 D9
Glenthorn Gv SALE M33 ....38 E5
Clenville Cl RUNC WA7 ....11 H7
Glenville Wy DTN/ASHW M34 ....29 N7
Glenwood Cl CH/BCN CH1 ....79 N7
Glenwood Gdns GTS/LS CH66 ....79 N7
Glenwood Gv OFTN SK2 ....57 H4
Glenwood Rd GTS/LS CH66 ....79 N7
Gleyve KNUT WA16 ....67 J1
Globe Cl WARRS WA4 ....29 P2
Globe Sq DUK SK16 ....29 N2
Glossop Rd MPL/ROM SK6 ....44 B9
Gloucester Av BNG/LEV M19 ....28 B9
  GTS/LS CH66 ....58 D1
Gloucester Cl GTS/LS CH66 ....102 A4
  MCFLDN SK10 ....13 L9
  WARR WA1 ....34 K9
Gloucester Dr SALE M33 ....38 A4
Gloucester Rd ALS/KID ST7 ....189 H6
  CHD/CHDH SK8 ....55 L8
  DTN/ASHW M34 ....29 N7
  KNUT WA16 ....90 D5
  POY/DIS SK12 ....73 K2
  WDN WA8 ....45 P4
Gloucester St CH/BCN CH1 ....2 E1
  WARR WA1 ....22 B7
Glover Rd COL/RIS/CU WA3 ....24 E3
Glover St GTS/LS CH66 ....143 K3
Glover St CW/HAS CW1 ....184 G3
  NEWLW WA12 ....23 N5
Glyn Av HALE/TIMP WA15 ....53 L5
Glynn Av CW/HAS CW1 ....140 B2
Goathland Wy MCFLDS SK11 ....117 K7
Godbert Av CCHDY M21 ....39 N4
Goddard Cl CW/HAS CW1 ....4 B1
Goddard Rd RUNC WA7 ....62 C3
Goddard St CW/HAS CW1 ....4 B1
Godfrey Range GTN M18 ....28 F5
Godfrey St WARRN/WOL WA2 ....19 H2
Godley Cl OP/CLY M11 ....28 C1
Godscroft La FROD/HEL WA6 ....83 L7
Godshill Cl WARRW/BUR WA5 ....32 A9
Godstow RUNC WA7 ....63 J2
Godward Rd NM/HAY SK22 ....59 M7
Godwin St GTN M18 ....28 E3
Goldbourne Dr ALS/KID ST7 ....201 J5
Goldcliffe Cl WARRW/BUR WA5 ....32 C6
Goldcrest Cl CW/HAS CW1 ....184 F1
  RUNC WA7 ....62 D9
  WSFD CW7 ....149 M2
  WYTH/NTH M22 ....55 H2
Goldfinch Cl CONG CW12 ....155 N9
Goldfinch Dr ALS/KID ST7 ....187 M5
Goldford La MALPAS SY14 ....34 F4
Goldie Av WYTH/NTH M22 ....55 H6
Goldsmith Av RDSH SK5 ....28 D8
Goldsmith Fold RAIN/WH L35 ....30 K5
Golf Links Cl BURS/TUN ST6 ....189 L9
  SALE M33 ....59 J4
Gongar La CHSE CH3 ....124 D2
Consley Ct CHNE CH2 ....121 N8
Conville Av MCFLDS SK11 ....117 M9
Gooch Dr NEWLW WA12 ....23 P7

Goodall St MCFLDS SK11 ... 9 H6
Goodban St STHEL WA9 ... 22 C9
Goodier St SALE M33 ... 38 D4
Goodleigh Pl STHEL WA9 ... 31 H3
Goodridge Av WYTH/NTH M22 ... 54 E5
Goodrington Rd WILM/AE SK9 ... 71 N4
Goodwin Crs CW/SHV CW2 ... 198 B3
Goodwood Av NTHM/RTH M23 ... 38 G8
SALE M33 ... 37 P4
Goodwood Cl CH/BCN CH1 ... 2 A2
MCFLDS SK11 ... 9 H7
NWCHW CW8 ... 109 K1
Goodwood Ct STHEL WA9 ... 30 C2
Goodwood Crs
HALE/TIMP WA15 ... 53 N1
Goodwood Gv GTS/LS CH66 ... 101 P1
Goodwood Ri MWCH CW10 ... 129 P9
Goodwood Rd MPL/ROM SK6 ... 58 C2
Goole St OP/CLY M11 ... 28 A1
Gooseberry La RUNC WA7 ... 63 H5
TPLY/KEL CW6 ... 125 K8
Goosebrook Cl NWCHE CW9 ... 87 L5
Goosebrook La NWCHE CW9 ... 87 H3
Goose Gn ALT WA14 ... 53 H3
Goose La WARRS WA4 ... 64 C4
Goosetrey Cl WILM/AE SK9 ... 71 N5
HOLMCH CW4 ... 131 M4
Goostrey La HOLMCH CW4 ... 132 D5
Gordale Cl CONG CW12 ... 156 A5
NWCHW CW8 ... 12 B1
WARRW/BUR WA5 ... 32 C9
Gordon Av BNG/LEV M19 ... 28 B8
BRAM/HZG SK7 ... 57 K4
RNFD/HAY WA11 ... 23 K2
WARR WA1 ... 34 C9
Gordon La CHNE CH2 ... 102 D7
Gordon Pl DID/WITH M20 ... 40 C3
Gordon Rd SALE M33 ... 38 E2
Gordon St GTN M18 ... 28 E3
HTNM SK4 ... 17 F2
Gorebrook Ct WGTN/LGST M12 ... 28 A5
Goredale Av GTN M18 ... 28 E6
Gore La KNUT WA16 ... 92 D2
Gorelan Rd GTN M18 * ... 28 D4
Goring Av GTN M18 ... 28 D3
Gorse Av MPL/ROM SK6 ... 58 C1
Gorse Bank Rd
HALE/TIMP WA15 ... 53 N8
Gorse Cl FROD/HEL WA6 ... 107 L6
Gorse Covert NWCHE CW9 ... 110 C1
Gorse Covert Rd
GOL/RIS/CU WA3 ... 35 J2
Gorsefield CHSE CH3 ... 163 P8
STHEL WA9 ... 30 C1
Gorsefield Hey WILM/AE SK9 ... 71 N6
Gorselands CHD/CHDH SK8 ... 72 B1
Gorse La CONG CW12 ... 174 E4
Gorse Sq PART M31 ... 36 C5
Gorse Stacks CH/BCN CH1 ... 2 E3
The Gorse ALT WA14 ... 52 F7
Gorse Wy CHSE CH3 ... 143 J5
Gorseway RDSH SK5 ... 42 A4
Gorsewood Rd RUNC WA7 ... 63 H8
Gorsey Av WYTH/NTH M22 ... 54 E3
Gorsey Bank Crs NANT CW5 ... 197 P7
Gorsey Bank Rd EDGY/DAV SK3 ... 41 J8
Gorsey Brow MPL/ROM SK6 ... 42 F6
STKP SK1 ... 17 J5
Gorsey Dr WYTH/NTH M22 ... 54 E3
Gorseyfields DROY M43 ... 28 G1
Gorsey La ALT WA14 ... 52 F2
LYMM WA13 ... 51 N1
STHEL WA9 ... 31 L4
WARRN/WOL WA2 ... 19 H1
WDN WA8 ... 46 C7
Gorsey Mount St STKP SK1 ... 17 H5
Gorsey Rd WILM/AE SK9 ... 71 H7
WYTH/NTH M22 ... 54 E3
Gorseywell La RUNC WA7 ... 63 K8
Gorsley Cl MWCH CW10 ... 151 J4
Gorstage La NWCHW CW8 ... 108 D7
Gorstons La NSTN CH64 ... 77 N7
Gorston Wk WYTH/NTH M22 ... 54 E7
Gorsty Hill Cl CW/SHV CW2 ... 199 L5
Gorton Crs DTN/ASHW M34 ... 29 J7
Gorton La WGTN/LGST M12 ... 28 A3
Gorton Rd RDSH SK5 ... 28 F9
Gorton Rd WGTN/LGST M12 ... 28 A2
Gosforth Pl CHNE CH2 ... 122 A8
Gosling Rd GOL/RIS/CU WA3 ... 34 C1
Gosling Wy CONG CW12 ... 155 J7
Gosport Cl WARRN/WOL WA2 ... 33 P7
Goss St CH/BCN CH1 ... 2 D4
Gotherage Cl MPL/ROM SK6 ... 43 K6
Gotherage La MPL/ROM SK6 ... 43 K6
Gothic Cl MPL/ROM SK6 ... 43 L6
Gough Av WARRN/WOL WA2 ... 33 L6
Gough's La KNUT WA16 ... 90 F6
Gough St EDGY/DAV SK3 ... 16 D5
Goulden Rd DID/WITH M20 ... 40 B3
Goulden St CW/HAS CW1 ... 184 G3
WARRW/BUR WA5 ... 48 A1
Goulder Rd GTN M18 ... 28 E6
Goulders Ct RUNC WA7 ... 62 F9
Gould St DTN/ASHW M34 ... 29 L6
Gourham Dr CHD/CHDH SK8 ... 55 P5
Govan St WYTH/NTH M22 ... 39 P7
Govett Rd STHEL WA9 ... 30 B1
Gower Av BRAM/HZG SK7 ... 57 J4
Gowerdale Rd RDSH SK5 ... 42 B3
Gower Rd HTNM SK4 ... 41 L4
Gower St STHEL WA9 ... 22 B8
Gowy Cl ALS/KID ST7 ... 187 K5
SBCH CW11 ... 171 K1
WILM/AE SK9 ... 71 N5
Gowy Ct GTS/LS CH66 ... 80 A5
TPLY/KEL CW6 ... 167 H7
Gowy Crs CHSE CH3 ... 145 H1
Gowy Rd CHNE CH2 ... 122 G2
Goyt Av MPL/ROM SK6 ... 58 D3
Goyt Crs STKP SK1 ... 42 A5
Goyt Rd MPL/ROM SK6 ... 58 D3
NM/HAY SK22 ... 59 N9
POY/DIS SK12 ... 75 H1
STKP SK1 ... 42 A5
Goyt Valley Rd MPL/ROM SK6 ... 42 E6
Goyt Vw NM/HAY SK22 ... 59 M9
MPL/ROM SK6 ... 43 L7
Goyt Wy MPL/ROM SK6 ... 58 F2
NM/HAY SK22 ... 59 N9
Grace Av WARRN/WOL WA2 ... 33 L8
Grace Cl CW/HAS CW1 ... 186 A4
Grace Rd EP CH65 ... 6 E2
Grace St STHEL WA9 ... 22 A9
Gradwell St EDGY/DAV SK3 ... 16 D6
Grafton Ms CHNE CH2 ... 2 E1
Grafton Rd EP CH65 ... 6 E1
The Graftons ALT WA14 * ... 53 H3
Grafton St ALT WA14 ... 53 H3
HTNM SK4 ... 41 M5
NEWLW WA12 ... 23 M6
WARRW/BUR WA5 ... 48 A1
Graham Av GTS/LS CH66 ... 79 P8
Graham Cl WDN WA8 ... 45 J7
Graham Crs IRL M44 ... 36 B4
Graham Dr HLWD L26 ... 44 A7
POY/DIS SK12 ... 58 G8
Graham Rd CH/BCN CH1 ... 121 H7
STKP SK1 ... 42 A8
WDN WA8 ... 45 J7
Graham St OP/CLY M11 ... 28 A1
STHEL WA9 ... 22 A5
Grainger Av WGTN/LGST M12 ... 28 A6
Grainger's Rd NWCHE CW9 ... 109 P7
Gralam Cl SALE M33 ... 39 H7
Grammar School Ct
WARRS WA4 * ... 49 H4
Grammar School Rd
LYMM WA13 ... 50 F5
WARRS WA4 ... 49 H4
Grampian Wy NSTN CH64 ... 77 L8
PS/BROM CH62 ... 79 J1
WSFD CW7 ... 149 J3
Granada Rd DTN/ASHW M34 ... 28 G6
Granary Wy SALE M33 ... 38 C6
Granby Cl RUNC WA7 * ... 62 G9
Granby Rd CHD/CHDH SK8 ... 56 B7
HALE/TIMP WA15 ... 38 D7
OFTN SK2 ... 57 H2
WARRS WA4 ... 48 D7
Grand Central Sq
EDGY/DAV SK3 * ... 17 F6
Grandford La NANT CW5 ... 207 N4
Grand Junction Wy
CW/HAS CW1 ... 5 H4
Granford Cl ALT WA14 * ... 38 A9
Grange Av CHD/CHDH SK8 ... 55 P4
HALE/TIMP WA15 ... 38 E9
HALE/TIMP WA15 ... 53 L5
HTNM SK4 ... 41 K3
NWCHW CW8 ... 109 J1
WARRS WA4 ... 48 G3
Grangebrook Dr WSFD CW7 ... 128 D8
Grange Cl CW/HAS CW1 ... 5 J4
GOL/RIS/CU WA3 ... 24 E3
SBCH CW11 ... 171 L2
Grange Ct BIDD ST8 ... 175 L7
Grange Crs GTS/LS CH66 ... 79 L4
Grange Dr NWCHW CW8 ... 109 J6
WARRW/BUR WA5 ... 47 L3
WDN WA8 ... 20 B1
Grange Farm Cl
WARRW/BUR WA5 ... 47 P1
Grangefields BIDD ST8 ... 175 M6
Grange Green Mnr
WARRS WA4 * ... 48 A8
Grangelands MCFLDN SK10 ... 116 F2
Grange La DID/WITH M20 ... 40 C6
MALPAS SY14 ... 191 L5
NWCHW CW8 ... 108 D6
NWCHW CW8 ... 128 B4
WSFD CW7 ... 128 D9
Grange Lea MWCH CW10 ... 151 H1
Grangemoor RUNC WA7 ... 62 B7
Grange Park Av CHD/CHDH SK8 ... 55 M2
RUNC WA7 ... 15 J3
WILM/AE SK9 ... 71 J6
Grange Park Dr BIDD ST8 ... 175 M6
Grange Park Rd CHD/CHDH SK8 ... 55 M2
RUNC WA7 ... 15 J3
Grange Pl IRL M44 ... 36 C3
Grange Rd ALT WA14 ... 52 G6
BIDD ST8 ... 175 M6
BRAM/HZG SK7 ... 56 G5
CHNE CH2 ... 121 N7
CHSE CH3 ... 122 C9
CHSE CH3 ... 124 F2
EP CH65 ... 6 E5
HALE/TIMP WA15 ... 38 E9
MCFLDS SK11 ... 8 D7
NWCHE CW9 ... 110 D6
NWCHW CW8 ... 108 B9
NWCHW CW8 ... 109 J1
RNFD/HAY WA11 ... 23 H4
RUNC WA7 ... 15 J3
SALE M33 ... 38 C4
Grange Rd North RUNC WA7 ... 15 J2
Grangeside CHNE CH2 ... 121 N4
The Grange NWCHW CW8 ... 109 K7
Grangethorpe Dr BNG/LEV M19 ... 40 F1
Grange Va RNFD/HAY WA11 ... 23 H3
Grangeway RUNC WA7 ... 62 A7
Grange Wy SBCH CW11 ... 171 L2
Grangeway WILM/AE SK9 ... 71 M2
Grangeway Ct RUNC WA7 ... 62 A7
Grangewood Dr KNUT WA16 ... 114 B1
Gransmoor Av OP/CLY M11 ... 28 F2
Gransmoor Rd OP/CLY M11 ... 28 F2
Granston Cl WARRW/BUR WA5 ... 33 H6
Granstone Cl BURS/TUN ST6 ... 189 P9
Grant Cl WARRW/BUR WA5 ... 32 G7
Grantham Av WARR WA1 ... 33 P9
WARRS WA4 ... 48 D7
Grantham Cl NWCHE CW9 ... 110 C5
Grantham Crs RNFD/HAY WA11 ... 22 A4
Grantham Rd HTNM SK4 ... 16 B3
Grant Rd WARRW/BUR WA5 ... 47 M1
Granville Dr GTS/LS CH66 ... 79 M6
Granville Gdns DID/WITH M20 ... 40 B6
Granville Rd CH/BCN CH1 ... 2 A1
CHD/CHDH SK8 ... 56 C2
HALE/TIMP WA15 ... 53 N1
NWCHE CW9 ... 110 A7
WILM/AE SK9 ... 71 H9
Granville Sq WSFD CW7 ... 149 M2
Granville St RUNC WA7 ... 15 F1
STHEL WA9 ... 22 B6
WARR WA1 ... 19 H3
WSFD CW7 ... 149 N2
Grapes St MCFLDS SK11 * ... 9 F6
WARRS WA4 ... 49 M9
Grappenhall Rd EP CH65 ... 102 B1
WARRS WA4 ... 48 F6
Grasmere MCFLDS SK11 ... 116 G6
Grasmere Av CONG CW12 ... 155 H8
CW/SHV CW2 ... 184 F3
HTNM SK4 ... 41 M2
WARRN/WOL WA2 ... 33 N5
Grasmere Cl WSFD CW7 ... 128 E9
Grasmere Crs BRAM/HZG SK7 ... 56 E7
MPL/ROM SK6 ... 58 C6
Grasmere Dr HOLMCH CW4 ... 131 M8
RUNC WA7 ... 62 B9
Grasmere Rd CHD/CHDH SK8 ... 55 K4
CHNE CH2 ... 122 A6
EP CH65 ... 102 E2
FROD/HEL WA6 ... 84 A5
HALE/TIMP WA15 ... 53 N1
LYMM WA13 ... 50 F3
NSTN CH64 ... 77 L7
PART M31 ... 36 D5
SALE M33 ... 38 F6
WILM/AE SK9 ... 93 J4
Grasmere St WGTN/LGST M12 ... 28 B6
Grason Av WILM/AE SK9 ... 71 L5
Grasscroft RDSH SK5 ... 42 B2
Grassfield Wy KNUT WA16 ... 90 E6
Grassholme Dr OFTN SK2 ... 57 N2
Grass Md DTN/ASHW M34 ... 29 N9
Grassygreen La ALS/KID ST7 ... 201 H6
Gratrix La SALE M33 ... 39 J5
Gratrix St GTN M18 ... 28 E5
Gravel Bank Rd MPL/ROM SK6 ... 42 G2
Gravel La WILM/AE SK9 ... 92 G1
Graveyard La KNUT WA16 ... 70 B9
Gray Av RNFD/HAY WA11 ... 23 H3
Graylag Cl RUNC WA7 ... 62 D9
Graymarsh Dr POY/DIS SK12 ... 73 L4
Graysands Rd HALE/TIMP WA15 ... 53 K4
Gray's Cl ALS/KID ST7 ... 189 K1
Grayston Av STHEL WA9 ... 31 J2
Grazing Dr IRL M44 ... 27 P6
Greasby Dr GTS/LS CH66 ... 80 A9
Great Ashfield WDN WA8 ... 45 K4
Great Delph RNFD/HAY WA11 ... 23 H2
Great Egerton St STKP SK1 ... 17 F3
Greatfield Rd WYTH/NTH M22 ... 54 D3
Great Jones St WGTN/LGST M12 ... 28 A3
Great King St MCFLDS SK11 ... 8 C4
Great Moor St OFTN SK2 ... 57 H2
Great Moreton Ter
CONG CW12 * ... 174 C7
Greatoak Rd ALS/KID ST7 ... 201 J3
Great Portwood St STKP SK1 ... 17 H2
Great Queen St MCFLDS SK11 ... 8 C4
Great Riding RUNC WA7 ... 62 G7
Great Underbank STKP SK1 ... 17 F4
Greave MPL/ROM SK6 ... 43 J4
Greave Fold MPL/ROM SK6 ... 43 H4
Greave Rd STKP SK1 ... 42 B8
Greaves La MALPAS SY14 ... 202 F7
Greaves La East MALPAS SY14 ... 202 F7
Greaves Rd WILM/AE SK9 ... 70 G7
Grebe Cl KNUT WA16 ... 90 F2
POY/DIS SK12 ... 73 H2
Greeba Av WARRS WA4 ... 48 D4
Greeba Rd NTHM/RTH M23 ... 54 A1
Greek St EDGY/DAV SK3 ... 17 F7
RUNC WA7 ... 14 D1
STKP SK1 ... 17 G6
Green Acre Cl KNUT WA16 ... 90 F5
Greenacre Rd CHSW/BR CH4 ... 142 B6
Greenacres CW/HAS CW1 ... 185 J2
FROD/HEL WA6 ... 84 A7
SBCH CW11 ... 171 M2
TPLY/KEL CW6 ... 145 N4
Greenacres Cl GOL/RIS/CU WA3 ... 25 K1
Greenacres Dr BNG/LEV M19 ... 40 F4
Greenacres Rd CONG CW12 ... 155 H8
The Greenacres LYMM WA13 ... 50 G3
Greenall Av WARRW/BUR WA5 ... 47 H3
Greenall Rd NWCHE CW9 ... 13 J2
Greenall's Av WARRS WA4 ... 48 E6
Green Av NWCHE CW9 ... 109 N9
Green Av NWCHW CW8 ... 109 J1
TPLY/KEL CW6 ... 166 G5
Greenbank CHSW/BR CH4 ... 142 G5
Green Bnk MKTDR TF9 ... 217 H8
Greenbank Av CHD/CHDH SK8 ... 55 J2
GTS/LS CH66 ... 79 N6
HTNM SK4 ... 40 F6
Greenbank Cl NANT CW5 ... 197 L1
Greenbank Crs MPL/ROM SK6 ... 58 D2
Greenbank Dr MCFLDN SK10 ... 95 N5
Greenbank Gdns WARRS WA4 ... 49 H5
NWCHW CW8 ... 109 H5
Greenbank Rd CHD/CHDH SK8 * ... 55 J1
CHNE CH2 ... 122 B7
MPL/ROM SK6 ... 43 N7
SALE M33 ... 38 B3
WARRS WA4 ... 49 H5
Greenbank St WARRS WA4 ... 48 E5
Green Bank Ter HTNM SK4 ... 17 F2
Greenbank Vls FLINT CH6 * ... 98 A6
Greenbeech Cl MPL/ROM SK6 ... 43 K9
Green Bridge Cl RUNC WA7 ... 62 E5
Greenbridge Rd RUNC WA7 ... 62 F4
Greenbrow Rd NTHM/RTH M23 ... 54 B4
Green Cl CHD/CHDH SK8 ... 55 J1
Green Coppice RUNC WA7 ... 62 G6
Green Cts ALT WA14 ... 52 F4
Green Cft MPL/ROM SK6 ... 43 J5
Greendale Dr MWCH CW10 ... 151 H3
NEWUL ST5 ... 201 N6
Greendale Gdns CW/HAS CW1 ... 185 L3
Greendale Gv DTN/ASHW M34 ... 29 P9
Greendale La MCFLDN SK10 ... 94 D5
Green Dr ALS/KID ST7 ... 187 P4
HALE/TIMP WA15 ... 38 D9
WILM/AE SK9 ... 71 M4
Green End BNG/LEV M19 ... 40 F3
DTN/ASHW M34 ... 29 P9
WHITCH SY13 ... 213 M6
Green End La STHEL WA9 * ... 22 A9
Green End Rd BNG/LEV M19 ... 40 F3
Greenfield Cl EDGY/DAV SK3 ... 56 E1
HALE/TIMP WA15 ... 53 N1
NM/HAY SK22 ... 59 L7
Greenfield Crs CHNE CH2 ... 122 C6
CHSE CH3 ... 144 B4
Greenfield Gdns CHNE CH2 ... 104 B1
Greenfield La CHNE CH2 ... 122 B6
FROD/HEL WA6 ... 83 P4
Greenfield Rd CHSE CH3 ... 144 B5
CHSW/BR CH4 ... 140 G6
CONG CW12 ... 155 K7
GTS/LS CH66 ... 79 M6
MCFLDN SK10 ... 95 N6
Greenfields CHNE CH2 ... 122 A2
WHITCH SY13 ... 213 L5
WSFD CW7 ... 150 B1
Greenfields Av CW/SHV CW2 ... 198 A3
WARRS WA4 ... 48 F7
Greenfields Cl NEWLW WA12 ... 23 N5
NSTN CH64 ... 77 M8
WARR WA1 ... 34 D9
Greenfields Cft NSTN CH64 ... 77 L8
Greenfields Dr ALS/KID ST7 ... 187 P5
NSTN CH64 ... 77 L9
Greenfields La CHSE CH3 ... 143 P5
MALPAS SY14 ... 204 A2
Greenfields Ms MALPAS SY14 * ... 204 A2
Greenfields Ri WHITCH SY13 ... 213 K5
Greenfield St DTN/ASHW M34 ... 29 K2
Greenfield Wy NWCHW CW8 ... 108 C8
Green Fold GTN M18 ... 28 F3
Greenfoot La WHITCH SY13 ... 213 M8
Greenford Cl CHD/CHDH SK8 ... 56 B3
Green Gables Cl CHD/CHDH SK8 ... 55 K6
Greengate HALE/TIMP WA15 ... 53 P8
Greengate Rd ALS/KID ST7 ... 188 B3
DTN/ASHW M34 ... 29 N5
Greengates MCFLDN SK10 * ... 116 E2
Greengates Crs NSTN CH64 ... 77 L8
Greenhalgh St HTNM SK4 ... 17 F2
Green Hall Ms WILM/AE SK9 ... 71 K8
Greenham Rd NTHM/RTH M23 ... 39 J6
Greenhaven Ct NANT CW5 ... 209 M1
Greenhill Av SALE M33 ... 38 D2
Greenhill La WARRS WA4 ... 64 C9
Greenhill Rd HALE/TIMP WA15 ... 53 N1
Greenhills Cl MCFLDS SK11 ... 9 H6
Green Hill St EDGY/DAV SK3 ... 41 L9
Green Hill Ter EDGY/DAV SK3 ... 41 L9
Greenhill Wk POY/DIS SK12 ... 59 H9
Greenhouse Farm Rd
RUNC WA7 ... 62 F8
Greenhow St DROY M43 ... 28 F1
Greenhythe Rd CHD/CHDH SK8 ... 55 L9
Greening Rd BNG/LEV M19 ... 28 B7
Green Jones Brow
WARRW/BUR WA5 ... 32 C2
Green Lake La CHSE CH3 ... 162 A6
Greenland Cl TPLY/KEL CW6 ... 147 H9
Greenlands CHSE CH3 ... 164 A6
Green La AUD/MAD/W CW3 ... 216 G4
BRAM/HZG SK7 ... 57 K4
CH/BCN CH1 ... 120 F5
CHNE CH2 ... 103 L9
CHSE CH3 ... 122 C9
CHSE CH3 ... 178 F3
CHSW/BR CH4 ... 142 A5
EP CH65 ... 6 E7
GTN M18 ... 28 D3
GTS/LS CH66 ... 79 N9
HALE/TIMP WA15 ... 53 M4
HTNM SK4 ... 16 C3
IRL M44 ... 36 C3
KNUT WA16 ... 89 L7
KNUT WA16 ... 90 B1
KNUT WA16 ... 113 P3
MALPAS SY14 ... 191 H7
MCFLDN SK10 ... 95 P4
MPL/ROM SK6 ... 42 G7
NANT CW5 ... 182 C1
NANT CW5 ... 197 M2
NWCHE CW9 ... 88 F9
NWCHE CW9 ... 109 P9
POY/DIS SK12 ... 74 A2
POY/DIS SK12 ... 75 H1
SALE M33 ... 38 B2
SBCH CW11 ... 170 F1
TPLY/KEL CW6 ... 125 J7
WARR WA1 ... 34 B8
WARRN/WOL WA2 ... 33 K1
WARRS WA4 ... 65 H1
WARRS WA4 ... 65 K2
WARRW/BUR WA5 ... 32 B1
WDN WA8 ... 45 L6
WILM/AE SK9 ... 71 K7
WILM/AE SK9 ... 93 H5
Green Lane Cl
WARRN/WOL WA2 ... 33 K1
Green La East CQ CH5 ... 120 A4
Green La North
HALE/TIMP WA15 ... 53 M3
Green Lane (West) CQ CH5 ... 100 F9
Greenlaw Cl NWCHE CW9 ... 110 A7
Green Lawns Dr GTS/LS CH66 ... 102 B4
Greenlea Av GTN M18 ... 28 D6
Greenlea Cl EP CH65 ... 102 D2
Green Mdw MPL/ROM SK6 ... 43 L9
Green Meadows Dr
MPL/ROM SK6 ... 43 L9
Green Meadows Wk
WYTH/NTH M22 ... 54 G6
Greenoak Dr SALE M33 ... 38 F7
Green Oaks Pth WDN WA8 ... 46 A7
Green Oaks Wy WDN WA8 ... 46 A7
Greenore Dr SPK/HALE L24 ... 60 D4
Greenough Av RAIN/WH L35 ... 30 B3
Green Pk NWCHW CW8 ... 108 G5
Greenpark Rd WYTH/NTH M22 ... 39 N7
Green Pastures HTNM SK4 ... 40 F7
Green Rd PART M31 ... 36 D5
Greensbridge La HLWD L26 ... 44 B6
Greenshall La POY/DIS SK12 ... 59 K9
Greenshank Cl NEWLW WA12 ... 23 N5
Greenside Av FROD/HEL WA6 ... 84 B6
Greenside Cl ALS/KID ST7 ... 189 J9
Greenside Ct NWCHE CW9 ... 111 K7
Greenside Dr HALE/TIMP WA15 ... 53 J6
IRL M44 ... 27 M8
NWCHE CW9 ... 110 G4
Greenside Pl DTN/ASHW M34 * ... 29 N9
Greenside St OP/CLY M11 ... 28 C1
Green Strawberry EP CH65 ... 102 C4
Green St EDGY/DAV SK3 ... 56 F1
KNUT WA16 ... 90 E3
MCFLDN SK10 ... 9 G5
RUSH/FAL M14 ... 40 F1
SBCH CW11 ... 171 N2
WARRW/BUR WA5 ... 48 B2
WILM/AE SK9 ... 93 J4
WRXS/E LL13 ... 176 G7
Greensway CHSW/BR CH4 ... 142 C3
The Green BEB CH63 ... 78 A1
CHD/CHDH SK8 ... 55 P7
CHSE CH3 ... 124 E9
CONG CW12 * ... 155 L7
EP CH65 ... 102 D2
HTNM SK4 ... 16 A2
MPL/ROM SK6 ... 58 E4
MWCH CW10 ... 151 K4
NANT CW5 ... 183 M8
The Green NSTN CH64 ... 77 K5
NSTN CH64 ... 77 M7
NWCHW CW8 ... 109 K7
RUNC WA7 ... 62 D5
WILM/AE SK9 ... 71 N3
Greenthorne Av HTNM SK4 ... 41 L1
Green Tree Gdns MPL/ROM SK6 ... 42 G6
Greenvale Dr CHD/CHDH SK8 ... 55 L1
Green Vw LYMM WA13 ... 51 H2
Greenview Dr DID/WITH M20 ... 40 D8
Green Villa Pk WILM/AE SK9 ... 92 G1
Green Vls CHSW/BR CH4 * ... 160 D2
Greenville Rd NSTN CH64 ... 77 M4
Green Wk ALT WA14 ... 52 E4
CHD/CHDH SK8 ... 55 J1
HALE/TIMP WA15 ... 38 C9
NWCHW CW8 ... 108 C8
Greenway ALS/KID ST7 ... 187 M3
ALT WA14 ... 52 E2
BRAM/HZG SK7 ... 56 D9
Green Wy CH/BCN CH1 ... 120 D2
Greenway CHSE CH3 ... 177 H7
CONG CW12 ... 155 K7
CW/HAS CW1 ... 185 K2
MALPAS SY14 ... 191 J4
MPL/ROM SK6 ... 43 K7
NSTN CH64 ... 77 H3
WARR WA1 ... 34 A9
WARRS WA4 ... 48 F8
WARRW/BUR WA5 ... 32 B9
WILM/AE SK9 ... 71 J8
WYTH/NTH M22 ... 39 P8
Greenway Av BNG/LEV M19 ... 28 B9
Greenway Cl ALS/KID ST7 ... 188 B1
FROD/HEL WA6 ... 105 H1
SALE M33 ... 38 A5
Greenway Dr NWCHE CW9 ... 110 C5
Greenway Rd BIDD ST8 ... 175 M7
CHD/CHDH SK8 ... 55 L9
HALE/TIMP WA15 ... 38 D7
RUNC WA7 ... 14 D5
SPK/HALE L24 ... 60 A3
WDN WA8 ... 45 P5
Greenways ALS/KID ST7 ... 201 J5
Greenway St CHSW/BR CH4 ... 2 E7
Greenwell Rd RNFD/HAY WA11 ... 22 G3
Greenwich Av WDN WA8 ... 46 B3
Greenwood Av CHSW/BR CH4 ... 142 F3
CONG CW12 ... 155 P7
OFTN SK2 ... 57 J1
Greenwood Cl GOL/RIS/CU WA3 ... 25 P7
HALE/TIMP WA15 ... 53 P2
NWCHW CW8 * ... 108 F3
Greenwood Ct STHEL WA9 ... 31 H4
Greenwood Crs
WARRN/WOL WA2 ... 33 N6
Greenwood Dr NEWLW WA12 ... 23 P7
WILM/AE SK9 ... 71 M6
Greenwood Rd LYMM WA13 ... 50 E5
WYTH/NTH M22 ... 54 E2
Greenwood St ALT WA14 ... 53 H3
Greenwood Ter KNUT WA16 * ... 91 L1
Greer St OP/CLY M11 ... 28 C1
Greg Av MCFLDN SK10 ... 95 L6
Greg Ms WILM/AE SK9 ... 71 K4
Gregory Av MPL/ROM SK6 ... 42 G7
Gregory Cl WARRW/BUR WA5 ... 32 F9
Gregory Wy RDSH SK5 ... 41 N2
Gregson Rd RDSH SK5 ... 41 M2
WDN WA8 ... 46 A6
Greg St RDSH SK5 ... 41 M2
Grendale Av BRAM/HZG SK7 ... 57 L6
STKP SK1 ... 42 A7
Grendon Wk WGTN/LGST M12 ... 28 A3
Grenfell Cl NSTN CH64 ... 77 J4
Grenfell Pk NSTN CH64 ... 77 J4
Grenfell Rd DID/WITH M20 ... 40 B5
Grenfell St WDN WA8 ... 21 J3
Grenville Cl CW/HAS CW1 ... 186 A3
Grenville Rd BRAM/HZG SK7 ... 57 J4
Grenville St EDGY/DAV SK3 ... 16 C6
Gresford Av CHNE CH2 ... 121 P8
Gresford Cl WARRW/BUR WA5 ... 33 H7
Gresham St DTN/ASHW M34 ... 29 M5
Gresham Wk HTNM SK4 ... 41 M5

Gresley Wy ALS/KID ST7 201 H5
Gresty Av WYTH/NTH M22 55 H6
Gresty Green Rd CW/SHV CW2 185 K8
Gresty La CW/SHV CW2 198 A1
CW/SHV CW2 5 G7
Gresty Side NANT CW5 196 D2
Gresty Ter CW/HAS CW1 5 J4
Greswell St DTN/ASHW M34 29 L5
Greta Av CHD/CHDH SK8 55 L9
Greville Dr WSFD CW7 150 A1
Grey Cl MPL/ROM SK6 42 F4
Grey Friars CH/BCN CH1 2 C5
Greyfriars Rd WYTH/NTH M22 54 D5
Greyhound Park Rd
CH/BCN CH1 121 J9
Greyhound Rd MCFLDN SK10 94 B8
Greylands Cl SALE M33 38 B4
Greylands Rd DID/WITH M20 40 D8
Greymist Av WARR WA1 34 D9
Grey Rd ALT WA14 52 G2
Greysan Av ALS/KID ST7 189 P8
Greys Ct WARR WA1 * 34 D7
Greystoke Av BNG/LEV M19 28 C8
HALE/TIMP WA15 53 P1
SALE M33 38 E5
Greystoke Dr WILM/AE SK9 93 J3
Greystoke Rd MCFLDN SK10 117 M2
Greystoke St STKP SK1 17 K5
Greystone Pk CW/HAS CW1 5 G2
Greystone Rd
WARRW/BUR WA5 47 K3
Greystones GTS/LS CH66 79 P9
Greystones Rd CHSE CH3 143 L1
Grey St DTN/ASHW M34 29 K6
WARR WA1 19 F4
Grice St WARRS WA4 48 E6
Griffin Cl CH/BCN CH1 121 J6
NM/HAY SK22 59 N9
WARRW/BUR WA5 32 B2
Griffin Gv BNG/LEV M19 28 A9
Griffin La CHD/CHDH SK8 55 M8
Griffin Ms WDN WA8 45 P4
Griffin St STHEL WA9 31 K1
Griffith Av GOL/RIS/CU WA3 34 F3
Griffiths Dr NWCHE CW9 110 C6
Griffiths Rd NWCHE CW9 110 E4
Griffiths St WARRS WA4 49 H3
Grig Pl ALS/KID ST7 187 N3
Grimsditch La WARRS WA4 64 C8
Grimshaw Av MCFLDN SK10 95 N6
Grimshaw Cl MPL/ROM SK6 42 F4
Grimshaw La MCFLDN SK10 95 N6
Grimshaw St STHEL WA9 31 H2
STKP SK1 17 K4
Grimstead Cl NTHM/RTH M23 54 A1
Grindley Av CCHDY M21 39 N3
Grindley Bnk CHNE CH2 122 G3
Grindley Gdns EP CH65 102 E2
Grisedale Av WARRN/WOL WA2 33 L5
Grisedale Cl RUNC WA7 62 C9
Grisedale Wy MCFLDS SK11 116 G7
Gritstone Dr MCFLDN SK10 116 G4
MCFLDS SK11 137 K2
MCFLDS SK11 157 N7
POY/DIS SK12 74 G7
Grizebeck Cl GTN M18 28 C3
Grizedale WDN WA8 45 H5
Grizedale Cl CW/SHV CW2 184 D6
Grizedale Rd MPL/ROM SK6 42 G4
Groarke Dr WARRW/BUR WA5 47 H2
Groby Rd ALT WA14 52 G3
CW/HAS CW1 170 C7
DTN/ASHW M34 29 L2
Groby Rd North
DTN/ASHW M34 29 K1
Grocotts Rw NANT CW5 10 C6
Grosvenor Av ALS/KID ST7 187 P3
GOL/RIS/CU WA3 24 F1
NWCHW CW8 109 J8
WARR WA1 33 P9
Grosvenor Cl WARRW/BUR WA5 47 N2
WILM/AE SK9 93 J1
Grosvenor Ct CHD/CHDH SK8 55 M1
CW/HAS CW1 185 H3
WSFD CW7 149 L3
Grosvenor Dr POY/DIS SK12 73 J3
Grosvenor Gdns NEWLW WA12 23 M7
WYTH/NTH M22 54 G1
Grosvenor Gra WARR WA1 34 C7
Grosvenor Park Rd CH/BCN CH1 3 G4
Grosvenor Park Ter CH/BCN CH1 3 G5
Grosvenor Pl CH/BCN CH1 2 E6
Grosvenor Prec CH/BCN CH1 2 E4
Grosvenor Rd ALT WA14 53 J1
CH/BCN CH1 2 D7
CHD/CHDH SK8 56 C3
CHSE CH3 123 P9
CHSW/BR CH4 142 E3
CONG CW12 155 J7
HTNM SK4 41 J5
MPL/ROM SK6 43 L9
RNFD/HAY WA11 22 F3
SALE M33 38 C3
WDN WA8 45 P3
Grosvenor Rbt CH/BCN CH1 2 D6
Grosvenor Sq SALE M33 38 C4
Grosvenor St BRAM/HZG SK7 57 K4
CH/BCN CH1 2 D6
CW/HAS CW1 4 B1
DTN/ASHW M34 29 K5
MCFLDN SK10 8 C3
RUNC WA7 15 H1
STKP SK1 17 G7
WSFD CW7 149 N2
Grotsworth La MALPAS SY14 193 K7
Grotto La KNUT WA16 113 L4
Grounds St WARRN/WOL WA2 18 E2
Grove Av ALS/KID ST7 188 C4
Grove Av ALS/KID ST7 188 G8
CHSE CH3 122 C8
LYMM WA13 50 C4
NWCHE CW9 110 G1
WILM/AE SK9 71 J7
Grove Cl WSFD CW7 149 K2
Grove Ct BRAM/HZG SK7 * 57 L4
SALE M33 38 G4
Grove Crs AUD/MAD/W CW3 219 H5
Grove Gdns CHSE CH3 122 F9
CHD/CHDH SK8 56 A9
DID/WITH M20 40 C6
Grove La HALE/TIMP WA15 53 L1
Grove La HALE/TIMP WA15 53 L4
Grovemount NWCHE CW9 128 G1
Grove Pk KNUT WA16 90 E4
Grove Park Av ALS/KID ST7 188 C4
Grove Ri LYMM WA13 50 E4
Grove Rd CH/BCN CH1 102 A7
HALE/TIMP WA15 53 J4
The Groves CH/BCN CH1 3 F6
EP CH65 102 C4
TPLY/KEL CW6 146 G8
Grove St BRAM/HZG SK7 * 57 L4
DROY M43 28 F1
NM/HAY SK22 59 M8
RUNC WA7 14 D1
WARRS WA4 48 E3
WILM/AE SK9 * 71 K7
The Grove ALS/KID ST7 188 C4
ALT WA14 * 53 H2
CHD/CHDH SK8 56 A9
DID/WITH M20 40 C7
EDGY/DAV SK3 41 M9
KNUT WA16 90 G1
LYMM WA13 50 E4
SALE M33 38 E5
WARRW/BUR WA5 47 K3
WHITCH SY13 213 L4
Grove Wy WILM/AE SK9 71 K7
Grovewood Ms MCFLDS SK11 8 D7
Grub La TPLY/KEL CW6 125 H6
Grundey St BRAM/HZG SK7 57 L5
Grundy Cl WDN WA8 45 M4
Grundy St GOL/RIS/CU WA3 24 C2
HTNM SK4 40 F6
Guardian Ms NTHM/RTH M23 * 38 F7
WARRW/BUR WA5 18 A4
Guernsey Cl BNG/LEV M19 * 41 A1
CONG CW12 156 A9
WARRS WA4 48 F7
Guernsey Dr EP CH65 102 E3
Guernsey Rd WDN WA8 46 C4
Guests Slack FROD/HEL WA6 106 F3
Guest St WDN WA8 21 G5
Guide La DTN/ASHW M34 29 L1
Guilden Gn CHSE CH3 122 F6
Guilden Sutton La CHSE CH3 122 D7
Guildford Av CHD/CHDH SK8 56 A9
Guildford Cl CHSW/BR CH4 142 B4
STKP SK1 42 A9
WARRN/WOL WA2 34 B7
Guildford Rd BNG/LEV M19 28 B7
Guillemot Cl CW/HAS CW1 185 M3
Gullane Cl MCFLDN SK10 95 H9
Gull Cl POY/DIS SK12 73 H3
The Gullet NANT CW5 10 C5
Gun Battery La BIDD ST8 175 P9
Gunco La MCFLDN SK10 95 J5
MCFLDS SK11 117 L6
Gunn Gv NSTN CH64 77 M5
Gunn St BIDD ST8 175 K9
Gutterscroft CW/HAS CW1 186 B3
Gutticar Rd WDN WA8 45 H7
Guy La CHSE CH3 144 B5
Guywood La MPL/ROM SK6 43 H5
Gwenbury Av STKP SK1 42 A7
Gwynedd Dr FLINT CH6 98 A6
Gypsy La OFTN SK2 57 K1
Gyte's La BNG/LEV M19 28 C7

H

Hackberry Cl ALT WA14 37 N8
Hacked Way La MCFLDS SK11 118 E6
Haddon Cl CW/SHV CW2 185 H9
HOLMCH CW4 131 N8
MCFLDS SK11 117 H7
MPL/ROM SK6 58 C9
WILM/AE SK9 93 H3
Haddon Dr WDN WA8 45 J4
Haddon Gv HALE/TIMP WA15 38 C9
RDSH SK5 41 M1
SALE M33 38 D5
Haddon La NSTN CH64 77 P9
Haddon Rd BRAM/HZG SK7 57 L6
CCHDY M21 39 N3
CHD/CHDH SK8 55 L8
NSTN CH64 100 B2
Hadfield Cl WDN WA8 46 C5
Hadfield St DUK SK16 29 N2
NWCHE CW9 13 J1
Hadleigh Cl WARRW/BUR WA5 47 H2
Hadley Cl CHD/CHDH SK8 55 P6
Hadlow Gn RDSH SK5 42 A2
Hadlow La NSTN CH64 78 D6
Hadlow Rd NSTN CH64 78 D7
Hadrian Dr CH/BCN CH1 121 H5
Hadrian Wy MWCH CW10 130 B9
NEWUL ST5 201 N9
NWCHW CW8 127 L1
Hadyn Jones NANT CW5 196 G4
Hadyn Jones Dr NANT CW5 196 G4
Hafod Cl CH/BCN CH1 120 G8
Hag Bank La POY/DIS SK12 59 H8
Haguebar Rd NM/HAY SK22 59 K7
Hague Fold Rd NM/HAY SK22 59 K7
Hague Rd DID/WITH M20 40 A8
Haig Av IRL M44 36 B4
WARRW/BUR WA5 47 L3
Haigh Av HTNM SK4 41 M3
Haigh Pk HTNM SK4 41 M3
Haig Rd KNUT WA16 90 B5
WDN WA8 21 G1
Haldon Rd DID/WITH M20 40 E3
Hale Av POY/DIS SK12 73 K4
Hale Bank Rd WDN WA8 60 E1
Hale Gate Rd WDN WA8 60 F3
Hale Gv WARRW/BUR WA5 47 L1
Hale Low Rd HALE/TIMP WA15 53 K4
Hale Rd HALE/TIMP WA15 53 J4
HTNM SK4 16 A1
WDN WA8 20 A3
Halesden Rd HTNM SK4 41 L3
Hale St WARRN/WOL WA2 18 D2
Hale Vw ALT WA14 * 53 H5
RUNC WA7 14 B6
Hale View Rd FROD/HEL WA6 83 J9
Haley Cl RDSH SK5 28 F9
Haley Rd North
WARRW/BUR WA5 32 B2
Haley Rd South
WARRW/BUR WA5 32 B2
Halfacre La WARRS WA4 49 N4
Halfacre Rd WYTH/NTH M22 54 E3
Half Moon La OFTN SK2 57 L1
Halifax Cl WARRN/WOL WA2 33 N6
Halkett Cl CHSW/BR CH4 142 A5
Halkyn Rd CHNE CH2 121 P8
Halkyn St FLINT CH6 98 A6
Hallam St OFTN SK2 56 G1
Hallas Gv NTHM/RTH M23 39 L7
Hallastone Rd FROD/HEL WA6 83 H9
Hall Av HALE/TIMP WA15 38 C9
Hall Av SALE M33 38 B2
WDN WA8 44 G6
Halla-way WARRS WA4 48 G4
Hall Cl MCFLDN SK10 95 K9
Hallcroft PART M31 36 E4
Hallcroft Pl WARRS WA4 49 J5
Hall Dr ALS/KID ST7 187 N5
NANT CW5 197 K1
NWCHE CW9 88 B7
WARRS WA4 48 F9
Hallefield Crs MCFLDN SK10 9 H5
Hallefield Dr MCFLDN SK10 9 G5
Hallefield Rd MCFLDS SK11 9 H5
Hall Farm Cl BRAM/HZG SK7 57 N4
Hallfield Dr CHNE CH2 104 B1
Hallfield Pk GTS/LS CH66 79 P9
Hallfields Rd CHSE CH3 124 B9
WARRN/WOL WA2 33 N8
Hallgate Dr CHD/CHDH SK8 55 J5
Hallgate Rd STKP SK1 42 A8
Hallgreen La CONG CW12 154 F2
Hall Hl MCFLDN SK10 95 L6
Halliday Cl GOL/RIS/CU WA3 34 G5
Halliwell's Brow KNUT WA16 67 H3
Hall La AUD/MAD/W CW3 209 J7
CHSE CH3 179 J9
KNUT WA16 89 H4
KNUT WA16 91 N1
MALPAS SY14 191 P6
MCFLDS SK11 117 M9
MPL/ROM SK6 42 G2
NTHM/RTH M23 54 D1
NWCHE CW9 87 H6
NWCHE CW9 88 E9
PART M31 36 E4
RAIN/WH L35 95 P4
SBCH CW11 170 G4
STHEL WA9 31 M4
TPLY/KEL CW6 125 J5
TPLY/KEL CW6 146 G5
TPLY/KEL CW6 181 M3
WARRS WA4 49 K7
WARRS WA4 63 P4
WARRS WA4 64 F6
WARRW/BUR WA5 23 M9
WDN WA8 45 K1
WSFD CW7 149 H8
The Hall La TPLY/KEL CW6 147 M7
Hall Meadow CHD/CHDH SK8 55 N6
Hall Moss La BRAM/HZG SK7 72 B2
Hall Nook WARRW/BUR WA5 47 K3
Hall O'shaw St CW/HAS CW1 5 H2
Hallows Av CCHDY M21 39 M3
WARRN/WOL WA2 33 N8
Hallows Cl TPLY/KEL CW6 125 H7
Hallows Dr TPLY/KEL CW6 125 H7
Hall Pool Dr OFTN SK2 42 D9
Hall Rd ALT WA14 52 G6
BRAM/HZG SK7 56 D6
RNFD/HAY WA11 23 J2
WARR WA1 34 E9
Hallsgreen La CHNE CH2 103 P5
Hallshaw Av CW/HAS CW1 5 J1
Hallside Pk KNUT WA16 90 G4
Halls Rd ALS/KID ST7 189 L2
BIDD ST8 175 K8
Hall St ALS/KID ST7 200 G5
CHD/CHDH SK8 55 M1
HYDE SK14 29 P6
MCFLDS SK11 8 C4
NM/HAY SK22 59 M7
STHEL WA9 31 K5
STKP SK1 42 A8
WARR WA1 19 F6
Hallsville Rd BNG/LEV M19 28 C8
Hall Ter WARRW/BUR WA5 32 B9
Hall View Cl NWCHW CW8 108 C5
Hall Wood Av RNFD/HAY WA11 23 K1
Hallwood Cl RUNC WA7 61 P8
Hallwood Dr GTS/LS CH66 78 G9
Hallwood Link Rd RUNC WA7 62 C8
Hallwood Park Av RUNC WA7 62 C8
Hallwood Rd NTHM/RTH M23 54 C1
Hall Wood Rd WILM/AE SK9 71 M4
WILM/AE SK9 71 N3
Halsall Av WARRN/WOL WA2 33 N8
Halsall Cl RUNC WA7 62 G9
Halstead Av CCHDY M21 39 K1
Halstead Dr IRL M44 27 P7
Halstead Gv CHD/CHDH SK8 55 H2
Halston Cl RDSH SK5 41 N4
Halstone Av WILM/AE SK9 92 G1
Halton Brook Av RUNC WA7 62 B5
Halton Brow RUNC WA7 62 C5
Halton Ct RUNC WA7 62 B4
Halton Crs GTS/LS CH66 102 B2
Halton Dr CW/SHV CW2 184 D3
HALE/TIMP WA15 38 E7
Halton Link Rd RUNC WA7 62 C6
Halton Lodge Av RUNC WA7 62 B7
Halton Rd CHNE CH2 122 A5
GTS/LS CH66 102 A3
RUNC WA7 15 H2
WARRW/BUR WA5 47 K1
Halton Station Rd RUNC WA7 84 D2
Halton St RNFD/HAY WA11 * 23 J3
Halton View Rd WDN WA8 46 A6
Halton Wy GTS/LS CH66 102 A3
Hambledon Cl GTS/LS CH66 79 L7
Hamble Dr WARRW/BUR WA5 47 K4
Hambleton Cl WDN WA8 * 45 J4
Hambleton Dr SALE M33 38 A3
Hambleton Rd CHD/CHDH SK8 55 L7
Hambleton Wy WSFD CW7 149 J3
Hambletts Hollow
FROD/HEL WA6 107 K6
Hamble Wy MCFLDN SK10 116 E3
Hamilton Av IRL M44 36 C4
Hamilton Cl CW/HAS CW1 186 A4
MCFLDN SK10 117 N4
NSTN CH64 77 H3
Hamilton Crs HTNM SK4 41 J7
Hamilton Pl CH/BCN CH1 2 D4
Hamilton Sq HTNM SK4 16 E1
Hamilton St CHNE CH2 122 A8
Hamlet Dr SALE M33 38 B2
Hammersley Av STHEL WA9 31 H5
Hammersley St STHEL WA9 * 31 H5
Hammerstone Rd GTN M18 28 C3
Hammond Av HTNM SK4 41 M3
Hammond Rd NEWUL ST5 201 P7
Hammond St CW/SHV CW2 4 D5
STHEL WA9 22 B7
Hamnett Ct GOL/RIS/CU WA3 34 F5
Hamon Rd HALE/TIMP WA15 53 J3
Hampden Crs GTN M18 28 C4
Hampden Rd SALE M33 38 D5
Hampshire Cl CONG CW12 155 M6
Hampshire Rd PART M31 36 C6
RDSH SK5 42 B3
Hampshire Wk MCFLDN SK10 116 F2
Hampson Av GOL/RIS/CU WA3 25 P6
Hampson Crs WILM/AE SK9 71 L2
Hampson St SALE M33 38 G4
STKP SK1 * 42 A8
Hampstead Ct WSFD CW7 149 J2
Hampstead Dr OFTN SK2 57 J2
Hampstead La OFTN SK2 57 H3
Hampton Cl NSTN CH64 77 L7
WDN WA8 46 C4
Hampton Crs MALPAS SY14 204 F2
NSTN CH64 77 L8
Hampton Dr WARRW/BUR WA5 47 N3
WDN WA8 45 J2
Hampton Gdns EP CH65 6 A4
Hampton Gv ALT WA14 38 B7
CHD/CHDH SK8 55 N5
Hampton Rd CHSW/BR CH4 142 B4
IRL M44 36 C4
Hamson Dr MCFLDN SK10 95 P4
Hamsterley Cl GOL/RIS/CU WA3 35 J2
Hanbury Cl CW/SHV CW2 185 H9
Hancock Rd CONG CW12 155 P6
Handa Dr EP CH65 102 E4
Handbridge CHSW/BR CH4 2 E7
Handel Ms SALE M33 38 F4
Handford Rd CHNE CH2 121 P5
Handforth Cl WARRS WA4 49 L3
Handforth La RUNC WA7 62 B8
Handforth Rd CW/SHV CW2 184 E5
RDSH SK5 41 N3
WILM/AE SK9 71 N5
Handley Cl EDGY/DAV SK3 56 C2
Handley Hl WSFD CW7 149 K2
Handley Rd BRAM/HZG SK7 56 E4
Hand St MCFLDS SK11 8 B4
Hangman's La NWCHE CW9 111 J5
Hankelow Cl MWCH CW10 151 J4
Hankey St RUNC WA7 14 D2
AUD/MAD/W CW3 217 P4
Hankinson Cl PART M31 36 D6
Hanley Cl POY/DIS SK12 75 H1
WDN WA8 45 J6
Hanley Rd WDN WA8 45 J6
Hannah St WGTN/LGST M12 28 A7
Hannesburg Gdns
NTHM/RTH M23 * 54 B3
Hannet Rd WYTH/NTH M22 54 F6
Hanns Hall Rd NSTN CH64 78 A5
Hanover Dr WSFD CW7 149 M4
Hanover Rd ALT WA14 37 N9
Hanover St WARR WA1 18 B7
Hanover St North
DTN/ASHW M34 29 L1
Hanover St South
DTN/ASHW M34 29 L1
Hanson Ms STKP SK1 42 A6
Hapsford Cl GOL/RIS/CU WA3 34 D4
Hapsford La CHNE CH2 82 D9
FROD/HEL WA6 104 E3
Hapton Pl HTNM SK4 16 E1
Hapton St BNG/LEV M19 28 A8
Harbbour Cl CHNE CH2 121 P4
Harbord St WARR WA1 19 G7
Harboro Gv SALE M33 38 C4
Harboro Rd SALE M33 38 C4
Harboro Wy SALE M33 38 C4
Harbour La MCFLDS SK11 135 K2
Harbury Crs WYTH/NTH M22 54 E2
Harcombe Rd DID/WITH M20 40 D2
Harcourt Cl GOL/RIS/CU WA3 34 F5
Harcourt Rd ALT WA14 53 H1
SALE M33 38 D2
Harcourt St RDSH SK5 28 F9
Hardberry Pl OFTN SK2 57 L1
Hardcastle Av CCHDY M21 39 M2
Hardcastle Rd EDGY/DAV SK3 41 L9
Harden Pk WILM/AE SK9 93 J2
Hardicker St BNG/LEV M19 41 J1
Hardie Cl STHEL WA9 30 F5
Harding Av CHSE CH3 164 B7
WARRN/WOL WA2 33 N7
Harding Rd CHNE CH2 121 L3
NANT CW5 196 D3
Hardings Meadow
ALS/KID ST7 188 G6
Harding St STKP SK1 42 A7
Hardingswood Rd ALS/KID ST7 188 G6
Hardman Av MPL/ROM SK6 42 F5
Hardman Rd RDSH SK5 28 F9
Hardman St EDGY/DAV SK3 16 D6
Hardwick Cl MPL/ROM SK6 58 D9
Hardwick Dr MCFLDS SK11 117 H7
Hardwicke Rd POY/DIS SK12 73 M2
Hardwick Gra WARR WA1 34 E8
Hardwick Rd PART M31 36 F5
RUNC WA7 62 B3
Hardy Cl CW/SHV CW2 184 F8
GTS/LS CH66 102 B1
Hardy Dr BRAM/HZG SK7 56 D8
HALE/TIMP WA15 38 C9
Hardy La CCHDY M21 39 M2
Hardy Rd LYMM WA13 50 C5
Hardy St WARRN/WOL WA2 18 E3
Hardywood Rd DTN/ASHW M34 42 F1
Harebell Cl CHSE CH3 143 J4
Harecastle Av ALS/KID ST7 188 F7
Harefield Dr DID/WITH M20 40 B6
WILM/AE SK9 71 J9
Harefield Rd WILM/AE SK9 71 N2
Hare La CHSE CH3 122 D7
Hare's La FROD/HEL WA6 83 L5
Harewood Av GTS/LS CH66 79 N9
SALE M33 38 A4
Harewood Cl NWCHE CW9 109 P7
WSFD CW7 149 J1
Harewood Gv RDSH SK5 28 E9
Harewood Rd IRL M44 27 P7
Harewood Wy MCFLDS SK11 117 H7
Harfield Gdns GTS/LS CH66 79 N8
Harford Cl BRAM/HZG SK7 56 G6
WARRW/BUR WA5 47 K3
Hargate Dr HALE/TIMP WA15 53 L6
IRL M44 27 N6
Hargrave Av CW/SHV CW2 184 F5
Hargrave Dr GTS/LS CH66 80 A8
Hargreaves Ct WDN WA8 46 B6
Hargreaves Rd
HALE/TIMP WA15 53 N1
NWCHE CW9 110 C4
Hargreaves St STHEL WA9 22 C5
Harington Cl CHNE CH2 121 M2
Harington Rd CHNE CH2 121 M3
Harlech Cl WARRW/BUR WA5 33 H6
Harlech Dr BRAM/HZG SK7 57 J6
Harlech Wy EP CH65 102 F1
Harleen Gv OFTN SK2 42 C9
Harley Rd SALE M33 38 F3
Harley St OP/CLY M11 28 D1
Harling Rd WYTH/NTH M22 39 N9
Harlow Cl STHEL WA9 30 E1
WARRS WA4 49 L4
Harlow Dr GTN M18 28 D6
Harlyn Av BRAM/HZG SK7 56 F8
Harlyn Gdns WARRW/BUR WA5 47 H4
Harmsworth Dr HTNM SK4 41 J3
The Harn GTS/LS CH66 101 N1
Harold Av GTN M18 28 F5
Haroldgate WHITCH SY13 213 L4
Harold Rd RNFD/HAY WA11 23 K2
Harold St STKP SK1 42 A8
Harper Cl GTS/LS CH66 79 P9
Harper Ct EDGY/DAV SK3 41 M9
Harper Gv CONG CW12 155 N6
Harper Rd WYTH/NTH M22 39 P9
Harpers Rd WARRN/WOL WA2 34 B7
Harper St EDGY/DAV SK3 * 41 M9
Harp St OP/CLY M11 28 D2
Harpur Cl MCFLDS SK11 9 F7
Harpur Crs ALS/KID ST7 187 M3
Harrier Cl CW/HAS CW1 184 F1
WYTH/NTH M22 54 G2
Harrier Rd WARRN/WOL WA2 34 A6
Harriet St IRL M44 36 D3
Harrington Dr MCFLDS SK11 135 L2
Harrington Rd ALT WA14 52 F2
Harrington St GTN M18 28 E4
Harris Av DTN/ASHW M34 29 H6
Harris Cl CW/HAS CW1 170 A8
DTN/ASHW M34 29 H6
Harriseahead La ALS/KID ST7 189 M4
Harrison Av BNG/LEV M19 28 B7
Harrison Cl ALS/KID ST7 200 G9
Harrison Dr HOLMCH CW4 131 N2
RNFD/HAY WA11 22 E3
Harrison's Dr MPL/ROM SK6 43 H3
Harrisons Pl NWCHW CW8 12 D3
Harrison St OFTN SK2 41 N9
WDN WA8 45 H9
Harrison Wy NEWLW WA12 23 N5
Harris Rd NWCHE CW9 110 G2
Harris St WDN WA8 46 A6
Harrogate Cl OP/CLY M11 28 E2
PS/BROM CH62 79 H1
WARRW/BUR WA5 32 D8
Harrogate Dr RDSH SK5 28 E9
Harrogate Rd PS/BROM CH62 79 H1
RDSH SK5 28 E8
Harrop La MCFLDN SK10 73 L9
Harrop Rd HALE/TIMP WA15 53 K5
MCFLDN SK10 96 A5
RUNC WA7 15 G5
Harrop St GTN M18 28 F3
Harrow Av BNG/LEV M19 41 H2
Harrow Cl CW/SHV CW2 184 G7
WARRS WA4 48 G9
Harrow Dr RUNC WA7 62 C4
SALE M33 38 D6
Harrow Rd EP CH65 7 G7
SALE M33 38 D6
Harrow Wy NWCHE CW9 109 N9
Harrycroft Rd MPL/ROM SK6 42 G3
Harry Lawson Ct MCFLDN SK10 9 G2

Harry Rd RDSH SK5 ....28 F9
Harry Rowley CI
  WYTH/NTH M22 * 54 E5
Harrytown MPL/ROM SK6 ....42 F6
Hart Av SALE M33 ....39 J5
Hartford Av HTNM SK4 ....41 L2
  WILM/AE SK9 ....71 H9
Hartford Br NWCHE CW9 ....109 M9
Hartford CI SBCH CW11 ....171 P2
Hartford CI EP CH65 ....80 B9
Hartford Gdns
  HALE/TIMP WA15 ....53 P2
Hartford Rd NWCHE CW9 ....128 F1
  SALE M33 ....38 A7
Hartford St DTN/ASHW M34 * 29 L4
Hartford Wy CH/BCN CH1 ....121 J3
Harthill CI NWCHE CW9 ....109 N7
Harthill La CHSE CH3 ....179 L4
Harthill Rd CH/BCN CH1 ....121 H5
  CHSE CH3 ....179 N2
Hartington Dr BRAM/HZG SK7 ......57 L7
Hartington Rd ALT WA14 ....38 A8
  BRAM/HZG SK7 ....56 E9
  CH/CHDH SK8 ....55 M7
  MPL/ROM SK6 ....58 C9
  OFTN SK2 ....57 K3
Hartington St CHSW/BR CH4 ......142 C3
Hartland St OFTN SK2 ....52 B8
  POY/DIS SK12 ....73 K1
  WDN WA8 ....45 N2
Hartland Gdns STHEL WA9 ....30 C2
Hartley CI LYMM WA13 ....50 F4
Hartley Gdns CONG CW12 ....175 J1
Hartley Gv MCFLDN SK10 * 96 A6
Hartley Gv IRL M44 ....27 P5
Hartley Rd ALT WA14 ....52 C2
Hartley St EDGY/DAV SK3 ....16 C7
Harton Av GTN M18 ....28 C6
Hartshead CI OP/CLY M11 ....28 G2
Hart St ALT WA14 ....41 J3
Hartswood CI DTN/ASHW M34 ......29 N5
  WARRS WA4 ....64 G3
Hartswood Rd DID/WITH M20 ......40 E2
Hartwell Gv WSFD CW7 ....128 C7
Harty Rd RNFD/HAY WA11 ....22 E4
Harvard Ct MPL/ROM SK6 ....42 E5
  RUNC WA7 ....63 H4
Harvard Ct WARRN/WOL WA2 ......33 K5
Harvest CI NWCHE CW9 ....128 G3
  SALE M33 ....39 K5
Harvest Rd MCFLDN SK10 ....117 J1
Harvest Wy STHEL WA9 ....31 H4
Harvey Av NANT CW5 ....14 B6
  NEWLW WA12 ....23 K6
Harvey Ct WARRN/WOL WA2 ....33 L5
Harvey Rd CONG CW12 ....156 A5
Harvey St STKP SK1 ....17 G4
Harvin Gv DTN/ASHW M34 ....29 N7
Harwich Dr BNG/LEV M19 * 42 B4
  RDSH SK5 ....42 B2
Harwood Gdns WARRS WA4 ....49 J5
Harwood Rd BNG/LEV M19 ....40 F2
Harwood Rd HTNM SK4 ....40 F6
Harwood St HTNM SK4 ....16 E1
Harwyton Av
  WARRW/BUR WA5 ....33 J9
Haseley CI POY/DIS SK12 ....73 L1
Haselhurst Wk NTHM/RTH M23 ....39 P4
Haslam CI EDGY/DAV SK3 ....56 E1
Haslemere Av HALE/TIMP WA15 ...54 B6
Haslemere Dr CHD/CHDH SK8 .....56 A6
  WARRW/BUR WA5 ....47 H3
Haslemere Rd DID/WITH M20 ....40 E2
Haslemere Wy CW/HAS CW1 ....185 K2
Haslin Crs CHSE CH3 ....143 M5
Haslington Gv NEWLL ST5 ....201 N6
Haslington Gv HLWD L26 ....44 A6
Haslington Rd WYTH/NTH M22 .....54 C5
Hasper Av DID/WITH M20 ....40 B1
Hassall Cross La SBCH CW11 ......171 L9
Hassall Rd ALS/KID ST7 ....187 M2
  SBCH CW11 ....171 P5
  SBCH CW11 ....186 E1
Hassals La CHNE CH2 ....105 P9
Hassop Rd RDSH SK5 ....28 G8
Hastings Av WARRN/WOL WA2 .....33 L4
Hastings CI CHD/CHDH SK8 ....56 C5
  STKP SK1 ....42 A9
Hasty La HALE/TIMP WA15 ....54 B8
Hatchery CI WARRS WA4 ....31 J2
Hatchett Rd WYTH/NTH M22 ....54 C6
Hatchmere CI HALE/TIMP WA15 ...53 P1
  SBCH CW11 ....171 L2
  WARRW/BUR WA5 ....48 A2
Hatchmere Dr CHSE CH3 ....143 K3
Hatchmere Rd CHD/CHDH SK8 ....55 P5
Hatfield Av BNG/LEV M19 ....40 C2
Hatfield CI STHEL WA9 ....30 E1
Hatfield CI HOLMCH CW4 ....131 M8
Hatfield Gdns WARRS WA4 ....64 G2
Hathaway Dr MCFLDS SK11 * 17 H7
Hathaway Gdns MPL/ROM SK6 ....40 E2
Hatherley Rd DID/WITH M20 ....40 D4
Hatherlow MPL/ROM SK6 ....42 E7
Hatherlow La BRAM/HZG SK7 ......57 K5
Hatherton CI NEWLL ST5 ....201 N5
  NWCHE CW9 ....121 H9
Hatley CI FROD/HEL WA6 ....83 M6
Hatters Rw WARR WA1 * 18 D5
Hatton Av PS/BROM CH62 ....79 J2
  NWCHW CW8 ....12 A7
  WARRS WA4 ....64 C5
Hatton Rd CH/BCN CH1 ....121 H6
Hatton St MCFLDS SK11 ....17 F3
  WGTN/LGST M12 ....28 A6
Haughton CI MPL/ROM SK6 ....42 E6
Haughton Dr WYTH/NTH M22 ......39 N7
Haughton Green Rd
  DTN/ASHW M34 ....29 N9
Haughton Hall Rd
  DTN/ASHW M34 ....29 M4
Haughton St DTN/ASHW M34 ....29 M4

Hauxwell Gv RNFD/HAY WA11 ....22 A3
  CONG CW12 ....155 P4
Havannah La CONG CW12 ....156 A5
Havannah St CONG CW12 ....155 P6
Haveley Rd WYTH/NTH M22 ....54 E2
Haven CI BRAM/HZG SK7 ....57 J6
The Haven CW/HAS CW1 ....185 K1
  HALE/TIMP WA15 ....53 J6
Havergal St RUNC WA7 ....14 D4
Haverhill CI CW/SHV CW2 ....198 C4
Havers Rd GTN M18 ....28 E4
Havisham CI ALS/KID ST7 ....24 E5
Hawarde CI NEWLW WA12 ....23 L5
Hawarden Gdns EP CH65 ....102 F1
Hawarden Rd ALT WA14 ....53 H1
Hawdraw Gn OFTN SK2 ....57 L1
Hawes Av RNFD/HAY WA11 ....22 A1
  RUSH/FAL M14 ....40 F1
Hawes CI OFTN SK2 ....56 G1
Haweswater Av CW/HAS CW1 ......170 A8
  RNFD/HAY WA11 ....22 E5
Haweswater CI
  DTN/ASHW M34 ....28 G7
  RUNC WA7 ....62 E9
Haweswater Dr WSFD CW7 ....128 E9
Hawick CI CHSL CH66 ....79 L8
Hawker CI CHSW/BR CH4 ....142 B5
Hawk Green Rd MPL/ROM SK6 .....58 D4
Hawkins La MCFLDN SK10 ....118 B1
Hawkins St NSTN CH64 ....77 M4
Hawkins St RDSH SK5 ....41 M4
Hawkridge Dr NTHM/RTH M23 .....39 H6
Hawk Vw CHSE CH3 ....123 M5
Hawkshaw Ct RUNC WA7 ....62 C8
Hawkshaw CI ALS/KID ST7 ....196 C4
Hawkshaw CI RUNC WA7 * 62 E9
Hawkshead Rd
  WARRW/BUR WA5 ....32 B2
Hawkshead Wy WSFD CW7 ....128 E9
Hawkstone Gv FROD/HEL WA6 .....83 J9
Hawk St SBCH CW11 ....171 N3
Hawkswick Dr NTHM/RTH M23 .....39 K5
Hawley Dr HALE/TIMP WA15 ....53 M7
Hawley La HALE/TIMP WA15 ....53 M7
Hawley's La WARRN/WOL WA2 .....33 K7
Haworth Av CONG CW12 ....155 P5
Haworth Ct MCFLDS SK11 ....117 H7
Haworth Rd GTN M18 ....28 C5
Hawthorn Av HALE/TIMP WA15 ....38 C9
  MPL/ROM SK6 ....58 B1
  NEWLW WA12 ....23 N6
  RUNC WA7 ....15 F4
  WDN WA8 ....45 P5
  WILM/AE SK9 ....71 J7
Hawthorn CI CONG CW12 ....155 J6
  NANT CW5 ....10 E5
  RNFD/HAY WA11 ....22 E4
Hawthorne Ct ALS/KID ST7 ....184 A4
Hawthorne Dr NSTN CH64 ....77 P3
  SBCH CW11 ....171 P3
Hawthorne Gv MPL/ROM SK6 ......42 D4
  POY/DIS SK12 ....74 A2
  WARR WA1 ....34 C9
  WSFD CW7 ....150 A1
Hawthorne Pk WILM/AE SK9 ....71 J7
Hawthorn Ri MCFLDN SK10 ....14 E7
Hawthorn Rd CHD/CHDH SK8 .....55 P3
  CHSE CH3 ....143 N5
  CHSW/BR CH4 ....142 B5
  DTN/ASHW M34 ....29 L3
  GTS/LS CH66 ....79 H7
  HALE/TIMP WA15 ....53 J4
  HTNM SK4 ....50 D4
  LYMM WA13 ....50 D4
  MCFLDN SK10 ....95 M4
  NEWLL ST5 ....201 P6
  NWCHW CW8 ....77 H3
The Hawthorns DTN/ASHW M34 ....29 K3
  NWCHW CW8 ....109 L5
  TPLY/KEL CW6 ....147 H9
  GTN M18 ....28 C5
  WILM/AE SK9 ....71 J7
Hawthorn Ter HTNM SK4 * 41 J5
Hawthorn Vw WILM/AE SK9 ....71 J7
Hawthorn Wk HOLMCH CW4 ....131 P8
Hawthorn Wk NWCHE CW9 ....110 C1
  WILM/AE SK9 ....71 J7
Hawthorn Wy MCFLDN SK10 ....117 L2
Haxby Rd GTN M18 ....28 D6
Haybarn Rd NTHM/RTH M23 ....39 L9

Hayburn Rd OFTN SK2 ....42 B8
Hay Cft CHD/CHDH SK8 ....55 N7
Haycroft CI GTS/LS CH66 ....101 P2
Haydock Av SALE M33 ....39 N6
Haydock CI CH/BCN CH1 ....2 A2
  MCFLDN SK10 ....117 J1
Haydock Dr BRAM/HZG SK7 ....57 M5
  HALE/TIMP WA15 ....53 M2
  RNFD/HAY WA11 ....22 C2
Haydock St NEWLW WA12 ....23 L5
  WARRN/WOL WA2 ....18 D4
Hayes CI NANT CW5 ....10 B2
  FROD/HEL WA6 ....83 P4
Hayes Crs FROD/HEL WA6 ....84 A4
Hayes Dr NWCHW CW8 ....109 K1
Hayes Rd CH/BCN CH1 ....121 M8
Haye's Rd IRL M44 ....36 D5
Hayeswood La ALS/KID ST7 ....201 H9
Hayfield Av MPL/ROM SK6 ....42 F4
Hayfield CI MCFLDN SK10 ....117 H1
Hayfield Rd MPL/ROM SK6 ....54 D8
  WARR WA1 ....34 C9
Hayfields KNUT WA16 ....90 G3
Hayfields
  AUD/MAD/W CW3 ....216 G2
Hayfield St SALE M33 ....38 D4
Hayfield Wk HALE/TIMP WA15 ......53 N1
Hayfield CI HLWD L26 ....44 A6
Hayhead CI ALS/KID ST7 ....189 K6
Hayhurst Av MWCH CW10 ....151 J2
Hayling CI CW/HAS CW1 ....170 B9
Hayle CI MCFLDN SK10 ....116 D3
Hayling Ct HALE/TIMP WA15 ....53 N1
Hayling Rd SALE M33 ....38 B3
Haymakers Ct CHNE CH2 ....142 B6
Haymakers Wy CH/BCN CH1 ....120 D3
Haymoor Green Rd NANT CW5 .....197 M5
Hayscastle CI
  WARRW/BUR WA5 ....33 H7
Hayside Wk MALPAS SY14 ....203 P3
Haythorp Av WYTH/NTH M22 ....54 G4
Hayton St KNUT WA16 ....90 D4
Haywood Crs RUNC WA7 ....63 H4
Hazel Av CHD/CHDH SK8 ....55 N2
  MCFLDS SK11 ....116 C7
  MPL/ROM SK6 ....58 C3
  RUNC WA7 ....14 B7
  SALE M33 ....38 E5
Hazelbadge CI POY/DIS SK12 ......73 J2
Hazelbadge Rd POY/DIS SK12 .....73 J2
Hazelbank CI DID/WITH M20 ....40 C1
Hazelborough CI
  GOL/RIS/CU WA3 ....35 J2
Hazel CI ALS/KID ST7 ....189 K5
  GTS/LS CH66 ....102 B5
  NSTN CH64 ....58 C3
Hazelcroft WILM/AE SK9 ....93 J5
Hazeldean CI NWCHW CW8 ....108 F5
  NWCHW CW8 ....108 G5
  OFTN SK2 ....57 K1
  POY/DIS SK12 ....73 M3
  WSFD CW7 ....149 L2
Hazelfield Ct STHEL WA9 * 31 H4
Hazel Gv ALS/KID ST7 ....188 C5
  CW/HAS CW1 ....185 J1
  GOL/RIS/CU WA3 ....24 D1
  WARR WA1 ....34 B8
Hazelhurst Dr MCFLDN SK10 ....95 N5
Hazelmere CI NWCHW CW8 * 109 K7
Hazelshaw La SBCH CW11 ....153 L6
Hazel St BRAM/HZG SK7 ....29 L3
  WARR WA1 ....19 J2
Hazelwell SALE M33 ....38 E5
Hazelwood CI STHEL WA9 ....30 C5
  WDN WA8 ....44 G7
Hazelwood Ms WARRS WA4 ....49 J9
Hazelwood Rd BRAM/HZG SK7 ....57 L5
  HALE/TIMP WA15 ....53 J6
  NWCHW CW8 ....87 K9
  OFTN SK2 ....57 L1
  WILM/AE SK9 ....71 M6
Hazlehurst Rd FROD/HEL WA6 .....84 B4
Hazlemere Av MCFLDS SK11 ......116 G6
Headingley CI RUSH/FAL M14 ......40 E1
Headland CI GOL/RIS/CU WA3 .....24 C3
Headlands Rd BRAM/HZG SK7 .....57 J5
The Headlands CH/BCN CH1 ....3 G4
Headworth CI NWCHE CW9 ....109 P7
Heald CI ALT WA14 ....52 C5
Heald Gv CHD/CHDH SK8 ....55 J8
Heald Rd ALT WA14 ....52 C5
Heald St NEWLW WA12 ....23 L5
  STKP SK1 ....17 J2
Healdwood Rd MPL/ROM SK6 .....43 H4
Healey CI CW/HAS CW1 * 169 P9
  NTHM/RTH M23 ....39 J6
Heanor Av DTN/ASHW M34 ....29 N9
Heapy St MCFLDS SK11 ....9 G7
Heapys La NANT CW5 ....195 H5
Heath Av ALS/KID ST7 ....188 B1
  GTS/LS CH66 ....102 C3
Heath Bnk CHSE CH3 ....122 E7
Heathbank Rd CHD/CHDH SK8 ....55 H8
  EDGY/DAV SK3 ....56 B1
  CHSE CH3 ....143 K2
Heath CI CHSE CH3 ....145 H4
  SBCH CW11 ....171 A5
Heathcote Av HTNM SK4 ....41 K5
Heathcote CI CHNE CH2 ....121 M7
Heathcote Gdns NWCHE CW9 .....110 D5
Heathcote Rd ALS/KID ST7 ....201 N1
  GTN M18 ....28 C5
Heathcote St ALS/KID ST7 ....189 H7
  NEWLL ST5 ....201 P7

Heath Ct ALS/KID ST7 ....188 A2
Heath Crs EDGY/DAV SK3 ....56 F2
Heath Dr CHSE CH3 ....145 H1
  RUNC WA7 ....61 N7
Heath End Rd ALS/KID ST7 ....187 M2
Heather Av IRL M44 ....36 C2
Heather Brae NEWLW WA12 ....23 L5
Heather CI GOL/RIS/CU WA3 ....34 E3
  GTS/LS CH66 ....102 A1
  MCFLDS SK11 ....117 J9
  RUNC WA7 ....62 F7
Heather Ct CHSE CH3 ....143 J2
Heatherfield CI WILM/AE SK9 ....71 N6
Heathergate PI CW/SHV CW2 ......185 H8
Heather Gv IRL M44 ....28 B5
Heather Lea DTN/ASHW M34 ....29 N7
Heatherleigh STHEL WA9 ....30 C2
Heather Rd ALT WA14 ....53 J6
Heatherside ALS/KID ST7 ....189 L3
  RDSH SK5 ....28 G8
The Heathers OFTN SK2 ....57 M2
Heather Wy MPL/ROM SK6 ....58 C2
Heatherway SALE M33 ....38 A3
Heatherways TPLY/KEL CW6 ....146 G7
Heath Farm La PART M31 ....35 P5
Heathfield WILM/AE SK9 ....71 J9
  ALS/KID ST7 ....4 C1
  DTN/ASHW M34 ....29 K7
  HTNM SK4 ....41 J5
Heathfield Av CHD/CHDH SK8 .....55 K2
  NANT CW5 ....10 E5
  SALE M33 ....53 J6
Heathfield Dr NEWLL ST5 ....201 N6
  WDN WA8 ....45 K4
Heathfield Rd
  AUD/MAD/W CW3 ....209 H9
  EP CH65 ....56 F9
  OFTN SK2 ....56 F1
Heathfields CI CHNE CH2 ....121 N8
Heathgate Av SPK/HALE L24 ....60 A4
Heath Gn TPLY/KEL CW6 ....146 G6
Heath Gv GTS/LS CH66 ....79 M6
Heathland Rd STHEL WA9 ....31 J9
Heathland Ter EDGY/DAV SK3 .....41 M9
Heath La CHNE CH2 ....102 C5
  CHSE CH3 ....143 J2
  GOL/RIS/CU WA3 ....25 J3
  GTS/LS CH66 ....79 L6
  KNUT WA16 ....112 D5
  NSTN CH64 ....78 C5
  NWCHE CW9 ....88 A4
  NWCHE CW9 ....88 A4
  WHITCH SY13 ....206 B8
Heathmoor Av
  GOL/RIS/CU WA3 ....24 E3
Heath Rd ALT WA14 ....53 H5
  CHNE CH2 ....121 N4
  CONG CW12 ....155 J5
  EDGY/DAV SK3 ....56 F1
  HALE/TIMP WA15 ....53 C8
  MCFLDN SK10 ....95 L7
  NWCHW CW8 ....108 G3
  RUNC WA7 ....15 H5
  WARRW/BUR WA5 ....47 K2
  WDN WA8 ....45 L6
  WHITCH SY13 ....213 N9
Heath Road Crs RUNC WA7 ....15 G5
Heathside NANT CW5 ....10 D4
Heathside Gdns ALS/KID ST7 ....49 H5
Heathside Park Rd
  EDGY/DAV SK3 ....40 G9
Heaths La TPLY/KEL CW6 ....125 P9
Heath St BURS/TUN ST6 ....189 K9
  CW/HAS CW1 ....5 F2
  GOL/RIS/CU WA3 ....24 C1
  STHEL WA9 ....30 C1
  WARRS WA4 ....48 E7
The Heath RUNC WA7 * 61 N7
Heath Vw ALS/KID ST7 ....188 A2
Heathview Rd WDN WA8 ....60 C2
Heath Wy TPLY/KEL CW6 ....166 A1
Heathwood Dr ALS/KID ST7 ....187 M3
Heathwood Gv WARR WA1 ....34 C9
Heathwood Rd BNG/LEV M19 ....40 F4
Heatley CI DTN/ASHW M34 ....29 P7
  LYMM WA13 ....50 C3
Heatley La NANT CW5 ....208 A2
Heaton Av BRAM/HZG SK7 ....56 D4
  HTNM SK4 ....41 H5
Heaton CI GOL/RIS/CU WA3 ....34 C2
  HTNM SK4 ....41 L9
Heaton Moor Rd HTNM SK4 ....41 J5
Heaton Rd DID/WITH M20 ....40 D1
  HTNM SK4 ....41 L5
Heaton Sq WSFD CW7 ....149 L2
Heaton St DTN/ASHW M34 ....29 N9
  MPL/ROM SK6 ....42 F4
Heaviley Ct AUD/MAD/W CW3 .....199 M9

The Heights FROD/HEL WA6 ....83 J9
Helena Ct KNUT WA16 ....90 C3
Helena Rd STHEL WA9 ....31 L1
Helen St WARR WA1 * * 18 C5
  WHEN NANT CW5 ....196 F5
Hellyar-brook Rd ALS/KID ST7 ......187 M4
Helmdon CI WSFD CW7 ....128 C8
Helmsdale CI CW/HAS CW1 ....185 L2
Helmsdale La
  WARRW/BUR WA5 ....47 N1
Helmsley CI WARRW/BUR WA5 ....33 H9
Helsby Av PS/BROM CH62 ....79 K2
Helsby Rd FROD/HEL WA6 ....105 J3
  SALE M33 ....39 H6
Helsby St STHEL WA9 ....30 A8
  WARR WA1 ....18 J5
Helston Av RNFD/HAY WA11 ....22 B2
Helston CI BRAM/HZG SK7 ....56 F8
  IRL M44 ....27 P7
  RUNC WA7 ....62 F9
  WARRW/BUR WA5 ....47 J2
Helton CI HOLMCH CW4 ....131 M8
Hembury Av BNG/LEV M19 ....40 G2
Hemingford CI GTS/LS CH66 ....101 P2
Hemlegh Vw FROD/HEL WA6 ....105 J7
Hemmingshaw La
  SBCH CW11 ....172 C1
Hemming St NWCHW CW8 ....109 M3
Hemmons Rd WGTN/LGST M12 ...28 F1
Hempcroft Rd
  HALE/TIMP WA15 ....53 N2
Hempshaw La STKP SK1 ....41 F9
Hempstead CI HTNM SK4 ....30 E1
Hemswell CI WSFD CW7 ....149 N2
Hemsworth Av GTS/LS CH66 ....79 N8
Hemsworth Rd GTN M18 ....151 J3
Henbury CI MWCH CW10 ....151 J3
Henbury Dr MPL/ROM SK6 ....42 G2
Henbury Gdns CHD/CHDH SK8 ....55 P9
Henbury PI RUNC WA7 ....61 P8
Henbury RI MCFLDS SK11 ....116 C4
Henbury Rd WILM/AE SK9 * 71 M2
Henbury St OFTN SK2 ....57 J5
Henderson CI
  WARRW/BUR WA5 ....47 H1
Henderson Rd WDN WA8 ....21 F2
Henderson St BNG/LEV M19 ....28 B9
  MCFLDS SK11 ....9 H5
Hendham CI BRAM/HZG SK7 ....52 F1
Hendham Dr ALT WA14 ....52 F1
Hendon Av CW/HAS CW1 ....185 M5
Hendon Dr EDGY/DAV SK3 ....41 H9
Hengist St GTN M18 ....28 D3
Henley Av CHD/CHDH SK8 ....36 D2
  IRL M44 ....36 D2
Henley CI MCFLDN SK10 ....95 J9
  WARRS WA4 ....77 L7
Henley Ct RUNC WA7 ....62 B4
Henley Dr HALE/TIMP WA15 ....38 C9
  WSFD CW7 ....149 P1
Henley PI BNG/LEV M19 ....41 N2
Henley Rd CHSW/BR CH4 ....142 B4
  RUNC WA7 ....77 L7
Henlian Gdns STHEL WA9 ....31 L1
Henry PI CH/BCN CH1 ....2 E2
  CW/HAS CW1 ....185 J1
  DTN/ASHW M34 * 29 P9
  LYMM WA13 ....50 B3
  TPLY/KEL CW6 ....146 G8
  WARR WA1 ....18 B6
Henry St CONG CW12 ....155 N7
  CW/HAS CW1 ....185 N5
  DTN/ASHW M34 ....29 N5
  EDGY/DAV SK3 ....41 L9
  STKP SK1 ....110 G2
  STHEL WA9 ....31 L1
  WARRW/BUR WA5 ....32 B2
Herdman St CW/SHV CW2 ....5 J3
Hereford Av GOL/RIS/CU WA3 * ...102 A4
  GTS/LS CH66 ....102 A4
  WARR WA1 ....34 E9
Hereford CI WILM/AE SK9 ....71 N3
Hereford PI CH/BCN CH1 ....121 K7
Hereford Rd CHD/CHDH SK8 ....54 E8
  RDSH SK5 ....28 F4
Hereford St SALE M33 ....38 B8
Hereford Wy MWCH CW10 ....130 C9
Hereward Rd CHSE CH3 ....143 K1
Heristone Av DTN/ASHW M34 ......29 L7
Heritage Gdns DID/WITH M20 ......40 C6
Herle Dr WYTH/NTH M22 ....54 E6
Hermitage Av HMLPN SK6 ....43 L6
Hermitage Ct CH/BCN CH1 ....120 D3
Hermitage Gdns MPL/ROM SK6 ...43 L6
Hermitage CI CH/BCN CH1 * 132 A3
Hermitage Green La
  WARRN/WOL WA2 ....24 C3

Hollybank Ct *WDN* WA8 * 45 M6
Holly Bank Gv *STHEL* WA9 22 A5
Hollybank Rd *RUNC* WA7 62 D6
Holly Bank Rd *WILM/AE* SK9 71 K5
Hollybrook Dene
MPL/ROM SK6 43 K6
Hollybush Crs *NANT* CW5 197 L2
Holly Bush La *GOL/RIS/CU* WA3 35 K7
Hollybush St *GTN* M18 28 E3
Holly Cl *CHNE* CH2 122 G3
HALE/TIMP WA15 53 L1
SPK/HALE L24 60 D5
Holly Ct *FROD/HEL* WA6 83 J8
Holly Cft *CONG* CW12 154 B4
Hollycroft Av *WYTH/NTH* M22 54 F1
Holly Dr *SALE* M33 38 D4
WSFD CW7 149 M2
Hollyfield Rd *EP* CH65 6 D4
Holly Gra *ALT* WA14 53 H5
BRAM/HZG SK7 56 F4
Holly Gv *DTN/ASHW* M34 29 N6
KNUT WA16 89 M2
SALE M33 38 G4
WARR WA1 34 B9
Holly Heath Cl *SBCH* CW11 171 P4
Hollyhedge Av *WYTH/NTH* M22 54 F2
Hollyhedge Court Rd
WYTH/NTH M22 54 G2
Holly Hedge La *WARRS* WA4 47 P9
Hollyhedge Rd *WYTH/NTH* M22 54 E2
Hollyhey Dr *NTHM/RTH* M23 39 L7
Hollyhouse Dr *MPL/ROM* SK6 42 F3
ALS/KID ST7 189 A5
Holly La *ALS/KID* ST7 189 N3
WILM/AE SK9 70 G1
Holly Mt *CW/SHV* CW2 198 D2
Hollymount Av *OFTN* SK2 57 J2
Hollymount Dr *OFTN* SK2 57 J2
Hollymount Gdns *OFTN* SK2 57 K2
Hollymount Rd *OFTN* SK2 57 J2
Holly Rd *BRAM/HZG* SK7 72 E1
CHSW/BR CH4 142 B5
EP CH65 7 F4
GOL/RIS/CU WA3 24 E1
HTNM SK4 41 K3
LYMM WA13 51 H2
MCFLDS SK11 8 B5
MPL/ROM SK6 58 C8
NEWUL ST5 201 N6
NWCHW CW8 108 E4
POY/DIS SK12 73 L3
RNFD/HAY WA11 22 D4
WARRW/BUR WA5 47 J2
Holly Rd North *WILM/AE* SK9 71 J8
Holly Rd South *WILM/AE* SK9 71 J9
Holly Royde Cl *DID/WITH* M20 40 B2
Holly St *STKP* SK1 17 K5
Holly Ter *WARRW/BUR* WA5 47 K2
Hollythorn Av *CHD/CHDH* SK8 56 C8
Holly Tree Dr *BIDD* ST8 175 K7
KNUT WA16 112 B5
Hollytree Rd *KNUT* WA16 111 M1
Holly Wk *NWCHW* CW8 109 L5
Hollyway *WYTH/NTH* M22 39 P8
Hollywood Wy *HTNM* SK4 16 C5
Holmcroft Rd *GTN* M18 28 D7
Holmcrofts *NSTN* CH64 77 L8
Holmdale Av *BNG/LEV* M19 40 F7
Holm Dr *CHNE* CH2 104 C1
Holme Beech Gv *OFTN* SK2 * 42 B8
Holme Cl *CHSE* CH3 143 N3
Holmefield *SALE* M33 38 E4
Holme Rd *DID/WITH* M20 40 A5
Holmes Chapel Rd *CONG* CW12 155 H7
HOLMCH CW4 153 L1
MCFLDS SK11 114 B7
MWCH CW10 130 E9
MWCH CW10 151 H3
NWCHE CW9 111 M8
SBCH CW11 172 B1
Holmes Ct *GOL/RIS/CU* WA3 34 D4
Holmes St *CHD/CHDH* SK8 55 N1
EDGY/DAV SK3 * 41 M9
Holme St *CHSE* CH3 123 M8
Holmesville Av *CONG* CW12 155 K8
Holmeswood Cl *WILM/AE* SK9 71 K6
Holmfield Av *RUNC* WA7 15 J3
Holmfield Cl *HTNM* SK4 41 L5
Holmfield Dr *CHD/CHDH* SK8 56 B7
GTS/LS CH66 101 P1
Holmlea Dr *CW/HAS* CW1 5 K4
Holmlee Wy *MCFLDN* SK10 94 D7
Holm Oak Wy *GTS/LS* CH66 102 A4
Holmpark Rd *OP/CLY* M11 28 E2
Holmsfield Rd *WARR* WA1 19 J6
Holmshaw La *CW/HAS* CW1 186 D2
Holmside Gdns *BNG/LEV* M19 40 E4
Holmwood *ALT* WA14 52 E4
Holmwood Dr *EP* CH65 102 D2
Holmwood Rd *DID/WITH* M20 40 A2
Holroyd St *OP/CLY* M11 * 28 A1
Holset Dr *ALT* WA14 52 F2
Holt Gdns *KNUT* WA16 * 70 A8
Holt Hey *NSTN* CH64 77 N8
Holt La *RUNC* WA7 62 D7
Holt's La *WILM/AE* SK9 71 H3
Holt St *ALT* WA14 37 P9
CW/HAS CW1 4 C2
DTN/ASHW M34 29 L1
STKP SK1 17 H7
Holwick Rd *NTHM/RTH* M23 39 J6
Holyhead Cl *WARRW/BUR* WA5 32 G5
Holyrood Av *WDN* WA8 45 N3
Holyrood Dr *CW/SHV* CW2 184 E8
Holyrood Wy *CHSE* CH3 122 C8
Holywell Cl *NSTN* CH64 77 H4
STHEL WA9 31 J2
Holywell La *CHSE* CH3 178 D6
Holywell Rd *FLINT* CH6 98 A5
Home Farm Av *MCFLDN* SK10 * 116 F3
Home Farm Pk *NANT* CW5 * 169 H1
Homelands Cl *SALE* M33 38 C6
Homelands Rd *SALE* M33 38 C6
Home Pk *CH/BCN* CH1 121 J2
Homer Dr *MPL/ROM* SK6 43 N8
Homestead Av
RNFD/HAY WA11 * 23 J2
Homestead Cl *PART* M31 36 F4
Homestead Crs *BNG/LEV* M19 40 E5
Homestead Rd *POY/DIS* SK12 58 G9
Homeway *FROD/HEL* WA6 105 H2
Homewood Av *WYTH/NTH* M22 39 N7
Homewood Crs
NWCHW CW8 109 K7
Homewood Rd
WYTH/NTH M22 39 M7
Honey Flds *TPLY/KEL* CW6 146 G9
Honey St *STHEL* WA9 * 30 B1
Honeysuckle Cl *CHSW/BR* CH4 140 G7
GTS/LS CH66 102 B4
MPL/ROM SK6 42 F3
NTHM/RTH M23 38 G7
WDN WA8 45 P3
Honford Rd *WYTH/NTH* M22 54 D3
Hong Kong Av *MANAIR* M90 54 C7
Honister Av *RNFD/HAY* WA11 22 A1
WARRN/WOL WA2 33 M6
Honister Gv *RUNC* WA7 62 C9
Honister Wk *NTHLY* L27 44 A4
Honiston Av *RAIN/WH* L35 30 A4
Honiton Wy *ALT* WA14 52 E1
WARRW/BUR WA5 47 J3
Hood La *WARRW/BUR* WA5 47 N2
Hood La North
WARRW/BUR WA5 47 N1
Hood Rd *WDN* WA8 21 F1
Hoofield La *CHSE* CH3 164 F1
Hoofield Rd *CHSE* CH3 * 145 N8
Hoogreen La *KNUT* WA16 67 K5
Hooker St *NWCHW* CW8 12 C5
Hookstone Dr *GTS/LS* CH66 79 N7
Hoole Br *CHNE* CH2 3 H1
Hoole Cl *CHD/CHDH* SK8 56 A2
Hoole Gdns *CHNE* CH2 122 C8
Hoole La *CHNE* CH2 3 K3
Hoole Pk *CHNE* CH2 3 K1
Hoole Rd *CHNE* CH2 122 A7
Hoole Wy *CH/BCN* CH1 3 G1
Hoole Way Rbt *CH/BCN* CH1 3 F2
Hooleyhey La *MCFLDN* SK10 119 H2
Hooley Range *HTNM* SK4 41 J5
Hoolpool La *FROD/HEL* WA6 82 F8
Hooper St *STKP* SK1 17 F5
Hooton Gn *GTS/LS* CH66 79 L3
Hooton La *GTS/LS* CH66 79 M4
Hooton Rd *NSTN* CH64 78 A4
Hooton Wy *GTS/LS* CH66 79 K3
Hope Av *WILM/AE* SK9 71 L3
Hope Cft *GTS/LS* CH66 102 B2
Hopedale Rd *RDSH* SK5 41 N2
Hope Farm Rd *GTS/LS* CH66 102 A3
Hopefield Rd *LYMM* WA13 51 H3
Hope Green Wy *POY/DIS* SK12 73 K4
Hope La *MCFLDN* SK10 73 L5
Hopelea St *DID/WITH* M20 40 C1
Hope Rd *CHSW/BR* CH4 140 F7
SALE M33 38 E5
Hopes Carr *STKP* SK1 17 H5
Hope St *ALS/KID* ST7 201 J4
BRAM/HZG SK7 57 K5
CHSW/BR CH4 142 B4
CW/SHV CW2 5 F7
DTN/ASHW M34 29 L4
DUK SK16 29 P1
HTNM SK4 16 D4
MCFLDN SK10 9 G4
NEWLW WA12 23 M6
NWCHW CW8 12 D4
SBCH CW11 171 N3
Hope St West *MCFLDN* SK10 8 C3
Hope Ter *DUK* SK16 * 29 P1
EDGY/DAV SK3 * 17 F7
Hopkins Cl *CONG* CW12 155 K7
Hopkins Fld *ALT* WA14 52 F6
Hopkinson Av *DTN/ASHW* M34 29 L4
Hopkin St *WGTN/LGST* M12 28 A6
Hopton Av *WYTH/NTH* M22 54 G4
Hopwood Cl *GOL/RIS/CU* WA3 25 H1
Hopwood St *WARR* WA1 19 F4
Horace Black Gdns *EP* CH65 6 E3
Horace Gv *HTNM* SK4 41 M4
Horatio St *GTN* M18 * 28 F3
Horatius Rd *NEWUL* ST5 201 N9
Horbury Av *GTN* M18 28 D6
Horbury Gdns *GTS/LS* CH66 79 N8
Hornbeam Av *GTS/LS* CH66 102 B3
Hornbeam Cl *HALE/TIMP* WA15 54 A2
RNFD/HAY WA11 22 D2
RUNC WA7 62 G4
SALE M33 37 P3
Hornbeam Dr *NWCHW* CW8 108 G8
Hornbeam Rd *BNG/LEV* M19 28 B7
HLWD L26 44 A8
Hornby Crs *STHEL* WA9 31 J4
Hornby Dr *CONG* CW12 155 J7
NANT CW5 11 F5
Hornby La *WARRN/WOL* WA2 33 K2
Horncastle Cl *GOL/RIS/CU* WA3 25 H1
Hornsea Rd *OFTN* SK2 57 N2
Horridge Av *NEWLW* WA12 23 N4
Horrocks La *WARR* WA1 18 D6
Horrocks Rd *CHNE* CH2 121 P6
Horsefield Cl *CCHDY* M21 39 P1
Horseshoe Cl *FROD/HEL* WA6 106 F2
Horseshoe Crs
WARRN/WOL WA2 33 P5
Horseshoe Dr *MCFLDS* SK11 8 B5
Horseshoe La *WILM/AE* SK9 93 J3
Horsfield Wy *MPL/ROM* SK6 42 E2
Horsham Av *BRAM/HZG* SK7 57 J6
Horsley La *TPLY/KEL* CW6 165 K8
Horstead Wk *BNG/LEV* M19 28 A7
Horstone Crs *GTS/LS* CH66 102 B2
Horstone Gdns *GTS/LS* CH66 102 B2
Horstone Rd *GTS/LS* CH66 102 B2
Horton St *OFTN* SK2 41 N9
Horton Wy *NANT* CW5 197 H3
Horwood Av *RAIN/WH* L35 30 A4
Horwood Crs *DID/WITH* M20 40 E3
Hoscar Ct *WDN* WA8 20 A4
Hoscar Dr *BNG/LEV* M19 40 F1
Hoskins Cl *WGTN/LGST* M12 28 A4
Hospital La *NANT* CW5 195 P5
Hospital St *CW/HAS* CW1 185 K2
NANT CW5 10 C6
Hospital Wy *RUNC* WA7 62 D7
Hotel Rd *MANAIR* M90 54 E8
Hotel St *NEWLW* WA12 23 M6
Hothersall Rd *RDSH* SK5 41 N1
Hothershall Cl *CW/HAS* CW1 * 170 A8
Hough Cl *MCFLDN* SK10 96 B8
Hough End Av *CCHDY* M21 39 M2
Houghend Crs *CCHDY* M21 39 P1
Hougher Wall Rd *ALS/KID* ST7 200 G5
Hough Gn *CHSW/BR* CH4 142 C4
HALE/TIMP WA15 69 J1
Hough Green Rd *WDN* WA8 44 G5
Hough La *FROD/HEL* WA6 107 K7
NWCHW CW8 87 J8
WILM/AE SK9 71 M9
Houghley Cl *MCFLDN* SK10 117 J2
Hough's La *WARRS* WA4 48 C9
Houghton Cl *CHNE* CH2 3 K2
NEWLW WA12 * 23 M6
NWCHE CW9 109 P8
WDN WA8 46 A5
Houghton Cft *WDN* WA8 45 J2
Houghton St *NEWLW* WA12 23 M6
RAIN/WH L35 * 30 B5
WARRN/WOL WA2 18 D3
WDN WA8 46 B5
Houldsworth Av *ALT* WA14 38 B9
Houldsworth St *RDSH* SK5 41 M1
Houndings La *SBCH* CW11 171 N4
Housesteads Dr *CHNE* CH2 3 K1
Housman Cl *CH/BCN* CH1 121 K6
Hove Cl *CW/HAS* CW1 170 A9
Hove Dr *RUSH/FAL* M14 40 F1
The Hove *RUNC* WA7 63 H8
Hovis St *OP/CLY* M11 28 C1
Howard Av *CHD/CHDH* SK8 56 A6
HTNM SK4 41 K2
LYMM WA13 50 G3
Howard Cl *MPL/ROM* SK6 42 F6
Howard Ct *HALE/TIMP* WA15 * 53 M1
Howard Dr *HALE/TIMP* WA15 53 L6
Howard La *DTN/ASHW* M34 29 M5
Howard Rd *CHSW/BR* CH4 141 P4
GOL/RIS/CU WA3 26 A7
WYTH/NTH M22 39 N7
Howard St *CW/HAS* CW1 185 M2
DTN/ASHW M34 29 M3
STKP SK1 17 G2
Howards Wy *NSTN* CH64 77 N7
Howarth Ct *RUNC* WA7 15 G2
Howarth Dr *IRL* M44 27 M8
Howbeck Crs *NANT* CW5 197 P7
Howbeck Wk *CW/SHV* CW2 185 K8
Howden Cl *RDSH* SK5 28 E7
Howden Rd *NM/HAY* SK22 59 N6
Howells Av *GTS/LS* CH66 101 N1
SALE M33 38 D3
Howe Rd *CHSW/BR* CH4 142 D3
Howe St *AULW* OL7 29 L1
MCFLDN SK10 9 J1
Howey Hl *CONG* CW12 155 M9
Howey La *CONG* CW12 155 M8
Howey La *FROD/HEL* WA6 83 N6
Howey Ri *FROD/HEL* WA6 83 N6
Howley La *WARR* WA1 19 H6
Howley Qy *WARR* WA1 * 19 H6
Howson Rd *WARRN/WOL* WA2 33 M6
Howton Cl *WGTN/LGST* M12 28 A5
Howty Cl *WILM/AE* SK9 71 M5
Hoxton Cl *MPL/ROM* SK6 42 F4
Hoylake Cl *RUNC* WA7 62 G8
Hoylake Gv *STHEL* WA9 31 H4
Hoylake Rd *EDGY/DAV* SK3 41 J8
SALE M33 39 J6
Hoyle St *WARRW/BUR* WA5 18 A2
Hubert Dr *MWCH* CW10 151 J2
Hucclecote Av *WYTH/NTH* M22 54 E5
Hucklow Av *NTHM/RTH* M23 54 C5
Hudson Cl *WARRW/BUR* WA5 32 G8
Hudson Rd *HYDE* SK14 43 K1
Hughes Av *WARRN/WOL* WA2 33 N6
Hughes Dr *CW/SHV* CW2 184 F4
Hughes Pl *WARRN/WOL* WA2 33 N6
Hughes St *STHEL* WA9 22 B9
WARRS WA4 48 E4
Hugh St *CHSW/BR* CH4 142 F3
Hulley Rd *MCFLDN* SK10 117 L1
Hullock's Pool Rd *ALS/KID* ST7 201 H2
Hulme Hall Av *CHD/CHDH* SK8 56 A7
Hulme Hall Cl *CHD/CHDH* SK8 56 A6
Hulme Hall Crs *CHD/CHDH* SK8 56 A7
Hulme Hall La *KNUT* WA16 111 P7
Hulme Hall Rd *CHD/CHDH* SK8 56 A5
Hulme La *KNUT* WA16 111 N5
Hulme Rd *DTN/ASHW* M34 29 H6
HTNM SK4 41 L3
SALE M33 38 G5
Hulme Sq *MCFLDS* SK11 117 J7
Hulme St *CW/HAS* CW1 184 F3
STKP SK1 42 A9
Hulseheath La *KNUT* WA16 67 N3
Hulse La *NWCHE* CW9 111 L6
Hulton Cl *CONG* CW12 156 B9
Humber Cl *WDN* WA8 46 D4
Humber Crs *STHEL* WA9 31 H3
Humber Dr *BIDD* ST8 175 M9
Humber Rd *GTS/LS* CH66 102 B2
WARRN/WOL WA2 33 P6
Hume St *BNG/LEV* M19 * 28 B9
WARR WA1 19 H3
Humphrey's Cl *RUNC* WA7 * 63 H7
Huncoat Av *HTNM* SK4 41 L2
Huncote Av *RNFD/HAY* WA11 22 B3
Hungerford Av *CW/HAS* CW1 5 J4
Hungerford Pl *SBCH* CW11 171 M4
Hungerford Rd *CW/HAS* CW1 5 J3
Hungerford Ter *CW/HAS* CW1 185 M5
Hunsterson Rd *NANT* CW5 210 C6
Hunston Rd *SALE* M33 38 C5
Hunt Cl *WARRW/BUR* WA5 * 32 E8
Hunter Av *CW/SHV* CW2 185 K9
WARRN/WOL WA2 33 L6
Hunters Cl *BIDD* ST8 175 K9
MPL/ROM SK6 42 E5
WILM/AE SK9 * 71 P5
Hunters Ct *FROD/HEL* WA6 83 K9
RUNC WA7 62 C8
Hunter's Crs *CHSE* CH3 145 H1
Hunter's Dr *CHSE* CH3 145 H1
Huntersfield *CW/SHV* CW2 198 A4
Hunters Fld *NWCHW* CW8 12 A4
Hunters Hl *FROD/HEL* WA6 106 G3
NWCHW CW8 108 E3
Hunters Ms *SALE* M33 38 D4
WILM/AE SK9 71 L7
Hunters Pointe *CONG* CW12 154 E4
Hunters Pool La *MCFLDN* SK10 94 B6
Hunters Ri *WSFD* CW7 149 L1
Hunter St *CH/BCN* CH1 2 D4
STHEL WA9 * 22 A7
Hunters Wk *CH/BCN* CH1 2 D4
Hunters Wy *ALS/KID* ST7 188 F8
NSTN CH64 77 J5
Huntingdon Crs *RDSH* SK5 * 42 B3
Huntington Av *DID/WITH* M20 40 B1
Huntley Gv *STHEL* WA9 31 H1
Huntley Rd *EDGY/DAV* SK3 41 J9
Huntley St *WARRW/BUR* WA5 47 N3
Huntly Cha *WILM/AE* SK9 71 L8
Hunt Rd *RNFD/HAY* WA11 23 J3
Huntsbank Dr *NEWUL* ST5 201 N6
Hunts Cl *CHSE* CH3 143 K1
Hunts Field Cl *LYMM* WA13 50 D5
Huntsham Cl *ALT* WA14 52 F1
Hunts La *WARRS* WA4 49 H5
Hunts Lock *NWCHE* CW9 12 E6
Huntsman Dr *IRL* M44 36 E1
Hurdsfield Cl *MWCH* CW10 151 J3
Hurdsfield Gn *MCFLDN* SK10 117 L2
Hurdsfield Rd *MCFLDN* SK10 9 H2
OFTN SK2 57 J3
Hurford Av *EP* CH65 80 B9
GTN M18 28 D3
Hurlbote Cl *WILM/AE* SK9 71 M1
Hurlestone Cl *CHNE* CH2 122 G2
Hurley Cl *WARRW/BUR* WA5 47 N2
Hurley Dr *CHD/CHDH* SK8 55 N5
Hurn Cl *CW/HAS* CW1 170 A9
Hurst Av *CHD/CHDH* SK8 56 C9
SALE M33 37 P5
Hurstbank Av *BNG/LEV* M19 * 40 E4
Hurst Cl *ALS/KID* ST7 201 N1
Hurstfold Av *BNG/LEV* M19 40 E5
Hursthead Rd *CHD/CHDH* SK8 56 B8
Hurst La *GOL/RIS/CU* WA3 26 B2
MCFLDN SK10 95 N5
Hurst Lea Ct *WILM/AE* SK9 93 J2
Hurst Lea Rd *NM/HAY* SK22 59 N8
Hurst Mill La *GOL/RIS/CU* WA3 26 C1
Hurst Rd *BIDD* ST8 175 P6
Hurst St *DUK* SK16 29 N3
RDSH SK5 41 M1
WDN WA8 61 N2
The Hurst *FROD/HEL* WA6 106 G2
Hurstvale Av *CHD/CHDH* SK8 55 K6
Hurstville Rd *CCHDY* M21 39 L2
Hurstwood *CHSE* CH3 144 A6
Hurstwood Rd *OFTN* SK2 57 M1
Huskisson Wy *NEWLW* WA12 23 M5
Hus St *DROY* M43 28 F1
Hutchins' Cl *MWCH* CW10 151 L4
Hutchinson St *WDN* WA8 21 G7
Huttfield Rd *SPK/HALE* L24 60 A2
Hutton Cl *GOL/RIS/CU* WA3 25 N4
Hutton Dr *CONG* CW12 156 A8
Huxley Cl *BRAM/HZG* SK7 56 E8
MCFLDN SK10 116 G2
Huxley Ct *GTS/LS* CH66 80 B5
Huxley Dr *BRAM/HZG* SK7 56 E8
Huxley La *TPLY/KEL* CW6 165 K3
Huxley St *ALT* WA14 38 A9
NWCHW CW8 12 C5
Huxley Ter *ALT* WA14 * 52 G6
Huxton Gn *BRAM/HZG* SK7 56 G5
Hyacinth Cl *EDGY/DAV* SK3 56 D2
RNFD/HAY WA11 23 K3
Hyde Bank Rd *NM/HAY* SK22 59 N7
Hyde Cl *EP* CH65 80 B9
RUNC WA7 * 62 B8
Hyde Fold Cl *BNG/LEV* M19 40 G2
Hyde Gv *SALE* M33 38 E4
Hyde Rd *DTN/ASHW* M34 29 M6
GTN M18 28 F5
MPL/ROM SK6 42 G3
WGTN/LGST M12 28 B4
Hydrangea Cl *SALE* M33 37 P3
Hyldavale Av *CHD/CHDH* SK8 55 K1
Hylton Ct *EP* CH65 102 G2
Hylton Dr *CHD/CHDH* SK8 56 C7
Hythe Av *CW/HAS* CW1 170 A9
Hythe Rd *EDGY/DAV* SK3 41 J8

I

Ian Rd *ALS/KID* ST7 189 M6
Ibis Ct *WARR* WA1 48 C4
Ikey La *NANT* CW5 195 J1
Ikins Dr *ALS/KID* ST7 201 J5
Ilex Av *WARRN/WOL* WA2 33 L2
Ilfracombe Rd *OFTN* SK2 42 C8
STHEL WA9 31 H3
Ilkley Crs *RDSH* SK5 28 E9
Imperial Av *CH/BCN* CH1 120 F7
Imperial Ms *EP* CH65 6 D2
Imperial Ter *SALE* M33 * 38 D2
Ince Av *PS/BROM* CH62 79 J2
Ince Cl *DID/WITH* M20 40 C1
HTNM SK4 16 E1
Ince Dr *CHSE* CH3 177 H7
CHNE CH2 82 B9
Ince La *CHNE* CH2 103 P8
Ince Orchards *CHNE* CH2 82 B9
Ince St *HTNM* SK4 41 M5
Indigo Rd *EP* CH65 81 H8
Ingersley Rd *MCFLDN* SK10 95 P5
Ingham Cl *CHSE* CH3 143 J1
Ingham Rd *ALT* WA14 38 A7
WDN WA8 45 M3
Ingle Dr *OFTN* SK2 42 B9
Inglehead Cl *DTN/ASHW* M34 29 N7
Inglenook Rd
WARRW/BUR WA5 47 K3
Ingle Rd *CHD/CHDH* SK8 56 A1
Inglesham Cl *NTHM/RTH* M23 54 D1
Ingleton Cl *CHD/CHDH* SK8 55 L1
HOLMCH CW4 131 M8
NEWLW WA12 * 23 M5
Ingleton Gv *RUNC* WA7 62 B9
EDGY/DAV SK3 16 A7
Inglewood Av *MWCH* CW10 151 K5
Inglewood Cl *GOL/RIS/CU* WA3 35 J2
PART M31 36 D4
Ingram Dr *HTNM* SK4 40 F5
Inman Av *STHEL* WA9 22 F7
Inman St *DTN/ASHW* M34 29 M6
Innes St *WGTN/LGST* M12 28 B6
Innisfree Cl *GTS/LS* CH66 79 N8
Insall Rd *WARRN/WOL* WA2 34 A6
Intack La *NWCHE* CW9 66 A3
Intake Cl *NSTN* CH64 78 E6
International Ap *MANAIR* M90 * 54 D8
Inveresk Rd *MALPAS* SY14 191 K4
Inward Wy *EP* CH65 80 D6
Ion Pth *WSFD* CW7 150 C1
Iqbal Cl *WGTN/LGST* M12 28 A4
Irby Cl *GTS/LS* CH66 80 A9
Ireland Rd *RNFD/HAY* WA11 22 G3
SPK/HALE L24 60 E5
Ireland St *WARRN/WOL* WA2 33 L8
WDN WA8 46 B5
Irene Av *RNFD/HAY* WA11 22 A2
Iris Cl *WDN* WA8 45 J5
Irlam Rd *SALE* M33 38 F3
URM M41 27 P8
Irlam Wharf Rd *IRL* M44 36 F2
Ironbridge Dr *HOLMCH* CW4 131 P9
Irons La *CHSE* CH3 123 N4
Iron St *DTN/ASHW* M34 * 29 M6
Irvin Dr *WYTH/NTH* M22 55 J7
Irving Cl *OFTN* SK2 56 G4
Irving's Crs *CHSW/BR* CH4 141 P4
Irwell La *RUNC* WA7 15 H1
Irwell Ri *MCFLDN* SK10 95 M6
Irwell Rd *WARRS* WA4 48 D5
Irwell St *WDN* WA8 61 N2
Irwin Dr *WILM/AE* SK9 71 L1
Irwin Rd *ALT* WA14 37 P8
STHEL WA9 31 H1
Irwin St *DTN/ASHW* M34 29 L6
Isabella Ct *CHSW/BR* CH4 142 A4
Isherwood Cl *WARRN/WOL* WA2 34 A5
Isherwood Dr *MPL/ROM* SK6 58 B1
Isherwood Rd *PART* M31 37 L2
Isis Cl *CONG* CW12 155 P9
Islay Cl *EP* CH65 102 E4
Islington Rd *OFTN* SK2 57 J3
Iveagh Cl *RUNC* WA7 62 E7
Iver Cl *WDN* WA8 45 J1
Iver Rd *CHNE* CH2 121 P4
Ivy Av *NEWLW* WA12 23 N7
Ivychurch Ms *RUNC* WA7 62 B4
Ivy Ct *CHSW/BR* CH4 160 G7
STHEL WA9 * 22 A6
Ivy Dr *NWCHW* CW8 127 K1
Ivy Farm Dr *NSTN* CH64 77 M7
Ivy Farm Gdns
GOL/RIS/CU WA3 25 M5
Ivy Farm La *CHSE* CH3 179 J8
Ivy Farm Rd *RAIN/WH* L35 30 A4
Ivy Gdns *CONG* CW12 155 L8
Ivy House Rd *BIDD* ST8 175 K7
Ivy La *ALS/KID* ST7 188 A6
MCFLDS SK11 116 G6
Ivylea Rd *BNG/LEV* M19 40 F4
Ivy Meade Rd *MCFLDS* SK11 116 F6
Ivy Ms *CHNE* CH2 122 B6
Ivy Rd *GOL/RIS/CU* WA3 24 D1
MCFLDS SK11 116 G5
POY/DIS SK12 73 L3
WARR WA1 34 F9
Ivy St *RUNC* WA7 15 G4

J

Jack Brady Cl *NTHM/RTH* M23 54 A3
Jack La *CW/SHV* CW2 199 J1
MWCH CW10 129 J6
Jack La *NWCHE* CW9 129 H4
Jackson Av *GOL/RIS/CU* WA3 25 N6
NANT CW5 10 E6
WARR WA1 34 A9
Jackson Cl *HALE/TIMP* WA15 38 F9
RAIN/WH L35 30 C7
Jackson Gdns *DTN/ASHW* M34 29 K7
Jackson La *MCFLDN* SK10 95 N6
Jackson Rd *CONG* CW12 155 N5
Jacksons Edge Rd
POY/DIS SK12 58 E8
Jacksons La *BRAM/HZG* SK7 57 H7
Jackson St *CHD/CHDH* SK8 55 N1
MCFLDS SK11 117 K6
RNFD/HAY WA11 * 22 E2
SALE M33 38 G3
STHEL WA9 22 A6
WARRW/BUR WA5 32 B2

Jacobs Wy *KNUT* WA16 ....88 F6
Jamage Rd *ALS/KID* ST7 ....201 N3
James Atkinson Wy
  CW/HAS CW1 ....184 F1
James Av *GTS/LS* CH66 ....101 N1
James Ct *WDN* WA8 ....61 N2
James Hall St *NANT* CW5 ....10 C3
James Pl *CHNE* CH2 ....3 K2
James St *CH/BCN* CH1 ....3 F2
  DTN/ASHW M34 * 29 M5
  EDGY/DAV SK3 ....41 M9
  MCFLDS SK11 ....8 E7
  MPL/ROM SK6 ....42 F3
  NWCHE CW9 ....110 C4
  SALE M33 ....38 G4
  STHEL WA9 ....31 J5
  WARR WA1 ....18 E5
Jamieson Cl *ALS/KID* ST7 ....188 A4
  CHSE CH3 ....122 B9
Jane St *STHEL* WA9 ....33 L1
Jan Palach Av *NANT* CW5 ....196 G3
Jarman *MCFLDS* SK11 ....117 M8
Jasmine Cl *NTHM/RTH* M23 ......39 H7
Jasmine Gdns *STHEL* WA9 ....31 N1
Jasmine Rd *WDN* WA8 ....20 A2
Jasmin Wy *ALS/KID* ST7 ....189 P6
Jay Cl *GOL/RIS/CU* WA3 ....35 H4
Jays Cl *RUNC* WA7 ....63 J7
Jayton Av *DID/WITH* M20 ....40 C8
Jean Cl *BNG/LEV* M19 ....28 A7
Jedburgh Av *GTS/LS* CH66 ....79 L7
Jellicoe Av *IRL* M44 ....36 D2
Jennings St *EDGY/DAV* SK3 ......41 L9
Jenniston Ct *WGTN/LGST* M12 ..28 B5
Jenny La *BRAM/HZG* SK7 ....72 E3
Jensen Ct *RUNC* WA7 ....15 K1
Jepson St *OFTN* SK2 ....56 C1
Jersey Av *EP* CH65 ....102 E3
Jersey Rd *RDSH* SK5 ....58 A5
Jersey St *STHEL* WA9 ....31 H5
Jersey Wy *MWCH* CW10 ....130 C9
Jervis Cl *WARRN/WOL* WA2 ....34 B5
Jesmond Crs *CW/SHV* CW2 ....4 B6
Jesmond Gv *CH/BCN* CH1 ....2 A2
Jesmond Rd *CH/BCN* CH1 ....2 A2
Jays Cl *MPL/ROM* SK6 ....48 L8
Jessop St *GTN* M18 ....28 D3
Jessop Wy *CW/HAS* CW1 ....186 A4
Jetson St *GTN* M18 ....28 C1
Jinnah St *OP/CLY* M11 ....28 C1
Jockey St *WARRN/WOL* WA2 ......18 D1
Jodrell Cl *HOLMCH* CW4 ....73 J1
  MCFLDS SK11 ....9 G6
Jodrell Meadow *CHF/WBR* SK23 ..75 P6
Jodrell St *MCFLDS* SK11 ....75 P6
  NM/HAY SK22 ....59 M8
Joel La *HYDE* SK14 ....43 L1
Johannesburg Gdns
  NTHM/RTH M23 ....55 K5
John Av *CHD/CHDH* SK8 ....55 N2
John Beeley Av *OP/CLY* M11 ......28 D1
John Brunner Crs *NWCHW* CW8 ..88 G8
John Fryer Av *NWCHE* CW9 ....88 C8
John Gresty Dr *NANT* CW5 ....197 L1
  EP CH65 ....6 E3
John Rd *LYMM* WA13 ....50 C4
Johns Av *RUNC* WA7 ....14 D5
Johnson Av *NEWLW* WA12 ....23 M4
Johnson Cl *CONG* CW12 ....156 B9
Johnsons Cl *CHSW/BR* CH4 ......142 D5
Johnson's La *WDN* WA8 ....46 C7
Johnson St *NEWLW* ST5 ....201 N8
  STHEL WA9 ....22 A5
John's Pl *APPL/ROM* SK6 ....43 H6
John Steet *MPL/ROM* SK6 ....43 H6
John St *ALT* WA14 ....53 H3
  BRAM/HZG SK7 ....57 K4
  CW/HAS CW1 ....4 D2
  DROY M43 ....29 M5
  DTN/ASHW M34 * 29 M5
  EP CH65 ....6 C2
  GOL/RIS/CU WA3 ....36 D3
  IRL M44 ....36 D3
  MCFLDS SK11 ....95 P5
  MPL/ROM SK6 ....42 F3
  MPL/ROM SK6 ....43 H6
  MPL/ROM SK6 ....58 E2
  SALE M33 ....38 G4
  STKP SK1 ....17 G6
  TPLY/KEL SK6 ....146 F3
  WARRN/WOL WA2 ....18 E5
  WSFD CW7 ....149 L1
John St West *AULW* OL7 ....29 M1
Join Rd *SALE* M33 ....38 A5
Jonathan's Wy *CH/BCN* CH1 .....121 H6
Jones's La *MWCH* CW10 ....152 B3
Jonson Sq *NTHM/RTH* M23 ....39 H8
Jonson Rd *NSTN* CH64 ....77 L4
Jordangate *MCFLDS* SK10 ....8 E3
Joseph Crs *ALS/KID* ST7 ....188 A6
Joseph Johnson Ms
  WYTH/NTH M22 ....39 P7
Joseph St *MPL/ROM* SK6 * 42 F3
  STHEL WA9 ....31 H1
  WDN WA8 ....46 A5
Joules Ct *STKP* SK1 ....17 H5
Joule St *GOL/RIS/CU* WA3 ....34 C3
Jowett St *RDSH* SK5 ....41 N1
Joyce Av *WSFD* CW7 ....128 D9
Joy La *STHEL* WA9 ....31 K6
  WARRW/BUR WA5 ....32 G4
Joynson St *SALE* M33 ....38 E3
Jubilee Av *CW/SHV* CW2 ....4 B4
  WARR WA1 ....18 G5
  WARRW/BUR WA5 ....62 A3
Jubilee Cl *HOLMCH* CW4 ....131 M8
Jubilee Crs *RNFD/HAY* WA11 ......23 K2
Jubilee Gdns *NANT* CW5 ....196 F3

  NM/HAY SK22 ....59 N8
Jubilee Gn *EP* CH65 ....7 G7
Jubilee Gv *LYMM* WA13 ....50 C3
Jubilee Rd *CONG* CW12 ....155 N8
Jubilee St *NM/HAY* SK22 ....59 N8
Jubilee Ter *NANT* CW5 ....10 C7
Jubilee Wy *WDN* WA8 ....45 L6
Jubits La *WDN* WA8 ....45 P6
Juddfield St *RNFD/HAY* WA11 .....22 E3
Judson Av *CCHDY* M21 ....39 M3
Judy La *MCFLDS* SK11 ....136 F1
Julian Wy *WDN* WA8 ....45 M5
Julius Cl *FLINT* CH6 ....98 C7
Julius St *BNG/LEV* M19 ....28 B9
Jumper La *MCFLDN* SK10 ....96 D6
Junction La *NEWLW* WA12 ....23 M7
  STHEL WA9 ....31 K1
Junction Rd *DTN* SK2 ....31 K1
June Av *HTNM* SK4 * 41 J6
Juniper Bnk *RDSH* SK5 ....28 G9
Juniper Cl *SALE* M33 ....38 C2
Juniper Ct *CHNE* CH2 ....122 C7
Juniper Dr *GTS/LS* CH66 ....102 A3
Juniper Gv *GTS/LS* CH66 ....102 B3
Juniper La *GOL/RIS/CU* WA3 ....35 H8
Juniper Ri *MCFLDN* SK10 ....116 E3
Jupiter Dr *CH/BCN* CH1 ....121 H9
  WARRN/WOL WA2 ....33 P7
Justice St *MCFLDN* SK10 ....8 E1
Justin Rd *RAIN/WH* L35 ....30 A5

K

Kaleyards *CH/BCN* CH1 ....2 E3
Karen Cl *WARRW/BUR* WA5 ....32 C2
Karen Wy *GTS/LS* CH66 ....101 P1
Katherine Rd *OFTN* SK2 ....57 J2
Kay Av *MPL/ROM* SK6 ....58 A5
Kay Cl *GOL/RIS/CU* WA3 ....25 P6
Kay La *LYMM* WA13 ....51 J7
Kay's Av *STKP* SK1 ....42 A7
Kays Wood Rd *MPL/ROM* SK6 ....58 B1
Kearton Dr *ECCL/OLD* M30 ....27 N5
Keary Cl *OTN* M18 ....28 D3
Keates Cl *STHEL* WA9 ....22 D9
Keats Av *ALS/KID* ST7 ....189 J8
  CW/SHV CW2 ....184 G3
  NWCHE CW9 ....116 E5
Keats Gdns *ALS/KID* ST7 ....189 J8
Keats Gv *WARRN/WOL* WA2 ....33 M6
Keats La *NWCHE* CW9 ....88 G8
Keaves Av *NTHM/RTH* M23 ....38 F8
Keble St *WDN* WA8 ....21 J6
Keckwick La *WARRS* WA4 ....63 M4
Kedleston Gn *OFTN* SK2 ....42 C9
Keele Crs *MCFLDS* SK11 ....8 A7
Keel Hey *NSTN* CH64 ....78 F4
Keepers La *NWCHE* CW9 ....87 M1
  NWCHW CW8 ....108 C4
Keeper's Rd *WARRS* WA4 ....49 J8
Keith Av *WARRW/BUR* WA5 ....47 J1
Keith Dr *EDGY/DAV* SK3 ....41 J9
Kelboro Av *DTN/ASHW* M34 ......29 K2
Kelbrook Cl *STHEL* WA9 ....31 J2
Kelbrook Ct *OFTN* SK2 ....57 L2
Kelbrook Rd *OP/CLY* M11 ....28 C2
Kelburn Ct *GOL/RIS/CU* WA3 ......34 G2
Kelby Av *NTHM/RTH* M23 ....39 L9
Kelfield Av *NTHM/RTH* M23 ....39 K9
Kelmarsh Cl *OP/CLY* M11 * 28 D2
Kelmscott Cl *GTS/LS* CH66 ......101 P2
Kelsall Av *PS/BROM* CH62 ....79 J7
  STHEL WA9 ....30 C4
Kelsall Ct *EDGY/DAV* SK3 ....34 D5
  PS/BROM CH62 ....79 J7
  WDN WA8 ....45 K5
Kelsall Grs *EDGY/DAV* SK3 ....56 D1
Kelsall Rd *HALE/TIMP* WA15 ....66 C2
Kelsall Rd *CHD/CHDH* SK8 ....56 A2
  CHSE CH3 ....124 D3
  CHSE CH3 ....124 E4
Kelsall St *CONG* CW12 ....155 N7
Kelsall Wy *ALS/KID* ST7 ....200 G6
Kelsborrow Cl *NWCHE* CW9 ......109 N9
Kelsborrow Wy *TPLY/KEL* CW6 ..125 J7
Kelso Wy *MCFLDN* SK10 ....95 J9
Kelstern Cl *WDN* WA8 ....13 J5
Kelsterton Rd *FLINT* CH6 ....98 G9
Kelvin Cl *RDSH* SK5 ....41 N5
Kelvin Av *SALE* M33 ....38 E4
Kelvindale Dr *HALE/TIMP* WA15 ..38 F9
Kelvin Gv *CHNE* CH2 ....121 P7
Kelvin Rd *WARRN/WOL* WA2 ......18 A6
  GOL/RIS/CU WA3 ....34 F2
Kemberton Dr *WDN* WA8 ....45 N2
Kemble Av *NTHM/RTH* M23 ....39 H7
Kemble Cl *CW/SHV* CW2 ....185 H8
Kemmel Av *WARRS* WA4 ....48 E5
  WYTH/NTH M22 ....54 C2
Kemp Rd *MPL/ROM* SK6 ....58 B5
Kempsell Wy *HLWD* L26 ....44 A8
Kempsey Gv *WARRS* WA4 ....30 D1
Kempsford Cl *NTHM/RTH* M23 ....54 D1
Kempton Av *CW/HAS* CW1 ....185 J1
  SALE M33 ....38 A5
Kempton Cl *BRAM/HZG* SK7 ....57 N5
  CH/BCN CH1 ....2 A4
  NEWLW WA12 ....23 M4
  RUNC WA7 ....62 A8
Kempton Wy *MCFLDN* SK10 ....8 E3
Kenchester Av *OP/CLY* M11 ....28 D1
Kendal Av *DTN/ASHW* M34 ....29 J3
  SALE M33 ....38 F5
Kerfoot Cl *WYTH/NTH* M22 ....39 P8

Kendal Cl *CHNE* CH2 ....122 B5
  GTS/LS CH66 ....101 P2
  HALE/TIMP WA15 ....53 P2
  MCFLDS SK11 ....116 E6
Kendal Ct *CONG* CW12 ....155 J8
Kendal Dr *BRAM/HZG* SK7 ....72 C1
  CHD/CHDH SK8 ....55 L3
  GTS/LS CH66 ....101 P2
  RNFD/HAY WA11 ....22 A1
Kendal Gdns *MPL/ROM* SK6 ....42 G4
Kendal Ri *RUNC* WA7 ....62 B9
Kendal Rd *MCFLDS* SK11 ....116 F6
  WDN WA8 ....45 J6
Kendal Rd West *MCFLDS* SK11 ..116 F6
Kendon Gv *DTN/ASHW* M34 ....29 L6
Kendrick Cl *NWCHW* CW8 * 108 F3
Kendricks Fold *RAIN/WH* L35 ......30 A5
Kendrick St *WARR* WA1 ....18 E5
Kenerew Av *CHD/CHDH* SK8 ....55 H1
  DID/WITH M20 ....50 A3
  RUNC WA7 ....15 F7
  WILM/AE SK9 ....71 M3
Kenilworth Av *CW/SHV* CW2 .....184 G9
  MCFLDS SK11 ....43 L8
  MPL/ROM SK6 ....43 L8
Kenilworth Dr *BRAM/HZG* SK7 ....57 K7
  WARR WA1 ....34 A8
Kenilworth Gdns *NEWLW* WA12 ..23 N7
Kenilworth Gn *MCFLDS* SK11 ....116 D6
Kenilworth Gv *DTN/ASHW* M34 ...29 L4
Kenilworth Rd *EDGY/DAV* SK3 ....34 G9
  GOL/RIS/CU WA3 ....24 C2
  MCFLDS SK11 ....116 F7
  NSTN CH64 ....77 L7
  SALE M33 ....38 F6
Kenley Av *WDN* WA8 ....45 K2
Kenmare Bnk *NWCHE* CW9 ......110 A7
Kenmore Dr *HALE/TIMP* WA15 ....53 L4
Kenmore Rd *SALE* M33 ....37 P7
  WYTH/NTH M22 ....39 M9
Kennedy Av *MCFLDN* SK10 ....116 E5
Kennedy Cl *CHNE* CH2 ....122 B6
Kennedy Wy *DTN/ASHW* M34 ......29 K7
  HTNM SK4 ....16 B3
Kennelwood Av *NWCHE* CW9 ......87 L6
Kennerley Rd *OFTN* SK2 ....56 C4
Kennerley's La *WILM/AE* SK9 ......71 J7
Kennet Cl *WILM/AE* SK9 ....71 M4
Kenneth Rd *WDN* WA8 ....45 J8
Kenneth Av *CONG* CW12 ....155 P9
Kennet Rd *RNFD/HAY* WA11 ....22 C3
Kennett Av *NTHM/RTH* M23 ....54 C4
Kennett Wy *MCFLDS* SK11 ....116 F4
Kenninghall Rd
  NTHM/RTH M22 ....54 F4
Kennington Pk *WDN* WA8 ....45 L4
Kenrick Cl *AUD/MAD* WA3 ....219 H4
Kensington Av *STHEL* WA9 ....31 H1
  GTS/LS CH66 ....101 P2
Kensington Cl *WDN* WA8 ....46 B3
Kensington Ct *ALS/KID* ST7 .....187 K5
  WILM/AE SK9 ....71 J8
  WSFD CW7 ....149 L3
Kensington Dr *CONG* CW12 ......155 P6
  NANT CW5 ....197 L3
Kensington Gdns
  HALE/TIMP WA15 ....53 K6
  CHSW/BR CH4 ....142 B4
Kensington Gn *CHSW/BR* CH4 ..142 B4
  ALT WA14 ....38 B8
Kensington Rd *EDGY/DAV* SK3 ...41 J9
  EP CH65 ....6 B4
Kensington Wy *NWCHE* CW9 ....109 N9
Kent Av *CHD/CHDH* SK8 ....56 C3
  MCFLDN SK10 ....8 F5
Kent Cl *WHITCH* SY13 ....213 N6
Kent Ct *CONG* CW12 ....155 M6
Kent Gv *NEWLW* ST5 ....201 N7
  RUNC WA7 ....15 H4
Kentmere Av *WSFD* CW7 ....128 E9
Kentmere Cl *CHD/CHDH* SK8 ......55 K4
Kentmere Pl *WARRN/WOL* WA2 ..18 A7
Kentmere Rd *HALE/TIMP* WA15 ...53 P1
Kentmere Cl *HTNM* SK4 ....40 F6
Kenton Av *GTN* M18 ....28 C6
Kenton Cl *DTN/ASHW* M34 ....29 K2
Kentridge Dr *GTS/LS* CH66 ....101 P1
Kent Rd *CHNE* CH2 ....122 A6
  DTN/ASHW M34 ....29 L6
  IRL M44 ....36 B3
  PART L24 ....36 D6
  STHEL WA9 ....22 A9
  WARRW/BUR WA5 ....47 N3
Kent's Green La *CW/HAS* CW1 ....14 F5
Kent's La *CW/HAS* CW1 ....170 B8
Kentstone Av *NTHM* SK4 ....40 F5
Kent St *WARRS* WA4 ....48 E3
  WDN WA8 ....21 J1
Kent Wk *MCFLDN* SK10 * 116 F5
Kentwell Cl *DUK* SK16 ....29 N6
Kentwell Dr *MCFLDN* SK10 ....117 J2
Kenview Cl *WDN* WA8 ....60 C2
Kenwick Cl *GTS/LS* CH66 ....101 N1
Kenwood Av *BNG/LEV* M19 ....40 G2
  BRAM/HZG SK7 ....72 D1
  CHD/CHDH SK8 ....55 K5
  HALE/TIMP WA15 ....53 L5
Kenwood Rd *RDSH* SK5 ....41 P5
Kenworthy La *WYTH/NTH* M22 ....39 N6
Kenwright Crs *STHEL* WA9 ....22 A9
Kenyon Av *SALE* M33 ....39 H6
  GOL/RIS/CU WA3 ....25 H3
Kenyons La North
  RNFD/HAY WA11 ....23 K1
Kenyon's La South
  RNFD/HAY WA11 ....23 K1
Kenyon St *DUK* SK16 ....29 N7
Kepwick Dr *WYTH/NTH* M22 ....54 G6
Kerfoot Cl *WYTH/NTH* M22 ....39 P8

Kerfoot St *WARRN/WOL* WA2 ......18 C1
Keristal Av *CHSE* CH3 ....143 J3
Kerne Gv *NTHM/RTH* M23 ....39 K7
Kerr Gv *STHEL* WA9 ....22 C6
Kerridge Cl *MWCH* CW10 ....151 J5
Kerridge Dr *MPL/ROM* SK6 ....42 E4
Kerridge Rd *MCFLDN* SK10 ....117 P1
Kerris Cl *WYTH/NTH* M22 ....54 F6
Kerry Cft *GTS/LS* CH66 ....102 A3
Kerrysdale Cl *STHEL* WA9 ....31 J1
Kersal Dr *HALE/TIMP* WA15 ....38 F9
Kerscott Rd *NTHM/RTH* M23 ....39 J6
Kersh Av *BNG/LEV* M19 ....28 B9
Kershaw Av *SALE* M33 ....39 G6
Kershaw Gv *DTN/ASHW* M34 ......29 H1
  MCFLDS SK11 ....8 A4
Kershaw La *DTN/ASHW* M34 ....29 J1
Kershaw St *AULW* OL7 ....29 M1
  WDN WA8 ....45 K6
Kershaw Wy *NEWLW* WA12 ....23 N7
Kerswell Cl *STHEL* WA9 ....31 J2
Kerwin Wk *OP/CLY* M11 * 28 A1
Keston Crs *RDSH* SK5 ....41 N5
Kestral Cl *CONG* CW12 ....155 N9
  MPL/ROM SK6 ....58 C1
  MWCH CW10 ....151 K5
  WSFD CW7 ....149 L5
Kestrel Dr *CW/HAS* CW1 ....185 H1
Kestrel La *GOL/RIS/CU* WA3 ....34 F6
Kestrel Rd *NWCHW* CW8 ....109 L5
Kestrels Wy *RUNC* WA7 ....62 D8
Kestrel Wk *WGTN/LGST* M12 ......28 A3
Keswick Av *BEB* CH65 ....78 G1
  CHD/CHDH SK8 ....55 K4
  CW/SHV CW2 ....184 E5
  IRL M44 ....36 C4
  MCFLDS SK11 ....8 B7
  WDN WA8 ....45 J6
  WSFD CW7 ....128 E9
Keswick Cl *CHNE* CH2 ....122 B6
Keswick Crs *WARRN/WOL* WA2 ...34 B5
Keswick Dr *BRAM/HZG* SK7 ....72 C1
  FROD/HEL WA6 ....86 F4
Keswick Rd *HALE/TIMP* WA15 .....53 P1
  HTNM SK4 ....41 L1
  MPL/ROM SK6 ....42 F3
Kettell Av *CW/HAS* CW1 ....184 F2
Kettering Rd *DTN/ASHW* M34 ......28 B7
Kettle La *AUD/MAD* CW3 ....211 J3
Kettleshulme Wy *POY/DIS* SK12 ..71 J4
Ketton Cl *OP/CLY* M11 ....28 C2
Kevin St *BNG/LEV* M19 ....28 B9
Kew Ct *DTN/ASHW* M34 * 58 N5
Key Ct *DTN/ASHW* M34 ....29 L4
Keyes Gdns *GOL/RIS/CU* WA3 .....34 G4
Keysbrook *CHSE* CH3 ....164 E7
Keysbrook Av *CW/HAS* CW1 ......184 E5
Kidderton Cl *NANT* CW5 ....182 A9
Kidderton La *NANT* CW5 ....182 B8
Kidsgrove Bnk *ALS/KID* ST7 .....189 K8
Kidsgrove Rd *BURS/TUN* ST8 ......38 J5
Kidstone Cl *STHEL* WA9 ....31 J1
Kilbuck La *RNFD/HAY* WA11 ....23 L1
Kilburn Cl *CHD/CHDH* SK8 ....55 K5
Kilburn Rd *EDGY/DAV* SK3 ....30 D1
Kildare Cl *DTN/ASHW* M34 ....60 D4
Kildonan Rd *WARRS* WA4 ....49 J5
Kilford Cl *WARRW/BUR* WA5 ....33 H2
Killingworth La
  GOL/RIS/CU WA3 ....35 J3
  CHNE CH2 ....121 P8
Kilmorey Park Rd *CHNE* CH2 ....122 A8
Kiln Cl *FLINT* CH6 ....98 A6
Kiln Cft *MPL/ROM* SK6 ....58 C1
Kilncroft *RUNC* WA7 * 62 F9
Kiln Croft La *WILM/AE* SK9 ....71 N2
Kiln La *NANT* CW5 ....182 A8
Kilnwick Cl *GTN* M18 ....28 B6
Kilshaw Rd *WARRW/BUR* WA5 ....32 C2
Kilsyth Cl *WARRN/WOL* WA2 ....34 A4
Kilvert Dr *SALE* M33 ....38 C5
Kimberley Av *MPL/ROM* SK6 ....58 D6
  STHEL WA9 ....30 E1
Kimberley Dr *WARRS* WA4 ....48 E6
Kimberley Rd *EDGY/DAV* SK3 .....41 M9
  WARRW/BUR WA5 ....48 A2
Kimberley Ter *CHSE* CH3 ....3 K3
Kimberley St *EDGY/DAV* SK3 ....7 M5
Kinder Av *DTN/ASHW* M34 ....29 L6
Kinder Cl *WSFD* CW7 ....149 N9
Kinder Dr *CW/SHV* CW2 ....184 A2
  MPL/ROM SK6 ....58 C1
Kinder Gv *MPL/ROM* SK6 ....42 F3
Kinderton Av *WSFD* CW7 ....151 K6
Kinderton Cl *WDN* WA8 ....45 N2
Kinderton St *MWCH* CW10 ....151 K1
King Edward Cl *NANT* CW5 ....102 F7
King Edward Dr *FLINT* CH6 ....109 P2
King Edward Rd *HYDE* SK14 ....43 K1
  KNUT WA16 ....88 F6
  MCFLDS SK10 ....8 F4
  RAIN/WH L35 ....30 A4
King Edward St *BNG/LEV* M19 ....28 B8
  MCFLDN SK10 ....8 F4
  MWCH CW10 ....151 J2
  WARR WA1 ....18 E5
Kingfisher Dr *WSFD* CW7 ....149 N9
Kingfisher Gv *NWCHE* CW9 ....88 E8
Kingfisher Rd *OFTN* SK2 ....57 M3

King George Av *NWCHE* CW9 ......13 J4
King George Crs *WARR* WA1 ....19 K2
King George Rd
  RNFD/HAY WA11 ....23 L2
Kingham Cl *WDN* WA8 ....46 B6
King James Ct *RUNC* WA7 ....10 C4
King Rd *NANT* CW5 ....10 C4
King's Acre *ALT* WA14 ....52 E6
Kings Cl *CHD/CHDH* SK8 ....55 J3
  FLINT CH6 ....98 B7
  GOL/RIS/CU WA3 ....25 H2
Kingsbridge Cl *MPL/ROM* SK6 .....43 K9
Kingsbridge Dr *DUK* SK16 ....29 P2
Kingsbury Cl *WARRS* WA4 ....64 F3
Kingsbury Rd *OP/CLY* M11 ....28 D2
Kingsclere Av *RAIN/WH* L35 ....30 C5
King's Cl *BRAM/HZG* SK7 ....56 F5
  CHSW/BR CH4 ....142 B5
  GTN M18 ....28 J8
  WILM/AE SK9 ....71 J8
King's Ct *NANT* CW5 ....196 E2
  RDSH SK5 ....17 G1
  RUNC WA7 ....63 H2
Kingsdale Av *RAIN/WH* L35 ....30 C5
Kingsdale Rd *DTN/ASHW* M34 .....28 C9
  WARRW/BUR WA5 ....32 C9
Kingsdown Rd
  WYTH/NTH M22 ....54 E6
  CHD/CHDH SK8 ....56 A4
  CW/SHV CW2 ....184 E8
  FROD/HEL WA6 ....105 H1
  HTNM SK4 ....41 H5
  MPL/ROM SK6 ....43 K9
Kingsfield Cl *CHSW/BR* CH4 ......142 B5
Kingsfield Crs *BIDD* ST8 ....175 L9
Kingsfield Dr *DID/WITH* M20 ....40 D6
Kingsgate Rd *WYTH/NTH* M22 .....54 E6
Kingshead Cl *RUNC* WA7 ....62 E4
Kingsholme Rd
  WYTH/NTH M22 ....54 E5
Kingsland Gra *WARR* WA1 ....34 E7
Kingsland Rd *EDGY/DAV* SK3 ....41 K9
King's La *MWCH* CW10 ....131 H2
  NANT CW5 ....196 E2
  TPLY/KEL SK6 ....147 P6
Kingslawn Cl *NTHM/RTH* M23 .....39 H8
Kingslea Rd *DID/WITH* M20 ....40 D3
Kingsleigh Rd *HTNM* SK4 ....41 M4
  PS/BROM CH62 ....79 J8
  WILM/AE SK9 ....71 L4
Kingsley Cl *ALS/KID* ST7 ....201 N1
  DTN/ASHW M34 ....29 H1
  NWCHW CW8 * 109 K7
Kingsley Crs *RUNC* WA7 ....15 F5
Kingsley Dr *CHD/CHDH* SK8 ....56 A4
  NWCHE CW9 ....13 G7
  WARRS WA4 ....48 E8
Kingsley Gdns *CHSE* CH3 ....143 J2
Kingsley Gv *DTN/ASHW* M34 ......29 H1
Kingsley Rd *ALS/KID* ST7 ....201 N1
  CHSE CH3 ....156 A7
  CW/HAS CW1 ....186 A4
  EP CH65 ....7 F4
  FROD/HEL WA6 ....84 C8
  HALE/TIMP WA15 ....38 E9
  NWCHW CW8 ....107 M3
  RUNC WA7 ....15 F4
  WYTH/NTH M22 ....39 N8
Kingsley Ter *CHSE* CH3 * 122 C5
King's Lynn Cl *DID/WITH* M20 .....40 C5
Kingsmead *CHNE* CH2 ....121 M4
  WYTH/NTH M22 ....13 F7
Kings Ms *WARRS* WA4 ....62 E7
Kingsmill Av *BNG/LEV* M19 ....28 B9
Kings Rd *BRAM/HZG* SK7 ....57 L4
  CHD/CHDH SK8 ....28 G4
  DTN/ASHW M34 ....28 C4
  GTS/LS CH66 ....24 C2
  IRL M44 ....36 D2
  MPL/ROM SK6 ....42 F5
  SALE M33 ....38 C4
  WARRN/WOL WA2 ....34 B6
  WDN WA8 ....70 G6
Kingston Av *DID/WITH* M20 ....40 D3
  MCFLDS SK11 ....9 K6
  WARR WA1 ....47 J1
Kingston Cl *RUNC* WA7 ....62 C4
  SALE M33 ....38 D6
Kingston Ct *CH/BCN* CH1 ....120 E1
Kingston Dr *SALE* M33 ....38 D6
Kingston Gdns *HYDE* SK14 ....29 F6
Kingston Hl *CHD/CHDH* SK8 ....55 M3
Kingston Rd *EDGY/DAV* SK3 * 16 C5
  WILM/AE SK9 ....71 L2
Kingston St *EDGY/DAV* SK3 ....16 D5
  ALS/KID ST7 ....189 J1
  ALS/KID ST7 ....200 C6
King's St *ALS/KID* ST7 ....201 N2
  BIDD ST8 ....175 K9
  CH/BCN CH1 ....2 D1
  CONG CW12 ....155 P6
  CW/HAS CW1 ....5 G3
  DROY M43 ....29 M3
  DTN/ASHW M34 ....29 H6
  DUK SK16 ....29 P2
  EP CH65 ....7 F2
  KNUT WA16 ....90 E3
  MCFLDN SK10 ....8 D3
  MWCH CW10 ....130 B9
  NEWLW WA12 ....23 M6
  NEWLW ST5 ....201 P8
  NWCHE CW9 ....110 E5

NWCHW CW8 ....109 K7
RUNC WA7 ....15 F1
SBCH CW11 ....171 K1
King St East STKP SK1 ....17 G2
King St West EDGY/DAV SK3 ....16 E5
Kings Vw HTNM SK4 * 16 B4
Kingsway AL 53 H2
BRAM/HZG SK7 ....56 F5
CHD/CHDH SK8 ....40 D9
CHNE CW2 ....122 D6
CW/SHV CW2 ....9 K6
Kingsway Ct DID/WITH M20 ....40 D8
FROD/HEL WA6 ....83 P6
HALE/TIMP WA15 ....53 J5
MCFLDN SK10 ....95 L6
MPL/ROM SK6 ....42 D5
NEWLW WA12 ....23 N7
NWCHE CW9 ....13 G3
STKP SK1 ....17 C3
WDN WA8 ....21 H2
WHITCH SY13 ....213M6
WSFD CW7 ....149 P1
Kingsway Ct WHITCH SY13 ....213M6
Kingsway Crs BNG/LEV M19 ....49 F5
Kingsway North WARR WA1 ....48 C2
Kingsway South WARRS 49 H5
Kingsway West CHTH CH2 ....121 P7
Kingswood ALS/KID ST7 ....189 J7
Kingswood Av CH/BCN CH1 ....120 F2
Kingswood Cl 198 C4
Kingswood Crs MWCH CW10 ....151 L5
Kingswood Gv RDSH SK5 ....28 F8
Kingswood La CH/BCN CH1 ....120 F5
Kingswood Rd RUSH/FAL M14 ....40 F1
WARRW/BUR WA5 ....32 E6
Kings Wood Wk
TPLY/KEL CW6 ....125 J6
Kinloch Cl CW/HAS CW1 ....185 H2
HLWD L26 ....44 A8
Kinmel Av RDSH SK5 ....42 B4
Kinmel St STHEL WA9 ....22 A9
Kinnaird Crs STKP SK1 ....42 A8
Kinnaird Rd DID/WITH M20 ....40 C3
Kinnerley Rd EP CH65 ....102 C1
Kinnersley Av ALS/KID ST7 ....189 H8
Kinnersley St ALS/KID ST7 ....189 J6
Kinnerton Cl CHSW/BR CH4 ....141 P5
Kinnerton La CHSW/BR CH4 ....141 M6
Kinnington Wy GTS/LS CH66 * 103 G2
Kinnock Pk WARRW/BUR WA5 ....32 B2
Kinross Av OFTN SK2 ....56 C4
Kinross Cl WARRN/WOL WA2 ....34 A4
Kinsale Dr GOL/RIS/CU WA3 ....34 B4
Kinsey Av NTHM/RTH M23 ....39 J9
Kinsey Rd EP CH65 ....102 C5
Kinsey's La EP CH65 ....81 P7
Kingsate Rd WYTH/NTH M22 ....54 E6
Kintore Av BRAM/HZG SK7 ....57 M5
Kintore Cl BEB CH63 ....78 C1
WSFD CW7 * 149 L5
Kintore Dr WARRW/BUR WA5 ....47 H1
Kintyre Cl EP CH65 ....102 E3
Kipling Av DTN/ASHW M34 ....42 F1
WARRN/WOL WA2 ....33 M7
Kipling Cl OFTN SK2 ....42 D9
Kipling Gv STHEL WA9 ....20 F5
Kipling Rd CH/BCN CH1 ....121 J6
Kipling Wy CW/HAS CW1 ....185 M4
Kirby Cl CHNE CW2 ....121 N6
Kirkacre Av NEWLW WA12 ....23 N9
Kirkbride Cl NTHLY L27 ....44 A5
Kirkby Av SALE M33 ....38 C6
Kirkby Dr SALE M33 ....38 C6
Kirkby Rd GOL/RIS/CU WA3 ....25 P6
Kirkfell Dr MPL/ROM SK6 ....58 C7
Kirkham Av GOL/RIS/CU WA3 * 28 D3
Kirkham Cl DTN/ASHW M34 ....29 M6
WARRW/BUR WA5 ....47 M3
Kirkham Rd CHD/CHDH SK8 ....55 L7
WDN WA8 ....46 A5
Kirklands SALE M33 ....38 C6
Kirkland Av GTN M18 ....28 C5
Kirkman Foan RAIN/WH L35 ....30 A5
Kirkmanshulme La GTN M18 ....28 B4
Kirk Rd BNG/LEV M19 ....41 J1
Kirkstall Cl MCFLDN SK10 ....117 N2
POY/DIS SK12 ....73 K2
Kirkstead Ct OP/CLY M11 ....28 A1
Kirkstead Rd CHD/CHDH SK8 ....56 C8
Kirkstone Av GOL/RIS/CU WA3 ....24 C1
Kirkstone Cl RNFD/HAY WA11 ....22 A1
WARRN/WOL WA2 ....33 M5
Kirkstone Ct CONG CW12 ....155 J9
Kirkstone Crs RUNC WA7 ....84 E1
Kirk St GTN M18 ....28 D4
Kirkwall Dr WARRW/BUR WA5 ....47 L4
Kirkwood Cl CHSE CH3 ....122 B9
Kishfield La CHF/WBR SK23 ....75 L9
Kitchener Av WARR WA1 ....36 B4
Kitchen St CH/BCN CH1 ....2 E5
Kite Gv ALS/KID ST7 ....189M5
Kitfield Av MWCH CW10 ....151 J3
Kitt's Moss La BRAM/HZG SK7 ....56 F8
Kitty Wheeldon Gdns
SALE M33 * 38 D3
Knaresborough Cl RDSH SK5 ....28 E9
Knebworth Ct CONG CW12 ....175 J1
Knight Rd WDN WA8 ....22 C2
Knightsbridge Av NWCHE CW9 * ...109 N9
WARRS 49 L4
Knightsbridge Cl WDN WA8 ....46 E5
WILM/AE SK9 ....77 H5
Knightsbridge Ct CH/BCN CH1 ....3 C5
WARR WA1 ....18 C6
Knight's Cl MCFLDS SK11 ....9 G5
Knights Grn FLINT CH6 ....98 A6
Knights La TPLY/KEL CW6 ....147 H1
Knights Meadow WSFD CW7 ....128 D6
Knight St DID/WITH M20 ....40 C6

MCFLDS SK11 ....9 G6
Knights Wy CW/SHV CW2 ....197 P4
Knightwake Rd NM/HAY SK22 ....59 L7
Knole Av POY/DIS SK12 ....73M2
Knoll St NM/HAY SK22 ....59 M7
Knottingley Dr GTS/LS CH66 ....79 N8
Knotty La CONG CW12 ....175 P1
Knowe Av WYTH/NTH M22 ....54 F6
The Knowe NSTN CH64 ....78 E5
Knowlbank Rd ALS/KID ST7 ....200 C9
Knowl Cl DTN/ASHW M34 ....28 C7
Knowle Cl GTS/LS CH66 ....102 A1
Knowle Pk WILM/AE SK9 ....71 L3
MPL/ROM SK6 ....58 C1
Knowles St WDN WA8 ....46 A5
Knowl Hey Rd HLWD L26 ....44 A9
Knowl La CHSE CH3 ....176 C3
The Knowl CHSE CH3 ....176 C3
Knowsley Crs STKP SK1 ....42 A8
Knowsley Expy RAIN/WH L35 ....44 D1
Knowsley Expy WDN WA8 ....44 E7
Knowsley La ALS/KID ST7 ....188 C4
Knowsley Rd BRAM/HZG SK7 ....57 M7
CHNE CW2 ....122 D7
MCFLDS SK11 ....117 J7
RAIN/WH L35 ....30 C6
STKP SK1 ....42 A8
Knowsley Ter STKP SK1 * 42 A8
Knutsford Old Rd WARRS WA4 ....49 J5
Knutsford Rd ALS/KID ST7 ....188 B3
GTN M18 ....28 C5
HOLMCH CW4 ....131 M6
KNUT WA16 ....91 H2
MCFLDS SK11 ....114 B1
NWCHE CW9 ....65 J9
NWCHE CW9 ....87 M1
Knutsford Rd WARRS WA4 ....48 E5
WILM/AE SK9 ....71 G6
Knutsford Wk MCFLDS SK11 ....9 H6
Knutsford Wy CH/BCN CH1 ....121 J9
Knypersley Av OFTN SK2 ....42 B9
Kohima Crs CHSE CH3 ....143 K5
Kronsbec Av GTS/LS CH66 ....79 P7
Kyle Rd BRAM/HZG SK7 * 57M6
Kynaston St CHSW/BR CH4 ....141 N5
Kynder St DTN/ASHW M34 ....29M6

L

Laburnum Cl ALS/KID ST7 ....188 G8
Laburnum Av CW/SHV CW2 ....184 E6
RNFD/HAY WA11 ....21 J7
WARR WA1 ....34 D9
Laburnum Cl CONG CW12 ....155 H6
HALE/TIMP WA15 ....53M2
Laburnum Crs NWCHW CW8 * 109 K1
Laburnum Farm Cl NSTN CH64 ....77 N8
Laburnum Gv CHSW/BR CH4 ....141 P4
CW/HAS CW1 ....185 K2
GTS/LS CH66 ....102 C4
NWCHW CW8 ....108 F4
RUNC WA7 ....10 A7
Laburnum La HALE/TIMP WA15 ....53 J7
WARRW/BUR WA5 ....45 J6
Laburnum Pl NEWUL ST5 ....201 N6
Laburnum Rd DTN/ASHW M34 ....28 F6
GOL/RIS/CU WA3 ....25 H1
GTN M18 ....28 D5
IRL M44 ....36 C3
MCFLDS SK11 ....117 L7
NWCHE CW9 ....109 P9
NWCHE CW9 ....110 C6
Laburnum Wy EDGY/DAV SK3 ....41 J8
WRXS/E LL15 ....176 F7
Lacey Av WILM/AE SK9 ....71 K6
Lacey Ct WDN WA8 ....21 J5
Lacey Gn WILM/AE SK9 ....71 K5
Lacey Gv WILM/AE SK9 ....71 L5
Lacey St WDN WA8 ....21 J5
Lache Hall Crs CHSW/BR CH4 ....142 A9
Lache La CHSW/BR CH4 ....142 A7
Lache Park Av CHSW/BR CH4 ....142 C4
Lacy St STKP SK1 ....17 G6
Ladies Mile KNUT WA16 ....90 D5
Lady Acre Cl LYMM WA13 ....25 L8
Ladybarn Crs BRAM/HZG SK7 ....56 F9
RUSH/FAL M14 ....40 E1
Ladybower CHD/CHDH SK8 ....56 C4
Ladybridge Rd CHD/CHDH SK8 ....56 C4
Ladybrook Av HALE/TIMP WA15 ...38 E9
Ladycroft Cl WARR WA1 ....54 F2
Ladyfield St WILM/AE SK9 ....71 K7
Ladyfield Ter WILM/AE SK9 ....71 J7
Ladygates AUD/MAD/W CW3 ....199M9
Lady Helen Wk NANT CW5 ....10 M4
Lady La GOL/RIS/CU WA3 ....25 L8
KNUT WA16 ....68 C3
Lady Marys Sq KNUT WA16 * 68 C3
Ladypool GOL/RIS/CU WA3 ....60 C5
Lady Richeld Cl RUNC WA7 ....63 K8
Ladys Cl POY/DIS SK12 ....73 L2
Ladysmith Rd DID/WITH M20 ....40 D6
Ladysmith St EDGY/DAV SK3 ....41 M9
Ladythorn Crs BRAM/HZG SK7 ....56 E2
Ladythorn Gv BRAM/HZG SK7 ....56 F9
Ladythorn Rd BRAM/HZG SK7 ....56 E3
Ladywell Cl BRAM/HZG SK7 ....56 C5
Ladywood Rd
WARRW/BUR WA5 ....32 F7
Lafrak Brd RNFD/HAY WA11 ....22 B1
Lagos Gv WSFD CW7 ....128 D9
Laidon Av CW/SHV CW2 ....184 G9

Laira Ct WARRN/WOL WA2 * 19 F2
Laira St WARRN/WOL WA2 ....19 F2
Laithwaite Cl STHEL WA9 ....30 C5
Lake House Cl NWCHW CW8 * 108 E3
Lakelands Cl MCFLDN SK10 ....9 J4
Lake La WARRS WA4 ....49 J8
Lakemoor Cl STHEL WA9 ....31 J1
Lake Rd DTN/ASHW M34 ....29M5
Lakeside AUD/MAD/W CW5 ....199M9
CHD/CHDH SK8 ....55 J4
CSBY/BAR CH44 ....142 D8
MCFLDS SK11 ....157 K2
Lakeside Cl CHNE CH2 ....121 P4
GTN M18 ....28 F3
WDN WA8 ....44 G8
Lakeside Gn OFTN SK2 ....57 J1
Lakeside Rd LYMM WA15 ....50 D6
Lakeside Vw NANT CW5 ....196 F4
Lakes St OFTN SK2 ....57 H2
Lake Vw CONG CW12 ....155 K8
Lakewood CHSW/BR CH4 ....142 D8
Laleham Gn BRAM/HZG SK7 ....56 D4
Laleston Cl WDN WA8 ....20 C3
Lambert Cl WDN WA8 ....21 J3
Lamberton Dr NTHM/RTH M23 ....54 A1
Lambert's La CONG CW12 ....174 C1
Lambeth Gv MPL/ROM SK6 ....109 J8
Lambeth Gv MPL/ROM SK6 ....42 F3
Lambeth Rd RDSH SK5 ....41 N1
Lamb La ALT WA14 ....189 J6
Lamborne Gv MWCH CW10 ....151 J1
Lambourn Av WDN WA8 ....45 J2
Lambourn Cl POY/DIS SK12 ....73 K2
Lambourn Dr CW/HAS CW1 ....170 A9
Lambourne GTS/LS CH66 ....102 B4
WYTH/NTH M22 ....54 F7
Lambourne Gv STHEL WA9 ....22 B8
Lambs Fold HTNM SK4 ....41 L5
Lambsickle Cl RUNC WA7 ....61 M8
Lambsickle La RUNC WA7 ....61 M8
Lambs La WARR WA1 ....34 B9
Lamb St ALS/KID ST7 ....189 J6
Lamerton Cl WARRW/BUR WA5 ...47 J5
Lamerton Wy WILM/AE SK9 ....71 N4
Lampeter Cl
WARRW/BUR WA5 * 33 H6
Lamport Cl WDN WA8 ....46 C4
Lampton Cl ALT WA14 ....43 L6
Lamsholme Cl BNG/LEV M19 ....28 A7
Lanark Av WYTH/NTH M22 ....39 N8
Lancashire Hl RDSH SK5 ....17 F1
Lancashire Rd PART M31 ....36 C6
Lancaster Av GOL/RIS/CU WA3 ...24 C1
RAIN/WH L35 ....43 M9
RUNC WA7 ....14 B7
Lancaster Cl BRAM/HZG SK7 ....57 K7
MPL/ROM SK6 ....42 F7
NEWLW WA12 ....23 K4
WARRN/WOL WA2 * 25 N7
WSFD CW7 ....149M4
Lancaster Dr CHSE CH3 ....122 D9
Lancaster Flds CW/HAS CW1 ....185M6
Lancaster Gdns EP CH65 ....102 F1
Lancaster Pk CHSW/BR CH4 ....140 C7
Lancaster Rd DID/WITH M20 ....40 B2
DTN/ASHW M34 ....29M8
IRL M44 ....23 P8
WDN WA8 ....45 N4
WILM/AE SK9 ....71 N5
Lancaster St STKP SK1 ....17 J2
WARRW/BUR WA5 ....33 H1
Lancelot Rd WYTH/NTH M22 ....55 H5
Lancelyn Dr WILM/AE SK9 ....71M6
Lancers Cft GTS/LS CH66 ....102 A3
Lancing Rd EP CH65 ....102 C1
Lancots La STHEL WA9 ....31M3
Land Cut La GOL/RIS/CU WA3 ....34 E5
Lander Cl WARRW/BUR WA5 ....32 C9
Landkey Cl NTHM/RTH M23 ....39 J3
Landl La WILM/AE SK9 ....71 L8
Landor Cl GOL/RIS/CU WA3 ....24 C1
Landrake Gv BURS/TUN ST6 ....189 N10
Landscape Dene
FROD/HEL WA6 ....83 K9
Landseer Av MCFLDN SK10 ....116 E4
MPL/ROM SK6 ....43 N9
Landswood Pk NWCHW CW8 ....109 K8
Lane End Rd BNG/LEV M19 ....40 E4
Lane Ends MPL/ROM SK6 ....43 J5
Lane Head Av GOL/RIS/CU WA3 ...24 C9
Lanehead Rd CHF/WBR SK23 ....75 N9
Laneside Dr BRAM/HZG SK7 ....56 G6
Laneside Rd DID/WITH M20 ....40 D8
Langcliffe Cl GOL/RIS/CU WA3 ....24 C1
Langdale WDN WA8 ....50 F4
Langdale Cl CHD/CHDH SK8 ....55 L4
DTN/ASHW M34 ....29 L8
HALE/TIMP WA15 ....53 J2
MCFLDS SK11 ....116 F7
MPL/ROM SK6 ....43 J8
WARRN/WOL WA2 ....33 N3
WDN WA8 ....45 J7
WSFD CW7 ....128 D9
Langdale Ct CONG CW12 ....155 J9
Langdale Rd BRAM/HZG SK7 ....72 C1
CW/HAS CW1 ....170 A7
HTNM SK4 ....41 K2
MPL/ROM SK6 ....43 J8
PART M31 ....36 D5

RUNC WA7 ....15 G4
SALE M33 ....38 B7
Langdale Wy FROD/HEL WA6 ....84 A4
Langden Cl GOL/RIS/CU WA3 ....25M5
Langfield GOL/RIS/CU WA3 ....25 N5
Langford SPK/HALE L24 ....60 C5
Langford Rd IRL M44 ....27 N8
Langford St DID/WITH M20 ....40 B2
HTNM SK4 ....41 K4
Langford St DTN/ASHW M34 * 29M6
MCFLDS SK11 ....8 C4
Langford Wy WARRS WA4 ....65M2
Langham Gv HALE/TIMP WA15 ...53 E8
Langham Rd ALT WA14 ....52 C5
HTNM SK4 ....41 J7
Langland Cl RDSH SK5 ....28 D7
WARRW/BUR WA5 ....33 H6
Langley Av BRAM/HZG SK7 ....57 H6
Langley Cl NEWUL ST5 ....201 N5
SBCH CW11 ....171 P4
Langley Ct EP CH65 ....102 G1
CW/SHV CW2 ....71 N5
WILM/AE SK9 ....71 N5
Langley Hall Cl MCFLDS SK11 ...117 P9
Langley Rd MCFLDS SK11 ....117 P9
NWCHE CW9 ....13 J6
SALE M33 ....38 B4
Langport Dr CHSE CH3 ....122 D9
Langston Gn BRAM/HZG SK7 ....56 G6
Langthorne St BNG/LEV M19 ....28 B9
Langton Cl NEWLW WA12 ....23 L5
WDN WA8 ....45 H4
Langton Gn WARR WA1 ....34 E9
Langtree St STHEL WA9 ....22 B6
Langwell Cl GOL/RIS/CU WA3 ....35 H5
Lanreath Cl MCFLDN SK10 ....116 D5
Lansbrook Ct RUNC WA7 ....15 J3
Lansbury Av STHEL WA9 ....22 C7
Lansdale Gdns BNG/LEV M19 ....40 F3
Lansdown Cl BRAM/HZG SK7 ....56 D8
Lansdowne FROD/HEL WA6 ....84 B7
GOL/RIS/CU WA3 ....25 N7
Lansdowne Av MPL/ROM SK6 ....43 J6
Lansdowne Rd BRAM/HZG SK7 ...56 D8
Lansdowne Rd ALT WA14 ....53 H1
CHSE CH3 ....122 D9
CW/HAS CW1 ....5 K2
SALE M33 ....38 D2
Lansdowne St MCFLDN SK10 ....9 H2
Lansdowne Ter CHSE CH3 ....122 D9
CW/HAS CW1 ....5 K2
Lantern Vw NM/HAY SK22 ....59M6
Lapwing Cl ALS/KID ST7 ....189 N6
GOL/RIS/CU WA3 ....24 F1
WSFD CW7 ....149 L5
Lapwing Gv RUNC WA7 ....62 E8
Lapwing La DID/WITH M20 ....40 B5
MCFLDS SK11 ....114 D5
RDSH SK5 ....42 A7
WARRS WA4 ....48 A8
Lapwing Rd ALS/KID ST7 ....189M6
Larch Av BRAM/HZG SK7 ....57 H6
CW/SHV CW2 ....184 E6
MCFLDS SK11 ....116 G7
NEWLW WA12 ....23 N7
WARRW/BUR WA5 ....45 P5
WDN WA8 ....45 P5
Larch Cl ALS/KID ST7 ....189 J8
GOL/RIS/CU WA3 ....25 H3
MPL/ROM SK6 ....58 D8
NTHM/RTH M23 ....38 F8
POY/DIS SK12 ....73M3
RUNC WA7 ....62 B7
Larchdale Cl GTS/LS CH66 ....102 B4
Larchfields CH/BCN CH1 ....120 D3
Larch Ri MCFLDN SK10 ....94 D7
Larch Rd CW/SHV CW2 ....184 E6
DTN/ASHW M34 ....29 H6
SALE M33 ....38 B7
Larchtree Cl NWCHW CW8 ....87 K9
Larchway BRAM/HZG SK7 ....56 D6
Larch Wy CHSW/BR CH4 ....142 A4
Larchway MPL/ROM SK6 ....58 D8
Larchways WARRS WA4 ....64 F1
Larchwood Cl SALE M33 ....37 P4
Larchwood Dr WILM/AE SK9 ....71 N6
Larke Ri MCFLDN SK10 ....116 B5
Larkfield Av ALS/KID ST7 ....189 J7
Larkfield Av WARR WA1 ....34 A9
Lark Hall Cl MCFLDN SK10 ....117 N4
Lark Hall Crs MCFLDN SK10 ....117 N5
Larkhall Ri WYTH/NTH M22 ....54 G2
Larkhill Cl HALE/TIMP WA15 ....53M1
Larkhill Rd CHD/CHDH SK8 ....56 C2
Lark Hill Rd EDGY/DAV SK3 ....16 B6
Larkhill Vw EDGY/DAV SK3 ....56 C2
Larkspur Cl CHSW/BR CH4 ....142 B6
NANT CW5 ....84 D1
Larkstoke Cl WARRS WA4 ....48 C9
Larkswood Dr OFTN SK2 ....57M2
Larmuth Av CCHDY M21 ....39M2
Larne Av EDGY/DAV SK3 ....41 J9
Larne Dr CHSW/BR CH4 ....141 H6
Larne St OP/CLY M11 ....28 A1
Larwood Av HTNM SK4 ....41 H7
Lascelles St STHEL WA9 ....22 A9
Laskey La WARRS WA4 ....49 P5
Lassell St OP/CLY M11 * 28 A1
Latchford St WARRS WA4 ....48 D4
Latham Av FROD/HEL WA6 ....105 H5
NEWLW WA12 ....23 N5
Latham Av RUNC WA7 ....14 H4
Latham Cl MPL/ROM SK6 ....42 E5
Latham Rd SBCH CW11 ....171M4
Latham St OP/CLY M11 ....28 A1
WSFD CW7 ....149 L2
Lathom Av WARRN/WOL WA2 ....33 J8
Lathom Gv SALE M33 ....39 H5

Lathom Rd DID/WITH M20 ....40 E5
IRL M44 ....27M9
Latimer Wy MCFLDN SK10 ....117M2
Latimer Dr CW/SHV CW2 ....184 G4
Latrobe St DROY WA8 ....28 G1
Launceston Cl BRAM/HZG SK7 ...56 F8
RUNC WA7 ....62 G8
WSFD CW7 ....149 K3
Launceston Dr
WARRW/BUR WA5 ....47 J4
Laundry Wy MCFLDN SK10 ....117M2
Laureate Wy DTN/ASHW M34 ....42 F1
Laurel Av CHD/CHDH SK8 ....55M2
NEWLW WA12 ....23 N7
WARR WA1 * 34 E9
Laurel Bnk WARRS WA4 ....49 L6
WDN WA8 ....45 N4
WSFD CW7 ....149M2
Laurel Cl MWCH CW10 ....130 A9
NWCHW CW8 ....87 J9
SBCH CW11 ....171 P4
Laurel Dr ALS/KID ST7 ....189 N5
EP CH65 ....102 D2
HALE/TIMP WA15 ....53M3
NSTN CH64 ....78 F4
Laurel End La HTNM SK4 ....41 H5
Laurel Gn DTN/ASHW M34 ....29 N7
Laurel Pk TPLY/KEL CW6 ....145 N4
Laurel Rd RNFD/HAY WA11 ....22 D4
Laurels Farm Ct CHNE CH2 * 104 B1
Laurel St KNUT WA16 ....16 E3
Laurel Wk PART M31 ....36 D6
Laurel Wy CHD/CHDH SK8 ....56 A4
Laurelwood Dr GTS/LS CH66 ....102 A4
Laurence Cl WGTN/LGST M12 ....28 A1
Laureston Av CW/HAS CW1 * 185M4
Lausanne Rd BRAM/HZG SK7 ....56 E4
DID/WITH M20 ....40 C1
Lavender Cl NTHM/RTH M23 ....39 F1
RUNC WA7 ....40 C1
SALE M33 ....37 P3
Lavender Dr NWCHE CW9 ....110 C6
Lavenders Brow STKP SK1 * 17 H4
Lavenham Cl BRAM/HZG SK7 ....56 F7
MCFLDN SK10 ....117 J2
Lavington Av CHD/CHDH SK8 ....56 A1
Lavington Gv GTN M18 ....28 A8
Lavister Av BNG/LEV M19 ....40 C5
Lavister Cl RUNC WA7 ....109 P8
Lavister Wks WRX/GR/LL LL12 ...160 F8
Lawford Dr CW/HAS CW1 ....185 L5
Lawn Av WARR WA1 ....34 A8
Lawn Dr CHNE CH2 ....121 N4
HALE/TIMP WA15 ....53 G8
Lawngreen Av CCHDY M21 ....107 P7
Lawnhurst Av NWCHW CW8 ....108 E1
Lawnside Ms DID/WITH M20 ....40 B8
The Lawns ALT WA14 ....52 C4
Lawnswood Gv CHNE CW2 ....104 B1
Lawrence Av MWCH CW10 ....151 J1
NWCHE CW9 * 128 F3
Lawrence Av West
MWCH CW10 * 151 J1
Lawrence Cl HOLMCH CW4 ....131M6
SBCH CW11 ....171 J3
Lawrence Pl POY/DIS SK12 ....73 K4
Lawrence Rd ALT WA14 ....52 D1
BRAM/HZG SK7 ....56 F7
Lawrence St CW/HAS CW1 ....4 E3
STKP SK1 ....17 F5
Laws Gdns CHSE CH3 ....143 J2
Lawson Av CHD/CHDH SK8 ....55 K2
Lawson Cl WARR WA1 ....34 F9
Lawson Cv SALE M33 ....38 D2
Law St CHNE CH2 ....3 J1
Lawton Av ALS/KID ST7 ....188 F5
BRAM/HZG SK7 ....56 F7
MPL/ROM SK6 ....42 E7
Lawton Coppice ALS/KID ST7 ....188 C4
Lawton Crs BIDD ST8 ....175 J9
Lawton Heath Rd ALS/KID ST7 ...188 A3
Lawton Moor Rd
NTHM/RTH M23 ....39 J7
Lawton Rd HTNM SK4 ....41 K4
Lawton St ALS/KID ST7 ....189 L4
BIDD ST8 ....175 K9
CONG CW12 ....155 N8
CW/SHV CW2 ....9 K1
OP/CLY M11 ....28 D2
Laxey Av WARR WA1 ....171 K2
Laxey Av WARR WA1 ....34 A9
Laxton Cl GTS/LS CH66 ....102 B4
Laxton Wy MWCH CW10 ....151 K2
Layland Gv GOL/RIS/CU WA3 ....25 N5
Layton Av HYDE SK14 ....29 P6
Layton Cl GOL/RIS/CU WA3 ....25 N5
STKP SK1 ....17 J6
Layton Dr MPL/ROM SK6 ....43 H5
Lea Av CW/HAS CW1 ....5 K4
HOLMCH CW4 ....131M6
Lea Bank CW1 ....5 K4
Lea Bank MCFLDS SK11 ....116 C4
Leabank Av ALS/KID ST7 ....189 H8
Leaburn Dr BNG/LEV M19 ....40 E6
Leach La STHEL WA9 ....31 J3
Leach St GTN M18 ....28 D8
Lea Cl SBCH CW11 ....171 P4
Leacroft Rd CCHDY M21 ....39 N3
GOL/RIS/CU WA3 ....35 H2
Leadbeaters Cl MCFLDS SK11 ...114 A2
Leadbeaters Rd MCFLDS SK11 ...9 G6
Leadbrook Dr FLINT CH6 ....98 B4
Leader Williams Rd IRL M44 ....27M8
Leadgate La CHSE CH3 ....145M8
Lea Dr MWCH CW10 ....196 D5
NANT CW5 ....196 D5
Leadsmithy St MWCH CW10 ....151 J1
Leadworks La CH/BCN CH1 ....3 G3

Leaf Gv WSFD CW7 ....149 K1
Leafield Av DID/WITH M20 ....40 E4
Leafield Dr CHD/CHDH SK8 ....55 P9
Leafield Rd POY/DIS SK12 ....58 G9
Leaf La WSFD CW7 ....129 H9
Leaford Av DTN/ASHW M34 ....29 K5
Leaford Cl DTN/ASHW M34 ....29 K5
Lea St RDSH SK5 ....41 M1
Lea Green Rd STHEL WA9 .....30 F4
Lea Hall Pk CH/BCN CW1 ....102 C9
Leahurst Cl CHNE CH2 ......122 A7
Lea La CHSE 162 C6
Leamington Av DID/WITH M20 ..40 A4
  NEWLW WA12 ....23 N8
Leamington Rd NSTN CH64 ....77 L7
  WARRW/BUR WA5 ....46 G1
Leamington Rd CONG CW12 ...155 H7
  MCFLDN SK10 ....116 F3
  RDSH SK5 ....41 M1
Leamington St OP/CLY M11 ...28 D2
Lea Rd CHD/CHDH SK8 ....184 F8
  HTNM SK4 ....47 J4
Leas Cl GTS/LS CH66 ....79 N3
Leaside Av RUNC WA7 ....62 B5
Leaside Rd CH/BCN CW1 .....121 H5
Leaside Wy WILM/AE SK9 .....71 L8
Lea's Pas MWCH CW10 ....151 H1
The Leas HALE/TIMP WA15 ...153 M4
Lea St NM/HAY SK22 ....59 L7
Leatham Cl GOL/RIS/CU WA3 ..77 L7
Leaton Av NTHM/RTH M23 .....54 C1
Lea Wy ALS/KID ST7 ....187 P5
Leawood Cl RUNC WA7 ....109 J6
Ledbury Dr CW/SHV CW2 .....184 G9
Ledge Ley CHD/CHDH SK8 .....55 N7
Ledger Rd RNFD/HAY WA11 ....22 E4
Ledley St MCFLDN SK10 ......90 B6
Ledsham Cl GOL/RIS/CU WA3 ..34 D5
Ledsham La GTS/LS CH66 ....101 K1
Ledsham Park Rd GTS/LS CH66 .79 L7
Ledsham Vlg GTS/LS CH66 ...101 K5
Ledston Cl RUNC WA7 ....63 H5
Ledward La ALT WA14 ....52 F5
Ledward St WSFD CW7 ....150 A1
Ledyard Cl WARRW/BUR WA5 ..32 G4
Lee Av ALT WA14 ....37 P9
Leech Brook Av
  DTN/ASHW M34 ....29 L4
Leech Rd MALPAS SY14 ......204 A3
Lee Cl IRL M44 ....27 M8
  KNUT WA16 ....90 D4
  RAIN/WL L35 ....30 C7
Lee Ct WARRN/WOL WA2 ......33 M6
  WYTH/NTH M22 * 39 P8
Lee Dale Cl DTN/ASHW M34 ...29 N7
Lee Dr NWCHW CW8 ....12 C5
Leegate Cl HTNM SK4 ....40 G4
Leegate Gdns HTNM SK4 .....40 G4
Leegate Rd HTNM SK4 ....41 H4
Lee Green La NANT CW5 .....150 A9
Leek Old Rd MCFLDN SK10 ...136 C4
Leek Rd CW/SHV CW2 ....175 H1
Lee La CH/BCN CH1 ....?
Lee Rd WARRW/BUR WA5 * 29 L7
  DTN/ASHW M34 ....29 L7
Leeside HTNM SK4 ....41 H7
Lees La CH/BCN CH1 ....?
  MCFLDN SK10 ....72 B7
  NSTN CH64 ....77 P5
Lees Rd BRAM/HZG SK7 ......72 D1
Lees St GTN M18 ....?
Leestone Rd WYTH/NTH M22 ..54 C1
Lee St STHEL WA9 ....22 C3
  STKP SK1 ....17 G5
Leesway Dr DTN/ASHW M34 ...29 M2
Leeswood Av CCHDY M21 .....39 M2
Legh Cl POY/DIS SK12 ....42 G2
Legh Rd MPL/ROM SK6 ....42 G2
Legh Rd KNUT WA16 ....90 F5
  MCFLDN SK10 ....94 G5
  POY/DIS SK12 ....58 E9
  RNFD/HAY WA11 ....22 E3
  SALE M33 ....39 H5
Legh St GOL/RIS/CU WA3 .....24 C1
  LYMM WA13 ....50 E4
  NEWLW WA12 ....23 L6
  WARRN/WOL WA2 ....18 C5
Leicester Av ALS/KID ST7 ...187 N3
  DTN/ASHW M34 ....29 M8
  HALE/TIMP WA15 ....53 M6
Leicester La CHSW/BR CH4 ..140 D8
Leicester Rd HALE/TIMP WA15 .53 J3
  SALE M33 ....38 E3
  NWCHW CW8 ....13 F1
  RDSH SK5 ....28 E9
  WARRW/BUR WA5 ....48 A2
Leigh Av KNUT WA16 ....90 C2
  MPL/ROM SK6 ....58 C1
  WDN WA8 ....21 G1
Leigh La NWCHW CW8 ....86 E8
Leigh Rd CONG CW12 ....156 B5
  HALE/TIMP WA15 ....53 J5
  WILM/AE SK9 ....70 F9
Leigh's Brow NWCHW CW8 ...109 H1
Leigh St MCFLDN SK11 ......?
Leighton Cha NSTN CH64 ....77 J4
Leighton Ct NSTN CH64 .....77 J3
Leighton Dr MPL/ROM SK6 ...43 P8
  NSTN CH64 ....77 J3
Leighton Rd NSTN CH64 .....77 J2
The Leightons NSTN CH64 ...77 J4
Leighton St CW/HAS CW1 ....185 H3
Leighton Vw CW/HAS CW1 ...185 H3
Leigh Wy NWCHW CW8 ....13 H5
Leinster Gdns RUNC WA7 ....14 C1
Leinster St RUNC WA7 ......14 C1
Leith Av SALE M33 ....39 H4
Leith Rd SALE M33 ....39 H4
Lenfield Dr RNFD/HAY WA11 ..22 H3

Lenham Cl RDSH SK5 ....42 A2
Lenton Gdns WYTH/NTH M22 ..54 G2
Leominster Dr WYTH/NTH M22 .54 G4
Leonard St CH/BCN CW1 * 2 B1
  RUNC WA7 ....61 K7
  STHEL WA9 ....31 L1
  WARRN/WOL WA2 ....19 F2
Leon Cl WARRW/BUR WA5 * ...48 E6
Leopold Av DID/WITH M20 ....32 A9
Leopold Gv STHEL WA9 ....40 D4
Lerryn Dr BRAM/HZG SK7 .....31 H5
Leslie Av DTN/ASHW M34 .....56 D6
Leslie Rd WSFD CW7 ....149 J3
Lester Cl ALS/KID ST7 .....187 P4
Leven Av WSFD CW7 ....128 G9
Levens Cl CHD/CHDH SK8 ....55 K3
Levenshulme Rd GTN M18 ....28 D5
Levenshulme Ter
  BNG/LEV M19 * 28 A8
Levens Rd BRAM/HZG SK7 ....57 J5
Levens Wk WDN WA8 ....80 C5
Leven Wk EP CH65 ....80 C5
Leverett Rd SPK/HALE L24 ...60 A3
Leverhulme Rd ALT WA14 ....52 E2
Leveret St BRAM/HZG SK7 ....57 K5
  STHEL WA9 ....31 J4
Levisham Gdns
  WARRW/BUR WA5 ....33 H9
Lewes Av DTN/ASHW M34 ....29 M3
Lewin St MWCH CW10 ....151 J1
Lewis Av WARRW/BUR WA5 ...33 J6
Lewis Cl CHNE CH2 ....102 E4
  NANT CW5 ....11 G5
Lewis Crs WDN WA8 ....21 G4
Lewis Rd RDSH SK5 ....28 F8
Lewis St CW/HAS CW1 * 4 C4
Lexden St WARRW/BUR WA5 ...4 C1
Leybourne Av BNG/LEV M19 ..28 B7
Leybrook Rd WYTH/NTH M22 ..54 E4
Leyburn Av OFTN SK2 ....57 J1
  RDSH SK5 ....28 F9
  WARRW/BUR WA5 ....17 H1
Leyburn Cl MPL/ROM SK6 ....43 M6
Leyburn Gv POY/DIS SK12 ...58 C3
Leyburn Rd NTHM/RTH M23 ..54 E5
Leycester Cl KNUT WA16 ....90 G5
Leycester Dr KNUT WA16 .....69 K7
Leycester Rd KNUT WA16 .....90 F6
Leycett La NTHM/RTH M23 ...39 K7
Leyct Cl STHEL WA9 ....31 H4
Leyfield Av MPL/ROM SK6 ....31 K4
Leyfield Ct CHSW/BR CH4 ...142 B5
Leygate Vw NM/HAY SK22 ....59 M7
Ley Hey Av MPL/ROM SK6 ....43 J5
Ley Hey Rd MPL/ROM SK6 ....43 J5
Leyland Av CHSW/BR CH4 ....141 M4
Leyland Gv CHSW/BR CH4 ...186 A4
  RNFD/HAY WA11 ....22 F3
Leyland St HTNM SK4 ....16 E4
Leyland Wk WSFD CW7 ......149 L4
Leys Rd ALT WA14 ....38 B8
Leyton Cl RUNC WA7 ....61 P8
Libson Cl WARRN/WOL WA2 ..34 B5
Lichfield Av GOL/RIS/CU WA3 ..24 F1
  HALE/TIMP WA15 ....53 N4
  RDSH SK5 ....41 M1
Lichfield Ct WSFD CW7 ....149 M5
Lichfield Dr GTS/LS CH66 ...102 A4
Lichfield Rd ALS/KID ST7 ...188 F9
  CH/BCN CW1 ....121 J6
Lichfield St MWCH CW10 ....130 C9
Lichfield Wk MPL/ROM SK6 ..31 H9
Lidgetts La MCFLDN SK10 ....96 A9
Liebig St WDN WA8 ....21 J3
Lift La Alders La POY/DIS SK12 .58 G8
Lightborne Rd SALE M33 .....38 A4
Lightburn St RUNC WA7 .....14 D5
Lightfoot La TPLY/KEL CW6 ..147 L6
Lightfoot St CHNE CH2 ......3 H1
Lighthorne Av EDGY/DAV SK3 .40 G9
Lighthorne Gv EDGY/DAV SK3 .40 G9
Lighthorne Rd EDGY/DAV SK3 .40 G9
Lighthouse Rd SPK/HALE L24 .62 F7
Lightley Cl SBCH CW11 .....171 M5
Light Oaks Rd GOL/RIS/CU WA3 .24 F7
Lightwood Green Av
  WRECM CW3 ....216 B3
Lightwood Rd NEWUL ST5 ...201 N6
Lilac Av KNUT WA16 ....90 C4
  WARRW/BUR WA5 ....47 L2
  WDN WA8 ....45 P5
Lilac Cl TPLY/KEL CW6 .....125 K9
Lilac Crs RUNC WA7 ....15 J6
Lilac Gv CHNE CH2 ....102 C4
  RNFD/HAY WA11 ....22 D4
  WARRS WA4 ....48 G6
Lilac Rd HALE/TIMP WA15 ....53 L4
Lilford Av WARRW/BUR WA5 ..33 J8
Lilford Dr WARRW/BUR WA5 ..33 H8
Lilford Sq MCFLDN SK11 * ..117 K7
Lilford St WARRW/BUR WA5 ..18 A2
Lilian Gv RDSH SK5 ....28 F9
Lily La MWCH CW10 ....130 F5
Limbrick Rd ALS/KID ST7 ....200 C6
Lime Av FROD/HEL WA6 .....84 A5
  NM/HAY SK22 ....59 M7
  NWCHW CW8 ....109 P7
  NWCHW CW8 ....108 F4
  WDN WA8 ....45 P5
Limebrook Cl OP/CLY M11 ....28 E2
Lime Cl GOL/RIS/CU WA3 .....35 P6

  MWCH CW10 ....130 A9
  SBCH CW11 ....171 M2
  TPLY/KEL CW6 ....147 H8
Lime Ct NWCHW CW9 ....109 P7
Limefield Av LYMM WA13 ....50 F5
Limefield Ter BNG/LEV M19 ..28 A8
Lime Gdns DUK SK16 ....29 P1
Lime Gv ALS/KID ST7 ......188 A6
  CHD/CHDH SK8 ....55 M1
  CHNE CH2 ....24 A1
  CHNE CH2 ....122 A8
  CHSW/BR CH4 ....141 P4
  CW/HAS CW2 ....198 B3
  DTN/ASHW M34 ....29 M5
  HALE/TIMP WA15 ....24 F3
  HALE/TIMP WA15 ....53 M1
  MCFLDN SK10 ....94 G7
  RUNC WA7 ....15 J6
  RDSH SK5 ....28 F9
  WSFD CW7 ....150 A1
Lime Kiln La ALS/KID ST7 ...188 G6
Limekiln La WARRW/BUR WA5 .32 B5
Limes Cl CW/HAS CW1 ......186 A4
Limes La WARRS WA4 ....64 E7
The Limes GOL/RIS/CU WA3 ..25 M5
  DUK SK16 ....29 P1
  EP CH65 ....6 E1
  SALE M33 ....38 B5
Lime Tree Av CW/HAS CW1 ..185 K1
Limetree Av WARRS WA4 ....34 A8
  WARRS WA4 ....48 G6
Lime Tree Cl GTS/LS CH66 ..102 B4
Lime Tree Dr CHSE CH3 .....177 H7
Limetree La KNUT WA16 .....51 K9
Limeways WARRS WA4 ......64 C1
Limewood Crs NWCHW CW8 ..87 K9
Limewood Gv NWCHW CW8 ...87 K9
Limley Gv CCHDY M21 ......39 M4
Lincoln Av BNG/LEV M19 ....28 B8
  CHD/CHDH SK8 ....55 K8
  DTN/ASHW M34 ....29 M8
  IRL M44 ....36 B4
Lincoln Cl CHNE CH2 ......122 B6
  HALE/TIMP WA15 ....53 M2
  WARR WA1 ....49 N1
Lincoln Dr ALS/KID ST7 ....188 B6
  CH/BCN CW1 ....121 J6
  GTS/LS CH66 ....101 P1
  WILM/AE SK9 ....71 N5
Lincoln Gv MPL/ROM SK6 ....43 H7
Lincoln Rd MCFLDN SK10 ...116 F2
  RAIN/WL L35 ....30 C7
Lincoln Sq WDN WA8 ....45 P5
Lincoln St CW/HAS CW1 ....185 J5
  GOL/RIS/CU WA3 ....25 L1
  RUNC WA7 ....62 A8
  WARR WA1 ....49 N1
Lincoln Wk MCFLDN SK10 ...116 F2
Lincombe Hey MCFLDN SK10 .95 J5
Lincombe Rd WYTH/NTH M22 .54 E6
Lindale Cl CONG CW12 .....156 A5
Lindale Dr STHEL WA9 ......31 H4
Lindbury Av OFTN SK2 .....42 B9
Linden Av DTN/ASHW M34 ...29 M6
  HALE/TIMP WA15 ....53 J2
  SALE M33 ....38 C4
  WHITCH SY13 ....213 L6
Linden Cl CONG CW12 .....175 H1
  DTN/ASHW M34 ....29 M6
  GTS/LS CH66 ....102 B4
  LYMM WA13 ....34 E9
Linden Ct MCFLDN SK10 ....117 H2
  SBCH CW11 ....171 L6
  WDN WA8 * 45 M3
Linden Dr BIDD ST8 ....122 C2
  CHNE CH2 ....122 C2
  CW/HAS CW1 ....186 A4
  FROD/HEL WA6 ....105 H5
Linden Gv BRAM/HZG SK7 ...72 D2
  CHNE CH2 ....122 A8
  CHSW/BR CH4 ....141 P4
  OFTN SK2 ....57 H3
Linden Rd CHD/CHDH SK8 ....56 A4
  DID/WITH M20 ....40 A6
  DTN/ASHW M34 ....29 M6
Linden Wy MPL/ROM SK6 ....58 E8
Lindeth Av GTN M18 ....28 D5
Lindfield Cl WARRS WA4 ....63 L1
Lindfield Est North
  WILM/AE SK9 ....71 J8
Lindfield Est South
  WILM/AE SK9 ....71 H8
Lindfield Rd RDSH SK5 ....28 F9
Lindi Av WARRS WA4 ....49 K6
Lindisfarne ALS/KID ST7 ...188 A6
Lindisfarne Cl MWCH CW10 ..151 H1
  SALE M33 ....38 E7
Lindisfarne Dr POY/DIS SK12 .73 K1
Lindley Av WARRS WA4 .....49 H5
Lindon Wy DROY WA5 ......28 D3
Lindop Rd HALE/TIMP WA15 ..53 K6
Lindow Cl MPL/ROM SK6 ....55 J9
Lindow Fold Dr WILM/AE SK9 .92 F1
Lindow La WILM/AE SK9 ....70 G8
Lindrick Cl MCFLDN SK10 ....95 J9
Lindrum Av MCFLDN SK11 ...136 C1
Lindsay Av CHD/CHDH SK8 ...56 A6
Lindsay St STHEL WA9 .....31 K5
Lindsay Wk NWCHW CW8 ....108 C8
Lindsay Wy ALS/KID ST7 ...188 A5
Lindsell Rd ALT WA14 .....37 P8
Lindsgate Dr HALE/TIMP WA15 .53 J6
Lindsworth Cl
  WARRW/BUR WA5 * 47 N1
Lindwall Cl NTHM/RTH M23 ..39 L6

Linear Vw NEWLW WA12 .....23 N9
Linehan Cl HTNM SK4 ......40 E6
Linen Hall Pl CH/BCN CW1 * ..2 D5
Lines Rd IRL M44 ....36 D3
Linford Gv RNFD/HAY WA11 ..22 A4
Lingard La BRAM/HZG SK7 ...57 N5
Lingard Rd WYTH/NTH M22 ..39 N7
Lingard St RDSH SK5 ......16 B3
Lingcrest Rd BNG/LEV M19 ..41 K1
Lingdale Rd CHD/CHDH SK8 ..55 P5
Lingfield Av BRAM/HZG SK7 ..57 N5
  SALE M33 ....37 N6
Lingfield Dr MCFLDN SK10 ...95 J9
Lingfield Rd RUNC WA7 ....185 J1
Lingford Rd IRL M44 ......27 M6
Lingley Green Av
  WARRW/BUR WA5 ....46 G1
Lingley Rd WARRW/BUR WA5 .47 H1
Linglongs Av CHF/WBR SK23 .75 N9
Linglongs Rd CHF/WBR SK23 .75 N9
Lingmell Gdns HOLMCK WA4 .131 L8
Lings Wk WYTH/NTH M22 ....54 G6
Lingwell Av WDN WA8 ......45 K5
Lingwood Rd
  WARRW/BUR WA5 ....47 N1
Linhope Cl HTNM SK4 ......40 F5
Link Av RNFD/HAY WA11 ....22 A4
Link Rd SALE M33 ....38 A4
Links Av GTS/LS CH66 .....102 A4
Linksfield DTN/ASHW M34 ...29 M4
Linkside Av WARRN/WOL WA2 .33 L2
Linkside Wy GTS/LS CH66 ...102 B4
  MPL/ROM SK6 ....43 J5
Links Rd BRAM/HZG SK7 ....57 M8
  WILM/AE SK9 ....92 C2
The Links GOL/RIS/CU WA3 * .34 E2
Linksway CHD/CHDH SK8 ....55 J5
  CHNE CH2 ....121 M4
  CONG CW12 ....174 F1
Linksway Cl CONG CW12 ....174 F1
  HTNM SK4 ....41 H3
The Link RDSH SK5 ....42 B2
Linkway RUNC WA7 ....15 J7
Linley Gv ALS/KID ST7 ....188 B5
Linley La ALS/KID ST7 ....188 C5
Linley Rd ALS/KID ST7 ....188 C5
  CHD/CHDH SK8 ....56 E7
  SALE M33 ....38 C3
Linnards La NWCHE CW9 ....89 J8
Linnet Cl NEWLW WA12 .....57 M2
  WARRN/WOL WA2 ....33 N5
  WSFD CW7 ....150 B2
Linnet Dr IRL M44 ....27 N6
Linnet Gv GOL/RIS/CU WA3 ..24 F1
  MCFLDN SK10 ....116 C3
Linnett Cl CW/HAS CW1 ....184 C1
Linnet Wy BIDD ST8 ....175 H9
Linney Rd BRAM/HZG SK7 ...56 D5
Linton Av DTN/ASHW M34 ...29 K6
Linton Rd SALE M33 ....38 F2
Linum Gdns STHEL WA9 .....31 N1
Linwood WSFD CW7 ....150 B2
Linwood Cl RUNC WA7 .....14 D4
Linwood Gv WGTN/LGST M12 .28 C2
Lionel St STHEL WA9 ......31 L1
Lion Gv NEWUL ST5 ....201 P7
Lion Hotel Yd WARR WA1 * ..17 J3
Lion St CONG CW12 ....155 M8
Lisburne Av OFTN SK2 .....57 H1
Lisburne Cl OFTN SK2 .....57 H1
Lisburne La OFTN SK2 .....57 H1
Liskeard Cl RUNC WA7 .....62 F8
Liskeard Dr BRAM/HZG SK7 ..56 F5
Lismore Av EDGY/DAV SK3 ...40 C9
Lisson Gv HALE/TIMP WA15 ..53 J5
Lister Cl MWCH CW10 .....151 K4
Lister Rd RUNC WA7 ....14 C8
Litherland Av WYTH/NTH M22 .54 G5
Litherland Crs RNFD/HAY WA11 .22 B3
Litherland Rd SALE M33 ...39 H5
Little Abbey Gtwy CH/BCN CW1 ..2 D3
Little Aston Cl MCFLDN SK10 .95 J9
Little Brook Rd SALE M33 ...37 P7
Littlecote Gdns WARRS WA4 ..62 C1
Littledale Rd
  WARRW/BUR WA5 ....32 G9
Littledales La WHITCH SY13 * .108 F7
Little Delph RNFD/HAY WA11 .22 C3
Little Ees La SALE M33 ....38 B1
Little Egerton St STKP SK1 * .17 F5
Littlegate RUNC WA7 ......62 G6
Little Gv GTS/LS CH66 ....101 P1
Little Heath La ALT WA14 ...52 B2
Little Heath Rd CHD/CHDH SK8 .?
Little Meadow Cl MCFLDN SK10 .95 H6
Little Meadow Rd ALT WA14 ..52 B2
Little Moss La ALS/KID ST7 ..188 C5
Little Moss La ALS/KID ST7 ..188 G7
Littler Grange Ct WSFD CW7 * .149 J7
Little St ALS/KID ST7 .....188 F9
Little Roodee CO CH5 ......?
Little Rw ALS/KID ST7 ....189 K6
Little St John St CH/BCN CW1 * ..3 G5
Little Stanney La CHNE CH2 ..102 A1
Littlestone Cl WDN WA8 ...45 L4
Littleton Cl NWCHE CW9 ...109 P5
  WARRW/BUR WA5 ....33 H8
Littleton La CHSE CH3 ....122 D9
Little Underbank STKP SK1 * .17 F4
Little Wissage GTS/LS CH66 .102 B2
Littlewood Rd WYTH/NTH M22 .54 E3
Littondale Cl RAIN/WL L35 * .30 C6

Littondale Cl CONG CW12 ...155 P5
Liverpool Cl RDSH SK5 ....41 M1
Liverpool Pl WDN WA8 ....45 J6
Liverpool Rd ALS/KID ST7 ..189 J7
  CH/BCN CW1 ....102 B5
  IRL M44 ....36 C5
  NEWUL ST5 ....201 N5
  NSTN CH64 ....77 M3
  RNFD/HAY WA11 ....22 F1
  WARRW/BUR WA5 ....20 E1
  WDN WA8 ....20 E1
Liverpool Rd East ALS/KID ST7 .188 F5
Liverpool Rd West ALS/KID ST7 .188 C4
Liverpool Rw NEWLW WA12 ..23 P9
Liverpool St CHSW/BR CH4 ..110 C4
Liverstudd Av RDSH SK5 ...28 F9
Livesey St BNG/LEV M19 ...28 B9
Livingstone Av MCFLDN SK10 .116 F4
Livingstone Rd WARRS WA4 ..32 G9
Livingstone St
  WARRW/BUR WA5 ....32 G9
Livingstone Wy MWCH CW10 .151 K4
Llanberis Rd CHD/CHDH SK8 .55 N6
Llandaff Cl GTS/LS CH66 ..102 A3
Llandovery Cl WARRS WA4 ..149 K5
Llanfair Rd EDGY/DAV SK3 ..16 B7
Lloyd Av CHD/CHDH SK8 ....55 L5
Lloyd Cl ALT WA14 ....53 H3
Lloyd Crs NEWLW WA12 .....23 K6
Lloyd Dr EP CH65 ....6 F9
Lloyd Rd BNG/LEV M19 ....41 J1
Lloyd Sq ALT WA14 ....53 H3
Lloyd St ALT WA14 ....53 H3
  FLINT CH6 ....98 B5
  HTNM SK4 ....16 D2
  RNFD/HAY WA11 ....22 D3
Llyndir La WRX/GR/LL LL12 ..160 E6
Llys Cadnant CHSW/BR CH4 ..141 H5
Llys Caer CHSW/BR CH4 ....140 E7
Loachbrook Av CONG CW12 ..155 J8
Lobelia Gv RUNC WA7 .....84 D1
Lochinvar Av GTS/LS CH66 ..79 K7
Lochmaben Cl CW/SHV CW2 ..184 G9
Lochmaden Cl HOLMCK WA4 ..131 N9
Lochmaddy Cl BRAM/HZG SK7 .57 M6
Loch St RUNC WA7 ....14 E2
Locker Av WARRN/WOL WA2 ..33 L6
Lockerbie Cl HOLMCK WA4 ..131 P9
Lockett Rd WDN WA8 ......33 H4
Lockett St WARRS WA4 ....49 H4
Lockgate East RUNC WA7 ...62 G4
Lockgate West RUNC WA7 ...62 G4
Lockhart Cl WGTN/LGST M12 .28 A4
Locking Stumps La
  WARRN/WOL WA2 ....34 C5
Lockitt St CW/HAS CW1 ....5 F5
Lock La PART M31 ....36 C5
Lock Rd ALT WA14 ....52 G1
  WARR WA1 ....34 A9
Lockside MPL/ROM SK6 ....58 E8
Locksley Cl HTNM SK4 ....16 B2
Lock St STHEL WA9 ....22 A4
Lockton Cl RDSH SK5 .....41 M2
Lockton La WARRW/BUR WA5 .48 A4
Lock Vis WARRS WA4 ......49 K4
Lockwood Vw WGTN/LGST M12 .28 B6
Lockwood Wy RUNC WA7 ...63 K9
Lodge Brow MCFLDN SK10 ...95 N4
Lodge Cl LYMM WA13 ......51 H3
Lodge Ct HTNM WA13 ......40 G6
Lodge Dr GOL/RIS/CU WA3 ..25 J1
  NWCHW CW9 ....128 C4
  WSFD CW7 ....150 A1
Lodge Farm Cl BRAM/HZG SK7 .56 E5
Lodgefields Dr CW/SHV CW2 .184 D4
Lodge Hollow FROD/HEL WA6 .105 H1
Lodge La CH/BCN CH1 .....120 D?
  MWCH CW10 ....209 P2
  NANT CW5 ....130 D2
  NWCHW CW8 ....66 A8
  NWCHW CW9 ....110 G2
  PART M31 ....109 K8
  RUNC WA7 ....85 N5
  WARRW/BUR WA5 ....33 H9
  WDN WA8 ....45 H5
  ALS/KID ST7 ....187 N4
Lodge Rd ALS/KID ST7 ....201 N1
  KNUT WA16 ....171 H1
  SBCH CW11 ....171 J4
  WDN WA8 ....45 H7
Lodmore La WHITCH SY13 ...215 M4
Lofthouse Ga WDN WA8 ....45 M4
Lomas La BNG/LEV M19 ....40 E5
Lomas Sq MCFLDN SK11 ....41 J9
Lomax St RUNC WA7 ......197 L1
Lomax Rd NANT CW5 ......197 L1
Lombard Cl MPL/ROM SK6 ...42 E4
Lombard Ct ALS/KID ST7 ...188 A4
Lomond Av HALE/TIMP WA15 .53 L4
Lomond Cl EP CH65 ....6 C6
Lomond Gv EP CH65 ....102 E1
Lomond Rd WYTH/NTH M22 ..55 H5
London Pl STKP SK1 ....17 G5
London Rd AUD/MAD/AV CW3 .219 H5
  FROD/HEL WA6 ....83 P5
  HALE/TIMP WA15 ....53 L1
  MCFLDN SK10 ....95 H2
  MCFLDN SK11 ....117 K9
  MKTDR TF9 ....218 G8
  NANT CW5 ....11 F7
  NANT CW5 ....210 E5
  NWCHW CW9 ....13 F4
  OFTN SK2 ....57 K3
  SBCH CW11 ....171 J1
  WARRS WA4 ....48 F7

WHITCH SY13 ....213 L5
WILM/AE SK9 ....93 J4
London Rd North
 POY/DIS SK12 ....57 L9
London Rd South
 MCFLDS SK11 ....73 K4
London Road Ter
 MCFLDS SK11 ....117 K7
London Rw NEWLW WA12 ...23 P9
London Sq STKP SK1 ....17 C5
London St MCFLDS SK11 .....8 C3
 NWCHW CW9 ....107 P8
Long Acre NWCHW CW8 ...108 L3
Longacres Rd HALE/TIMP WA15 ...53 N8
Long Acres Rd NSTN CH64 ...77 L3
Longacre St MCFLDS SK11 ...8 C4
Longbarn Bvd
 WARRN/WOL WA2 ....34 D6
Long Barn La WARR WA1 ...34 E8
Long Barn La WARRN/WOL WA2 ...34 C6
Longburgh Cl CHNE CH2 ...3 K1
Longbutt La LYMM WA13 ...50 F5
Longbutts La MCFLDS SK11 ...135 K2
Longclough Rd NEWLW ST5 ...201 N5
Longcroft Dr ALT WA14 ...52 F3
Longcroft Dr DTN/ASHW M34 ...29 H1
 NTHM/RTH M23 ....39 K9
Longdale Dr CH/BCN CH1 ...120 F6
Longden La MCFLDS SK11 ...117 N6
Longden Rd WGTN/LGST M12 ...28 A7
Longden St MCFLDS SK11 ...9 H5
Longdin St WARRS WA4 ...49 H4
Longdon Ct BRAM/HZG SK7 * ...72 C5
Longdown Rd CONG CW12 ...155 H6
Longfield Av CHD/CHDH SK8 ...5 L8
 CHNE CH2 ....121 P4
 HALE/TIMP WA15 ....53 N1
Longfield Rd NTHM/RTH M23 ...39 J8
 WARRN/WOL WA2 ....33 M7
Longford Rd RDSH SK5 ...28 F8
Longford Rd West RDSH SK5 ...28 D8
Longford St CW/SHV CW2 ...5 F7
 GTN M18 ....28 D3
 WARRN/WOL WA2 ....18 D1
Long Grain Pl OFTN SK2 ...57 K2
Longham Cl BRAM/HZG SK7 ...56 C6
Long Hey HALE/TIMP WA15 ...54 C3
Longhey Rd WYTH/NTH M22 ...54 F2
Longhill La AUD/MAD/W CW5 ...209 L7
Longhope Rd WYTH/NTH M22 ...54 F4
Longhorn Cl MWCH CW10 ...130 C9
Longhurst La MPL/ROM SK6 ...43 N9
Longlands Dr NM/HAY SK22 ...59 M7
Longlands Rd NM/HAY SK22 ...59 M7
Long La ALS/KID ST7 ....189 N4
 CH/BCN CH1 ....120 E1
 CHNE CH2 ....122 B5
 CHSE CH3 ....144 C7
 CONG CW12 ....155 N6
 KNUT WA16 ....112 G5
 MALPAS SY14 ....179 M8
 MALPAS SY14 ....191 J5
 MCFLDN SK10 ....95 P4
 MWCH CW10 ....151 J3
 TPLY/KEL CW6 ....167 H6
 TPLY/KEL CW6 ....158 F1
 WARRN/WOL WA2 ....33 M7
 WHITCH SY13 ....212 D9
 OFTN SK2 ....167 P2

Lonsdale Rd BNG/LEV M19 ...28 B7
Lon y Capel FLINT CH6 ...98 A6
Looe Cl WDN WA8 ....45 L5
The Looms NSTN CH64 ...77 H5
Loonies Ct STKP SK1 * ...17 G6
The Loont WSFD CW7 ...149 L8
Lord Derby Rd HYDE SK14 ...43 K2
Lord Nelson St WARR WA1 ...19 F6
Lordship La FROD/HEL WA6 ...82 F7
Lordshire Pl ALS/KID ST7 ...189 P7
Lords La GOL/RIS/CU WA3 ...34 D4
Lords Mill Rd CW/SHV CW2 ...198 A3
Lord's St IRL M44 ....36 B3
Lord St CHSE CH3 ....3 K4
 CW/SHV CW2 ....5 F5
 DTN/ASHW M34 ....28 C5
 GOL/RIS/CU WA3 ....25 J9
 MCFLDN SK10 ....95 P5
 MCFLDS SK11 ....9 F7
 NEWLW WA12 ....23 L6
 RUNC WA7 ....14 D1
 STKP SK1 ....17 G5
 WARRS WA4 ....48 D3
Lorgill Cl EDGY/DAV SK3 ...56 F5
Lorland Rd EDGY/DAV SK3 ...56 E3
Lorna Av CHD/CHDH SK8 ...55 H1
Lorna Rd CHD/CHDH SK8 ...56 E3
Lorne Gv EDGY/DAV SK3 ...56 E1
Lorraine Rd HALE/TIMP WA15 ...53 L2
Lorraine St ALS/KID ST7 ...189 P7
Lostock Av BNG/LEV M19 ...28 B8
 BRAM/HZG SK7 ....57 H6
 POY/DIS SK12 ....73 H2
 SALE M33 ....39 H4
 WARRW/BUR WA5 * 33 J8
Lostock Cl RUNC WA7 ...15 C7
Lostock Hall Rd POY/DIS SK12 ...73 H3
Lostock Hollow MALPAS SY14 ...110 C3
Lostock Rd POY/DIS SK12 ...73 J4
Lostock Wy WILM/AE SK9 ...71 M2
Lottery St EDGY/DAV SK3 ...16 D5
Lotus Gdns STHEL WA9 ...31 M1
Loughborough Cl SALE M33 ...38 A5
Louisa St OP/CLY M11 ...28 D1
Louise St CH/BCN CH1 ...2 B2
Loushers La WARRS WA4 ...48 F5
Lovage Cl WARRN/WOL WA2 ...34 D6
Lovat Dr KNUT WA16 ...90 F6
Lovatt Cl LYMM WA13 ...50 F5
Love La HTNM SK4 ....16 E2
 NANT CW5 ....10 B6
 SBCH CW11 ....172 F8
Lovel Ter WDN WA8 ....61 H1
Lovely La WARRW/BUR WA5 ...48 A1
Love St CH/BCN CH1 ....3 F4
Lowcross La MALPAS SY14 ...191 L4
 WARRS WA4 ....49 H5
Lowe Av CONG CW12 ....155 H5
Lowe Cl KNUT WA16 ....90 F5
Lower Appleton Rd WDN WA8 ...45 P6
Lower Aph Rd ALS/KID ST7 ...188 G8
Lowerbank DTN/ASHW M34 ...29 M4
Lower Bank St MCFLDS SK11 * ...9 G6
Lower Bents La MPL/ROM SK6 ...42 E4
Lower Bridge St CH/BCN CH1 ...2 E5
Lower Bury St HTNM SK4 ...16 C5
Lower Carrs STKP SK1 ....17 H5
Lower Church St WDN WA8 ...61 N1
Lower Cliffe NM/HAY SK22 * ...59 J5
Lower Cl HLWD L26 ....44 A7
Lower Darwin St NWCHW CW8 ...12 D6
Lower Exchange St
 MCFLDS SK11 * 8 E5
Lowerfield Dr OFTN SK2 * ...57 M2
Lower Field Rd CHSW/BR CH4 ...142 C5
Lowerfield Rd MCFLDN SK10 ...9 G1
Lower Fold DTN/ASHW M34 ...29 N7
 MPL/ROM SK6 ....43 N8
Lower Greenhall La
 POY/DIS SK12 ....59 J8
Lower Hague NM/HAY SK22 ...59 J7
Lower Haigh St WSFD CW7 ...149 L2
Lower Hall La MALPAS SY14 ...178 C6
Lower Heath CONG CW12 ...155 H6
Lower Heath Av CONG CW12 ...155 N5
Lower High St ALS/KID ST7 ...189 M1
Lower Hillgate STKP SK1 ...17 H5
Lower House La WDN WA8 ...21 F4
Lower La CHSE CH3 ....162 B7
Lower Macclesfield St
 MCFLDS SK11 * 147 L7
Lowerlea POY/DIS SK12 ...58 G9
Lower Macclesfield St
 CHF/WBR SK23 ....75 P8
Lower Meadow Dr
 WILM/AE SK9 ....71 N2
Lower Meadow Rd
 WILM/AE SK9 ....71 N2
Lower Mersey St EP CH65 ...80 E6
Lower Moat Cl HTNM SK4 ...41 M5
Lower Mountain Rd
 CHSW/BR CH4 ....140 A8
Lower Mumfort St
 FLINT CH6 * 98 B5
Lower Park Crs POY/DIS SK12 ...57 H9
Lower Park Rd CHSW/BR CH4 ...3 G6
 POY/DIS SK12 ....73 H1
Lower Rake La FROD/HEL WA6 ...85 H9
Lower Rd HLWD L26 ....44 B7
Lower Robin Hood La
 FROD/HEL WA6 ....105 H1
Lower Sandy La CHSE CH3 ...179 J9
Lower Strines Rd
 MPL/ROM SK6 ....58 E2
Lower Sydney St FLINT CH6 * ...98 B5
Lower Wash La WARRS WA4 ...48 C4
Lowes La MCFLDS SK11 ...135 M2
The Lowes ALT WA14 ....52 F6
Lowe St DTN/ASHW M34 ...29 P6
 GOL/RIS/CU WA3 ....24 C1
 MCFLDS SK11 ....9 F6
 STKP SK1 ....17 G5

Loweswater Crs
 RNFD/HAY WA11 ....22 E3
Loweswater Rd
 CHD/CHDH SK8 ....55 K4
Lowfield Gdns
 GOL/RIS/CU WA3 ....26 C2
Lowfield Gv OFTN SK2 ...41 N9
Lowfield La STHEL WA9 ...30 E3
Lowfield Rd EDGY/DAV SK3 ...56 E1
Lowfields Av WARRW/BUR CH62 ...79 H2
Lowfields Cl PS/BROM CH62 ...79 J2
Low Hi FROD/HEL WA6 ...104 D7
Lowick Cl BRAM/HZG SK7 ...57 K5
Lowick Gn MPL/ROM SK6 ...42 E3
Lowlands Rd RUNC WA7 ...14 D3
Lowland Wy KNUT WA16 ...90 D6
Low Lea Rd MPL/ROM SK6 ...43 N9
Low Leighton Rd NM/HAY SK22 ...59 P8
Low Meadow CHF/WBR SK23 ...75 P6
Lowndes Cl OFTN SK2 ...42 A9
Lowndes La OFTN SK2 ...42 A9
Lownorth Rd WYTH/NTH M22 ...54 C7
Lowside Av MPL/ROM SK6 ...43 H3
Lowther Av ALS/KID ST7 ...173 H9
 GOL/RIS/CU WA3 ....25 B6
Lowther Dr RAIN/WH L35 ...30 A5
Lowther Rd WILM/AE SK9 ...95 P5
Lowton Gdns GOL/RIS/CU WA3 ...24 D4
Low Wood Cl BRAM/HZG SK7 ...56 C6
Low Wood Rd DTN/ASHW M34 ...28 C5
Loxdale Dr EP CH65 ....80 B9
Loxley Cl MCFLDS SK11 ...8 B5
Loyola Hey RAIN/WH L35 ...30 D8
Lucerne Cl CHSE CH3 ....143 K4
Lucerne Rd BRAM/HZG SK7 ...56 E4
Lucy St EDGY/DAV SK3 ...16 E7
Ludford Cl NEWU ST5 ....201 N5
Ludford Gv SALE M33 ...38 C6
Ludford St CW/HAS CW1 ...4 E1
Ludlow Av CW/HAS CW1 ...5 J5
Ludlow Cl MCFLDN SK10 ...117 L2
 WARR WA1 ....34 C8
 WSFD CW7 ....149 K5
Ludlow Crs RUNC WA7 ...15 C7
Ludlow Dr EP CH65 ....102 C1
Ludlow Rd CH/BCN CH1 ...121 K6
Ludworth Av WYTH/NTH M23 ...39 J8
Lugano Rd BRAM/HZG SK7 ...56 E4
Lugsdale Rd WDN WA8 ...21 H4
Luke Rd DTN/ASHW M34 ...29 M5
Lulworth Cl WSFD CW7 ...149 L8
Lulworth Gdns NTHM/RTH M23 ...39 J8
 WARRS WA4 ....48 B9
Lumb Cl BRAM/HZG SK7 ...56 E9
Lumber La WARRW/BUR WA5 ...23 J9
Lumb La BRAM/HZG SK7 ...56 E9
 DTN/ASHW M34 ....29 J2
Lumley Cl PH CH/BCN CH1 ...2 E5
Lumley Rd CHAD CW7 ....121 M7
 MCFLDS SK11 ....116 F5
Lundy Av CCHDY M21 ...39 M3
Lundy Dr EP CH65 ....102 E4
Lune Cl CONG CW12 ....156 B3
Lunedale Cn OFTN SK2 ...57 L1
Lunehurst GOL/RIS/CU WA3 ...24 C1
Lune Wy RDSH SK5 ....41 N3
Lunn Av GTN M18 ....28 F5
Lunt Av CW/SHV CW2 ....4 F2
Lunts Heath Rd WDN WA8 ...45 M5
Lupin Dr RNFD/HAY WA11 ...22 F2
Lupus Wy GTS/LS CH66 ...102 B1
Lurgan Av SALE M33 ....38 C6
Luscombe Cl HLWD L26 ...44 A7
Lutener Av ALT WA14 ....52 C3
Luther Gv STHEL WA9 ....22 F7
Luton Dr WYTH/NTH M23 ...54 C3
Luton Rd RDSH SK5 ....28 F9
 EP CH65 ....6 A5
Luton St WDN WA8 ....21 H5
Lutyens Cl MCFLDN SK10 ...116 F4
Luxor Gv DTN/ASHW M34 ...28 E5
Lyceum Cl CW/HAS CW1 ...169 P9
Lyceum Wy CW/HAS CW1 * ...169 P9
Lychgate WARRS WA4 ....48 B8
Lychgate Ms HTNM SK4 * ...40 F6
Lycroft Cl RUNC WA7 ....62 D6
Lydbury Ct WARRW/BUR WA5 ...22 F6
Lydden Cl CW/SHV CW2 ...184 D1
 DTN/ASHW M34 ....29 P8
Lydgate Rd SALE M33 ...38 D3
Lydgate La NSTN CH64 ...78 C5
Lydiat La NSTN CH64 ...77 N5
 RUNC WA7 ....188 B4
Lydiat La WILM/AE SK9 ...93 J5
Lydney Av CHD/CHDH SK8 ...55 J3
Lydstep Cl WARRW/BUR WA5 * ...33 H6
Lydyett La NWCHW CW8 ...109 K1
Lymcote Dr NWCHW CW8 ...109 J3
Lyme Av WILM/AE SK9 ...117 K7
 WILM/AE SK9 ....93 J4
Lymefield Gv OFTN SK2 ...57 H1
Lyme Green Pk MCFLDS SK11 * ...136 C9
Lyme Gv ALT WA14 ....52 C3
 DROY M43 ....28 G1
 LYMM WA13 ....50 F5
 MPL/ROM SK6 ....43 J6
 MPL/ROM SK6 ....58 D2
 OFTN SK2 ....41 N9
Lyme Rd BRAM/HZG SK7 ...57 H7
 POY/DIS SK12 ....72 G4
 POY/DIS SK12 ....73 J3
Lymes ALT WA14 ....52 C6
Lyme St BRAM/HZG SK7 ...57 K4

HTNM SK4 ....40 F6
Lyme Vw RNFD/HAY WA11 ...23 J5
Lyme Vw MCFLDS SK11 ...136 C1
Lymewood Dr POY/DIS SK12 ...58 F9
 WILM/AE SK9 * 71 N6
Lymington Dr NTHM/RTH M23 ...38 G8
Lymm Cl EDGY/DAV SK3 ...56 D1
Lymmhay La LYMM WA13 ...50 E3
Lymmington Av LYMM WA13 ...52 A6
 LYMM WA13 ....51 M6
 WARRS WA4 ....49 P4
Lynalls Cl CONG CW12 ...155 H7
Lynbrook Cl CW/HAS CW1 ...5 K3
Lyncastle Rd WARRS WA4 ...65 M2
Lyncastle Wy WARRS WA4 ...65 M2
Lyncombe Cl CHD/CHDH SK8 ...56 B9
Lyncroft Cl CW/HAS CW1 ...185 M5
Lyndale Av PS/BROM CH62 ...79 J1
 RDSH SK5 ....28 E7
Lyndale Cl WSFD CW7 ...149 H8
Lyndene Gdns CHD/CHDH SK8 ...55 K1
Lyndene Rd WYTH/NTH M22 ...54 F2
Lyndhurst Av BRAM/HZG SK7 ...57 J6
 DTN/ASHW M34 * 29 L6
 IRL M44 ....27 N6
 MPL/ROM SK6 ....42 C5
 SALE M33 ....38 C5
Lyndhurst Cl WILM/AE SK9 ...70 F9
Lyndhurst Dr HALE/TIMP WA15 ...53 L5
Lyndhurst Rd DID/WITH M20 ...40 B4
 RDSH SK5 ....28 E7
Lyndon Gv RUNC WA7 ...15 G6
Lyndon Rd IRL M44 ....27 M8
Lyneal Av GTS/LS CH66 ...101 N2
Lyngard Cl WILM/AE SK9 ...71 M5
Lyngate Cl STKP SK1 ....17 J6
Lynham Av WARRW/BUR WA5 * ...47 M2
Lynmouth Av DID/WITH M20 ...40 B2
 RDSH SK5 ....41 M1
Lynn Av GOL/RIS/CU WA3 ...25 N8
 SALE M33 ....38 G2
Lynn Cl RUNC WA7 ....62 A7
Lynndene CCHDY M21 ...39 P6
Lynn Gv ALS/KID ST7 ....188 E8
Lynton Av GOL/RIS/CU WA3 ...25 N8
 HALE/TIMP WA15 ....53 L2
 STHEL WA9 ....31 H5
Lynton Cl CHSW/BR CH4 * ...142 B4
 KNUT WA16 ....90 C4
 WARRW/BUR WA5 ....47 J3
Lynton Crs WDN WA8 ....45 L5
Lynton Dr BNG/LEV M19 ...40 G1
 MPL/ROM SK6 ....58 C7
Lynton Gdns WARRS WA4 ...64 F2
Lynton Gv CW/HAS CW1 ...188 D3
 HALE/TIMP WA15 ....53 L2
 STHEL WA9 ....31 H5
Lynton La WILM/AE SK9 ...93 J3
Lynton Ms WILM/AE SK9 ...93 J3
Lynton Park Rd CHD/CHDH SK8 ...55 P7
Lynton Pl CHSW/BR CH4 ...140 G6
Lynton Rd CHD/CHDH SK8 ...55 L2
 HTNM SK4 ....41 J5
Lyntonvale Av CHD/CHDH SK8 ...55 J1
Lynton Wy CW/SHV CW2 ...184 G8
Lynway Dr DID/WITH M20 ...40 C3
Lynwood HALE/TIMP WA15 ...53 G3
Lynwood Av GOL/RIS/CU WA3 ...24 C3
 WARRS WA4 ....48 B8
Lynwood Gv HTNM SK4 ...41 K2
 SALE M33 ....38 F3
Lynwood Rd CH/BCN CH1 ...121 J6
Lyon Rd ALT WA14 ....52 B4
Lyons Fold SALE M33 ....38 E2
Lyon's La WARRS WA4 ....48 F9
Lyons Rd WARRW/BUR WA5 ...47 J3
Lyon St CW/HAS CW1 ....3 F2
 CW/HAS CW1 ....5 G3
 MCFLDS SK11 ....9 H4
 WARRS WA4 ....49 H4
Lyster Cl GOL/RIS/CU WA3 ...34 G5
Lytham Av CCHDY M21 ...39 M1
Lytham Dr BRAM/HZG SK7 ...56 G8
 WSFD CW7 ....128 D9
Lytham Rd CHD/CHDH SK8 ...55 K6
 WDN WA8 ....20 E9
Lytham St EDGY/DAV SK3 ...56 F1
Lytherton Av IRL M44 ....36 B2
Lythgoes La WARRN/WOL WA2 ...18 E4
Lyth St RUSH/FAL M14 ....40 E1

M

Mableden Cl CHD/CHDH SK8 ...55 M7
Mablins La CW/HAS CW1 ...170 A9
Macarthur Cl
 WARRW/BUR WA5 * 47 M1
Macauley Rd RDSH SK5 ...28 D8
Macclesfield Main Rd
 ....139 J2
Macclesfield Rd
 BRAM/HZG SK7 ....57 M7
 CHF/WBR SK23 ....75 N8
 CONG CW12 ....155 P4
 HOLMCH CW4 ....132 A8
 MCFLDN SK10 ....96 C6
 MCFLDN SK10 ....98 F5
 WILM/AE SK9 ....71 L8
Macdermott Rd WDN WA8 ...61 M1
Macdonald Av RAIN/WH L35 ...41 M4
Macdonald Rd IRL M44 ...36 D1
Macefin Av CCHDY M21 ...39 N4
Macfarren St WGTN/LGST M12 ...28 A6

Mackenzie St WGTN/LGST M12 ...28 A6
Macnair Cl MPL/ROM SK6 ...58 C7
Macnair Ms MPL/ROM SK6 * ...58 C7
Macnair Ms MPL/ROM SK6 ...58 C5
Macon Ct CW/HAS CW1 ...5 H5
Macon Wy CW/HAS CW1 ...5 H5
Maddocks Hl FROD/HEL WA6 ...107 K1
Maddock St ALS/KID ST7 ...200 C6
Madeley Cl ALT WA14 ....53 J7
 CHSW/BR CH4 ....140 G6
Madeley St CW/SHV CW2 ...185 J7
Madeline McKenna Ct
 WDN WA8 ....45 A5
Madison Av CHD/CHDH SK8 ...56 A5
 DTN/ASHW M34 ....29 J1
Madison St GTN M18 ....28 J3
Madras Rd EDGY/DAV SK3 * ...41 K9
Madron Av MCFLDN SK10 ...116 D3
Maelor Wy WHITCH SY13 ...212 D8
Maerway La MKTDR TF9 ...219 N8
Maes Alaw FLINT CH6 ....98 C7
Maes Gwyn FLINT CH6 ...98 C7
Maes-Hyfryd FLINT CH6 ...98 A4
Maes Teg FLINT CH6 ....98 A8
Maes-y-Coed CHSW/BR CH4 ...142 A4
Maes-y-Dre Av FLINT CH6 ...98 B7
Magdala Pl NWCHE CW9 ...110 C4
Magdalen Cl WYTH/NTH M22 ...54 B3
Magda Rd OFTN SK2 ....57 J2
Magecroft CW/HAS CW1 ...170 A8
Magenta Av IRL M44 ....36 D2
Mag La LYMM WA13 ....50 F8
Magna Cl WHITCH SY13 ...214 D9
Magnolia Cl GTS/LS CH66 ...102 E5
 RNFD/HAY WA11 ....22 C4
 SALE M33 ....37 P3
 WARR WA1 ....34 F9
Magnolia Dr RUNC WA7 ...84 D1
Magnolia Ri MCFLDN SK10 ...94 D7
Magpie Crs ALS/KID ST7 ...189 K6
Mahood St EDGY/DAV SK3 ...41 J9
Maida St BNG/LEV M19 ...28 C2
Maiden Gdns EP CH65 ...102 F1
Maidenhills MWCH CW10 ...151 K2
Maidstone Cl MCFLDN SK10 ...117 H2
Maidstone Rd HTNM SK4 ...40 D5
Maidwell Cl WSFD CW7 ...129 H7
Main Av BNG/LEV M19 ...40 C1
Main Cl RNFD/HAY WA11 ...22 E3
Main La GOL/RIS/CU WA3 ...24 C4
Main Rd AUD/MAD/W CW5 ...199 M9
 CHSW/BR CH4 ....140 F6
 CW/SHV CW2 ....186 A9
 CW/SHV CW2 ....198 A3
 HOLMCH CW4 ....132 A2
 MCFLDS SK11 ....118 A8
 NANT CW5 ....183 P3
 NANT CW5 ....197 F7
 NWCHE CW9 ....25 J3
Main St CHSE CH3 ....123 L6
 FROD/HEL WA6 ....83 N5
 RUNC WA7 ....14 C3
Maintree Crs SPK/HALE L24 ...60 A2
Mainwaring Cl NANT CW5 ...13 L6
Mainwaring Dr CHSW/BR CH4 ...141 N3
 WILM/AE SK9 ....71 M6
Mainwaring Rd KNUT WA16 ...113 L4
Mainwaring Ter
 NTHM/RTH M23 ....39 K6
Mainwood Rd HALE/TIMP WA15 ...53 K6
Mairesfield Av WARRS WA4 ...49 K5
Maismore Rd WYTH/NTH M22 ...54 C6
Maisterson Ct NANT CW5 ...10 C5
Maitland Av CCHDY M21 ...39 M4
Maitland Cl STKP SK1 ....17 J6
Maitland Wy CH/BCN CH1 ...120 C7
Maitland-wood Ct
 NWCHE CW9 ....110 D3
Major Cross St WDN WA8 ...21 H4
Makepeace Cl CHSE CH3 ...122 D8
Makerfield Dr NEWLW WA12 ...23 H1
Malaga Av MANAIR M90 ...54 D8
Malbank NANT CW5 ....10 D4
Malbank Rd CW/HAS CW1 ...184 D4
Malcolm Av WARRN/WOL WA2 ...33 N7
Malcolm St RUNC WA7 ...14 F5
Malden Gv NTHM/RTH M23 ...39 K9
Maldon Cl OFTN SK2 ....57 L1
Malgam Dr DID/WITH M20 ...40 C8
Malham Cl OFTN SK2 ....57 K1
Malhamdale Av RAIN/WH L35 ...30 C6
Malhamdale Rd CONG CW12 ...156 A5
Malin Cl SPK/HALE L24 ...60 B2
Maliston Rd WARRW/BUR WA5 ...47 M2
Mallaig Cl HOLMCH CW4 ...131 P9
Mallard Cl OFTN SK2 ....62 D2
 RUNC WA7 ....62 D3
 WARRN/WOL WA2 ....33 N5
Mallard Crs POY/DIS SK12 ...72 C2
Mallard Gdns STHEL WA9 ...30 D2
Mallard Gn ALT WA14 ....37 N8
Mallard La GOL/RIS/CU WA3 ...34 G5
Mallards Reach MPL/ROM SK6 ...42 A4
Mallard Wy CW/SHV CW2 * ...185 N6
 WSFD CW7 ....
Malling Rd NTHM/RTH M23 ...54 C3
Mallory Cl CW/HAS CW1 ...185 M3
Mallory Ct CONG CW12 ...155 H7
Mallory Gv RNFD/HAY WA11 ...22 B3
Mallory Rd EP CH65 ....6 D6
Mallory Wk CHSW/BR CH4 ...160 D2
Mallow Cl CHSE CH3 ....143 J4
Mallowdale Rd OFTN SK2 ...57 L1
Mallowdale Rd CONG CW12 ...73 K2
Malmesbury Cl MWCH CW10 ...151 K2
 POY/DIS SK12 ....73 K2
Malmesbury Pk RUNC WA7 ...78 A1
Malmesbury Rd CHD/CHDH SK8 ...56 A4
 CONG CW12 ....13 L6
 WILM/AE SK9 ....
Malpas Cl CHD/CHDH SK8 ...56 A2
Malpas Dr ALT WA14 ....38 E8
 WARRW/BUR WA5 ....47 N3
Malpas Rd EP CH65 ....80 B9

NWCHE CW9.................................13 K4
RUNC WA7..................................61 P7
Malpas St WGTN/LGST M12 ....28 A3
Malpas Wy WARRW/BUR WA5 * ...47 N5
Malrae HALE/TIMP WA15 *..............53 J6
Malsham Rd NTHM/RTH M23 ....39 J6
Maltby Rd NTHM/RTH M23 ....54 B1
Malt Kiln Rd KNUT WA16 ....89 M9
Maltmans Rd LYMM WA13.............50 D4
Malton Av GOL/RIS/CU WA3...........24 C6
Malton Cl WDN WA8 ....45 J2
Malton Dr ALT WA14 ....52 E1
BRAM/HZG SK7.........................57 K8
Malton Rd HTNM SK4....................41 H4
Malt St KNUT WA16 ....90 E3
Malvern Av CHD/CHDH SK8 ....55 H2
EP CH65 ....102 E1
Malvern Cl CONG CW12................155 H7
CW/SHV CW2 ....198 A3
HTNM SK4 ....16 D1
WARRW/BUR WA5......................32 D8
Malvern Dr ALT WA14 ....52 F2
MCFLDN SK10............................95 L9
Malvern Gv DID/WITH M20............60 B2
Malvern Rd CH/BCN CH1 ....121 K7
KNUT WA16................................90 D5
STHEL WA9 ....89 H3
Malvern Wy WSFD CW7 ....149 J2
Manby Rd GTN M18 ....28 B5
Manby Sq GTN M18.......................28 B5
Manchester New Rd PART M31 ......36 E5
ALT WA14..................................38 A9
CHD/CHDH SK8 ....40 E8
CONG CW12.............................155 N5
DTN/ASHW M34.........................29 L6
Manchester Rd
GOL/RIS/CU WA3.......................35 J9
GOL/RIS/CU WA3.......................36 A6
HTNM SK4 ....41 L3
HYDE SK14 ....29 P6
MCFLDN SK10..........................117 K2
PART M31 ....36 F4
WARR WA1 ....34 C9
WILM/AE SK9 ....71 L6

Manchester Rd North
DTN/ASHW M34.........................29 J5

Manchester Rd South
DTN/ASHW M34.........................29 J6
Mancroft Cl WARR WA1 ....34 F9
Manchester Rw NEWLW WA12 ......23 P9
Mancunian Rd DTN/ASHW M34 .....29 N9
Mandalay Gdns MPL/ROM SK6 .....43 J1
Mandarin Cn ALT WA14................37 N8
Mandeville St BNG/LEV M19 ....28 B9
Manifold Cl SBCH CW11 ....171 K1
Manifold Dr MPL/ROM SK6 ....58 D9
Manley Cl HOLMCH CW4 ....131 M8
NWCHE CW9..............................87 L1
NWCHE CW9............................110 A7
Manley Gdns WARRW/BUR WA5 ...68 D2
Manley Gv BRAM/HZG SK7 ....56 E9
FROD/HEL WA6 ....105 L8
Manley La FROD/HEL WA6...........105 L8
Manley Pl STHEL WA9 ....30 D1
Manley Rd FROD/HEL WA6...........105 K4
Manley Rd FROD/HEL WA6...........105 N6
MCFLDS SK11 ....116 C7
SALE M33 ....38 C7
Manley Vw CHNE CH2..................104 C1
Manna Dr CHNE CH2 ....104 C1
Mannings La South
CHNE CH2................................122 C6
Mannings La South
CHNE CH2................................122 B6
Manning St CW/SHV CW2 ....185 K7
Manora Rd NWCHE CW9...............13 H3
Manor Av CW/SHV CW2 ....184 G7
GOL/RIS/CU WA3......................24 E1
HOLMCH CW4 ....132 C2
NEWLW WA12 ....23 K5
NWCHE CW9.............................88 D7
RAIN/WH L35 ....30 B6
SALE M33 ....38 A4
Manor Cl CHD/CHDH SK8 ....56 C7
CHSE CH3 ....123 M5
CHSW/BR CH4 ....140 G3
CONG CW12.............................156 A9
DTN/ASHW M34.........................29 P7
WARR WA1 ....34 E9
WILM/AE SK9 ....70 G6
Manor Ct CW/SHV CW2 ....185 H7
GOL/RIS/CU WA3......................24 E1
Manor Crs CHSW/BR CH4 ....140 G4
KNUT WA16................................90 F3
MCFLDN SK11 ....117 K1
MWCH CW10 ....151 J3
Manor Dr CHCHDY M21................39 N4
CHSE CH3 ....143 K1
NWCHE CW9............................110 C5
NWCHE CW9............................109 K2
Manor Farm Cl CHNE CH2 ....122 F3
Manor Farm Crs CH/BCN CH1 ....101 M4
Manor Farm Rd RUNC WA7 ....68 F2
Manor Fld RUNC WA7 ....62 F7
Manorfield Cl CH/BCN CH1 ....101 L4
Manor Flds MWCH CW10 ....151 J3
Manor Gdns NANT CW5 ....10 B4
WILM/AE SK9 ....71 M7
Manor Gv NWCHW CW8 ....109 L6
Manor Hill Rd MPL/ROM SK6 ....43 J7
Manorial Rd NSTN CH64................77 J5
Manorial Rd South NSTN CH64 .....77 J5
Manor La CHSW/BR CH4 ....140 F5
GTS/LS CH66 ....101 P7
HOLMCH CW4 ....132 A9
KNUT WA16................................91 J7
MWCH CW10 * 151 J2
NWCHE CW9............................129 L1
Manor Pk CHSE CH3 ....123 M5
Manor Park Av RUNC WA7 ....62 G2
Manor Pk Crs DTS/LS CH66 ....101 P2
Manor Pk North KNUT WA16 ....90 G3
Manor Park Rd CONG CW12 ....135 L9

Manor Pk South KNUT WA16.........90 F4
Manor Rd ALS/KID ST7 ....189 M1
BNG/LEV M19.............................28 B7
CHD/CHDH SK8 ....56 C6
DTN/ASHW M34.........................29 H2
DTN/ASHW M34.........................29 P8
FROD/HEL WA6 ....84 A4
HALE/TIMP WA15 ....53 J5
LYMM WA13...............................50 E5
MPL/ROM SK6............................42 C3
NANT CW5 ....43 J9
NANT CW5 ....10 D4
NWCHW CW8 ....127 J1
RDSH SK5 ....42 A3
RNFD/HAY WA11 ....23 L2
RUNC WA7 ....62 B4
SALE M33 ....38 E3
SBCH CW11 ....172 A3
WDN WA8 ....45 H6
WILM/AE SK9 ....70 G6
Manor Sq WSFD CW7 ....149 J2
Manor St DTN/ASHW M34 ....29 M2
NWCHW CW8 ....109 L3
STHEL WA9 ....22 A7
Manor Wy CW/SHV CW2 ....185 J7
Mansbury Cl NANT CW5 ....43 G2
Manse Field Rd
FROD/HEL WA6 ....106 F5
Manse Gdns NEWLW WA12 ....23 P5
Mansell Cl WDN WA8 ....46 A2
Mansfield Av DTN/ASHW M54 ....29 K4
Mansfield Cl DTN/ASHW M54 ....29 K4
Mansfield Rd EP CH65 ....102 C2
Mansfield St AULW OL7 ....29 L1
Manshaw Crs DTN/ASHW M34 ......29 N6
Manshaw Rd OP/CLY M11..............28 D2
Mansion Ct NANT CW5 *................10 D6
Mansion Dr KNUT WA16 ....90 F5
Manston Dr CHD/CHDH SK8 ....55 M1
Manston Rd WARRW/BUR WA5......47 K4
Manton Av DTN/ASHW M34...........28 C6
Manuel Perez Rd
WARRW/BUR WA5......................47 M1
Manvers St RDSH SK5 ....41 M5
Manville St STHEL WA9 ....22 A8
Manx Rd WARR WA1 ....48 D4
Maori Dr FROD/HEL WA6...............83 N5
Maple Av ALS/KID ST7 ....188 A6
Maple Av ALS/KID ST7 ....188 F8
GOL/RIS/CU WA3.......................55 P5
DTN/ASHW M34.........................29 L6
GOL/RIS/CU WA3.......................25 H2
GTS/LS CH66 ....79 N7
HALE/TIMP WA15 ....54 A2
MCFLDS SK11 ....117 K7
MPL/ROM SK6............................58 D3
NEWLW WA12 ....23 P7
NEWLW WA12 ....23 P7
POY/DIS SK12............................59 L9
POY/DIS SK12............................73 M5
RNFD/HAY WA11 ....22 F2
RUNC WA7 ....15 K6
RUNC WA7 ....84 E1
WDN WA8 ....45 P6
Maple Cl CONG CW12 ....155 H6
HOLMCH CW4 ....132 A7
OFTN SK2 ....57 H1
SBCH CW11 ....171 P5
Maple Crs WARRW/BUR WA5........47 K3
Maple Gv CHNE CH2 ....122 C7
Maple Gv CHNE CH2 ....122 C7
Maplecroft STKP SK1 ....42 A8
CH/BCN CH4 ....141 P5
CW/HAS CW1 ....185 L2
GTS/LS CH66 ....102 C3
NWCHW CW8 * 87 K9
NWCHW CW8 ....109 L5
WARRS WA4 ....48 F4
WSFD CW7 ....93 K3
Maple La NWCHW CW8 ....127 J1
Maple Pl ALS/KID ST7 ....188 B1
Maple Rd BRAM/HZG SK7 ....72 E1
NTHM/RTH M23.........................38 F8
PART M31 ....36 D5
WARR WA1 ....34 F9
WARRW/WOL WA2.....................33 L2
WILM/AE SK9 ....93 K3
Maple Rd West
NTHM/RTH M23.........................38 F8
The Maples WSFD CW7 ....129 H8
Mapleton Dr RUNC WA7 ....84 D2
Maplewood Cl WDN WA8 ....45 J6
Maplewood Gv CH/BCN CH1 ......120 E3
Mapley Av WYTH/NTH M22 ....39 N8
Maplin Dr OFTN SK2 ....57 N2
Mapplewell Crs
WARRW/BUR WA5......................47 L1
Marbury Dr EDGY/DAV SK3 ....41 H9
Marbury Gdns EP CH65 ....80 B7
Marbury La NWCHE CW9 ....87 N3
Marbury Rd CHSE CH3 ....122 D9
HTNM SK4 ....41 L1
NWCHW CW9............................87 N3
WILM/AE SK9 ....71 J5
Marbury St WARRS WA4 ....48 E5
March Av HTNM SK4 ....41 J6
Marchbank Dr CHD/CHDH SK8 .....55 L1
Marches Wy CH/BCN CH1 .... 2 E3
MALPAS SY14 ....203 H1
Marches Wy MALPAS SY14 ....204 C4
WHITCH SY13 ....213 H4
Marchioness St GTN M18 * 28 B5
March St CW/HAS CW1 * 5 G2
Marchwiel Rd EP CH65 ....7 H6
Marcien Wy WDN WA8 ....45 M4
Marcliffe Dr BNG/LEV M19.............28 C8

Marcliff Gv HTNM SK4 ....41 J6
Marcross Cl WARRW/BUR WA5 ......33 H7
Mardale Av DID/WITH M20.............40 D3
WARRN/WOL CW2....................156 A5
NTHLY L27 ....44 A5
Mardale Ct HOLMCH CW4 ....131 M9
Mardale Crs LYMM WA13..............50 F4
Mardale Dr CHD/CHDH SK8 ....55 K1
Mardale Lawn NTHLY L27..............44 A4
Marden Rd NTHM/RTH M23...........54 C2
Mardon Cl KNUT WA16 ....91 H1
Marford Cl NWCHE CW9 ....109 N7
WYTH/NTH M22.........................54 F1
Marford Crs SALE M33 ....38 C6
Margaret Av STHEL WA9................31 H1
WARR WA1 ....34 C9
Margaret Ct WDN WA8 * 21 J5
Margaret Rd DTN/ASHW M34 ....29 N5
Margaret's La GTS/LS CH66 ....79 L6
Margaret St RDSH SK5 ....41 M1
Margate Rd RDSH SK5 ....41 N1
Margery Av ALS/KID ST7 ....188 C1
Marham Cl CCHDY M21 * 39 P2
Marian FLINT CH6 ....98 B8
Marian Av RAIN/WH L35 ....23 J6
Marian Cl RAIN/WH L35 ....30 B6
Marian Dr CHSE CH3 ....143 K2
RAIN/WH L35 ....30 A6
Marian Rd RNFD/HAY WA11 ....23 J2
Marie Cl DTN/ASHW M54 ....29 M7
NANT CW5 ....207 J2
Marie Dr WARRS WA4 ....49 M5
Marigold Cl MCFLDS SK11 ....116 F5
Marigold Wy STHEL WA9 ....31 M1
Marina Av DTN/ASHW M34...........29 N8
STHEL WA9 ....31 H1
WARRW/BUR WA5......................47 M3
Marina Cl WILM/AE SK9 ....71 M1
Marina Dr CHNE CH2 ....121 P4
EP CH65 ....6 E5
MPL/ROM SK6............................43 M6
RUNC WA7 ....33 M7
Marina Gv RUNC WA7 ....15 H3
Marina Rd MPL/ROM SK6 ....42 D4
Mariner Av WARR WA1 ....36 C5
Mariner Cl RUNC WA7 ....63 N8
Marion Dr RUNC WA7 ....61 M8
Maritime Cl NEWLW WA12 ....23 N4
Marjorie Cl GTN M18 ....28 B3
Mark Av GTS/LS CH66 ....79 N9
Mark Cl CHNE CH2 .... 3 K2
Market Av NWCHE CW9..................13 J7
Market Ct TPLY/KEL CW6 ....146 G8
Market Ga WARR WA1...................18 D6
Market Pl MALPAS SY14 ....192 C8
MCFLDN SK10...........................10 B8
SBCH CW11 ....90 P5
STKP SK1 ....17 J3
WSFD CW7 ....149 P1
Market Sq CW/HAS CW1 ....4 E3
Market Sq ALS/KID ST7 ....189 J7
ALT WA14..................................54 B3
CONG CW12.............................155 M8
CW/HAS CW1 * 5 F5
DTN/ASHW M34.........................29 M6
EP CH65 ....6 D6
NANT CW5 ....10 B5
NEWLW WA12 ....23 L5
NM/HAY SK22 ....59 M8
NWCHE CW9..............................13 J8
POY/DIS SK12............................59 H9
WDN WA8 ....21 H4
Market Wk SALE M33 ....38 E4
Market Wy NWCHE CW9 ....13 F2
Markfield Crs RNFD/HAY WA11 ......22 A4
Markland Av CHD/CHDH SK8 ....55 P5
Marl Cl SBCH CW11 ....171 L6
Marlborough Av
CHD/CHDH SK8 ....56 B6
WILM/AE SK9 ....93 K3
WSFD CW7 ....128 D8
Marlborough Cl AULW OL7 ....29 L1
CW/SHV CW2 ....184 E8
DTN/ASHW M34.........................29 M6
KNUT WA16...............................90 C1
MCFLDN SK10...........................95 M9
MPL/ROM SK6............................43 J9
Marlborough Crs WARRS WA4........49 H5
STKP SK1 ....17 J1
Marlborough Dr
FROD/HEL WA6 ....105 H2
HTNM SK4 * 41 L4
MCFLDN SK10...........................95 M9
Marlborough Rd ALT WA14 ....53 H5
EP CH65 ....102 C2
IRL M44 ....27 P6
SALE M33 ....38 E4
Marlborough Wk EP CH65 ....102 E1
Marl Edge MCFLDN SK10 ....94 D8
Marley Av CW/HAS CW1 ....185 H2
Marley Av CW/HAS CW1 ....38 C9
RAIN/WH L35 ....30 D7
Marley Cl SALE M33 ....38 D2
Marley Rd BNG/LEV M19 ....28 C8
POY/DIS SK12............................73 L4
Marley Wy CHSW/BR CH4 ....142 A5
Marlfield Rd HALE/TIMP WA15 ....53 P8
WARR WA1 ....49 J5
Marl Heys CHNE CH2...................121 P4
Marling Cl DTN/ASHW M54 ....29 N5
Marling Pk WDN WA8 ....45 H6
Marlor Rd DTN/ASHW M54 ....29 L5
Marlow Av CHNE CH2 ....122 A4
Marlow Cl CHD/CHDH SK8 ....55 P5
GOL/RIS/CU WA3.......................34 D3
Marlow Ct DTN/ASHW M20............40 D4
Marton Cl CONG CW12................155 N5
CW/SHV CW2 ....198 C4
GOL/RIS/CU WA3.......................25 N5

WILM/AE SK9 ....71 L1
CW/SHV CW2 ....184 G8
SBCH CW11 ....171 J4
WDN WA8 ....45 H6
Marlowe Cl CH/BCN CH1 ....121 K6
Marlowe Ct MCFLDS SK11 * 117 J7
Marlowe Dr DID/WITH M20.............40 C4
NANT CW5 ....196 F4
Marlowe Rd NSTN CH64................77 L5
NWCHE CW9............................110 C6
Marlowe Wks MPL/ROM SK6 ....42 D6
Marlston Av CHSW/BR CH4 ....142 A9
Marlston Ct CHSW/BR CH4 ....142 A9
Marlston Pl RUNC WA7 ....61 P8
Marlwood Pl CHSW/BR CH4 ....140 E7
Marne Av WYTH/NTH M22.............54 G2
Maroon Rd WYTH/NTH M22 ....55 H8
Marple Crs CW/SHV CW2 ....184 E8
Marple Hall Dr MPL/ROM SK6 ....43 J9
Marple Old Rd OFTN SK2 ....57 N1
Marple Rd NWCHE CW9 ....110 C5
OFTN SK2 ....42 C9
Marquis Dr CHD/CHDH SK8 ....55 M8
Marquis St BNG/LEV M19 ....28 C8
Marrick Av CHD/CHDH SK8...........55 L2
Marriott Rd SBCH CW11 ....171 L6
Marriott St DID/WITH M20..............40 C2
STKP SK1 ....17 H7
Marron Av WARRW/WOL WA2........33 L6
Marryat Cl WARRN/WOL WA2........33 J5
Marsden Av WARRS WA4 ....49 J5
Marsden Cl WDN WA8 ....46 L3
Marsden Dr HALE/TIMP WA15.......53 N1
Marsden Rd MPL/ROM SK6 ....43 H5
Marsden Ter MCFLDS SK11 * 8 D5
Marshall Av STHEL WA9 * 29 J8
WARRW/BUR WA5......................33 J6
Marshall Gv CONG CW12 ....156 D9
NWCHW CW8 ....12 B6
Marshall Rd BNG/LEV M19 ....28 A8
WARR WA1 ....34 E9
Marshalls Ct NWCHW CW8 ....109 L7
NWCHW CW9.............................87 L5
Marshalls Cross Rd STHEL WA9 ....30 C2
Marshall St DTN/ASHW M34..........29 L5
Marsham Dr MPL/ROM SK6 ....58 E2
Marsham Pl BRAM/HZG SK7 ....57 H6
Marsh Av ALS/KID ST7 ....189 M6
Marsh Cl ALS/KID ST7 ....187 L5
EDGY/DAV SK3 ....56 D1
Marshfield Av WARRW/WOL WA2 ...18 F3
Marshfield Bnk CW/SHV CW2 ......184 D3
Marshfield La BIDD ST8 ....175 L6
Marshfield Rd
HALE/TIMP WA15 ....53 N2
Marshgate WDN WA8 ....45 H9
Marshgate Pl FROD/HEL WA6 ....84 A3
Marsh Green Cl BIDD ST8 ....175 L5
Marsh Green Rd BIDD ST8 ....175 L6
Marsh Hall Rd WDN WA8 ....45 P3
Marsh House La
WARRN/WOL WA2....................19 G2
Marshlands Rd NSTN CH64 ....77 L8
Marsh La ALS/KID ST7 ....187 L5
CHNE CH2.................................87 A7
CHNE CH2................................104 B1
CHSE CH3 ....177 K4
FLINT CH6 ....104 B1
FROD/HEL WA6 ....83 N5
FROD/HEL WA6 ....107 L6
HOLMCH CW4 ....132 B9
KNUT WA16...............................68 D5
NANT CW5 ....196 D5
NM/HAY SK22 ....59 P9
RUNC WA7 ....62 D3
WARRS WA4 ....85 P2
WARRW/BUR WA5......................46 G5
Marsh Rd WARRS WA4..................46 G2
Marsh St WARR WA1 ....19 J2
WDN WA8 ....21 G7
Marshway Dr NEWLW WA12 ....23 M5
Marsland Av HALE/TIMP WA15 ......38 E8
Marsland Cl DTN/ASHW M54 ....29 H6
Marsland Gv STHEL WA9 ....22 C6
Marsland Rd HALE/TIMP WA15 ......53 M1
MPL/ROM SK6............................95 M9
Marsland St BRAM/HZG SK7 * 57 K5
STKP SK1 ....17 J5
Marsland Ter STKP SK1 * 42 A8
Marson St WARRN/WOL WA2 ....18 C4
Marston Cl PS/BROM CH62 ....79 J2
Marston Gdns EP CH65 ....27 P7
Marston La NWCHE CW9 ....88 D8
Martens Rd IRL M44 ....27 N6
Marthall Dr SALE M33 ....39 H6
Marthall La KNUT WA16 ....91 L7
Martham Ct WARRS WA4 ....49 J4
Martham Dr OFTN SK2 ....57 N1
Martin Av NEWLW WA12 ....23 M4
Martin Cl CHNE CH2 ....121 M3
DTN/ASHW M54.........................29 M4
OFTN SK2 ....57 M2
RUNC WA7 ....84 A2
Martindale Gv RUNC WA7 ....62 B9
Martin Dr IRL M44 ....27 M6
Martin Rd CHNE CH2 ....121 M5
FROD/HEL WA6 ....83 P9
Martinscroft Rd
NTHM/RTH M23.........................54 C2
Martinsfields NWCHW CW8 ....88 A9
Martin's La CHNE CH2 ....184 F6
Martland Av GOL/RIS/CU WA3........24 B6
Martlet Av POY/DIS SK12...............58 C9
Martock Av WYTH/NTH M20...........40 C4
Marton Av DTN/ASHW M34 ....29 L6
Marton Cl CONG CW12................155 N5
CW/SHV CW2 ....198 C4
GOL/RIS/CU WA3.......................25 N5

MCFLDN SK10...........................116 F3
Marton Gn EDGY/DAV SK3 ....56 D2
Marton Gv HTNM SK4....................17 J7
Marton Hall La MCFLDS SK11 ......134 B8
Marton La MCFLDS SK11.............134 E4
Marton La MCFLDS SK11.............134 G8
Marton Pl SALE M33 ....38 D7
Marton La MCFLDS SK11.............135 L2
Marwood Cl ALT WA14..................52 G6
Marwood Dr NTHM/RTH M23 ....54 B4
Maryfield Cl GOL/RIS/CU WA3.......24 D2
Maryhill Cl ALS/KID ST7 ....189 J5
Maryhill Rd RUNC WA7 ....14 E7
Marylebone Av STHEL WA9 ....30 E2
Marylon Dr WYTH/NTH M22 ....39 P8
Marys Ga CW/SHV CW2 ....184 E8
CW/HAS CW1 ....5 J1
DTN/ASHW M34 * 29 M5
DUK SK16 ....29 P1
STHEL WA9 ....22 A9
STKP SK1 ....17 J5
WDN WA8 ....46 B8
Maryville Cl EP CH65 ....6 B3
Marywell Cl STHEL WA9 ....31 J1
Masefield Dr CH/BCN CH1 ....121 H5
CW/HAS CW1 ....5 K3
HTNM SK4 ....41 L4
Masefield Gv RDSH SK5 ....28 E8
Maskery Pl CONG CW12 ....155 M7
Mason Av WARR WA1....................33 P8
WDN WA8 ....45 N3
Mason Cl GTS/LS CH66................101 P2
Mason Dr BIDD ST8 ....175 J9
Masons La MCFLDN SK10 ....7 J3
Mason St CH/BCN CH1 .... 2 J2
RUNC WA7 ....15 J1
WARR WA1 ....19 G6
Massey Av LYMM WA13 ....50 A5
NWCHW CW8 ....109 J8
WARRW/BUR WA5......................12 J8
WSFD CW7 ....149 P1
Massey Brook La LYMM WA13 ....50 B5
Masseyfield Rd RUNC WA7 ....62 E9
Massey Rd HALE/TIMP WA15 ....53 J3
Massey St EP CH65 ....39 H4
STKP SK1 ....17 G5
WILM/AE SK9 ....93 J4
Massey Wk WYTH/NTH M22...........55 H6
Massie St CHD/CHDH SK8 ....55 M1
Masters Cl KNUT WA16 * 90 C1
Mates La MALPAS SY14 ....192 A9
Mather Av GOL/RIS/CU WA3..........24 C3
STHEL WA9 ....22 C6
Mather Cl MWCH CW10 ....151 J2
Mather La NWCHW CW8 ....87 L5
Mather Rd NWCHE CW9 ....110 D5
Mathers Cl WARRN/WOL WA2 ....54 B4
Matley Cl WARRW/BUR WA5 ....32 D8
Matley Gn RDSH SK5 ....42 B2
Matlock Av DID/WITH M20.............40 A2
DTN/ASHW M54.........................29 N9
Matlock Cl SALE M33 ....38 F4
WARRW/BUR WA5......................32 D8
Matlock Dr BRAM/HZG SK7 ....57 L7
RDSH SK5 ....28 B3
Matterdale Cl FROD/HEL WA6........84 B6
Matthew Cl CHNE CH2 .... 3 K2
Matthew Henry Ct
WHITCH SY13 ....213 L1
Matthews La BNG/LEV M19 ....28 B7
Matthews Pl CONG CW12 ....156 A8
Matthews St WARR WA1 ....19 H2
Maud Av GOL/RIS/CU WA3............58 E1
Mattison St OP/CLY M11 ....28 E2
Matty's La FROD/HEL WA6 ....83 N6
Mauldeth Cl HTNM SK4 ....41 H5
Mauldeth Rd BNG/LEV M19 ....40 F7
Mauldeth Rd DID/WITH M20 ....40 F5
HTNM SK4 ....41 H5
Mauldeth Rd RUSH/FAL M14 ....40 F7
Maunders Ct SALE M33 ....55 G5
Mavor Ct CW/HAS CW1 .... 4 C2
Mawdsley Av WARR WA1 ....34 F9
Maw Green Cl CW/HAS CW1 ....185 L1
Maw Cl CW/HAS CW1 * 185 N1
Mawson Cl WARRW/BUR WA5........32 G8
Maxfield Cl MCFLDS SK11 ....116 F4
Maxwell Av EP CH65 ....102 C2
Maxwell St CW/SHV CW2 ....184 E8
GOL/RIS/CU WA3.......................34 F2
May Av CHD/CHDH SK8 ....56 B9
WARR WA1 ....16 A3
Mayberry Gv WARRN/WOL WA2 ....34 B7
Maybury St GTN M18 ....28 E3
Maycroft Av DID/WITH M20 ....40 D3
Maycroft Av CHSW/BR CH4 ....141 N5
Mayer St OFTN SK2 * 40 G2
Mayer St OFTN SK2 * 42 B9
Mayfair Cl POY/DIS SK12 ....73 L1
WARRW/BUR WA5......................32 A9
Mayfair Dr IRL M44 ....27 N6
NWCHE CW9............................109 N3
SALE M33 ....38 B6
Mayfair Gv WDN WA8 ....45 K6
Mayfair Ms DID/WITH M20 * 40 A4
Mayfield Av DTN/ASHW M34..........41 H6
WARRN/WOL WA2.....................54 G5
Mayfield Av DTN/ASHW M54 ....42 F1
MCFLDS SK11 ....117 J7
RDSH SK5 ....41 N3
SALE M33 ....39 H4
Mayfield Cl HALE/TIMP WA15 ....53 M1
HOLMCH CW4 ....132 A8

Mayfield Dr *GOL/RIS/CU* WA3 ....25 L1
NWCHW CW8 ....108 C8
Mayfield Gv *GTN* M18 ....28 F6
NWCHW CW8 ....108 C8
RDSH SK5 ....41 N3
WILM/AE SK9 ....70 G9
Mayfield Ms *CW/HAS* CW1 ....184 F2
Mayfield Rd *BRAM/HZG* SK7 ....72 E2
CH/BCN CW1 ....120 C6
HALE/TIMP WA15 ....53 M1
KNUT WA16 ....91 K1
MPL/ROM SK6 ....43 N7
NWCHE CW9 ....13 K3
WARRS WA4 ....49 J5
Mayfield St *DTN/ASHW* M34 ....29 L4
Mayfield Ter *MCFLDS* SK11 ....117 J7
Mayfield Vw *LYMM* WA13 ....50 E5
Mayflower Rd *NANT* CW5 ....196 F5
Mayford Rd *BNG/LEV* M19 ....28 A7
May Gv *BNG/LEV* M19 ....39 N5
Mayhurst Av *GOL/RIS/CU* WA3 ....39 M5
Mayorlowe Av *RDSH* SK5 ....42 B4
Mayor's Rd *HALE/TIMP* WA15 ....53 J3
Maypool Dr *RDSH* SK5 ....41 N2
May Rd *CH/CHDH* SK8 ....56 A9
Maythorn Av *CW/SHV* CW2 ....34 E1
Maytree Av *OP/CLY* M11 ....28 E1
Maytree Av *CHSE* CH3 ....122 C9
Mayville Dr *DID/WITH* M20 ....40 C3
Maywood Dr *DID/WITH* M20 ....40 C8
McCarthy CI *GOL/RIS/CU* WA3 ....35 H5
McClellan PI *WDN* WA8 ....22 C5
McCormack Av *STHEL* WA9 ....22 A6
McCulloch St *STHEL* WA9 ....22 A6
EP CH65 ....6 E7
McGough CI *STHEL* WA9 ....30 F5
McKee Av *WARRN/WOL* WA2 ....53 L6
McKellin CI *ALS/KID* ST7 ....201 H5
McLaren St *CW/HAS* CW1 ....185 H5
McLean Dr *IRL* M44 ....27 N5
McMinnis Av *STHEL* WA9 ....22 E7
McNeill Av *CW/HAS* CW1 ....184 F3
Meachin Av *CCHDY* M21 ....39 M2
Mead Av *ALS/KID* ST7 ....188 C1
Mead CI *KNUT* WA16 ....90 D5
Meade CI *RAIN/WH* L35 ....30 C7
The Meade *WILM/AE* SK9 ....71 K6
Meadfoot Rd *GTN* M18 ....28 D3
Meadow Av *CONG* CW12 ....155 L9
CW/SHV CW2 ....198 G2
HALE/TIMP WA15 ....53 L4
HOLMCH CW4 ....131 P2
STHEL WA9 ....31 J5
WARRS WA4 ....48 C5
Meadow Bnk *CCHDY* M21 ....39 K1
HALE/TIMP WA15 ....53 D9
HTNM SK4 ....41 J4
MKTDR TF9 ....217 H9
MPL/ROM SK6 ....42 E5
TPLY/KEL CW6 ....125 H7
Meadowbank Gdns
GOL/RIS/CU WA3 ....26 C2
Meadow Brook Wy
CHD/CHDH SK8 ....56 B3
Meadow Brow *WILM/AE* SK9 ....93 J3
Meadow CI *BRAM/HZG* SK7 ....57 L4
CHF/WBR SK23 ....75 N6
CHSE CH3 ....124 A9
CHSE CH3 ....3 G7
CW/SHV CW2 ....198 C2
DTN/ASHW M34 ....42 F1
FROD/HEL WA6 ....105 H2
HALE/TIMP WA15 ....53 M4
HOLMCH CW4 ....132 B2
MPL/ROM SK6 ....48 D7
NSTN CH64 ....77 L7
WDN WA8 ....45 K4
Meadow Cft *ALS/KID* ST7 ....189 N6
CH/BCN CW1 ....121 J2
MALPAS SY14 ....204 F2
Meadow Cft *ALS/KID* ST7 ....188 A6
BRAM/HZG SK7 ....57 L4
Meadow Cft *CH/BCN* CH1 ....120 D2
Meadow Crft *NSTN* CH64 ....78 C5
WHITCH SY13 ....213 K5
Meadow Dr *CW/SHV* CW2 ....184 F9
KNUT WA16 ....90 D5
MCFLDN SK10 ....95 N6
NWCHW CW8 ....109 J1
Meadowfield *CHF/WBR* SK23 ....75 N6
TPLY/KEL CW6 ....146 C9
Meadow Field Rd
CHSW/BR CH4 ....142 C5
Meadow Ga *NWCHE* CW9 ....88 F9
Meadowgate CI *SBCH* CW11 ....171 J4
Meadow Gv *NWCHW* CW8 ....110 B7
WSFD CW7 ....128 F6
Meadow La *ALT* WA14 ....51 N3
CHSE CH3 ....143 J5
DTN/ASHW M34 ....42 F1
EP CH65 ....6 C5
NSTN CH64 ....78 C4
NWCHE CW9 ....87 L6
NWCHW CW8 ....128 G4
RDSH SK5 ....59 H9
WARRN/WOL WA2 ....34 B6
Meadow Ri *MALPAS* SY14 * 178 D6
WSFD CW7 ....149 J1
Meadow Rd *CHSW/BR* CH4 ....140 F6
NWCHW CW8 ....108 G4
Meadows Gn *GOL/RIS/CU* WA3 ....24 C4
Meadowside *BRAM/HZG* SK7 ....75 P6
CHF/WBR SK23 ....75 P6
MCFLDN SK10 ....73 P6
MCFLDS SK11 * 8 D4
NM/HAY SK22 ....59 L9
NWCHW CW8 ....12 A4

Meadowside Av *ALS/KID* ST7 ....200 F6
IRL M44 ....27 N7
WYTH/NTH M22 ....54 G3
Meadowside La *ALS/KID* ST7 ....189 N1
Meadowside Ms *CH/BCN* CH1 ....121 L7
Meadows La *CH/BCN* CH1 ....120 D3
CHSW/BR CH4 ....3 G7
Meadows PI *CHSW/BR* CH4 ....3 G7
Meadows Rd *ALS/KID* ST7 ....189 H7
Meadows Rd *CHD/CHDH* SK8 ....55 K6
CHD/CHDH SK8 ....55 P7
HTNM SK4 ....41 K2
SALE M33 ....38 F2
The Meadows *FLINT* CH6 ....98 A6
IRL M44 ....36 C2
MPL/ROM SK6 ....42 G4
NSTN CH64 ....77 M7
RAIN/WH L35 ....30 B6
Meadow St *NM/HAY* SK22 ....59 M7
SWIN M27 ....37 J2
OFTN SK2 ....57 J2
Meadowsway *CHNE* CH2 ....121 N3
The Meadow *HOLMCH* CW4 ....132 A3
Meadowvale CI *NANT* CW5 ....10 C1
Meadow Vw *CHNE* CH2 ....104 A1
CHNE CH2 ....130 A9
Meadow View Dr
FROD/HEL WA6 ....83 N6
Meadow View Rd
WHITCH SY13 ....213 H6
Meadow Wk *RUNC* WA7 * 62 D7
Meadow Wy *ALS/KID* ST7 ....188 C3
HALE/TIMP WA15 ....53 M4
MCFLDN SK10 ....93 G1
WILM/AE SK9 ....92 G1
Mead Rd *WARR* WA1 ....34 B8
Meadscroft Dr *WILM/AE* SK9 ....93 H4
Mead St *ALS/KID* ST7 ....187 P4
The Mead *MCFLDS* SK11 * 39 L1
Meadway *BRAM/HZG* SK7 ....72 E1
GOL/RIS/CU WA3 ....24 F1
GTS/LS CH66 ....79 M6
MCFLDN SK10 ....94 C8
MPL/ROM SK6 ....58 H1
POY/DIS SK12 ....73 H1
RUNC WA7 ....62 D5
SALE M33 ....38 B6
WDN WA8 ....44 C6
Meadway CI *SALE* M33 ....38 B5
Meadway Rd *CHD/CHDH* SK8 ....56 B4
Meakin CI *CONG* CW12 ....156 B9
Mealhouse Brow *STKP* SK1 ....17 G4
Meal St *HTNM* SK4 ....41 H4
NM/HAY SK22 ....59 N7
Measham CI *RNFD/HAY* WA11 * 22 J2
Meddings CI *WILM/AE* SK9 ....93 J5
Medina Av *WSFD* CW7 ....128 C9
Medina CI *CHD/CHDH* SK8 ....56 E3
Medina Wy *ALS/KID* ST7 ....189 K6
Medlar CI *CHSW/BR* CH4 ....142 B5
Medway CI *LEIGH* WN7 ....25 L1
WARRN/WOL WA2 ....33 P6
WARRS WA4 ....71 M4
Medway Crs *ALT* WA14 ....52 C1
Medway Dr *BIDD* ST8 ....175 L8
Medway Rd *GOL/RIS/CU* WA3 ....26 A7
Meeanee Dr *NANT* CW5 ....196 E3
Meech St *OP/CLY* M11 ....28 C1
Meerbrook Rd *EDGY/DAV* SK3 ....57 H8
Mee St *MCFLDS* SK11 ....117 L1
Meeting La *WARRW/BUR* WA5 ....47 H2
Megacre *ALS/KID* ST7 ....201 K5
Meg La *MCFLDN* SK10 ....116 E4
MCFLDS SK11 ....137 J1
Melande Dr *RDSH* SK5 ....28 F9
Melba St *OP/CLY* M11 ....28 E1
Melbecks Wk *NTHM/RTH* M23 ....39 J6
Melbourne Av *MANAIR* M90 ....54 C7
Melbourne Gv *CW/HAS* CW1 ....186 A3
Melbourne Rd *BRAM/HZG* SK7 ....56 E9
CH/BCN CH1 ....111 P6
Melbourne St *DTN/ASHW* M34 ....29 L7
RDSH SK5 ....28 F9
Melbury Av *DID/WITH* M20 ....40 E4
Melbury Ct *GOL/RIS/CU* WA3 ....34 G2
Melbury Rd *CHD/CHDH* SK8 ....56 B9
Melchett Crs *NWCHE* CW9 ....110 D5
Melford CI *CW/SHV* CW2 ....185 J8
Melford Ct *WARR* WA1 * 54 E8
Melford Dr *MCFLDN* SK10 ....117 J2
RUNC WA7 ....15 J5
Melford Rd *BRAM/HZG* SK7 ....57 M6
Melibon Crs *WYTH/NTH* M22 ....54 G5
Meliden Gdns *STHEL* WA9 ....31 L1
Meliden Gv *FROD/HEL* WA6 ....65 H6
Melkridge CI *CHNE* CH2 ....122 B8
Melksham CI *MCFLDS* SK11 ....8 A6
Meiland Av *CCHDY* M21 ....39 M3
Melland Rd *GTN* M18 ....28 C6
Mellard St *ALS/KID* ST7 ....200 C6
Melling Av *HTNM* SK4 ....41 M2
Melling St *WGTN/LGST* M12 ....28 A1
Mellington Av *DID/WITH* M20 ....40 D8
Mellock CI *NSTN* CH64 ....77 M7
Mellock La *NSTN* CH64 ....77 M7
Mellor CI *RUNC* WA7 ....63 H6
Mellor Ct *OFTN* SK2 ....42 D9
Mellor Crs *KNUT* WA16 ....90 C4
Mellor Rd *CHD/CHDH* SK8 ....56 B6
NM/HAY SK22 ....59 M4
Mellors Bnk *ALS/KID* ST7 ....189 L2
Mellor St *ALS/KID* ST7 ....189 P7
EDGY/DAV SK3 ....12 B8
Melrose Av *CHSE* CH3 ....122 C9
SALE M33 ....38 E5
WARRS WA4 ....48 F7
WARRW/BUR WA5 ....32 C1
Melrose Crs *EDGY/DAV* SK3 ....12 B7
HALE/TIMP WA15 ....53 M6
POY/DIS SK12 ....73 L3
Melrose Dr *CW/HAS* CW1 ....169 P9
GTS/LS CH66 ....102 B4
Melsomby Rd *NTHM/RTH* M23 ....39 K6
Meltham Av *DID/WITH* M20 ....40 B2

Meltham CI *HTNM* SK4 ....40 F7
Meltham Rd *HTNM* SK4 ....40 F7
Melton Av *DTN/ASHW* M54 ....28 C6
WARRS WA4 ....48 D7
Melton CI *CONG* CW12 ....155 H7
Melton Dr *CONG* CW12 ....155 H7
Melton Rd *RUNC* WA7 ....61 P8
Melton St *RDSH* SK5 ....41 N4
Melverly Dr *CH/BCN* CW1 ....120 F7
Melville CI *OP/CLY* M11 ....28 E2
WARRN/WOL WA2 ....18 D2
WDN WA8 ....46 B6
Melville Rd *IRL* M44 ....36 B5
Melvin Av *WYTH/NTH* M22 ....54 G3
Menai Gv *CHD/CHDH* SK8 ....55 H5
Menai Rd *EDGY/DAV* SK3 ....56 E1
Mendip Av *WARRN/WOL* WA2 ....33 L5
WYTH/NTH M22 ....55 H3
Mendip CI *CHD/CHDH* SK8 ....55 K8
CHSE CH3 ....102 A1
HTNM SK4 ....41 J5
WSFD CW7 ....149 K2
Mendip Gv *STHEL* WA9 ....22 D6
Menin Av *WARRS* WA4 ....48 E4
Menlow CI *WARRS* WA4 ....49 L6
Mentmore Gdns *WARRS* WA4 ....48 D9
Mentmore Crs *WYTH/NTH* M22 ....56 L5
Mentmore Rd *HTNM* SK4 ....41 J5
Meols CI *GTS/LS* CH66 ....80 A9
Mercer CI *MALPAS* SY14 ....204 A5
Mercer Rd *GTN* M18 ....28 D4
RNFD/HAY WA11 ....22 C5
Mercer St *BNG/LEV* M19 ....28 B8
NEWLW WA12 ....23 P5
WARRW/BUR WA5 ....32 B2
Mercer Wy *CH/BCN* CH4 ....142 B4
NANT CW5 ....10 B1
Merchants Ct *CW/HAS* CW1 ....185 J1
Mercian CI *CW/SHV* CW2 ....198 A3
Mercian Wy *EDGY/DAV* SK3 ....41 M9
Mercury CI *CH/BCN* CW1 ....121 H6
Mere Bnk *NWCHE* CW9 ....129 H5
Merebank Rd *CW/SHV* CW2 ....185 H7
Merebrook Rd *MCFLDS* SK11 ....116 F4
Mere Brook Wk *CW/SHV* CW2 ....185 J7
Mere CI *CW/HAS* CW1 ....186 B4
DTN/ASHW M34 ....29 H7
GTS/LS CH66 ....101 P2
KNUT WA16 ....88 F8
SALE M33 ....39 J5
Merecliff *RUNC* WA7 ....63 H7
Merecroft *CHSE* CH3 ....143 J1
Meredith Av *WARRS* WA4 ....49 K5
Meredith St *CW/HAS* CW1 ....4 D1
RUSH/FAL M14 ....40 E1
Mere Dr *DID/WITH* M20 ....40 C8
Merefield Rd *HALE/TIMP* WA15 ....88 F6
Merehaven CI *KNUT* WA16 ....68 F3
Merehatham Pk *KNUT* WA16 ....90 D2
Merelake Rd *ALS/KID* ST7 ....188 C8
Mereland Av *DID/WITH* M20 ....40 D7
Mereland Wy *STHEL* WA9 ....30 D7
Mere La *KNUT* WA16 ....88 F7
NWCHW CW8 ....127 K1
Meremore Dr *NEWLW* WA12 ....45 H9
Merepool CI *MPL/ROM* SK6 ....43 H9
Mere Rd *CW/SHV* CW2 ....198 G2
NEWLW WA12 ....24 B5
NWCHE CW9 ....88 B7
WARRN/WOL WA2 ....34 A9
Mereside Av *CONG* CW12 ....155 K8
Mereside CI *CHD/CHDH* SK8 ....55 C5
MCFLDN SK10 ....73 N2
Mereside Gdns *CHF/WBR* SK23 ......75 P8
Mereside Rd *KNUT* WA16 ....68 A5
Mere St *CW/HAS* CW1 ....186 B4
The Mere *CHD/CHDH* SK8 ....55 P5
Merewood Av *WYTH/NTH* M22 ....54 F1
Merewood CI
WARRN/WOL WA2 ....33 N5
Mereworth Dr *NWCHE* CW9 ....109 P7
Merganser CI *CW/HAS* CW1 ....18 C6
Meriden CI *RNFD/HAY* WA11 ....22 D3
Meridian PI *DID/WITH* M20 ....40 B4
Meriton Rd *WILM/AE* SK9 ....71 L2
Merlewood Av *BNG/LEV* M19 ....28 A7
Merlin Av *KNUT* WA16 ....90 F2
Merlin CI *OFTN* SK2 ....57 N1
Merlin Rd *IRL* M44 ....27 N5
Merlin Wy *ALS/KID* ST7 ....189 M5
CW/HAS CW1 ....169 P9
Merlyn Av *DID/WITH* M20 ....40 D4
DTN/ASHW M34 ....29 J7
Merlyn St *CW/SHV* CW2 ....185 K4
Merrick Av *WYTH/NTH* M22 ....54 G3
Merrick CI *WARRN/WOL* WA2 ....33 P6
The Merridale *HALE/TIMP* WA15 .....53 K7
Merrilees Rd *MCFLDN* SK10 ....117 H2
Merrill's Av *CW/HAS* CW1 ....184 E3
Merriman Av *KNUT* WA16 ....90 C4
Merrivale Rd *CW/SHV* CW2 ....185 H6
Merrybent CI *OFTN* SK2 ....57 N1
Merrydale CI *MCFLDN* SK10 ....116 F3
Merryman's La *WILM/AE* SK9 ....92 D6
Merseybank Av *CCHDY* M21 ....39 N4
Mersey Bank Rd *STHEL* WA9 ....18 E7
Mersey Dr *PART* M31 ....46 G1
Mersey Mdw *DID/WITH* M20 ....40 A5
Mersey PI *WSFD* CW7 ....150 B1
Mersey Rd *HTNM* SK4 ....40 A5
Mersey Rd *HTNM* SK4 ....41 G8
RUNC WA7 ....14 E1
SALE M33 ....38 F2
WDN WA8 ....61 M2
STKP SK1 ....16 E4
Mersey St *OP/CLY* M11 ....28 E6
STHEL WA9 ....22 E6
STKP SK1 ....17 K2

WARR WA1 ....18 E7
Merseyton Rd *EP* CH65 ....80 E6
Mersey Vw *RUNC* WA7 ....61 K7
Mersey View Rd *WDN* WA8 ....61 H2
Mersey View South Rd
RUNC WA7 ....61 K6
Mersey Wy *STKP* SK1 ....7 F3
Mersey Wy *WARRW/BUR* WA5 ....47 H3
Mersham Ct *WDN* WA8 ....45 M5
Merston Dr *DID/WITH* M20 ....40 D9
Merton Av *BRAM/HZG* SK7 ....57 M7
MPL/ROM SK6 ....42 F4
Merton Bank Rd *STHEL* WA9 ....22 E2
Merton CI *CW/HAS* CW1 ....77 L8
Merton Dr *CHSW/BR* CH4 ....142 C6
Merton Rd *EDGY/DAV* SK3 * 41 J9
GTS/LS CH66 ....102 A1
POY/DIS SK12 ....79 M2
SALE M33 ....38 D3
Merton St *STHEL* WA9 ....22 A4
Mertoun Rd *WARRS* WA4 ....48 D4
Mervyn Rd *NWCHW* CW8 ....108 C5
Merwood Av *CHD/CHDH* SK8 ....55 M7
Meshaw CI *NTHM/RTH* M23 ....39 H6
Message La *CONG* CW12 ....133 K7
Meteor Crs *WARRN/WOL* WA2 ....33 N6
Methuen St *WGTN/LGST* M12 ....28 B6
Mevagissey Rd *RUNC* WA7 ....62 D9
The Mews *CHD/CHDH* SK8 ....56 B3
HOLMCH CW4 ....131 P8
NWCHW CW8 ....109 K2
SALE M33 * 38 F5
WARRW/BUR WA5 * 32 B2
Meyer St *EDGY/DAV* SK3 ....41 J9
Meyneil CI *CW/SHV* CW2 ....184 C7
Meynell PI *CH/BCN* CW1 ....121 K6
Micawber Rd *POY/DIS* SK12 ....73 L4
Micklegate *CONG* CW12 ....122 F3
RUNC WA7 ....63 H7
Micklehurst Av *DID/WITH* M20 ....39 P4
Micklehurst Gn *OFTN* SK2 ....57 N1
Mickley Hall La *NANT* CW5 * 185 K3
Mickley Hall La *NANT* CW5 ....208 A2
Middlecroft *CHSE* CH3 ....122 F6
Middlefields *HALE/TIMP* WA15 ....53 L1
Middle Hillgate *STKP* SK1 ....17 H5
Middlehills *MCFLDS* SK11 ....117 N6
Middlehurst Av *NWCHW* CW8 ....108 C4
Middlehurst Rd *WARRS* WA4 ....49 J6
Middle La *CHSE* CH3 ....162 A6
CONG CW12 ....156 C6
FROD/HEL WA6 ....105 K2
Middle Wk *FROD/HEL* WA6 ....83 P6
KNUT WA16 ....90 F3
Middlesex Rd *RDSH* SK5 ....42 B2
Middlewalk *WARRS* WA4 ....28 F7
Middle Wk *CHD/CHDH* SK8 ....55 P7
Middlewich Rd *CW/SHV* CW2 ....184 C5
HOLMCH CW4 ....131 K5
HOLMCH CW4 ....131 N8
HOLMCH CW4 ....111 D2
MWCH CW10 ....129 N9
NANT CW5 ....13 G2
NWCHE CW9 ....110 C4
SBCH CW11 ....171 K3
WSFD CW7 ....150 C1
Middlewich St *CW/HAS* CW1 ....185 K3
Middlewood *GOL/RIS/CU* WA3 ....24 C1
Middlewood Dr *HTNM* SK4 ....40 F7
POY/DIS SK12 ....73 N2
POY/DIS SK12 ....73 N8
Midfield CI *BIDD* ST8 ....175 K7
Midgley Av *DTN/ASHW* M34 ....28 E5
Midhurst CI *ALS/KID* ST7 ....189 P7
CHD/CHDH SK8 ....55 P7
Midland Av *BRAM/HZG* SK7 ....56 E4
Midland St *WDN* WA8 ....21 K1
Midland Ter *ALT* WA14 * 53 H5
NM/HAY SK22 ....54 B4
Midland Wy *BRAM/HZG* SK7 ....56 E4
Midland Wy *WARR* WA1 ....18 B5
Midway *CHD/CHDH* SK8 ....72 B1
Midway St *WGTN/LGST* M12 ....28 A7
Midwood St *WDN* WA8 ....21 H3
Milborne CI *CHNE* CH2 ....177 D9
Milburn Av *NTHM/RTH* M23 ....39 L6
Milden CI *DID/WITH* M20 * 40 D4
WHITCH SY13 ....213 N4
Mile End La *OFTN* SK2 ....57 H2
Miles CI *GOL/RIS/CU* WA3 ....34 G5
Miles Green Rd *ALS/KID* ST7 ....199 J1
Miles St *WYTH/NTH* M22 ....28 A2
Milford Dr *BNG/LEV* M19 ....41 K1
Milford Gdns *WARRS* WA4 ....64 F2
Milford Gv *OFTN* SK2 ....42 B9
Milk St *CONG* CW12 ....155 M7
Milkwood Crs *GTN* M18 ....28 D5
Millar Crs *WDN* WA8 ....21 L9
Mill Av *WARRW/BUR* WA5 ....32 B9
Millbank *LYMM* WA13 ....51 N4
Millbank CI *MCFLDS* SK11 ....114 C1
Millbank St *FROD/HEL* WA6 ....85 N5
Mill Bridge CI *CW/HAS* CW1 ....185 M5
Millbrook Av *DTN/ASHW* M34 ....29 K8
Millbrook La *GOL/RIS/CU* WA3 ....26 C4
Millbrook Rd *NTHM/RTH* M23 ....54 C4
Millbrook St *STKP* SK1 ....17 C6
Mill Brow *STHEL* WA9 ....31 J3
Mill Brow CI *STHEL* WA9 ....31 J3

Millbuck Wy *SBCH* CW11 ....171 J3
Mill CI *CHNE* CH2 ....121 N5
EP CH65 ....102 E5
KNUT WA16 ....91 H1
WARRN/WOL WA2 ....33 P4
Mill Cft *FLINT* CH6 ....98 C7
Millcroft *SBCH* CW11 ....171 J9
Milford Gdns *ALS/KID* ST7 ....200 F2
Millers CI *CHSE* CH3 ....39 K5
SALE M33 ....39 K5
Millers Ct *MCFLDN* SK10 * 37 H9
Millersdale *STHEL* WA9 ....31 H4
Millersdale Gv *RUNC* WA7 ....62 D7
Millerscroft La *LYMM* WA13 ....51 H2
Millers Meadow *MCFLDN* SK10 ....96 C8
Miller St *WARRS* WA4 ....48 E3
Millers Vw *ALS/KID* ST7 ....189 J8
Millers Whf *ALS/KID* ST7 ....188 A1
Milley La *KNUT* WA16 ....55 J8
Mill Farm CI *WARRN/WOL* WA2 ....33 P5
Mill Field CI *CHSE* CH3 ....177 H6
Millfield La *CHSE* CH3 ....143 P9
RNFD/HAY WA11 ....23 K1
Millfield Rd *WDN* WA8 ....46 A5
Millfield CI *CHNE* CH2 ....121 N6
Millfield La *TPLY/KEL* CW6 ....146 G8
Millgate *NWCHW* CW8 ....108 B8
STKP SK1 ....17 H3
Millgate La *DID/WITH* M20 ....40 C7
Mill Gn *CONG* CW12 ....155 M7
Mill Green La *WDN* WA8 ....46 B2
Mill Gv *ALS/KID* ST7 ....188 F7
MALPAS SY14 ....180 B6
Mill Hey RAIN/WH L35 ....30 D7
Mill Hill Av *POY/DIS* SK12 ....57 K8
Mill Hill La *SBCH* CW11 ....171 M4
Mill Hill Hollow *POY/DIS* SK12 ....32 K8
Mill Hill La *SBCH* CW11 ....171 M5
Millhouse Av *NTHM/RTH* M23 ....54 A5
Millhouse La *GOL/RIS/CU* WA3 ....34 B2
Milliner Ct *OFTN* SK2 * 42 C9
The Millingfield *HOLMCH* CW4 ....131 P9
Millington CI *RUNC* WA7 ....84 B6
WDN WA8 ....20 E2
Millington Hall La *ALT* WA14 ....67 P1
Millington La *ALT* WA14 ....51 P9
NWCHW CW8 ....108 C6
Mill La *ALS/KID* ST7 ....200 F2
AUD/MAD M* CW3 ....216 F3
AUD/MAD M* CW3 ....217 H1
BRAM/HZG SK7 ....57 M7
CHD/CHDH SK8 ....55 M1
CHD/CHDH SK8 ....56 B4
CHNE CH2 ....121 N6
CHSE CH3 ....123 M6
CHSE CH3 ....135 L1
CHSE CH3 ....145 J9
CONG CW12 ....154 G1
CW/SHV CW2 ....196 G3
CW/SHV CW2 ....198 D5
DTN/ASHW M34 ....29 M3
FROD/HEL WA6 ....107 H1
FROD/HEL WA6 ....107 H1
GTS/LS CH66 ....79 P9
HALE/TIMP WA15 ....70 E2
HOLMCH CW4 ....153 J1
KNUT WA16 ....91 M1
KNUT WA16 ....113 P3
LYMM WA13 ....51 J2
MALPAS SY14 ....180 B6
MCFLDN SK10 ....72 C9
MCFLDN SK10 ....96 A5
MCFLDS SK11 ....114 C6
MPL/ROM SK6 ....42 G5
MWCH CW10 ....151 J1
NANT CW5 ....210 F3
NEWLW WA12 ....78 A4
NSTN CH64 ....78 B3
NSTN CH64 ....108 A3
NWCHW CW8 ....100 B3
RAIN/WH L35 ....30 B7
RDSH SK5 ....41 P1
SBCH CW11 ....152 A9
SBCH CW11 ....177 B9
STHEL WA9 ....41 L5
TPLY/KEL CW6 ....145 M3
TPLY/KEL CW6 ....146 C1
TPLY/KEL CW6 ....147 M8
TPLY/KEL CW6 ....148 C2
WARRN/WOL WA2 ....33 H3
WARRS WA4 ....48 A5
WARRS WA4 ....48 G5
WDN WA8 ....46 B2
WILM/AE SK9 ....92 D7
WSFD CW7 ....128 D5
WYTH/NTH M22 ....55 J9
Millmead *ALS/KID* ST7 ....188 A1
Millom Av *NTHM/RTH* M23 ....54 A5
RAIN/WH L35 ....30 A4
Mill Pk *HALE/TIMP* WA15 * 53 P4
Millom PI *CHD/CHDH* SK8 ....55 P7
Mill Park Dr *PS/BROM* CH62 ....79 J2
Mill Pond Av *NM/HAY* SK22 ....59 N7
Mill Pool La *NANT* CW5 ....182 F2
Millrace Dr *CW/SHV* CW2 ....185 H8
Mill Ri *ALS/KID* ST7 ....9 H7
Mill Rd *MCFLDS* SK11 ....9 F7
Millstone Av *ALS/KID* ST7 ....188 C7
Millstone CI *POY/DIS* SK12 ....73 M1
Millstone La *NANT* CW5 ....11 G4

Millstone Pas MCFLDS SK11 ....9 G7
Mill Stream Cl HOLMCH CW4 ..132 B2
Mill St ALT 53 J2
 BRAM/HZG SK7 ....57 K4
 CHSW/BR CH4 ....8 F7
 CONG CW11 ....155 M7
 CONG CW12 ....155 P6
 CW/SHV CW2 ....5 F5
 GOL/RIS/CU WA3 ....24 C1
 MCFLDS SK11 ....10 B6
 NANT CW5 ....77 L5
 NSTN CH64 ....77 L5
 OP/CLY CH1 ....28 A1
 WHITCH SY13 ....213 M6
 WILM/AE SK9 ....71 K7
Mill Street MI MCFLDS SK11 *.....8 E4
Mill Vw Cl CW/HAS CW1 ....170 A9
Mill View Cl MALPAS SY14 ....180 C6
Millwall Cl GTN M18 ....28 D4
Millway CHSE CH3 ....144 B5
 HALE/TIMP WA15 ....53 N8
Mill Wy NANT CW5 ....196 G5
Millwood Av SPK/HALE L24 ....60 A2
Millwood RUNC WA7 ....170 A9
Millwood Cl CHD/CHDH SK8 ....55 N7
Millwood Ct SPK/HALE L24 * 60 A2
Milne Cl CW/SHV CW2 ....184 F8
 WGTN/LGST M12 ....28 A3
 WILM/AE SK9 ....37 N9
Milner Rd NWCHW CW8 ....109 L6
Milner St WARRW/BUR WA5 ....18 A6
Milnthorpe Rd
 WARRW/BUR WA5 ....32 B2
Milton Av IRL M44 ....36 D2
 NEWLW WA12 ....23 M5
 SALE M33 ....39 G6
 WDN WA8 ....20 C5
Milton Cl MPL/ROM SK6 ....38 C8
 MWCH CW10 ....151 K5
 NWCHE CW9 ....88 C8
Milton Ct FROD/HEL WA6 ....20 F4
Milton Crs ALS/KID ST7 ....188 E8
 CHD/CHDH SK8 ....55 L2
Milton Dr CW/SHV CW2 ....184 F8
 HALE/TIMP WA15 ....38 D7
 POY SK12 ....73 K2
 SALE M33 ....39 G6
Milton Gv FROD/HEL WA6 ....104 G3
 SALE M33 ....39 G6
 WARRS WA4 ....18 C6
Milton Rd CH/BCN CH1 ....121 J5
 EP CH65 ....7 H7
 GOL/RIS/CU WA3 ....24 C2
 WDN WA8 ....20 C5
Milton Rough NWCHW CW8 ....108 A2
Milton St CH/BCN CH1 ....3 F3
 DTN/ASHW M34 ....21 P5
 STHEL WA9 ....30 F6
 WDN WA8 ....20 C5
Milton Wy SBCH CW11 ....171 J3
Milvain Dr WARRN/WOL WA2 ......9 K7
Milverton Dr CHD/CHDH SK8 .....72 B1
Milwain Dr HTNM SK4 ....K1 K2
Min Awel FLINT CH6 ....98 B9
Minden Cl DID/WITH M20 ....D4 D4
Minehead Av DID/WITH M20 ....40 A1
Minehead Gv STHEL WA9 ....31 J3
Miners Wy SPK/HALE L24 ....60 C4
 WDN WA8 ....20 C5
 CH/BCN CH1 ....120 G9
Minerva Cl WARRS WA4 ....48 F5
Mine Wy RNFD/HAY WA11 *.........23 K2
Minfield Cl ALS/KID ST7 ....189 J8
Minn-end-lane ALS/KID SK11 ....157 N4
Minor Av MCFLDS SK11 ....136 C1
Minshull La WSFD CW7 ....149 M5
Minster Cl WDN WA8 ....20 E2
Minster Ct CW/SHV CW2 ....184 E8
 RUNC WA7 ....17 J9
Minster Dr ALT WA14 ....52 E6
 CHD/CHDH SK8 ....56 A2
Minton Cl CONG CW12 ....156 B9
Minton Wy WDN WA8 ....45 P2
Mirfield Av HTNM SK4 ....41 J6
Mirfield Cl GOL/RIS/CU WA3 ......25 M4
Mirion St CW/HAS CW1 ....5 G2
Misty Cl WDN WA8 ....46 C4
Mitchell Av ALS/KID ST7 ....188 F7
 WARRS WA4 ....32 B3
Mitchell Cl CHD/CHDH SK8 *......55 H1
Mitchell St GOL/RIS/CU WA3 .....24 C2
 WARRS WA4 ....48 E7
Mitford Cl RUSH/FAL M14 ....40 C1
Mithril Cl WDN WA8 ....46 C4
Mitton Cl GOL/RIS/CU WA3 ....25 M4
Moadlock MPL/ROM SK6 ....48 H4
Moat Av WYTH/NTH M22 ....54 E3
Moat Gdns WYTH/NTH M22 ....54 E3
Moat La ALS/KID ST7 ....200 D5
 GOL/RIS/CU WA3 ....35 M7
Moat Rd WYTH/NTH M22 ....54 E4
 WARRS WA4 ....48 F4
Mobberley Rd BNG/LEV M19 .....189 L9
 KNUT WA16 ....69 J4
 KNUT WA16 ....90 C2
 WILM/AE SK9 ....70 E5
Modbury Cl BRAM/HZG SK7 ....56 E6
Modfire Dr CHD/CHDH SK8 ....55 J1
Moel Parc FLINT CH6 ....98 B8
Moggle La MCFLDS SK10 ....73 M5
Mold Rd CHD/CHDH SK8 ....140 D7
Mollets Wd DTN/ASHW M34 ....35 N4
Mollington Rd WYTH/NTH M22 ....54 G7
Molly Pitcher Wy
 WARRW/BUR WA5 ....47 M2
Molly Potts Cl KNUT WA16 ....90 F5
Molyneux Av
Molyneux Rd BNG/LEV M19 ....28 E6
Monaco Av CHD/CHDH SK8 ....55 M6
Monaco Dr WYTH/NTH M22 ....39 N6

Monarch Cl CW/SHV CW2 ....184 F4
 IRL M44 ....36 D2
Monarch Dr NWCHE CW9 ....109 N7
Monastery La STHEL WA9 ....31 J1
Monastery Rd STHEL WA9 ....31 K1
Monck Dr NANT CW5 ....196 E1
Mond Rd IRL M44 ....27 P5
 WDN WA8 ....21 G3
Mond St NWCHW CW8 ....109 K2
Money Ash Rd
 HALE/TIMP WA15 ....53 H4
Monfa Av EDGY/DAV SK3 ....56 G3
Monica Dr WDN WA8 ....45 D3
Monks Gv EP CH65 ....6 D3
Monk's La AUD/MAD/W CW3 ......184 F7
 CW/HAS CW1 ....184 F2
Monks Orch NANT CW5 ....10 C5
Monks St WARRW/BUR WA5 *......48 A1
Monk St CW/HAS CW1 ....4 A1
Monks Wy NWCHW CW8 ....109 K8
Monkswood Cl
 WARRW/BUR WA5 ....33 H6
Monmouth Av GTN M18 ....28 C6
Monmouth Av SALE M33 ....38 C5
Monmouth Cl WARR WA1 ....34 F9
Monmouth Gv STHEL WA9 ....31 J1
Monmouth Rd CHD/CHDH SK8 ....56 B6
Monroe Cl WARR WA1 ....28 E3
Monroe St GTN M18 ....28 C3
Monsal Av OFTN SK2 ....42 C9
Monsall Cl MCFLDS SK11 ....9 K5
Monsall Rd SALE M33 ....38 E4
Montague Rd WILM/AE SK9 ....38 E4
Montagu Rd OFTN SK2 ....42 C9
Montague St MPL/ROM SK6 ....43 N6
Montana Sq OP/CLY M11 ....28 B2
Montclare Crs WARRS WA4 ....48 C6
Montcliffe Cl GOL/RIS/CU WA3 ...34 D3
Montgomery Cl KNUT WA16 ....90 C1
Montgomery Rd WDN WA8 ....20 A4
Montgomery Wy WSFD CW7 ......149 K3
Mont Morency Rd KNUT WA16 ....91 H1
Monton Rd RDSH SK5 ....42 B4
Montpelier Av RUNC WA7 ....61 M8
Montpellior Rd WYTH/NTH M22 ...54 F5
Montreal St BNG/LEV M19 ....28 E8
Montrose Av CW/SHV CW2 ....198 A4
 MCFLDS SK11 ....116 C3
 WARRN/WOL WA2 ....34 A4
Montrose Cl CHSW/BR CH4 ......142 B3
 HOLMCH CW4 ....131 N9
Montrose Crs BNG/LEV M19 ......28 B8
Monument Rd ALS/KID ST7 ....201 N1
Monument Vw ALS/KID ST7 ....201 J5
Moody St CONG CW12 ....155 M8
Moorby Av BNG/LEV M19 ....40 F4
Moor Cl BIDD ST8 ....175 M8
Moorcroft KNUT WA16 ....51 H9
Moorcroft Av CHSE CH3 ....143 K1
Moorcroft Crs CHSE CH3 ....122 D7
Moorcroft Dr BNG/LEV M19 ....40 E3
Moorcroft Rd KNUT WA16 ....90 F3
Moordale Rd KNUT WA16 ....90 F3
Moordale Av STHEL WA9 ....22 B7
Moorditch La FROD/HEL WA6 .....83 M4
Moore Av STHEL WA9 ....22 B6
 WARRS WA4 ....49 M4
Moore Cl WDN WA8 ....46 B5
Moore Dr RNFD/HAY WA11 ....23 K3
Moore Cl LYMM WA13 ....51 H2
Moore La WARRS WA4 ....47 M8
Moore End WYTH/NTH M22 ....39 N8
Moor End Rd MPL/ROM SK6 ....59 L2
Mooreway RAIN/WH SL5 ....30 D7
Moorfield Av BIDD ST8 ....175 K9
 RUSH/FAL M14 ....39 N1
Moorfield Cl IRL M44 * 27 P6
Moorfield Dr NSTN CH64 ....77 J3
 WILM/AE SK9 ....70 G9
Moorfield Gv HTNM SK4 ....38 G5
 SALE M33 ....38 D5
Moorfield Rd DID/WITH M20 ....40 A4
 IRL M44 ....27 N6
Moorfield Rd WDN WA8 ....46 B3
Moorfields NANT CW5 ....197 M1
Moorfield Ter WYTH/NTH M22 ....40 C8
Moorfoot Rd STHEL WA9 ....31 J1
Moorgate Av DID/WITH M20 ......40 A2
Moorhead La WDN WA8 ....153 N7
Moorhill Rd MCFLDS SK11 ....117 J8
Moorhouse Av ALS/KID ST7 ......188 A4
Moorhouse Ct CHNE CH2 ....121 N6
Mooring Cl RUNC WA7 ....9 K8
Moorings CONG CW12 ....155 N9
Moorings Cl NSTN CH64 ....77 H4
The Moorings MWCH CW10 ......151 J1
 POY SK12 ....59 J9
Moorland Av SALE M33 ....38 F5
Moorland Dr CHD/CHDH SK8 .....55 P7
 RUNC WA7 ....8 B2
Moorland Rd ALS/KID ST7 ....189 M1
 BIDD ST8 ....175 J8
 DID/WITH M20 ....40 A5
 OFTN SK2 ....56 C3
Moorlands Av NWCHW CW8 ......108 C8
Moorlands Cl MCFLDS SK10 ......117 J1
Moorlands Pk NWCHW CW8 ......108 C8
Moor La BRAM/HZG SK7 ....72 D3
 CHSE CH3 ....144 A5
 CHSW/BR CH4 ....160 A1
 CQ CH5 ....140 C2
 FROD/HEL WA6 ....85 P5
 FROD/HEL WA6 ....104 E3
 NTHM/RTH M23 ....39 K6
 WILM/AE SK9 ....21 G5
Moor La South WDN WA8 ....21 F5

Moor Nook SALE M33 ....38 G5
Moor Park Rd DID/WITH M20 ......40 D8
Moor-park Wy NWCHE CW9 ....109 P8
Moor Rd NTHM/RTH M23 ....39 H8
Moorsfield Av
 AUD/MAD/W CW3 ....216 G2
Moorside HALE/TIMP WA15 *.......38 F9
 KNUT WA16 ....90 E1
Moorside Av NSTN CH64 ....77 J5
Moorside Ct DTN/ASHW M34 ......29 M5
 WDN WA8 ....21 F4
Moorside Dr DTN/ASHW M34 ......29 N5
 MCFLDN SK10 ....95 J4
 NSTN CH64 ....77 J6
Moorside Rd HTNM SK4 ....41 H6
Moors La SPK/HALE L24 ....149 L5
Moorson Av ALS/KID ST7 ....174 A9
Moorton Av BNG/LEV M19 ....40 C1
Moorton Pk BNG/LEV M19 ....40 C1
Moor Top Pl HTNM SK4 ....41 J5
Moorview Gdns ALS/KID ST7 ....189 N3
Moorwood Crs STHEL WA9 ....31 H4
Moorwood Dr SALE M33 ....38 B5
Moor Av STHEL WA9 ....71 H4
Moran Crs MCFLDS SK11 ....8 B6
Moran Rd MCFLDS SK11 ....8 B6
Moravian Fld DROY M43 * 28 G1
Morcott La SPK/HALE L24 ....60 D4
Moresby Cl RUNC WA7 ....63 J7
Moresby Dr DID/WITH M20 ....40 C8
Moreton Av BRAM/HZG SK7 ....71 J1
 SALE M33 ....38 B5
 STHEL WA9 ....31 H4
Moreton Cl WILM/AE SK9 ....189 K8
Moreton Dr ALS/KID ST7 ....187 M5
 HOLMCH CW4 ....131 N8
 POY/DIS SK12 ....73 M2
 SBCH CW11 ....171 P2
 WILM/AE SK9 ....71 N5
Moreton La OFTN SK2 ....42 B9
Moreton Rd BNG/LEV M19 ....28 E8
Moretons Meade
 NWCHW CW9 * 108 C5
Moreton St NWCHW CW9 ....12 B2
Moreville Cl NWCHE CW9 ....109 N9
Morgan Av WARRW/WOL WA2 ....33 M6
Morgan Cl CH/BCN CH1 ....121 J6
 CW/SHV CW2 ....184 G4
Morgan Pl RDSH SK5 ....41 N1
Morgan St STHEL WA9 ....22 B7
Morillon Rd IRL M44 ....27 N5
Morland Av NSTN CH64 ....77 M6
Morley Br FROD/HEL WA6 ....104 C8
Morley Cl CHNE CH2 ....122 C3
Morley Dr CONG CW12 ....155 M8
Morley Green Rd WILM/AE SK9 ...70 E5
Morley Rd RUNC WA7 ....14 E5
 WARRS WA4 ....48 C6
Morley St WARR WA1 ....19 G4
Mornant Av NWCHW CW8 ....109 J9
Morningside Cl DROY M43 * 28 E2
Morningside Dr DID/WITH M20 ....40 D8
Mornington Av CHD/CHDH SK8 ...55 M5
 EP CH65 ....7 H5
Mornington Cl SBCH CW11 ......171 J2
Mornington Rd CHD/CHDH SK8 ...55 M3
 SALE M33 ....38 C5
Morphany La WARRS WA4 ....64 A8
Morrell Rd WYTH/NTH M22 ....39 P8
Morreys La TPLY/KEL CW6 ....125 L5
Morris Av WARRS WA4 ....49 H5
Morris Cl RNFD/HAY WA11 ....22 E4
Morris Dr NWCHW CW8 ....108 F5
Morris Oak CHSW/BR CH4 * 142 G9
Morrison Cl WARRW/BUR WA5 ....47 L2
Morris Pk NWCHW CW8 ....109 K8
Morris St WDN WA8 ....40 C1
 STHEL WA9 ....22 C8
Morten Av WYTH/NTH M22 ....54 C2
Mortimer Av WARRN/WOL WA2 ...33 L8
Mortimer Dr SBCH CW11 ....171 P4
Mortlake Cl WDN WA8 ....143 J1
Mortlake Crs CHSE CH3 ....143 J1
Morton Av FROD/HEL WA6 ....105 H3
Morton Cl WARRW/BUR WA5 ......32 F8
Morton Rd MCFLDS SK11 ....9 H7
Morton St HTNM SK4 ....41 M4
Morven Av BRAM/HZG SK7 ....57 M4
Morven Cl WARRN/WOL WA2 ......33 P8
Morven Dr NTHM/RTH M23 ....54 C2
Moscow Rd EDGY/DAV SK3 ....41 L9
Moscow Rd East EDGY/DAV SK3 ..41 L9
Mosedale Cl NTHM/RTH M23 ......54 A1
Mosedale Gv RUNC WA7 * 63 K7
Moseldene Rd OFTN SK2 ....57 K2
Moseley Av RUNC WA7 ....49 J5
Moseley Rd CHD/CHDH SK8 ......55 P4
Moseley St EDGY/DAV SK3 ....16 E7
Mosley Cl HALE/TIMP WA15 ....38 C9
Mosley Rd HALE/TIMP WA15 ......53 M1
Mossack Av WYTH/NTH M22 ......54 F6
Moss Bnk CH/BCN CH1 ....121 H7
 CHD/CHDH SK8 ....72 C1
 WSFD CW7 ....149 K1
Moss Bank Rd WDN WA8 ....46 B8
Moss Bower Rd MCFLDS SK11 ...117 J8
Mossbray Av BNG/LEV M19 ....40 C1
Moss Brow MCFLDN SK10 ....95 L6
Moss Brow La KNUT WA16 ....66 D2
Moss Cl NSTN CH64 ....78 E5
 CW/HAS CW1 ....48 G5
Moss Cft CW/HAS CW1 ....169 P9
Mossdale Cl NTHM/RTH M23 ......54 A1
Mossdale Gv RUNC WA7 * 63 K7
 WARRW/BUR WA5 ....32 D9
Mossdale Rd NTHM/RTH M23 .....39 J7
 SALE M33 ....38 B7
Moss Dr MWCH CW10 ....151 K4
Mossfields ALS/KID ST7 ....189 K6
Mossfield Rd HALE/TIMP WA15 ...53 P1

Moss Flds ALS/KID ST7 ....187 L5
 CW/HAS CW1 ....169 P8
Mossford Av CW/HAS CW1 ....185 H1
Moss Ga GOL/RIS/CU WA3 ....35 H3
Moss Gn PART M31 ....37 L2
Moss Green Wy STHEL WA9 ....22 E8
Moss Gv CHSW/BR CH4 ....141 P4
 LYMM WA13 ....51 H3
 NEWUL ST5 ....201 N4
Mossgrove Rd
 HALE/TIMP WA15 ....53 K1
Moss Hall La TPLY/KEL CW6 ......147 N5
 WARRS WA4 ....48 C6
Moss Hey Dr NTHM/RTH M23 .....39 L7
Mosslands Cl GTS/LS CH66 ......102 A2
Moss La ALS/KID ST7 ....188 G4
 BRAM/HZG SK7 ....72 D7
 CONG CW12 ....154 B5
 CONG CW12 ....155 N4
 CW/HAS CW1 ....170 B6
 FROD/HEL WA6 ....105 M8
 FROD/HEL WA6 ....107 L7
 GOL/RIS/CU WA3 ....24 D4
 GOL/RIS/CU WA3 ....35 H5
 HALE/TIMP WA15 ....38 C9
 HALE/TIMP WA15 ....53 J3
 IRL M44 ....36 C3
 KNUT WA16 ....51 L9
 KNUT WA16 ....66 E9
 KNUT WA16 ....90 B1
 KNUT WA16 ....91 M9
 KNUT WA16 ....92 B2
 LYMM WA13 ....51 M9
 MCFLDN SK10 ....94 A3
 MCFLDS SK10 ....95 L5
 MCFLDS SK11 ....117 H7
 MCFLDS SK11 ....133 N1
 MWCH CW10 ....197 P6
 NANT CW5 ....197 P6
 NWCHE CW9 ....198 A6
 NWCHE CW9 ....8 E7
 NWCHW CW9 ....111 J5
 PART M31 ....36 B4
 SALE M33 ....38 C4
 SBCH CW11 ....171 J2
 STHEL WA9 ....22 B7
 TPLY/KEL CW6 ....146 F8
 WARRS WA4 ....54 L9
 WILM/AE SK9 ....93 K4
Mossley Ct CONG CW12 ....174 C1
Mossley Garth Cl CONG CW12 ...156 A9
Mossmere Rd CHD/CHDH SK8 ....55 M5
Moss Pl ALS/KID ST7 ....189 K5
Moss Rd CONG CW12 ....174 F3
 IRL M44 ....36 G2
 IRL M44 ....36 E1
 NWCHW CW8 ....12 B2
 PART M31 ....37 N4
 WARRS WA4 ....49 J4
 WARRS WA4 ....47 J8
Moss Side La GOL/RIS/CU WA3 ...35 M5
 NWCHE CW9 ....10 C2
 WARRS WA4 ....47 J8
Moss Side Rd IRL M44 ....36 C3
Moss Sq CW/HAS CW1 ....5 H3
 MCFLDS SK11 ....117 K8
Moss St NWCHW CW8 ....46 B8
 WDN WA8 ....46 B8
The Moss NWCHE CW9 ....109 N8
Mossvale GTS/LS CH66 ....79 P5
Moss View Rd MCFLDS SK11 .....116 C8
Moss Wy ALS/KID ST7 ....187 L5
 SALE M33 ....38 B4
Mosswood Pk DID/WITH M20 .....40 C8
Mosswood Rd HALE/TIMP WA15 ..71 N5
Moston Gv CHNE CH2 ....121 N5
 RDSH SK5 ....41 N3
 SBCH CW11 ....171 J3
Mostyn Av CHD/CHDH SK8 ....55 P4
Mostyn Pl CH/BCN CH1 ....121 H5
Mostyn Rd BRAM/HZG SK7 ....57 M4
Mostyn Sq NSTN CH64 ....77 M6
Motcombe Farm Rd
 CHD/CHDH SK8 ....55 K6
Motcombe Gv CHD/CHDH SK8 ....55 J5
Motcombe Rd CHD/CHDH SK8 ....55 J5
Mothershead Cl WDN WA8 ....21 G5
Mothershead St WDN WA8 ....21 G5
Mottershead Av
 WYTH/NTH M22 ....54 C2
Mottram Av CCHDY M21 ....39 M3
Mottram Cl CHD/CHDH SK8 ......56 A2
 WARRS WA4 ....48 F4
Mottram Dr HALE/TIMP WA15 ....53 L2
 NANT CW5 ....196 E1
Mottram Fold STKP SK1 ....17 G6
Mottram Rd SALE M33 ....39 G6
 WILM/AE SK9 ....93 K4
Moughland La RUNC WA7 ....14 E6
Moulders La WARR WA1 ....18 E6
Mouldsworth Av DID/WITH M20 ..40 A1
 HTNM SK4 ....41 L6
Mouldsworth Cl NWCHE CW9 ...109 N8
Moulton Cl NWCHE CW9 ....88 C1
 RUNC WA7 ....48 F9
Mountain Ash Cl SALE M33 ....38 C4
Mountain Cl STKP SK1 ....17 K3
Mountain Vw CHSW/BR CH4 ....142 A4
 FROD/HEL WA6 ....105 H1
Mountbatten Cl CW/SHV CW2 ....4 A9
Mountbatten St GTN M18 ....28 C4
Mountbatten Wy CONG CW12 ...155 M7

Mount Cl NANT CW5 ....10 E4
Mount Dr MPL/ROM SK6 ....58 D2
Mount Farm Wy GTS/LS CH66 ...101 N2
Mountfield Rd BRAM/HZG SK7 ....72 E1
 EDGY/DAV SK3 ....41 K9
Mount Gv WYTH/NTH M22 ....54 E3
Mount Pl CHSE CH3 ....14 H3
Mount Pleasant ALS/KID ST7 ....189 J7
 AUD/MAD/W CW3 ....217 J1
 BRAM/HZG SK7 ....57 K4
 CHSE CH2 ....82 A9
 CHSW/BR CH4 * 160 D2
 CW/HAS CW1 ....170 A9
 CW/HAS CW1 ....186 B4
 MCFLDN SK10 ....8 A1
 MCFLDN SK10 ....95 P4
 NEWUL ST5 ....201 P9
 WDN WA8 ....20 A9
 WILM/AE SK9 ....93 K4
Mount Pleasant Av FLINT CH6 ....98 A7
 STHEL WA9 ....22 B7
Mount Pleasant Dr WSFD CW7 ...149 J5
Mount Pleasant Rd
 ALS/KID ST7 ....189 K1
 DTN/ASHW M34 ....29 M7
 NWCHE CW9 ....128 C1
Mount Pleasant St
 DTN/ASHW M34 ....29 M7
Mount Pleasant CHSW/BR CH4 ..142 B3
Mount Rd ALS/KID ST7 ....189 K7
 GTN M18 ....16 B2
 HYDE SK14 ....43 M2
 RUNC WA7 ....62 D6
Mount St NEWUL ST5 ....201 P9
 WDN WA8 ....45 P5
Mount Ter MCFLDS SK11 ....9 N4
 ALS/KID ST7 ....180 C1
The Mount ALS/KID ST7 ....189 J7
 ALT WA14 ....53 H2
 CHSE CH3 ....3 K4
 CONG CW12 ....155 J8
 HALE/TIMP WA15 ....53 N7
 NEWUL ST5 ....201 P9
 WDN WA8 ....88 A6
Mount Wy CHSE CH3 ....144 A6
Mourne Cl GTS/LS CH66 ....79 N5
Mowbray Av RNFD/HAY WA11 .....22 A4
 SALE M33 ....38 G5
Mow Cop Rd ALS/KID ST7 ....189 L7
Mow Cop Trail MCFLDS SK11 ....157 N7
Mowcroft
 WARRW/BUR WA5 ....46 F4
Mow La ALS/KID ST7 ....189 H7
 CONG CW12 ....174 F3
Mowpen Brow KNUT WA16 ....51 H9
Moxon Av WARRS WA4 ....45 K5
Moyles Cl WDN WA8 ....45 K5
Mudhouse La KNUT WA16 ....100 C2
Mudhurst La POY SK12 ....75 J5
Muirfield Av MPL/ROM SK6 ....42 F4
Muirfield Cl NWCHE CW9 ....110 A7
 WARRN/WOL WA2 ....34 B5
 WILM/AE SK9 ....71 M6
Muirfield Dr MCFLDN SK10 ....95 J9
 WSFD CW7 ....128 D9
Muir Rd CH/BCN CH1 ....121 H8
Mulberry Cl GOL/RIS/CU WA3 ....25 H7
Mulberry Cl CHD/CHDH SK8 ......55 L8
 CHNE CH2 ....104 C1
Mulberry Gv WARRS WA4 * 48 F6
Mulberry Rd MCFLDN SK10 ....9 H2
Mulberry Rd CW/SHV CW2 ......184 E6
 SALE M33 ....38 A2
Mulcaster Ct CW/HAS CW1 ....186 B5
Mulcrow Cl STHEL WA9 ....22 C8
Mullace Rd WYTH/NTH M22 ....54 E5
Mullein Cl GOL/RIS/CU WA3 ......24 F1
 WARRW/BUR WA5 * 48 B9
Mullins Av NEWLW WA12 ....23 N4
Mullion Cl RDSH SK5 ....41 N3
Mullion Dr HALE/TIMP WA15 .....38 B9
Mullion Gv WARRN/WOL WA2 .....34 B7
Mulsford La MALPAS SY14 ....202 A8
Munro Av WYTH/NTH M22 ....55 H5
Murdishaw Av RUNC WA7 ....63 J8
Murray Gv STHEL WA9 ....31 J1
 HALE/TIMP WA15 ....53 J5
Murphy Gv STHEL WA9 ....22 C5
Murray Cl MCFLDN SK10 ....116 C3
Murrayfield Dr NANT CW5 ....197 L2
Murrayfield Rd NANT CW5 ....197 L2
Mursery Av BURS/TUN ST6 ......189 L9
Musbury Av CHD/CHDH SK8 ......56 A5
Museum St WARR WA1 ....18 E4
Musgrave Rd WYTH/NTH M22 ....54 F1
Mustard La GOL/RIS/CU WA3 .....25 K9
Muter Av WYTH/NTH M22 ....55 H5
Mycdleton La
 WARRN/WOL WA2 ....33 L2
Myrica Gv CHNE CH2 ....122 C3
Myrtle Av NANT CW5 ....23 N7
 RNFD/HAY WA11 ....22 F2
Myrtle Gv CHNE CH2 ....122 D8
 DTN/ASHW M34 ....28 F6
 WARRS WA4 ....48 F4
Myrtle Rd PART M31 ....36 C6
 CW/SHV CW2 ....4 E5
 EDGY/DAV SK3 ....41 J8
 EP CH65 ....80 E6
Mythorne Av IRL M44 ....36 B5
Mytton Dr NANT CW5 ....196 H1

N

RUNC WA7 85 H1
WARRS WA4 64 G6
WARRS WA4 85 P5
Northwood Av CHD/CHDH SK8 56 A4
MWCH CW10 151 L5
NEWLW WA12 24 B5
Northwood Gv SALE M33 38 E4
Northwood La KNUT WA16 66 F5
Northwood Rd RUNC WA7 62 C4
Norton Av CHSW/BR CH4 141 P4
DTN/ASHW M34 28 G6
SALE M33 38 A3
WARRW/BUR WA5 47 J2
WGTN/LGST M12 28 B6
Norton Ga RUNC WA7 62 G6
Norton Gv HTNM SK4 41 J7
STHEL WA9 30 C1
Norton Hl RUNC WA7 62 G5
RUNC WA7 62 G6
Norton Rd CHSE CH3 122 D9
Norton's La CHSE CH3 105 H9
TPLY/KEL CW6 125 L4
Norton Station Rd RUNC WA7 63 H6
Norton St MCFLDN SK10 9 G3
Norton Vw RUNC WA7 62 E6
Norton Village RUNC WA7 63 H6
Norton Wy SBCH CW11 171 J2
Nortonwood La RUNC WA7 62 G5
Norview Dr DID/WITH M20 40 C9
Norville GTS/LS CH66 79 P6
Norway Gv RDSH SK5 * 41 N4
Norwell Rd WYTH/NTH M22 54 G2
Norwich Av DTN/ASHW M34 29 M8
GOL/RIS/CU WA3 24 F1
Norwich Dr GTS/LS CH66 102 A4
Norwood Av BRAM/HZG SK7 72 C1
DID/WITH M20 40 E4
GOL/RIS/CU WA3 24 G2
MPL/ROM SK6 58 B8
Norwood Dr CHSW/BR CH4 142 D5
HALE/TIMP WA15 53 P2
Norwood Rd CHD/CHDH SK8 55 K1
OFTN SK2 57 H3
Nottingham Av RDSH SK5 42 B2
Nottingham Cl RAIN/WH L35 30 B3
RDSH SK5 42 B2
WARR WA1 49 M1
Nottingham Dr RDSH SK5 42 B2
Nova Ct CW/HAS CW1 4 C1
Nuffield Rd WYTH/NTH M22 54 G3
Nuneham Av DID/WITH M20 40 D1
Nun House Cl WSFD CW7 129 J9
Nun House Dr WSFD CW7 150 B1
Nunn St STHEL WA9 22 B6
Nunsmere Cl WSFD CW7 150 B1
Nun's Rd CH/BCN CH1 2 C5
Nursery Av HALE/TIMP WA15 53 J7
Nursery Cl ALS/KID ST7 188 F7
OFTN SK2 42 C9
SALE M33 38 G4
WDN WA8 46 B4
Nursery Dr BIDD ST8 175 K7
POY/DIS SK12 73 K2
Nursery Gv PART M31 36 E4
Nursery La CONG CW12 155 N8
EDGY/DAV SK3 41 H9
MCFLDN SK10 92 F8
MCFLDS SK11 115 J9
WILM/AE SK9 71 H8
Nursery Rd ALS/KID ST7 188 G3
CHD/CHDH SK8 55 P6
CW/HAS CW1 187 H6
HTNM SK4 16 A2
MCFLDN SK10 * 95 L6
NWCHW CW8 109 K1
STHEL WA9 30 C1
The Nursery NWCHW CW8 109 L6
Nutfield Av CW/HAS CW1 185 H1
Nutgrove Av STHEL WA9 * 30 C1
Nutgrove Hall Dr STHEL WA9 30 C1
Nutgrove Rd STHEL WA9 30 B2
Nuthurst Gdns NANT CW5 10 D6
Nutsford V WGTN/LGST M12 28 A5
Nut St STHEL WA9 30 C1
Nuttall Ct GOL/RIS/CU WA3 34 D4
Nuttall St IRL M44 36 D2
OP/CLY M11 28 A2

O

Oadby Cl WGTN/LGST M12 28 A5
Oak Av ALS/KID ST7 188 A6
CHD/CHDH SK8 55 P5
GOL/RIS/CU WA3 24 D1
GTN M18 28 F5
HTNM SK4 41 J6
IRL M44 36 C3
MCFLDS SK11 116 G7
MPL/ROM SK6 43 H6
NEWLW WA12 23 N6
POY/DIS SK12 59 L9
RNFD/HAY WA11 23 J2
WILM/AE SK9 71 H9
WSFD CW7 149 M3
Oak Bank Cl NANT CW5 197 M3
Oak Bank Dr MCFLDN SK10 95 P4
Oak Bank La CHNE CH2 122 D4
Oak Cl WILM/AE SK9 71 H8
Oakcroft Wy WYTH/NTH M22 54 G1
Oakdale Av FROD/HEL WA6 84 B7
WARRS WA4 48 F6
Oakdale Cl CHSW/BR CH4 140 F7
CW/SHV CW2 198 G5
Oakdale Dr CHD/CHDH SK8 55 K5
DID/WITH M20 40 D7
Oakdene Av CHD/CHDH SK8 55 K8
GTS/LS CH66 79 N8
HTNM SK4 41 L3
WARR WA1 34 D9
Oakdene Ct SBCH CW11 * 171 N3
Oakdene Crs MPL/ROM SK6 43 L9
Oakdene Gdns MPL/ROM SK6 43 L9
Oakdene Rd HALE/TIMP WA15 38 E8
MPL/ROM SK6 43 L9
Oakdene Wy TPLY/KEL CW6 166 A1
Oak Dr ALS/KID ST7 188 G2
BRAM/HZG SK7 56 C8
DTN/ASHW M34 28 G5
MPL/ROM SK6 58 B1
MWCH CW10 151 K3
RUNC WA7 62 A7
WHITCH SY13 213 L7
Oakenbank La MCFLDN SK10 96 A5
Oakenclough Cl WILM/AE SK9 71 M4
Oaker Av DID/WITH M20 39 P4
Oakfield SALE M33 38 D3
Oakfield Av CHD/CHDH SK8 55 N1
CHNE CH2 121 P3
KNUT WA16 90 G2
NANT CW5 207 J3
Oakfield Cl BRAM/HZG SK7 72 E2
NANT CW5 207 J3
STHEL WA9 30 C1
WILM/AE SK9 93 K2
Oakfield Dr CHNE CH2 121 P3
WDN WA8 44 G7
Oakfield Gv GTN M18 28 D5
Oakfield Ri HOLMCH CW4 131 N8
Oakfield Rd CH/BCN CH1 120 F7
DID/WITH M20 40 B5
EDGY/DAV SK3 56 F2
GTS/LS CH66 79 J5
HALE/TIMP WA15 53 J2
KNUT WA16 111 M1
POY/DIS SK12 73 M2
WILM/AE SK9 93 K3
Oakfield St HALE/TIMP WA15 53 J2
Oak Gv CHD/CHDH SK8 55 N2
EP CH65 102 C1
NANT CW5 196 F4
POY/DIS SK12 73 K2
Oakham Rd DTN/ASHW M34 * 29 N8
Oakhill Cl MCFLDN SK10 95 H9
Oakhouse Dr CCHDY M21 39 L1
Oak House La WSFD CW7 149 K2
Oakhurst Cha WILM/AE SK9 93 J3
Oakhurst Dr CHD/CHDH SK8 56 B2
CW/SHV CW2 185 H9
Oakland Av BNG/LEV M19 40 F4
CW/HAS CW1 186 A4
OFTN SK2 57 J1
Oaklands CHSE CH3 122 G6
RAIN/WH L35 30 B5
Oaklands Av CHD/CHDH SK8 56 A5
CHSE CH3 164 A7
MPL/ROM SK6 43 P8
Oaklands Cl WILM/AE SK9 71 N5
Oaklands Ct STHEL WA9 31 H4
Oaklands Crs CHSE CH3 164 A6
Oaklands Dr BRAM/HZG SK7 57 L6
LYMM WA13 50 D5
SALE M33 38 D3
Oaklands Rd GOL/RIS/CU WA3 25 H2
KNUT WA16 91 K7
Oakland St WARR WA1 33 P9
WDN WA8 61 N2
Oak La MCFLDN SK10 95 N7
MCFLDS SK11 134 D6
NWCHW CW8 127 J1
WILM/AE SK9 71 H8
Oaklea Av CHNE CH2 122 A7
Oak Lea Av WILM/AE SK9 71 J9
Oaklea Rd SALE M33 38 B2
Oakleigh KNUT WA16 90 G6
Oakleigh Av BNG/LEV M19 40 G1
HALE/TIMP WA15 38 D9
Oakleigh Ct CONG CW12 155 H7
Oakleigh Ri NWCHW CW8 12 C1
Oakleigh Rd CHD/CHDH SK8 55 N7
Oakley Cl SBCH CW11 171 M1
Oakley St CW/HAS CW1 4 E1
Oakley Vls HTNM SK4 41 J5
Oak Ldg BRAM/HZG SK7 * 56 F8
Oak Meadow NWCHW CW8 108 G5
Oak Meadows Ct RAIN/WH L35 30 D7
Oakmere Cl SBCH CW11 171 L2
WYTH/NTH M22 54 F3
Oakmere Dr CHSE CH3 143 K2
GTS/LS CH66 102 B4
WARRW/BUR WA5 47 K4
Oakmere Rd CHD/CHDH SK8 55 P3
WILM/AE SK9 71 M1
WSFD CW7 149 K2
Oakmere St RUNC WA7 14 E3
Oak Ms WILM/AE SK9 71 L5
Oakmoore RUNC WA7 63 K2
Oakmoor Rd NTHM/RTH M23 54 C1
Oak Mt DID/WITH M20 * 40 C6
Oak Rd CHD/CHDH SK8 55 N1
CHSW/BR CH4 142 B4
DID/WITH M20 40 C3
GTS/LS CH66 79 J4
HALE/TIMP WA15 53 J4
LYMM WA13 50 C4
MCFLDN SK10 94 B4
MCFLDS SK11 114 C2
PART M31 36 C6
SALE M33 38 G4
WARRW/BUR WA5 47 K4
Oaks Cl STHEL WA9 31 J5
The Oaks Dr CHNE CH2 121 M4
Oaks Pl WDN WA8 21 G4
The Oaks CHD/CHDH SK8 55 J5
HOLMCH CW4 132 A3
Oakston Av RAIN/WH L35 30 C6
Oak St ALS/KID ST7 173 H9
BRAM/HZG SK7 57 K4
CW/SHV CW2 5 F4
DTN/ASHW M34 29 M3
EDGY/DAV SK3 41 J8
EP CH65 80 E6
GOL/RIS/CU WA3 34 B1
NWCHE CW9 13 H1
SBCH CW11 171 J1
STHEL WA9 22 C9
Oakthorn Gv RNFD/HAY WA11 22 G3
Oak Tree Cl CW/HAS CW1 5 K1
OFTN SK2 42 C8
Oaktree Cl NWCHW CW8 87 K9
TPLY/KEL CW6 147 H8
Oak Tree Ct CHD/CHDH SK8 55 M1
Oaktree Ct CHNE CH2 122 B8
Oak Tree Dr CW/HAS CW1 5 K1
Oak Tree Ga AUD/MAD/W CW3 216 G2
Oaktree La ALS/KID ST7 201 N2
Oak Tree La MWCH CW10 131 K4
Oak Vw KNUT WA16 90 G4
MCFLDS SK11 134 D6
SPK/HALE L24 60 A3
Oakway DID/WITH M20 40 D8
Oakways WARRS WA4 64 F1
Oak Wharf Ms WARRS WA4 * 48 E7
Oakwood SALE M33 37 P4
Oakwood Av CHD/CHDH SK8 55 K2
DTN/ASHW M34 29 K2
WARR WA1 19 J2
WILM/AE SK9 70 G8
Oakwood Ct ALT WA14 52 F7
Oakwood Crs CW/SHV CW2 184 E4
SBCH CW11 172 B3
Oakwood Dr MCFLDN SK10 95 J7
Oakwood Ga GOL/RIS/CU WA3 34 E4
Oakwood La ALT WA14 52 E6
NWCHW CW8 109 J2
SBCH CW11 170 G1
Oak Wood Rd KNUT WA16 67 M4
Oakwood Rd MPL/ROM SK6 43 J7
POY/DIS SK12 * 59 H9
Oatfield Cl WHITCH SY13 213 M7
Oathills MALPAS SY14 204 A1
Oathills Cl TPLY/KEL CW6 147 H9
Oathills Dr TPLY/KEL CW6 147 H9
Oatlands WILM/AE SK9 93 K5
Oatlands Rd WYTH/NTH M22 54 E5
Oat Market NANT CW5 196 D1
Oat St STKP SK1 41 P9
Oban Crs EDGY/DAV SK3 56 D3
Oban Dr SALE M33 39 H5
Oban Gv WARRN/WOL WA2 34 B5
Obelisk Wy CONG CW12 155 L7
O'brien Gv STHEL WA9 22 C5
Occlestone Cl SALE M33 39 H7
Occupiers La BRAM/HZG SK7 * 57 P6
Ocean St ALT WA14 52 F1
O'connell Cl RNFD/HAY WA11 22 G3
Odell St OP/CLY M11 * 28 B2
Odette St GTN M18 28 C5
Offerton Dr OFTN SK2 42 C9
Offerton Fold OFTN SK2 42 B9
Offerton Gn OFTN SK2 57 N1
Offerton La OFTN SK2 42 B8
Offerton Rd BRAM/HZG SK7 57 N4
Offerton St STKP SK1 42 A6
Offley Av SBCH CW11 171 N2
Offley Rd SBCH CW11 171 N2
Ogden Gv CHD/CHDH SK8 * 55 H3
Ogden La OP/CLY M11 28 D2
Ogden Rd BRAM/HZG SK7 72 D1
Ogden Sq DUK SK16 29 P1
Ogden St DID/WITH M20 40 C5
Oil Sites Rd EP CH65 7 G2
O'keeffe Rd STHEL WA9 22 A5
Okehampton Crs SALE M33 38 A3
Okell St RUNC WA7 14 E3
Old Applecroft SBCH CW11 171 H4
Old Bank Cl MPL/ROM SK6 42 F5
Old Boston RNFD/HAY WA11 23 L2
Old Broadway DID/WITH M20 40 C3
Oldbrook Fold
HALE/TIMP WA15 53 M3
Old Butt La ALS/KID ST7 188 F6
Oldcastle Av DID/WITH M20 40 B1
Oldcastle La MALPAS SY14 202 F6
Old Chads La WHITCH SY13 205 H6
Old Chapel St EDGY/DAV SK3 41 L9
Old Cherry La LYMM WA13 50 A9
Old Chester Ct NANT CW5 182 F2
Old Chester Rd
FROD/HEL WA6 105 H1
GTS/LS CH66 79 P9
NANT CW5 182 E2
WARRS WA4 48 B8
Old Church Cl EP CH65 * 7 F1
Old Coach Rd CHSE CH3 * 179 H6
MALPAS SY14 192 B1
TPLY/KEL CW6 125 J6
Oldcott Crs ALS/KID ST7 189 L8
Oldcott Dr ALS/KID ST7 189 L8
The Old Ctyd WYTH/NTH M22 * 55 H2
Old Croft Ms STKP SK1 42 A9
Old Farm Cl NSTN CH64 78 E5
Old Farm Crs DROY M43 28 F1
Old Farm Dr OFTN SK2 57 M1
Oldfield Crs CHSW/BR CH4 142 B5
Oldfield Dr CHSE CH3 122 D9
HALE/TIMP WA15 53 K1
KNUT WA16 91 L1
Oldfield Gv SALE M33 38 F3
Oldfield Rd ALT WA14 52 E2
EP CH65 6 D5
LYMM WA13 50 C3
SALE M33 38 F3
SBCH CW11 171 L6
Old Gardens St STKP SK1 17 H6
The Old Gdn HALE/TIMP WA15 38 E9
Oldgate WDN WA8 45 J9
Old Gate Cl MWCH CW10 151 H3
Old Gorse Cl CW/SHV CW2 184 E5
Old Hall Cl WARRS WA4 48 C7
Old Hall Ct CHSE CH3 124 E4
MALPAS SY14 204 A3
Old Hall Crs WILM/AE SK9 71 N3
Old Hall Dr EP CH65 6 D7
GTN M18 28 D5
OFTN SK2 57 L1
Old Hall Gdns CHNE CH2 121 P8
Old Hall La BRAM/HZG SK7 72 D5
CHNE CH2 104 B1
KNUT WA16 89 L2
MPL/ROM SK6 58 G2
Old Hall Pk CHSE CH3 122 G6
Old Hall Pl CH/BCN CH1 * 2 D5
Old Hall Rd CHD/CHDH SK8 55 J1
NWCHE CW9 110 A7
SALE M33 39 H4
WARRW/BUR WA5 32 G8
Old Hall St DUK SK16 29 N2
Oldhall St MALPAS SY14 204 A3
Old Hall St MCFLDN SK10 8 E2
OP/CLY M11 * 28 E2
Oldham Av STKP SK1 42 A7
Oldham Dr MPL/ROM SK6 42 F4
Oldhams Hl NWCHW CW8 12 E1
Oldham Sq NM/HAY SK22 * 59 N8
Oldham's Ri MCFLDN SK10 95 K9
Oldham St DTN/ASHW M34 29 J7
MCFLDN SK10 95 P5
RDSH SK5 * 41 M1
WARRS WA4 48 F4
Old Higher Rd WDN WA8 60 D1
Oldhill Cl ALS/KID ST7 201 P2
Old Hutte La SPK/HALE L24 60 A1
Oldknow Rd MPL/ROM SK6 58 E1
Old La CHSW/BR CH4 160 G7
NWCHE CW9 87 L2
NWCHE CW9 129 L1
NWCHW CW8 108 B2
OP/CLY M11 28 D2
RAIN/WH L35 30 A6
Old Lansdowne Rd
DID/WITH M20 40 A4
Old Liverpool Rd
WARRW/BUR WA5 48 A3
Old Malt La DID/WITH M20 40 B1
Old Market Pl ALT WA14 53 H2
WARR WA1 18 C5
Old Meadow Dr
DTN/ASHW M34 29 M4
Old Meadow La
HALE/TIMP WA15 53 M4
Old Mill Av STHEL WA9 31 J3
Old Mill Cl LYMM WA13 51 J1
Old Mill La BRAM/HZG SK7 57 N7
MCFLDS SK11 9 G7
WARRS WA4 65 J9
Old Mill Rd SBCH CW11 171 P3
Old Moat La DID/WITH M20 40 C2
Oldmoor Rd MPL/ROM SK6 42 D3
Old Moss La GOL/RIS/CU WA3 26 D3
TPLY/KEL CW6 145 K4
Old Nook La RNFD/HAY WA11 22 C3
Old Oak Dr DTN/ASHW M34 29 N6
Old Oak St DID/WITH M20 40 C5
Old Orch NWCHE CW9 87 L1
WILM/AE SK9 71 J7
The Old Orch HALE/TIMP WA15 38 E8
The Old Paddock
HOLMCH CW4 132 C3
Old Paper Mill La FLINT CH6 98 E9
Old Park Rd CW/HAS CW1 186 B9
Old Pasture Cl OFTN SK2 42 D9
Old Pearl La CHSE CH3 143 K1
Old Pewterspear La
WARRS WA4 64 G2
Old Port Sq CH/BCN CH1 * 2 B3
Old Quay Cl NSTN CH64 77 J6
Old Quay La NSTN CH64 77 K6
Old Quay St RUNC WA7 15 H1
Old Rectory Gdns
CHD/CHDH SK8 55 M2
Old River Cl IRL M44 27 N7
Old Rd ALS/KID ST7 201 H4
AUD/MAD/W CW3 211 M3
CHD/CHDH SK8 55 P1
HTNM SK4 41 M5
NWCHE CW9 109 M1
WARRS WA4 48 D3
WILM/AE SK9 71 K6
WILM/AE SK9 71 M3
Old School Cl NSTN CH64 77 M8
Old School House La
WARRN/WOL WA2 33 K1
Old Seals Wy CH/BCN CH1 121 K9
Old Smithy La LYMM WA13 50 C5
Old Stack Yd CHSE CH3 123 M6
Old Upton La WDN WA8 45 L3
Old Vicarage Gdns
AUD/MAD/W CW3 216 G1
Old Vicarage La NWCHW CW8 109 L7
Old Vicarage Rd NSTN CH64 78 E5
Old Wargrave Rd NEWLW WA12 23 M6
Old Warrington Rd
NWCHE CW9 110 A2
Old Whint Rd RNFD/HAY WA11 22 E3
Oldwood Rd NTHM/RTH M23 54 C4
Old Wool La CHD/CHDH SK8 55 P3
Old Wrexham Rd
CHSW/BR CH4 142 E3
O'leary St WARRN/WOL WA2 19 G1
Olga Rd STHEL WA9 31 H1
Olive Dr NSTN CH64 77 L5
Oliver Cl MCFLDN SK10 95 L6
Oliver La GTS/LS CH66 79 P9
Olive Rd HALE/TIMP WA15 38 D8
NSTN CH64 77 L5
Oliver St EDGY/DAV SK3 17 G7
WARRN/WOL WA2 18 D3
Olive Shapley Av DID/WITH M20 40 C5
Ollerbarrow Rd
HALE/TIMP WA15 53 J5
Ollersett Av NM/HAY SK22 59 N7
Ollersett La NM/HAY SK22 59 P7
Ollershaw La NWCHE CW9 88 C9
Ollerton Av SALE M33 38 A3
Ollerton Cl WARRS WA4 49 K4
Ollerton Rd WILM/AE SK9 71 M1
Ollier Av WGTN/LGST M12 28 A7
Ollier St WDN WA8 21 G5
Olney Av WYTH/NTH M22 54 F1
Olwen Crs RDSH SK5 28 F9
Omega Bvd WARRW/BUR WA5 32 B8
Omer Dr BNG/LEV M19 40 F1
One Oak La WILM/AE SK9 71 P7
Onslow Rd CH/BCN CH1 120 G7
EDGY/DAV SK3 16 A7
Onston La NWCHW CW8 108 A3
Opal St BNG/LEV M19 28 B9
Openshaw La IRL M44 36 D2
Orange Gv WARRN/WOL WA2 33 P6
Orbital Wy DTN/ASHW M34 29 K6
Orchard Av CHF/WBR SK23 75 P7
GTN M18 28 E5
LYMM WA13 50 F4
NWCHW CW8 86 A9
PART M31 36 E4
Orchard Brow GOL/RIS/CU WA3 35 P6
Orchard Cl CHD/CHDH SK8 56 C8
CHNE CH2 121 N6
FROD/HEL WA6 83 N7
GTS/LS CH66 102 B3
HOLMCH CW4 132 B2
MCFLDS SK11 8 B7
MWCH CW10 151 J3
NWCHE CW9 88 G7
NWCHW CW8 108 F3
NWCHW CW8 109 K1
POY/DIS SK12 73 L3
RNFD/HAY WA11 22 B2
TPLY/KEL CW6 166 C9
WILM/AE SK9 71 H9
WSFD CW7 149 M3
Orchard Ct CHSE CH3 143 J1
CW/HAS CW1 186 B3
OFTN SK2 * 57 K1
Orchard Crs ALS/KID ST7 188 F7
MCFLDN SK10 93 H7
NANT CW5 196 F4
Orchard Cft CHSE CH3 122 F6
Orchard Dene NWCHW CW8 107 P7
Orchard Dr HALE/TIMP WA15 53 L4
NSTN CH64 77 L8
NWCHW CW8 86 F8
WILM/AE SK9 71 N3
Orchard Gdns NWCHW CW8 108 D3
TPLY/KEL CW6 166 A1
Orchard Gn WILM/AE SK9 93 K4
Orchard Gv CHSE CH3 177 H7
DID/WITH M20 40 A3
Orchard Hvn GTS/LS CH66 102 A3
Orchard La GTS/LS CH66 79 L5
Orchard Park La CHNE CH2 82 B9
Orchard Pl FROD/HEL WA6 83 J9
HALE/TIMP WA15 38 E9
POY/DIS SK12 * 73 K2
SALE M33 38 E3
Orchard Ri NWCHE CW9 128 F3
Orchard Rd CHF/WBR SK23 75 P7
EP CH65 102 C2
HALE/TIMP WA15 53 J2
LYMM WA13 51 H2
MPL/ROM SK6 43 N6
Orchard Rd East
WYTH/NTH M22 39 N6
Orchard Rd West
WYTH/NTH M22 39 N6
The Orchards CW/SHV CW2 198 B3
KNUT WA16 88 F7
Orchard St CH/BCN CH1 2 B2
CW/HAS CW1 4 D1
DID/WITH M20 40 A3
NANT CW5 197 L1
NWCHE CW9 13 J2
STKP SK1 17 H4
WARR WA1 19 F5
WARRN/WOL WA2 34 B6
WARRS WA4 48 E7
The Orchard CHSE CH3 143 J2
FROD/HEL WA6 104 G2
NWCHW CW8 * 109 K1
Orchard V EDGY/DAV SK3 56 C1
Orchard Wk RUNC WA7 * 62 D7
Orchard Wy TPLY/KEL CW6 125 J6
WDN WA8 44 G4
Orchid Cl CHSE CH3 143 J4
IRL M44 27 L9
Orchid Wy STHEL WA9 31 N1
Orchil Cl GTS/LS CH66 79 L7
Ordnance Av GOL/RIS/CU WA3 34 G4
Ordsall Cl SBCH CW11 171 L6
Orford Av POY/DIS SK12 59 H9
WARRN/WOL WA2 19 F1
Orford Cl MPL/ROM SK6 58 C8
Orford Gn WARRN/WOL WA2 33 N7
Orford La WARRN/WOL WA2 18 E2
Orford Rd WARRN/WOL WA2 33 N8
Orford St WARR WA1 18 E5
Oriel Cl OFTN SK2 57 H1
Oriel Rd DID/WITH M20 40 B4
Oriole Cl ECCL WA10 30 A1
Orion Bvd WARRW/BUR WA5 32 B7
Orkney Av ALS/KID ST7 189 P8
Orkney Cl EP CH65 102 E3
NTHM/RTH M23 54 C3
RNFD/HAY WA11 22 B2
WDN WA8 46 C4
MCFLDN SK10 94 G5
Orme Cl MCFLDN SK10 117 K1
Orme Crs MCFLDN SK10 117 K1
Ormerod Cl MPL/ROM SK6 42 E7
SBCH CW11 171 P4
Orme St STKP SK1 * 42 A6
WILM/AE SK9 93 J4
Ormonde Rd CHNE CH2 121 M7
Ormonde St CH/BCN CH1 * 3 G2
Ormsby Av GTN M18 28 B5
Ormsby Cl EDGY/DAV SK3 56 E3
Orms Gill Pl OFTN SK2 * 57 L1
Ormside Gv HTNM SK4 31 J1
Ormskirk Av DID/WITH M20 40 A2
Ormskirk Rd RDSH SK5 41 N2
Orphanage St HTNM SK4 17 F1
Orrell Cl WARRW/BUR WA5 47 L1
Orrell St OP/CLY M11 * 28 D1
STHEL WA9 22 A6
Orrishmere Rd CHD/CHDH SK8 55 P4

Orthes Gv HTNM SK4 ....41 L3
Orton Av NTHM/RTH M25 ....39 K7
Orton Cl WSFD CW7 * 129 H7
Orton Rd NTHM/RTH M23 ....39 K7
Orville Dr BNG/LEV M19 ....40 G1
Orville St STHEL WA9 ....31 L1
Orwell Av DTN/ASHW M34 ....28 G6
  NTH/NTH M22 ....54 F1
Orwell Cl STHEL WA9 ....30 F5
  WILM/AE SK9 ....71 H8
Osborne Av WARRN/WOL WA2 ....33 N7
Osborne Cl SBCH CW11 ....171 J4
Osborne Ct CW/CHDH SK8 ....55 J4
  CW/SHV CW2 ....198 B3
Osborne Rd DTN/ASHW M34 ....29 H5
  GOL/RIS/CU WA3 * 25 M6
  HALE/TIMP WA15 ....53 J2
  OFTN SK2 ....41 N9
  WARRS WA4 ....48 D6
Osborne Ter SALE M33 ....42 B5
Osbourne St MPL/ROM SK6 ....38 E4
Osbourne Pl ALT WA14 ....53 H3
Osbourne St DID/WITH M20.... ....40 B5
Osier Cl CHNE CH2 ....104 C1
Osmere Cl WHITCH SY13 ....213 N4
Osprey Av WSFD CW7 ....149 L5
Osprey Cl MWCH CW10 ....151 K5
  RUNC WA7 ....
  WARRN/WOL WA2 ....33 P5
Osprey Dr IRL M44 ....27 N6
  WILM/AE SK9 ....71 L6
Osprey Vw ALS/KID ST7 ....189M5
Ossett Cl RUNC WA7 ....63 J6
Osmere Cl SALR CW11 ....171 L1
Ostler's La KNUT WA16 ....70 A7
O'Sullivan Crs RNFD/HAY WA11....22 C4
Oswald St RDSH SK5 ....28 F6
Otley Gv EDGY/DAV SK3 ....56 D3
Ottawa Ct NTHM/RTH M23 ....54 D3
Otterburn Pl OFTN SK2 ....57 K1
Otters Bnk WSFD CW7 ....149 J1
Otterspool Rd MPL/ROM SK6 ....42 G7
Oughterton Crs LYMM WA13 ....51 H4
Oughtrington La LYMM WA13 ....50 C5
Oughtrington Vw LYMM WA13...51 H5
Oulton Av CHSE CH5 ....121 P5
  SALE M33 ....39 H3
Oulton Dr CONG CW12 ....155 H7
Oulton Mill La TPLY/KEL CW6 ...147 L3
Oulton Pl CH/BCN CH1 ....2 E5
Ousel Nest NWCHW CW8 ....107 P8
Out La CHSE CH5 ....58 D3
Outram Cl MPL/ROM SK6 * 58 D3
Outram Rd DUK SK16 ....29 P5
Outram Sq DROY M43 * 28 G1
Outrington Dr OP/CLY M11 ....28 A1
Outwood Dr CHD/CHDH SK8 ....55 J7
Outwood La MANAIR M90 ....54 D7
Outwood La West MANAIR M90..54 D7
Outwood Rd CHD/CHDH SK8....55 K7
Oval Dr DUK SK16 ....29 P2
The Oval CHD/CHDH SK8 ....55 K7
  EP CH65 ....102 E1
Ovenhouse La MACCLN SK10 ....
Overdale La NWCHW CW8 ....126 C2
Overdale Rd MPL/ROM SK6 ....42 F8
  NSTN CH64 ....78 E4
  POY/DIS SK12 ....59 K9
Overdene Rd WSFD CW7 ....149M2
Overfields KNUT WA16 ....90 G2
Over Hall Dr WSFD CW7 ....149 L3
Overhill La WILM/AE SK9 ....71 N7
Overhill Rd WILM/AE SK9 ....71 N7
Overhill Rd WILM/AE SK9 ....71M7
Overlea Dr BNG/LEV M19 ....40 F3
Overleigh Ct CHSW/BR CH4 ....142 F5
Overleigh Rd CHSW/BR CH4 ....142 E5
Overleigh Ter CHSW/BR CH4 ...142 E5
Overpool Gdns GTS/LS CH66 ...102 B1
Overpool Rd EP CH65 ....80 B8
Over Rd MANT CW5 ....
Over the Hi BIDD ST8 ....175 P7
Overton Av WYTH/NTH M22 ....54 F2
Overton Cl CONG CW12 ....155 L7
  MWCH CW10 ....151 H2
Overton Crs BRAM/HZG SK7 ....57 L3
  SALE M33 ....
Overton Dr FROD/HEL WA6 ....38 A7
Overton Rd CONG CW12 ....175 N2
  WYTH/NTH M22 ....54 F2
Overway WSFD CW7 ....149 N1
Overwood Av CH/BCN CH1 ....121 H3
Overwood La CH/BCN CH1 ....121 H3
Overwood La CH/BCN CH1 ....120 G2
Overwood Pl WYTH/NTH M22....189 P2
Overwood Rd WYTH/NTH M22 ...39 N8
Ovington Cl RUNC WA7 ....84 D1
Owen Cl CH/BCN CH1 ....121 H5
Owen Rd RAIN/WH L35 ....30 B6
Owens Farm Dr OFTN SK2 ....42 D9
Owen St CW/SHV CW2 ....4 D6
  EDGY/DAV SK3 ....16 D5
  NWCHW CW9 ....13 K2
  WARRN/WOL WA2 ....18 C2
Owley Wood Rd NWCHW CW8 ..108 G3
Owlsfield NEWLW WA12 ....
Oxborough Cl WDN WA8 ....45 M4
Oxbridge Cl SALE M33 ....38 A5
Oxenham St SALE M33 ....38 A8
Oxenhurst Gn OFTN SK2 ....57 L2
Oxford Av SALE M33 ....38 A4
Oxford Cl GTS/LS CH66 ....102 A4
Oxford Ct MCFLDN SK10 ....9 C3
Oxford Gv IRL M44 ....43 H4
Oxford Ms MPL/ROM SK6 ....43 H4
Oxford Gv IRL M44 ....36 B2
Oxford Rd AULW OL7 * 29M1
Oxford Rd ALT WA14 ....53 H4
  CHSW/BR CH4 ....142 B4
  MCFLDS SK11 ....
  RUNC WA7 ....14 E5
  CW/HAS CW1 ....
  NEWLW WA12 ....23 L6

WARRS WA4 ....48 E3
WDN WA8 ....21 J4
Oxford St East AULW OL7....29M1
Oxford St West AULW OL7 ....29M1
Ox-hey La RAIN/WH L35 ....16 D1
Ox-hey Dr BIDD ST8 ....175 L8
Oxheys RUNC WA7 ....62 G6
Ox-hey Dr BIDD ST8 ....175 L7
Oxley St STHEL WA9 ....31 J1
Oxmead Ct WARRN/WOL WA2 ...34 C7
Oxmoor Cl RUNC WA7 ....62 E9
Oxney Cl MCFLDN SK10 ....
Oxton Av WYTH/NTH M22 ....54 E3
Oxton Cl WDN WA8 ....45 J3
Oxton Gn GTS/LS CH66 ....79 P9
Oxton St OP/CLY M11 ....28 F2

P

Pacific Rd ALT WA14 ....52 E1
Packsaddle Pk MCFLDN SK10 ....94 E8
Padarn Cl CHSW/BR CH4 ....141 P5
Padden Brk MPL/ROM SK6 ....42 G6
Paddington Bnk WARR WA1 ....49 H1
Paddock Brow WARR SK10 ....94 G8
Paddock Cha POY/DIS SK12 ....57 N1
Paddock Cl CHF/WBR SK23 ....97 K1
Paddock Dr NSTN CH64 ....63 H6
Paddock Gv STHEL WA9 ....31 J5
Paddock Hl KNUT WA16 ....92 C2
Paddock La AUD/MAD/W CW3 ..217 J2
  CHF/WBR SK23 ....97 K1
  LYMM WA13 ....36 C9
  LYMM WA13 ....51 N2
Paddock Ri RUNC WA7 ....84 C1
Paddock Rd CHSW/BR CH4 ....142 G8
Paddock Rw CH/BCN CH1 * 2 E5
The Paddocks BRAM/HZG SK7 ..56 D6
  CHD/CHDH SK8 ....55 N2
  CHNE CH2 ....104 A1
  CHSW/BR CH4 ....142 D3
  FROD/HEL WA6 ....105 J2
  GTS/LS CH66 ....101 P1
  HALE/TIMP WA15 ....53 K3
  LYMM WA13 ....51 J4
  NANT CW5 ....197 L3
  NWCHW CW8 ....109 L8
  SBCH CW11 ....172 C8
  TPLY/KEL CW6 ....147 H4
Paddock Vw NWCHW CW8 * ....
Padgbury Cl CONG CW12 ....155 G9
Padgbury La CONG CW12 ....155 J9
Padge La CHSE CH5 ....179 J6
Padmore Cl CW/HAS CW1 ....184 C1
Padston Dr ALS/KID ST7 ....187 L5
Padstow Cl CW/HAS CW1 ....170 B9
  MCFLDN SK10 ....116 A4
  WARRN/BUR WA5 ....47 J8
Padstow Dr BRAM/HZG SK7 ....56 F8
Padworth Pl CW/HAS CW1 ....170 A8
Page Gv CW/SHV CW2 ....198 A4
Page La WDN WA8 ....46 A6
Paignton Cl WARRW/BUR WA5 ...47 J3
Paignton Dr SALE M33 ....38 A1
Paignton Gv HTNM SK4 ....41M1
Painswick Rd GTS/LS CH66 ....102 A2
  WYTH/NTH M22 ....54 D6
Paisley Av PS/BROM CH62 ....79 J1
  RNFD/HAY WA11 ....22 B2
Palace Fields Av RUNC WA7 ....62 E9
Palace Hey NSTN CH64 ....77 N8
Palace Rd SALE M33 ....38 D3
Palatine Av DID/WITH M20 ....40 C2
  CH/BCN CH1 ....120 C5
  IRL M44 ....27 M8
Palatine Crs DID/WITH M20 ....40 C3
Palatine Rd NTHEN M22 ....201 N9
Palatine Rd DID/WITH M20 ....40 A5
Palatine Rd DID/WITH M20 ....40 A5
Palatine Rd WYTH/NTH M22 ....39 N7
Palgrave Cl CH/BCN CH1 ....120 D5
Palin Dr WARRW/BUR WA5 ....47 K1
Paliser Cl GOL/RIS/CU WA3 ....35 H5
Pall Ml NANT CW5 ....10 B6
Palma Av MANAIR M90 ....54 E8
Palmyra Sq North WARR WA1...18 C6
Palmyra Sq South WARR WA1...18 C7
Pandora Cl DID/WITH M20.... ....40 B3
Panfield Rd WYTH/NTH M22 ....54 E5
Pangbourne Cl EDGY/DAV SK3 ..56 C1
  WARRS WA4 ....48 B6
Panton Rd CHNE CH2 ....122 A8
Panton Pl CHNE CH2 ....3 K1
Paper Mill La FLINT CH6 ....98 E9
Parade St MANAIR M90 ....54 E8

The Parade CH/BCN CH1 ....121 H6
  GOL/RIS/CU WA3 * 25 N6
  NSTN CH64 ....77 J5
Paradise Cl CHSW/BR CH4 ....3 F7
Paradise St NANT CW5 ....168 F1
Paradise St DTN/ASHW M34 ....29 M2
  MCFLDS SK11 ....8 D5
Paragon Cl WDN WA8 ....45 P2
Parbold Av DID/WITH M20.... ....40 B1
  RNFD/HAY WA11 ....22 B4
Parbold Ct WDN WA8 ....20 A3
Parbutts La MALPAS SY14 ....204 A3
The Parchments NEWLW WA12 ..23 P5
Parish Cl ALS/KID ST7 ....187M4
Park Av ALS/KID ST7 ....188 G8
  ALT WA14 ....53 H4
  BRAM/HZG SK7 ....72 C1
  CH/BCN CH1 ....120 D1
  CHD/CHDH SK8 ....55 P6
  CHF/WBR SK23 ....75 P3
  CHSE CH5 ....164 A7
  CHSW/BR CH4 ....142 A4
  EDGY/DAV SK3 ....16 B7
  FLINT CH6 ....98 A6
  HALE/TIMP WA15 ....53 K6
  MPL/ROM SK6 ....43 H6
  NWCHW CW8 ....108 F3
  POY/DIS SK12 ....73 L2
  RAIN/WH L35 ....30 B4
  SALE M33 ....38 F4
  WARRS WA4 ....48 F4
  WDN WA8 ....45 P5
  WHITCH SY13 ....213 M6
  WILM/AE SK9 ....71 L6
  WSFD CW7 ....129 H8
Park Av North NEWLW WA12 ....23 N7
Park Av South NEWLW WA12 ....23 N7
Park Bnk CONG CW12 ....155 P8
Park Bvd WARR WA1 ....48 C3
Park Brook Rd NTHM/RTH M23 ..39 M1
Parkbrooke Rd NTHM/RTH M23 ..39 L9
Park Brow Cl CCHDY M21 ....39 M1
Park Cl ALT WA14 ....38 C8
  CHSE CH5 ....124 A9
Park Ct NEWLW ST5 * 201 P8
  RUNC WA7 ....14 E7
Park Court Ms CHD/CHDH SK8 ...55 N3
Park Crs CHF/WBR SK23 ....75 P3
  NWCHW CW8 ....108 B8
  WARRS WA4 ....48 A4
  WILM/AE SK9 ....71 K5
Parkdale Av DTN/ASHW M34 ....29 K2
  GTN M18 ....28 C4
Parkdale Rd WDN WA8 ....34 B9
Park Dr CHNE CH2 ....122 B7
  CW/SHV CW2 ....184 F7
  CHSE CH5 ....102 E1
  HALE/TIMP WA15 ....53 K6
  HALE/TIMP WA15 ....53 K6
  HTNM SK4 ....41 J6
Park Dr South CHNE CH2 ....122 B8
Parkend Rd NTHM/RTH M23 ....39 M1
Parker Av NWCHW CW8 ....109 J6
Parker Dr CHSE CH5 ....176 G7
Parker Dr South CHSE CH5 ....177 H7
Parkers Ct RUNC WA7 ....62 C4
  CW/HAS CW1 ....169 P9
Park St MCFLDS SK11 ....9 F5
Parkett Heyes Rd
  MCFLDS SK11 ....116 A5
Park Farm Vw BURS/TUN ST6 ..189M9
Park Fold CW/HAS CW1 ....169 P9
Parkfield Av MPL/ROM SK6 ....58 D1
  WARRS WA4 ....49 J3
Parkfield Dr EP CH65 ....102 C2
  FROD/HEL WA6 ....105 H1
  NANT CW5 ....196 F5
Parkfield Rd ALT WA14 ....52 G3
  CHD/CHDH SK8 ....56 C6
  CHSW/BR CH4 ....140 G7
  KNUT WA16 ....
  NWCHW CW9 ....13 K3
Parkfield Rd South
  DID/WITH M20 ....40 C4
Parkfield St La WARRN/WOL WA2..34 A6
Parkgate KNUT WA16 ....90 C2
Park Gate Av DID/WITH M20 ....40 C2
Parkgate Av KNUT WA16 ....113 L4
Park Gate Cl MPL/ROM SK6 ....42 D3
Parkgate Dr OFTN SK2 ....57 H3
Park Gate La NWCHW CW8 ....90 C2
Parkgate Rd CH/BCN CH1 ....121M7
  GTS/LS CH66 ....100 C2
  MCFLDS SK11 ....117 J8
  NSTN CH64 ....77 J7
  WARRS WA4 ....48 F6
Park Gates CHD/CHDH SK8 ....55 N6
Park Gates Dr CHD/CHDH SK8 ..55 N6
Parkgate Wy RUNC WA7 ....62 C7
Park Gn MCFLDS SK11 ....9 F6
Park Gv BNG/LEV M19 ....41 J4
  CW/BCN CH1 ....120 D2
Parkland Av NM/HAY SK22 ....59 N6
Park Hill Cl NM/HAY SK22 ....59 N6
Parkhill Ct KNUT WA16 ....90 C2
Park Hill Rd HALE/TIMP WA15 ..53 L6
Park House Dr MCFLDN SK10 ...94 H5
  SBCH CW11 ....171 P1
Park House La West
  NEWLW ST5 ....201 P6
Parkhouse La CW/SHV CW2 ....184 F7
Parkin St WGTN/LGST M12 ....28 A6
Parkland Av NM/HAY SK22 ....59 N6
Parkland Dr CHNE CH2 ....104 D1
Parkland Gv FROD/HEL WA6 ....105 J2
Parklands ALS/KID ST7 ....189 K7
  GTS/LS CH66 ....79 P8
  WDN WA8 ....45 J8
Parklands Dr SALE M33 ....38 A6

Parklands Gdns GTS/LS CH66 ....79 P7
Parklands Rd NTHM/RTH M25 ...39 J9
The Parklands CONG CW12 ....156 A8
Parklands Vw GTS/LS CH66 ....79 P7
Parklands Wy POY/DIS SK12 ....73 L2
Park La ALS/KID ST7 ....200 F3
  ALT WA14 ....
  CHSE CH5 ....145 L7
  CONG CW12 ....155 P8
  FROD/HEL WA6 ....83 P5
  HALE/TIMP WA15 ....53 L6
  HTNM SK4 ....88 E5
  MCFLDS SK11 ....8 C7
  NANT CW5 ....169 P9
  NWCHE CW8 ....
  NWCHW CW8 ....109 K8
  POY/DIS SK12 ....73 L2
  CW/HAS CW1 ....186 B3
  DTN/ASHW M34 ....29 K1
  EP CH65 ....6 B8
  HALE/TIMP WA15 ....53 K6
  HALE/TIMP WA15 ....53 K6
  HTNM SK4 ....41 J8
  LYMM WA13 ....36 B8
  MANT CW5 ....51 K7
  MPL/ROM SK6 ....42 D2
  NEWLW WA12 ....11 K4
  NANT CW5 ....197 L3
  NSTN CH64 ....78 F5
  PART M31 ....
  POY/DIS SK12 ....58 D9
  RUNC WA7 ....14 D7
  SALE M33 ....38 D2
  STHEL WA9 ....31 J5
  TPLY/KEL CW6 ....146 G8
  WARR WA1 ....18 D7
  WARRN/WOL WA2 ....33 N7
  WARRS WA4 ....47 J1
  WDN WA8 ....45 P6
  WHITCH SY13 ....213 L6
  WILM/AE SK9 ....71 H7
Park La North WARRW/BUR WA5 ..47 L4
Park La South WARRW/BUR WA5 ...23 P7
Park Rd NTHM/RTH M23 ....39 K5
Parkside Av STHEL WA9 ....30 G5
  NSTN CH64 ....78 F5
Parkside La MPL/ROM SK6 ....58 D1
Parkside Rd NEWLW WA12 ....24 D8
  SALE M33 ....38 G5
Parkside Wk BRAM/HZG SK7 ....56 E4
Park St CH/BCN CH1 ....3 G5
  DTN/ASHW M34 ....29 K6
  MCFLDN SK10 ....95 P5
  MCFLDS SK11 ....9 F6
  NSTN CH64 ....77 J5
  NWCHW CW9 ....12 C4
  STHEL WA9 ....22 A3
  STKP SK1 ....17 G5
Parksway WARR WA1 ....54 J9
The Park CHSE CH5 ....143 N2
  WARRW/BUR WA5 ....47 H4
Park Vale Rd MCFLDS SK11 ....8 C7
Park Vw CONG CW12 * 155 N7
  DTN/ASHW M34 ....29 K1
  EDGY/DAV SK3 ....40 C9
  MCFLDN SK10 ....10 D4
  NANT CW5 ....169 P9
  STKP SK1 ....42 A9
  WARRN/WOL WA2 ....33 P5
  WILM/AE SK9 ....71 L6
Parkview Pk LYMM WA13 ....51 K6
Park View Ri NM/HAY SK22 ....59 N6
Park View Rd ALS/KID ST7 ....189 J5
Parkville Rd DID/WITH M20.... ....40 D3
Park Wk CHNE CH2 ....121 N7
Parkway BRAM/HZG SK7 ....56 E5
Park Wy CH/BCN CH1 ....120 D2
Parkway DTN/ASHW M34 ....29 G9
  HOLMCH CW4 ....131 P8
  NM/HAY SK22 ....59 N6
  WILM/AE SK9 ....71 K6
Parkwood Cl LYMM WA13 ....50 D5
Parkwood Rd NTHM/RTH M23 ...39 M1
Parlane St STHEL WA9 ....22 A5
Parliament St NWCHW CW8 ....12 B4
Parliament Wy GTS/LS CH66 ....102 B4
Parlington Cl WDN WA8 ....45 J8
Parnell Av WYTH/NTH M22 ....39 N8
Parr Gv RNFD/HAY WA11 ....
Parr Mount Ct STHEL WA9 ....22 A6
Parr Mount St STHEL WA9 ....22 A6
Parrs Mount Ms HTNM SK4 * 40 G6

Parr Stocks Rd STHEL WA9 ....22 B6
Parr St MCFLDS SK11 ....8 C5
  OP/CLY M11 * 28 E2
  STHEL WA9 ....22 A6
  WARR WA1 ....18 E7
  WDN WA8 * 20 A1
Parrs Wood Av DID/WITH M20 ...40 D7
Parrs Wood La DID/WITH M20 ....40 E7
Parrs Wood Rd DID/WITH M20 ...40 D7
Parrs Wood View WARRS WA4 ..48 J6
Parry Dr WARRS WA4 ....48 A6
Parry Md MPL/ROM SK6 ....42 F4
Parry Rd WGTN/LGST M12 ....28 A5
Parsonage Gdns MPL/ROM SK6 ..58 E3
Parsonage Rd DID/WITH M20 ....40 D1
  HTNM SK4 ....41 J8
  WDN WA8 ....61 N2
Parsonage St HTNM SK4 ....16 E3
  MCFLDS SK11 * ....
Parsonage Wy CHD/CHDH SK8 ..56 A2
  WARRW/BUR WA5 ....47 L2
Parsons La CHNE CH2 ....121 L4
Parson St CONG CW12 ....155 L8
Partington Pl SALE M33 ....38 E3
Partridge Av CONG CW12 ....155 N9
  GOL/RIS/CU WA3 ....34 F4
  WSFD CW7 ....149 L5
Partridge Ct OFTN SK2 * 57 K1
Partridge Wy NWCHE CW9 ....88 F7
Parvey La MCFLDN SK11 ....136 D2
Pascal St BNG/LEV M19 ....28 A4
Paston Rd WYTH/NTH M22 ....39 N9
Pasture Cl MCFLDN SK10 ....117 J1
  STHEL WA9 ....31 H4
  TPLY/KEL CW6 ....125 H7
Pasture Dr GOL/RIS/CU WA3 ....34 B1
Pasturefield Cl SALE M33 ....39 J3
Pasture Field Rd
  WYTH/NTH M22 ....55 H6
Pasturegreen Wy IRL M44 ....27 N6
Pasture La WARRN/WOL WA2 ....34 F7
The Pastures STHEL WA9 ....31M1
Patch Croft Rd WYTH/NTH M22 ..55 H6
Patch La BRAM/HZG SK7 ....72 A3
Patmos La KNUT WA16 ....111 N4
Patrivale Cl WARR WA1 ....34 A9
Patten La WARR WA1 * 18 D6
Patten St DID/WITH M20.... ....40 C2
Patterdale Av
  WARRN/WOL WA3 ....33 N6
Patterdale Cl CW/SHV CW2 ....184 D5
Patterdale Rd MPL/ROM SK6 ....42 G4
  OFTN SK2 ....57 H1
  PART M31 ....
  WYTH/NTH M22 ....39 P8
Patterson Cl GOL/RIS/CU WA3 ...34 F5
Patterson St DTN/ASHW M34 ....29M5
  NEWLW WA12 ....
Paul Cl WARRW/BUR WA5 ....54 C1
Paulden Av NTHM/RTH M23 ....54 D1
Paulden Rd NWCHE CW9 ....110 C2
Paulhan Rd DID/WITH M20 ....40 D3
Pauls Moss Ct WHITCH SY13 ....213M6
Paul St WARRN/WOL WA2 ....18 C2
Pavement La KNUT WA16 ....91 K2
The Pavilions CHD/CHDH SK8 ...55M3
  NWCHE CW9 ....128 F1
Pavilion Wy CONG CW12 ....155 K7
  MCFLDN SK10 ....116 F5
Paxford Pl WILM/AE SK9 ....71 J9
Payne Cl WARRW/BUR WA5 ....47 P1
Paythorne Cl GOL/RIS/CU WA3 ..25 P6
Paythorne Gn OFTN SK2 ....57 L2
Peace Dr WARRW/BUR WA5 ....58 C2
Peacefield MPL/ROM SK6 ....58 C2
Peach Fld CHSE CH5 ....143 K3
Peach Gv RNFD/HAY WA11 * 23 J2
Peach La NANT CW5 ....184 C1
Peacock Av WARR WA1 ....48 C1
  WSFD CW7 ....149 L4
Peacock Cl GTN M18 ....28 C3
Peacock Dr CHD/CHDH SK8 ....55 N1
Peacock Gv GTN M18 ....28 C3
Peacock Hay Rd ALS/KID ST7 ....201 P3
Peacock La KNUT WA16 ....51 J9
Peak Bnk MPL/ROM SK6 ....42 F6
Peak Dale Av BURS/TUN ST6 ....189 K9
Peakdale Av CHD/CHDH SK8 ....55 J6
Peakdale Rd MPL/ROM SK6 ....58 E5
Peak Rd NM/HAY SK22 ....59 P7
Peak St STKP SK1 ....17 J4
Pearle St MCFLDN SK10 ....8 E2
Pearl La CHSE CH5 ....143 K1
Pearl St BRAM/HZG SK7 ....57 L3
  DTN/ASHW M34 ....
  MCFLDN SK10.... ....94 G6
Pearl Yd WHITCH SY13 ....213M6
Pearn Rd BNG/LEV M19 ....40 G3
Pearson Av WARRS WA4 ....48 A4
Pearson Cl PART M31 ....
Pearson St MCFLDS SK11 ....9 H1
  RDSH SK5 ....
Peart Av MPL/ROM SK6 ....43 H2
Pear Tree Av CW/HAS CW1 ....185 J1
  RUNC WA7 ....62 A7
Peartree Cl FROD/HEL WA6 ....84 E4
Pear Tree Cl SBCH CW11 ....172 B3
Pear Tree Dr NWCHE CW9 ....88 F7
Pear Tree Rd WYTH/NTH M22 ...39 N9
Pear Tree La NEWLW ST5 ....201 N3
  NWCHW CW8 ....
  WHITCH SY13 ....213 K4
Peartree Pl WARR WA1 ....48 C4
  WARRS WA4 ....48 F4
Pear Tree Rd ALS/KID ST7 ....201 N3
Pear Tree Wy CHNE CH2 ....122 A6
  GTS/LS CH66 ....102 A3
Peart St DTN/ASHW M34 ....29 K6
Pearwood Cl TPLY/KEL CW6 ....147 H9
Peaslake Cl MPL/ROM SK6 ....43 H3

Peasley Cl WARRN/WOL WA2	34 C7
Peckers Hill Rd STHEL WA9	31 K1
Peckfield Cl RUNC WA7	62 E9
Peckforton Cl CHD/CHDH SK8	55 J2
SBCH CW11	171 K2
RUNC WA7	84 D1
Peckforton Hall La
TPLY/KEL CW6	180 G2
Peckforton Rd TPLY/KEL CW6	165 M8
Peckforton Wa ALS/KID ST7	189 J9
Peckforton Wy CHNE CH2	121 P4
NWCHW CW8	12 D4
Peckmill Cl WILM/AE SK9	71 N4
Peck Mill La FROD/HEL WA6	104 G5
MCFLDN SK10	73 M7
Pedley Hl MCFLDN SK10	96 C9
Pedley House La WARR WA16	92 A4
Pedley La CONG CW12	156 E6
KNUT WA16	91 N6
Pedley St CW/SHV CW2	5 C8
Peebles Av RNFD/HAY WA11	22 B3
Peebles Cl GTS/LS CH66 *	79 K7
Peel Av ALT WA14	53 H5
Peel Cl WARR WA1	49 M1
Peel Crs CHSE CH3	124 D4
Peel Dr CONG CW12	174 C2
SALE M33	39 H4
Peelgate Dr CHD/CHDH SK8	55 J5
Peel Hall La CHSE CH3	124 D4
Peel Hall Rd WYTH/NTH M22	28 A5
Peel Hollow ALS/KID ST7	200 D6
Peel La CONG CW12	174 D2
Peel Moat Rd HTNM SK4	J3
Peel Rd HALE/TIMP WA15	53 J4
Peel Sq CW/HAS CW1	4 B1
Peel St CW/HAS CW1	4 B1
DROY M43	28 F1
DTN/ASHW M34	29 L3
DTN/ASHW M34	29 L5
MCFLDS SK11	8 E7
NEWLW WA12	23 L6
OFTN SK2	56 F1
RUNC WA7	C8
Peel Ter CH/BCN CH1	3 G2
Peersword Ct NSTN CH64	77 L8
Peewit Cl WSFD CW7	149 M5
Peggie's La MCFLDN SK10	93 M5
Pelham Cl CW/HAS CW1	21 K2
Pelham Rd WARR WA4	49 J4
Pelham St AULW OL7	29 L1
Pelican Cl CW/HAS CW1	185 M3
Pemberton Cl NSTN CH64	78 E5
Pemberton Rd CH/BCN CH1 *	2 D3
Pembridge Gdns EP CH65	102 C1
Pembroke Av SALE M33	38 C3
Pembroke Ct CHSW/BR CH4	142 C4
Pembroke Ct BRAM/HZG SK7 *	55 L1
Pembroke Dr EP CH65	102 C1
Pembroke Gdns WARRS WA4	62 F2
Pembroke Gv IRL M44	36 B2
Pembroke Rd MCFLDS SK11	116 F5
Pembroke Wy WSFD CW7	149 K4
Pembry Cl RDSH SK5	42 A2
Pembury Cl WYTH/NTH M22	54 E4
Penare Gorran Hvn RUNC WA7	62 E8
Penbrook Cl CW/SHV CW2	184 D5
Pencarrow Cl DID/WITH M20	40 A5
Pencombe Cl WGTN/LGST M12	28 A5
Pendeen Cl WYTH/NTH M22	54 F4
Pendennis Rd HTNM SK4	16 B1
Pendine Cl WARRW/BUR WA5	32 F6
Pendlebury Rd CHD/CHDH SK8	55 L4
Pendlebury St STHEL WA9	31 H4
WARRS WA4	49 H4
Pendle Cl CW/HAS CW1	185 N3
Pendle Gdns GOL/RIS/CU WA3	25 N6
Pendle Rd DTN/ASHW M34	29 M8
Penfold Hey CHNE CH2	121 N4
Penfolds RUNC WA7	62 B5
Pengrove Cl BURS/TUN ST6	189 N8
Penhale Ms BRAM/HZG SK7	56 F8
Penistone Dr GTS/LS CH66	79 M8
Penketh Av GTN M18	28 B5
WARRW/BUR WA5	33 J8
Penketh Cl RUNC WA7	15 F2
Penketh's La RUNC WA7	15 F1
Penkford La WARRW/BUR WA5	44 A7
Penkmans La FROD/HEL WA6	31 K1
Penlake La STHEL WA9	10 E4
Penlington Ct NANT CW5	10 E4
Penmark Cl WARRW/BUR WA5	52 G6
Penmere Gv SALE M33	38 B7
Pennon Cha BRAM/HZG SK7	57 H6
Pennant Cl GOL/RIS/CU WA3	35 H5
Penn Gdns EP CH65	6 D4
Penn House Cl BRAM/HZG SK7	54 B6
Pennine Cl MCFLDN SK10	112 L2
Pennine Dr ALT WA14	52 F2
STHEL WA9	22 D6
Pennine Rd BRAM/HZG SK7	57 H2
MPL/ROM SK6	43 H2
WARRW/WOL WA2	33 P6
Pennine Wy BIDD ST8	175 M7
WSFD CW7	149 K2
Pennington Cl FROD/HEL WA6	84 A4
Pennington Dr NEWLW WA12	A6
Pennington Gn GTS/LS CH66	101 N1
Pennington La
WARRW/BUR WA5	22 G6
Penningtons La MCFLDS SK11	116 G7
Pennington St WGTN/LGST M12	28 A7
Penny Av RUNC WA7	14 C4
Penny Bank Cl CHSW/BR CH4	140 D7
Pennyfields ALS/KID ST7	189 M6
Penny La MCFLDN SK10	118 B1
RUNC WA7	17 G1
RNFD/HAY WA11	22 L2
Penny La WARRW/BUR WA5	23 H9
Pennymoor Dr ALT WA14	52 F1
Pennypleck La NWCHE CW9	66 A4
Penny's La NWCHE CW9	110 E5
NWCHE CW9	110 G6
Penrhos Av CHD/CHDH SK8	55 H5
Penrhyn Av CHD/CHDH SK8	55 H5
Penrhyn Crs BRAM/HZG SK7	57 J7
RUNC WA7	61 N7
Penrhyn Dr BRAM/HZG SK7	57 J6
EDGY/DAV SK3	16 A7
Penrith Av MCFLDS SK11	116 F7
RDSH SK5	28 F8
WARRN/WOL WA2	33 M5
Penrith Cl FROD/HEL WA6	84 B5
KNUT WA16	91 J8
Penrith Ct CONG CW12	155 J8
Penrose Gdns
WARRS WA4	47 H4
Pensarn Gv RDSH SK5	41 N4
Pensby Av CHNE CH2	121 N6
Pensby Dr GTS/LS CH66	79 L7
Pensford Rd NTHM/RTH M23	54 B4
Penshaw Ct RUNC WA7	62 C7
Penshurst Rd RDSH SK5	42 A2
Pentland Av STHEL WA9	22 D6
Pentland Cl BRAM/HZG SK7	55 J2
CHSE CH3	122 B9
WSFD CW7	149 K2
Pentland Pl WARRN/WOL WA2	33 L1
Penton Cl CHSE CH3	124 E4
Pentwyn Gv NTHM/RTH M23	39 L6
Pen-y-Bryn CHNE CH2	98 B9
Peony Gdns STHEL WA9	31 N1
Peover Av SALE M33	39 H4
Peover La CONG CW12	158 C3
Peover Rd WILM/AE SK9	71 N1
Pepper Av NTHM/RTH M23	39 L6
Pepper Rd BRAM/HZG SK7	57 H5
The Peppers LYMM WA13	50 F4
Pepper St CH/BCN CH1	2 E5
CHSE CH3	143 M2
KNUT WA16	93 J6
LYMM WA13	50 F4
MCFLDS SK11	114 A2
MCFLDS SK11	116 B4
MWCH CW10	151 J1
SPK/HALE L24	10 B5
WARRS WA4	65 J3
WHITCH SY13	213 M5
Percival Cl CHNE CH2	121 M4
Percival La RUNC WA16	113 H1
Percival Rd CHNE CH2	121 M4
EP CH65	6 D5
Percival St WARR WA1	19 F6
Percy James Cl ALS/KID ST7	188 A4
Percy Rd CHSW/BR CH4	142 F3
Percy St NWCHE CW9	13 G2
STHEL WA9	31 L1
STKP SK1	17 G3
WARRW/BUR WA5 *	48 A2
Peregrine Cl WSFD CW7	149 M5
Peregrine Dr IRL M44	27 N6
Peregrine Rd OFTN SK2	57 P8
Perimeter Rd CHNE CH2	82 C8
Perkins St BURS/TUN ST6	189 L9
Perrey St RUNC WA7	15 H2
Perrin Av RUNC WA7	14 B7
Perrins Rd WARRW/BUR WA5	32 C2
Perry Flds CW/HAS CW1 *	170 A4
Perrygate Av DID/WITH M20	40 B2
Perry Rd HALE/TIMP WA15	53 M1
Perth Av STHEL WA9	30 C1
Perth Cl BRAM/HZG SK7	72 E1
HOLMCH CW4	131 N9
WARRN/WOL WA2	32 C4
Peterborough Ct GTS/LS CH66	102 B5
Peterborough St GTN M18	116 C2
Peter Destapleigh Wy
WARRS WA4	196 G4
Peterhouse Gdns
MPL/ROM SK6	43 H4
Peter House Rd MCFLDS SK11	117 H7
Peters Cl STHEL WA9	30 L1
Peter Moss Wy BNG/LEV M19	28 C8
Peter Pl CW/HAS CW1 *	4 C1
Peter Salem Dr
WARRW/BUR WA5	47 M1
Petersburg Rd EDGY/DAV SK3	56 C1
Peters Cl MCFLDN SK10	94 G6
Petersfield Dr NTHM/RTH M23	38 G9
Petersfield Gdns
WARRW/BUR WA5	25 N5
Petersgate RUNC WA7	63 H7
Petersham Dr WARRS WA4	64 C1
Peterstone Cl
WARRW/BUR WA5	32 G6
Peter St ALT WA14	53 H4
BRAM/HZG SK7	73 K4
DTN/ASHW M34	29 N6
GOL/RIS/CU WA3	24 C1
MCFLDS SK11	13 J5
NWCHE CW9	13 K1
STKP SK1	17 J2
Peter St West MCFLDS SK11 *	8 C7
Peterswood Cl WYTH/NTH M22	54 D4
Petheridge Dr WYTH/NTH M22	54 D6
Petrel Cl EDGY/DAV SK3	56 D1
WSFD CW7	149 M5
Petunia Cl MCFLDS SK11	117 H7
STHEL WA9	31 H1
Petworth Av WARRN/WOL WA2	33 L5
Petworth Cl CW/SHV CW2	185 H6
WYTH/NTH M22	54 C2
Pevensey Dr KNUT WA16	90 E5
Peveril Av NM/HAY SK22	59 N6
Peveril Cl WARRS WA4	48 F8
Peveril Dr BRAM/HZG SK7	57 M7
Peveril Gdns POY/DIS SK12	59 L9
Peveril Rd ALT WA14	37 P9
Peveril Wk MCFLDS SK11	116 F5
Pewit La NANT CW5	210 A6
Pewterspear Gn Rd
WARRS WA4	55 H4
Pewterspear La WARRS WA4	64 C3
Pexall Rd CONG CW12	135 K8
Pexhall Dr MCFLDS SK10	116 E5
Pexhill Rd MCFLDN SK10	134 D1
MCFLDS SK11	116 B3
Pheasant Cl GOL/RIS/CU WA3	34 G4
Pheasant Dr CCHDY M21	39 N1
Pheasant Fld SPK/HALE L24	60 C4
Pheasant Ri ALT WA14	53 H6
Pheasant Wk KNUT WA16	67 J2
Pheasant Wy WSFD CW7	149 M5
Philip Av WITH/ASHW M34	29 K4
Philip Dr SALE M33	38 E6
Philip Gv STHEL WA9	31 H1
Philips Dr WARRW/BUR WA5	47 J1
Philips La GTS/LS CH66	79 N9
Phillips Rd CH/BCN CH1	120 C8
Phillip St CHNE CH2	3 H1
Phipps' La WARRW/BUR WA5	32 B1
Phoenix Av WARRW/WOL WA2	32 F1
Phoenix Cl ALS/KID ST7	189 L6
Phythian Crs WARRW/BUR WA5	47 K5
Phythian St WARRW/BUR WA5	47 K4
Piccadilly STKP SK1	17 G5
Pichael Nook WARRS WA4	64 B3
Pickenham Cl MCFLDS SK11	116 F6
Pickering Cl HALE/TIMP WA15	58 D9
Pickering Ct WARRS WA4	49 M4
Pickering Crs WARRS WA4	61 H1
Pickering Cl RUNC WA7	62 B8
Pickering St CHNE CH2	3 H1
Pickford's Brow STKP SK1	17 G4
Pickford St MCFLDS SK11	13 J5
Pickfords Yd ALS/KID ST7 *	188 F5
SALE M33	39 J6
MCFLDS SK11	171 L2
Pickmere Ct CW/HAS CW1	185 J3
Pickmere Gdns CHD/CHDH SK8	55 P7
KNUT WA16	88 C7
Pickmere Rd WILM/AE SK9	71 M1
Pickmere St WARRW/BUR WA5	33 J7
Pickwick Cl SBCH CW11	171 P1
Pickwick Pl ALS/KID ST7	188 F6
Pickwick Rd POY/DIS SK12	73 K3
Picow St WARR WA1	14 A5
Picton Av EP CH65	6 C5
RUNC WA7	15 H4
Picton Cl GOL/RIS/CU WA3	34 D4
CW/SHV CW2	109 P8
PS/BROM CH62	79 H2
Picton Dr WILM/AE SK9	71 H1
Picton Gorse La CHNE CH2	122 C3
Picton La CHNE CH2	103 J5
Piele Rd RNFD/HAY WA11	23 J2
Pierce St MCFLDS SK11	8 C4
Pierpoint Ct CH/BCN CH1	2 D5
Pierpoint St NEWLW WA12	24 C2
WARRW/BUR WA5	18 A3
Pigot Pl WARRS WA4	49 H2
Pike La FROD/HEL WA6	106 E1
Pikemere Rd ALS/KID ST7	187 M3
Pikenall La NWCHW CW8	107 N1
Pike Rd MCFLDN SK10	96 E7
Pike St WARRS WA4	48 D6
The Pike NANT CW5	196 F4
Pilgrim's La WARRN/WOL WA2	33 K2
Pillar Box La SBCH CW11	152 E7
Pilling St DTN/ASHW M34	29 M6
Pillmoss La WARRS WA4	64 C7
Pillory St NANT CW5	205 M3
Pine Av NEWLW WA12	25 H7
WARRN/WOL WA2	33 M5
Pine Cl ALS/KID ST7	188 E9
DTN/ASHW M34	29 L3
MCFLDS SK11	171 M2
Pine Gdns CHNE CH2	121 M5
Pine Gv CHNE CH2	121 C7
DTN/ASHW M34	29 N6
GOL/RIS/CU WA3	24 C1
GTS/LS CH66	102 C3
Pinehey NSTN CH64	77 K4
Pinehurst MCFLDN SK10	94 E7
Pinellas RUNC WA7	15 H1
Pine Ldg BRAM/HZG SK7 *	56 C8
Pine Rd BRAM/HZG SK7	56 F7
DID/WITH M20	40 B4
MCFLDN SK10	73 M3
POY/DIS SK12	73 M3
Pine Trees Cl CHSW/BR CH4	140 F7
Pinetree Cl NWCHW CW8	7 H7
WSFD CW7	150 A1
Pine Trees KNUT WA16	95 H8
Pinetree St GTN M18	28 C3
Pine Wk NANT CW5	196 F5
SALE M33	38 A4
Pinewood ALT WA14	52 E5
Pinewood Av WARR WA1	19 K1
CW/SHV CW2	185 N9
CW/SHV CW2	185 H9
HALE/TIMP WA15	53 J6
SALE M33	38 A4
Pinewood Gv NEWLW WA12 *	201 P6
Pinewood Rd CCHDY M21 *	39 K1
WARRW/BUR WA5	71 N6
WSFD CW7	149 K1
The Pinewoods MPL/ROM SK6	39 G4
Pinfold Cl HALE/TIMP WA15	53 P8
Pinfold Ct CHSW/BR CH4	142 C4
Pinfold Dr CHD/CHDH SK8	56 A9
Pinfold La CHSW/BR CH4	142 C5
KNUT WA16	92 A7
KNUT WA16	94 B9
MANAIR M90	54 B9
MCFLDS SK11	151 H1
TPLY/KEL CW6	148 A4
Pinfold St WARRW/BUR WA5	8 D4
Pinfold Wy NWCHW CW8	108 C3
Pingard's La NWCHW CW8	107 N6
Pingate Dr CHD/CHDH SK8	56 A9
Pingate La CHD/CHDH SK8	56 A9
Pingate La South
CHD/CHDH SK8	56 A9
Pingot Av NTHM/RTH M23	39 L6
Pingot Cft CHSE CH3	143 K3
The Pingot IRL M44	27 P6
Pink Bank La WGTN/LGST M12	28 A3
Pinmill Brow FROD/HEL WA6	83 P6
Pinmill Cl FROD/HEL WA6	83 P6
Pinner Pl BNG/LEV M19	41 P2
Pinners Brow
WARRN/WOL WA2	18 B3
Pinners Fold RUNC WA7	62 F5
Pinnington Rd GTN M18	28 D5
Pinsley Green Rd NANT CW5	207 H4
Pinsley Vw NANT CW5	207 H2
Pintail Av EDGY/DAV SK3	56 C1
Pintail Pl WSFD CW7	149 M4
Piperhill Av WYTH/NTH M22	39 N7
Pipers Ash WSFD CW7	149 J1
Pipers Cl CHNE CH2	122 C7
Pipers La CHNE CH2	122 C7
NSTN CH64	100 D4
The Pipers GOL/RIS/CU WA3	34 F5
Pipewell Av GTN M18	28 C4
Pipit Av NEWLW WA12	23 N5
Pipit La GOL/RIS/CU WA3	34 F5
Pippin Cl NANT CW5	151 J3
Pippits Rw RUNC WA7	63 H7
Pirie Cl CONG CW12	156 A5
Pirie Rd CONG CW12	156 A5
Pitchcombe Rd WYTH/NTH M22	54 D6
Pitfield Gdns NTHM/RTH M23	39 J9
Pit La ALS/KID ST7	201 M2
CW/SHV CW2	198 A8
WDN WA8	61 H1
Pitville Ter WDN WA8	45 P3
Place Rd ALT WA14	52 C1
Plaistow Ct RUNC WA7	62 C7
Plane Gv NEWLW WA12	201 P6
Plane Tree Dr CW/HAS CW1	185 L2
Plane Tree Gv
RNFD/HAY WA11	23 L2
Planetree Rd HALE/TIMP WA15	53 L5
Plane Tree Rd PART M31	36 B3
Planet Wy DTN/ASHW M34	29 L4
Plantagenet Cl WSFD CW7	149 M4
Plantation Cl RUNC WA7	62 E5
Plantation Dr GTS/LS CH66	80 E8
Plant Cl SALE M33	38 B8
Plas Newton La CHNE CH2	122 A5
Platt Av CW/SHV CW2	171 M2
Platts Dr IRL M44	27 N7
Platts La CHSE CH3	145 K3
CHSE CH3	162 H4
CHSE CH3	145 J3
Platts St RNFD/HAY WA11	23 H1
Platt St CHD/CHDH SK8	55 N1
Pleachway HTNM SK4	40 G6
Pleasance Wy NEWLW WA12	23 N5
Pleasant St MCFLDN SK10	94 C6
NWCHW CW8	12 C4
Pleasant Wy CHD/CHDH SK8	56 C9
Pleck Rd EP CH65	102 C2
Plemstall Cl CHNE CH2	122 G3
Plemstall La CHNE CH2	123 H2
Plemstall Wy CHNE CH2	123 L1
Plemstall Wy CHNE CH2	122 G2
Plex GTS/LS CH66	80 B5
The Plex ALS/KID ST7	187 P4
Plinston Av WARRS WA4	49 H3
Ploughbank Dr CCHDY M21	39 N1
Plough Cft ALS/KID ST7	187 L5
Plough La CHSE CH3	143 P3
Ploughmans Wy GTS/LS CH66	102 A4
MCFLDN SK10	117 H1
Plover Av WSFD CW7	149 M5
Plover Cl CHSE CH3	177 H7
NEWLW WA12	23 N5
Plover Dr ALT WA14	37 N8
BIDD ST8	175 M9
IRL M44	27 N5
RUNC WA7	63 H6
Plovers La FROD/HEL WA6	83 J8
Plover Wy GOL/RIS/CU WA3	35 H4
Plowden Rd WYTH/NTH M22	54 D5
Plucksbridge Rd
MPL/ROM SK6	58 E4
Plumbley St OP/CLY M11 *	28 C2
Plumley Cl CHSE CH3	143 L1
EDGY/DAV SK3	56 A8
Plumley Gdns RAIN/WH L35	44 C6
SALE M33	89 L8
Plumley Rd WILM/AE SK9	71 M1
Plumley La FROD/HEL WA6	83 P4
Plumptons La FROD/HEL WA6	83 P4
Plum Ter CH/BCN CH1	2 C2
Plumtre Av WARRW/BUR WA5	33 J8
Plumville Gv BNG/LEV M19	41 J9
Plymouth Cl RUNC WA7	63 J8
Plymouth Dr BRAM/HZG SK7	56 A8
Plymouth Gv EDGY/DAV SK3	41 J9
Plymouth Rd SALE M33	39 K8
Plymyard Av PS/BROM CH62	79 H7
Poachers' La WARRS WA4	49 H4
Pochard Av WSFD CW7	149 M4
POY/DIS SK12	72 C2
Pochard Ri RUNC WA7	63 H6
Pochin Wy MWCH CW10	151 L2
Pocket Nook La
GOL/RIS/CU WA3	25 J1
Pocklington Ct
WARRN/WOL WA2	34 A7
Pocklington Dr
NTHM/RTH M23	39 J9
Podmore Av ALS/KID ST7	201 H9
Podmore La ALS/KID ST7	201 H9
Podnor La MPL/ROM SK6	59 L1
Podsmead Rd WYTH/NTH M22	54 D6
Poise Brook Dr OFTN SK2	57 M2
Poise Brook Rd OFTN SK2	57 N2
Poise Cl BRAM/HZG SK7	57 N4
Poland St DTN/ASHW M34	29 L1
Poleacre Dr WDN WA8	46 A5
Poleacre La MPL/ROM SK6	43 H2
Polesworth Cl WGTN/LGST M12	53 H2
Police St ALT WA14	53 H2
Pollard Av RUNC WA7	11 H7
Pollard Sq PART M31	36 F5
Pollen Cl SALE M33	38 F6
Pollin Rd ALT WA14	52 C1
Polletts Av RDSH SK5	42 E2
Pollitt Crs STHEL WA9	31 H5
Polperro Cl MCFLDN SK10	116 D3
WARRW/BUR WA5	47 J4
Pomfret St WGTN/LGST M12	28 A3
Pond Green Wy STHEL WA9	22 D3
Pond St GOL/RIS/CU WA3	25 J1
Pond Wk STHEL WA9	22 D3
Poolcroft SALE M33	39 J9
Poole Av WARRN/WOL WA2	33 L6
Poole Cl BRAM/HZG SK7	56 C6
Poole Crs WARRN/WOL WA2	33 L6
Poole Hall La GTS/LS CH66	80 A5
Poole Hall Rd EP CH65	80 B5
Poole Hill Rd NANT CW5	183 K6
Poole La CHNE CH2	103 H2
Pool End Cl MCFLDN SK10	95 K3
Pool End Rd MCFLDN SK10	95 K3
Pooles La SBCH CW11	173 K2
Poole St WSFD CW7	149 N1
Pool House Rd POY/DIS SK12	12 H2
Pool La CHNE CH2	103 P7
CHSE CH3	124 B7
LYMM WA13	127 L1
NWCHW CW8	15 C1
RUNC WA7	186 D1
SBCH CW11	186 D1
WARRS WA4	64 A3
Pool Rd GTS/LS CH66	35 P5
Pools Platt La NWCHE CW9	65 N7
Pool St MCFLDS SK11	4 A9
WDN WA8	21 K4
EP CH65	6 C7
Pooltown Rd EP CH65	80 B7
Pool Vw CW/HAS CW1	186 D1
Poplar Av ALT WA14	53 H1
GOL/RIS/CU WA3	35 P6
NEWLW WA12	59 P6
NM/HAY SK22	59 N6
NWCHE CW9	128 C3
RUNC WA7	62 A7
Poplar Cl CHD/CHDH SK8	55 L2
CONG CW12	155 J6
EP CH65	6 C7

NWCHW CW8 * 108 C9
RUNC WA7 ....62 A7
WHITCH SY13 ....213 K6
WSFD CW7 ....149 K2
Poplar Ct DTN/ASHW M54 * 29M5
EDGY/DAV SK3 * 56 F7
ALS/KID ST7 ....188 A6
MWCH CW10 ....151 K3
Poplar Gv CHNE CH2 ....104 A1
CTN M18 ....28 D5
IRL M44 ....36 C2
MCFLDN SK10 ....95 N5
OFTN SK2 ....57 J3
RNFD/HAY WA11 ....22 G3
Poplar La MKTDR TF9 ....218 E7
Poplar Rd BNG/LEV M19 ....40 E5
CHSW/BR CH4 ....142 B5
MCFLDS SK11 ....8 D7
NWCHW CW8 ....108 H4
RNFD/HAY WA11 ....22 G3
Poplars Av WARRN/WOL WA2 .....33 N6
The Poplars CW/SHV CW2 ....184 F9
LEIGH WN7 ....25 L1
LYMM WA13 ....50 D3
Poplar Vw WARRS WA4 * 47 L8
The Poppies NWCHW CW9 ....128 C4
Poppy Cl NTHM/RTH M23 ....39 H7
Poppyfields ALS/KID ST7 ....187 M5
Porlock Av DTN/ASHW M54 ....29 J1
STHEL WA9 ....31 H3
Porlock Cl STKP SK1 ....42 B8
WARRW/BUR WA5 ....47 J3
Porlock Rd NTHM/RTH M23 ....54 D1
Portal Gv DTN/ASHW M54 ....29 P8
Porter Av NEWLW WA12 ....23 N4
Porter Cl RAIN/WH L35 ....30 C7
Porter Dr NWCHE CW9 ....110 C6
Porter St RUNC WA7 ....15 K2
Porter Wy NWCHE CW9 ....110 C5
Portford Cl MCFLDN SK10 ....116 F3
Porthacawl Cl WDN WA8 ....45 J4
Porthleven Dr NTHM/RTH M23 .....54 A1
Porthleven Rd RUNC WA7 ....62 F9
Portland Cl BRAM/HZG SK7 ....57 H6
Portland Dr ALS/KID ST7 ....188 G2
BIDD STB 175 L7
Portland Gv CW/HAS CW1 ....186 A5
HTNM SK4 ....41 J4
Portland Houses
MPL/ROM SK6 * 58 C2
Portland Pl FROD/HEL WA6 ....83 J9
Portland Rd ALT WA14 ....52 C4
NM/HAY SK22 ....99 P6
RUNC WA7 ....14 C1
Portland Wk MCFLDS SK11 ....116 F5
Portland Wy STHEL WA9 ....22 D8
Portloe Rd CHD/CHDH SK8 ....55 K8
Portmarnock St MCFLDN SK10 .....17 J7
Portola Cl WARRS WA4 ....49 L5
Portrea Cl EDGY/DAV SK3 ....56 E2
Portree Dr HOLMCH CW4 ....131 N9
Portrush Cl MCFLDN SK10 ....95 J9
Portrush Rd WYTH/NTH M22 ....54 G5
Portside North EP CH65 ....80 F5
Portsmouth Pl RUNC WA7 ....63 J8
Port St STKP SK1 ....16 E3
Portugal St AULW OL7 ....29M1
Portville Rd BNG/LEV M19 ....28 A8
Portway WYTH/NTH M22 ....54 F7
Portwood Pl RDSH SK5 ....17 G2
Posnett St EDGY/DAV SK3 ....16 A6
Post Office Cl NWCHE CW9 ....199 L6
Post Office St ALT WA14 ....53 H3
FROD/HEL WA6 ....107 H7
MALPAS SY14 ....192 C8
RUNC WA7 ....61 K7
Potter Cl NANT CW5 ....197 L3
Potters End BIDD STB 175 J8
Potters La WDN WA8 ....60 F2
Pottery La OP/CLY M11 ....28 A1
Pottinger St AULW OL7 ....29M1
Poulton Crs WARR WA1 ....42 E8
Poulton Dr WDN WA8 ....20 A4
Poulton St OP/CLY M11 ....28 E2
Pound Rd GTS/LS CH66 ....79 N6
Poundswick La WYTH/NTH M22 ...54 F4
Powy Rd WARRN/WOL WA2 ....33 P1
Powderham Ct BURS/TUN ST6 ....189 P7
Powell Av GOL/RIS/CU WA3 ....34 F4
Powell's Orch CHSW/BR CH4 ......142 E3
Powell St STHEL WA9 ....31 K1
WARRS WA4 ....42 F1
Powey La CH/BCN CW1 ....101M7
Powick Dr MPL/ROM SK6 ....42 E7
Powicke Wk RAIN/WH L35 ....42 E7
Pownall Av BRAM/HZG SK7 ....56 F9
Pownall Rd ALT WA14 ....53 H4
CHD/CHDH SK8 ....56 A6
WILM/AE SK9 ....71 H6
Pownall Sq MCFLDS SK11 ....8 E3
Pownall St BRAM/HZG SK7 ....57 K4
WILM/AE SK9 ....71 H6
Powy Dr ALS/KID ST7 ....189 J6
Powys Ct STHEL WA9 ....2 C3
Powys St WARRW/BUR WA5 ....48 D2
Poynings St WYTH/NTH M22 ....54 F7
Poynter St DTN/ASHW M34 ....30 D2
Poynton Cl WARRS WA4 ....49 K4
Poynton St MCFLDS SK11 * 8 E4
Pratchitts Rw NANT CW5 ....10 C1
The Precinct CW/SHV CW2 *........184 F6
EDGY/DAV SK3 ....41M9
OFTN SK2 * 57 K2
Preece Cl WDN WA8 ....45 K4
Preece Ct CW/HAS CW1 ....4 C1

Preesall Av CHD/CHDH SK8 ....55 K7
Prees Rd WHITCH SY13 ....213 N7
Premier Gdns ALS/KID ST7 ....189 H6
Prenton Av STHEL WA9 ....30 C4
Prenton Dr CW/SHV CW2 ....142 G5
Prenton St OP/CLY M11 ....28 D1
Prescot Rd HALE/TIMP WA15 ....53 K5
WDN WA8 ....44 F2
WDN WA8 ....45 K5
Prescot St CHNE CH2 ....3 J1
Prescott Rd WILM/AE SK9 ....71 K5
Prescott St WARRS WA4 ....48 G4
Press St OP/CLY M11 ....28 D2
Prestbury Av HALE/TIMP WA15 .....53 J1
Prestbury Cl NWCHE CW9 ....109 P8
OFTN SK2 ....57 K3
WDN WA8 ....57 J8
Prestbury Dr MPL/ROM SK6 ....42 D5
WARRS WA4 ....49M4
MCFLDN SK10 ....94 G6
MCFLDN SK10 ....8 C3
MCFLDN SK10 ....93 P7
WILM/AE SK9 ....71 H9
Preston Av IRL M44 ....23 N7
Preston on the Hl WARRS WA4 .....63 K8
Preston Rd BNG/LEV M19 ....28 A7
Preston St GTN M18 ....28 C3
STHEL WA9 ....31 N3
Preston St West MCFLDS SK11 * 8 B2
Prestwich Av GOL/RIS/CU WA3 .....25 N6
Prestwich Cl OFTN SK2 ....57 K3
Prestwich Dr DTN/ASHW M34 ....29 L5
Prestwich Cl MCFLDN SK10 ....95 J8
WSFD CW7 ....128 D9
Pretoria St CHSW/BR CH4 ....142 F3
Price Av WARRS WA4 ....171M4
Price Dr SBCH CW11 ....171M4
Price Gv STHEL WA9 ....22 E7
Pride Cl NEWLW WA12 ....24 A7
Pridmouth Rd DID/WITH M20 ....40 D2
Priest Av CHD/CHDH SK8 ....55 J3
Priestfield Rd EP CH65 ....6 D4
Priest La MCFLDN SK10 ....94 B4
Priestley Ct NANT CW5 ....10 C1
Priestley St
WARRW/BUR WA5 * 48 B2
Priestnall Rd HTNM SK4 ....40 G5
Priest St STKP SK1 ....41 N9
Priestway La NSTN CH64 ....100 C3
Priesty Ct CONG CW12 ....155M8
Priesty Flds CONG CW12 ....155M8
Primitive St ALS/KID ST7 ....189 L1
Primrose Av CW/HAS CW1 ....186 A4
HYDE SK14 ....43 J1
MCFLDS SK11 ....117 H6
MPL/ROM SK6 * 58 C1
Primrose Bnk ALT WA14 ....52 C6
Primrose Cha HOLMCH CW4 ....131 P5
Primrose Cl CHSE CH3 ....143 J4
RUNC WA7 ....14 C5
WARRN/WOL WA2 ....33M7
WDN WA8 ....19 J8
Primrose Cots ALT WA14 ....52 C6
Primrose Gv RNFD/HAY WA11 ....23 J2
Primrose Hl CW/SHV CW2 ....184 E3
NWCHW CW8 ....108 B8
TPLY/KEL CW6 ....165 M2
Primrose La FROD/HEL WA6 ....104 G3
Primula Dr ALS/KID ST7 ....189 J6
Prince Albert Av BNG/LEV M19 * .28 A7
Prince Albert St CW/HAS CW1 ....5 F3
Prince Edward Av
DTN/ASHW M34 ....29M7
Prince Edward St NANT CW5 ....10 B3
Prince of Wales Av FLINT CH6 ....6 B8
Prince Rd POY/DIS SK12 ....74 A1
Princedom St CH/BCN CH1 ....3 H3
DID/WITH M20 ....40 D4
MPL/ROM SK6 ....42 J7
NWCHE CW9 ....13 J2
Princes Dr FLINT CH6 ....6 B8
MPL/ROM SK6 ....43 J9
Princes Pk NWCHW CW8 ....109 J2
Princes Pl WDN WA8 ....45 L6
Princes Rd ALT WA14 ....53 H1
EP CH65 ....80 B7
HTNM SK4 ....41 H4
SALE M33 ....42 F5
SALE M33 ....38 F5
Princess Av ALS/KID ST7 ....200 F6
CHD/CHDH SK8 ....56 A4
DTN/ASHW M34 ....29M7
RNFD/HAY WA11 ....23 L2
WARR WA1 ....49 H1
WARRW/BUR WA5 ....47 J1
Princess Dr CW/SHV CW2 ....198 E5
MCFLDN SK10 ....95 L7
NANT CW5 ....171M2
SBCH CW11 ....171M2
Princess Gv CW/SHV CW2 ....198 E5
Princess Pkwy WYTH/NTH M22 ...39 M8
Princess Rd DID/WITH M20 ....39 N5
KNUT WA16 ....112 C9
LYMM WA13 ....50 C4
WILM/AE SK9 ....71 H7
Princess St ALS/KID ST7 ....201 N2
ALT WA14 ....37 H7
CH/BCN CH1 ....2 D4
CONG CW12 ....155M7
CW/HAS CW1 * 185 J2
KNUT WA16 ....90 E3
MCFLDN SK10 ....95 L7
NWCHE CW9 ....110 C2
RUNC WA7 ....14 E1
WARRW/BUR WA5 ....47 P3
WSFD CW7 ....150 A1
Princes St FLINT CH6 * 6 B8
NEWLW WA12 ....23M6

STKP SK1 ....17 F4
WDN WA8 ....21 H2
Princes Wk BRAM/HZG SK7 ....56 C8
Princes Wy MCFLDS SK11 ....116 E5
Princeway FROD/HEL WA6 ....85 P5
Prinknash Rd WYTH/NTH M22 ....54 F6
Printer St OP/CLY M11 * 28 D1
Printworks La BNG/LEV M19 ....28 C8
Prior Cl CW/SHV CW2 ....184 F7
Priors Cl NWCHE CW9 ....109 P8
Priory Cl CH/BCN CH1 ....171M7
CONG CW12 ....175 J2
CW/HAS CW1 ....169 P9
SALE M33 ....38 G2
WSFD CW7 ....128 D8
Priory Ct MCFLDN SK10 ....116 F5
RDSH SK5 ....17 G5
RUNC WA7 * 63 J9
Priory Dr MCFLDN SK10 ....116 E2
Priory La MCFLDN SK10 ....116 E3
OFTN SK2 ....57 K3
Priory Rd ALT WA14 ....52 E6
CHD/CHDH SK8 ....56 A2
RUNC WA7 ....62 G4
SALE M33 ....38 C3
WILM/AE SK9 ....70 C6
Priory St WA14 ....52 C7
NWCHE CW9 ....13 G3
WARRS WA4 ....48 D4
The Priory NSTN CH64 ....77 K4
RAIN/WH L35 ....30 B5
WARRN/WOL WA2 ....33 K1
Priory Wy NWCHW CW8 ....109 K8
Pritchard Dr NWCHE CW9 ....128 F1
Private Wk CHSE CH3 ....143 J2
Probert Cl CW/SHV CW2 ....184 G4
Proctors Cl WDN WA8 ....46 A5
Proctors La SBCH CW11 ....171 J4
Promenade
WARRS WA4 * 47 L8
Promised Land La CHSE CH3 ......143 N5
Prospect Av IRL M44 ....36 D2
Prospect Dr HALE/TIMP WA15 ....53 L4
NWCHE CW9 ....128 F1
Prospect La GOL/RIS/CU WA3 ....35 K5
Prospect Rd IRL M44 ....36 D2
STHEL WA9 ....22 B5
Prospect Rw RUNC WA7 ....61 M7
WARR WA1 * 42 C7
Prosperity La MWCH CW10 ....10 K1
Prosper Rd CHNE CH2 ....121M7
Prout St WGTN/LGST M12 ....28 A6
Provan Wy CH/BCN CH1 ....120 C6
Providence St DTN/ASHW M34 ....29M2
Provident Av BNG/LEV M19 ....28 C8
Provident Wy HALE/TIMP WA15 ....22 E6
Provident Wy
HALE/TIMP WA15 ....38 D9
Provis Rd CCHDY M21 ....39 L1
Prubella Av DTN/ASHW M34 ....29 L4
Prunus Rd CW/HAS CW1 ....185 L2
The Pryors CHSE CH3 ....124 B8
Parmigan M WSFD CW7 ....149M5
Public Hall St RUNC WA7 ....15 F1
Pudding La TPLY/KEL CW6 ....165M2
Puddington La NSTN CH64 ....100 B4
Puddle Bank La CONG CW12 ......174 C4
Pudsey Cl RUNC WA7 ....62 B5
Puffin Cl EP CH65 ....80 F5
Puffin Cl EP CH65 ....102 E4
CHSW/BR CH4 ....160 C7
Pulford Av NWCHE CW9 ....109 N4
RUNC WA7 ....62 B8
Pulford Cl CHSW/BR CH4 ....160 C5
Pulford La CHSW/BR CH4 ....160 D5
Pulford Rd CH/BCN CH1 ....121 H6
EP CH65 ....80 D9
SALE M33 ....38 F6
WSFD CW7 ....149 L1
Pullman Cl BNG/LEV M19 ....28 A8
Pullman Dr NWCHE CW9 ....110 C4
CHSE CH3 ....17 J3
Pump La CHSE CH3 ....178 C2
RUNC WA7 ....62 D6
Pump Tree Ms MCFLDS SK11 ......116 E5
Puncorn St WYTH/NTH M22 ....54 E6
Purcell St WGTN/LGST M12 ....28 A6
Purdy U WARRW/BUR WA5 ....32 G7
Purley Av NTHM/RTH M23 ....39 L7
Purley Dr IRL M44 ....36 B3
Purser La MALPAS SY14 ....202 F2
Putney Ct RUNC WA7 ....62 C8
Pwll y Hwyaden FLINT CH6 ....98 B9
Pye Cl RNFD/HAY WA11 ....23M1
Pyecroft Cl WARRW/BUR WA5 ....47 H1
Pyecroft La WARRW/BUR WA5 ......47 H1
Pyecroft St CHSW/BR CH4 ....142 F5
Pymgate Dr CHD/CHDH SK8 ....55 J5
Pymgate La CHD/CHDH SK8 ....55 J5
Pyrus Av CW/HAS CW1 ....184 E2
Pyrus Gv FROD/HEL WA6 * 83 J9
Pytcheley Hollow
FROD/HEL WA6 ....107 K6
Pytha Fold Rd DID/WITH M20 ....40 E5

Quadrant Cl RUNC WA7 ....63 H8
The Quadrant MPL/ROM SK6 ....42 J7
The Quadrant STKP SK1 ....42 A7
Quail Cl WARRN/WOL WA2 ....33 N1
Quail Dr IRL M44 ....36 D2
Quaintways NWCHW CW8 ....109 L8
Quakers Coppice CW/HAS CW1 ..185 N6

Quakers Wy WRXS/E LL13 ....176 G7
Quantock Cl GTS/LS CH66 ....79 L7
HTNM SK4 ....16 E2
Quarmby Rd GTN M18 ....28 E5
Quarry Av CHSE CH3 ....177 H7
Quarry Bnk TPLY/KEL CW6 ....146 F3
Quarrybank RNFD/HAY WA6 ....180 D2
Quarry Bank Rd WILM/AE SK9 ......71 H3
Quarry Cl WDN WA8 ....45 J6
Quarry Hl RNFD/HAY WA11 ....62 B5
Quarry La CHSE CH3 ....143M3
TPLY/KEL CW6 ....146 F3
WARRS WA4 ....48 F9
Quarry Ri MPL/ROM SK6 ....42 G5
Quarry Rd CW/SHV CW2 ....184 G4
NM/HAY SK22 ....59 P8
NSTN CH64 ....77 P4
Quarry Ter ALS/KID ST7 ....189 J7
Quay Fold WARRS WA4 ....48 A3
Quayle Cl RNFD/HAY WA11 ....22 F3
Quay Pl RUNC WA7 ....63 J7
Quayside CONG CW12 ....155 N9
Quay Side FROD/HEL WA6 ....84 B4
Quayside NSTN CH64 ....77 K8
Quayside Ms LYMM WA13 ....50 F4
Quayside Wy MCFLDN SK10 ....9 H6
The Quay FROD/HEL WA6 ....84 B3
Queastybirch La WARRS WA4 ......64 C6
Quebec Rd WARRN/WOL WA2 ....19 H1
Quebec St DTN/ASHW M34 ....28 A7
Queen Annes Ct MCFLDS SK11 * ...8 B7
Queenhill Rd WYTH/NTH M22 ....59 P7
Queen's Av CH/BCN CH1 ....3 H3
EP CH65 ....102 C1
FLINT CH6 ....98 B7
GOL/RIS/CU WA3 ....26 C2
MCFLDN SK10 ....95 J7
MPL/ROM SK6 ....42 F5
WARR WA1 ....33 P9
WARRS WA4 ....45 H7
Queensbury Cl WILM/AE SK9 ....71 M6
Queensbury Wy WDN WA8 ....45 K4
Queens Cl HTNM SK4 ....41 K1
MCFLDN SK10 ....95 L7
RUNC WA7 ....14 D5
Queens Crs CHNE CH2 ....169M7
CW/HAS CW1 ....184 E4
WARR WA1 * 42 E5
Queens Dr CHD/CHDH SK8 ....56 A4
CHSW/BR CH4 ....105 H1
GOL/RIS/CU WA3 ....24 E1
HYDE SK14 ....43 L1
MWCH CW10 ....151 K4
NEWLW WA12 ....23 N5
NWCHE CW9 ....171M1
WARRS WA4 ....49 H5
Queens Gdns EP CH65 ....6 C4
Queensgate BRAM/HZG SK7 ....72 E1
NWCHW CW8 ....109 J2
Queen's Gv ALS/KID ST7 ....128 A5
Queensland Av STHEL WA9 ....30 D1
Queensland Pl STHEL WA9 ....30 D1
Queensland Rd GTN M18 ....28 B4
Queen's Park Dr
CW/SHV CW2 ....184 F5
Queen's Park Gdns
CHSW/BR CH4 ....3 F7
Queen's Park Vw
CHSW/BR CH4 ....3 F7
Queen's Rd BRAM/HZG SK7 ....57 L4
CHD/CHDH SK8 ....55 P4
CHSE CH3 ....177 M1
GTS/LS CH66 ....79 N6
HALE/TIMP WA15 ....42 F5
RNFD/HAY WA11 ....23 L2
SALE M33 ....38 C4
WHITCH SY13 ....213 N6
WILM/AE SK9 ....71 J8
Queenston Rd DID/WITH M20 ....40 A4
ALS/KID ST7 ....189 J6
Queen St ALS/KID ST7 ....200 F6
CHD/CHDH SK8 ....55 N1
CONG CW12 ....155 P6
CW/HAS CW1 ....5 H2
CW/SHV CW2 ....198 B5
DTN/ASHW M34 ....29 L5
DTN/ASHW M34 ....29 L5
FLINT CH6 ....98 C7
GOL/RIS/CU WA3 * 24 D1
KNUT WA16 ....90 D3
MCFLDN SK10 ....95 J8
MCFLDS SK11 ....8 D5
MPL/ROM SK6 * 151 J1
MWCH CW10 ....151 J1
NEWLW WA12 ....23 N5
NEWLW WA12 ....23 M6
NEWLW ST5 ....201 P8
NWCHE CW9 ....128 E1
RUNC WA7 ....14 E1
STKP SK1 * 16 D4
TPLY/KEL CW6 ....166 B9
Queen St West
DID/WITH M20 ....39 N4
Queensway ALS/KID ST7 ....187 M3
BNG/LEV M19 ....40 E6
CHSE CH3 ....122 A6
CHNE CH2 ....122 A6
Queen's Wy CHSW/BR CH4 ....140 F6
Queensway CW/HAS CW1 ....5 F3

Raby Cl WDN WA8 ....46 B5
Raby Gdns NSTN CH64 ....77 L5
Raby Park Cl NSTN CH64 ....77 L5
Raby Park Rd NSTN CH64 ....77 L5
Raby Rd NSTN CH64 ....77 L5
Raby Rd NSTN CH64 ....77 P2
Racecourse La TPLY/KEL CW6 ....126 D9
Racecourse Pk WILM/AE SK9 ....71 G4
Racecourse Rd WILM/AE SK9 ....70 C8
Racefield Cl LYMM WA13 ....50 F3
Racefield Rd ALT WA14 ....52 C4
The Race WILM/AE SK9 ....71M4
Rackhouse Rd NTHM/RTH M23 .....39 L7
Radbourne Cl WGTN/LGST M12 ...28 A3
Radbroke Cl SBCH CW11 ....172 A1
Radcliffe Av GOL/RIS/CU WA3 .....26 C2
Radcliffe Rd MCFLDS SK11 ....136 C4
Radcliffe St OP/CLY M11 ....171 L6
Raddel La WARRS WA4 ....64 B7
Raddon Pl WARRS WA4 * 48 C4
Radford Cl OFTN SK2 ....42 C9
WDN WA8 ....45 J8
Radford Dr IRL M44 ....27 N6
Radlet Dr HALE/TIMP WA15 ....38 D8
Radlett Cl WARRW/BUR WA5 ....47 J4
Radley Cl SALE M33 ....38 B2
Radley La WARRN/WOL WA2 ....33 N5
Radley St DROY M43 ....29 P1
STHEL WA9 ....30 D1
Radnor Av DTN/ASHW M34 ....29 H4
Radnor Cl CONG CW12 ....155 J5
SBCH CW11 ....171 K2
WDN WA8 ....45 K5
Radnormere Dr
CHD/CHDH SK8 ....55 P3
Radnor St DTN M18 ....28 B5
WARRW/BUR WA5 ....48 C1
Radstock Gv STHEL WA9 ....31 J3
Radway Gn GTS/LS CH66 ....88 A4
CW/SHV CW2 ....187 J3
Radway Green Rd
WARRN/WOL WA2 ....200 A1
Raeburn Av NSTN CH64 ....77 M6
Rae St EDGY/DAV SK3 ....16 B6
Raglan Cl GOL/RIS/CU WA3 ....34 D2
Raglan Dr ALT WA14 ....38 B8
Raglan Rd MCFLDS SK11 ....117M2
SALE M33 ....38 C5
Ragley Cl POY/DIS SK12 ....73M2
Railbrook Ct CW/SHV CW2 * 5 E5
Railton Av CW/HAS CW1 ....184 C1
RAIN/WH L35 ....30 C6
Railton Rd EDGY/DAV SK3 ....17 F6
GOL/RIS/CU WA3 * 24 D1
Railway St ALT WA14 ....53 H5
CW/SHV CW2 ....29 F1
DUK SK16 ....29 P1
GTN M18 ....28 C2
HTNM SK4 ....16 C3
NEWLW WA12 ....23M6
Rainbow Cl CCHDY M21 ....39 L1
MWCH CW10 ....151 H5
WDN WA8 ....45 J8
Rainford Av HALE/TIMP WA15 ....53 L2
Rainford Cl ALS/KID ST7 ....189 P7
Rainham Wy RDSH SK5 ....42 A2
Rainhill Rd RAIN/WH L35 ....30 B3
Rainow Av DROY M43 ....28 E1
Rainow Rd EDGY/DAV SK3 * 56 F7
Rainow Wy MCFLDN SK10 * 96 C4
MCFLDN SK10 ....117 N2
Rake La CHNE CH2 ....102 F7
CHSE CH3 ....144 A2
CHSW/BR CH4 ....142 D3
CQ CH5 ....140 A9
FROD/HEL WA6 ....104 B5
FROD/HEL WA6 ....104 B5
MCFLDN SK10 ....95 H8
MPL/ROM SK6 * 58 D6
MWCH CW10 * 151 H5
NSTN CH64 ....88 B6
NWCHE CW9 ....109 N6
RUNC WA7 ....14 E2
STKP SK1 * 17 H3
TPLY/KEL CW6 ....166 B9
Rake Wy CH/BCN CH1 ....171 L6
Raleigh Cl DID/WITH M20 ....39 M8
WARRW/BUR WA5 ....32 G7
Raleigh Rd RDSH SK5 ....41M4
Raleigh St WDN WA8 ....20 E6
Ralph Av HYDE SK14 ....43 K1
Ramford St STHEL WA9 ....56 B6
Ramillies Av CHD/CHDH SK8 ....56 B6
Rampit Cl RNFD/HAY WA11 ....180 D2
Ramp Rd East MANAIR M90 ....54 D8
Ramp Rd South MANAIR M90 ....54 D8
Ramp Rd West MANAIR M90 ....54 D8
Ramps Ga NWCHW CW8 ....127 K1
Ramsay Cl GOL/RIS/CU WA3 ....34 F5
Ramsbottom St CW/HAS CW1 ....4 F1
Ramsdale La SPK/HALE L24 ....60 C3
Ramsdale Rd BRAM/HZG SK7 ....57 L8

R

Ramsden Ct CHSW/BR CH4 ....142 B6
Ramsey Av BNG/LEV M19....28 D8
Ramsey Rd WDN WA8 ......45 J4
Ramsey Rd EP CH65 .....102 E5
Ramsfield Rd SPK/HALE L24 ....60 A2
Ramsgate Rd RDSH SK5....41 N1
Ramsgill St NTHM/RTH M23....39 H7
Randle Meadow CHS/LS CH66 ..102 B2
Randle's Vw CONG CW12 .....3 J5
Randolph Pl EDGY/DAV SK3 ....41 M9
Randolph St BNG/LEV M19 ....28 A7
Ranford Rd BNG/LEV M19 ....28 A9
Range Ct MCFLDN SK10 ......9 H1
Range Dr MPL/ROM SK6....43 H2
Rangemoor Cl GOL/RIS/CU WA3 ..35 H2
Rangemore Av
 WYTH/NTH M22 * 39 N8
Range Rd EDGY/DAV SK3 .....56 E1
Range St OP/CLY M11 .....28 C1
Rannoch Cl GTS/LS CH66 ..102 B1
Ranulph Cl FROD/HEL WA6....84 B4
Ranworth Ct CHNE CH2 ....121 N8
Ranworth Av HTNM WA4 .....40 G6
Ranworth Dr GOL/RIS/CU WA3 ..24 C2
Ranworth Rd
 WARRW/BUR WA5 ......47 J1
Rappax Rd HALE/TIMP WA15 ....53 L7
Raspberry La IRL M44 .....27 N7
Ratcliffe Av IRL M44 .....27 N7
Ratcliffe St BNG/LEV M19 ....28 B8
 STKP SK1 .....17 G7
Ratcliff Pl RAIN/WH L35 .....30 A4
Rathbone Pk TPLY/KEL CW6 ..147 H8
Rathen Rd DID/WITH M20 ....40 C5
Rathlin Cl WDN WA8 .....46 C4
Rathmell Cl GOL/RIS/CU WA3 ..25 N6
Rathmel Rd NTHM/RTH M23 ....39 J6
Rathvale Dr WYTH/NTH M22 ....54 E7
Raven Cl SBCH CW11 ....171 M1
Ravendale Cl WSFD CW7 .....149 M4
Raven Dr IRL M44 .....27 N6
Ravenfield Dr WDN WA8 ....45 J4
Ravenho La MCFLDN SK10 ....118 B1
Ravenhurst Ct GOL/RIS/CU WA3 ..34 G3
Ravenna Av NTHM/RTH M23 ....38 G9
Ravennoak Av BNG/LEV M19....28 B9
Ravenoak Park Rd
 CHD/CHDH SK8 .....56 B7
Ravenoak Rd CHD/CHDH SK8 ..56 C7
Ravenoak Rd EDGY/DAV SK3 ..56 C3
Raven Rd HALE/TIMP WA15 ....53 E7
Ravenscar Crs WYTH/NTH M22 ..54 F7
Ravenscliffe Rd ALS/KID ST7 ..189 J8
Ravens Cl ALS/KID ST7 .....201 H4
Ravenscroft HOLMCW4 .....131 M8
Ravenscroft Cl SBCH CW11 ..171 P2
Ravenscroft Rd CW/SHV CW2 ..184 E5
Ravensdale Cl
 WARRN/WOL WA2 .....33 N5
Ravensfield NWCHW CW8 ....107 P8
Ravensholme Ct CHSE CH3 ....163 P7
Ravensholme La CHSE CH3 ..163 P7
Raven's La ALS/KID ST7 .....201 J4
Ravens La NANT CW5 .....195 P1
Ravenstone Dr SALE M33 .....55 J4
 STHEL WA9 .....31 J1
Ravenswood NWCHW CW8 ..109 K8
Ravenswood Av HTNM SK4 ....41 H7
Ravenswood Dr CHD/CHDH SK8..56 B7
 WILM/AE SK9 .....92 C1
Ravenswood Dr DTN/ASHW M34 ..29 L3
 HALE/TIMP WA15 .....53 P8
Rawcliffe Cl WDN WA8 .....45 M3
Rawdon Cl BNG/LEV M19 ....28 B8
 RUNC WA7 .....62 E7
Rawlings Cl GOL/RIS/CU WA3 ..34 C5
Rawlinson Crs NLWD L26 ....42 E8
Rawpool Gdns NTHM/RTH M23 ..39 K9
Rawson Rd CH/BCN CH1 ....121 H8
Ray Av NANT CW5 .....10 D1
Rayleigh Wy MCFLDN SK10 ..116 E3
Raymond Av WARRS WA4 ....48 F5
Raymond Rd NTHM/RTH M23 ..39 L6
Raymond St CH/BCN CW1 .....2 C3
Raymond Wy NSTN CH64 .....77 N6
Rayner St STKP SK1 .....42 A8
Raynham Av DID/WITH M20 ..40 C5
Rays Brow NWCHW CW8 * ..109 K2
Readesdale Av CW/SHV CW2 ..184 F6
Reades La CCDHY CW12 ....175 J1
Reading Cl OP/CLY M11 .....28 C1
Reading Dr SALE M33 .....38 A4
Reading Room La CHSE CH3 ..179 K8
Reaney Wk WGTN/LGST M12 * ..28 A3
Rean Meadow CHSE CH3 ....164 A7
Reaper Cl WARRW/BUR WA5 ..47 P1
Reay St WDN WA8 .....46 A5
Rebecca Gdns STHEL WA9 ....31 H1
Recreation St STHEL WA9 ....31 J1
Rectory Cl GOL/RIS/CU WA3 ..24 E1
Rectory Cl CHSE CH3 .....176 G2
 CW/SHV CW2 * 184 E8
 DTN/ASHW M34 .....29 N7
 FLINT CH6 .....98 A7
 NANT CW5 .....13 G2
 WARRN/WOL WA2 .....33 C2
Rectory Flds STKP SK1 .....17 J4
Rectory Gdns ALS/KID ST7 ..201 N1
 LYMM WA13 .....50 E5
 STHEL WA9 .....31 H2
Rectory Gn STKP SK1 .....17 J4
Rectory La CH/BCN CW1 ....101 K3
 CO CH5 .....140 B2
 LYMM WA13 .....50 E5
 MKTDR TF9 .....217 H9
Rectory Vw ALS/KID ST7 ....201 N1
Redacre POY/DIS SK12 .....57 M9
Redacre La POY/DIS SK12 ....57 M9
Redacre Rd GTN M18 .....28 E4
Red Bank Av NEWLW WA12 ....24 B8
Redbarn Cl MPL/ROM SK6 ....42 E4

Redbourne Dr WDN WA8 .....45 H3
Redbrook Rd HALE/TIMP WA15 ..53 L7
Redbrook Rd MCFLDN SK10 ..75 J9
Red Brow La RUNC WA7 .....63 J6
Redburn Rd NTHM/RTH M23 ..39 H6
Redby St OP/CLY M11 * 28 B2
Redcar Av DID/WITH M20 ....40 C2
Redcar La GOL/RIS/CU WA3 ..36 C4
Redcliffe Rd DID/WITH M20 ..40 B3
Redcourt Av DID/WITH M20 ..40 C4
Red Cow Yd KNUT WA16 .....90 E3
Redcroft Gdns BNG/LEV M19 ..40 F4
Redcroft Rd SALE M33 .....38 B2
Reddish Av CHF/WBR SK23 ..75 N8
Reddish Crs LYMM WA13 ....50 F5
Reddish La CHF/WBR SK23 ..75 P8
 GTN M18 .....28 E6
 LYMM WA13 .....50 C2
Reddish Rd CHF/WBR SK23 ..75 P8
 RDSH SK5 .....41 N2
Reddish Vale Rd RDSH SK5 ..41 P1
Reddy La ALT WA14 .....51 P7
Redesdale Cl
 WARRN/WOL WA2 .....33 P6
Redesmere Cl
 HALE/TIMP WA15 .....53 P1
 MCFLDN SK10 .....116 C3
 NWCHE CW9 .....108 A1
 SBCH CW11 .....171 L2
Redesmere Dr CHD/CHDH SK8 ..55 P3
 WILM/AE SK9 .....93 H4
Redesmere La MCFLDS SK11 ..115 K9
Redesmere Rd WILM/AE SK9 ..71 M1
Redfern Av CONG CW12 .....155 P6
 SALE M33 .....39 H5
Redford Dr BRAM/HZG SK7 ..56 G5
Redgate NWCHW CW8 .....43 J5
Redgate La WGTN/LGST M12 ..28 A4
Redhill Dr MPL/ROM SK6 ....42 C5
Redhill Ms EP CH65 .....6 D2
Redhill Rd CHSW/BR CH4 ....142 B4
 TPLY/KEL CW6 .....125 H6
Redland Av RDSH SK5 .....41 N3
Redland Crs CCHDY M21 .....39 L1
Red La CHSE CH3 .....164 C3
 FROD/HEL WA6 .....74 F1
 POY/DIS SK12 .....58 G5
 SBCH CW11 .....171 H5
 WARRS WA4 .....48 A5
 WARRS WA4 .....86 E4
Red Lion Cl ALS/KID ST7 ....188 F9
 NANT CW5 .....196 E1
Redmain Cl GOL/RIS/CU WA3 ..24 C1
Redmayne Cl NEWLW WA12 ..23 M5
Redmond Cl DTN/ASHW M34 ..29 L2
Redmoor La NM/HAY SK22 ..59 M9
 POY/DIS SK12 .....58 G6
Red Pike GTS/LS CH66 .....79 P6
Redpoll La GOL/RIS/CU WA3 ..34 F4
Red Rose Crs BNG/LEV M19 ..41 K1
Redruth Av MCFLDN SK10 ..116 E3
 RNFD/HAY WA11 .....51 K2
Redruth Cl RUNC WA7 .....62 G8
Redshank Av WSFD CW7 ....149 L5
Redshank Cl NEWLW WA12 ..23 N5
Redshank La GOL/RIS/CU WA3 ..34 G4
Redshaw Cl NWCH CW10 ....151 J4
Redstart Cl GOL/RIS/CU WA3 ..24 C1
Redstone Dr WSFD CW7 ....149 J1
Red Stone Hl FROD/HEL WA6 ..83 H9
Redstone Rd BNG/LEV M19 ..40 E5
Redthorn Av BNG/LEV M19 ..40 G1
Redvales Ct GOL/RIS/CU WA3 ..79 L3
Redvers Av GTS/LS CH66 ....79 L3
Redway La MCFLDN SK10 ..95 P6
Redwing Cl ALS/KID ST7 ..189 N7
Redwing Dr BIDD ST8 .....175 P4
Redwood SALE M33 .....37 P4
Redwood Cl CHSW/BR CH4 ..142 A4
 NWCHW CW8 .....87 K9
 WARR WA1 .....49 N1
Redwood Ct MCFLDN SK10 ....95 L8
Redwood Dr CHNE CH2 .....42 D4
 DTN/ASHW M34 .....29 L3
 GTS/LS CH66 .....102 B3
 MPL/ROM SK6 .....43 H2
 WARR WA1 .....47 D4
Reece Cl CHNE CH2 .....122 F5
Reedgate La NWCHE CW9 ....65 N5
Reed La NWCHE CW9 .....65 N5
Reedham Bnk OFTN SK2 .....57 K2
Reedsmere Cl WARRS WA4 ..48 C5
Reedsmere Wk NWCHE CW9 ..37 N5
Reed St GTN M18 .....28 D3
Reeman Cl MPL/ROM SK6 ....42 F4
Rees Crs HOLMCH CW4 .....131 P7
Reeve Cl OFTN SK2 .....57 M7
Reeves Rd CCHDY M21 .....39 L1
 CHSE CH3 * 145 K5
Reeves St STHEL WA9 .....22 C6
Reeve St GOL/RIS/CU WA3 ..25 K1
Reevey Av BRAM/HZG SK7 ..57 J5
Reform Wk OP/CLY M11 .....28 B2
Regal Cl GTS/LS CH66 .....102 A1
 WDN WA8 .....46 A3
Regal Crs WDN WA8 .....45 H7
Regan Av CCHDY M21 .....39 N1
Regency Cl ALS/KID ST7 ..201 N2
Regency Ct CHNE CH2 .....122 F3
 HALE/TIMP WA15 * 53 M6
Regency Gdns CHD/CHDH SK8 ..57 H9
Regency Wy NWCHW CW8 ..109 N8
Regent Av MCFLDN SK10 .....8 B7
 RNFD/HAY WA11 .....22 F2
 WARR WA1 .....34 B8

Regent Cl BRAM/HZG SK7 ....72 D2
 CHD/CHDH SK8 .....56 C3
 CW/SHV CW2 .....198 A4
 WILM/AE SK9 .....71 P4
Regent Ct HTNM SK4 .....41 K3
Regent Dr DTN/ASHW M34 ..29 K8
Regent Rd ALT WA14 .....53 H1
 OFTN SK2 .....56 G1
 WDN WA8 .....45 N5
Regents Cl CHSE CH3 .....122 C9
Regents Ga NANT CW5 .....11 F6
Regent St NEWLW WA12 .....23 L6
 NWCHE CW9 .....128 G3
 RUNC WA7 .....14 E1
 WARR WA4 .....18 C6
Reginald Rd CHNE CH2 .....18 C6
Reginald St OP/CLY M11 .....28 F2
Registry Cl NWCHE CW9 ....109 N8
Reid Av WARRW/BUR WA5 ..33 J8
Reid Cl DTN/ASHW M34 .....29 N9
Reid Ct GTS/LS CH66 .....79 N6
Reins Shaw CW/SHV CW2 ..185 J2
Rembury Pl RUNC WA7 .....85 K2
Remer St CW/HAS CW1 ....185 K1
Rena Cl HTNM SK4 .....41 H2
Renaissance Cl CW/HAS CW1 ..185 N5
Renaissance Wy CW/HAS CW1 ..185 N5
Rendlesham Cl
 GOL/RIS/CU WA3 .....35 J2
Renfrew Av RNFD/HAY WA11 ..22 C7
Renfrew Cl MCFLDN SK10 ..116 F2
Renown Cl GOL/RIS/CU WA3 ..34 E4
Renshaw St NWCHE CW9 ....110 C2
Renshards Pl KNUT WA16 ....67 J1
Renton Av RUNC WA7 .....62 B4
Repton Av NTHM/RTH M22 ..54 F7
Repton Cl KNUT WA16 .....67 J2
Repton Dr CW/HAS CW1 ..186 D5
Repton Rd EP CH65....7 J1
Reservoir Rd CHF/WBR SK23 ..75 P8
 EDGY/DAV SK3 .....41 L9
Reservoir St STHEL WA9 ....30 B1
Reservoir Ter CHSE CH3 .....3 K5
The Retreat CW/HAS CW1 ..185 J2
Revesby Cl WDN WA8 .....45 K5
Reveton Av BRAM/HZG SK7 ..56 G5
Reynard Rd CCHDY M21 .....39 L1
Reynolds Av GOL/RIS/CU WA3 ..34 F3
 NEWLW L35 .....201 P9
 STHEL WA9 .....28 D3
Reynolds Dr GTN M18 .....28 D3
Reynolds Ms WILM/AE SK9 ..71 N6
 WARRS WA4 .....48 A5
Reynolds St WARRS WA4 ....49 J5
Rhoden St CW/HAS CW1 ..185 N2
Rhodes Av BNG/LEV M19 ..186 B4
Rhodes St WARRN/WOL WA2 ..71 P3
Rhona Cl BEB CH63 .....78 C1
Rhona Dr WARRW/BUR WA5 ..47 L9
Rhos Av CHD/CHDH SK8 ..56 B6
Rhos Dr BRAM/HZG SK7 ....57 K6
Rhoswen FLINT CH6 .....98 B8
Rhuddlan Ct EP CH65 .....102 F2
Rhuddlan Rd CH/BCN CH1 ..120 C7
Rhum Cl EP CH65 .....102 E5
Rhyl St WDN WA8 * 71 J5
Ribble Av RAIN/WH L35 ....30 B5
 WSFD CW7 .....150 B1
Ribble Cl GOL/RIS/CU WA3 ..25 P7
 WDN WA8 .....46 D4
Ribble Dr BIDD ST8 .....175 M9
Ribble Pl WSFD CW7 .....150 B1
Ribblesdale Cl EP CH65 ....102 C1
Ribblesdale La CONG CW12 ..156 A5
Ribchester Gdns
 GOL/RIS/CU WA3 .....26 A6
Rickard Moon St CW/HAS CW1 ..4 B2
Richards Ct DTN/ASHW M34 ..29 N7
Richards Crs CHSE CH3 ....143 J3
Richardson Cl CW/SHV CW2 ..198 C2
 SBCH CW11 .....171 J3
Richardson St OP/CLY M11 ..28 F2
 STKP SK1 .....41 P7
 WARRN/WOL WA2 .....33 M8
Richard St CW/HAS CW1 * ..4 E5
 NWCHE CW9 .....110 C5
 STKP SK1 .....17 H2
Richmond Av RNFD/HAY WA11 ..36 D1
 RUNC WA7 .....62 C8
Richmond Av WARRS WA4 ..49 H5
 WARRS WA4 .....49 L4
 WILM/AE SK9 .....71 M1
Richmond Cl CW/SHV CW2 ..199 J6
 GOL/RIS/CU WA3 .....34 G5
 LYMM WA13 .....51 H5
 SALE M33 .....38 B5
 SBCH CW11 .....171 K2
Richmond Crs CHSE CH3 ....143 L1
Richmond Dr LYMM WA13 ..51 H3
 NWCHE CW9 .....110 A8
Richmond Gdns NEWLW WA12 ..23 L2
 BRAM/HZG SK7 * 72 C5
Richmond Hill MCFLDS SK11 ..9 G5
Richmond Hill Rd
 CHD/CHDH SK8 .....55 L2
 ALT WA14 .....51 N2
Richmond Pl MCFLDS SK11 ..9 H2
Richmond Rd CCHDY M21 ..39 P2
 CW/HAS CW1 .....187 H2
 DTN/ASHW M34 * 29 J1
 HTNM SK4 .....41 H4
 MPL/ROM SK6 .....43 H5

Richmond St DTN/ASHW M34 ..29 L3
 WARRS WA4 .....49 J4
Ricroft Rd MPL/ROM SK6 ....46 A6
Ridding Av WYTH/NTH M22 ..54 C4
Ridding Cl OFTN SK2 .....57 K1
Ridding La RUNC WA7 .....62 F9
Riddings Ct HALE/TIMP WA15 ..53 C8
Riddings La NANT CW5 .....109 K8
 NWCHW CW8 .....109 K8
 HALE/TIMP WA15 .....38 D8
Riddings Rd HALE/TIMP WA15 ..53 K6
The Riddings EP CH65 * 6 C7
Ridge Av HALE/TIMP WA15 ..53 N9
 MPL/ROM SK6 .....58 E3
Ridgebourne Cl
 WARRW/BUR WA5 .....32 C6
Ridge Crs MPL/ROM SK6 ....43 K6
Ridge End Fold MPL/ROM SK6 ..58 E6
Ridge Hl MCFLDS SK11 ....117 N9
Ridgemont Av RUNC WA7 ....41 J6
Ridge Pk BRAM/HZG SK7 ..56 E3
Ridgeway GOL/RIS/CU WA3 ..24 E2
 WILM/AE SK9 .....71 P7
Ridgeway Cl GTS/LS CH66 ..101 N2
Ridgeway Gdns LYMM WA13 ..50 D4
Ridgeway Rd
 HALE/TIMP WA15 .....53 N2
 RUNC WA7 .....62 A7
Ridgeway CHSE CH3 .....124 B8
 FROD/HEL WA6 .....105 N2
 POY/DIS SK12 .....58 C8
 WDN WA8 .....45 J1
Ridgewell Av GOL/RIS/CU WA3 ..24 F1
Ridgewood Dr STHEL WA9 ....9 C1
Ridgmont Rd BRAM/HZG SK7 ..72 E2
Ridgway St CW/HAS CW1 ..185 K3
 WARRN/WOL WA2 .....19 H1
The Ridgway MPL/ROM SK6 ..42 F7
Riding Cl STHEL WA9 * 31 H4
Ridings St OP/CLY M11 .....28 F2
The Ridings CH/BCN CH1 ..120 E5
Ridley Cl CW/SHV CW2 ....198 D4
Ridley Dr ALT WA14 .....38 B7
 WARRW/BUR WA5 .....47 N3
Ridley Gv SALE M33 .....39 J5
Ridley Rd MCFLDN SK10 ....95 J5
Ridsdale WDN WA8 .....45 J1
Ridsdale Av DID/WITH M20 ..40 C3
Rifle Rd SALE M33 .....39 J3
Rigby Av CW/HAS CW1 ....184 C1
Rigby Rd ALS/KID ST7 .....189 K5
Rigbys Rw NANT CW5 .....10 C6
Rigby St ALT WA14 .....53 H4
 GOL/RIS/CU WA3 .....24 C1
Rigg St CW/HAS CW1 * 4 C1
Rigton Cl WGTN/LGST M12 ..28 A4
Riley Cl SALE M33 .....37 N7
 SBCH CW11 .....171 J4
Riley Av ALS/KID ST7 .....188 F9
Riley Wy ALS/KID ST7 .....189 J8
Riley Wood Cl MPL/ROM SK6 * ..42 E7
Rilshaw La WSFD CW7 .....150 A2
Rilston Av WYTH/NTH M22 ..53 M6
Rimington Cl GOL/RIS/CU WA3 ..25 N6
Rimmer Gv STHEL WA9 .....22 C6
Rimsdale Cl CHD/CHDH SK8 ..55 J4
 CW/SHV CW2 .....184 C9
Rindle Rd TYLD M29 .....25 J1
Ringmer Dr WYTH/NTH M22 ..54 E6
Ringmore Rd BRAM/HZG SK7 ..56 C5
Ring O'Bells La LYMM WA13 ..50 C2
Ring Rd CHSE CH3 .....143 L1
Ringsfield Rd SPK/HALE L24 ..60 A3
Ringstead Cl WILM/AE SK9 ..71 M5
Ringstead Dr WILM/AE SK9 ..71 M5
Ringstone Wy CHF/WBR SK23 ..75 N8
Ringway Cl CHSE CH3 .....144 B5
 GTS/LS CH66 .....80 A9
 NSTN CH64 .....77 M3
Ringway Gv SALE M33 .....39 H6
Ringway Rd West
 MANAIR M90 .....54 E8
 RUNC WA7 .....62 B4
 WYTH/NTH M22 .....54 E8
Ringway Rd West MANAIR M90 ..54 F7
 WGTN/LGST M12 .....28 B7
Ringwood Av BRAM/HZG SK7 ..57 H6
 WGTN/LGST M12 .....28 B7
Ripley Av CHD/CHDH SK8 ..72 B1
 OFTN SK2 .....57 H3
Ripley Cl BRAM/HZG SK7 ....57 L7
Ripley St WARRW/BUR WA5 ..33 H9
Ripon Av GOL/RIS/CU WA3 ..34 F3
 NEWLW ST5 .....201 P8
Ripon Cl HALE/TIMP WA15 ..53 N6
 MCFLDN SK10 .....117 J1
 NEWLW WA12 .....23 N5
 STHEL WA9 .....17 G7
Ripon Crs CHD/CHDH SK8 ..55 J1
Ripon Gv SALE M33 .....39 H6
Rippingham Rd DID/WITH M20 ..40 C1
Rippleton Rd WYTH/NTH M22 ..54 F7
Rippon Av GTS/LS CH66 .....79 N8
Riseley St MCFLDN SK10 .....8 C3
The Rise CHF/WBR SK23 ..75 N9
Rishworth Cl OFTN SK2 .....57 L2
Rising Sun Rd MCFLDS SK11 ..116 C8
Risley Rd GOL/RIS/CU WA3 ..34 A1
Rissington Av NTHM/RTH M23 ..39 H9
Ritherup La RAIN/WH L35 ....30 B5
Ritson Cl GTN M18 .....28 D3
Rivacre Rd EP CH65 .....79 L1
 GTS/LS CH66 .....80 A9
 PS/BROM CH62 .....79 L1
Riva Rd BNG/LEV M19 .....40 E6

Riverbank Cl MCFLDN SK10 ....95 M5
 NANT CW5 .....10 B1
Riverdale Dr BURS/TUN ST6 ..199 N8
Riverdane Rd CONG CW12 ..155 P6
River La CHSE CH3 .....176 G6
 CHSW/BR CH4 .....142 A3
 CHSW/BR CH4 .....142 E3
 PART M31 .....37 G6
Rivermead Av HALE/TIMP WA15 ..53 M9
Rivermead Cl DTN/ASHW M34 ..42 F1
Rivermead Rd DTN/ASHW M34 ..42 F1
Riverpark Cl NANT CW5 ....183 N8
River Rd WARR WA1 .....34 A8
 WARR WA1 .....34 G9
Riversdale Rd CHD/CHDH SK8 ..55 L2
 RUNC WA7 .....62 C5
Riversdale Vw MPL/ROM SK6 ..42 F3
Rivershill SALE M33 .....38 D2
Rivershill Gdns
 HALE/TIMP WA15 .....55 N9
Riverside Av IRL M44 .....10 A7
 NWCHE CW9 .....110 B7
Riverside Cl WARR WA1 .....19 C2
Riverside Ct MCFLDS SK11 ..118 A8
 MPL/ROM SK6 * 43 H8
Riverside Dr MCFLDN SK10 ..90 C8
 NWCHW CW8 .....108 A1
Riverside Gdns SALE M33 ....38 D2
Riverside Gv CW/SHV CW2 ..184 D5
Riverside STHEL WA9 .....31 J1
Riverside Wk NWCHW CW8 ..12 C8
Riverside Wk NSTN CH64 ....77 M3
Riversmead CHSE CH3 .....143 J5
Riverstone Dr NTHM/RTH M23 ..38 F3
River St CONG CW12 .....155 M7
 MCFLDS SK11 .....9 G3
 WILM/AE SK9 .....71 K6
Riverton Rd DID/WITH M20 ..40 C3
River Vw RDSH SK5 .....41 P1
 WSFD CW7 .....149 N1
Riverview Rd NSTN CH64 ....77 M8
River Wk RUNC WA7 * 62 B8
Rivington Ct WARR WA1 * ..34 F8
Rivington Gv DTN/ASHW M34 ..29 J1
 IRL M44 .....36 C2
Rivington Rd EP CH65 .....6 D5
 HALE/TIMP WA15 .....53 K5
 RUNC WA7 .....62 B8
The Roaches MCFLDS SK11 * ..117 J4
Roachill Cl ALT WA14 .....52 F2
Road Beta WSFD CW7 .....129 K9
Road Five WSFD CW7 .....129 K9
Road Four WSFD CW7 .....129 J7
Road One WSFD CW7 .....129 J7
Roadside Ct GOL/RIS/CU WA3 ..24 E1
Road St TPLY/KEL CW6 .....146 D7
Road Three WSFD CW7 .....129 J9
Road Two WSFD CW7 .....129 J9
Road Ten MCFLDS SK11 .....9 K6
Riley Rd RUNC WA7 .....14 C2
Roan House Wy MCFLDS SK11 ..9 J6
Roan Ms MCFLDS SK11 .....9 K5
Roan Wy WILM/AE SK9 .....93 K5
Roaring Gate La
 HALE/TIMP WA15 .....54 A4
Robert Moffat KNUT WA16 ..67 H7
Robert Owen Gdns
 WYTH/NTH M22 * 39 N8
Roberts Cl RNFD/HAY WA11 ..22 E4
Roberts Cl ALS/KID ST7 .....201 J9
Roberts Ct RUNC WA7 .....62 C8
Roberts Ct II WYTH/NTH M22 ..54 E1
Roberts Gn NWCHE CW9 ....110 C6
Robertshaw Av CCHDY M21 ..39 L2
Roberts Rd NWCHW CW8 ....110 C2
Roberts St DUK SK16 .....29 P1
 NWCHW CW8 .....15 J2
 RUNC WA7 .....15 J2
 SALE M33 .....39 M4
 WARRW/BUR WA5 .....33 K5
 WDN WA8 .....21 K1
Robeson Wy WYTH/NTH M22 ..55 H1
Robina Rd STHEL WA9 .....22 C6
Robin Cl MCFLDN SK10 .....96 C8
 RUNC WA7 .....62 B8
 SBCH CW11 .....171 M1
Robin Crs CW/SHV CW2 * ..184 C8
Robin Cft MPL/ROM SK6 ....42 C5
Robin Dr IRL M44 .....36 C2
Robin Hood Av MCFLDS SK11 ..117 J7
Robin Hood La FROD/HEL WA6 ..105 H2
 MCFLDS SK11 * 136 C1
Robin La NEWLW WA12 ....136 C1
Robinsbay Rd WYTH/NTH M22 ..54 E8
Robins Cft GTS/LS CH66 ....102 B3
Robin's La BRAM/HZG SK7 ..56 E8
 GOL/RIS/CU WA3 .....36 M7
 STHEL WA9 .....22 D5
Robinson Pl STHEL WA9 .....22 B5
Robinsons Cft CHSE CH3 ....143 L9
Robinson St EDGY/DAV SK3 ..41 L9
Robinsway ALT WA14 .....53 L8
Robinswood Rd
 WYTH/NTH M22 .....54 F6
Roblet Dr IRL M44 .....36 C2
Robson Wy GOL/RIS/CU WA3 ..25 H1
Roby Cl RAIN/WH L35 .....30 B5
Roby Gv WARRW/BUR WA5 ..47 L1
Roche GOL/RIS/CU WA3 * ..25 M7
Rochester Av CCHDY M21 ..39 N1
Rochester Cl GOL/RIS/CU WA3 ..47 N2
 WARRW/BUR WA5 .....47 N2
Rochester Dr ALT WA14 .....38 B7
 EP CH65 .....102 F1
Rochester Gv BRAM/HZG SK7 ..57 L4

Rochford Av WYTH/NTH M22 ......54 F7
Rock Dr FROD/HEL WA6 ......84 A4
Rock Farm Cl NSTN CH64 ......77 N7
Rock Farm Dr NSTN CH64 ......77 N7
Rock Farm Rd NSTN CH64 ......77 N7
Rockfield Dr WDN WA8 ......43 K5
Rockfield Dr FROD/HEL WA6 ...105 J2
Rockford Ldg KNUT WA16 ......90 G4
Rockhouse La ALS/KID ST7 ...188 E8
Rockingham Ct
GOL/RIS/CU WA3 ......35 J2
Rock La CHSE CH3 ......180 A2
WDN WA8 ......45 M3
Rocklee Gdns NSTN CH64 ......77 N7
Rocklynes MPL/ROM SK6 ......42 G6
Rocksavage Expy RUNC WA7 ...62 A9
Rockside ALS/KID ST7 ......189 L2
Rock St HYDE SK14 ......43 K1
NM/HAY SK22 ......59 M8
OP/CLY M11 ......28 E2
The Rock FROD/HEL WA6 ...105 H2
Rockwood Av CH/SHV CW2 ......4 A4
Rockwood Cl CW/SHV CW2 ......4 A4
Rocky La CHS CH5 ......178 F1
Rodborough Rd
NTHM/RTH M23 ......54 B4
Roddy La FROD/HEL WA6 ...107 N2
Rodehealth Cl WILM/AE SK9 ...71 M7
Rode House Cl ALS/KID ST7 ...188 D2
Rodepool Cl WILM/AE SK9 ......71 M4
The Rode ALS/KID ST7 ......187 P4
Rodger Av AUD/MAD/W CW5 ...199 M9
Rodgers Cl FROD/HEL WA6 ......83 P4
Rodgers Ct BURS/TUN ST6 *..189 L9
Rodgers St BURS/TUN ST6 ......55 J3
Rodmill Dr CHD/CHDH SK8 ......55 L8
Rodney Dr MPL/ROM SK6 ......42 F5
Rodney St MCFLDS SK11 ......8 E6
WARRN/WOL WA2 ......18 D3
Roebourne Rd CH/BCN CH1 ..120 C7
Roebuck Cl WARRN/WOL WA2 ..18 B4
Roebuck La SALE M33 * 38 D4
Roebuck St CW/HAS CW1 ......4 D1
Roeburn Wy WARRW/BUR WA5 ..47 H4
Roedean Wk CW/HAS CW1 ...185 K2
Roehampton Dr RUNC WA7 ......62 C7
Roehurst La WSFD CW7 ......62 C8
Roemarsh Ct RUNC WA7 ......62 C8
Roe Pk CONG CW12 ...174 F8
Roe St MCFLDS SK11 ......8 D5
Roewood La MCFLDN SK10 ..117 N3
MCFLDN SK10 ......117 P4
Rogate Dr NTHM/RTH M23 ......54 C2
Roger Cl MPL/ROM SK6 ......42 E1
Rokeby Ct RUNC WA7 ......63 H1
Rokeden NEWLW WA12 ......23 P5
Roker Park Av DTN/ASHW M34 ..29 K2
Roland Av RNFD/HAY WA11 ......22 A2
RUNC WA7 ......14 D5
Roland Rd RDSH SK5 ......44 E1
Rolleston St WARRN/WOL WA2 ..18 B4
Rolling Mill La STHEL WA9 ......22 D9
Rollins La MPL/ROM SK6 ......43 M7
Rolls Av CW/HAS CW1 ...184 C2
Roman Cl NEWLW WA12 ......23 K7
RUNC WA7 ......62 C5
Roman Ct NSTN CH64 ......77 M6
Roman Dr CH/BCN CH1 ..120 C5
Romanes St NWCHW CW8 ......12 C5
Roman Rd HTNM SK4 ......17 F3
WARRS WA4 ......16 B7
Roman Wy SBCH CW11 ...171 K2
WHITCH SY13 ...213 L5
Romford Av DTN/ASHW M34 ..29 N5
Romford Rd SALE M33 ......38 B2
Romiley Rd GTS/LS CH66 ......80 A7
Romiley St STKP SK1 ......9 J4
Romney Av NEWLW WA12 ..201 P9
Romney Ct WDN WA8 ......46 B5
Romney Wy NSTN CH64 ......77 M6
RDSH SK5 ......42 A2
Romsey Dr CHD/CHDH SK8 ......56 B9
Romsley Ct WGTN/LGST M12 ..28 A3
Rona Av EP CH65 ......102 E3
Ronald Dr WARRN/WOL WA2 ..34 C6
Ronaldshay WDN WA8 ......46 C5
Ronaldsway HLWD L26 ......44 A7
Ronan Hl CONG CW12 ......1 C6
Rood La CONG CW12 ...155 M6
Rookery Av GTN M18 ......28 F5
Rookery Cl NANT CW5 ......10 D6
SBCH CW11 ......171 H4
Rookery Dr CHSE CH3 ...164 A7
NANT CW5 ......196 F3
Rookery Gdns NWCHE CW9 ..108 F1
Rookerypool Cl WILM/AE SK9 ..71 M4
Rookery Ri WSFD CW7 ...150 B2
Rookery Rd ALS/KID ST7 ...189 L5
MALPAS SY14 ...191 J4
The Rookery CHSW/BR CH4 ..140 F7
NEWLW WA12 ......23 P5
Rookfield Av SALE M33 ......38 F3
Rook Rd WARRS WA4 ......48 C3
Rookwood Av NTHM/RTH M23 ..39 M9
Rooley St WARRN/WOL WA2 ......1 K4
Rooth St HTNM SK4 ......16 C3
Rope Bank Av CW/SHV CW2 ..184 D3
Rope La CW/SHV CW2 ......184 D3
Rope Walk CONG CW12 ...155 M7
Roper St STHEL WA9 ......22 A5
The Ropewalk NSTN CH64 ......77 J5
Rosam Ct RUNC WA7 ......62 G8
Roscoe Av NEWLW WA12 ......24 A6
WARRN/WOL WA2 ......33 N8
Roscoe Crs RUNC WA7 ......61 L7
Roscoe Rd IRL M44 ......27 L8
Roscoe St EDGY/DAV SK3 ......9 E5
Roseacre Dr CHD/CHDH SK8 ..55 L6
Rose Av IRL M44 ......27 M8

RNFD/HAY WA11 ......23 J3
STHEL WA9 ......31 H1
Rose Bank LYMM WA13 ......50 E4
MCFLDN SK10 ......95 M6
Rosebank Cl WSFD CW7 ...149 P2
Rosebank Rd IRL M44 ......36 B5
Roseberry St OFTN SK2 ......57 K5
Rosebery Cl BIDD ST8 ...175 M9
Rosebery Wy CW/HAS CW1 ..186 A4
Rose Cl HTNM SK4 ......63 H9
Rose Cottage Rd
......40 C1
Rose Cottages LYMM WA13 *..54 E1
Rose Crs IRL M44 ......27 M8
WDN WA8 ......21 F4
Rosecroft Cl EDGY/DAV SK3 ..56 E3
Rosedale Av GOL/RIS/CU WA3 ..24 E2
Rosedale Dr DTN/ASHW M54 *..29 L6
Rosedale Rd SALE M33 ......41 L3
Rosedene Cl CHNE CH2 ...121 P5
Rosefield Cl EDGY/DAV SK3 ..39 H4
Rosegarth Av DID/WITH M20 ..39 N4
Rosehay Av DTN/ASHW M34 ..29 M7
Rose Hl DTN/ASHW M34 ......29 K6
Rosehill Av STHEL WA9 ......31 N3
Rosehill Rd CW/SHV CW2 ......184 D9
Roseland Dr DID/WITH M20....40 C4
Roselands Av SALE M33 ......41 L4
Roselands Ct WRX/GR/LL LL12 ..160 F8
Rose La MPL/ROM SK6 ......58 C2
Rose Lea Cl WDN WA8 ......45 N5
Rosemary Av RUNC WA7 ......84 D1
WARRS WA4 ......48 C5
Rosemary Cl CHSW/BR CW4 ..140 C2
WARRW/BUR WA5 * 47 J1
Rosemary Dr HYDE SK14 ......43 J1
NEWLW WA12 ......24 B6
Rosemary La STKP SK1 ......17 J5
WHITCH SY13 ...213 M6
Rosemere Dr CH/BCN CH1 ..102 B5
Rosemoor Gdns WARRS WA4 ..65 H1
Rose Mt RUNC WA7 * 65 H1
Roseneath BRAM/HZG SK7 ......56 D6
Roseneath Av BNG/LEV M19 ..28 C3
Rose St RDSH SK5 ......41 N5
WDN WA8 ......21 F4
Rose Ter CW/HAS CW1 ...185 J3
Rose V CHD/CHDH SK8 ......55 K6
Rosevale Av BNG/LEV M19 ......40 F3
Rosevale Ct NEWLW ST5 ......201 P7
Rosevale Rd NEWLW ST5 ......201 P7
Rose View Av WDN WA8 ......45 N5
Roseville Dr CONG CW12 ...175 J1
Roseway BRAM/HZG SK7 ......56 E6
MCFLDS SK11 ......117 K7
Rose Wd DTN/ASHW M34 ......29 K6
Rosewood Av CHNE CH2 ...121 N6
FROD/HEL WA6 ......84 B6
WARR WA1 ......41 H7
WARR WA1 * 19 K1
Rosewood Cl CW/HAS CW1 *..185 L2
Rosewood Dr WSFD CW7 ...149 J2
Rosewood Gdns
CHD/CHDH SK8 ......55 P5
Rosewood Gv CH/BCN CH1 ..120 C8
Rosgill Cl HTNM SK4 ......40 F6
Rosina St OP/CLY M11 ......28 D1
Roslyn Rd EDGY/DAV SK3 ......56 E2
Rossall Dr BRAM/HZG SK7 ......56 F9
Rossall Rd WARRW/BUR WA5 ..47 M3
WDN WA8 ......46 B5
Ross Av EDGY/DAV SK3 ......56 D3
Rossbank Rd EP CH65 ......6 A1
Rosscliffe Rd EP CH65 ......6 A2
Ross Cl WARRN/WOL WA2 ......18 B4
Ross Dr GTS/LS CH66 ......79 N8
Rossenclough Rd WILM/AE SK9 ..71 M5
Rossendale Dr GOL/RIS/CU WA3 ..35 H2
Rossendale Rd CHD/CHDH SK8 ..55 L7
Rosett Av HALE/TIMP WA15 ..38 D8
WYTH/NTH M22 ......54 F6
Rossett Cl NWCHE CW9 ......109 N8
WARRW/BUR WA5 ......33 H6
Rossett Gv ALS/KID ST7 ...189 P9
Rossett Pk WRX/GR/LL LL12 ..160 F8
Rossett Rd WRX/GR/LL LL12 *..176 A2
Rossett Rd WRXS/E LL13 * ..176 C6
Rossfield Rd EP CH65 ......6 A1
Rosslare Rd WYTH/NTH M22 ..54 G5
Ross Lave La DTN/ASHW M34 ..29 J9
Rosslyn Gv HALE/TIMP WA15 ..53 L1
Rosslyn La NWCHW CW8 ......108 C9
Rosslyn Rd CHD/CHDH SK8 ..55 M6
CHS CH3 ......122 C8
Rossmill La HALE/TIMP WA15 ..53 N8
Rossmore Gdns GTS/LS CH66 ..79 P7
Rossmore Rd East EP CH65 ..80 B6
Rossmore Rd West
GTS/LS CH66 ......79 P6
Rossmount Rd EP CH65 ......6 P6
Ross Rd EP CH65 ......6 A8
Ross St STHEL WA9 ......22 A5
WDN WA8 ......21 F1
Rosswood Rd EP CH65 ......6 A8
Rostherne Av
GOL/RIS/CU WA3 ......24 F1
Rostherne Cl WILM/AE SK9 ..80 A9
MPL/ROM SK6 ......58 G9
Rostherne Cl WARRW/BUR WA5 ..45 K5
Rostherne La ALT WA14 ......68 B1
Rostherne Rd EDGY/DAV SK3 ..56 E2
SALE M33 ......39 J5
WILM/AE SK9 ......70 G9
Rostherne St ALT WA14 ......53 H4
Rostherne Wy SBCH CW11 ..171 L2
Rosthernmere Rd
CHD/CHDH SK8 ......55 P5
Rostrevor Rd EDGY/DAV SK3 ..56 E4
Rothay Dr RDSH SK5 ......28 F3
WARRW/BUR WA5 ......47 H4

Rothbury Cl RUNC WA7 ......62 B8
Rothbury Ct STHEL WA9 ......30 C6
Rotherby Rd WYTH/NTH M22 ..54 G3
Rotherdale Av
HALE/TIMP WA15 ......53 P2
Rother Dr EP CH65 ......80 C6
Rotherhead Dr MCFLDS SK11 ..117 H7
Rotherwood Rd WILM/AE SK9 ..70 F9
Rothesay Crs SALE M33 ......37 P6
Rothesay Dr PS/BROM CH62 ..79 H1
Rothesay Rd CHSW/BR CH44 ..142 C3
Rothley Av WYTH/NTH M22 ..54 F2
Rothsay Cl RNFD/HAY WA11 ..22 C2
Rottingdene Dr
WYTH/NTH M22 ......54 E6
Rough Bnk CONG CW12 ...175 M1
Roughdale Av STHEL WA9 ......30 G4
Roughey Gdns WYTH/NTH M22 ..54 E3
Rough Heys La MCFLDS SK11 ..116 A4
Roughlea Av GOL/RIS/CU WA3 ..25 M5
Roughley Av
WARRW/BUR WA5 ......47 P5
Roughwood La SBCH CW11 ...172 D8
The Roundabout WDN WA8 ......45 K1
Roundcroft MPL/ROM SK6 ......43 J5
Round Gdns MCFLDS SK10 ......95 N5
Round Hill Meadow CHSE CH3 ..143 K5
Round Meadow MCFLDN SK10 ..96 B8
Round Thorn GOL/RIS/CU WA3 ..34 H1
Roundthorn Rd
NTHM/RTH M23 ......54 B1
Roundway BRAM/HZG SK7 ......56 D9
Round Wy NM/HAY SK22 ......59 P7
Roundwood Rd
NTHM/RTH M23 ......39 N9
Routledge St WDN WA8 ......45 P6
Rowan Av GOL/RIS/CU WA3 ..25 H2
SALE M33 ......38 F6
Rowan Cl ALS/KID ST7 ...187 N2
ALS/KID ST7 ...187 P5
ALS/KID ST7 ...189 J8
MWCH CW10 ......151 L4
RNFD/HAY WA11 ......22 B2
RNFD/HAY WA11 ......22 D4
SBCH CW11 ......171 L5
WARRW/BUR WA5 ......47 K1
WSFD CW7 ......128 D8
Rowan Dr CHD/CHDH SK8 ......56 C7
Rowan Pk CHSE CH3 ...143 M5
Rowan Pl CHNE CH2 ...122 C7
Rowan Ri NWCHW CW8 ......109 J1
Rowan Rd NWCHW CW8 ......108 E4
Rowanside Rd MCFLDN SK10 ..94 E7
Rowanside Dr WILM/AE SK9 ..71 N6
The Rowans CHSW/BR CH4 ..140 F7
Rowan Tree Dr SALE M33 ......38 B9
Rowarth Av DTN/ASHW M34 ..29 N9
Rowarth Rd NTHM/RTH M23 ..54 B5
Rowcliffe Av CHSW/BR CH4 ..142 C6
Rowden Rd DTN/ASHW M34 ..29 L4
Rowe Gn DTN/ASHW M34 ......29 M6
Rowe St NWCHE CW9 ......108 C6
Rowhurst Cl NEWLW ST5 ......201 M8
Rowland Cl WARRN/WOL WA2 ..34 B5
Rowlandsway WYTH/NTH M22 ..54 F5
Rowley Bank La KNUT WA16 ..67 J5
Rowley Rd BRAM/HZG SK7 ......57 L7
Rowley Wy KNUT WA16 ......90 F6
Rowood Av RDSH SK5 ......29 H6
Rowsley Av DID/WITH M20 ..39 P4
Rowson Dr IRL M44 ......36 C3
Rowson Ct SALE M33 * 38 G4
Rowson St IRL M44 ......27 N7
The Row WSFD CW7 ......149 M1
Rowthorn Cl WDN WA8 ......46 B9
Rowton Bridge Rd CHSE CH3 ..143 N5
Rowton Cl NWCHE CW9 ......109 P8
Rowton La CHSE CH3 ...143 P4
Rowton St CW/SHV CW2 ......184 D5
Roxborough Ct
WARRW/BUR WA5 ......32 D2
Roxburgh Cl MCFLDN SK10 ..116 C3
Roxburgh Rd GTS/LS CH66 ......79 K7
Roxby St GTN M18 ......28 D4
Roxby Wy KNUT WA16 ......90 E6
Roxholme Wk WYTH/NTH M22 ..54 F7
Roxton Av HTNM SK4 ......41 J4
Roxton Rd HTNM SK4 ......41 J4
Royal Av CW/HAS CW1 * 4 E2
Royal Av CCHDY M21 ......39 K1
WDN WA8 ......45 H7
Royal Ct MCFLDS SK11 ......9 F5
Royal Gdns ALT WA14 ......52 D5
NWCHE CW9 ......109 N9
Royal George St EDGY/DAV SK3 ..17 F7
Royal Mdw MCFLDN SK10 ..116 C3
Royal Oak Dr NTHM/RTH M23 ..39 P9
Royal Oak Rd POY/DIS SK12 ..75 H1
Royalthorn Dr WYTH/NTH M22 ..54 F1
Royalthorn Rd
WYTH/NTH M22 ......54 F1
Royce Av HALE/TIMP WA15 ......53 J2
Royce Cl CW/SHV CW2 ......184 C1
Royden Av IRL M44 ......27 N7
Royds Cl NWCHW CW8 ......109 K7
Roylance Dr MWCH CW10 ..151 J2
Royle Cl OFTN SK2 ......56 G2
Royleen Dr FROD/HEL WA6 ..84 B7
Royle Green Rd
WYTH/NTH M22 ......39 P8
Royle's Pl NWCHW CW8 ......12 A6
Royle St CONG CW12 ...155 M7
DTN/ASHW M34 ......29 M4
NWCHE CW9 ......108 C6
RUSH/FAL M14 ......40 E1
STKP SK1 ......9 K5
WSFD CW7 ......149 N1

Royon Dr EDGY/DAV SK3 ......41 J9
Roysten Gdns STHEL WA9 ......22 B7
Royston Av DTN/ASHW M34 ..28 F6
WARR WA1 ......34 A9
Royston Cl GOL/RIS/CU WA3 ..24 G1
GTS/LS CH66 ......102 B2
Royton Av SALE M33 ......39 H6
Rozel Crs WARRW/BUR WA5 ..47 M3
Ruabon Rd DID/WITH M20 ..40 D6
Rubens Cl MPL/ROM SK6 ......43 P8
Ruby St DTN/ASHW M34 ......29 L6
Rudd Av STHEL WA9 ......22 E7
Ruddpark Rd WYTH/NTH M22 ..54 E6
Rudheath Cl CW/SHV CW2 ..184 D5
Rudheath La RUNC WA7 ......12 B2
Rudheath Wy NWCHE CW9 ..110 D7
Rudloe Ct WARRN/WOL WA2 ..34 A7
Rudstone Cl GTS/LS CH66 ......79 M8
Rudyard Cl MCFLDS SK11 ..117 H6
Rudyard Gv HTNM SK4 ......17 H1
SALE M33 ......38 B6
Rufford Cl CW/SHV CW2 ......185 H8
WARR WA1 ......45 J5
Rufford Pl GTN M18 * 28 F5
Rufus Court Rw CH/BCN CH1 ..2 D3
Rufus St RUSH/FAL M14 ......40 F1
Rugby Cl MCFLDN SK10 ..117 L1
Rugby La SALE M33 ......38 A6
SALE M33 ......38 B6
Rugby Rd EP CH65 ......102 F1
Rugby Wk EP CH65 ......102 F1
Ruislip Ct WARRN/WOL WA2 ..34 A7
Runcorn Docks Rd RUNC WA7 ..14 B3
Runcorn Rd NWCHW CW8 ..109 K2
Runcorn Spur Rd RUNC WA7 ..15 H4
Runger La MANAIR WA91 ......54 B7
Runhall Cl WGTN/LGST M12 ..28 A3
The Runnell NSTN CH64 ......77 K1
Runnymede WARR WA1 ......34 D9
Runnymede Ct BNG/LEV M19 ..28 B8
Runnymede Dr
RNFD/HAY WA11 * 22 E3
Runnymede Wk WDN WA8 * ..46 A5
Rupert St BIDD ST8 ...175 K9
RDSH SK5 ......41 K9
Ruscoe Av SBCH CW11 ...171 K5
Ruscombe Cl WARRW/BUR WA5 ..32 A9
Rushden Rd BNG/LEV M19 ..28 B7
Rushes Meadow LYMM WA13 ..51 H2
Rushey Cl HALE/TIMP WA15 ..53 P8
Rushey Rd WYTH/NTH M22 ..54 E2
Rushfield Crs RUNC WA7 ......62 F9
Rushfield Rd CHD/CHDH SK8 ..56 A9
CHSW/BR CW4 ......142 D5
Rushford Av BNG/LEV M19 ..28 A7
Rushford St WGTN/LGST M12 ..28 A5
Rush Gdns LYMM WA13 ......51 H2
Rushgreen Rd LYMM WA13 ..50 F5
Rushmere Av BNG/LEV M19 ..28 B8
Rushmere La MCFLDN SK10 ..95 N3
Rushmere La CHSE CH3 ...162 A6
Rushmoor Cl IRL M44 ......27 J5
Rushmore Gv WARR WA1 ......34 B9
Rushmore Gv WARR WA1 ......34 B9
Rusholme Cl HLWD L26 ......44 A9
Rushside Rd CHD/CHDH SK8 ..55 P9
Rushton Av WARRN/WOL WA2 ..33 M5
Rushton Cl MPL/ROM SK6 ......58 D3
NWCHE CW9 ......110 C5
WDN WA8 ......45 M4
Rushton Dr BRAM/HZG SK7 ..56 D4
CHSW/BR CW4 ......142 D5
CW/SHV CW2 ......198 D5
MPL/ROM SK6 ......43 H5
MWCH CW10 ......151 J3
Rushton Fold MCFLDN SK10 ..94 A3
Rushton La TPLY/FEL CW6 ..147 N5
EDGY/DAV SK3 ......41 J9
Rushton Rd CHD/CHDH SK8 ..56 A9
Rushton St DID/WITH M20 ..40 C6
Rushworth Ct HTNM SK4 ......41 K3
Rushyfield Crs MPL/ROM SK6 ..43 J5
Rushy Vw NEWLW WA12 ......23 L5
Ruskin Av DTN/ASHW M34 ..29 J2
Ruskin Ct KNUT WA16 ......90 E5
NEWLW WA12 ......23 N5
WARRN/WOL WA2 ......33 M6
SALE M33 ......38 D5
Ruskin Dr GTS/LS CH66 ......79 M8
Ruskin Gdns MPL/ROM SK6 ..42 F5
Ruskin Gv MPL/ROM SK6 ......42 F5
Ruskin Rd CONG CW12 ...155 L8
CW/SHV CW2 ......184 A3
IRL M44 ......27 N7
Russell Av ALS/KID ST7 ...187 N3
Russell Gdns HTNM SK4 ......41 J7
Russell La PART M31 ......36 F5
RUNC WA7 ......14 A6
Russell St CHSE CH3 ...164 C6
CW/SHV CW2 ......184 A3
IRL M44 ......27 N7
Russell St CHSE CH3 ...164 D6
Russet Cl MWCH CW10 ..130 A9
Russet Rd NWCHW CW8 ......108 F4
Rutherford Dr KNUT WA16 ..90 F6
Ruthin Av CHD/CHDH SK8 ......55 N5
Ruthin Cl WARRW/BUR WA5 ..33 H5
Ruth St GTN M18 ......28 D6
Rutland Cl DID/WITH M20 ..40 B3
GOL/RIS/CU WA3 ......24 D7
WARRS WA4 ......48 B7
Rutland Ct CHD/CHDH SK8 ..55 K1
CONG CW12 ...155 N6

SBCH CW11 ......171 H4
Rutland Crs RDSH SK5 ......42 C3
Rutland Dr MWCH CW10 ..151 J3
NWCHW CW9 * 108 C3
Rutland La SALE M33 ......38 C3
Rutland Rd CHNE CH2 ......122 B6
Rutland Rd ALS/KID ST7 ..189 J6
ALT WA14 ......53 H1
BRAM/HZG SK7 ......57 L7
IRL M44 ......27 N7
MCFLDS SK11 ......117 J8
PART M31 ......36 D5
Rutland St GTN M18 ......28 D3
RUNC WA7 ......14 D2
Rutter Av WARRW/BUR WA5 ..33 J6
Rutter's La BRAM/HZG SK7 ......57 J5
Ryan St OP/CLY M11 ......28 E2
Ryburn Rd MCFLDS SK11 ..116 G7
Rydal Av BRAM/HZG SK7 ......57 J4
MPL/ROM SK6 ......58 C3
SALE M33 ......38 C3
WARRS WA4 ......48 C5
WHITCH SY13 ...213 N7
Rydal Cl CHD/CHDH SK8 ......56 A9
DTN/ASHW M34 ......29 L2
EP CH65 ......102 E2
HOLMCH CW4 ......131 N9
NSTN CH64 ......77 M7
Rydal Ct CONG CW12 ...155 J8
Rydal Dr HALE/TIMP WA15 ..53 P7
FROD/HEL WA6 ......105 H3
RUNC WA7 ......15 H7
Rydal Mt CW/HAS CW1 ...170 A8
Rydal Pl MCFLDS SK11 ..116 C6
Rydal St NEWLW WA12 ......23 L2
Rydal Wy ALS/KID ST7 ...187 N3
WDN WA8 ......45 J7
Ryde Av DTN/ASHW M34 ......29 P9
WHITCH SY13 ...213 N7
Ryde Cl CW/HAS CW1 ...170 A9
Ryder Av ALT WA14 ......38 B9
Ryder Brow GTN M18 ......28 D5
Ryderbrow Rd GTN M18 ......28 D5
Ryder Rd WARR WA1 ......34 D8
WARRS WA4 ......45 P3
Ryders St NWCHW CW8 ......12 C5
Ryebank Av CW/HAS CW1 ..185 H1
Ryebank Wy MCFLDN SK10 ..117 J1
Ryebrook Gv BURS/TUN ST6 ..189 P9
Ryeburn Av WYTH/NTH M22 ..54 F5
Rye Cl ALS/KID ST7 ...187 M5
STHEL WA9 ......31 H4
Ryecroft CHNE CH2 ...122 A3
Ryecroft Av GOL/RIS/CU WA3 ..25 L2
DTN/ASHW M34 ......29 J1
Ryecroft Gv NTHM/RTH M23 ..39 N9
Ryecroft La CHSE CH3 ...145 H4
DTN/ASHW M34 ......29 L2
WARR WA1 ......91 J1
TPLY/FEL CW6 ......145 H4
Ryecroft Vw DTN/ASHW M34 ..29 J1
Ryedale Cl HTNM SK4 ......41 J5
Ryedale Wy CONG CW12 ...175 J1
Ryefield Cl HALE/TIMP WA15 ..53 P7
Ryefield St WHITCH SY13 ...213 J7
Ryefield Wy WHITCH SY13 ...213 J7
Ryehills ALS/KID ST7 ...201 H6
Rylands Cl MALPAS SY14 ...204 A3
Rylands St GTN M18 * 18 D6
WARR WA1 ......21 J2
Ryles Cl MCFLDS SK11 ..117 J6
Ryles Crs MCFLDS SK11 ..117 J7
Ryle's Park Rd MCFLDS SK11 ..117 J7
Ryle St MCFLDS SK11 ......8 F8
Ryleys La WILM/AE SK9 ......93 H4
Rylstone Av CCHDY M21 ......39 N5
Ryton Av GTN M18 ......28 C6

S

Sabre Cl RUNC WA7 * 63 H7
Sack La NWCHE CW9 ......66 F8
Saddleback Dr MCFLDN SK10 ..94 F6
Saddleries Ri RUNC WA7 ......62 A6
Saddlewood Av BNG/LEV M19 ..40 E6
Sadler Cl WSFD CW7 ......149 M1
Sadler Rd WSFD CW7 ......149 M1
Sadler's Cl HOLMCH CW4 ......131 N8
Sadler Cl TPLY/FEL CW6 ......147 L1
Sadler St WDN WA8 ......46 A6
Sadlers Wls TPLY/FEL CW6 ..169 B9
Saffron Cl GOL/RIS/CU WA3 ..34 C7
WARRN/WOL WA2 ......34 C7
Saffron Gdns STHEL WA9 ......22 B7
Sagars Rd WILM/AE SK9 ......34 G6
Saighton La CHSE CH3 ...143 P8
St Agnes St RDSH SK5 ......28 F6
St Alban Rd WARRW/BUR WA5 ..47 J2
St Alban's Av HTNM SK4 ......41 K3
St Albans Ct ALT WA14 ......37 P8
St Albans Crs ALT WA14 ......37 P8
St Albans Pl NANT CW5 ......196 C4
St Albans Pl NM/HAY SK22 ..59 N7
St Aldates MPL/ROM SK6 ......42 G6
St Andrew's Av
MPL/ROM SK6 ......42 G7
St Andrew's CH/SHV CW2 ..185 J7
HALE/TIMP WA15 ......38 B9
St Andrews Cl ALT WA14 ......37 P7
HTNM SK4 ......41 K3
St Andrew's Cl
MPL/ROM SK6 ......42 G7

St Andrews Cl NWCHE CW9 ....110 E5
  WARRN/WOL WA2 ....34 B4
St Andrews Dr ALS/KID ST7 ..189 L5
  HOLMCH CW4 ....131 N9
St Andrews Gdns ALS/KID ST7 ..188 A6
St Andrews Rd CHD/CHDH SK8 ...56 A6
  EP CH65 ....102 F1
  HTNM SK4 ....41 J4
  MCFLDS SK11 ....8 B6
St Anns CHD/BCN CH1 ....2 E2
St Anne's Av MWCH CW10 ....151 J2
  WARRS WA4 ....49 K5
St Annes Av East WARRS WA4 ...49 K5
St Anne's Ct DTN/ASHW M34 * ...29 M3
  SALE M33 ....38 F4
St Anne's Dr DTN/ASHW M54 ....29 M5
St Annes Rd CCHDY M21 ......39 L1
St Annes Rd ALS/KID ST7 ....57 J6
  DTN/ASHW M54 ....29 M5
  WDN WA8 ....45 P5
St Anne St CH/BCN CH1 ......2 E2
St Ann Pl RAIN/WH L35 ....30 B7
St Anne's La NANT CW5 ....30 A6
St Ann's Rd CCHDY M21 ....39 J1
St Ann's Rd ALS/KID ST7 .....151 J1
St Ann's Rd North
  CHD/CHDH SK8 ....55 K6
St Ann's Rd South
  CHD/CHDH SK8 ....55 L6
St Ann Sq CHD/CHDH SK8 .....55 L7
St Anns St SALE M33 ....39 J5
St Anthony Pl
  WARRN/WOL WA2 ....33 L2
St Asaph Dr WARRW/BUR WA5 ..32 G6
St Asaph Rd CLS CH66 ....102 A4
St Augustine's Av WARRS WA4 ..49 H3
St Augustine's Rd
  EDGY/DAV SK3 ....41 J8
St Austel Cl WARRN/WOL WA2 ...47 J4
St Austell Av MCFLDN SK10 ...116 D3
St Austell Cl RUNC WA7 ......62 F8
St Austell Dr CHD/CHDH SK8 ...55 K7
St Austins La WARR WA1 ......18 C7
St Barnabas Ct MCFLDS SK11 * .117 K6
St Barnabas Pl
  WARRW/BUR WA5 ....48 A1
St Barnabas Sq OP/CLY M11 ...28 B3
St Bartholomew's Ct CO CH5 ..120 B5
St Bede's Av NWCHW CW8 .....108 F5
St Bees Cl CHD/CHDH SK8 ....55 K4
St Benedicts Cl
  WARRN/WOL WA2 ....18 E2
St Brannocks Rd
  CHD/CHDH SK8 ....56 B8
St Brendan's Rd
  DID/WITH M20 ....40 C1
St Brendan's Rd North
  DID/WITH M20 ....40 C1
St Brides Cl WARRW/BUR WA5 ...47 J4
St Bridget's Cl
  WARRN/WOL WA2 ....33 K2
St Catherine Dr NWCHW CW8 ...109 H8
St Catherine's Cl FLINT CH6 ....98 A6
St Catherine's Rd
  DID/WITH M20 ....40 C1
St Chad's Av MPL/ROM SK6 ....43 H6
St Chads Cl NANT CW5 ....197 P7
St Chad's Flds WSFD CW7 ....149 L5
St Chad's Gv MPL/ROM SK6 ....43 H6
St Chad's Rd CH/BCN CH1 ....121 J7
  DID/WITH M20 ....40 C1
St Christophers Cl CHNE CH2 ..121 M5
  DID/WITH M20 ....40 A2
St Christopher's Dr
  MPL/ROM SK6 ....43 K1
St Clairs Cl CW/SHV CW2 ....185 K7
St Clements Cl MCFLDS SK11 * 8 E7
St Crewood Cl CW/SHV CW2 ...185 H9
St Davids Av CHD/CHDH SK8 ...56 A6
  MPL/ROM SK6 ....43 G6
St Davids Cl FLINT CH6 ......98 B8
  RAIN/WH L35 ....30 B4
St Davids Dr GTS/LS CH66 ...102 B4
  WARRW/BUR WA5 ....32 G4
St David's Rd BRAM/HZG SK7 ...57 J6
  CHD/CHDH SK8 ....56 A1
St David's Ter CHSW/BR CH44 ..141 N3
St Edwards Cl MCFLDS SK11 * .117 K6
St Elisabeth's Wy RDSH SK5 ...41 M1
St Elmo Av OFTN SK2 ....14 C9
St Elmo Pk POY/DIS SK12 .....14 A2
St Elphins Cl WARR WA1 ......19 G5
St Gabriels Ct ALS/KID ST7 ...187 N5
St Georges CH/BCN CH1 ......2 E4
St Georges Av GTS/LS CH66 ...102 B4
  HALE/TIMP WA15 ....38 E8
St George's Ct KNUT WA16 ....90 C5
  WARRS WA4 ....64 C3
St George's Cr ALT WA14 .....37 N9
  WDN WA8 ....40 A4
St George's Crs CHSE CH3 ....144 A5
  CHSW/BR CH44 ....1 G7
  HALE/TIMP WA15 ....38 E8
St George's Gdns
  DTN/ASHW M54 ....29 N8
St Georges Pl MCFLDS SK11 * 9 F7
St Georges Rd NM/HAY SK22 ...59 N7
  PART M31 ....31 M3
  RUSH/FAL M14 ....40 F7
  WSFD CW7 ....149 L2
St George's Wy NWCHE CW9 ..109 P7
St Helens Linkway
  RAIN/WH L35 ....30 E7
St Helens Linkway STHEL WA9 ...30 E1
St Helens Rd NWCHE CW9 ......13 H2
St Hilda's Dr FROD/HEL WA6 ....84 A4
St Hilda's Rd DTN/ASHW M54 ...29 L3
St Hilda's Vw DTN/ASHW M54 * ...29 L4
St Hugh's Cl ALT WA14 ....38 B8
St Ives CHD/CHDH SK8 ....56 A1
St Ives Cl MCFLDN SK10 .....116 E3

St Ives Crs SALE M33 ....38 D7
St James Cl
  AUD/MAD/W CW3 * 217 H1
St James Ct BIDD ST8 * 175 M6
  HALE/TIMP WA15 ....53 J3
St James Dr SALE M33 ....38 D5
  WILM/AE SK9 ....71 J8
St James Mt RAIN/WH L35 ....30 B5
St James Rd HTNM SK4 ......41 J3
St James Rd RAIN/WH L35 ....30 B6
St James's Gv ALT WA14 .....38 C7
St James St CH/BCN CH1 .....3 F2
St James Ter WSFD CW7 * 149 J2
St James Wk NWCHW CW8 ....12 D4
St James' Wy CHD/CHDH SK8 ...55 P9
St John's Av WARRS WA4 .....48 D5
St John's Av KNUT WA16 .....90 D4
  NWCHE CW9 ....110 F1
St John's Brow RUNC WA7 * 15 G1
St John's Cl CH/BCN CH1 .....2 E3
St John's Cl MPL/ROM SK6 ....42 G6
  NWCHE CW9 ....110 D5
St Johns Dr WSFD CW7 ......149 J2
St John's Pk WHITCH SY13 ...213 M5
St John's Rear Rd
  CHSW/BR CH44 ....3 G7
St John's Rd ALT WA14 ......52 C4
  BRAM/HZG SK7 ....57 H6
  CHSW/BR CH44 ....3 G6
  CONG CW12 ....155 P5
  DTN/ASHW M54 ....29 M4
  HTNM SK4 ....40 F6
  KNUT WA16 ....90 D4
  MCFLDS SK11 ....8 D6
  WILM/AE SK9 ....92 G2
St John's St RUNC WA7 ......15 G1
  WHITCH SY13 ....213 M5
St John St CH/BCN CH1 ......2 E4
  NEWLW WA12 ....23 L6
St Johns Wk EDGY/DAV SK3 * ...41 J8
St John's Wy NWCHW CW8 ....127 L1
  SBCH CW11 ....172 B3
St John's Wd ALS/KID ST7 ...189 H7
St Joseph's Cl
  WARRW/BUR WA5 ....47 J2
St Joseph St BURS/TUN ST6 * .189 L9
St Josephs Wy NANT CW5 .....11 G6
St Katherines Wy WARR WA1 ...19 H5
St Kilda Cl EP CH65 ....102 E5
St Lawrence Ct NANT CW5 ....10 D4
St Lawrence Rd
  DTN/ASHW M54 ....29 M6
  FROD/HEL WA6 ....83 P6
St Leonard's Ct SALE M33 ....38 C4
St Leonards Dr
  HALE/TIMP WA15 ....53 K1
St Leonard's Rd HTNM SK4 ....41 L3
St Leonard's Wy
  AUD/MAD/W CW3 ......219 H5
St Lesmo Rd EDGY/DAV SK3 * ...24 F1
St Luke's Av GOL/RIS/CU WA3 ..24 F1
St Lukes Cl HOLMCH CW4 ....132 A8
St Luke's Wy FROD/HEL WA6 ...83 P4
St Margaret's Av BNG/LEV M19 ..40 C2
  WARRN/WOL WA2 ....33 N7
St Margarets Ct
  AUD/MAD/W CW3 ......199 M9
St Margaret's Rd ALT WA14 ...52 C3
  CHD/CHDH SK8 ....56 A1
St Mark's Av ALT WA14 ......52 E2
St Marks Crs GTS/LS CH66 ...102 B5
St Mark's Dr CHSW/BR CH44 ..142 B4
St Mark's St BNG/LEV M19 ....28 C8
  MPL/ROM SK6 ....42 F4
  RNFD/HAY WA11 ....22 C5
St Martin's Av HTNM SK4 .....16 A3
St Martins Dr GTS/LS CH66 ...101 P7
St Martins La ALS/KID ST7 ....63 H7
St Martin's Rd ALS/KID ST7 ...201 P2
  CHD/CHDH SK8 ....56 E1
  SALE M33 ....38 C3
St Martin's Wy CH/BCN CH1 ....2 C5
St Mary's Av DTN/ASHW M34 ...29 N9
  NWCHW CW8 ....108 F3
St Marys Cl ALS/KID ST7 ....187 N5
  CHSW/BR CH44 ....1 G7
  WARRS WA4 ....48 D3
St Marys Ct NANT CW5 ......183 J9
St Mary's Dr CHD/CHDH SK8 * ..55 P1
  NWCHW CW8 ....128 A3
  RDSH SK5 ....41 N5
St Mary's Hl CH/BCN CH1 .....2 E5
St Mary's Rd ALT WA14 ......52 F5
  CHSW/BR CH44 ....160 D2
  NANT CW5 ....59 J6
  NM/HAY SK22 ....75 H1
  POY/DIS SK12 ....62 D5
  RUNC WA7 ....62 G5
  SALE M33 ....38 B3
  WARRW/BUR WA5 ....47 K2
  WDN WA8 ....61 N2
St Mary's St CW/HAS CW1 * 4 D3
  WARRS WA4 ....48 E3
  WHITCH SY13 ....213 M5
St Mary's Wy CHSW/BR CH44 ..148 A5
  STKP SK1 ....17 J7
St Matthews Cl CW/HAS CW1 * ..186 B4
  WARRS WA4 ....48 H3
St Matthew's Pl
  EDGY/DAV SK3 ....16 D7
St Matthews Ter
  EDGY/DAV SK3 * 16 D7
St Mawes Cl WDN WA8 ......45 L5
St Mawgan Ct
  WARRN/WOL WA2 ....34 A7
St Michael's Av BRAM/HZG SK7 ..56 E8
St Michaels Cl NWCHW CW8 ....86 F5
  WDN WA8 ....45 J8
St Michaels Cl SALE M33 .....38 B2
St Michaels Rd STHEL WA9 ....30 F5

WDN WA8 ....45 J8
St Michaels Rw CH/BCN CH1 * 2 E5
St Michaels Sq CH/BCN CH1 * 2 E5
St Michaels Ter MCFLDS SK11 * 9 F4
St Michael's Wy MWCH CW10 ..151 J1
St Monicas Cl WARR WA1 .....48 F8
St Nicholas Gv STHEL WA9 * ...31 J1
St Olave St CH/BCN CH1 ......2 E2
St Oswalds Cl CHD/CHDH SK8 ...2 E2
St Oswalds Cl MALPAS SY14 ...202 A3
St Oswald's Gv SBCH CW11 ...153 K5
St Oswald's Rd BNG/LEV M19 ..28 B7
  CH/BCN CH1 ....2 B7
St Paul's Cl CW/HAS CW1 .....4 D2
St Pauls Gdns GTS/LS CH66 ...79 M6
St Paul's Ms RUNC WA7 ......52 G4
St Paul's Rd DID/WITH M20 ....40 D2
  HTNM SK4 ....41 J4
  WDN WA8 ....21 H4
St Paul's St CW/HAS CW1 .....4 D2
  STKP SK1 ....17 K1
St Peter's Av KNUT WA16 .....90 D4
St Peter's Cl LYMM WA13 .....33 G5
St Peter's Dr TPLY/KEL CW6 ..148 B3
St Peters Ri SBCH CW11 .....17 C4
St Peters Rd CONG CW12 ....155 N9
St Peters Sq STKP SK1 ....17 F4
St Peters Wy CHNE CH2 ......122 C3
  WARRW/BUR WA5 ....18 A4
St Philip's Rd GTN M18 ......28 D5
St Saviour's Rd EDGY/DAV SK3 ..57 J2
St Saviour's St ALS/KID ST7 ..188 F7
Saintsbridge Rd
  WYTH/NTH M22 ....54 E5
St Simons Cl OFTN SK2 ......42 B8
St Stephen Rd
  WARRW/BUR WA5 ....47 K2
St Stephen's Av
  DTN/ASHW M54 ....29 L1
  WARRN/WOL WA2 ....33 L5
St Stephens Ct SBCH CW11 ...171 J2
St Thomas Pathway
  CH/BCN CH1 ....3 F3
St Thomas St STKP SK1 ......17 G7
St Thomas St ALS/KID ST7 ...189 M1
St Thomas' Vw EP CH65 ......6 C7
St Vincent Dr NWCHW CW8 ...109 H8
St Vincent Rd
  WARRW/BUR WA5 ....47 K2
St Vincent St HALE/TIMP WA15 ..53 J3
St Wenefredes MALPAS SY14 ...53 J3
St Werburgh St CH/BCN CH1 * 2 E4
St Wilfrids Cl WSFD CW7 * ...109 P9
St Wilfrid's Dr WARRS WA4 ....49 L6
St Winifred Rd RAIN/WH L35 ...30 A3
Salander Crs CW/SHV CW2 * ...185 J5
Salcombe Cl SALE M33 ......38 B8
Salcombe Rd OFTN SK2 ......42 B6
  OP/CLY M11 ....28 D1
Sale Heys Rd SALE M33 ......38 C5
Sale Rd NTHM/RTH M23 ......39 K6
Salesbrook La NANT CW5 ....207 M8
  AUD/MAD/W CW3 ......207 F8
Salisbury Av PART M31 ......141 P4
  WARRN/WOL WA2 ....17 J2
Salisbury Cl CW/SHV CW2 ....185 J7
  GTS/LS CH66 ....102 B4
Salisbury Pl MCFLDN SK10 .....95 L9
Salisbury Rd ALT WA14 ......38 A5
  CH/BCN CH1 ....2 A5
  WHITCH SY13 ....213 N5
Salisbury St CH/BCN CH1 ....121 L8
  GOL/RIS/CU WA3 ....24 C1
  RDSH SK5 ....28 F9
  RUNC WA7 ....14 E4
  WDN WA8 ....21 J2
Salkeld St NWCHE CW9 ....13 K3
Salmon Leap CHSW/BR CH44 ....3 F6
Salop Pl ALS/KID ST7 ....189 J5
Salop Wk MCFLDN SK10 ......116 F2
Saltash Cl RUNC WA7 ....62 F6
  WYTH/NTH M22 ....54 E6
Saltdene Rd NTHM/RTH M23 ...54 E6
Saltersgate GTS/LS CH66 ....102 B2
Salter's La CHNE CH2 ....122 D3
  CHSE CH3 ....179 L7
  MCFLDS SK11 ....179 L7
Salthill Dr WYTH/NTH M22 ....54 C5
Salt Line Wy SBCH CW11 ....171 J3
Salt Mdw NANT CW5 ....196 D2
Saltney Av DID/WITH M20 ....40 A1
Saltney Ferry Rd
  CHSW/BR CH44 ....141 M3
Salton Gdns WARRW/BUR WA5 ..33 H9
Saltrush Rd WYTH/NTH M22 ...54 F5
Saltwood Dr RUNC WA7 ......62 D9
Saltworks Cl FROD/HEL WA6 ...84 B3
Salusbury St FLINT CH6 ......98 B5
Samian Cl MWCH CW10 ......151 J1
Samlesbury Cl DID/WITH M20 ..40 A5
Samphire Gdns WARR WA1 ....31 N1
Samuel St ALS/KID ST7 .....189 P7
  BNG/LEV M19 ....28 B9
  CH/BCN CH1 ....3 G2
  HTNM SK4 ....41 L5
  MCFLDS SK11 ....8 E5
  STHEL WA9 ....30 C1
  WARRW/BUR WA5 ....48 A3
Sanbec Gdns WDN WA8 ......45 A2
Sanby Av GTN M18 ....28 C5
Sanby Rd GTN M18 ....28 C5
Sandacre Rd NTHM/RTH M23 ...39 L9
Sandalwood RUNC WA7 ......62 F5
Sandalwood Cl
  WARRN/WOL WA2 ....33 N6
Sandalwood Gdns STHEL WA9 ..31 H1
  ALS/KID ST7 ....187 P2
  ALS/KID ST7 ....187 P2
  CONG CW12 ....154 G8
  CONG CW12 ....155 H7

RDSH SK5 * 28 E7
  SALE M33 ....39 J5
  SBCH CW11 ....172 C8
Sandbach Rd North
  ALS/KID ST7 ....187 N3
Sandbach Rd South
  ALS/KID ST7 ....187 P5
Sandbrook Wy DTN/ASHW M54 ..29 M4
Sandby Dr MPL/ROM SK6 ......43 M8
Sanderling Rd OFTN SK2 ......42 A8
Sanders Hey Cl RUNC WA7 ....62 E9
Sanderson Cl CW/SHV CW2 ...185 J8
  WARRW/BUR WA5 ....47 H1
Sanders Sq MCFLDS SK11 * ...117 K7
Sandfield Av NANT CW5 ......207 N9
Sandfield Cl GOL/RIS/CU WA3 ..24 C1
Sandfield Cl FROD/HEL WA6 ...83 P5
  NANT CW5 ....26 C2
Sandfield Crs GOL/RIS/CU WA3 ..26 C2
  NWCHW CW8 ....108 A3
Sandfields La NWCHW CW8 ...109 L8
Sandfields FROD/HEL WA6 ....83 P5
Sandford Av NANT CW5 * 29 P4
Sandford Rd NANT CW5 ......207 N5
  SALE M33 ....39 J5
Sandford Station La RDSH SK5 ..28 C9
Sandford St NEWLW ST5 .....20 P7
Sandham Gv MCFLDN SK10 ...117 M2
Sandham Rd ALS/KID ST7 .....60 A3
Sandheys DTN/ASHW M54 .....29 M4
  NSTN CH64 ....77 J4
Sandheys Gv GTN M18 ......28 E5
Sandhill Wk WYTH/NTH M22 ...54 E6
Sandhole La KNUT WA16 ....113 P1
  NWCHW CW8 ....107 M5
Sandhurst Av DID/WITH M20 ...40 B2
  DID/WITH M20 ....40 B2
  HALE/TIMP WA15 ....53 K4
  KNUT WA16 ....90 D3
  RDSH SK5 ....42 A3
Sandileigh Dr HALE/TIMP WA15 ..53 J3
Sandington Dr NWCHW CW8 ..127 J1
Sandiway BRAM/HZG SK7 .....56 E5
  IRL M44 ....27 N7
  KNUT WA16 ....90 D3
  MPL/ROM SK6 ....42 E5
Sandiway Av WDN WA8 ......45 L8
Sandiway Cl NWCHW CW8 ....127 K1
Sandiway Dr DID/WITH M20 ...40 B5
Sandiway La NWCHE CW9 .....23 J2
Sandiway Pk NWCHW CW8 ...108 D3
Sandiway Pl ALT WA14 ......53 H1
Sandiway Rd ALT WA14 ......53 H1
  CW/HAS CW1 ....184 G2
  SALE M33 ....38 B5
  WILM/AE SK9 ....71 M1
Sand La MCFLDN SK10 ....93 H8
Sandle Bridge La KNUT WA16 ..92 B8
Sandle Bridge Ri WILM/AE SK9 ..92 B6
Sandon Cl RAIN/WH L35 ......30 A4
Sandon Crs NSTN CH64 ......77 L8
Sandon Park Gdns
  CW/SHV CW2 ....184 D4
Sandon Pl WDN WA8 ....46 A6
Sandon Rd CHNE CH2 ....121 N7
Sandon St CW/HAS CW1 ....5 F3
Sandown Cl GOL/RIS/CU WA3 * ..25 P5
  MWCH CW10 ....151 J1
  RUNC WA7 ....62 A8
  WILM/AE SK9 ....71 M6
Sandown Ct GTN M18 ....28 C8
  NWCHW CW8 ....127 K1
Sandown Dr DTN/ASHW M54 ...29 P9
  HALE/TIMP WA15 ....38 E8
  SALE M33 ....38 B5
Sandown Pl MCFLDN SK10 ....95 L9
Sandown Rd BRAM/HZG SK7 ...57 N6
  CW/HAS CW1 ....185 J1
  EDGY/DAV SK3 ....41 K8
Sandown Ter CHSE CH3 ......121 M7
Sandpiper Cl CW/HAS CW1 ...184 F1
  SALE M33 ....23 N5
Sandpiper Ct CHSW/BR CH44 ..142 D8
Sandpiper Dr EDGY/DAV SK3 ...56 D1
Sandra Dr NEWLW WA12 .....23 P1
Sandringham Av CHSE CH3 ...122 B9
  DTN/ASHW M54 ....29 K3
  FROD/HEL WA6 ....105 H1
  NWCHE CW9 ....109 N8
  WSFD CW7 ....149 P7
Sandringham Ct
  CW/SHV CW2 ....184 E9
  HTNM SK4 ....28 C5
  POY/DIS SK12 ....73 K3
  STHEL WA9 ....31 H1
Sandringham Dr
  CW/SHV CW2 ....184 E9
  POY/DIS SK12 ....73 K3
  STHEL WA9 ....31 H1
  WSFD CW7 ....47 N1
Sandringham Gdns EP CH65 * ...6 C5
Sandringham Rd
  BRAM/HZG SK7 ....57 M5
  CHD/CHDH SK8 ....56 A4
  CONG CW12 ....155 P6
  HYDE SK14 ....43 J1
  MCFLDN SK10 ....9 J2
  MPL/ROM SK6 ....43 H5
  WDN WA8 ....45 M3
Sandringham St GTN M18 ....28 C5

Sandringham Wy
  WILM/AE SK9 ....71 J8
Sandrock Rd CHSE CH3 .....143 N5
Sandsdown Cl BIDD ST8 .....175 K8
Sandside Rd ALS/KID ST7 ....187 L5
Sands Rd ALS/KID ST7 ......189 N2
Sandstone Cl RAIN/WH L35 ....30 B7
Sandstone Trail
  FROD/HEL WA6 ....105 M2
  MALPAS SY14 ....179 L9
  NWCHW CW8 ....125 M2
Sandstone Trail
  TPLY/KEL CW6 ....165 L7
Sandwell Dr SALE M33 ......38 E2
Sandwood Av CHSW/BR CH44 ..140 F7
Sandy Brow La
  GOL/RIS/CU WA3 ....24 C3
Sandy Cl MCFLDN SK10 ......95 M6
Sandyhill Pl WSFD CW7 ....149 M3
Sandylands Crs ALS/KID ST7 ..188 B5
Sandylands Pk CW/SHV CW2 ..184 D9
  CHSE CH3 ....124 B8
Sandy La CHSE CH3 ....143 J2
  CHSE CH3 ....143 L7
  CHSE CH3 ....179 J9
  CHSW/BR CH44 ....133 H8
  CONG CW12 ....153 H8
  CONG CW12 ....154 F7
  CONG CW12 ....155 K8
  GOL/RIS/CU WA3 ....25 P1
  HOLMCH CW4 ....131 P2
  IRL M44 ....27 N6
  KNUT WA16 ....112 C4
  KNUT WA16 ....112 C1
  LYMM WA13 ....179 P7
  MALPAS SY14 ....202 F6
  MCFLDN SK10 ....116 C2
  MPL/ROM SK6 ....43 H5
  NANT CW5 ....207 M4
  NANT CW5 ....209 N2
  NEWLW WA12 ....23 K6
  NTHM/RTH M23 ....39 G2
  NTHM/RTH M23 ....77 N7
  NWCHW CW8 ....108 D1
  NWCHW CW8 ....127 M5
  RDSH SK5 ....41 N5
  RUNC WA7 ....63 J8
  SBCH CW11 ....171 J4
  SBCH CW11 ....186 E1
  WARRN/WOL WA2 ....33 M6
  WARRS WA4 ....48 F7
  WDN WA8 ....45 L3
  WDN WA8 ....45 L3
  WILM/AE SK9 ....70 F6
Sandy La West
  WARRN/WOL WA2 ....33 K5
Sandy Moor La RUNC WA7 ....63 H3
Sandymoor La RUNC WA7 .....63 H3
Sandy Rd BIDD ST8 ....175 K7
  BURS/TUN ST6 ....189 M9
Sandywell Cl OP/CLY M11 ....28 D2
Sandywell St OP/CLY M11 ....28 D1
Sankey La BNG/LEV M19 .....28 C8
Sankey's WARRS WA4 ....64 B6
Sankey Mnr
  WARRW/BUR WA5 * 47 J1
Sankey Rd RNFD/HAY WA11 ...22 C5
Sankey St GOL/RIS/CU WA3 ...24 C1
  NEWLW WA12 ....23 B7
  STHEL WA9 ....22 B7
  WARR WA1 ....2 C6
  WDN WA8 ....21 G7
Santey St WGTN/LGST M12 ...28 C1
Santon Dr GOL/RIS/CU WA3 ...24 C1
Santon St CHSE CH3 ....38 A6
Sapling La TPLY/KEL CW6 ....147 J3
Sargent Rd MPL/ROM SK6 ....43 K5
Sark Av EP CH65 ....102 D3
Sarn Av WYTH/NTH M22 .....54 C5
Sarn Bank Rd MALPAS SY14 ..202 F8
Sarn Rd MALPAS SY14 ......202 F8
Sarra La CHSE CH3 ....179 P9
Sarsfield Av GOL/RIS/CU WA3 ..24 F1
Saughall Cl NWCHE CW9 ....109 N8
Saughall Hey CH/BCN CH1 ...120 C6
  CH/BCN CH1 ....120 C6
Saughall Rd CH/BCN CH1 ....121 J8
Saundersfoot Cl
  WARRW/BUR WA5 ....33 H6
Saunders St CW/HAS CW1 ....4 E3
Saunderton Dr RNFD/HAY WA11 ..22 C2
Saunton Rd OP/CLY M11 .....28 D1
Sauncey Av MPL/ROM SK6 ....43 K5
Saville Av WARRW/BUR WA5 ...18 A4
Saville Cl CHD/CHDH SK8 ....55 L1
Savoy Rd CW/HAS CW1 .....185 N8
Sawley Cl GOL/RIS/CU WA3 ...26 A7
  RUNC WA7 ....63 J7
Sawley Dr CHD/CHDH SK8 ....56 B9
Sawpit St LYMM WA13 ......36 F9
Sawyer Dr BIDD ST8 ....175 K8
Saxfield Dr NTHM/RTH M23 ...54 E1
Saxon Cl WARRS WA4 ....64 B2
Saxon Crossway WSFD CW7 ..149 L1
Saxon Dr DTN/ASHW M54 .....29 L2
Saxons La NWCHW CW8 ......12 C6
Saxon Rd RUNC WA7 ....15 J3
Saxon St MCFLDN SK10 ......31 K1
Saxon Wy CH/BCN CH1 .....121 H5
  GTS/LS CH66 ....102 B4
Saxthorpe Cl SALE M33 .....38 A3

Sayce St WDN WA8 .....21 J1
Scafell Av WARRN/WOL WA2 ...33 M5
Scafell Cl BEB CH63 ...96 B4
MPL/ROM SK6 ...58 C7
Scafell Lawn NTHLY L27 ...44 A4
Scaife Rd NWCHW CW9 ...10 D5
Scaliot Cl NM/HAY SK22 ...59 M7
Scarcroft Rd WGTN/LGST M12 ...28 A4
Scarisbrick Av DID/WITH M20 ...40 E5
Scar La MALPAS SY14 ...191 N5
Sceptre Cl NEWLW WA12 ...23 L6
Scholars Cl MCFLDN SK10 ...116 D4
Scholars Dr DID/WITH M20 ...40 D5
Scholars Green La LYMM WA13 ...50 F4
Scholes La ECCL WA10 ...30 A1
Scholes Pk ECCL WA10 ...30 A1
School Av NSTN CH64 ...77 M7
School Bnk FROD/HEL WA6 ...107 L7
School Cl ALS/KID ST7 ...201 K6
KNUT WA16 ...90 C4
POY/DIS SK12 ...73 M3
WHITCH SY13 ...206 B6
School Ct EDGY/DAV SK3 ...56 F1
School Crs CW/HAS CW1 ...5 J3
School Dr NWCHW CW9 ...109 J1
School Field Cl
AUD/MAD/W CW3 ...217 N1
Schoolfold La HOLMCO L ...73 N7
School Gn DID/WITH M20 ...40 E2
School Gv West
DID/WITH M20 * ...40 D2
School La ALT WA14 ...52 B3
AUD/MAD/W CW3 ...217 H1
AUD/MAD/W CW3 ...219 L1
CHD/CHDH SK8 ...56 A7
CHNE CH2 ...104 A1
CHSE CH3 ...122 F6
CHSE CH3 ...162 A7
CHSE CH3 ...179 P3
CONG CW12 ...155 M2
CONG CW12 ...174 C1
DID/WITH M20 ...40 D5
FROD/HEL WA6 ...84 A6
FROD/HEL WA6 ...105 N7
FROD/HEL WA6 ...107 H7
GOL/RIS/CU WA3 ...35 K3
GOL/RIS/CU WA3 ...35 P6
GTS/LS CH66 ...79 L5
HTNM SK4 ...41 K5
HYDE SK14 ...43 K1
IRL M44 ...27 M7
IRL M44 ...36 C3
KNUT WA16 ...89 J5
MCFLDN SK10 ...113 L1
MCFLDN SK10 ...93 P7
MCFLDS SK11 ...115 P6
MCFLDS SK11 ...134 D6
MKTDR TF9 ...219 M6
MPL/ROM SK6 ...43 H5
NANT CW5 ...16 B4
NSTN CH64 ...77 H4
NSTN CH64 ...77 M7
NSTN CH64 ...77 P3
NWCHE CW9 ...87 K2
NWCHE CW9 ...88 B5
NWCHE CW9 ...110 C2
NWCHE CW9 ...128 F3
NWCHW CW8 ...109 L8
PART M31 ...37 K2
POY/DIS SK12 ...73 M3
RAIN/WH L35 ...60 D7
RUNC WA7 ...62 C6
SBCH CW11 ...153 K5
SBCH CW11 ...170 C2
SBCH CW11 ...171 J2
SBCH CW11 ...172 B3
SBCH CW11 ...172 C1
TPLY/KEL CW6 ...166 A8
WARRS WA4 ...64 C8
WDN WA8 ...31 K9
WHITCH SY13 ...206 B6
School Rd EP CH65 ...6 C4
HALE/TIMP WA15 ...53 H4
NWCHE CW9 ...110 D7
SALE M33 ...38 E3
WARRN/WOL WA2 ...33 M7
WILM/AE SK9 ...71 M2
WSFD CW7 ...128 E6
WSFD CW7 ...129 H9
School Rd North NWCHE CW9 ...110 D6
School Rd South NWCHE CW9 ...110 E6
Schools Hl CHD/CHDH SK8 ...55 M4
Schools Rd GTN M18 ...28 E4
School St BRAM/HZG SK7 ...121 P8
CHNE CH2 ...121 P8
CW/HAS CW1 ...190 D8
GOL/RIS/CU WA3 ...24 C1
NEWLW WA12 ...23 M6
RNFD/HAY WA11 ...22 D3
WARRS WA4 * ...48 D5
School Ter GOL/RIS/CU WA3 * ...24 C1
School Wy NWCHE CW9 ...109 J1
WDN WA8 ...46 B4
Schooner Cl RUNC WA7 ...63 H8
Scilly Cl EP CH65 ...102 E3
The Score STHEL WA9 ...30 F2
Scotch Hall La NWCHE CW9 ...87 H2
Scotland Bd WARR WA1 ...3 G3
Scotland St WHITCH SY13 ...213 L6
Scott Av CW/HAS CW1 ...185 M4
WDN WA8 ...20 E2
Scott Cl ALS/KID ST7 ...173 H9
MCFLDN SK10 * ...117 N5
RDSH SK5 ...45 J8
SBCH CW11 ...171 J5
Scott Dr HALE/TIMP WA15 ...53 K3
MPL/ROM SK6 ...43 N8
Scott Ga DTN/ASHW M34 ...29 L2
Scotthope Cl MCFLDS SK11 ...116 F6

Scotton Av GTS/LS CH66 ...79 M8
Scott Rd DTN/ASHW M34 ...29 L8
MCFLDN SK10 ...94 G6
Scotts Av STHEL WA9 ...30 F5
Scott St WARRN/WOL WA2 ...18 E5
Scout Dr NTHM/RTH M23 ...54 B3
Scragg St ALS/KID ST7 ...189 P8
Scroggins La PART M31 ...36 E4
Sea Bnk MWCH CW10 ...151 K1
Seabury St WARRS WA4 ...49 J4
Seacombe Av CW/HAS CW1 ...185 P5
Seacombe Dr GTS/LS CH66 ...102 A1
Seaford Cl RUNC WA7 ...63 H5
Seaford Pl WARRN/WOL WA2 ...33 K4
Seagrave Cl NWCHE CW9 ...109 N7
Seagull Cl CW/HAS CW1 ...185 M5
Seahill Rd CH/BCN CH1 ...120 C5
Sealand Cl SALE M33 ...39 H6
WARRN/WOL WA2 ...33 P8
Sealand Rd CH/BCN CH1 ...121 H9
NTHM/RTH M23 ...39 J6
Sea La RUNC WA7 ...62 B4
Seale Av DTN/ASHW M34 ...29 K2
Sea Rd BRAM/HZG SK7 ...56 G8
Seamon's Dr ALT WA14 ...52 E2
Seamon's Rd ALT WA14 ...52 E1
Searby Rd GTN M18 ...28 B5
Seathwaite Wy RUNC WA7 ...22 C5
Seathwaite Grove Cl RUNC WA7 ...62 C9
Seaton Cl BRAM/HZG SK7 ...57 K6
CW/HAS CW1 ...170 A9
Seaton Gv STHEL WA9 ...30 C2
Seaton Pk RUNC WA7 ...63 J3
Seaton St WSFD CW7 ...150 D1
Sea Vw NSTN CH64 ...77 H3
Seaville St CHSE CH3 ...3 H3
Sebastian Cl MPL/ROM SK6 ...43 N5
Secker Cl WARRS WA4 ...48 F5
Secker Cl WARRS WA4 ...48 F5
Second Av ALS/KID ST7 ...188 C7
CO CH5 ...100 D9
CW/HAS CW1 ...185 M7
FLINT CH6 ...98 A7
MCFLDN SK10 ...73 K5
RAIN/WH L35 ...30 A4
RUNC WA7 ...62 D6
SBCH CW11 ...171 J4
Second Dig La NANT CW5 ...197 K8
Second Wood St NANT CW5 ...10 A4
Sedbergh Cl HOLMCH CW4 ...131 M8
Sedbergh Gv RUNC WA7 ...62 C9
Sedburgh Cl SALE M33 ...38 A5
Sedbury Cl NTHM/RTH M23 ...39 J7
Seddon Av GTN M18 ...28 B5
Seddon Rd ALT WA14 ...53 H5
Seddon St BNG/LEV M19 ...28 B7
MWCH CW10 ...130 B9
Sedge Cl RDSH SK5 ...45 J8
Sedgefield Cl MCFLDN SK10 ...95 J9
Sedgefield Rd CH/BCN CH1 ...2 A2
Sedgeford Cl WHITCH SY13 ...213 M7
Sedgeford Cl CHD/CHDH SK8 ...71 L5
Sedgemoor Cl CHD/CHDH SK8 ...56 B5
Sedgewick Crs
WARRW/BUR WA5 ...32 B2
Sedgmere Av CW/HAS CW1 ...169 P9
Sedum Cl CHSE CH3 ...143 J4
Sefton Av CONG CW12 ...156 A9
WDN WA8 ...45 N4
Sefton Cl SALE M33 ...38 E2
Sefton Dr WILM/AE SK9 ...71 J1
Sefton Rd CHNE CH2 ...122 E7
SALE M33 ...38 E2
Sefton St NEWLW WA12 ...23 K6
Selbourne Dr BURS/TUN ST6 ...189 N9
Selby Cl POY/DIS SK12 * ...73 J1
RUNC WA7 ...63 H6
Selby Gdns CHD/CHDH SK8 ...56 C9
Selby Gn GTS/LS CH66 ...79 M8
Selby St HTNM SK4 ...41 J8
OP/CLY M11 ...28 A1
WARRW/BUR WA5 ...48 A2
Selkirk Av PS/BROM CH62 ...79 J3
WARRS WA4 ...49 J4
Selkirk Cl GTS/LS CH66 * ...79 K8
MCFLDN SK10 ...116 F2
Selkirk Dr CHSW/BR CH4 ...142 C5
HOLMCH CW4 ...131 N9
Selkirk Rd CHSW/BR CH4 ...142 C5
Sellars Sq DROY M43 ...28 C1
Seller St CH/BCN CH1 ...3 G3
Selside Ct CHSW/BR CH4 ...142 C5
Selsey Cl CW/HAS CW1 ...170 D8
Selsey Dr DID/WITH M20 ...40 D8
Selside Wk NTHLY L27 ...44 A4
Selstead Rd WYTH/NTH M22 ...54 E6
Selworth Av SALE M33 ...53 J1
Selworthy Dr CW/HAS CW1 ...185 H5
WARRS WA4 ...49 J4
Selwyn Cl WARRW/BUR WA5 ...48 B3
WDN WA8 ...12 F4
Selwyn Dr CHD/CHDH SK8 ...56 C8
MCFLDS SK11 ...117 M9
Semper Cl CONG CW12 ...156 A6
Seneschal Ct RUNC WA7 ...62 F8
Senior Av RUSH/FAL M14 ...102 A1
Senna La NWCHE CW9 ...87 K5
Sennen Cl RUNC WA7 ...62 F8
Sens Cl CH/BCN CH1 ...2 C5
Septal Rd RDSH SK5 ...24 D8
Sephton Av GOL/RIS/CU WA3 ...25 N6
Sergeant York Loop
WARRW/BUR WA5 ...47 M2
Serin Cl NEWLW WA12 ...23 N6
The Serpentine CHSW/BR CH4 ...142 D3
Service St HTNM SK4 ...41 J8
Servite Cl EP CH65 ...102 E3
Sevenoaks Av HTNM SK4 ...41 H3
Sevenoaks Cl MCFLDN SK10 ...117 H2
Sevenoaks Rd CHD/CHDH SK8 ...55 K1

Seven Sisters La KNUT WA16 ...90 G9
Seven Stiles Dr MPL/ROM SK6 ...43 K9
Severn Cl ALT WA14 ...175 M9
BIDD ST8 ...175 M9
CONG CW12 ...155 P9
STHEL WA9 ...31 H3
WARRN/WOL WA2 ...33 P6
WDN WA8 ...46 D4
Severn Dr BRAM/HZG SK7 ...56 C9
Severn Rd GOL/RIS/CU WA3 ...25 P7
RAIN/WH L35 ...30 A5
Severnvale EP CH65 ...102 C1
Severn Wy RDSH SK5 ...41 N3
Sewell St RUNC WA7 ...15 H5
Sexa St OP/CLY M11 ...28 D1
Sextant Cl RUNC WA7 ...63 H8
Sexton Av STHEL WA9 ...31 H2
Seymore Cha KNUT WA16 ...90 E5
Seymour Dr GTS/LS CH66 ...80 A7
NANT CW5 ...53 J2
Seymour Gv HALE/TIMP WA15 ...53 J2
OFTN SK2 ...57 H1
Seymour St DTN/ASHW M34 ...29 K6
DTN/ASHW M34 ...28 D3
Sgt York Loop
WARRW/BUR WA5 ...47 M1
Shackleton Cl
WARRW/BUR WA5 ...32 G8
Shadewood Crs WARRS WA4 ...49 J5
Shadewood Rd MCFLDS SK11 ...116 C6
Shadowmoss Rd
DTN/ASHW M34 ...29 M9
Shady Brook La NWCHW CW8 ...108 C3
Shady Gv ALS/KID ST7 ...187 P4
Shady La NTHM/RTH M23 ...38 C9
Shady Oak Rd OFTN SK2 ...57 M1
Shaftesbury Av CHD/CHDH SK8 ...56 B6
CHSE CH3 ...3 L7
HALE/TIMP WA15 ...53 M2
WARRW/BUR WA5 ...47 J5
Shaftesbury Dr EDGY/DAV SK3 ...56 F1
Shaftesbury Wy
DTN/ASHW M34 ...32 C1
Shaftway Cl RNFD/HAY WA11 ...23 K2
Shakerley Av CONG CW12 ...155 P7
Shakespeare Av
DTN/ASHW M34 ...29 M9
Shakespeare Cl ALS/KID ST7 ...189 H8
NWCHE CW9 ...110 C5
Shakespeare Dr
CHD/CHDH SK8 ...55 P1
CW/HAS CW1 ...185 N4
Shakespeare Gv
WARRN/WOL WA5 ...33 M6
Shakespeare Rd MPL/ROM SK6 ...42 D5
NSTN CH64 ...77 L8
WARRS WA4 ...30 F6
Shalcombe Cl ALS/KID ST7 ...189 H8
Shalcomb Hll HLWD L26 ...44 A8
Shalford Dr WYTH/NTH M22 ...54 F7
Shallacres EP CH65 ...102 C1
The Shambles KNUT WA16 ...90 F4
Shandon Av NTHM/RTH M23 ...39 N7
Shanklin Cl DTN/ASHW M34 * ...29 P7
WARRW/BUR WA5 ...46 G1
Shannon Cl CHSW/BR CH4 ...142 A5
NANT CW5 ...197 L2
Shannon Ct BURS/TUN ST6 ...189 L9
Shannon Dr BURS/TUN ST6 ...189 K9
Shannon Rd WARRW/BUR WA5 ...54 C4
Shap Av HALE/TIMP WA15 ...53 P2
Shard St STHEL WA9 ...31 K1
Shargate Cl WILM/AE SK9 ...71 M2
Sharnbrook Dr CW/HAS CW2 ...184 E5
Sharnford Sq WGTN/LGST M12 ...28 A1
Sharon Park Cl WARRS WA4 ...49 L6
Sharples Cl HTNM SK4 ...41 M5
Sharpley St MCFLDN SK10 * ...8 C3
Sharps Dr WHITCH SY13 ...213 K6
Sharp St WARRN/WOL WA2 ...18 D7
Sharston Av WARRW/BUR WA5 ...46 G4
Sharston Crs KNUT WA16 ...90 F4
Sharston Rd WYTH/NTH M22 ...39 P9
Shavington Av CHNE CH2 ...122 A7
Shavington Wy NWCHE CW9 ...109 N8
Shawbrook Rd BNG/LEV M19 ...41 H5
Shawbury Cl SALE M33 ...38 C6
WARR WA1 ...34 B8
Shawbury Rd NTHM/RTH M23 ...54 D3
Shawcroft Cl NWCHE CW9 ...110 B6
Shawcross Fold STKP SK1 * ...17 L3
Shawcross La WYTH/NTH M22 ...40 A8
Shawcross St STKP SK1 ...17 H7
Shawdene Rd WYTH/NTH M22 ...39 M8
Shaw Dr KNUT WA16 ...90 G2
Shawell Ct WDN WA8 ...46 C5
Shaw Entry
EDGY/DAV SK3 ...16 E7
Shawe Av BNG/LEV M19 ...54 F2
Shaw Hall Bnk WYTH/NTH M22 ...41 J3
Shaw Rd South EDGY/DAV SK3 ...56 E1
Shaw's Av WARRN/WOL WA2 ...33 L8
Shaw St GOL/RIS/CU WA3 ...26 A6
MCFLDS SK11 ...117 K8
RNFD/HAY WA11 ...23 J3
RUNC WA7 ...14 D5
Shay La HALE/TIMP WA15 ...54 F2
Shayfield Av WYTH/NTH M22 ...54 F2
Shayfield Dr WYTH/NTH M22 ...54 F2
Shayfield Rd WYTH/NTH M22 ...54 F2
Shay La CHSE CH3 ...124 D8
CHSE CH3 ...124 E4
Shay La CHSE CH3 ...124 B9
HALE/TIMP WA15 ...54 A6
MALPAS SY14 ...192 F6
Shay's La TPLY/KEL CW6 ...127 H7
Sheaf Cl CHSE CH3 ...124 B9

Shearbrook La HOLMCH CW4 ...132 A2
Sheardhall Av POY/DIS SK12 ...75 J1
Shearer Rd OFTN SK2 ...57 M2
Sheath St NWCHE CW9 ...11 F2
Shed La CHSE CH3 ...122 B9
Sheepfield Cl GTS/LS CH66 ...79 N6
Sheerness St GTN M18 ...28 D4
Sheerwater Cl WARR WA1 ...34 A9
Sheffield Cl WARRW/BUR WA5 ...47 N2
Sheffield St WARR WA1 ...3 H4
Shelagh Av WDN WA8 ...12 C3
The Sheilings GOL/RIS/CU WA3 ...25 H1
Shelagh Av WDN WA8 ...12 C3
Shelbourne Ms MCFLDN SK10 ...116 F4
Shelburne Dr CW/HAS CW1 ...186 A3
Sheldon Av CHSE CH3 ...122 C9
CONG CW12 ...156 A9
Sheldon Cl PART M31 ...36 D5
POY/DIS SK12 ...74 A4
Sheldrake Rd ALT WA14 ...53 H6
Shelford Av GTN M18 ...28 B5
Shelley Av NWCHE CW9 ...88 F8
ALS/KID ST7 ...173 H9
CW/HAS CW1 ...185 J5
MWCH CW10 ...151 J5
Shelley Cl SBCH CW11 ...171 J5
Shelley Dr CW/SHV CW2 ...184 F7
Shelley Gv WARRS WA4 ...49 H3
Shelley Rd CH/BCN CH1 ...121 J6
RDSH SK5 ...28 D8
Shelley St NSTN CH64 ...45 N6
Shellow La MCFLDS SK11 ...135 K6
Shellway Rd EP CH65 ...103 J1
Shelton Av SALE M33 ...38 A4
Shelton Cl WDN WA8 ...46 D4
Shenhurst Cl WILM/AE SK9 ...92 G1
Shenton Av RNFD/HAY WA11 ...22 B3
Shentonfield Rd
WYTH/NTH M22 ...54 G1
Shenton Park Av SALE M33 ...37 P7
Shepcroft La WARRS WA4 ...64 E4
Shepherds Fold Dr WSFD CW7 ...128 A8
Shepherd's La CHNE CH2 ...121 N6
Shepley Cl BRAM/HZG SK7 ...57 K7
Shepley Dr BRAM/HZG SK7 ...57 K6
Shepley La MPL/ROM SK6 ...58 D3
Shepley St DTN/ASHW M34 ...29 M3
Sheppard Cl CW/HAS CW1 ...5 G2
Sheppenhall Gv NANT CW5 ...207 M5
Sheppenhall La NANT CW5 ...207 M5
Shepperton Cl WARRS WA4 ...48 F9
Shepsides Cl GTS/LS CH66 ...101 N1
Shepton Dr NTHM/RTH M23 ...55 H8
Shepton Rd GTS/LS CH66 ...102 A3
Sheraton Rd CHSE CH3 ...144 B5
Sherborne Cl RUNC WA7 ...63 K3
Sherborne Rd CW/HAS CW1 ...185 K2
EDGY/DAV SK3 ...41 K9
Sherborne Av CHSW/BR CH4 ...142 D5
Sherbourne Cl CHD/CHDH SK8 ...56 B8
Sherbourne Rd EP CH65 ...102 F1
MCFLDS SK11 ...116 F5
Sherbourne Wy
WARRW/BUR WA5 ...32 C5
Sherbrook Cl SALE M33 ...38 C5
Sherbrooke Rd POY/DIS SK12 ...59 H9
Sherbrook Ri WILM/AE SK9 ...93 L8
Sherdley Park Dr STHEL WA9 ...30 G2
Sherdley Rd STHEL WA9 ...30 E1
Sherford Cl BRAM/HZG SK7 ...56 G5
Sheridan Av GOL/RIS/CU WA3 ...24 F2
Sheridan Cl CW/HAS CW1 ...170 A8
Sheridan Pl WARRN/WOL WA2 ...33 N5
Sheri Dr NEWLW WA12 ...23 P7
Sheringham Cl CHSW/BR CH4 * ...142 A5
STHEL WA9 ...22 B6
Sheringham Dr CW/HAS CW1 ...185 H1
Sheringham Rd RUSH/FAL M14 ...40 E1
WARRW/BUR WA5 ...47 J1
Sherlock Av RNFD/HAY WA11 ...23 J2
Sherlock St RUSH/FAL M14 ...40 E1
Sherman Dr RNFD/HAY WA11 ...23 J2
Sherratt Cl CONG CW12 ...155 N8
Sherston Cl CHSE CH3 ...179 K3
Sherwell Cl WGTN/LGST M12 ...28 A8
Sherrymill Hl WHITCH SY13 ...213 L5
Sherway Dr HALE/TIMP WA15 ...53 N1
Sherwin St DTN/ASHW M34 ...29 L2
Sherwood Av HTNM SK4 ...4 E7
SALE M33 ...38 F3
Sherwood Cl MPL/ROM SK6 ...58 D5
RAIN/WH L35 ...30 A5
WDN WA8 ...46 J6
Sherwood Crs
WARRW/BUR WA5 ...32 B2
Sherwood Gv FROD/HEL WA6 ...104 G1
Sherwood Rd CH/BCN CH1 ...121 J6
DTN/ASHW M34 ...29 H6
MCFLDS SK11 ...117 K8
MPL/ROM SK6 ...58 C4
Shetland Cl WARRN/WOL WA2 ...33 M4
WDN WA8 ...46 C4
Shetland Dr EP CH65 ...102 E3
Shevington Cl STHEL WA9 ...30 C4
WDN WA8 ...46 C4
Shevington Gdns
NTHM/RTH M23 ...39 L7
Shield St EDGY/DAV SK3 ...16 E6
Shiers Dr CHD/CHDH SK8 ...55 N3
Shiggins Cl WARRW/BUR WA5 ...47 P1
Shillingford Ct WARRS WA4 ...49 L5
Shilton Cl MWCH CW10 ...151 L5
Shipbrook Rd CHNE CH2 ...122 B8
Shipbrook Rd NWCHE CW9 ...110 B9
NWCHE CW9 ...110 C9
Shippats Ct CH/BCN CH1 ...2 E6
Shippey St RUSH/FAL M14 ...40 E1
Shipton Cl WARRW/BUR WA5 ...32 E8

WDN WA8 ...45 K4
Shira Cl ALS/KID ST7 ...188 B3
Shire Gn STHEL WA9 ...31 H2
Shireoak Rd DID/WITH M20 ...40 E1
DTN/ASHW M34 ...29 J1
MPL/ROM SK6 ...58 C1
Shirley Cl BRAM/HZG SK7 ...57 J5
WARRS WA4 ...49 J5
Shirley Gv EDGY/DAV SK3 ...56 E2
Shirleys Cl MCFLDN SK10 ...94 G7
Shirleys Dr MCFLDN SK10 ...94 G7
Shirwell Gv STHEL WA9 ...31 H4
Shocklach Rd CHNE CH2 ...121 P5
Shoecroft Av DTN/ASHW M34 ...29 L7
Shones Ct CH/BCN CH1 ...96 A7
Shop La CONG CW12 ...155 N9
TPLY/KEL CW6 ...127 J9
Shoredon Gdns
CHD/CHDH SK8 ...56 B5
Shoreham Dr
WARRW/BUR WA5 ...47 L4
Shores Green Dr NWCHE CW9 ...88 F3
Shores La NANT CW5 ...182 F9
Short Av DROY M43 ...28 F1
Short Cl NEWLW WA12 ...23 L6
Shortland Crs BNG/LEV M19 ...40 C1
Short St BRAM/HZG SK7 ...57 K4
HTNM SK4 ...16 E1
NEWLW WA12 ...23 L6
Short St East HTNM SK4 ...17 F1
Shorwell Cl WARRW/BUR WA5 ...47 M5
Shorwell Gv BURS/TUN ST6 ...189 N8
Shotwick La CH/BCN CH1 ...101 J6
Shotwick Rd CO CH5 ...100 C8
Shraleybrook Rd ALS/KID ST7 ...200 D8
Shrewbridge Crs NANT CW5 ...197 L4
Shrewbridge Rd NANT CW5 ...201 N5
Shrewsbury Dr NEWLW WA12 ...23 P7
Shrewsbury Gdns
CHD/CHDH SK8 ...55 P5
Shrewsbury Rd SALE M33 ...38 D6
Shrewsbury St WARRS WA4 ...48 F3
Shrewsbury Wy SBCH CW11 * ...171 M6
Shrigley Cl WILM/AE SK9 ...71 M5
Shrigley Ri MCFLDN SK10 * ...73 P9
MCFLDN SK10 ...73 P9
Shrigley Rd MCFLDN SK10 ...96 A3
POY/DIS SK12 ...75 H6
Shropshire Av RDSH SK5 ...42 B2
Shropshire Cl MWCH CW10 ...151 J2
WARR WA1 ...34 C6
Shropshire La WHITCH SY13 ...214 G4
Shropshire Rd EP CH65 ...103 H1
Shropshire Wy WHITCH SY13 ...213 J7
Shrowbridge Wk
WGTN/LGST M12 ...28 H5
Shuldham Cl KNUT WA16 ...67 J2
Shurlach Rd NWCHE CW9 ...110 D7
Shutley La WHITCH SY13 ...213 J6
Shuttingslow Wy MCFLDN SK10 ...116 C4
Sibberstield La CHSE CH3 ...177 M5
Sibbering Cl STHEL WA9 ...31 G2
Sibell St CH/BCN CH1 ...3 G2
Sibley Rd HTNM SK4 ...41 J5
Sibley St GTN M18 ...28 C5
Sidcup Rd NTHM/RTH M23 ...54 B2
Siddall St NEWLW WA12 ...28 A7
WGTN/LGST M12 ...28 A7
Siddeley Cl CHSW/BR CH4 ...140 G6
Siddeley Dr NEWLW WA12 ...23 K6
Siddington Av EDGY/DAV SK3 ...56 C4
NWCHE CW9 ...110 A8
Siddington Bnk MCFLDS SK11 ...115 H9
Siddington Rd POY/DIS SK12 ...73 M1
WILM/AE SK9 ...71 M1
Siddorn St WSFD CW7 ...149 N1
Side Av ALT WA14 ...52 C6
Side La CHSW/BR CH4 ...142 C5
Side La TPLY/KEL CW6 ...145 L4
Sidlaw Av STHEL WA9 ...22 B6
Sidmouth Cl WARRW/BUR WA5 ...47 J3
Sidmouth Gv CHD/CHDH SK8 ...55 P8
Sidmouth Rd SALE M33 ...38 A5
Sidmouth St DTN/ASHW M34 ...29 K2
Sidney Rd NSTN CH64 ...77 M4
Siemens Rd IRL M44 ...36 D2
Sienna Cl IRL M44 ...36 D2
Sierra Rd IRL M44 ...36 D3
Silcock Cl GOL/RIS/CU WA3 ...24 C1
Silk Mill St KNUT WA16 ...90 E3
MCFLDN SK10 ...
The Silk Rd MCFLDN SK10 ...95 L9
Silkstone Crs RUNC WA7 ...62 F7
Silkstone St OP/CLY M11 ...28 G2
Silsden Av GOL/RIS/CU WA3 ...25 K1
Silver Av RNFD/HAY WA11 ...22 E4
Silverbirch Cl SALE M33 ...38 A6
Silver Birches DTN/ASHW M34 ...29 P8
Silverbirch Wy GTS/LS CH66 ...175 K9
Silver Cl BIDD ST8 ...
DUK SK16 ...29 P2
Silverdale NWCHE CW9 ...12 B4
Silverdale Av DTN/ASHW M34 ...29 L7
IRL M44 ...27 P5
Silverdale Cl FROD/HEL WA6 ...84 A6
RNFD/HAY WA11 ...22 E4
Silverdale Dr WILM/AE SK9 ...93 J1
Silverdale Rd CHD/CHDH SK8 ...55 N3
HTNM SK4 ...41 K4
WARR WA1 ...34 M5
Silverdale St OP/CLY M11 ...28 F2
Silvergate Ct CONG CW12 ...174 F1
Silver La GOL/RIS/CU WA3 ...35 H1

Silver La GOL/RIS/CU WA3 ....35 K1
Silvermine Gdns STHEL WA9 ....30 B1
Silvermine Cl ALS/KID ST7 ....189 K6
Silverne Dr EP CH65 ....102 C2
Silverstone Crs BURS/TUN ST6 ..189 N9
Silver St IRL M44 ....27 P5
  MCFLDN SK10 ....95 P5
  WARRN/WOL WA2 ....18 D3
Silverwood ALS/KID ST7 ....189 K7
Simkin Av WARRS WA4 ....49 H5
Simmonds Cl NWCHE CW9 ....109 N9
Simms Av STHEL WA9 ....22 C6
Simon Freeman Cl
  BNG/LEV M19 ....41 K2
Simons Cl SALE M33 ....38 D5
Simonside WDN WA8 ....45 J5
Simons La FROD/HEL WA6 ....83 P7
Simonstone Gv STHEL WA9 ....33 J1
Simonstone Rd CHSW/BR CH4 ...141 H6
Simonsway NTHM/RTH M23 ....54 C4
Simonsway WYTH/NTH M22 ....54 E5
Simonswood Cl MWCH CW10 .....151 H2
Simpson Cl CW/HAS CW1 ....121 M2
Simpson Cl CW/HAS CW1 ....170 A8
Simpson La ALS/KID SK10 ....74 B7
Simpson La CHNE CH2 ....121 M3
Simpson St EDGY/DAV SK3 * 17 F7
  WILM/AE SK9 ....71 H8
Simpsons Wy CHSW/BR CH4 .....140 F7
Sinclair Av ALS/KID ST7 ....187 M5
  WARRN/WOL WA2 ....33 L6
  WDN WA8 ....21 F5
Sinderland La ALT WA14 ....37 H7
  LYMM WA13 ....36 G8
Sinderland Rd ALT WA14 ....37 N8
Sinderland Rd PART M31 ....37 H5
Singapore Av MANAIR M90 ....54 C7
Singleton Av CW/HAS CW1 ....170 A8
Singleton Cl FROD/HEL WA6 ....84 A5
Singleton Rd EP CH65 ....80 B9
  HTNM SK4 ....41 J4
Sirdar St OP/CLY M11 * 28 F2
Sir Richard Fairey Rd
  HTNM SK4 ....41 J2
Siskin Cl NEWLW WA12 ....23 N6
Siskin Dr SK2 DROY 57 M2
Sisters' St DROY M43 ....28 C1
Six Acre Gdns WARRS WA4 ....63 L1
Six Acre La WARR WA1 ....63 L1
Sixth Av FLINT CH6 ....98 A7
Skaife Rd SALE M33 ....39 H4
Skeath Cl SBCH CW11 ....172 A3
Skellern St ALS/KID ST7 ....188 F6
Skellorn Green La MCFLDN SK10 ..73 M6
Skelton Rd ALT WA14 ....38 B9
Skiddaw Cl RUNC WA7 ....48 E1
Skip's La CHSE CH5 ....143 N3
Skipton Cl BRAM/HZG SK7 ....57 J7
  RDSH SK5 ....101 P2
Skipton Dr GTS/LS CH66 ....79 N9
Skye Cl EP CH65 ....102 E3
  WDN WA8 ....46 C4
Skye Cft MPL/ROM SK6 ....43 J5
Skylark Cl CW/HAS CW1 ....184 F1
Slack La ALS/KID ST7 ....188 F6
Slack St MCFLDS SK11 ....117 L7
Slade Hall Rd WGTN/LGST M12 ...28 A7
Slade La ALT WA14 ....69 K7
  MCFLDN SK10 ....93 N8
Slade St NWCHE CW9 ....13 K2
Slag La RNFD/HAY WA11 ....22 F2
Slateacre Rd HYDE SK14 ....43 L1
Slate La DTN/ASHW M34 ....29 J1
Slate La DTN/ASHW M34 ....29 J1
Slater St MCFLDS SK11 ....4 E1
  WARR WA1 ....48 E3
Sleddale Cl OFTN SK2 ....57 K2
Sledmoor Rd NTHM/RTH M23 ....39 J7
Sleeper's Wy MCFLDS SK11 ....118 C5
Slindon Cl NEWLW WA12 ....201 N6
Slutchers La WARR WA1 ....48 C4
Small Av WARRN/WOL WA2 ....33 H6
Smallbrook Rd WHITCH SY13 .....213 K6
Smallbrook Wk CW/HAS WA4 .....185 J8
Small Crs WARRN/WOL WA2 ....33 M6
Small La WILM/AE SK9 ....69 K6
Smallman Rd CW/SHV CW2 ....198 B7
Smallwood Cl NEWUL ST5 ....201 N6
Smart St WGTN/LGST M12 ....28 A6
Smethwick La SBCH CW11 ....154 A4
Smith Cl ALS/KID ST7 ....187 M4
Smith Dr WARRN/WOL WA2 ....33 N8
Smithfield Dr WRXS/E LL15 ....176 F3
Smithfield La SBCH CW11 ....11 P3
Smithfields CHSE CH3 ....164 B7
Smithfield St STHEL WA9 ....22 A7
  WRXS/E LL15 ....176 F8
Smith Gv CW/HAS CW1 ....198 B7
Smithills Cl GOL/RIS/CU WA3 ....24 E1
Smith La CH/BCN CH1 ....77 G2
Smith La KNUT WA16 ....69 K7
  MCFLDN SK10 ....18 E6
Smith Rd WDN WA8 ....21 F4
Smith's Lawn WILM/AE SK9 ....71 J9
Smiths Ter MCFLDS SK11 ....9 H7
Smith St CHD/CHDH SK8 * 55 N5
Smith St DUK SK16 ....16 E1
  MCFLDS SK11 ....117 K6
  WARR WA1 ....31 K1
Smithy Bnk WSFD SW7 ....149 J7
Smithy Brow GOL/RIS/CU WA3 ......34 A1
  MCFLDN SK10 ....96 A5
Smithy Cl CH/BCN CH1 ....120 D2
  NSTN CH64 ....98 A9
  WILM/AE SK9 ....45 J1
Smithy Fold MCFLDS SK11 * 157 P9
Smithy Gn CHD/CHDH SK8 * 42 G3
  MPL/ROM SK6 ....42 G3
Smithy La ALT WA14 ....52 B4
  BIDD ST8 ....175 L7

CHSE CH3 ....124 E1
CONG CW12 ....155 K3
CW/HAS CW1 ....169 M9
CW/SHV CW2 ....192 C1
CW/SHV CW2 ....199 P1
FROD/HEL WA6 ....83 J8
FROD/HEL WA6 ....106 F2
GOL/RIS/CU WA3 ....34 B1
GTS/LS CH66 ....79 N7
MALPAS SY14 ....203 D4
MCFLDN SK10 ....94 C3
MCFLDN SK10 ....96 C8
MCFLDS SK11 ....157 L4
MKTDR TF9 ....218 G8
NSTN CH64 ....78 E5
NWCHE CW9 ....88 A5
NWCHW CW8 ....110 G2
NWCHW CW8 ....86 D7
NWCHW CW8 ....108 C7
PART M31 ....36 E5
TPLY/KEL CW6 ....146 F4
WDN WA8 ....45 J2

Smithy Pathway
  CHSW/BR CH4 ....142 B6
Smithy Wk SBCH CW11 ....171 L6
Smokehall La NWCHE CW9 ....128 C5
Smokey La WHITCH SY13 ....212 A5
Smokies Wy BIDD ST8 ....175 K6
Smyth Rd WDN WA8 ....46 B5
Snab La NSTN CH64 ....74 M9
Snabwood Cl NSTN CH64 ....77 L8
Snaefell Ri WARRS WA4 ....48 E8
Snape La CW/SHV CW2 ....199 J5
Snape Rd CW/SHV CW2 ....185 K8
  MCFLDN SK10 ....117 L2
  KNUT WA16 ....113 P1
Snelson La KNUT WA16 ....114 A5
Snipe La POY/DIS SK12 ....72 G3
Snipe Wy DTN/ASHW M34 ....29 K1
Snowberry Cl WDN WA8 ....46 C5
Snowdon Cl GTS/LS CH66 ....79 L7
  WARRW/BUR WA5 ....47 J1
Snowdon Cresent
  CHSW/BR CH4 ....142 C5
Snowdon Dr CW/SHV CW2 ....184 D5
Snowdon Gv STHEL WA9 ....31 H1
Snowdonia Wy WSFD SW7 ....149 K3
Snowdon St NWCHW CW8 ....109 H1
Snowdrop Cl RUNC WA7 ....84 D1
Snow Hl MCFLDS SK11 ....9 G7
Soapstone Wy IRL M44 ....27 N9
Solly Crs CONG CW12 ....155 J8
Solvay Rd NWCHW CW8 ....109 M2
Solway Cl WARRN/WOL WA2 ....34 A4
Solway Gv WARRN/WOL WA2 ....62 B9
Somerby Dr WYTH/NTH M22 ....54 E6
Somerford Av CW/SHV CW2 ....184 G5
Somerford Cl SBCH CW11 ....40 A1
Somerford Rd CHSW/BR CH4 ......140 G6
  RDSH SK5 ....28 G7
Somerley Cl CW/HAS CW1 ....170 A9
Somerset Av ALS/KID ST7 ....189 H6
Somerset Cl CONG CW12 ....155 M6
  IRL M44 ....36 C2
Somerset Pl SALE M33 ....38 E2
Somerset Rd ALT WA14 ....53 H1
  CHNE CH2 ....122 A6
Somerset St CHNE CH2 ....3 J5
Somers Rd RDSH SK5 ....28 F8
Somerton Av SALE M33 ....38 F5
Somerton Cl MCFLDS SK11 ....116 F5
Somerton Rd MCFLDS SK11 ....116 F6
Somerville Cl KNUT WA16 ....67 J2
  NSTN CH64 ....77 L8
Somerville Gdns
  HALE/TIMP WA15 ....38 C9
Somerville Rd WDN WA8 ....20 B3
Somerville St CW/SHV CW2 ....4 C7
Soot Hl NWCHW CW8 ....109 L1
Sorbus Cl CHNE CH2 ....104 C1
Sorbus Dr CW/HAS CW1 ....185 L2
Sorby Rd IRL M44 ....36 F1
Sorogold St STHEL WA9 ....22 B2
Sorrel Cl CHST CH3 ....143 J4
  WARRN/WOL WA2 ....34 D6
Sorrell Bnk RDSH SK5 ....28 G8
Sorrel Sussex La MCFLDN SK10 ...92 F7
Soudan Rd OFTN SK2 ....57 K4
Sound La NANT CW5 ....195 N9
Souter's La CH/BCN CH1 ....3 F5
South Acre Dr MCFLDS SK11 ......117 N5
  WILM/AE SK9 ....71 M3
Southampton Wy RUNC WA7 ....63 J8
South Av BNG/LEV M19 ....40 C1
  CHNE CH2 ....104 A1
  CW/HAS CW1 ....186 B4
  WARRN/WOL WA2 ....18 E1
  WARR WA1 ....48 E6
South Bnk CH/BCN CH1 ....121 M7
Southbank NWCHE CW9 ....88 A5
Southbank Av CW/SHV CW2 ....198 B2
Southbank Cl WILM/AE SK9 ....93 K3
Southbank Gv CONG CW12 ....155 P9
Southbank Rd BNG/LEV M19 ....40 E3
  NANT CW5 ....207 K4
  RUNC WA7 ....14 D1
South Cheshire Wy
  ALS/KID ST7 ....173 H8
  CW/SHV CW2 ....198 E5
  NANT CW5 ....207 K4
  WHITCH SY13 ....206 A9
Southcliffe Rd RDSH SK5 ....41 N2
South Cliffe St OP/CLY M11 ....28 C2
South Cl TPLY/KEL CW6 ....146 G8
  WILM/AE SK9 ....71 H8
South Crescent Rd
  CHSW/BR CH4 ....3 G6

South Cft TPLY/KEL CW6 ....181 H1
South Crofts NANT CW5 ....10 C5
Southcross Rd GTN M18 ....28 D6
South Dr WARRW/BUR WA5 ....47 K2
Southdale Rd WARR WA1 ....34 B9
Southdene Av CHD/WITH M20 ....38 P4
Southdown Cl HTNM SK4 ....16 D2
Southdown Crs CHD/CHDH SK8 ...55 P7
South Downs Dr ALT WA14 ....53 H7
  ALT WA14 ....53 H7
South Dr CCHDY M21 ....39 L2
  CHD/CHDH SK8 ....55 J3
  HALE/TIMP WA15 ....38 D7
  KNUT WA16 ....111 N1
  NWCHE CW9 ....110 D6
Southern Cl BRAM/HZG SK7 ....56 F6
Southern Rd SALE M33 ....38 D2
Southern St WARRS WA4 ....48 E6
  WDN WA8 ....20 E2
Southfield MCFLDN SK10 ....10 A1
Southfield Rd GTS/LS CH66 ....79 N7
Southfields KNUT WA16 ....90 G2
Southfields
  WARRW/BUR WA5 ....47 K1
South La NANT CW5 ....197 P7
Southgate Rd
  HALE/TIMP WA15 ....38 E9
  HTNM SK4 ....41 K3
South Gv SALE M33 ....38 E5
  WILM/AE SK9 ....93 J4
South Heath Rd RUNC WA7 ....88 G1
South John St STHEL WA9 ....22 A6
Southlands HOLMCH CW4 ....131 P9
Southlands Av
  WARRW/BUR WA5 ....47 K4
Southlands Ct RUNC WA7 ....14 C5
Southlands Ms RUNC WA7 ....14 D6
South Lanc CONG CW12 ....156 A9
  HOLMCH CW4 ....132 B2
South La WDN WA8 ....46 C2
South La WDN WA8 ....46 E3
Southlea Rd CHD/WITH M20 ....40 E3
South Md POY/DIS SK12 ....65 L9
South Meade CCHDY M21 ....39 L1
South Meadway MPL/ROM SK6 ....58 D8
  HALE/TIMP WA15 ....38 D9
  NTHM/RTH M23 ....39 J9
South Oak La WILM/AE SK9 ....71 H8
South Pde BRAM/HZG SK7 ....57 K7
  RUNC WA7 ....14 C6
South Park Dr POY/DIS SK12 ....73 L2
South Park Rd CW/HAS CW1 ....55 K1
  NWCHW CW8 ....8 D6
South Pier Rd EP CH65 ....80 F6
Southpool Cl BRAM/HZG SK7 ....56 E6
Southport St STHEL WA9 ....22 E6
South Rdg DTN/ASHW M34 ....29 K4
  ALT WA14 ....52 G5
South Rd ALT WA14 ....53 H7
  CHD/WITH M20 ....38 G8
  EP CH65 ....81 H8
  EP CH65 ....102 E1
  SPK/HALE L24 ....60 A2
Southsea St OP/CLY M11 ....28 D2
Southside MPL/ROM SK6 ....42 D2
  WILM/AE SK9 ....70 D2
South St ALS/KID ST7 ....189 K2
  AULW OL7 ....29 L1
  CHSE CH3 ....143 J1
  CW/SHV CW2 ....5 G7
  OP/CLY M11 ....28 C2
  STHEL WA9 ....30 C1
  WDN WA8 ....21 J2
  WILM/AE SK9 ....93 J4
South Vale Crs
  HALE/TIMP WA15 ....53 K2
South Vw BIDD ST8 ....175 K9
  CHSW/BR CH4 ....142 F3
  HALE/TIMP WA15 ....56 A5
  RDSH SK5 ....28 F6
South View Av MCFLDS SK11 ......135 L1
South View Gdns
  CHD/CHDH SK8 ....55 L4
South View La WSFD SW7 ....168 A7
South View Rd CHD/CHDH CH1 ......2 B5
Southward Rd RNFD/HAY WA11 ....22 F1
Southway Pl WSFD SW7 ....149 J2
Southway ALT WA14 ....53 J1
South Wy CH/BCN CH1 ....121 H7
Southway DROY M43 ....28 G1
  RUNC WA7 ....62 C7
  WDN WA8 ....62 C9
Southway Av WARRS WA4 ....48 F8
Southwell Cl GOL/RIS/CU WA3 ......24 C1
  MPL/ROM SK6 ....42 F7
South West Av MCFLDN SK10 ......95 M7
Southwood Av RUNC WA7 ....62 G4
Southwood Rd OFTN SK2 ....57 H3
Southworth Av
  WARRW/BUR WA5 ....33 J8
Southworth La
  WARRN/WOL WA2 ....33 N1
Southworth Rd NEWLW WA12 ....28 B3
Southyard St BNG/LEV M19 ....28 B9
Sovereign Cl GOL/RIS/CU WA3 ......24 E1
  NWCHE CW9 ....110 E6
  RUNC WA7 ....63 H6
Sovereign St GOL/RIS/CU WA3 .....34 D4
Sovereign Wy CH/BCN CH1 ....120 E7
Spa Cl RDSH SK5 ....28 E9
Spalding Dr NTHM/RTH M23 ....54 C5
Sparkford Av NTHM/RTH M23 ....38 G7
Spark Hall Cl WARRS WA4 ....64 G4
Spark La RUNC WA7 ....62 D5
Spark Rd NTHM/RTH M23 ....153 N9
Sparks Cl CHSE CH3 ....143 K3
Sparrowbutts Gv ALS/KID ST7 .....189 L6

Sparrow Cl RDSH SK5 ....28 E7
Sparrowhawk Cl RUNC WA7 ....62 E7
Sparrow La KNUT WA16 ....90 F4
Sparta Wk OP/CLY M11 ....28 A1
Spartanfield Rd HTNM SK4 ....16 C1
  HTNM SK4 ....16 C1
Spath La WILM/AE SK9 ....71 M1
Spath La East CHD/CHDH SK8 .....72 B1
Spath La CHD/CHDH SK8 ....40 B5
Spath Wk CHD/CHDH SK8 ....72 B1
Speakman Av NEWLW WA12 ....23 M4
Speakman St RUNC WA7 ....14 B4
Spedding Wy EDGY/DAV SK3 .....175 M9
Speed's Wy CHSE CH3 ....176 G6
Speedwell Cl CHSE CH3 ....143 J5
  GOL/RIS/CU WA3 ....24 C1
Speke Rd HLWD L26 ....24 D6
  DTN/ASHW M34 ....29 J2
  WDN WA8 ....48 A9
  WDN WA8 ....45 H9
Spencer Brk MCFLDN SK10 ....58 F7
Spencer Cl CW/SHV CW2 ....187 K4
  CW/SHV CW2 ....184 G8
Spencer Gdns STHEL WA9 ....20 E1
Spencer Ms MCFLDN SK10 ....94 F7
Spencer Pl NEWUL ST5 ....201 P9
  NWCHW CW8 ....12 D5
  RDSH SK5 ....28 F8
Spenlow Cl MCFLDN SK10 ....54 C5
Spennymoor Ct RUNC WA7 ....62 C7
Spenser Av DTN/ASHW M34 ....39 H3
Spenser Rd NSTN CH64 ....77 L5
Spey Cl ALT WA14 ....52 G1
  WSFD SW7 ....128 G9
Spey Dr ALS/KID ST7 ....189 L6
Spink La KNUT WA16 ....88 G7
Spinnaker Cl RUNC WA7 ....63 H6
Spinner Crs NWCHE CW9 ....87 M6
Spinners La POY/DIS SK12 ....73 J2
Spinney Av HOLMCH CW4 ....132 C2
  WSFD SW7 ....149 P2
Spinney Cl STHEL WA9 ....33 H1
Spinney Dr CW/SHV CW2 ....198 C2
  GTS/LS CH66 ....101 P2
  SALE M33 ....38 D3
Spinney End CHSE CH3 ....163 P6
Spinney Gdns CHSW/BR CH4 ......162 G4
Spinney La DTN/ASHW M34 ....29 M4
Spinney La KNUT WA16 ....90 C3
Spinney Md MCFLDN SK10 ....117 L2
Spinney Rd NTHM/RTH M23 ....37 L8
The Spinney ALS/KID ST7 ....188 C4
  CHD/CHDH SK8 ....55 N4
  FROD/HEL WA6 ....100 J7
  NANT CW5 ....197 L1
  NWCHW CW8 ....107 P5
  SALE M33 ....38 B6
Spires Cl WARRN/WOL WA2 ....33 K1
Spirewood Gdns MPL/ROM SK6 .....58 D8
Spital Wk CHSE CH3 ....3 K4
Spodegreen La ALT WA14 ....52 A7
Spout La KNUT WA16 ....91 M1
Spragg St CONG CW12 ....155 N7
Spring Bnk ALS/KID ST7 ....189 J1
Spring Bank MCFLDN SK10 ....95 L6
Spring Bank Rd ALS/KID ST7 ....189 J6
Springbank Cl MPL/ROM SK6 ....43 H2
  RUNC WA7 ....61 P8
Springbank Crs WSFD SW7 ....149 K1
Springbank Gdns LYMM WA13 .....51 H2
Spring Bank Pl EDGY/DAV SK3 * ...17 F6
Spring Bank Rd MPL/ROM SK6 ......43 H2
Spring Bank Rd NM/HAY SK22 ....59 N7
Springbourne FROD/HEL WA6 ....84 A7
Springburn Gdns
  WARRN/WOL WA2 ....33 N8
Spring Ct RUNC WA7 ....15 F2
Springcroft NSTN CH64 ....77 J4
Springdale Gdns DID/WITH M20 ....40 D9
Springe La NANT CW5 ....195 K2
Springfield Av BRAM/HZG SK7 ......57 K4
  FROD/HEL WA6 ....105 H1
  HTNM SK4 ....41 H2
  LYMM WA13 ....51 H2
  MALPAS SY14 ....204 A3
  MPL/ROM SK6 ....58 D7
  WARR WA1 ....49 K4
  WARRS WA4 ....48 E9
Springfield Crs NWCHW CW8 ......109 H1
Springfield Dr ALS/KID ST7 ....188 F6
  CHNE CH2 ....121 P7
  CW/SHV CW2 ....192 C1
Springfield La IRL M44 ....27 M7
Springfield Pk RNFD/HAY WA11 ....22 C2
Springfield Rd ALT WA14 ....53 H2
  CHD/CHDH SK8 ....56 E6
  KNUT WA16 ....91 K1
  MCFLDS SK11 ....116 A4
  SALE M33 ....38 E3
  WDN WA8 ....19 F2
Springfields CHNE CH2 ....122 F3
  MCFLDN SK10 ....96 F2
Springfields Dr CONG CW12 ....155 P8
Springfield St DTN/ASHW M34 .....29 N8
  WARR WA1 ....18 E6
Spring Gdns BRAM/HZG SK7 ....57 K4
  CW/HAS CW1 ....170 B8
  HALE/TIMP WA15 ....38 E1
  NANT CW5 ....207 K4
  STKP SK1 ....17 J5
Springhead Av CHD/WITH M20 .....40 B9
Springhead Cl ALS/KID ST7 ....201 N1
Spring Hill MCFLDN SK10 ....117 N3
Spring Hl TPLY/KEL CW6 ....165 P1
Springholm Dr WARRS WA4 ....64 F3

Spring La CHSE CH3 ....177 M2
  GOL/RIS/CU WA3 ....34 C2
  LYMM WA13 ....51 L4
Spring Meadow NWCHW CW8 ......12 C1
Springmount GOL/RIS/CU WA3 ......24 G2
Spring Mt NM/HAY SK22 ....59 N7
Springs La ALS/KID ST7 ....31 J1
Spring Rd ALT WA14 ....53 M5
  POY/DIS SK12 ....73 M4
Springside HTNM SK4 ....41 L1
The Springs ALT WA14 ....52 F5
Spring St CW/SHV CW2 ....155 N8
  WDN WA8 ....21 H6
  WGTN/LGST M12 ....28 A7
  WILM/AE SK9 ....71 J8
Spring V BRAM/HZG SK7 * 57 L5
Springwell Cl CW/SHV CW2 ....185 J8
Springwood Av NWCHW CW8 ......90 G2
Springwood Cl CH/BCN CH1 ....120 F7
Springwood Crs MPL/ROM SK6 .....43 K6
Springwood Rd NEWUL ST5 ....201 M7
Springwood Wy MCFLDN SK10 .....95 K8
Sprink La CONG CW12 ....156 D5
Sproston Wy NWCHE CW9 ....109 N8
Spruce Cl GOL/RIS/CU WA3 ....25 H2
  WARR WA1 ....34 F9
Spruce Av ALS/KID ST7 ....188 D1
Spuley La MCFLDN SK10 ....96 B2
Spunhill Av GTS/LS CH66 ....101 N1
Spurling Rd WARRW/BUR WA5 ......34 E9
Spurston Cl KNUT WA16 ....12 J2
Square St MCFLDS SK11 ....117 L6
The Square CHSE CH3 ....143 N2
  CHSW/BR CH4 ....160 D2
  HALE/TIMP WA15 ....53 N7
  HTNM SK4 ....16 A1
Squires Av WDN WA8 ....45 J5
Squires Cl RNFD/HAY WA11 ....22 F3
Squirrel Cl NWCHW CW8 ....109 L5
Squirrel Dr ALT WA14 ....37 P8
Squirrels Cha MCFLDN SK10 ....94 G8
Squirrel's Jump WILM/AE SK9 ....71 J9
Stable La CHSE CH3 ....105 P5
  TPLY/KEL CW6 ....147 K1
Stable Ms NWCHW CW8 * 127 K1
The Stablings WILM/AE SK9 ....71 J9
Stadium Wy CH/BCN CH1 ....121 L6
Stadmorslow La ALS/KID ST7 ......189 P4
Staffin Av EP CH65 ....102 D4
Stafford Cl MCFLDN SK10 ....116 F2
Stafford Gdns EP CH65 ....102 D4
Stafford Rd WARRS WA4 ....48 E9
Staffordshire Moorland Wks
  CONG CW12 ....175 H6
Stafford St ALS/KID ST7 ....174 F9
Stafford St AUD/MAD/W CW3 ......217 H1
  CW/HAS CW1 ....4 D1
  NM/HAY SK22 ....59 N7
Stafford Wk MCFLDN SK10 ....116 F2
Stage Lass WHITCH SY13 ....213 K5
Stainburne Rd OFTN SK2 ....57 J4
Stainburn Rd OP/CLY M11 ....28 B1
Stainer Cl NEWLW WA12 ....23 M4
Stainsby Rd WGTN/LGST M12 ....28 A6
Staines Cl WARRS WA4 ....64 C1
Stainthorn Cl GOL/RIS/CU WA3 ...25 M5
Stainmoor Ct OFTN SK2 ....57 J3
Stainton Av GOL/RIS/CU WA3 ....35 J2
Stainton Av GTN M18 ....28 E5
Staithes Rd WYTH/NTH M22 ....54 F7
Stalbridge Rd CW/SHV CW2 ....4 E6
Stalham Wy MWCH CW10 ....151 J2
Stalmine Av CHD/CHDH SK8 ....55 J1
Stamford Av ALT WA14 ....52 E1
  CW/SHV CW2 ....4 D5
Stamford Cl MCFLDS SK11 ....117 J3
  NWCHW CW8 ....109 N7
Stamford Ct LYMM WA13 ....50 E4
  CHSE CH3 ....123 J9
Stamford Park Rd
  HALE/TIMP WA15 ....53 N3
Stamford Pl SALE M33 ....38 F4
  WILM/AE SK9 ....51 F5
Stamford Rd ALT WA14 ....53 H2
  CH/BCN CH1 ....121 H5
  DTN/ASHW M34 ....29 K2
  MCFLDS SK11 ....117 J8
  PART M31 ....37 J1
  WILM/AE SK9 ....93 J4
Stamford St ALT WA14 ....53 H2
  EP CH65 ....6 A4
  SALE M33 ....38 D2
Stamford Wy ALT WA14 ....21 G2
Stamp Av CW/HAS CW1 ....185 J2
Stanbank St HTNM SK4 ....41 J1
Stanbrook St BNG/LEV M19 ....28 C8
Stancliffe Rd WYTH/NTH M22 ....54 G2
Stancross Rd NTHM/RTH M23 .....110 A7
Standford Dr NWCHE CW9 ....109 N8
Standish Ct WDN WA8 ....20 A3
Stanford Cl NWCHE CW9 ....13 L2
Stanhope Av CW/HAS CW1 ....5 J5
  DTN/ASHW M34 ....29 L4
Stanhope Cl WILM/AE SK9 ....71 M6
Stanhope Pl ALT WA14 ....52 E5
Stanhope St BNG/LEV M19 ....28 B8
  DTN/ASHW M34 ....29 L4
  RDSH SK5 ....41 M1
Stanier Cl NWCHE CW9 ....185 N4
Stan Jolly Wk OP/CLY M11 ....28 C1
Stanlaw Rd EP CH65 ....7 F6
Stanley Av CW/HAS CW1 ....57 K4
  MPL/ROM SK6 ....43 K4
  WARRS WA4 ....49 H5
  WARRW/BUR WA5 ....33 A9
Stanley Bank Rd
  RNFD/HAY WA11 ....22 E2
Stanley Cl NWCHW CW8 ....98 A5
  WDN WA8 ....46 A5
Stanley Ct ALS/KID ST7 ....187 K4

Stanley Dr CHD/CHDH SK8 ...55 M9
HALE/TIMP WA15 ...53 L2
NEWLL ST5 * ...201 M6
Stanley Gv GTN M18 ...28 B5
CHD/CHDH SK8 ...41 J4
HTNM SK4 ...41 J4
NWCHE CW9 ...110 E2
WGTN/LGST M12 ...28 B5
Stanley Park Ct
CHSW/BR CH4 * ...142 M15
Stanley Park Ms CHSW/BR CH4 ..142 M5
Stanley Pl CH/BCN CH1... ...2 C4
WARRS WA4 * ...18 D7
Stanley Place Ms CH/BCN CH1 * ..2 C4
Stanley Rd BIDD ST8 ...175 K7
CHD/CHDH SK8 ...55 M9
DTN/ASHW M34 ...29 H6
EP CH65 ...80 E6
HTNM SK4 ...41 J4
Stanley St BIDD ST8 ...175 K9
CH/BCN CH1 ...2 C4
CW/HAS CW1 ...4 D2
MCFLDS SK11 ...83 E4
NEWLW WA12 * ...25 L6
NWCHE CW9 ...110 C4
OP/CLY M11 ...28 E2
RUNC WA7 ...15 G1
STKP SK1 ...17 J3
WARR WA1 ...18 D7
Stanley Ter WILM/AE SK9 * ...7 J5
Stanley Vls RUNC WA7 * ...14 D5
Stannage La CHSE CH3... ...177 H3
Stanner Cl WARRW/BUR WA5 ...32 C6
Stannerhouse La SBCH CW11 ..172 B6
Stannybrook Cl
FROD/HEL WA6 ...107 L6
Stanney Cl PS/BROM CH62 ...79 J2
Stanneylands Cl WILM/AE SK9 ...71 L4
Stanneylands Dr WILM/AE SK9 ...71 L4
Stanneylands Rd WILM/AE SK9 ...71 K2
EP CH65 ...6 D7
Stanney Mill La CHNE CH2 ...104 C8
Stanney Mill Rd EP CH65 ...103 H2
Stanney Woods Av EP CH65 ...102 E3
Stansbury Pl OFTN SK2... ...57 L1
Stansfield Av WARR WA1 ...49 H1
Stansfield St OP/CLY M11 ...28 D1
Stanstead Av
WARRW/BUR WA5 ...47 K4
Stanthorne Av CW/SHV CW2 ..184 F5
DID/WITH M20... ...40 B1
Stanton Av DID/WITH M20 ...39 P4
Stanton Cl NSTN CH64 ...77 L5
Stanton Ct NSTN CH64... ...77 L5
Stanton Dr CHNE CH2... ...121 N6
Stanton Rd WARRS WA4 ...49 M4
Stanway Dr HALE/TIMP WA15 ...53 K4
Stapeley Cl NWCHE CW9... ...109 N8
Stapeley Gdns HLWD L26... ...48 A9
Stapeley Ter NANT CW5 ...11 F7
Stapleford La NTHM/RTH M23 ..54 B3
SALE M33 ...39 H5
Stapleford Ct GTS/LS CH66 ...80 B5
Stapleton Av RAIN/WH L35 ...30 B4
WARRN/WOL WA2 ...24 C3
Stapleton Cl RAIN/WH L35 ...30 B4
Stapleton Rd MCFLDN SK10 ...117 H2
RAIN/WH L35 ...30 A3
Stapley Cl RUNC WA7 ...14 C4
Starbeck Dr GTS/LS CH66 ...79 M7
Starkey Gv WARRS WA4 * ...16 B5
Star La LYMM WA13 ...50 C3
MCFLDS SK11 ...117 K8
Starling La ALS/KID ST7 ...189 M5
RUNC WA7 ...63 H7
Start La CH/TWF/WBR SK23 ...75 N7
Stash Gv NTHM/RTH M23 ...54 A1
Statham Av LYMM WA15 ...50 C4
WARRN/WOL WA2 ...33 M6
Statham Cl DTN/ASHW M34 ...29 N6
LYMM WA13 ...50 D4
Statham Dr LYMM WA13 ...50 C4
Statham St MCFLDS SK11 ...8 D6
Station Av FROD/HEL WA6 ...83 H9
GTS/LS CH66 ...79 N6
Station Cl NSTN CH64 ...77 M6
Station Gn GTS/LS CH66 ...108 B3
Station In NWCHW CW8 ...108 D3
Station La CHNE CH2... ...122 C5
CO CH5 ...140 A2
MCFLDS SK11 ...157 P9
ALS/KID ST7 ...187 N5
ALS/KID ST7 ...188 C1
Station Rd ALS/KID ST7 ...189 H7
ALS/KID ST7 ...200 C8
ALT WA14 ...51 P2
AUD/MAD/W CW3 ...219 M3
BIDD ST8 ...175 K8
CH/BCN CH1... ...3 G1
CHD/CHDH SK8 ...55 M1
CHF/WBR SK23 ...75 P2
CHNE CH2 ...82 A8
CHSE CH3 ...105 N9
CONG CW12 ...135 P9
CO CH5 ...140 A2
EDGY/DAV SK3... ...7 F5
GTS/LS CH66 ...79 N7
HOLMCH CW4 ...132 A9
HTNM SK4 ...40 F7
IRL M44 ...56 D1
MCFLDN SK10 ...114 C2
MKTDR T9 ...217 H8
MPL/ROM SK6 ...42 G3
MPL/ROM SK6 ...58 G6
MPL/ROM SK6 ...58 G6
NANT CW5 ...10 C6

NANT CW5 ...183 N2
NANT CW5 ...207 J3
NM/HAY SK22 ...59 M8
NSTN CH64 ...77 J5
NSTN CH64 ...77 L6
NSTN CH64 ...99 N2
NWCHE CW9 ...13 J1
NWCHW CW8 ...107 N2
NWCHW CW8 ...108 C3
NWCHW CW8 ...126 A3
RAIN/WH L35 ...30 B5
RDSH SK5 ...28 E7
RNFD/HAY WA11 ...22 C5
RUNC WA7 ...14 D2
RUNC WA7 ...84 F1
SBCH CW11 ...171 J2
STHEL WA9 ...31 K1
TPLY/KEL CW6 ...167 H7
WARRS WA4 ...48 C5
WARRW/BUR WA5 ...47 K2
WARRW/BUR WA5 ...47 K2
WHITCH SY13 ...213 N6
WILM/AE SK9 ...71 J3
WILM/AE SK9 ...71 K7
WILM/AE SK9 ...71M3
WSFD SW7 ...150 B1
Station Rd North
WARRN/WOL WA2 ...34 B6
Station Rd South
WARRN/WOL WA2 ...34 B7
Station St BRAM/HZG SK7 ...57 K5
EDGY/DAV SK3 ...8 E2
RAIN/WH L35 * ...30 B5
Station Vw BNG/LEV M19 ...28 A8
CHNE CH2... ...3 J5
NANT CW5 ...10 C7
Station Wks ALS/KID ST7 ...200 C8
Staton Id NM/HAY SK22 * ...59 M9
WARRN/WOL WA2 * ...34 B8
Staton St OP/CLY M11 ...28 C1
Staveley Dr WSFD CW7 ...128 E9
Staveton Cl BRAM/HZG SK7 ...56 F4
Steadings Rd KNUT WA16 ...68 B8
Steam Mill St CHSE CH3 ...3 H3
Stearns Ct CHNE CH2... ...121 K6
Steele Rd MWCH CW10 ...151 K5
Steele St CH/BCN CH1... ...2 E5
Steel St WARR WA1 ...19 J1
Steeple Cl NSTN CH64 ...77 L6
Steeple St MCFLDN SK10 ...9 G2
Steer Br WHITCH SY13 ...205 P5
Steth Av GOL/RIS/CU WA3 ...24 G1
Stelfox Av HALE/TIMP WA15 ...53 N8
Stelfox La DTN/ASHW M34 * ...29M2
Stelling St GTN M18... ...28 D4
Stendall Rd CH/BCN CH1... ...121 K9
Stennills Crs RUNC WA7 ...15 J4
Stenner La DID/WITH M20 ...39 N5
Stephenson Dr CW/HAS CW1 ..185 N4
Stephenson Rd NEWLW WA12 ..23 N7
Stephens Rd WSFD CW7 ...149 J2
Stephens Wk WSFD CW7 ...149 J2
Stephens Wy ALS/KID ST7 ...201 J5
Stephen Wk STKP SK1 * ...17 J3
Stephen Wy RAIN/WH L35 * ...30 A3
Sterling Cl CONG CW12 ...155 L7
NWCHE CW9 ...109 P7
Sterndale Rd EDGY/DAV SK3 ...56 E2
MPL/ROM SK6 ...42 D2
Sterne Cl SBCH CW11 ...171 J3
Stetchworth Rd WARRS WA4 ..48 D6
Stevenage Cl MCFLDS SK11 ...8 B6
STHEL WA9 ...30 E1
Stevenage Dr MCFLDS SK11.....8 B6
Steven Ct CHSE CH3 ...3 H3
Stevens St WILM/AE SK9 ...93 J4
Steventon WGTN/LGST M12 ...63 J2
Steward's Av WDN WA8 ...20 E2
Stewart St CW/SHV CW2 ...4 A5
Stile End CHNE CH2 ...122 C3
Stiles Av MPL/ROM SK6 ...43 K9
The Stiles NWCHW CW8 ...108 A7
Stilton Dr OP/CLY M11 ...28 A1
Stiperstones Cl GTS/LS CH66 ...79 K7
Stirling Av BRAM/HZG SK7 ...57 K6
MPL/ROM SK6 ...58 C2
Stirling Cl CHSE CH3 ...122 B9
EDGY/DAV SK3 ...56 E1
MCFLDN SK10 ...116 F2
WARR WA1 ...34 F9
WSFD CW7 ...149 J3
Stirling Ct HOLMCH CW4 ...131 N9
Stirling Crs STHEL WA9 ...30 C2
Stirrup Cl WARRN/WOL WA2 ...34 B5
Stitch La HTNM SK4 ...16 C7
Stockdale Rd EDGY/DAV SK3 ...56 F2
Stockham Cl RUNC WA7 ...62 E6
Stockham La RUNC WA7 ...62 F7
Stockham La RUNC WA7 ...62 G9
Stockholm Rd EDGY/DAV SK5 ...56 D1
Stock La NANT CW5 ...197 P6
Stockley La WARRS WA4 ...48 B8
Stockport Rd AULW WA2 ...29M1
CHD/CHDH SK8 ...55M1
DTN/ASHW M34 ...29 M6
EDGY/DAV SK3 ...41 H9
HALE/TIMP WA15 ...53 K3
HYDE SK14 ...63 M2
MPL/ROM SK6 ...42 G6
MPL/ROM SK6 ...58 G6
WARRS WA4 ...49M4
WGTN/LGST M12 ...28 A7
Stockport Rd East
MPL/ROM SK6 ...42 E4
Stockport Rd West
MPL/ROM SK6 ...42 B5
Stocks Av CHSE CH3 ...143 J2
STHEL WA9 ...32 C6
Stocks HI WSFD CW7 ...149 J4
Stocks La CHSE CH3 ...143 J1
KNUT WA16 ...113 H2

MCFLDN SK10 ...96 C8
WARRW/BUR WA5 ...47 H2
Stockwell Rd RAIN/WH L35 ...44 F3
Stockton Av EDGY/DAV SK3 ...41 J8
Stockton Gv STHEL WA9 ...30 C2
Stockton La WARRS WA4 ...48 C6
Stockton Rd WILM/AE SK9 ...93 H1
Stoke Abbott Cl BRAM/HZG SK7 ..56 E8
Stoke Cl PS/BROM CH62 ...79 J2
Stoke Gdns EP CH65 ...2 F7
Stokehall La NANT CW5 ...182 F2
Stokesay Cl EP CH65 ...102 C4
Stokesay Dr BRAM/HZG SK7 ...57 J6
Stokesay Rd SALE M33 ...38 B3
Stokes St GOL/RIS/CU WA3 ...34 F3
Stoke Wk EP CH65 ...2 F6
Stokoe Av ALT WA14 ...52 E1
Stoneacre Gdns WARRS WA4 ...48 C2
Stoneacre Rd WYTH/NTH M22 ..54 E5
Stonebank Dr NSTN CH64 ...77 N7
Stone Bank Rd ALS/KID ST7 ...189 J8
Stone Barn La RUNC WA7 ...62 D8
Stonebeck Rd NTHM/RTH M23 ..54 B2
Stonebridge Rd NANT CW5 ...196 E4
Stone Chair La ALS/KID ST7 ...173 P9
Stonechat Cl CW/HAS CW1 * ..184 F1
GOL/RIS/CU WA3 ...24 C1
Stone Cft CHSE CH3 ...143 K2
Stonecrog Cl GOL/RIS/CU WA3 ..34 D4
RUNC WA7 ...84 D1
Stonecross Dr RAIN/WH L35 ...30 C7
Stone Cross La North
WARRS WA4 ...24 E2
Stone Cross La South
WARRS WA4 ...28 E3
Stonehaven Dr
WARRN/WOL WA2 ...34 B5
Stoneheads Ri CHF/WBR SK23 ..75 P6
Stone Heyes La NWCHW CW8 ...87 H8
Stonehill Cl WARRS WA4 ...64 F2
Stonehills La RUNC WA7 ...15 K5
Stone House La CONG CW12 ..157 M7
Stone House La MALPAS SY14 ..180 B6
Stonehurst St WGTN/LGST M12 ..28 A3
Stoneleigh Cl MCFLDN SK10 ...117 H2
Stoneleigh Gdns WARRS WA4 ..49M6
Stoneley Av CW/HAS CW1 * ..185 J1
Stoneley Rd CW/HAS CW1 * ..185 K1
Stone Md MPL/ROM SK6 ...43 K5
Stone Mead Av
HALE/TIMP WA15 ...53 N8
Stonepail Cl CHD/CHDH SK8 ...55 H2
Stonepail Rd CHD/CHDH SK8 ...55 J2
Stone Pit La GOL/RIS/CU WA3 ..25 H7
Stone Pl WYTH/NTH M22 ...54 C6
Stone Rw MPL/ROM SK6 ...58 E1
Stones Manor La
NWCHW CW8 ...109 L7
Stoneyfold La MCFLDS SK11 ..117 N6
Stoneyford La NWCHW CW8 ...86 B7
Stoneygate Wk OP/CLY M11 ...28 D2
Stoney Holt RUNC WA7 ...62 G6
Stoneyland Dr NM/HAY SK22 ..59 L7
Stoneylands La TPLY/KEL CW6 ..125 P5
WILM/AE SK9 ...71 H9
Stonyford Rd SALE M33 ...38 C4
Stonyhurst Crs
GOL/RIS/CU WA3 ...25 M4
Stony La CONG CW12 ...155 L9
Stopford St EDGY/DAV SK3 ...16 D7
OP/CLY M11 ...28 E2
Stopsley Cl CONG CW12 ...155 M6
Store St MCFLDN SK10 ...95 P5
OFTN SK2 ...57 J3
OP/CLY M11 * ...28 B2
Storeton Cl WGTN/LGST M12 ..28 A3
Stortford Dr NTHM/RTH M23 ..39 L6
Stour Av RAIN/WH L35 ...30 B5
Stour Cl ALT WA14 ...52 G1
Stour Ct EP CH65 ...6 D1
Stourport Cl MPL/ROM SK6 ...42 F7
Stovell Av WGTN/LGST M12 ...28 A7
Stow Gdns DID/WITH M20 ...40 B7
Stradbroke Cl GOL/RIS/CU WA3 ..28 B4
GTN M18 ...28 B4
Straight Length FROD/HEL WA6 ..83 L6
Straight Mile CHSW/BR CH4 ..161 J4
Straker Av EP CH65 ...80 B7
Stratfield Av NTHM/RTH M23 ..39 L7
Stratford Av DID/WITH M20 ...40 A3
Stratford Gdns MPL/ROM SK6 ..42 E3
Stratford Rd CH/BCN CH1... ...121 H7
NSTN CH64 ...77 K7
Stratford Wy MCFLDS SK11 ...117 J5
Strathaven Av CW/SHV CW2 ..184 E8
Strathblane Cl DID/WITH M20 * ..40 C1
Strathmore Cl DTN/ASHW M34 ..29 P7
Strathmore Ct HOLMCH CW4 ..131 N9
Strathmore Gv WSFD CW7 ...31 H2
Stratton Cl RUNC WA7 ...62 F8
Stratton Pk WDN WA8 ...45M2
Stratton Rd OFTN SK2 ...42 B8
WARRW/BUR WA5 ...48 A3
Strawberry Cl ALT WA14 ...37 N9
GOL/RIS/CU WA3 ...34 C4
Strawberry Cross
CO CH5 * ...102 C4
Strawberry Dr EP CH65 ...102 C4
Strawberry Flds CHSE CH3 ...143 K5
Strawberry La CH/BCN CH1... ..101 N7
NWCHW CW8 ...108 B1
WILM/AE SK9 ...71 J8
Stray St OP/CLY M11 ...28 D1
Streamside Cl HALE/TIMP WA15..53M3
Stream Ter STKP SK1... ...17 J2
Street Hey La NSTN CH64 ...78 F3
Street La MCFLDN SK10 ...173 H7
SBCH CW11 ...173 H1
WARRS WA4 ...86 E3
The Street CHNE CH2 ...122 D4
MCFLDN SK10 ...97M7

Stretton Av DID/WITH M20 ...40 D5
GOL/RIS/CU WA3 * ...24 F2
SALE M33 ...38 A8
STHEL WA9 ...22 D6
Stretton Cl PS/BROM CH62 ...79 J2
Stretton Rd WARRS WA4 ...49 J8
Stretton Wk NWCHE CW9 ...109 P8
Strickland Cl WARRS WA4 ...49 J8
Striling Ct HOLMCH CW4 ...131 N9
Strines Rd MPL/ROM SK6 ...58 E2
Stringer Av CW/HAS CW1 * ..171 P3
Stringer Ct WARRS WA4 ...48 C5
Stringer's La WAV/CR/LL LL12 ..160 A7
Stringer St BIDD ST8 ...175 K9
Stringer St STKP SK1 ...17 J3
Stroma EP CH65 ...102 D4
Stromness Cl WARRN/WOL WA2 ..34 C5
Stuart Av IRL M44 ...27 H7
Stuart Cl CHSE CH3 ...122 D8
WSFD CW7 ...149 L5
Stuart Ct MCFLDN SK10 ...117 H2
Stuart Dr MPL/ROM SK6 ...43 H9
WARRS WA4 ...48 F6
Stuart Pl CH/BCN CH1 * ...3 F2
Stuart Rd ALT WA14 ...37 N9
MPL/ROM SK6 ...42 C2
RUNC WA7 ...62 G6
Stubbins Cl NTHM/RTH M23 ...39 H7
Stubbs La KNUT WA16 ...91 P1
RUNC WA7 ...110 C2
Stubbs Pl CH/BCN CH1 ...121 H8
Stubbs Ter MCFLDS SK11 * ...9 G6
Stubley La MCFLDN SK10 ...114 C3
Studland Rd WYTH/NTH M22 ..55 H4
Sturgess St NEWLW WA12 ...23 N7
Styal Av RDSH SK5 ...41 H3
Styal Cl NWCHE CW9 ...109 P8
Styal Gv CHD/CHDH SK8 ...55 J4
Styal Rd WILM/AE SK9 ...71 J1
WYTH/NTH M22 ...39 P9
Styal Vw WILM/AE SK9 ...71 J1
Styperson Wy POY/DIS SK12 ...73 L3
Sudbourne Cl ALS/KID ST7 ...189 N8
Sudbrook Cl GOL/RIS/CU WA3 * ..24 C1
Sudbury Dr CHD/CHDH SK8 ...55 L8
Sudbury Rd BRAM/HZG SK7 ...57 L4
Sudlow La KNUT WA16 ...89 P6
Suez St NEWLW WA12 ...23 L6
WARR WA1 ...18 C6
Suffolk Av EP CH65 ...80 B8
Suffolk Cl CONG CW12 ...155M6
MCFLDN SK10 ...116 F3
WILM/AE SK9 ...71 K5
Suffolk Dr RDSH SK5 ...41 L5
WILM/AE SK9 ...71 K5
Suffolk Rd ALT WA14 ...52 F5
Suffolk St RUNC WA7 ...14 C1
Sugar La FROD/HEL WA6 ...105 L7
MCFLDN SK10 ...96 B8
MCFLDN SK10 ...96 C8
Sugar Pit La KNUT WA16 ...90 C2
Sugar St MCFLDS SK11 ...158 A9
Sulby Av WARRS WA4 ...48 D4
Sulgrave Av POY/DIS SK12 ...73M2
Sullivan St WGTN/LGST M12 ...28 A4
Summerfield ALS/KID ST7 ...189 K7
WARR WA1 ...18 E6
Summerfield Av
WARRW/BUR WA5 ...33 J6
Summerfield Cl CHSW/BR CH4 ..140 E7
Summerfield Dr NWCHE CW9 ..128 C5
Summerfield Pl WILM/AE SK9 ...71 J8
Summerfield Rd CHSE CH3 ...122 C6
WYTH/NTH M22 ...54 E5
Summerhill Rd MCFLDN SK10 ..96 D8
Summer La RUNC WA7 ...62 D5
WARRS WA4 ...64 C6
Summerlea CHD/CHDH SK8 ...56 B7
Summerlees Rd GTS/LS CH66 ..102 A2
Summerville Gdns WARRS WA4 ..64 G5
Summit St WARRS WA4 ...30 C7
Sumner Rd CH/BCN CH1... ...121 H7
Sumner St RNFD/HAY WA11 ...22 C5
Sumpter Pathway CHNE CH2 ..122 A8
Sunart Cl CW/SHV CW2 ...184 D8
HALE/TIMP WA15 ...53 P9
Sunbeam St NEWLW WA12 ...23 N6
Sunbury Cl WILM/AE SK9 ...71 N4
Sunbury Crs CHSW/BR CH4 ...142 B4
Sunbury Gdns WARRS WA4 ...48 C8
Suncroft Cl WARR WA1 ...36 C6
Sundale Dr CW/SHV CW2 ...184 D5
Sunderland St MCFLDS SK11 ...9 F5
Sundial Rd OFTN SK2 ...57 K1
Sundown Cl NM/HAY SK22 ...59 L7
Sunfield WILM/AE SK9 ...42 G5
Sunfield Cl EP CH65 ...101 P1
Sunfield Crs STHEL WA9 ...31M1
Sunflower Meadow IRL M44 ...27 P7
Sunningdale Av SALE M33 ...39 H5
WDN WA8 ...45 H6
Sunningdale Cl NWCHE CW9 ..110 E5
WARRW/BUR WA5 ...32 C9
WDN WA8 ...57 H7
Sunningdale Dr BRAM/HZG SK7 ..56 A8
IRL M44 ...27M6
MCFLDS SK11 ...116 G6
Sunningdale Gv NSTN CH64 ...77 L9
Sunningdale Rd CHD/CHDH SK8 ..55 P5
Sunny Bank WILM/AE SK9 ...92 F1
Sunny Bank Cl MCFLDS SK11 ..117 K7
Sunnybank Cl NEWLW WA12 ...23 N5
Sunny Bank Rd ALT WA14 ...37 N8
Sunnybank Rd CW/SHV CW2 ..184 E3
Sunny Brow Rd GTN M18 ...28 C4

Sunnydale RAIN/WH L35 ...30 C5
Sunnyfield Rd HTNM SK4 ...40 G5
Sunnygate Av BNG/LEV M19 ...40 F5
Sunnymill Dr SBCH CW11 ...171M5
Sunnyside ALS/KID ST7 ...187 L4
EP CH65 ...47 J1
WARRW/BUR WA5 ...47 J1
Sunnyside La RUNC WA7 ...63 J2
Sunset Av WYTH/NTH M22 ...39 N6
Sunwell Ter MPL/ROM SK6 ...58 C4
Surrey Dr CONG CW12 ...155 N6
Surrey Rd ALS/KID ST7 ...189 J6
CHNE CH2 ...122 B6
MCFLDS SK11 ...116 C8
Surrey St CW/HAS CW1 ...5 H2
RUNC WA7 ...14 E3
Surrey Wy RDSH SK5 ...42 B3
Surridge KNUT WA16 ...67 J1
Surtees Rd WYTH/NTH M23 ...39 K6
Susan Dr WARRW/BUR WA5 ...47 H2
Susan St WDN WA8 ...46 A5
Sussex Av DID/WITH M20 ...40 C4
MCFLDS SK11 ...116 C7
Sussex Cl ALS/KID ST7 ...189 H6
Sussex Gv STHEL WA9 ...22 A7
Sussex Pl CONG CW12 ...155 N5
Sussex Rd CHNE CH2 ...122 A7
GTS/LS CH66 ...80 B6
Sussex St WDN WA8 ...46 A5
PART M31 ...36 D6
Sutcliffe Av WGTN/LGST M12 ...28 A7
Sutherland Cl RUNC WA7 ...15 G2
Sutherland Dr MCFLDN SK10 ..116 G3
WYTH/NTH M22 ...54 E5
Sutherland Wy CHSE CH3 ...122 C8
Sutton Av GOL/RIS/CU WA3 ...25 N5
NSTN CH64 ...77 L7
Sutton Cswy FROD/HEL WA6 ...84 C5
Sutton Cl CHNE CH2 ...3 J5
MCFLDS SK11 ...117 K7
NANT CW5 ...196 D2
NWCHE CW9 ...88 F7
PS/BROM CH62 ...79 J2
Sutton Dr CHNE CH2 ...121 P6
Sutton Fld NWCHW CW8 ...88 F9
Sutton Hall Dr GTS/LS CH66 ...79 L7
Sutton Hall Gdns GTS/LS CH66 ..79 L7
Sutton Heath Rd STHEL WA9 ...30 D2
Sutton La MWCH CW10 ...151 J4
Sutton Moss Rd STHEL WA9 ...22 D4
Sutton Oak Dr STHEL WA9 ...22 A8
Sutton Park Dr STHEL WA9 ...31 H1
Sutton Rd GTN M18 ...28 C4
HTNM SK4 ...41 K5
POY/DIS SK12 ...73M4
WILM/AE SK9 ...93 H4
Suttons La MPL/ROM SK6 ...58 E2
WDN WA8 ...57 J1
Sutton St NEWLL ST5 ...201 P9
RUNC WA7 ...14 C1
WARR WA1 ...19 F7
EP CH65 ...80 B9
Sutton Wy EP CH65 ...80 B9
GTS/LS CH66 ...80 A9
Swaine St EDGY/DAV SK3 ...16 E5
Swale Av RAIN/WH L35 ...30 B5
Swalecliff Av NTHM/RTH M23 ..38 F7
Swale Rd ALS/KID ST7 ...71 N4
Swaledale Av CONG CW12 ...156 A5
RAIN/WH L35 ...30 C5
Swaledale Cl WARRW/BUR WA5 ..32 C9
Swale Dr ALT WA14 ...52 F1
Swale Rd EP CH65 ...80 C6
Swallow Cl ALS/KID ST7 ...189 J6
GOL/RIS/CU WA3 ...34 C4
MCFLDN SK10 ...117 N5
Swallow Ct WSFD CW7 ...149M5
IRL M44 ...27 N6
SBCH CW11 ...171M1
TPLY/KEL CW6 ...167 H7
Swallowfield Cl CW/SHV CW2 ..184 G8
Swallowfield Gdns WARRS WA4 ..65 H1
Swallowfields CHSE CH3 ...176 G6
Swallowmore Vw
ALS/KID ST7 ...188 B8
Swallow Rd ALS/KID ST7 ...189 N7
Swallow St STKP SK1 ...17 J4
WGTN/LGST M12 * ...28 A7
Swanage Cl WARRS WA4 ...48 G5
Swanage Ct WSFD CW7 ...149M5
Swan Av STHEL WA9 ...22 E7
Swan Bank ALS/KID ST7 ...188 E9
Swanbourne Gdns
EDGY/DAV SK3 ...56 C5
Swan Cl ALS/KID ST7 ...188 F8
GTS/LS CH66 ...101 N2
POY/DIS SK12 ...73 H3
Swan Ct NWCHW CW8 ...108 A5
Swan Farm La
AUD/MAD/W CW3 ...218 G4
Swan Gdns STHEL WA9 ...30 D2
Swan Gv KNUT WA16 ...112 B5
Swanhill Cl GTN M18 ...28 F3
Swan La TPLY/KEL CW6 ...166 B9
Swanley Av NANT CW5 ...195 J7
Swanlow Av WSFD CW7 ...149M5
Swanlow Dr WSFD CW7 ...149 L3
Swann Gv CHD/CHDH SK8 ...56 B6
Swann La CHD/CHDH SK8 ...56 B6
NEWLW WA12 ...25 J5
Swan Rd HALE/TIMP WA15 ...53 J5
Swanscoe Av MCFLDS SK10 ...96 G4
Swanscoe Cl MWCH CW10 ...151 K5
Swanscoe La MCFLDS SK10 ...117 P1
Swan St CONG CW12 ...155 L7
Swanwick Cl HOLMCH CW4 ...131 P2
Swaylands Dr SALE M33 ...38 E7
Sweet Briar Cl STHEL WA9 * ...31 J5

Sweet Briar Crs CW/SHV CW2 ...184 F5
Sweet Brier Cl NWCHW CW8 *...87 K9
Sweet Brier St WARR WA1 ......31 J6
Sweetfield Gdns GTS/LS CH66...79 P6
Swettenham Rd GTS/LS CH66...79 P6
Swettooth La SALE M33 *....171 M2
Swettenham Cl ALS/KID ST7 ...187 N5
    SBCH CW11 ....171 P2
Swettenham St MCFLDS SK11...H5
Swift Cl ALS/KID ST7 ....189 K6
    CW/SHV CW2 ....184 F7
    MPL/ROM SK6 ....43 H3
    WARRN/WOL WA2 ....33 P5
Swift Dr BIDD ST8 ....175 M9
Swinburne Dr DID/WITH M20...40 D1
Swinburne Dr HALE/TIMP WA15..185 M4
Swinburne Gn RDSH SK5 ....28 D8
Swinchiard La FLINT CH6 ....98 A6
Swindale Av WARRN/WOL WA2...33 L5
Swindell's St OP/CLY M11 * 28 F2
Swinden Cl RUNC WA7 ....63 H4
Swindon Cl GTN M18 ....28 C4
Swine Market NANT CW5 ....10 B5
Swineyard La NWCHE CW9 ....6 C5
Swinford Av WDN WA8 ....46 C5
Swinley Cha WILM/AE SK9 ....5 H5
Swinleys Hey CHSE CH5 ....143 J3
Swinnerton St CW/SHV CW2 .....4 E7
Swireford Rd FROD/HEL WA6 ...106 B1
Swiss Hi WILM/AE SK9 ....93 K4
Swisspine Gdns WARR WA9 .....30 B1
Swithin Rd WYTH/NTH M22 ....54 C2
Swn-y-Gwynt FLINT CH6 ....96 B8
Swynnerton Wy WDN WA8 ....45 P2
Swythamley Cl EDGY/DAV SK3 ..41 H8
Swythamley Rd
    EDGY/DAV SK3 ....41 H8
Sycamore Av ALS/KID ST7 .....188 B1
Sycamore Av ALS/KID ST7 .....188 B1
    ALT WA14 ....52 E2
    CONG CW12 ....155 H6
    CW/HAS CW1 ....185 K2
    DTN/ASHW M34 ....29 M7
    NEWLW WA12 ....23 N6
    RNFD/HAY WA11 ....22 E4
    WDN WA8 ....45 P5
    WSFD CW7 ....149 L2
Sycamore Crs GOL/RIS/CU WA3 ..35 P6
    MCFLDS SK11 ....116 G6
    NEWHW CW8 ....87 K9
Sycamore Dr CHSW/BR CH4 ...142 B6
    GTS/LS CH66 ....102 B3
    LYMM WA13 ....50 D3
    MWCH CW10 ....151 K5
    RUNC WA7 ....84 E1
Sycamore Dr CHSW/BR CH4 ...140 F7
    SBCH CW11 ....171 M1
Sycamore Gdns WARR WA9 .....47 M2
    SBCH CW11 ....171 M1
Sycamore Ldg BRAM/HZG SK7 *..56 F8
Sycamore Ri BRAM/HZG SK7 ...57 K6
Sycamore Rd MPL/ROM SK6 ....42 F4
    PART M31 ....56 C5
    RUNC WA7 ....15 K6
Sycamore St EDGY/DAV SK3 ....41 J8
    SALE M33 ....39 H4
Sycamore Wk CHD/CHDH SK8...55 M1
Sydali St DTN/ASHW M34 ....29 M6
Sydal Cl BRAM/HZG SK7 ....72 D1
Syddal Crs BRAM/HZG SK7 ......72 D1
Syddal Gn BRAM/HZG SK7 ....72 D1
Syddall Av CHD/CHDH SK8 ......55 M7
Syddal Rd BRAM/HZG SK7 ....72 D1
Sydney Av MANAIR M90 ....54 C7
    CH/BCN CH1 ....2 B1
    CW/HAS CW1 ....185 L2
Sydney St NWCHW CW8 ....109 L5
    OFTN SK2 ....42 B9
    RUNC WA7 ....61 K7
Sydney Wk FLINT CH6 ....98 A5
    WARR WA1 ....31 K1
Sykes Meadow EDGY/DAV SK3 ..56 C1
Sykes St RDSH SK5 ....28 F9
Sylvan Av HALE/TIMP WA15....185 L8
    M33 ....38 F5
    WILM/AE SK9 ....93 M1
Sylvan Cl NWCHW CW8 ....109 L6
Sylvandale Av BNG/LEV M19 ....28 A8
Sylvan Gv ALT WA14 ....52 G6
Sylvester Av STKP SK1 ....57 H1
Sylvia Crs WARRN/WOL WA2 ...33 N3
Sylvia Gv RDSH SK5 ....41 M1
Symondley Rd MCFLDS SK11 ..136 E1
Symons Rd SALE M33 ....53 H3
Synge St WARRN/WOL WA2 .....19 F1
Syston Av RNFD/HAY WA11 ......77 L5
Sytch Cft NSTN CH64 ....77 L5

T

Tabley Av WDN WA8 ....45 K3
Tabley Cl KNUT WA16 ....90 C2
    MCFLDS SK10 ....116 C4
    SBCH CW11 ....171 K2
Tabley Gdns MPL/ROM SK6 .....43 H3
    STHEL WA9 ....30 C2
Tabley Gv HALE/TIMP WA15 ....185 L8
    KNUT WA16 ....90 C5
    RDSH SK5 ....41 M1

Tabley Hill La KNUT WA16 ....89 P2
Tabley La KNUT WA16 * 89 N4
Tabley Mere Gdns
    CHD/CHDH SK8 ....55 P4
Tabley Ms ALT WA14 ....53 H2
Tabley Rd CW/SHV CW2 ....184 E5
    KNUT WA16 ....90 B2
    SALE M33 * 39 H6
    WILM/AE SK9 ....71 M1
Tabley St NWCHE CW9 ....13 G1
Tabor St MCFLDS SK11 ....9 H7
Tadgers La FROD/HEL WA6 ......83 K4
Tadman Gv ALT WA14 * 52 F6
Tailors Vw NANT CW5 * 10 C3
Talbot Av NSTN CH64 ....77 M7
Talbot Ct CW/SHV CW2 ....198 A3
    GOL/RIS/CU WA3 ....34 F5
    NSTN CH64 ....77 M7
Talbot Crs WHITCH SY13 ....213 N5
Talbot Gdns NSTN CH64 ....77 M7
Talbot Rd ALT WA14 ....52 F5
    FROD/HEL WA6 ....104 E5
    GTS/LS CH66 ....102 B1
    RNFD/HAY WA11 ....22 C4
    SALE M33 ....39 H4
    WILM/AE SK9 ....93 K4
Talbot St BRAM/HZG SK7 ....57 K3
    CH/BCN CH1 ....3 F1
    WILM/AE SK9 ....24 C1
    WHITCH SY13 ....213 N5
Talford Gv DID/WITH M20 ....40 B5
Talisman Cl RUNC WA7 ....63 H7
Talke Rd ALS/KID ST7 ....188 A5
    NEWLU ST5 ....201 N4
    NEWLU ST5 ....201 P4
Tallarn Cl DID/WITH M20 ....40 D1
Tall Ash Av CONG CW12 ....156 A6
Tallis St WGTN/LGST M12 ....29 H2
Tallow Wy IRL M44 ....27 N9
Tall Trees Cl NWCHW CW8 ......109 L5
Tall Trees Pl OFTN SK2 ....57 J1
Tamar Cl CONG CW12 ....155 P9
    MCFLDN SK10 ....116 E3
Tamar Dr NTHM/RTH M23 ....116 C5
Tamarisk Gdns STHEL WA9 ......30 B1
Tamar Rd ALS/KID ST7 ....189 K6
    RNFD/HAY WA11 ....22 C3
Tamar Wk WSFD CW7 * 129 H9
Tame Cl BIDD ST8 ....175 L8
    SBCH CW11 ....171 K1
Tameside Ct DUK SK16 * 29 P2
Tame Rd DTN/ASHW M34 ....29 M2
Tame St DTN/ASHW M34 ....29 M5
Tamworth Cl BRAM/HZG SK7 * ..57 J7
Tamworth Gn STKP SK1 ....42 H6
Tamworth St STKP SK1 ....42 A6
Tanfield Rd DID/WITH M20 ....40 C9
Tamworth Cl OFTN SK2 * 57 L1
Tan House La
    WARRW/BUR WA5 ....32 D4
    WDN WA8 ....46 A7
Tankersley Gv
    WARRW/BUR WA5 ....47 L2
Tanner's La GOL/RIS/CU WA3 ...24 D1
    WARRN/WOL WA2 ....18 C4
Tanners Wy NANT CW5 ....196 F5
Tannery La NSTN CH64 ....77 L5
    WARRW/BUR WA5 ....46 G4
Tanning Wy ALT WA14 ....38 B9
Tanning Ct WARR WA1 ....18 E6
Tannock Rd BRAM/HZG SK7 .....57 M6
Tan Yard Brow GTN M18 ....28 E5
Tanyard Dr HALE/TIMP WA15...53 N9
Tanyard Gn RDSH SK5 ....41 M1
Tanyard La HALE/TIMP WA15 ....69 K1
Tapley Av POY/DIS SK12 ....73 L4
Taplin Dr GTN M18 ....28 C4
Taplow Cl WARRS WA4 ....48 G9
Taplow Gv CHD/CHDH SK8 ....55 P5
Tarbolton Crs
    HALE/TIMP WA15 ....53 N4
Target Cl ALS/KID ST7 ....201 P1
Tarnbeck RUNC WA7 ....62 G7
Tarn Cl WARR WA1 ....128 D8
Tarn Ct WARR WA1 ....34 G9
Tarn Ms MCFLDS SK11 ....116 C7
Tarnside Cl OFTN SK2 ....57 M1
The Tarns CHD/CHDH SK8 ....55 K4
Tarnway GOL/RIS/CU WA3 ....25 H2
Tarporley Cl EDGY/DAV SK3 .....56 C2
    GTS/LS CH66 ....124 B9
Tarporley Rd CHSE CH5 ....145 J1
    GTS/LS CH66 ....145 G5
    TPLY/KEL CW6 ....145 L3
    TPLY/KEL CW6 ....147 J5
    WARRS WA4 ....48 C8
    WHITCH SY13 ....213 L5
Tarran Gv DTN/ASHW M34 ....29 P8
Tarran Pl ALT WA14 ....53 J1
Tarrant Cl CH/BCN CH1 ....121 H7
Tarrington Cl WGTN/LGST M12 ..28 A4
Tarvin Av CW/SHV CW2 ....184 D4
    DID/WITH M20 ....40 B1
Tarvin Cl EP CH65 ....7 F7
    GOL/RIS/CU WA3 ....24 G2
    MCFLDS SK11 ....117 L7
    MWCH CW10 ....151 K5
    NWCHE CW9 ....109 P7
    RUNC WA7 ....63 H4
    STHEL WA9 ....30 C4
Tarvin Dr MPL/ROM SK6 ....42 D4
Tarvin Rd CHD/CHDH SK8 ....56 A3
    CHSE CH5 ....143 J1
    FROD/HEL WA6 ....105 M1
    FROD/HEL WA6 ....105 N1
    PS/BROM CH62 ....79 K1
Tasker Ter WARR/WH L35 ....30 B4
Tasman Cl WARRW/BUR WA5 ..32 F8
Tasman Gv STHEL WA9 ....30 D1
Tate St WDN WA8 * 45 K5
Tate Dr CW/HAS CW1 ....186 A4
Tatland Dr WYTH/NTH M22 ....55 H4
Tattenhall La CHSE CH3 ....164 E7

TPLY/KEL CW6 ....165 L7
Tattenhall Rd CHSE CH5 ....164 A7
Tatton Cl ALS/KID ST7 * 187 N5
    BRAM/HZG SK7 ....57 M3
    CHD/CHDH SK8 ....56 A3
    CHSW/BR CH4 ....102 A6
    NWCHE CW9 ....109 P8
    WSFD CW7 ....149 K1
Tatton Ct WARR WA1 * 34 E8
Tatton Dr SBCH CW11 ....171 P2
Tatton Gdns MPL/ROM SK6 ......43 J3
Tattonmere Gdns
    CHD/CHDH SK8 ....56 A3
Tatton Pl SALE M33 ....38 E3
Tatton Rd CW/SHV CW2 ....184 E6
    DTN/ASHW M34 ....29 N8
    SALE M33 ....38 E3
    WILM/AE SK9 ....71 N1
Tatton Rd North HTNM SK4 ......41 K3
Tatton Rd South HTNM SK4 ......41 K4
Tatton St HYDE SK14 ....43 K1
    KNUT WA16 ....90 E5
    STKP SK1 ....17 G4
Taunton Av RDSH SK5 ....31 J5
Taunton Cl BRAM/HZG SK7 .....57 N5
    SALE M33 ....38 A4
Taurus Pk WARRW/BUR WA5...32 G4
Tavistock Rd SALE M33 ....38 A5
    WARRW/BUR WA5 ....45 J2
Tavlin Av WARRW/BUR WA5 .....33 J7
Tawney Cl ALS/KID ST7 ....189 K6
Tawny Ct RUNC WA7 ....62 C7
Taxal Moor Rd CHF/WBR SK23 ..97 N2
Taxi Rd MANAIR M90 ....54 B9
Taxmere Cl SBCH CW11 ....171 L2
Tay Cl BIDD ST8 ....175 M8
Tayfield Rd WYTH/NTH M22 ......54 E5
Tayleur Ter NEWLW WA12 * 23 P7
Taylor Cl STHEL WA9 ....22 C9
Taylor La DTN/ASHW M34 ....29 K5
Taylor Rd ALT WA14 ....23 K3
    RNFD/HAY WA11 ....33 H5
Taylor's La CW/HAS CW1 ....186 C5
    WARRW/BUR WA5 ....46 E5
Taylors Rw RUNC WA7 ....15 K3
Taylor St BURS/TUN ST6 ....189 L9
    DTN/ASHW M34 ....29 L8
    GTN M18 ....29 G2
    WARRS WA4 ....48 C6
    WDN WA8 ....45 K3
Teal Av KNUT WA16 ....90 F5
Tedder Dr WYTH/NTH M22 ....55 H8
Tedder Sq WARRS WA4 ....48 B3
Teddington Cl WARRS WA4 ......64 G1
Tees Ct EP CH65 ....80 C6
Teesdale Cl OFTN SK2 ....57 L1
Teesdale Rd RNFD/HAY WA11 ..22 C2
Teggsnose La MCFLDS SK11 ...118 A6
Tegid Wy CHSW/BR CH4 ....141 P5
Tegsnose Mt MCFLDS SK11 ....118 A8
Telfer Ct MWCH CW10 ....151 L4
Telford Cl ALS/KID ST7 ....188 G8
    CONG CW12 ....156 B8
    DTN/ASHW M34 ....29 L2
    WDN WA8 ....45 K3
Telford Gdns SBCH CW11 ....171 L4
Telford Pl NANT CW5 ....196 D2
Telford Rd EP CH65 ....7 J7
    MPL/ROM SK6 ....58 D8
Telford Wy AUD/MAD/W CW3...216 G2
    CHSW/BR CH4 ....142 B6
    MWCH CW10 ....151 L1
Tempest Rd WILM/AE SK9 ....93 L4
Temple Cl GOL/RIS/CU WA3 .....35 K5
Temple Rd SALE M33 ....38 E2
Templeton Cl ALT WA14 * 52 F1
Tenbury Cl WARRW/BUR WA5 ..32 D7
Tenbury Rd DID/WITH M20 ....40 C2
Tenby Av DID/WITH M20 ....23 J6
    WARRW/BUR WA5 ....56 B6
Tenby Dr CHD/CHDH SK8 ....56 B6
    RUNC WA7 ....62 E6
Tenby Gv NEWLU ST5 ....201 P8
Tenby Rd EDGY/DAV SK3 ....41 J9
    MCFLDS SK11 ....116 E6
Tenchersfield NANT CW5 ....11 F7
Tenement La BRAM/HZG SK7 ....56 D5
Tennyson Av ALS/KID ST7 ....188 A6
    CW/HAS CW1 * 5 K2
    DTN/ASHW M34 * 42 F1
    CW/SHV CW2 ....184 G7
    HTNM SK4 ....41 K4
    MCFLDS SK11 ....116 E5
    STKP SK1 ....42 A8
    WDN WA8 ....45 N6
Tennyson St STHEL WA9 ....30 F6
Tennyson Wk CH/BCN CH1 .....121 K6
Tensing Cl WARRW/BUR WA5 ...32 E8
Tenth Av CQ CH5 ....100 C9
Terence Av WARR WA1 ....31 K8
Terminal Rd East MANAIR M90...54 D8
Terminal Rd North
    MANAIR M90 ....54 D8
Terminal Rd South
    MANAIR M90 ....54 D8
Tern Av ALS/KID ST7 ....189 L6
Tern Cl ALT WA14 ....37 N8
    BIDD ST8 ....175 M9

WDN WA8 ....45 P3
Tern Dr POY/DIS SK12 ....73 H2
Terrace Rd WDN WA8 ....61 N1
Terrick Rd WHITCH SY13 ....213 N5
Terrington Cl CCHDY M21 ....39 P1
Terry Rd WYTH/NTH M22 ....54 D6
Tetchill Cl GTS/LS CH66 ....101 P2
    RUNC WA7 ....63 H6
Tetton La MWCH CW10 ....151 L8
Tewkesbury Av
    HALE/TIMP WA15 ....53 L2
Tewkesbury Cl CHD/CHDH SK8...56 A2
    CHNE CH2 ....122 A4
    GTS/LS CH66 ....102 A5
    MWCH CW10 ....151 L1
    POY/DIS SK12 ....73 K2
Tewkesbury Dr MCFLDN SK10...95 L9
Tewkesbury Rd EDGY/DAV SK3...56 B1
    GOL/RIS/CU WA3 ....24 C1
Textile St WGTN/LGST M12 ....28 A2
Thackeray Dr CHSE CH3 ....122 D9
Thackery Cl SBCH CW11 ....171 J5
Thames Cl CONG CW12 ....155 P9
    OP/CLY M11 * 28 B1
    EP CH65 ....80 C7
Thames Dr BIDD ST8 ....175 L8
Thames Gdns EP CH65 ....102 C1
Thames Pl WSFD CW7 ....150 B1
Thames Rd GOL/RIS/CU WA3 ...25 P7
    STHEL WA9 ....31 H2
Thames Side EP CH65 ....102 D1
Thatcher Cl ALT WA14 ....52 D7
Thatcher Gv BIDD ST8 ....175 J9
Thaxted Dr OFTN SK2 ....57 N2
Theatre Ct NWCHE CW9 ....13 G3
Thelwall Cl HALE/TIMP WA15 ....53 L4
Thelwall La WARRS WA4 ....49 J4
Thelwall New Rd WARRS WA4 ...49 K4
Thelwall New Rd WARRS WA4 ...49 M4
Thelwall Rd GTS/LS CH66 ....80 A3
    SALE M33 ....39 H5
Theobald Rd ALT WA14 ....53 H6
The Roaches LEEK ST13 ....159 N7
Thetford Cl MCFLDN SK10 ....117 J1
Thetford Rd WARRW/BUR WA5...47 J1
The Uplands RUNC WA7 ....63 J6
Thewlis St WARRW/BUR WA5 ...48 A2
Third Av ALS/KID ST7 ....188 C7
    CW/HAS CW1 * 185 M7
    POY/DIS SK12 ....73 K5
    RUNC WA7 ....62 D7
    SBCH CW11 ....77 L7
Thirlby Dr WYTH/NTH M22 ....54 F6
Thirlmere Rd STKP SK1 ....42 A9
Thirlmere MCFLDS SK11 ....116 C7
Thirlmere Av WARRN/WOL WA2...33 M5
    HOLMCH CW4 ....131 M8
    WILM/AE SK9 ....93 H4
    WSFD CW7 ....128 G8
Thirlmere Ct CONG CW12 ....155 J8
Thirlmere Dr LYMM WA13 ....50 F4
Thirlmere Rd CHNE CH2 ....122 B6
    CW/SHV CW2 ....184 G9
    EP CH65 ....102 E2
    NSTN CH64 ....77 L7
    PART M31 ....56 C4
    WYTH/NTH M22 ....54 D5
Thirlmere Wy WDN WA8 ....45 K3
Thirsk Av SALE M33 ....37 P5
Thirsk Cl RUNC WA7 ....62 A8
Thirsk Wy MCFLDN SK10 ....117 J1
Thistle Cl KNUT WA16 ....90 B3
Thistle Sq PART M31 ....56 D6
Thistleton Cl MCFLDS SK11 .....117 K6
Thistlewood Dr WILM/AE SK9 ....71 M7
Thomas Brassey Cl CHNE CH2...3 H1
Thomas Cl ALS/KID ST7 ....188 A4
    CH/BCN CH1 ....121 J5
    CHNE CH2 ....122 C3
    DTN/ASHW M34 ....29 L5
    EP CH65 ....102 D2
Thomas Rw NANT CW5 ....10 B4
Thomas St ALS/KID ST7 ....188 B1
    ALS/KID ST7 ....188 B1
    BIDD ST8 ....175 M8
    CW/HAS CW1 * 4 E1
    GOL/RIS/CU WA3 ....24 C1
    HALE/TIMP WA15 ....53 J5
    MPL/ROM SK6 ....42 F5
    RUNC WA7 ....15 G1
    STKP SK1 ....17 J5
    WDN WA8 ....45 K4
Thomas St West OFTN SK2 ....57 N9
Thompson Av GOL/RIS/CU WA3...25 N6
Thompson Cl DTN/ASHW M34 ...29 H6
Thompson Dr WHITCH SY13 ....213 K6
Thompson Rd DTN/ASHW M34...29 M6
Thompson St GOL/RIS/CU WA3...35 H5
Thomson Gdns CONG CW12 ...155 J7
Thomson Rd GTN M18 ....28 C5
Thomson St EDGY/DAV SK3 ......17 F7
Thoralby Cl WGTN/LGST M12 ....28 A3
Thoresway Rd WILM/AE SK9 .....71 H9
Thoriby Rd GOL/RIS/CU WA3 ....35 H6
Thorley Dr HALE/TIMP WA15 ...185 M1
Thorley Gv CW/SHV CW2 ....184 G1
    HALE/TIMP WA15 ....53 M4
Thorley La HALE/TIMP WA15 .....54 B6
Thorley La HALE/TIMP WA15 .....54 B6
Thornaby Gv STHEL WA9 ....30 C2
Thornberry Cl CH/BCN CH1 .....120 E3
Thornbrook Wy SBCH CW11 ....171 J4
Thornbury Av WILM/AE SK9 ....71 H9
Thornbury Cl CHD/CHDH SK8 ...56 C6
Thornbury Wy GTN M18 ....28 C4

Thorncliffe Gv BNG/LEV M19 .....28 C8
Thorn Cl RUNC WA7 ....62 A7
    WARRW/BUR WA5 ....47 K4
Thorndale Gv
    HALE/TIMP WA15 ....53 L2
Thorn Dr WYTH/NTH M22 ....55 J7
Thorndyke Cl RUNC WA7 ....63 J7
Thorndyke Cl RUNC WA7 ....30 C7
Thorne Cl MCFLDN SK10 ....94 C8
Thorne Dr GTS/LS CH66 ....79 P6
Thornedale Dr SBCH CW11 ....30 D6
Thorneycroft Av CCHDY M21 .....39 L3
Thorneycroft Rd
    HALE/TIMP WA15 ....53 M2
Thorney Dr BRAM/HZG SK7 ......56 C9
Thorneyholme Dr KNUT WA16 ..90 F4
Thornfield Cl GOL/RIS/CU WA3...24 E1
Thornfield Dr CHD/CHDH SK8 ...56 A3
Thornfield Hey WILM/AE SK9 .....71 N6
Thornfield Houses
    CHD/CHDH SK8 ....56 A5
Thorn Gv CHD/CHDH SK8 ....56 B8
    HALE/TIMP WA15 ....53 J4
    SALE M33 ....39 F5
Thorngrove Av NTHM/RTH M23...38 C9
Thorngrove Dr WILM/AE SK9 .....71 L8
Thorngrove Hi WILM/AE SK9 .....71 L8
Thornham Av GOL/RIS/CU WA3...22 A9
Thornham Rd SALE M33 ....38 C3
Thornhill Cl CHSW/BR CH4 ......140 D7
    DTN/ASHW M34 ....28 C7
Thornholme Cl GTN M18 ....28 B6
Thornholme Rd MPL/ROM SK6...58 D3
Thorn La NWCHW CW8 ....109 L7
Thornleigh Av PS/BROM CH62...79 K2
Thornleigh Dr GTS/LS CH66 .....79 N6
Thornley Crs MPL/ROM SK6 .....42 F4
Thornley La North RDSH SK5 ....28 F6
Thornley Rd DTN/ASHW M34 ....29 N5
    LYMM WA13 ....50 C4
Thorn Rd BRAM/HZG SK7 ....56 F7
    RUNC WA7 ....62 A7
    WARR WA1 ....34 B8
Thornsett NM/HAY SK22 ....59 P5
Thornsgreen Rd
    WYTH/NTH M22 ....54 F7
The Thorns CCHDY M21 ....39 L1
Thornton WDN WA8 ....20 C5
Thornton Av WARRS WA4 ....29 J1
    MCFLDS SK11 ....116 C7
Thornton Bnk TPLY/KEL CW6 ..166 G5
Thorntondale Dr
    WARRW/BUR WA5 ....32 C9
Thornton Dr CHNE CH2 ....121 N6
    CW/SHV CW2 ....184 G9
    SALE M33 ....39 N8
Thornton Ga CHD/CHDH SK8 ....55 J1
Thornton Green La CHNE CH2 ..103 N3
Thornton Pl HTNM SK4 ....41 J4
Thornton Rd GTS/LS CH66 ....55 L6
    EP CH65 ....7 J7
    WARRW/BUR WA5 ....47 M3
Thorn Tree Dr CW/HAS CW1 ...169 P6
Thorntree Gn WARRS WA4 ....65 K1
Thornway BRAM/HZG SK7 ....56 C9
    MCFLDN SK10 ....95 N6
    MPL/ROM SK6 ....58 D8
Thornwood Av GTN M18 ....28 C5
Thornwythe Gv GTS/LS CH66 ...80 A9
Thornycroft WSFD CW7 ....149 J1
Thornycroft Cl MCFLDS SK11 ..135 M2
Thornycroft St MCFLDS SK11 ....9 J2
Thorold Gv SALE M33 ....39 H4
Thorpe Cl CW/HAS CW1 ....169 N9
    DTN/ASHW M34 ....29 M5
Thorpe Gv HTNM SK4 ....41 L2
Thorpeness Sq GTN M18 ....28 D5
Thorpe St MCFLDN SK10 ....9 F5
Thorp St MCFLDN SK10 ....9 F5
Thorsby Rd HALE/TIMP WA15 ...53 J2
Thowler La ALT WA14 ....51 M9
Threaphurst La BRAM/HZG SK7...58 A5
Threapwood Rd
    WYTH/NTH M22 ....54 C6
Three Fields Cl CONG CW12 ....155 J7
Threeways NWCHW CW8 ....107 P8
Thresher Cl ANS 39 J5
Threshfield Dr
    HALE/TIMP WA15 ....38 F9
Throstle Gv KNUT WA16 ....58 C2
Thrush Wy WSFD CW7 ....128 C7
Thurleigh Rd DID/WITH M20 .....40 C4
Thurlestone Dr BRAM/HZG SK7...57 H5
Thurlestone Rd ALT WA14 ....52 F1
Thurlow Gol/RIS/CU WA3 ....24 E2
Thurlwood Av DID/WITH M20 .....40 B1
Thursfield Av ALS/KID ST7 ....189 L5
Thurston Cl WARRW/BUR WA5...47 P1
Thurston Gn WILM/AE SK9 ....93 J4
Thurston Rd CHSW/BR CH4 ....142 A5
Thyme St WARR WA1 ....18 E8
Tibbs Cross La WDN WA8 ....31 J7
Tibb St ALS/KID ST7 ....201 J5
Tib St DTN/ASHW M34 ....29 M4
Tickle Av STHEL WA9 ....22 B6
Tidal La WARRN/WOL WA2 ....34 A8
Tidebrook Pl BUDS/TON SK8 ....55 M7
Tideswell Cl CHD/CHDH SK8 ....55 P6
Tideswell Rd BRAM/HZG SK7 ....57 L7
Tidnock Av CONG CW12 ....155 M5
Tiffield Ct WSFD CW7 ....129 H7
Tilbrook Dr STHEL WA9 ....31 J2
Tildsley Crs RUNC WA7 ....61 M8
Tilewright Cl ALS/KID ST7 ....189 K6
Tillard Av EDGY/DAV SK3 ....56 C1
Tilley St WARR WA1 ....19 F4
Tilley Rd WYTH/NTH M22 ....54 F5
Tilman Cl WARRW/BUR WA5 .....32 E8
Tilson Rd NTHM/RTH M25 ....54 D8

Tilstock Cl *HLWD* L26 ....44 A5
Tilstock Rd *WHITCH* SY13 ......213 M8
Tilston Av *WARRS* WA4 ....49 J3
Tilstone Cl *ALS/KID* ST7 ....189 J8
  CW/SHV CW2 ....198 D5
  NWCHE CW9 ....110 A7
Tilston Rd *MALPAS* SY14 ....191 P9
Timberfields Rd *CH/BCN* CH1 ....120 D3
Timber La *NWCHE* CW9 ....13 F2
Timberscombe Gdns
  WARR WA1 ....49 N1
Timber St *MCFLDN* SK10 ....9 J1
Timbrell Av *CW/HAS* CW1 ....184 G2
Timmis Cl *WARRN/WOL* WA2 ......34 B5
Timmis Crs *WDN* WA8 ....21 G1
Timperley Av *WARRS* WA4 ....49 J3
Timperley St *OP/CLY* M11 * 21 J3
  WDN WA8 * 21 J3
Timpson Rd *NTHM/RTH* M23 ......39 H9
Tindall St *RDSH* SK5 ....28 F6
Tinkersfield *NANT* CW5 * 197 H3
Tinkwood La *MALPAS* SY14 ....202 G6
Tinningham Cl *OP/CLY* M11 ....28 E2
Tinshill Cl *WGTN/LGST* M12 ....28 A4
Tinsley St *WARRS* WA4 ....49 H4
Tintagel Cl *MCFLDN* SK10 ....116 E4
  WARR WA1 ....62 G8
Tintern Av *CHNE* CH2 ....122 A5
  DID/WITH M20 ....40 A3
Tintern Cl *POY/DIS* SK12 ....73 K1
  WARRW/BUR WA5 * 47 N3
Tintern Dr *HALE/TIMP* WA15 ......53 N5
Tintern Gv *STKP* SK1 ....42 A7
Tintern Rd *CHD/CHDH* SK8 ....56 B9
Tipping St *ALT* WA14 ....53 H4
Tipton Cl *CHD/CHDH* SK8 ....58 E3
Tipton Dr *NTHM/RTH* M23 ....59 K6
Tiree Cl *BRAM/HZG* SK7 ....57 M6
Tirley La *TPLY/KEL* CW6 ....125 L8
Tirza Av *BNG/LEV* M19 ....40 G1
Tithebarn Dr *NSTN* CH64 ....77 H3
Tithebarn Rd *HALE/TIMP* WA15 ...54 B3
Tithe Barn Rd *HTNM* SK4 ....40 C4
Tithington Cl *RDSH* SK5 * 28 D8
The Tithings *RUNC* WA7 ....62 C5
Tiverton Av *SALE* M33 ....38 C5
Tiverton Cl *CHNE* CH2 ....121 P6
  SBCH CW11 ....171 P2
  WDN WA8 ....45 J4
Tiverton Dr *SALE* M33 ....58 C5
  WILM/AE SK9 ....71 M5
Tiverton Sq *WARRW/BUR* WA5 ...47 J3
Tiviot Dl *STKP* SK1 ....17 G3
Tiviot Wy *RDSH* SK5 ....4 D3
Tobermory Cl *RNFD/HAY* WA11 ...22 E4
Tobermory Rd *CHD/CHDH* SK8 ...55 J5
Todbrook Cl *CHF/WBR* SK23 ....75 N3
Toft Cl *CHSW/BR* CH4 ....142 A5
  WDN WA8 ....20 E1
Toft Rd *GTN* M18 ....28 C5
  KNUT WA16 ....96 N6
Toftwood Av *RAIN/WH* L35 ....30 D7
Tolland La *HALE/TIMP* WA15 ....53 K7
Tollard Cl *CHD/CHDH* SK8 ....56 B8
Toll Bar Av *MCFLDN* SK11 * 9 J5
Toll Bar Rd *CHSE* CH3 ....143 L1
  MCFLDN SK11 * 9 J5
  WARRN/WOL WA2 ....34 A5
Toll Bar St *STKP* SK1 ....17 H6
Tollemache Dr *CW/HAS* CW1 ......169 P9
Tollemache Ter *CHNE* CH2 ....3 K3
Tollgate Cl *ALS/KID* ST7 ....188 E8
Tollgate Dr *AUD/MAD/W* CW5 ....216 C1
Tollitt St *CW/HAS* CW1 ....4 A4
Tomcroft La *DTN/ASHW* M34 ....29 K7
Tomfields *WSFD* CW7 ....201 J7
Tomkinson St *CHNE* CH2 ....3 H1
Tom La *ALT* WA14 ....52 C9
Tomlinson Av
  WARRN/WOL WA2 ....33 N8
Tommy's La *CONG* CW12 ....155 P6
  CW/HAS CW1 ....5 H6
Tonbridge Cl *CW/SHV* CW2 ....184 D8
Tonbridge Rd *BNG/LEV* M19 ....28 B9
Tonbridge Rd *RDSH* SK5 ....28 B8
Toogood Cl *CHNE* CH2 ....122 G3
Topcroft Cl *WYTH/NTH* M22 ....39 P8
Top Farm La *WSFD* CW7 ....168 A7
Topfield Rd *WYTH/NTH* M22 ....39 N7
Topping Cl *POY/DIS* SK12 ....34 C4
The Toppings *MPL/ROM* SK6 ......42 F5
  FROD/HEL WA6 ....106 F5
Top Rd *FROD/HEL* WA6 ....106 F3
Top Station Rd *ALS/KID* ST7 ....189 L1
Torbay Dr *OFTN* SK2 ....42 A9
Torkington La *BRAM/HZG* SK7 .....58 B4
Torkington Rd *BRAM/HZG* SK7 .....57 H3
  CHD/CHDH SK8 ....55 K2
  WILM/AE SK9 ....71 L8
Torkington St *EDGY/DAV* SK3 ......41 L9
Toronto Av *MANAIR* M90 ....54 D8
Toronto St *RUNC* WA7 ....56 G1
Torquay Gv *OFTN* SK2 ....57 H3
Torridon Gv *GTS/LS* CH66 ....102 D1
Torrin Cl *EDGY/DAV* SK3 ....56 F2
Torrse TPLY/KEL* CW6 ....147 H9
Torr Rd *MCFLDS* SK11 ....117 J8
Torrs Va *NM/HAY* SK22 ....59 N8
Torr Top St *NM/HAY* SK22 ....59 N7
Torrvale Rd *NM/HAY* SK22 ....59 M8
Torville Dr *BIDD* ST8 ....175 M9
Totland Cl *WARRW/BUR* WA5 ......31 P9
  WGTN/LGST M12 ....28 A6
Totnes Av *BRAM/HZG* SK7 ....56 G5
Totnes Cl *SALE* M33 ....38 A3
Totridge Cl *OFTN* SK2 ....57 K2
Tottenham Dr *NTHM/RTH* M23 ....38 G9
Tours Av *NTHM/RTH* M23 ....39 K6
Towergate *CH/BCN* CH1 ....2 B4
Tower Hi *MCFLDN* SK10 ....96 B9
Tower Hill Rd *ALS/KID* ST7 ....174 F9
  BIDD ST8 ....189 P2

Tower La *LYMM* WA13 ....50 F5
  NWCHW CW8 ....108 D3
  RUNC WA7 ....62 G7
Tower Rd *CH/BCN* CH1 ....2 B3
Towers Cl *CH/HAS* CW1 ....184 G9
  POY/DIS SK12 ....73 M1
Tower Wy *CW/HAS* CW1 ....4 E3
Towey Cl *GTN* M18 ....28 D3
Towncroft *DTN/ASHW* M54 ....29 M5
Towneley Ct *WDN* WA8 ....21 G1
Town Farm La *FROD/HEL* WA6 ...107 J6
Townfield Av *CHSE* CH3 ....176 G6
Townfield Cl *ALS/KID* ST7 ....188 E9
Townfield Ct *NWCHW* CW8 ....109 J1
Townfield Gdns *ALT* WA14 ....53 H2
Townfield La *CH/BCN* CH1 ....121 J3
  CHSE CH3 ....123 P9
  CHSE CH3 ....176 F5
  FROD/HEL WA6 ....84 A6
  KNUT WA16 ....112 D7
  LYMM WA13 ....36 B9
  NWCHW CW8 ....87 J9
  TPLY/KEL CW6 ....165 P3
Townfield Rd *ALT* WA14 * 53 H2
  KNUT WA16 ....91 L2
  RUNC WA7 ....62 G4
Townfields *KNUT* WA16 ....90 G5
Town Fids *SBCH* CW11 ....171 M4
Townfields Dr *WSFD* CW7 ....149 L4
Townfields Gdns *WSFD* CW7 ......149 M5
Townfields Rd *WSFD* CW7 ....149 M3
Townfield Vw *RUNC* WA7 * 62 G4
Town Fold *MPL/ROM* SK6 ....43 N9
Town Hi *WARR* WA1 ....18 D5
Town La *DTN/ASHW* M34 ....29 K8
  KNUT WA16 ....91 K1
  NSTN CH64 ....91 M1
  SPK/HALE L24 ....60 E4
Townley Pl *MCFLDS* SK11 * 9 F5
Townley St *MCFLDS* SK11 ....9 F5
Townley Ter *MPL/ROM* SK6 * 58 E1
Townscliffe La *MPL/ROM* SK6 ......58 F1
Townsend La *ALS/KID* ST7 ....173 K9
Townsend Rd *CONG* CW12 ....155 N8
Townsfield Dr *TPLY/KEL* CW6 .....148 B5
Townshend Rd *NWCHE* CW9 ......110 G1
Township Cl *MALPAS* SY14 ....178 C7
Town Sq *NWCHE* CW9 ....13 F2
Town St *MPL/ROM* SK6 ....43 N9
Town Wk *RUNC* WA7 * 62 D7
Town Well *FROD/HEL* WA6 ....106 G2
Townwell Ct *NANT* CW5 * 10 A5
Toxteth St *OP/CLY* M11 ....28 A3
Tracy Dr *NEWLW* WA12 ....32 B3
Trafalgar Av *DTN/ASHW* M34 ....29 J2
  POY/DIS SK12 ....73 N3
Trafalgar Cl *NWCHE* CW9 ....109 N9
  POY/DIS SK12 ....73 N3
Trafalgar Ct *WDN* WA8 ....21 G7
Trafalgar Pl *DID/WITH* M20 ....40 B4
Trafalgar Rd *SALE* M33 ....38 D2
Trafford Av *WARRW/BUR* WA5 .....33 H8
Trafford Crs *RUNC* WA7 ....62 A8
Trafford Dr *HALE/TIMP* WA15 ....38 E8
Trafford Pl *WILM/AE* SK9 * 71 M8
  WILM/AE SK9 ....71 M8
Trafford St *CH/BCN* CH1 ....2 E2
Tragan Cl *OFTN* SK2 ....57 K1
Tragan Dr *OFTN* SK2 ....57 K1
  WARRW/BUR WA5 ....47 H4
Tram St *OP/CLY* M11 ....28 A3
Tramway Rd IRL M44 ....38 E1
Tranby Cl *WYTH/NTH* M22 ....55 H3
Tranmere Cl *GTN* M18 ....28 B4
Tranmere Rd *EDGY/DAV* SK3 ......41 J8
Trans Pennine Trail
  WARRW/BUR WA5 ....47 H6
  WDN WA8 ....60 G5
Trap Rd *CONG* CW12 ....133 M7
Trap St *MCFLDS* SK11 ....133 K4
Travers' Entry *STHEL* WA9 ....31 M2
Traverse St *STHEL* WA9 ....22 A6
Travis Brow *HTNM* SK4 ....16 D4
Travis St *WDN* WA8 ....21 J2
Trawden Gn *OFTN* SK2 ....57 K3
Treborth Rd *CH/BCN* CH1 ....120 D8
Tree Bank Cl *RUNC* WA7 ....14 E6
Treen Cl *MCFLDN* SK10 ....116 D3
Tree Tops *NSTN* CH64 ....77 J8
Treetops Cl *WARR* WA1 ....34 A9
Tree Wy *KNUT* WA16 ....90 E6
Trefoil La *CHSE* CH3 ....143 K4
Trelawny Av *FLINT* CH6 ....98 B6
Trelawny Sq *FLINT* CH6 ....98 A5
Trenance Cl *RUNC* WA7 ....62 F9
Trenchard Dr *WYTH/NTH* M22 .....55 H8
Trent Av *WSFD* CW7 ....150 B1
Trent Cl *BRAM/HZG* SK7 ....56 C9
  RAIN/WH L35 ....30 A1
  RDSH SK5 ....42 B5
  STHEL WA9 ....31 H5
  WDN WA8 ....45 P3
  WSFD CW7 ....150 B1
Trentdale EP CH65 ....102 D1
Trentham Av *HTNM* SK4 ....40 C5
Trentham Cl *WDN* WA8 ....45 J3
Trentham St *RUNC* WA7 ....14 C1
Trent Rd *RAIN/WH* L35 ....30 A5
Trent Wk *DROY* M43 ....29 H1
Tresham Dr *WARRS* WA4 ....49 J7
Tressel Dr *STHEL* WA9 ....30 F5
Trevithick Cl *CW/HAS* CW1 ....185 M4
Trevone Cl *KNUT* WA16 ....90 E4
Trevor Av *SALE* M33 ....38 C6

Trevor Gv *STKP* SK1 ....17 K6
Trevor St *OP/CLY* M11 ....28 E2
The Triangle *HALE/TIMP* WA15 .....38 E9
Tribune Av *ALT* WA14 ....37 M9
Trickett La *WARRW/BUR* WA5 ......108 C9
Tricketts La *NANT* CW5 ....197 M2
Trident Pk *RUNC* WA7 * 62 C7
Trinity Av *CW/SHV* CW2 ....184 C7
Trinity Ct *GOL/RIS/CU* WA3 ....54 G3
Trinity Gdns *EDGY/DAV* SK3 ....56 F4
Trinity La *MCFLDS* SK11 ....117 M9
Trinity Pl *CONG* CW12 ....175 J1
  WARR WA1 ....21 J4
Trinity Sq *MCFLDN* SK10 ....9 J2
Trinity St *CH/BCN* CH1 ....2 D4
  MPL/ROM SK6 ....58 D1
  STHEL WA9 ....22 A5
Trinity Ter *NWCHW* CW8 ....12 D4
Troon Cl *BRAM/HZG* SK7 ....56 B9
  HOLMCH CW4 ....131 N9
  RNFD/HAY WA11 ....22 E4
Troon Dr *CHD/CHDH* SK8 ....55 L6
Troon Rd *NTHM/RTH* M23 ....54 B1
Trossachl Cl *WARRN/WOL* WA2 ...33 P6
Troutbeck Av *CONG* CW12 ....155 J8
  NEWLW WA12 ....32 A5
  WARRW/BUR WA5 ....33 J9
Troutbeck Cl *RUNC* WA7 ....62 E9
Troutbeck Gv *WSFD* CW7 ....128 E9
Troutbeck Rd *CHD/CHDH* SK8 .....55 K4
  HALE/TIMP WA15 ....53 P2
Trouthall La *KNUT* WA16 ....111 M1
Troutbridge Rd *DTN/ASHW* M34 ..29 N8
Trubshaw Pl *ALS/KID* ST7 ....189 K5
Trueman's La *CO* CH5 ....140 A2
Trueman's Wy *CO* CH5 ....140 A1
Trumans La *GTS/LS* CH66 ....79 N6
Truro Av *RDSH* SK5 ....42 B5
Truro Cl *BRAM/HZG* SK7 ....38 A4
Trust Rd *GTN* M18 ....28 C6
Tudor Av *FLINT* CH6 ....98 A8
Tudor Cl *GTS/LS* CH66 ....102 B4
  NWCHE CW9 ....110 C6
  RDSH SK5 ....45 M1
  WARRS WA4 ....49 J5
  WSFD CW7 ....149 M4
Tudor Ct *WARRS* WA4 * 48 C6
Tudor Dr *MCFLDN* SK10 ....94 D6
Tudor Gn *WILM/AE* SK9 ....71 K5
Tudor Rd *ALT* WA14 ....37 N9
  RUNC WA7 ....62 F5
  WILM/AE SK9 ....71 K5
Tudor Wy *CHSE* CH3 ....143 J5
  CONG CW12 ....155 M9
  NANT CW5 ....196 F4
Tue La *WDN* WA8 ....45 H1
Tuffley Rd *NTHM/RTH* M23 ....54 C3
Tulip Cl *EDGY/DAV* SK3 ....56 D2
  SALE M33 ....37 P4
Tulip Dr *HALE/TIMP* WA15 ....53 K1
  RNFD/HAY WA11 ....23 K3
Tully Av *NEWLW* WA12 ....23 J6
Tulworth Rd *POY/DIS* SK12 ....73 K2
Tumbleweed Dr
  CHD/CHDH SK8 ....55 N3
Tunbridge Cl *CW/SHV* CW2 ....184 G8
  WARRW/BUR WA5 ....32 D8
Tunnel Rd *NWCHW* CW8 ....109 K2
Tunnel Top North *WARRS* WA4 .....45 J5
Tunnicliffe Rd *MCFLDS* SK11 ......117 M9
Tunnicliffe St *MCFLDN* SK10 ....8 E2
Tunstall Rd *CONG* CW12 ....175 M1
Tunstall St *HTNM* SK4 ....17 M1
  OP/CLY M11 * 28 E2
Tunstall's Wy *STHEL* WA9 ....31 J4
Tunstead Av *DID/WITH* M20 ....40 A2
Turf La *MCFLDS* SK11 ....117 J9
Turf Lea Rd *MPL/ROM* SK6 ....58 F6
Turnall Rd *WDN* WA8 ....45 H8
Turnberry Cl *HALE/TIMP* WA15 ....50 C5
  MCFLDN SK10 ....95 J9
  NWCHE CW9 ....110 C5
  WSFD CW7 ....128 D9
Turnberry Dr *WILM/AE* SK9 ....71 M5
Turnberry Rd *CHD/CHDH* SK8 .....55 L6
Turnbull Rd *GTN* M18 ....28 F6
Turnbury Cl *SALE* M33 ....38 E2
Turnbury Rd *WYTH/NTH* M22 ......54 C2
Turncliff Crs *MPL/ROM* SK6 ....43 J9
Turncroft La *STKP* SK1 ....17 K5
Turner Av *ALS/KID* ST7 ....201 K6
  IRL M44 ....38 C1
Turner Cl *CW/HAS* CW1 ....169 P9
  WDN WA8 ....45 J3
Turner Crs *NEWLW* ST5 ....201 P9
Turner La *MPL/ROM* SK6 ....42 E2
Turner Rd *WILM/AE* SK9 ....58 D1
Turner St *DTN/ASHW* M34 ....29 M4
  GTN M18 ....28 B6
  MCFLDN SK10 ....95 P5
  NANT CW5 ....10 B2
Turnfield Rd *CHD/CHDH* SK8 ......55 L4
Turnhurst Rd *BURS/TUN* ST6 .....189 P9
Turnock St *MCFLDN* SK10 ....9 G6
The Turnpike *MPL/ROM* SK6 ....58 F6
Turnstone Av *NEWLW* WA12 ....23 N5
Turnstone Rd *OFTN* SK2 ....57 N2
Turret Hall Dr
  GOL/RIS/CU WA3 ....24 C1
Turret Hall Dr
  GOL/RIS/CU WA3 ....24 C1
Turriff Dr *BEB* CH63 ....78 G1
Turrocks Cl *NSTN* CH64 ....77 L8
Turrocks Cft *NSTN* CH64 ....77 L8

Turton Cl *GOL/RIS/CU* WA3 ....34 D3
Turton St *GOL/RIS/CU* WA3 ....24 C1
  OP/CLY M11 * 28 D2
Turves Rd *CHD/CHDH* SK8 ....55 P6
Tuscan Cl *WDN* WA8 ....45 P2
Tuscan Rd *DID/WITH* M20 ....40 C8
Tuscan Wy *NEWLU* ST5 ....201 N9
Tushingham Cl *CHSE* CH3 ....143 K3
Tuson Dr *WDN* WA8 ....45 M5
Tutor Bnk *NEWLW* WA12 ....23 P6
Tutwall Cl *ALT* WA14 ....52 C1
Tweedsmuir Cl
  WARRN/WOL WA2 ....34 B4
Tweenbrook Av
  NTHM/RTH M23 ....54 C4
Twelve Yards Rd *IRL* M44 ....27 J5
Twemlow Av *SBCH* CW11 ....171 N1
Twemlow La *HOLMCH* CW4 ....131 N5
Twenty Acre Rd
  WARRW/BUR WA5 ....32 F8
Twigworth Rd *WYTH/NTH* M22 ....54 E5
Twining Brook Rd
  CHD/CHDH SK8 ....56 B4
Twinnies Rd *WILM/AE* SK9 ....71 K5
Twiss Green Dr
  GOL/RIS/CU WA3 ....25 N5
Twiss Green La
  GOL/RIS/CU WA3 ....24 E1
Two Acre Gv *GTS/LS* CH66 ....102 B5
Two Trees La *DTN/ASHW* M34 ......29 N8
Twyford Cl *DID/WITH* M20 ....40 A5
  WDN WA8 ....45 P5
Twyford La *WDN* WA8 ....46 B1
Tyler St *WILM/AE* SK9 ....93 J4
Tyne Cl *STHEL* WA9 ....30 C2
  WARRN/WOL WA9 ....33 P6
Tynedale Av *CW/SHV* CW2 ....4 C7
Tynedale Cl *MCFLDS* SK11 ....9 C4
  RDSH SK5 ....41 M5
Tynemouth Rd *RUNC* WA7 ....62 G8
Tynesdale EP CH65 ....102 D1
Tynwald Crs *WDN* WA8 ....45 M2
Tynwald Dr *WARRS* WA4 ....48 E8
Tyrer Rd *NEWLW* WA12 ....23 N8
Tyrone Cl *NTHM/RTH* M23 ....38 G8
Tyrrel Rd *RDSH* SK5 ....28 F8
Tytherington Cl *MNWCH* CW10 ...151 J4
Tytherington Dr *MCFLDN* SK10 ....95 K9
  RDSH SK5 ....28 D8
Tytherington La *MCFLDN* SK10 ....95 K9
Tytherington Park Rd
  MCFLDN SK10 ....117 K2

Ullapool Cl *GTS/LS* CH66 ....79 K7
Ullswater *MCFLDS* SK11 ....116 F7
Ullswater Av *CW/SHV* CW2 ....184 E5
  WARRN/WOL WA2 ....33 M5
  WSFD CW7 ....128 D9
Ullswater Crs *CHNE* CH2 ....122 B5
Ullswater Dr *WILM/AE* SK9 ....92 B6
Ullswater Gv *RUNC* WA7 ....62 E9
Ullswater Rd *CONG* CW12 ....155 J8
  EP CH65 ....102 E2
  STKP SK1 ....42 A9
  WILM/AE SK9 ....71 L2
  WYTH/NTH M22 ....54 D5
Ulverston Av *DID/WITH* M20 ....40 A1
  WARRN/WOL WA2 ....33 J5
Ulverston Ct *RNFD/HAY* WA11 ....22 E5
Ulviet Ga *KNUT* WA16 ....67 J2
Underbridge La *WARRS* WA4 ....48 A9
Underhill *MPL/ROM* SK6 ....43 H6
Under Rainow Rd *CONG* CW12 ....156 E9
Under the Hi *BIDD* ST8 ....175 P6
The Underway *RUNC* WA7 ....62 D6
Underwood Cl *GTN* M18 ....28 F3
Underwood Ct
  MCFLDN SK10 ....116 F9
Underwood Dr EP CH65 ....102 E2
Underwood La *CW/HAS* CW1 ......185 H5
Underwood Rd *WILM/AE* SK9 ....93 L4
Underwood St *DUK* SK16 ....100 F1
Unicorn Gtwy *MCFLDN* SK10 ....8 E3
Union Bank La *WDN* WA8 ....30 C7
Union Rd *MCFLDS* SK11 ....9 F1
  MPL/ROM SK6 ....58 D1
  NM/HAY SK22 ....59 P8
Union St *CH/BCN* CH1 ....3 C4
  CONG CW12 ....155 M7
  CW/SHV CW2 ....2 F5
  MCFLDS SK11 ....9 J3
  RUNC WA7 ....15 H3
  SBCH CW11 ....171 M3
  STKP SK1 ....17 J2
Union Ter *CH/BCN* CH1 ....3 F5
Unity Wy *ALS/KID* ST7 ....188 F8
  STKP SK1 ....17 J7
Unsworth Ct
  WARRN/WOL WA2 * 34 A7
Unwin Av *GTN* M18 ....28 D5
Upavon Rd *WYTH/NTH* M22 ....55 H4
Upcast La *WILM/AE* SK9 ....92 F2
Uplands *NWCHW* CW8 ....107 P8
Uplands Rd *HYDE* SK14 ....43 M2
Upper Brook St *STKP* SK1 ....17 H5
Upper Cambrian Rd
  CH/BCN CH1 ....2 B2
Upper Downs *ALT* WA14 ....52 C4
Upper Haigh St *WSFD* CW7 ....149 L2
Upper Hibbert La
  MPL/ROM SK6 ....58 D3

Upper Mersey Rd *WDN* WA8 ....61 N1
Upper Mersey St EP CH65 ....7 F1
Uppermill Dr *BNG/LEV* M19 ....40 E5
Upper Northgate St
  CH/BCN CH1 ....2 C1
Upper Raby Rd *NSTN* CH64 ....177 K3
Upton Av *CHD/CHDH* SK8 ....56 A7
  HTNM SK4 ....40 F4
Upton Bridle Pth *WDN* WA8 ....45 K4
Upton Cl *GOL/RIS/CU* WA3 ....24 E1
  WSFD CW7 ....128 C7
Upton Dr *ALT* WA14 ....38 B8
  CHNE CH2 ....121 M5
  WARRW/BUR WA5 ....47 K2
Upton Gra *WDN* WA8 ....45 K4
Upton La *CHNE* CH2 ....121 M5
  WDN WA8 ....45 M3
Upton Pk *CHNE* CH2 ....121 N5
Upton Rd *GTS/LS* CH66 ....79 P9
Upwood Rd *GOL/RIS/CU* WA3 ......24 F2
Urban Dr *HALE/TIMP* WA15 ....53 J3
  SALE M33 ....38 D4
Ure Ct EP CH65 ....80 C6
Urmston Av *NEWLW* WA12 ....23 M4
Urwick Rd *MPL/ROM* SK6 ....42 G7
Utkinton La *TPLY/KEL* CW6 ....147 H4
Utkinton Rd *TPLY/KEL* CW6 ....146 F5

V

Vahler Ter *RUNC* WA7 ....15 J2
Valance Cl *WGTN/LGST* M12 ....28 A3
Vale Av *SALE* M33 ....39 H3
  WARRN/WOL WA2 ....33 L8
Valebrook Dr *NANT* CW5 ....197 P7
Vale Cl *BRAM/HZG* SK7 ....57 L3
  CHSW/BR CH4 ....140 C7
  HTNM SK4 ....43 L6
  MPL/ROM SK6 ....43 L6
Vale Ct *WARRS* WA4 ....65 L2
Vale Crs *CHD/CHDH* SK8 ....55 P5
Vale Gdns *ALS/KID* ST7 ....188 A4
  EP CH65 ....6 B3
  FROD/HEL WA6 ....63 H9
Vale Head *WILM/AE* SK9 ....71 M4
Valentine Rd *ALS/KID* ST7 ....189 J7
  ALS/KID ST7 ....23 K6
Vale Owen Rd
  WARRN/WOL WA2 ....33 N7
  EP CH65 ....52 F6
  HALE/TIMP WA15 ....53 L2
  HTNM SK4 ....42 G8
  MPL/ROM SK6 ....42 G8
  NWCHE CW9 ....109 L3
  NWCHW CW8 ....108 L3
  TPLY/KEL CW6 ....166 D5
  WILM/AE SK9 ....71 K4
Vale Royal Dr *NWCHW* CW8 ....128 A4
  NWCHW CW8 ....108 C3
Vale St *NEWLU* ST5 ....201 P7
Vale Vw *ALT* WA14 * 52 C9
  NWCHE CW9 ....110 C3
Valewood Av *HTNM* SK4 ....41 H7
Valiant Cl *WARRN/WOL* WA3 ....34 B4
Valley Cl *ALS/KID* ST7 ....187 K5
  CHD/CHDH SK8 ....55 N4
  KNUT WA16 ....90 E6
Valley Ct *WARRN/WOL* WA2 ....34 A7
Valley Dr *CHNE* CH2 ....121 M6
Valley La *NWCHW* CW8 ....108 B9
  WILM/AE SK9 ....71 L5
Valley Gv *DTN/ASHW* M54 ....29 P7
Valley La *NWCHW* CW8 ....108 B9
Valley Rd *BRAM/HZG* SK7 ....56 F6
  CHD/CHDH SK8 ....56 F6
  CW/SHV CW2 ....184 F7
  MCFLDS SK11 ....116 C7
  MPL/ROM SK6 ....42 G8
  NWCHW CW8 ....108 L3
Valley Vw *CONG* CW12 ....115 J3
  GTS/LS CH66 ....79 P8
  NEWLW WA12 ....23 N3
  NWCHE CW9 ....110 C5
Valley Wy *KNUT* WA16 ....90 F6
Vanguard Ct *CW/SHV* CW2 ....2 E8
Varden Gv *EDGY/DAV* SK3 ....56 D2
Varden Rd *POY/DIS* SK12 ....73 L3
Vardon Dr *WILM/AE* SK9 ....71 H8
Varey Cl *CONG* CW12 ....155 P6
Varey St *GTN* M18 ....28 D4
Varley Rd *STHEL* WA9 ....22 A5
Varna St *OP/CLY* M11 ....28 D2
Vaudrey Crs *CONG* CW12 ....155 P7
Vaudrey Dr *BRAM/HZG* SK7 ....57 L5
  CHD/CHDH SK8 ....56 A4
  HALE/TIMP WA15 ....38 D8
  WARR WA1 ....34 A4
Vaudrey La *DTN/ASHW* M34 ....29 N7
Vaudrey Rd *MPL/ROM* SK6 ....42 D2
Vaughan Av *HTNM* SK4 ....41 L5
Vaughans La *CHSE* CH3 ....175 L3
Vauxhall Cl *WARRW/BUR* WA5 ....47 K3
Vauxhall Rd *NANT* CW5 ....10 B2
Vauxhall Wy *WSFD* CW7 ....149 L4
Vawdrey Dr *NTHM/RTH* M23 ....39 J6
Venable's Rd *CH/BCN* CH1 ....121 J7
  NWCHE CW9 ....4 C8
Venables Wy *KNUT* WA16 ....96 D6
  MWCH CW10 ....151 L5
Venlow Gdns *CHD/CHDH* SK8 .....55 L6
  WARRN/WOL WA2 ....19 H1
Ventnor Av *BNG/LEV* M19 ....28 F3
  SALE M33 ....32 A3
Ventnor Cl *DTN/ASHW* M34 ....29 P7
  MWCH CW10 ....151 J2
  WARRW/BUR WA5 ....32 D4
Ventnor Rd *DID/WITH* M20 ....40 D5

HTNM SK4..........................41 H6
Venture Wy POY/DIS SK12 ....73 M3
Verbena Cl PART M31 ....36 E5
RUNC WA7 ....2 D4
Verdin Av NWCHW CW8 ....1 D1
Verdin Cl NWCHE CW9 ....128 C4
Verdin Cl WSFD CW7 ....128 D9
Verdin Ct CW/HAS CW1 ....169 P9
Verdin Gv HALE/TIMP WA15 ....110 C4
Vere St CW/HAS CW1 ....38 F7
Verity Cl CW/HAS CW1 ....186 A4
DID/WITH M20 ....40 C2
Vermont Cl WARRW/BUR WA5 ...32 F9
Vernon Av ALS/KID ST7 ....200 C5
CONG CW12 ....174 G1
GTS/LS CH66 ....79 L3
STKP SK1 ....41 P9
Vernon Cl ALS/KID ST7 ....200 G5
CH/BCN CH1 ....120 D3
CHD/CHDH SK8 ....55 N6
Vernon Dr AUD/MAD/W CW3 ....217 N1
MPL/ROM SK6 ....43 H9
Vernon Gv SALE M33 ....39 H5
Vernon Pk HALE/TIMP WA15 ....38 D9
Vernon Rd CH/BCN CH1 ....2 B3
POY/DIS SK12 ....73 L4
Vernon St BRAM/HZG SK7 ....57 K4
CW/HAS CW1 * 185 H3
MCFLDN SK10 ....9 J4
STHEL WA9 ....22 A5
STKP SK1 * 17 G3
WARR WA1 ....19 F5
Vernon Wy CW/SHV CW2 ....5 F4
Veronica Rd DID/WITH M20 ......40 D5
Veronica Wy GTS/LS CH66 ......79 P6
Verrill Av NTHM/RTH M23 ....39 M7
Vetch Cl GOL/RIS/CU CW9 ....36 A3
The Vetches CHSE CH3 ....122 C6
Viaduct Rd ALT WA14 ....38 A9
Viaduct St EDGY/DAV SK3 ....16 E5
NEWLW WA12 ....21 H3
Vicarage Av CHD/CHDH SK8 .....56 B7
Vicarage Cl CHSE CH3 ....122 C6
SPK/HALE L24 ....60 E5
Vicarage Ct WRRS/E LL13 ....176 C8
Vicarage Dr RNFD/HAY WA11 ....22 E2
Vicarage Gdns EDGY/DAV SK3 * .16 E7
SBCH CW11 ....171 J1
Vicarage Gv WSFD CW7 ....149 M5
Vicarage Hl FROD/HEL WA6 .....83 J9
Vicarage La ALT WA14 ....52 C6
AUD/MAD/W CW3 ....217 H1
FROD/HEL WA6 ....84 A6
NSTN CH64 ....100 B2
POY/DIS SK12 ....73 L1
SBCH CW11 ....171 K1
TPLY/KEL CW6 ....148 E5
TPLY/KEL CW6 ....166 C9
Vicarage Rd CHNE CH2 ....122 A8
CW/HAS CW1 ....186 B2
EDGY/DAV SK3 ....56 E1
IRL M44 ....27 N7
NWCHE CW9 ....13 J3
RNFD/HAY WA11 ....22 F2
WDN WA8 ....21 H4
Vicarage Wk NWCHE CW8 ....13 F5
Vicarage Wy MCFLDS SK11 .....116 F5
Vicar's Cl CHSE CH3 ....124 E4
Vicars Cross Rd CHSE CH3 ......122 C9
Vicar's La CH/BCN CH1 ....3 F5
Vicker Cl WDN WA8 ....40 A3
Vickers Rd WDN WA8 ....61 L2
Vickers Wy NWCHE CW9 ....13 G4
ALS/KID ST7 ....189 H6
Victoria Av ALS/KID ST7 ....15 M2
BNG/LEV M19 ....28 A9
BRAM/HZG SK7 * 57 L4
CHD/CHDH SK8 ....56 A5
CW/HAS CW1 ....186 A4
CW/SHV CW2 ....7 J4
DID/WITH M20 ....40 D5
HALE/TIMP WA15 ....38 B9
HOLMCH CW4 ....131 P9
MPL/ROM SK6 ....42 E5
WARRS/E LL13 * 28 A5
WARRW/BUR WA5 ....49 J5
WDN WA8 ....45 N5
Victoria Ct BRAM/HZG SK7 ......56 D8
EDGY/DAV SK3 * 41 M9
WHITCH SY13 ....213 M6
Victoria Crs CHSW/BR CH4 * 20 C5
CHNE CH2 * 121 M8
Victoria Dr SALE M33 ....38 G5
Victoria Gv HTNM SK4 ....41 N9
RUSH/FAL M14 ....40 D1
WDN WA8 ....45 N4
Victoria Mill Dr NANT CW5 .....197 L1
Victoria Pk NWCHW CW8 ....12 D1
STKP SK1 * 42 A8

WARRS WA4 ....48 F6
WARRS WA4 ....49 H5
WARRW/BUR WA5 ....47 H3
WARRW/BUR WA5 ....47 M3
WDN WA8 ....21 H4
WILM/AE SK9 ....71 J8
WYTH/NTH M22 ....39 N8
Victoria Sq WDN WA8 ....21 H4
WSFD CW7 ....149 J2
Victoria St ALT WA14 ....53 H7
CW/HAS CW1 ....4 E2
DTN/ASHW M34 ....29 L5
KNUT WA16 ....90 D3
NEWUL ST5 ....201 P8
NM/HAY SK22 ....59 M9
NWCHE CW9 ....110 E2
OP/CLY M11 ....28 C1
RAIN/WH L35 ....30 B5
SBCH CW11 ....171 M2
WARR WA1 ....19 F5
WDN WA8 ....21 J4
Victoria Ter RAIN/WH L35 ....30 B5
Victoria Wk MCFLDN SK10 ......10 D2
Victor Mann St OP/CLY M11 ....28 C2
Victory Rd DTN/ASHW M34 .....29 J2
IRL M44 ....36 B4
Victory Rd IRL M44 ....36 B4
Vienna Rd EDGY/DAV SK3 ......56 D1
Vienna Rd East EDGY/DAV SK3 .56 E1
Viewlands Dr WILM/AE SK9 .....71 M4
View Rd RAIN/WH L35 ....30 B6
Villa Farm SBCH CW11 ....155 M9
Villagate La WARRS WA4 ....65 L1
Village Cl NWCHE CW9 ....110 G4
NEWUL ST5 ....201 P8
WARRS WA4 ....49 N5
Village La WARRS WA4 ....86 F2
Village Ms MCFLDN SK10 * 94 G9
CHSE CH3 ....123 M6
CHSE CH3 ....143 N2
Village Rd CHSE CH3 ....144 D6
Village St RUNC WA7 ....63 J4
The Village CONG CW12 ....174 B1
MCFLDN SK10 ....94 C7
NSTN CH64 ....100 B3
Village Wy WILM/AE SK9 ....71 M5
MCFLDN SK10 ....94 C7
Villars St WARR WA1 ....19 C6
Villdale Av OFTN SK2 ....42 B9
Villiers Russell Cl CW/HAS CW1 .5 L1
Vincent Cl WARRW/BUR WA5 ...32 E8
Vincent Dr CHSW/BR CH4 ......142 D4
Vincent Rd WILM/AE SK9 ....30 A4
Vincent St CW/HAS CW1 ....5 L5
MCFLDS SK11 ....11 H8
OP/CLY M11 ....28 C1
Vine Bank Rd ALS/KID ST7 .....189 J6
Vine Cl MCFLDS SK11 ....116 C7
SALE M33 ....37 P3
Vine Crs WARRW/BUR WA5 .....47 J1
Vine Gv OFTN SK2 ....57 J1
Vine Rd GTS/LS CH66 ....102 B4
Vinery Gv DTN/ASHW M34 ......29 L6
Vine St BRAM/HZG SK7 ....57 L4
MCFLDN SK10 ....95 P5
OP/CLY M11 ....28 E1
RUNC WA7 ....14 E3
WDN WA8 ....21 H4
Vine Ter RAIN/WH L35 * 44 C5
CW/SHV CW2 ....4 C7
Vine Tree Av CW/SHV CW2 .....198 A2
Violet Cl GOL/RIS/CU WA3 ......34 D4
Violet St OFTN SK2 ....56 F1
WDN WA8 ....21 G5
Virginia Cha CHD/CHDH SK8 ....55 P7
Virginia Cl NTHM/RTH M23 ......38 G9
Virginia Dr CH/BCN CH1 ....120 F6
Virginia Gdns
WARRW/BUR WA5 ....32 E8
Viscount Dr CHD/CHDH SK8 ....55 M8
MANAIR M90 * 54 B8
Viscount Rd WARRN/WOL WA2 .33 P6
Vista Av NEWLW WA12 ....23 L5
Vista Rd NEWLW WA12 ....23 L5
RUNC WA7 ....15 F6
The Vista IRL M44 ....36 B4
Vista Wy NEWLW WA12 ....23 L5
Vixen Cl CONG CW12 ....39 P1
Volunteer Av NANT CW5 ....10 C4
Volunteer Flds NANT CW5 ....10 C4
Volunteer St CH/BCN CH1 ....2 C5
FROD/HEL WA6 ....84 A4
Vose Cl WARRW/BUR WA5 ......47 P1
Vulcan Cl NEWLW WA12 ....23 N8
Vyner Gv SALE M33 ....38 C2
Vyrnwy Rd CHSW/BR CH4 ......141 P4

STHEL WA9 ....22 B5
Wainwright Av DTN/ASHW M34 .28 F6
Wainwright Cl OFTN SK2 ....41 P9
Wainwright Rd ALT WA14 ....52 F2
Wakefield Cl CW/HAS CW1 ......184 F1
Wakefield Ct NWCHE CW9 ......110 A7
Wakefield Crs MPL/ROM SK6 ...42 F7
Wakefield Dr CHD/CHDH SK8 ..102 A3
Wakeham Cha MCFLDS SK11 ...116 F5
Wakefield Rd GTS/LS CH66 ......24 C2
Wakeham Cha MCFLDS SK11 ...116 F5
Wakeman Dr CW/HAS CW1 .....29 L9
Wakes Meadow
TPLY/KEL CW6 ....166 B9
Wald Av RUSH/FAL M14 ....40 F1
Walden Cl WARRS WA4 ....49 M4
Walden Crs BRAM/HZG SK7 .....57 J4
Walden Dr CH/BCN CH1 ....101 H4
Waldon Av CHD/CHDH SK8 ......55 M2
Waldron Rd MCFLDS SK11 .....116 C7
Waldron Gdns CW/HAS CW1 ....184 F7
Waldron's La CW/HAS CW1 .....170 B8
Walfield Av CONG CW12 ....155 M5
Walford Av CW/SHV CW2 ....4 A3
Walgrave Cl CONG CW12 ....155 J6
Walker Av STHEL WA9 ....30 C5
Walker Dr MWCH CW10 ....101 J2
Walker La MCFLDS SK11 ....136 D1
Walker Rd IRL M44 ....36 A6
Walkersgreen Rd NEWUL ST5 ..201 N5
Walkers La ALS/KID ST7 ....173 L7
CHSE CH3 ....177 H7
GTS/LS CH66 ....79 N7
STHEL WA9 ....30 F5
TPLY/KEL CW6 ....147 H9
WARRW/BUR WA5 ....47 J4
Walker St CHNE CH2 ....3 H1
CW/HAS CW1 ....185 H3
DTN/ASHW M34 ....29 L5
MCFLDN SK10 ....8 C3
STKP SK1 * 17 F3
WARRN/WOL WA2 ....18 B4
Wallace St NWCHW CW8 ....12 C5
WDN WA8 ....21 H2
Wallbank Rd BRAM/HZG SK7 ...56 C6
Wallcroft NSTN CH64 ....78 E6
Wallerscote Cl NWCHW CW8 ...108 C4
Wallerscote Rd NWCHW CW8 ..108 F5
Waller St MCFLDS SK11 * 9 G7
Walleys La NANT CW5 ....182 E9
Walley La BIDD ST8 ....175 K9
Wall Fields Cl NANT CW5 ....10 C2
Wall Fields Rd NANT CW5 ......10 B2
Wallhill La CONG CW12 ....154 F6
Wall Hill Wy NWCHW CW8 ......108 B1
Wallingford Rd WILM/AE SK9 ...71 L1
Wallis St CW/HAS CW1 ....5 L4
WARRS WA4 ....48 D4
Wall La NANT CW5 ....10 B5
Walls Av CH/BCN CH1 ....44 F7
Walsend Ct WDN WA8 ....45 L4
Wall Wy WDN WA8 ....28 E5
Wallwork Cl OP/CLY M11 ....28 E1
Wallworth Av OFTN SK2 ....41 N9
Wallworth's Bnk CONG CW12 ..155 N8
Walmer Dr BRAM/HZG SK7 .....56 C6
Walmer Pl WSFD CW7 * 149 L4
Walmer St BRAM/HZG SK7 .....57 K4
Walmoor Pk CHSE CH3 ....143 J1
Walmsley St NEWLW WA12 .....23 P5
RDSH SK5 ....56 A3
WDN WA8 ....46 A7
Walney Rd WYTH/NTH M22 ....54 F3
Walnut Av NWCHW CW8 ....108 F4
Walnut Cl CHNE CH2 ....121 N4
WARR WA1 ....34 F9
WSFD CW7 ....150 A1
Walnut Gv GTS/LS CH66 ....24 A4
Walnut Rd PART M31 ....36 C5
Walnut St OFTN SK2 ....56 F2
Walnut Tree La SBCH CW11 ...152 E7
Walnut Tree Rd EDGY/DAV SK3 .41 H9
Walpole Cl CW/HAS CW1 ....186 A3
Walpole Av WARRN/WOL WA2 .33 M6
Walpole Rd RUNC WA7 ....61 P8
Walpole St CH/BCN CH1 ....2 C1
Walsh Cl NEWLW WA12 ....23 L5
Walsingham Av DID/WITH M20 .40 A4
Walsingham Dr RUNC WA7 ......63 H4
Walsingham Rd
WARRW/BUR WA5 ....47 K2
Walter Gv STHEL WA9 ....31 L1
Walter St CH/BCN CH1 ....3 F1
WARR WA1 ....19 K1
WDN WA8 ....46 B6
Walthall St CW/SHV CW2 ....4 D6
Waltham Av GOL/RIS/CU WA3 ..26 D2
Waltham Dr CHD/CHDH SK8 ....56 B9
Waltham PI CHSW/BR CH4 * ...142 C4
Walton Av WARRW/BUR WA5 ...47 J3
Walton Gn MPL/ROM SK6 ....48 J9
Walton Gv ALS/KID ST7 ....188 E8
Walton Hall Dr RDSH SK5 ....28 D8
Walton Heath Dr WILM/AE SK9 .67 H9
Walton Heath Rd WARRS WA4 ..48 C8
Walton New Rd WARRS WA4 ....48 E7
Walton PI CH/BCN CH1 ....121 H7
Walton Rd ALT WA14 ....52 F2
GOL/RIS/CU WA3 ....25 P6
GOL/RIS/CU WA3 ....38 C7
SALE M33 ....38 E7
WARRS WA4 ....48 E7
The Waltons CHSW/BR CH4 ...142 G4
Walton St RUNC WA7 ....15 F3

STKP SK1 * 41 N9
Walton Wy ALS/KID ST7 ....188 E8
WDN WA8 ....46 E8
Wansfell Pl WARRN/WOL WA2 ..33 K5
Warbeck Cl RUNC WA7 ....35 P7
Warbreck Gv SALE M33 ....38 G5
Warburton Bridge Rd
GOL/RIS/CU WA3 ....35 P7
Warburton Cl HALE/TIMP WA15 .53 P9
LYMM WA13 ....50 C2
MPL/ROM SK6 ....42 F7
Warburton Dr
HALE/TIMP WA15 ....53 P9
Warburton Hey RAIN/WH L35 ...30 A4
Warburton La LYMM WA13 .....36 D8
Warburton La PART M31 ....36 E5
Warburton Rd WILM/AE SK9 ....71 M2
Warburton St DID/WITH M20 ....40 D5
WARRS WA4 ....49 J5
Warburton Vw
HALE/TIMP WA15 ....38 F9
Warburton Wy
HALE/TIMP WA15 ....38 F9
Warburton Cl HALE/TIMP WA15 .95 N5
Ward Cl WARRW/BUR WA5 ......32 E7
Ward La POY/DIS SK12 ....55 J2
Wardle Av NANT CW5 ....182 E1
Wardle Crs MCFLDS SK11 ......135 L1
Wardle Br CW/HAS CW1 ....151 K9
Wardle Ms MWCH CW10 * 151 J2
Wardle Rd SALE M33 ....38 E5
Wardle St MCFLDS SK11 * 39 K4
Wardour Cl MCFLDS SK11 ......116 F5
Wardour St WARRW/BUR WA5 ..48 B5
Ward Rd DID/WITH M20 ....40 C5
Wards Cl CW/HAS CW1 ....175 L1
SBCH CW11 ....152 C5
Wards Ter CHNE CH2 ....3 J1
Ward St MPL/ROM SK6 ....43 J9
STKP SK1 ....41 P9
Wareham Cl WARR WA1 ....34 D8
Warford Av DTN/ASHW M34 ....170 A9
Warford Crs WILM/AE SK9 ......92 D6
Warford Hall Dr WILM/AE SK9 ..92 D7
Warford La WILM/AE SK9 ....92 C4
Warford Pk KNUT WA16 * 92 A4
Wargrave Ms NEWLW WA12 ...23 N6
Wargrave Rd NEWLW WA12 ....23 N6
Warham St WILM/AE SK9 ....71 H5
Waring Av STHEL WA9 ....30 F5
WARRS WA4 ....49 H1
Warkick Rd CH/BCN CH1 ....121 J6
Warkworth Cl WDN WA8 ....45 J4
Warley Cl CHD/CHDH SK8 ......55 N1
Warmingham La MWCH CW10 ..151 K4
SBCH CW11 ....170 C1
Warmley Rd NTHM/RTH M23 ....38 G8
Warmley Cl WDN WA8 ....45 K4
KNUT WA16 ....90 D5
NWCHE CW9 ....110 G3
Warren Cl BRAM/HZG SK7 ......56 D5
DTN/ASHW M34 ....29 K7
NWCHE CW9 ....90 D3
MWCH CW10 ....151 H9
POY/DIS SK12 ....73 H2
Warren Ct CW/HAS CW1 ....84 B7
GTS/LS CH66 ....101 P1
Warren Cft RUNC WA7 ....62 C7
Warren Dr CHSW/BR CH4 ......142 E6
GTS/LS CH66 ....80 A6
HALE/TIMP WA15 ....135 C2
MCFLDS SK11 ....135 L2
NEWLW WA12 ....23 L5
WARRS WA4 ....48 E7
Warren Gv MCFLDS SK11 ....38 G5
Warren Hey WILM/AE SK9 ......71 N6
Warren La NWCHW CW8 ....109 J3
WARR WA1 ....34 E8
Warren Lea MPL/ROM SK6 .....43 N6
WARRS WA4 ....48 E7
Warren St SALE M33 ....38 C5
Warren Cv MCFLDS SK11 * 9 J5
Warren Hey WILM/AE SK9 ......71 N6
WARR WA1 ....34 E8
Warren St STKP SK1 ....17 G3
The Warren NWCHW CW8 ......107 P7
Warren Wy TPLY/KEL CW6 ....147 H9
Warriiowheath Rd NEWUL ST5 .201 N6
Warrington Av CW/HAS CW1 * ..185 J2
EP CH65 ....6 E5
Warrington La LYMM WA13 .....51 K4
Warrington Rd CHNE CH2 ....122 C4
GOL/RIS/CU WA3 ....34 C5
KNUT WA16 ....90 B3
LYMM WA13 ....50 E3
NEWLW WA12 ....24 C3
NWCHE CW9 ....87 M6
NWCHE CW9 ....108 C4
RAIN/WH L35 ....30 A4
RUNC WA7 ....62 A2
WARRS WA4 ....48 B6
WARRW/BUR WA5 ....31 J9
WDN WA8 ....45 N8
Warsall Rd WYTH/NTH M22 ....39 P9
Warsop Av WYTH/NTH M22 ....54 B4
Warton Cl BRAM/HZG SK7 ......56 C8
WARR WA1 * 34 D9
Warton Dr NTHM/RTH M23 .....54 C2
Warwick Av DID/WITH M20 .....40 A4
DTN/ASHW M34 ....29 M8
NEWLW WA12 ....23 K6
WILM/AE SK9 ....71 J8
Warwick Cl ALS/KID ST7 ....189 J6
CHD/CHDH SK8 ....55 M8
HTNM SK4 ....41 K4
KNUT WA16 ....90 C4
MCFLDS SK11 ....116 F6
NSTN CH64 ....77 J8

Warwick Ct EP CH65 ....102 G2
Warwick Dr BRAM/HZG SK7 ....57 K7
HALE/TIMP WA15 ....53 J6
SALE M33 ....38 C4
Warwick Gv DTN/ASHW M34 ...29 J5
Warwick PI WSFD CW7 ....149 L4
Warwick Rd HALE/TIMP WA15 ..53 K6
HTNM SK4 ....36 C3
IRL M44 ....36 C3
MCFLDS SK11 ....116 E6
MPL/ROM SK6 ....42 F6
WDN WA8 ....45 N8
Warwick St NEWUL ST5 ....201 P9
Warwick Wk MCFLDS SK11 ....116 F6
Wasdale Cl GTS/LS CH66 ....80 A6
Wasdale Dr CHD/CHDH SK8 * ..102 A3
Wasdale Gv NWCHE CW9 ....108 G8
Washford Dr NTHM/RTH M23 ..38 G8
Washington Cl BIDD ST8 ....175 K7
Washington Dr
WARRW/BUR WA5 ....47 M1
Wash La KNUT WA16 ....112 D8
WARRS WA4 ....48 C5
Washway Rd ALT WA14 ....38 B7
Wasley Cl WARRN/WOL WA2 ...34 A5
Wastdale Rd WILM/AE SK9 .....54 B5
NWCHW CW8 ....108 A9
Waste La NWCHW CW8 ....126 C5
TPLY/KEL CW6 ....125 K6
Watburn Rd NM/HAY SK22 .....59 N6
Watch La SBCH CW11 ....170 F3
Waterbank Rw NWCHE CW9 ....13 C4
Waterbridge Ct WARRS WA4 ...48 A7
Waterdale Crs STHEL WA9 ......31 J1
Waterdale PI STHEL WA9 ....31 J1
Waterfoot La CHF/WBR SK23 ...75 P8
Waterford Av DID/WITH M20 ...39 N5
WARRS WA4 ....43 K6
Waterford Dr NSTN CH64 ....6 E6
Waterford Wy RUNC WA7 ....62 G8
Watergate Rw North
CH/BCN CH1 ....2 D4
Watergate Rw South
CH/BCN CH1 ....2 D5
Watergate Sq CH/BCN CH1 .....2 D5
Watergate St CH/BCN CH1 ......2 D5
Waterhouse Av MCFLDN SK10 ..95 M5
Waterhouse Rd DTN/ASHW M34 28 E5
Waterland La STHEL WA9 ....31 J1
Water La RAIN/WH L35 ....44 D3
WILM/AE SK9 ....71 J7
Water-lode NANT CW5 ....10 A5
Waterloole NANT CW5 ....196 D1
Waterloo Cl EP CH65 ....6 D4
Waterloo Gv ALS/KID ST7 ......189 J6
Waterloo La RAIN/WH L35 .....106 D3
Waterloo PI STKP SK1 * 17 H5
Waterloo Rd BRAM/HZG SK7 ...56 F6
CHNE CH2 ....121 M7
CW/HAS CW1 * 186 B4
MPL/ROM SK6 ....43 K6
NWCHW CW8 ....12 D4
POY/DIS SK12 ....73 N4
RUNC WA7 ....14 D2
STKP SK1 ....17 H1
Waterloo St West MCFLDS SK11 .3 D4
Watermead Cl EDGY/DAV SK3 ..56 E3
Watermead Dr RUNC WA7 ......63 K9
Watermeetings La
MPL/ROM SK6 ....43 K6
Watermill Dr MCFLDS SK11 .....9 J5
Waters Edge CH/BCN CH1 ......43 M8
NWCHE CW9 ....109 M1
Watersedge FROD/HEL WA6 ....84 B3
Watersedge Cl CHD/CHDH SK8 ..54 B8
Watersfield Cl CHD/CHDH SK8 ..55 P7
Waters Gn MCFLDS SK11 ....9 G6
MPL/ROM SK6 ....58 D2
WARRS WA4 ....48 F7
Waterside MPL/ROM SK6 ....58 D2
Waterside Cl CCHDY M21 ......213 L5
WHITCH SY13 ....213 L5
Waterside Dr FROD/HEL WA6 ..84 B3
Waterside Ms SBCH CW11 ......171 L6
Waterside Rw POY/DIS SK12 ...59 J8
NWCHE CW9 ....110 E5
Waterside Wy MWCH CW10 ....130 A9
Waters Reach POY/DIS SK12 ...73 M1
Waters Reams CHSE CH3 ....143 K2
Water St DTN/ASHW M34 ....29 M2
MCFLDN SK10 ....95 N5
NEWLW WA12 ....23 N5
NEWUL ST5 ....201 N5
RUNC WA7 ....15 F1
STKP SK1 ....17 H1
Water Tower Rd NSTN CH64 ...77 L3
Water Tower St CH/BCN CH1 ...2 D3
Watertower Vw CHNE CH2 ......3 K3
Waterway CHSE CH3 ....144 B5
Waterworks Dr NEWLW WA12 ..47 P1
Waterworks La GTS/LS CH66 ...79 J5
WARRN/WOL WA2 ....33 L1
Watery La CONG CW12 ....174 D4
FROD/HEL WA6 ....84 C8
STHEL WA9 ....33 H2
Watford Bridge Rd
NM/HAY SK22 ....59 P6
Watford La NM/HAY SK22 ......59 N5
Watford Rd NM/HAY SK22 ......59 N5
Watkins Av NEWLW WA12 ....23 K6
Watkin St WARRN/WOL WA2 ...18 D2
WARR WA1 ....19 G5
Watlands Rd ALS/KID ST7 ......201 N6

Watling Crs *CHSW/BR* CH4......142 G3
Watling Dr *TPLY/KEL* CW6......125 P5
Watling St *NWCHE* CW9......13 F2
NWCHW CW8......12 E2
Watson's Cl *CHSW/BR* CH4......140 C7
Watson Sq *STHEL* WA9......17 H5
Watson St *DTN/ASHW* M34......29 P6
Watton Cl *WARRS* WA4......49 L4
Watts St *BNG/LEV* M19......28 B9
Wavell Av *WDN* WA8......45 J7
Wavell Rd *WYTH/NTH* M22......54 F3
Wavells Wy *CHSE* CH5......143 K5
Waveney Dr *ALT* WA14......52 C1
WILM/AE SK9......71 M4
Waveney Rd *WYTH/NTH* M22......54 G3
Waverley Av *WARRS* WA4......48 F7
Waverley Cl *MCFLDN* SK10......117 N4
Waverley Crs *WRX/GR/LL* L12....160 F9
Waverley Dr *CHD/CHDH* SK8......56 B9
Waverley Rd *EDGY/DAV* SK3......41 K9
SALE M33......38 F2
Waverley Ter *CHNE* CH2......121 P8
Waverton Ap *CHSE* CH3......142 A4
Waverton Cl *NTHM* SK4......41 L1
Waverton Cl *CW/SHV* CW2......198 D5
NWCHE CW9......109 N3

Waverton Mill Quays
CHSE CH3......144 B5
Wavertree Av *GTS/LS* CH66......80 A3
Wavertree Av *CH/BCN* CH1......188 G1
WDN WA8......21 G2
Wavertree Cl *CHNE* CH66......80 B6
Wavertree Dr *MWCH* CW10......151 H3
Wavertree Rd *CH/BCN* CH1......120 F6
CW/SHV CW2......198 G6
Wayfarers Dr *NEWLW* WA12....94 J4
Wayford Cl *FROD/HEL* WA6......83 P4
Wayland Cl *WHITCH* SY13......213 N7
Wayland Rd *GTN* M18......28 D6
WHITCH SY13......213 N6
Wayland Rd South *RDSH* SK5....28 D6
Waymills *WHITCH* SY13......213 P6
Wayne St *OP/CLY* M11......28 E1
Way's Grn *WSFD* CW7......149 N2
Wayside Cl *LYMM* WA13......50 D5
Wayside Ct *CHNE* CH2......122 G3
Wayside Dr *POY/DIS* SK12......73 J2
Wayside Gdns *BRAM/HZG* SK7....7 M3
Wayside Linley *ALS/KID* ST7....188 B6
Wayside Rd *MCFLDN* SK10......9 K5
Waystead Cl *NWCHE* CW9......109 P8
Waywell Cl *WARRW/WOL* WA2....34 A5
Weald Dr *GTS/LS* CH66......79 L7
Weald Stone La *CHNE* CH2......121 P6
Weal Stone La *CHNE* CH2......121 P6
Weardale Cl *GOL/RIS/CU* WA3....24 C2
Weardale Rd *STHEL* WA9......31 J1
Weaste La *WARRS* WA4......49 M5
Weates Cl *WDN* WA8......46 C5
Weathercock La *CONG* CW12....155 P8
Weatherley Dr *MPL/ROM* SK6....58 F1
Weaver Av *RAIN/WH* L35......30 A5
Weaver Cl *ALS/KID* ST7......187 L5
ALT WA14......52 C6
BIDD ST8......175 L8
SBCH CW11......171 K2
Weaver Ct *MCFLDS* SK11......4 A5
Weaver Crs *FROD/HEL* WA6......84 B4
Weaver Gra *NWCHE* CW9......128 F3
Weaver Gv *CHNE* CH2......122 G2
STHEL WA9......22 E6
Weaver Valley La *WSFD* CW7....128 G9
Weaverham Rd *NWCHW* CW8...127 K1
Weaver La *FROD/HEL* WA6......83 P3
Weaver Rd *EP* CH65......102 E1
FROD/HEL WA6......84 B4
GOL/RIS/CU WA3......26 A7
NANT CW5......10 C3
NWCHE CW9......128 F4
NWCHW CW8......12 D2
RUNC WA7......61 N8
Weaverside *NANT* CW5......196 F5
Weaverside Av *RUNC* WA7......84 D1
Weavers La *BRAM/HZG* SK7......56 D9
Weaver St *CH/BCN* CH1......2 A2
WSFD CW7......149 N2
Weaver Valley Rd *WSFD* CW7....128 G9
Webb Av *NWCHE* CW9......12 E2
Webb Dr *WARRW/BUR* WA5....32 C2
Webb La *STKP* SK1......17 K5
Webb's La *MWCH* CW10......130 B9
Webb St *STHEL* WA9......22 B8
Webber Cl *CHSW/BR* CH4......140 C7
Websters La *GTS/LS* CH66......102 B2
Weddell Cl *WARRW/BUR* WA5....32 C9
Wedge Av *RNFD/HAY* WA11....12 E4
Wedgewood Av *ALS/KID* ST7....201 J6
Wedgwood Gdns *STHEL* WA9....24 B2
Wedgwood Dr *WDN* WA8......45 P3
Wedgwood Rd *ALS/KID* ST7....201 N1
Wednesbury Dr
WARRW/BUR WA5......47 K1
Weedon Av *NEWLW* WA12......23 M4
Weighbridge Ct *IRL* M44......27 P6
Weighbridge Rd *CQ* CH5......99 M8
Weighbridge Rd *CQ* CH5......99 P7
Weir Gv *ALS/KID* ST7......189 J6
Weir La *WARR* WA1......49 N1
Weir St *NWCHE* CW9......13 F5
WARRS WA4......48 C6
Welbeck Av *NEWLW* WA12......23 P7
Welbeck Cl *MWCH* CW10......150 C1
Welbeck Rd *RDSH* SK5......28 F7
Welbeck St *GTN* M18......28 D9
Welburn Av *WYTH/NTH* M22....54 C4
Welbury Rd *NTHM/RTH* M23....37 P3
Welcomb Cl *MPL/ROM* SK6......42 E1
Welcomb St *OP/CLY* M11......28 E2
Welcroft St *STKP* SK1......17 H6
Weldon Crs *EDGY/DAV* SK3......56 E3

Weldon Rd *ALT* WA14......52 G1
Weld Rd *DID/WITH* M20......40 E1
Welford Av *GOL/RIS/CU* WA3....24 E2
Welford Cl *WILM/AE* SK9......71 N6
Welford Gn *RDSH* SK5......41 N3
Welkin Rd *MPL/ROM* SK6......42 B5
Welland Cl *SBCH* CW11......171 H4
Welland Rd *WILM/AE* SK9......71 N4
Welland St *OP/CLY* M11......28 D1
Welland St *RDSH* SK5......28 F8
Well Av *MALPAS* SY14......204 A3
Well Bnk *SBCH* CW11......171 N3
Wellbank Ct *CW/SHV* CW2 *....155 N8
Wellbank Dr *HLWD* L26......44 A6
Wellbrook Cl *RUNC* WA7......77 N9
Well Cl *NSTN* CH64......77 M6
Wellcroft Cl *CHSW/BR* CH4......185 J4
Weller Av *CCHDY* M21......39 N1
POY/DIS SK12......73 K4
Weller Cl *POY/DIS* SK12......73 K4
Wellesbourne Cl
MCFLDN SK10......116 F3
Wellesbourne Dr
NTHM/RTH M23......39 J9
Wellesley Av *CW/HAS* CW1......186 A6
EP CH65......103 H4
GTN M18......28 D3
Wellesley Cl *NEWLW* WA12....23 M4
Wellesley Wk *EP* CH65......103 H4
Welles St *SBCH* CW11......171 N2
Well Farm Cl *MALPAS* SY14....204 A3
WARR WA1......34 E8
Wellfield *RUNC* WA7......63 J9
Wellfield *WDN* WA8......45 N3
WSFD CW7......128 C9
Wellfield Cl *WILM/AE* SK9......71 N6
Wellfield La *HALE/TIMP* WA15...53 N3
Wellfield Rd *GOL/RIS/CU* WA3...25 N5
NTHM/RTH M23......39 K9
OFTN SK2......57 J1
Wellfield St
WARRW/BUR WA5......48 A2
Wellfield Wy *WHITCH* SY13....213 L4
Wellgate Av *BNG/LEV* M19......28 B9
Wellgreen Cl *HALE/TIMP* WA15...53 N4
Wellhouse La *MPL/ROM* SK6....42 C2
Wellington Circ *MCFLDN* SK10....9 G4
Wellington Cl *CONG* CW12....155 M6
EP CH65......7 F4
KNUT WA16......90 G1
SALE M33......38 F2
WARRN/WOL WA2......34 A6
Wellington Ga *SPK/HALE* L24....60 D4
Wellington Gv *OFTN* SK2......41 N9
Wellington Pl *ALT* WA14......53 H4
CH/BCN CH1......2 E2
Wellington Rd *ALS/KID* ST7....189 J7
BRAM/HZG SK7......7 K4
CHSW/BR CH4......140 F7
EP CH65......8 D6
HALE/TIMP WA15......53 K1
MCFLDN SK10......9 M5
NANT CW5......196 F3
RUSH/FAL M14......40 D1
Wellington Rd North *EP* CH65....7 F5
Wellington Rd North
HTNM SK4......41 J1
Wellington Rd South
OFTN SK2......41 N9
STKP SK1......17 G7
Wellington St *BRAM/HZG* SK7....57 M4
DTN/ASHW M34......29 M3
GTN M18......28 D4
MCFLDS SK11......8 D5
NEWLW WA12......23 L6
NWCHW CW8......12 D4
STKP SK1......17 G5
WARR WA1......19 F6
WDN WA8......20 B5
Well La *ALS/KID* ST7......187 N5
BIDD ST8......175 K7
CHNE CH2......121 P6
FROD/HEL WA6......106 C2
MCFLDN SK10......95 H4
NSTN CH64......77 M8
NWCHE CW9......87 J1
TPLY/KEL CW6......148 E3
WARRS WA4......64 G6
WARRW/BUR WA5......47 J4
Well Mdw *MPL/ROM* SK6......42 D5
Wells Av *CW/HAS* CW1......186 B5
Wells Cl *BIDD* ST8......175 J8
CHD/CHDH SK8......55 L8
CHNE CH2......122 C3
GTS/LS CH66......102 A4
OP/CLY M11......28 F1
WARR WA1......34 C8
Wells Dr *HTNM* SK4......41 H4
Wellside Wk *ALS/KID* ST7....189 M1
MALPAS SY14......204 A3
NM/HAY SK22......59 M7
Wellswood Dr *CW/SHV* CW2....184 F9
Wellswood Rd *GTS/LS* CH66......80 A6
Welman Wy *HALE/TIMP* WA15...54 A5
Welsby Cl *WARRN/WOL* WA2....34 A5
Welshampton Cl *GTS/LS* CH66...101 P2
Welsh La *WSFD* CW7......149 M4
Welshmen's La *NANT* CW5......183 L8
Welshpool Cl *NTHM/RTH* M23...39 L6
WARRS WA4......34 E6
Welton Av *DID/WITH* M20......40 D6
Welton Cl *WILM/AE* SK9......93 H1
Welton Dr *WILM/AE* SK9......92 G1
Welton Gv *WILM/AE* SK9......92 G1

Welwyn Cl *STHEL* WA9......30 D2
WARRS WA4......49 L4
Wembley Rd *GTN* M18......28 C5
Wem Gv *NEWLL* ST5......201 P5
Wemyss Av *RDSH* SK5......28 F8
Wemyss Rd *CH/BCN* CH1......120 C7
Wendon Rd *NTHM/RTH* M23....54 D2
Wendover Rd *NTHM/RTH* M23...38 F9
Wenger Rd *WDN* WA8......45 P2
Wenlock Cl *MCFLDN* SK10......117 H2
NEWUL ST5......201 P5
OFTN SK2......57 N1
WARR WA1......34 B8
Wenlock Gdns *GTS/LS* CH66....102 B2
Wenlock La *GTS/LS* CH66......102 B2
Wenlock Rd *RUNC* WA7......84 E1
SALE M33......38 D6
Wenlock Wy *CHSW/BR* CH4....142 B4
WGTN/LGST M12......28 A3
Wensleydale Av
CHD/CHDH SK8......55 L1
CONG CW12......156 A5
MPLN M35......30 C5
Wensleydale Cl
NTHM/RTH M23......54 B4
WARRW/BUR WA5......32 C8
Wensley Dr *BRAM/HZG* SK7....57 K8
DID/WITH M20......40 C3
Wensley Rd *CHD/CHDH* SK8......55 L3
GOL/RIS/CU WA3......24 G2
RDSH SK5......41 N4
Wentworth Av *GTN* M18......28 E4
HALE/TIMP WA15......53 L1
IRL M44......27 N6
MCFLDS SK11......116 F6
WARR WA1......34 C9
Wentworth Cl *MPL/ROM* SK6....45 L8
NWCHE CW9......110 E5
WDN WA8......45 N7
Wentworth Dr *ALS/KID* ST7....189 L5
BRAM/HZG SK7......57 L8
SALE M33......38 C3
Wentworth Gv *WSFD* CW7......128 B9
Wentworth Rd *RDSH* SK5......28 F8
Wereton Rd *ALS/KID* ST7......200 C2
Werneth Cl *BRAM/HZG* SK7 *....57 L5
DTN/ASHW M34......29 M7
Werneth Hollow *MPL/ROM* SK6...42 G2
Werneth Low Rd *MPL/ROM* SK6...43 J4
Werneth Ri *HYDE* SK14......43 J1
Werneth Rd *MPL/ROM* SK6......43 L8
Werneth St *DTN/ASHW* M34......29 M4
HTNM SK4......41 J5
Wervin Rd *CHNE* CH2......122 A2
Wesley Av *ALS/KID* ST7......187 P4
RNFD/HAY WA11......23 J2
SBCH CW11......171 N3
Wesley Cl *NANT* CW5......10 C6
CHNE CH4......77 K6
NWCHE CW9......13 H2
Wesley Pl *ALS/KID* ST7......200 C8
CW/SHV CW2......42 A5
NWCHE CW9......13 H2
Wesley St *ALS/KID* ST7......201 K7
BRAM/HZG SK7......57 L4
NSTN CH64......77 M8
STKP SK1......17 H5
Wessenden Bank East
OFTN SK2......57 K2
Wessenden Bank West
OFTN SK2......57 K2
Wessex Cl *CW/SHV* CW2......198 B4
WARR WA1......34 E9
Wessex Dr *NWCHE* CW9......111 J5
Westage Gdns *NTHM/RTH* M23...39 K9
West Av *ALS/KID* ST7......188 E7
ALT WA14......52 E2
BNG/LEV M19......28 B9
CHD/CHDH SK8......55 L6
CW/HAS CW1......186 A5
CW/SHV CW2......198 C2
GTN M18......28 D3
MWCH CW10......130 B9
NWCHE CW9......110 D6
WARRN/WOL WA2......33 L8
WARRS WA4......48 E6
West Bnk *CH/BCN* CH1......121 M7
OP/CLY M11......28 C2
WILM/AE SK9......93 J6
West Bank Dock Av *WDN* WA8...45 P7
West Bank Dock Est *WDN* WA8...61 K1
Westbank Rd *DID/WITH* M20....40 E5
Westbank Rd *MCFLDN* SK10......8 A2
West Bank St *WDN* WA8......61 N1
West Bond St *MCFLDS* SK11......8 C5
Westbourne Av *CW/HAS* CW1...184 C2
Westbourne Gv *DID/WITH* M20...40 G2
RDSH SK5......28 F9
SALE M33......38 E5
Westbourne Ms *CONG* CW12 *...155 K8
Westbourne Range *GTN* M18....28 F6
Westbourne Rd *CH/BCN* CH1...121 K7
DTN/ASHW M34......29 L7
WARRS WA4......48 F5
Westbrook Av *WARRS* WA4......48 F5
WHITCH SY13......213 L5
Westbrook Cen
WARRW/BUR WA5......32 F7
Westbrook Crs
WARRW/BUR WA5......32 F7
Westbrook Dr *FROD/HEL* WA6...106 C7
Westbrook Sq *WGTN/LGST* M12...28 A3
Westbury Cl *CHSW/BR* CH4......140 F6
WARRW/BUR WA5......32 F7
Westbury Av *SALE* M33......37 P7
Westbury Cl *CW/SHV* CW2......185 J8
MWCH CW10......151 H2
WARR WA1......34 B8
Westbury Dr *MCFLDS* SK11......116 C5
MPL/ROM SK6......58 B9
Westbury Wy *CHSW/BR* CH4....142 B4
Westby Cl *BRAM/HZG* SK7......56 G8
Westcliffe Gdns *WARRS* WA4....64 G3

West Cl *MCFLDN* SK10......95 L6
Westcott Av *DID/WITH* M20......40 B2
Westcourt Rd *SALE* M33......38 D5
Westcroft Rd *DID/WITH* M20....40 C4
Westdale Gdns *BNG/LEV* M19....41 H5
Westdale Rd *WARR* WA1......34 B9
Westdean Ct *BNG/LEV* M19......40 C3
West Downs Rd
CHD/CHDH SK8......55 P4
West Dr *CHD/CHDH* SK8......55 J5
NSTN CH64......77 K7
WARRW/BUR WA5......47 M5
WSFD CW7......128 C9
West Dudley St *WSFD* CW7....149 P1
West End *CHSE* CH3......124 C4
West End Av *CHD/CHDH* SK8....55 J1
West End Gv *RNFD/HAY* WA11...22 D5
West End Rd *RNFD/HAY* WA11...22 D5
Westena Av *EP* CH65......80 B7
Westerham Cl *MCFLDS* SK10....117 H2
Western Ap *CHNE* CH2......121 P7
Western Av *CH/BCN* CH1......120 F7
MCFLDS SK11......117 J7
NANT CW5......196 F4
Western Cir *BNG/LEV* M19......40 C2
Western Rd *SALE* M33......38 D5
Western St *GTN* M18......28 D3
Westfield Av *ALS/KID* ST7......200 F6
WSFD CW7......149 L5
Westfield Crs *RUNC* WA7......14 C5
Westfield Dr *CW/SHV* CW2......184 F8
KNUT WA16......90 D6
MPL/ROM SK6......43 H5
Westfield Gv *DTN/ASHW* M34....29 L4
NWCHW CW8......87 H9
Westfield Ms *RUNC* WA7......14 C4
Westfield Rd *ALS/KID* ST7......189 L1
CHD/CHDH SK8......55 P7
NWCHE CW9......12 A3
RUNC WA7......14 B5
Westfields *HALE/TIMP* WA15....53 K7
Westfields Av *MCFLDN* SK10......8 A1
Westfields Ri
AUD/MAD/W WA5......219 H4
Westford Rd *WARRS* WA4......48 C6
Westgate *HALE/TIMP* WA15......53 J5
SALE M33......38 D4
WILM/AE SK9......71 J9
Westgate Av *WSFD* CW7......149 J1
Westgate Pk *CW/SHV* CW2......198 C5
West Gv *ALS/KID* ST7......188 E5
SALE M33......38 E5
West Hall Cl *KNUT* WA16......67 J1
Westhay Crs *GOL/RIS/CU* WA3...35 K1
Westhead Av *GOL/RIS/CU* WA3...24 F3
West Heath Gv *LYMM* WA13......50 C5
West Heath Rd *RNFD/HAY* WA11...12 E6
Westholme Cl *CONG* CW12....155 K7
CW/SHV CW2......185 J8
Westholme Ct *WILM/AE* SK9....93 J5
West House Ct *MCFLDN* SK10...116 E5
West Hyde *LYMM* WA13......50 C3
Westlake Av *STKP* SK1......42 A7
Westlands *ALS/KID* ST7......201 J5
Westlands Rd *MWCH* CW10....151 H1
The Westlands *CONG* CW12....155 L8
West La *KNUT* WA16......108 B9
NWCHW CW8......62 C7
RUNC WA7......62 C7
West Lea *DTN/ASHW* M34......29 N6
Westlea Dr *GTN* M18......28 D6
Westleigh Pl *STHEL* WA9......31 H3
West Lorne St *CHSW/BR* CH4......2 C1
West Mains *SPK/HALE* L24......60 A5
Westmead Dr *HALE/TIMP* WA15...38 E9
West Meade *CCHDY* M21......39 K1
West Meadow *RDSH* SK5......28 G8
Westmere Cl *CW/SHV* CW2......198 C2
Westmere Ct *CW/HAS* CW1 *...185 M6
Westmere Dr *CW/HAS* CW1....185 M6
Westminster Av *CHSW/BR* CH4...142 M2
HTNM SK4......41 M1
Westminster Cl *MPL/ROM* SK6...43 J7
OP/CLY M11......151 H1
SALE M33......38 A5
WDN WA8......45 H7
Westminster Ct
CHD/CHDH SK8......56 B9
RNFD/HAY WA11......23 K2
WILM/AE SK9......93 H1
Westminster Dr
CHSW/BR CH4......142 F7
EP CH65......6 E3
HALE/TIMP WA15......54 L4
MCFLDN SK10......9 L5
Westminster Gv *EP* CH65......6 E5
Westminster Pl *WARR* WA1......34 C8
Westminster Rd *CHNE* CH2......3 J1
EP CH65......6 E3
HALE/TIMP WA15......54 L4
MCFLDN SK10......9 L5
Westminster St *BNG/LEV* M19 *...28 B8
CW/SHV CW2......4 E5
Westminster Ter
HOLMCH CW4......131 N8
West Oak Pl *CHD/CHDH* SK8....55 P6
Weston Ct *MWCH* CW10......151 J3
NWCHE CW9......109 P7
Weston Court Ms
WHITCH SY13......213 M5

Weston Crs *RUNC* WA7......61 N8
Weston Dr *CHD/CHDH* SK8......56 D3
DTN/ASHW M34......29 N6
Weston Gv *CHNE* CH2......121 L5
HLWD L26......44 A9
HTNM SK4......41 K2
WYTH/NTH M22......39 P8
Weston La *CW/SHV* CW2......198 C2
Weston Point Dock *RUNC* WA7....14 A4
Weston Point Expy *RUNC* WA7....14 A4
CW/HAS CW1......27 N7
IRL M44......27 N7
RUNC WA7......61 L7
WILM/AE SK9......71 M8
Weston Rd *GTS/LS* CH66......102 B4
Weston St *RDSH* SK5......42 A8
Westover Av *WARR* WA1......34 A9
Westover Rd *WARR* WA1......34 A9
West Pk *HYDE* SK14......43 K1
West Park Av *DTN/ASHW* M34...29 P7
POY/DIS SK12......72 C2
West Park Dr *GTS/LS* CH66....102 B4
West Park Rd *BRAM/HZG* SK7....42 A6
STKP SK1......42 A6
West Pl *BNG/LEV* M19......40 G1
West Quay Rd
WARRN/WOL WA2......33 J3
Westres *NWCHW* CW8......107 P7
West Rd *ALT* WA14......52 C5
CONG CW12......155 K7
EP CH65......102 E1
NWCHW CW8......108 D4
RUNC WA7......61 K7
West Side *STHEL* WA9......22 A7
West Side Av *RNFD/HAY* WA11...22 E3
West St *ALS/KID* ST7......189 K2
CHNE CH2......121 P8
CONG CW12......155 L7
CW/HAS CW1......11 L4
CW/HAS CW1......186 A3
CW/SHV CW2......184 G4
EDGY/DAV SK3......16 C5
MCFLDS SK11......116 A3
MWCH CW10......151 J1
WARRN/WOL WA2......18 E1
WILM/AE SK9......92 F5
Westune *WHITCH* SY13......213 L7
West V *NSTN* CH64......77 L7
West Vale Rd
HALE/TIMP WA15......53 K2
West Vw *WARRN/WOL* WA2......34 B7
WILM/AE SK9......70 G7
West View Rd
FROD/HEL WA6......107 L6
WYTH/NTH M22......39 P8
Westville Dr *MCFLDS* SK11......155 J8
Westville Gdns *BNG/LEV* M19....40 F3
Westward Rd *CHSE* CH3......143 J2
WILM/AE SK9......70 G7
West Wy *CW/SHV* CW2......198 C2
Westway *DROY* M43......28 D2
West Wy *HOLMCH* CW4......131 N8
RUNC WA7 *......62 A7
SBCH CW11......171 L5
Westwood *RUNC* WA7 *......62 A7
Westwood Av
HALE/TIMP WA15......38 D7
Westwood Ct *NSTN* CH64......77 L3
Westwood Dr *SALE* M33......38 L5
Westwood Rd *CHD/CHDH* SK8....55 P7
Westy La *WARRS* WA4......48 G3
Wet Gate La *LYMM* WA13......51 K3
Wetherall St *BNG/LEV* M19......28 B8
Wetheral Rd *MCFLDN* SK10......117 H2
Wetherby Cl *CH/BCN* CH1......2 A2
NEWLW WA12......23 N4
NEWUL ST5......201 P8
Wetherby Dr *BRAM/HZG* SK7 *...57 N5
Wetherby St *OP/CLY* M11......28 E2
Wetherby Wy *GTS/LS* CH66......79 K6
Wetreins La *CHSE* CH3......177 K9
Wetterhald Rd *NANT* CW5......183 L7
Weston La *NWCHW* CW8......86 A8
Wexford Av *SPK/HALE* L24......60 A5
Weybourne Cl *CHSW/BR* CH4 *...142 A5
Weybourne Dr *MPL/ROM* SK6....58 C1
Weybridge Cl *WARRS* WA4......48 G8
Weybridge Dr *MCFLDN* SK10...117 H1
Weybrook Rd *HTNM* SK4......41 J1
Wey Gates Dr *HALE/TIMP* WA15...53 N9
Weyhill Rd *NTHM/RTH* M23......54 C3
Weymouth Cl *STHEL* WA9......22 C8
Weymouth Cl *RUNC* WA7......63 J8
Weymouth Rd
WARRN/BUR WA5......32 C2
Whaddon Dr *CHSW/BR* CH4....142 B6
Whaley La *WHITCH* SY13......75 N5
Whalley Av *BNG/LEV* M19......28 B7
CCHDY M21......39 M1
GOL/RIS/CU WA3......24 C5
SALE M33......38 F3
Whalley Cl *HALE/TIMP* WA15....38 C8
Whalley Gv *WDN* WA8......46 B4
Whalley Hayes *MCFLDN* SK10....8 D3
Whalley Rd *HALE/TIMP* WA15...53 L5
NWCHE CW9......110 E6
OFTN SK2......57 N1
Whalley St *WARR* WA1......19 J4
Wharams Bnk *SBCH* CW11......173 J4
The Wharfage *WHITCH* SY13...213 M6
Wharfdale Av *CW/HAS* CW1....170 A8
Wharfdale Cl
WARRW/BUR WA5......32 B8
Wharfe Cl *CONG* CW12......155 P9
Wharfedale *RUNC* WA7......62 F8
Wharfedale Cl *RAIN/WH* L35....30 A7
Wharfedale Rd *CONG* CW12....155 M4
RDSH SK5......28 C6
Wharf La *CW/SHV* CW2......198 C2
Wharfe La *CONG* CW12......155 N6
Wharford La *RUNC* WA7......63 J3
Wharf Rd *ALT* WA14......53 H2
BIDD ST8......175 K9

NEWLW WA12 ....23 J7
SALE M33 ....38 F3
Wharfside Ct WARRS WA4 ....48 F3
Wharf St HTNM SK4 ....17 F1
  WARR WA1 ....19 H7
The Wharf CW/HAS CW1 * 5 G2
Wharmby Rd RNFD/HAY WA11 ....23 J5
Wharton Av CCHDY M21 ....39 N1
Wharton Dr WSFD CW7 ....129 H7
Wharton Gdns WSFD CW7 ....129 H8
Wharton Park Rd WSFD CW7 ....128 G9
  WSFD CW7 ....129 H8
Wharton Rd WSFD CW7 ....149 P1
Whatcroft Cl RUNC WA7 ....62 B8
Whatcroft La NWCHE CW9 ....129 M2
Wheat Cr EDGY/DAV SK3 ....56 F2
  WARRW/BUR WA5 * 47 N1
Wheatfield Cl GTS/LS CH66 ....101 N1
  MPL/ROM SK6 ....42 F4
Wheatfield Rd WDN WA8 ....43 J2
Wheatland Cl STHEL WA9 ....31 H4
Wheatlands RUNC WA7 ....62 C5
Wheatley Av NEWLW WA12 ....23 N4
Wheatley Rd CW/HAS CW1 ....185 L2
Wheat Moss MCFLDS SK11 ....114 D1
Wheatsheaf Av STHEL WA9 ....32 A2
Wheatsheaf Dr WISTASTON K13 ....213 L7
Wheatsheaf La NWCHE CW9 ....87 K2
Wheelman Rd CW/HAS CW1 ....184 G1
Wheelock Cl ALS/KID ST7 ....187 L5
  WILM/AE SK9 ....45 J5
Wheelock Dr WSFD CW7 ....71 B5
Wheelock St MWCH CW10 ....151 J1
Wheelock Wy ALS/KID ST7 * 189 K6
Whelan Gdns STHEL WA9 ....30 D2
Wheldon Cl CHNE CW2 ....121 P3
Wheldrake Cl GTS/LS CH66 ....78 B7
Whelier St OP/CLY M11 ....28 D1
Whernside WA6 ....45 J5
Whernside Cl HTNM SK4 ....17 F2
Whetmorhurst Rd
  NEWLW WA12 ....59 J3
Whetstone Hey GTS/LS CH66 ....79 P8
Whetstone Rd BIDD ST8 ....175 K1
Whickham Cl WA6 ....45 M4
Whimbrel Av NEWLW WA12 ....23 N6
Whimbrel Cl RUNC WA7 ....62 D7
Whimbrel Rd OFTN SK2 ....57 N2
Whinberry Rd ALT WA14 ....37 N9
Whinbury Ct STHEL WA9 ....31 H5
Whinchat Av NEWLW WA12 ....23 N5
Whinchat Gv GOL/RIS/CU WA3 ....24 C2
  OFTN SK2 ....57 N3
Whinchat Dr GOL/RIS/CU WA3 ....24 C9
Whinfell Gv RUNC WA7 ....62 C9
Whipcord La CH/BCN CH1 ....2 A2
Whitley Cl HTNM SK4 ....41 L3
  MWCH CW10 ....151 J3
Whiston Cl KNUT WA16 ....67 J2
  WSFD CW7 ....129 H7
Whiston St MCFLDS SK11 ....8 C5
Whitbarrow Rd LYMM WA13 ....50 C3
Whitbread Dr BIDD 175 M9
Whitbread Rd RTHM/RTH M23 ....14 C3
Whitby Av CHNE CH2 ....121 N6
  WARRN/WOL WA2 ....33 N6
Whitby Cl CHD/CHDH SK8 ....55 L1
  CW/HAS WA4 ....170 A9
  POY/DIS SK12 ....73 J1
Whitby La CH/BCN CH1 ....102 C5
  EP CH65 ....6 D6
  RUNC WA7 ....15 F5
Whitby's La WSFD CW7 ....149 K1
Whitchurch Cl WARR WA1 ....34 A8
Whitchurch Gv NEWUL ST5 ....201 P5
Whitchurch Rd
  AUD/MAD/W CW3 ....216 B2
  CHSE CH3 ....143 L2
  CHSE CH3 ....163 L9
  CHSE CH3 ....178 G9
  DID/WITH M20 ....40 A1
  MALPAS SY14 ....192 C7
  WHITCH SY13 ....207 K9
Whitchurch Wy RUNC WA7 ....62 B8
White Av CW/SHV CW2 ....184 F4
White Bank Rd RDSH SK5 ....42 B9
Whitebarn Rd WILM/AE SK9 ....93 K5
Whitebeam Cl GTS/LS CH66 ....102 B3
Whitebeam Cl
  HALE/TIMP WA15 ....54 A2
  RUNC WA7 ....71 B5
Whitebeam Gdns STHEL WA9 ....30 B2
White Bear Yd KNUT WA16 * 90 E5
White Broom LYMM WA13 ....51 H5
  HALE/TIMP WA15 ....53 P4
Whitechapel St DID/WITH M20 ....40 C5
Whitecroft Gdns BNG/LEV M19 ....40 F4
Whitecroft Heath Rd
  MCFLDS SK11 ....114 D9
Whitecroft Rd GTS/LS CH66 ....102 A2
  MPL/ROM SK6 ....58 C5
Whitecross Rd
  WARRW/BUR WA5 ....48 A2
  LYMM WA13 * 50 C3
Whitefield HTNM SK4 ....41 L5
Whitefield Cl LYMM WA13 ....50 C3
  CH/BCN CH1 ....101 K9
Whitefield La RAIN/WH L35 ....36 E8
Whitefield Rd MPL/ROM SK6 ....42 D4
  WARRS WA4 ....48 D7
Whitefields CHNE CW2 ....104 B1
White Friars CH/BCN CH1 ....2 D5
Whitegate Av GOL/RIS/CU WA3 ....25 P7
Whitegate Cl NWCHW CW10 ....151 J4
Whitegate Flds WRXS/E LL15 ....176 F7
Whitegate La CHSE CH3 ....124 D4
Whitegate Rd WSFD CW7 ....128 A7

Whitegates Cl
  HALE/TIMP WA15 ....53 M2
  NSTN CH64 ....78 C4
Whitegates Crs NSTN CH64 ....78 C5
Whitegates Rd CHD/CHDH SK8 ....55 M2
  NWCHW CW8 ....126 C1
Whitehall Av ALS/KID ST7 ....189 H6
Whitehall Cl NWCHW CW8 ....87 J9
  WILM/AE SK9 ....71 J9
Whitehall Dr NWCHW CW8 ....29 M4
White Hall La SBCH CW11 ....151 L9
Whitehall La TPLY/KEL CW6 ....147 P2
Whitehall Rd PROD/HEL WA6 ....83 P5
White Hall Rd ALS/KID ST7 ....189 H6
Whitehall Rd DID/WITH M20 ....40 D5
  SALE M33 ....38 E6
White Hart Gdns NWCHW CW8 ....109 H8
White Hart La NWCHW CW8 ....184 E8
Whitehaven Gdns
  DID/WITH M20 ....40 B6
Whitehaven La NANT CW5 ....182 C9
Whitehaven Rd
  BRAM/HZG SK7 ....72 C1
Whitehill Rd ALS/KID ST7 ....189 K6
Whitehill St HTNM SK4 ....41 M4
Whitehill St West HTNM SK4 ....41 L4
Whiteholme Av CCHDY M21 ....39 M2
White House Cl
  RNFD/HAY WA11 ....29 N4
Whitehouse Dr
  HALE/TIMP WA15 ....53 M7
  NTHM/RTH M23 ....54 C2
White House Dr WARR WA1 ....34 F9
Whitehouse Gn RUNC WA7 ....62 D9
Whitehouse La ALT WA14 ....37 J9
  KNUT WA16 ....89 L8
  NANT CW5 ....10 E2
Whitehouse Rd KNUT WA16 ....67 P3
Whitehouse V RUNC WA7 * 63 K9
Whitehurst Rd HTNM SK4 ....40 G4
White La CHSE CH3 ....143 M2
Whitelea Dr EDGY/DAV SK3 ....56 D2
Whiteleas Rd CHF/WBR SK23 ....97 P3
Whiteleggs La LYMM WA13 ....50 G6
Whitelley Pl ALT WA14 ....53 H1
White Lodge Ms
  NWCHW CW8 ....108 C9
Whitelow Rd HTNM SK4 ....41 H5
Whitemead St DTN/ASHW M34 ....29 M2
Whitemere Rd MWCH CW10 ....151 J4
White Park Cl MWCH CW10 ....130 C9
Whiteridge Rd ALS/KID ST7 ....189 J6
White Rd NM/HAY SK22 ....59 N6
Whitesands Rd LYMM WA13 ....50 C3
Whiteside Av RNFD/HAY WA11 ....22 C4
Whiteside Rd RNFD/HAY WA11 ....22 C4
Whites La CW/SHV CW2 ....198 C1
Whitesmead Ct POY/DIS SK12 ....75 H1
White Meadow CHSE CH3 ....143 J3
White St MCFLDS SK11 ....117 K6
  WARR WA1 ....16 E2
  WARRS WA4 ....48 E6
  WDN WA8 * 61 N1
  BNG/LEV M19 ....40 D7
  WARRW/BUR WA5 ....47 K2
Whitethorn Cl NWCHW CW8 ....108 C9
Whitethorn Wy NEWLW ST5 ....201 P6
Whitethroat Cl NANT CW5 ....10 C5
Whitewell Rd WHITCH SY13 ....212 B6
Whitewood La MALPAS SY14 ....191 L9
Whitfield Av WARR WA1 ....34 A8
Whitfield Rd ALS/KID ST7 ....189 K6
  CHSE CH3 ....143 K4
The Whitfields MCFLDN SK10 ....116 C3
Whitfield Rd NM/HAY SK22 ....59 N6
Whitley Av NWCHW CW8 ....109 J1
  WARRS WA4 ....49 J3
Whitley Cl MWCH CW10 ....151 H3
  RUNC WA7 ....14 D3
Whitley Gdns
  HALE/TIMP WA15 ....38 E9
Whitley La KNUT WA16 ....66 G7
Whitley Pl HALE/TIMP WA15 ....38 E9
  HALE/TIMP WA15 ....41 J5
Whitlow Av ALT WA14 ....37 N8
  WARRS WA4 ....196 G5
Whitlow La NWCHE CW9 ....128 C5
Whitmoor Cl RAIN/WH L35 ....30 D7
Whitney Cft MCFLDN SK10 ....117 N4
Whitsand Rd WYTH/NTH M22 ....54 C2
Whitsbury Av GTN M18 ....28 C6
Whitson Cl KNUT WA16 ....67 J2
Whitstable Pk WDN WA8 ....45 L3
Whittaker Av
  WARRN/WOL WA2 ....33 N6
Whittaker Cl CW/HAS CW1 ....184 G1
Whittington Gdns
  WARRW/BUR WA5 ....47 L2
Whittle Av RNFD/HAY WA11 ....22 E4
  WARRW/BUR WA5 ....47 L2
Whittle Hall La
  WARRW/BUR WA5 ....47 K1
Whittles Av DTN/ASHW M34 ....29 N6
Whittlewood Cl
  GOL/RIS/CU WA3 ....35 H3
Whitton Dr CHNE CH2 ....121 P6
Whitwell Cl WARRW/BUR WA5 ....32 A8
Whitwell Wy GTN M18 ....28 C4
Whitworth Cl GOL/RIS/CU WA3 ....34 F5
Whitworth St East OP/CLY M11 ....28 C2
Wickenby Dr SALE M33 ....38 D4
Wicken St OFTN SK2 ....42 B9
Wicker La CHSE CH3 ....123 H7
  HALE/TIMP WA15 ....53 M7
Wicklow Av EDGY/DAV SK3 ....56 D2
Wicklow Cl GTS/LS CH66 ....79 L7
Wicklow Dr WYTH/NTH M22 ....54 C5
Wickson La CHSE CH3 ....165 J6
Wickstead Av NANT CW5 ....11 G7

Wicksten Dr RUNC WA7 ....15 J5
Widdale Av RAIN/WH L35 * 30 C5
Widdale Cl WARRW/BUR WA5 ....32 C9
Widgeon Cl POY/DIS SK12 ....73 H2
Widgeon Rd ALT WA14 ....37 N8
Widnes Rd WARRW/BUR WA5 ....46 G4
  WDN WA8 ....21 J3
Widnes St OP/CLY M11 * 28 C2
The Wiend CHNE CH2 ....121 N7
The Wigdale CD CW5 ....140 A2
Wight Cl EP CH65 ....6 E4
Wightman Av NEWLW WA12 ....23 N4
Wigmore Cl GTS/LS/CU WA3 ....35 H2
Wigsey La LYMM WA13 ....35 M9
Wigshaw La GOL/RIS/CU WA3 ....25 N6
Wigwam Ct POY/DIS SK12 ....73 J2
Wilbraham Cl NANT CW5 ....183 J9
Wilbraham Rd CONG CW12 ....155 P7
  NANT CW5 ....183 J9
  NANT CW5 ....108 G3
Wilbraham St STHEL WA9 ....31 K5
Wilbraham's Wk ALS/KID ST7 ....200 C5
Wilbrahams Wy ALS/KID ST7 ....187 G4
Wilbur St STHEL WA9 ....31 K1
Wilcock Rd RNFD/HAY WA11 ....23 L1
Wilcote Cl WDN WA8 ....46 A3
Wilcott Dr SALE M33 ....38 B5
  WILM/AE SK9 ....93 H1
Wilcott Rd CHD/CHDH SK8 ....55 H5
Wild Arum Cl NWCHW CW8 ....24 C1
Wildcherry Gdns STHEL 30 A1
Wilderhope Cl CW/SHV CW2 ....185 J9
Wilderspool Cswy WARRS WA4 ....48 D4
Wilderswood Cl DID/WITH M20 ....40 D5
Wilde St DTN/ASHW M34 ....29 M6
Wild Goose Av ALS/KID ST7 ....189 M5
Wilding Av RUNC WA7 ....15 H2
Wildings Old La
  GOL/RIS/CU WA3 ....25 J9
Wildmoor Av CHSE CH3 ....123 L2
Wild St BRAM/HZG SK7 ....57 K5
  MPL/ROM SK6 ....42 E6
Wildwood Gv WARR WA1 ....34 C9
Wilford Av SALE M33 ....38 D6
Wild Cl CHD/CHDH SK8 ....55 M5
Wilkins La WILM/AE SK9 ....70 G1
Wilkinson Av WARR WA1 ....49 H1
Wilkinson Rd HTNM SK4 ....16 E2
Wilkinson St HTNM SK4 ....16 E2
  SALE M33 ....38 G4
  WARRN/WOL WA2 ....2 D1
Wilkinson Street Ms EP CH65 ....6 E2
Wilkinson St North EP CH65 ....6 E2
Wilks Av WYTH/NTH M22 ....55 H5
Willan Rd CH/BCN CH1 ....120 C7
Willard St BRAM/HZG SK7 * 57 K4
Willaston Cl CCHDY M21 ....39 M3
Willaston Hall Gdns NANT CW5 ....197 K1
Willaston La DROY M43 ....28 D5
Willbank La NANT CW5 ....194 C2
Willder Gv EDGY/DAV SK3 ....56 B1
Willenhall Rd NTHM/RTH M23 ....36 M6
Willerby Cl MCFLDN SK10 ....8 C5
Willeymoor La WHITCH SY13 ....205 J7
William Penn Cl
  WARRW/BUR WA5 ....47 J3
William Rd ALS/KID ST7 ....189 J6
  RNFD/HAY WA11 ....22 D4
Williams Av NEWLW WA12 ....23 N4
Williams Cl CHNE CH2 ....121 M7
Williamson Crs CHF/WBR SK23 ....75 P6
Williamson La DROY M43 ....29 H1
Williamson Rd CHF/WBR SK23 ....75 P6
Williams Rd GTN M18 ....28 C5
Williams Rd RDSH SK5 ....41 N1
Williams St CHNE CH2 ....2 C2
  CONG CW12 ....156 A2
  DID/WITH M20 ....40 B6
  MCFLDN SK10 ....9 J4
  NWCHE CW9 ....13 K2
  STKP SK1 ....42 A9
  WDN WA8 ....A5
Williams Wy MCFLDS SK11 ....116 C4
Willington Av PS/BROM L62 ....75 J9
  TPLY/KEL CW6 ....125 J7
Willington La NWCHE CW9 ....85 G4
Willington Rd CHSE CH3 ....125 J8
  TPLY/KEL CW6 ....125 J8
Willink Rd RNFD/HAY WA11 ....22 A2
Willis Rd EDGY/DAV SK3 ....56 E1
Willis St WARR WA1 ....19 H3
Willmer Crs ALS/KID ST7 ....189 K2
Willotts Hill Rd NEWUL ST5 ....201 N6
Willoughby Av DID/WITH M20 ....40 B4
Willoughby Cl SALE M33 ....39 D5
  WARRW/BUR WA5 ....32 F7
Willoughby St BURS/TUN ST6 * 189 M9
Willow Av CHD/CHDH SK8 ....55 P5
  NEWLW WA12 ....23 P5
  RDSH SK5 ....41 N9
  WDN WA8 ....45 P5
Willow Bank Cl OFTN SK2 ....42 G9
Willowbank Dr MCFLDN SK10 ....96 A4
Willow Bank Est NEWLW WA12 ....24 B6
Willowbrow Rd BEB L63 ....78 B2
Willow Cl ALS/KID ST7 ....188 D6
  CHNE CH2 ....121 N3
  POY/DIS SK12 ....73 J3
  RUNC WA7 ....61 J7
  WSFD CW7 ....128 E8
Winchester Cl CW/SHV CW2 ....198 A4

MWCH CW10 ....130 B9
  NANT CW5 ....10 E2
  SALE M33 ....39 H3
Willow Crs CHNE CH2 ....122 E6
  CW/SHV CW2 ....198 A4
  WARR WA1 ....34 C8
  WARRS WA4 ....47 L8
Willowcroft Wy ALS/KID ST7 ....189 N4
Willowdale NEWLW WA12 ....24 A6
Willowdale Av CHD/CHDH SK8 ....55 K5
Willowdale Wy GTS/LS CH66 ....102 A2
Willow Dr CH/BCN CH1 ....120 G6
  SBCH CW11 ....172 B2
  TPLY/KEL CW6 ....166 B9
  WARRS WA4 ....48 F6
  WILM/AE SK9 ....71 M3
Willow Fold DROY M43 * 29 H1
Willow Gn KNUT WA16 ....90 D2
  NWCHW CW8 ....108 G3
Willowgreen La NWCHW CW8 ....86 D8
Willow Lawn CHD/CHDH SK8 * 56 A5
Willow Lea CH/BCN CH1 ....121 J1
Willowmead Dr MCFLDN SK10 ....96 G8
Willow Rd CHSW/BR CH4 ....142 B4
  MPL/ROM SK6 ....58 D8
  NEWLW WA12 ....36 D6
  PART M31 ....36 D5
Willows Cl CW/SHV CW2 ....185 J9
Willow Sq WSFD CW7 ....71 B5
The Willows CCHDY M21 ....39 K1
  FROD/HEL WA6 ....84 A5
  NWCHE CW9 ....88 F8
  PART M31 ....36 E5
  SBCH CW11 ....171 N2
  STHEL WA9 ....31 K5
  WARRW/BUR WA5 ....47 K2
Willow St CW12 ....155 N7
Willow Tree Av STHEL WA9 ....31 J4
Willow Tree Gv ALS/KID ST7 * 188 B1
Willow Tree Ms CHD/CHDH SK8 ....55 J5
Willow Tree Rd ALT WA14 ....53 H5
Willow Wy BRAM/HZG SK7 ....58 A2
  CHSW/BR CH4 ....140 F7
  DID/WITH M20 ....40 D3
  MCFLDN SK10 ....94 D8
Wilmere La WDN WA8 ....45 N1
Wilmot Av WARRW/BUR WA5 ....47 K1
Wilmot Dr GOL/RIS/CU WA3 ....24 C9
Wilmslow Crs WARRS WA4 ....49 M4
Wilmslow Dr GTS/LS CH66 ....80 A8
Wilmslow Old Rd
  HALE/TIMP WA15 ....54 B9
  MCFLDN SK10 ....55 N6
Wilmslow Park Rd WILM/AE SK9 ....71 L7
Wilmslow Rd BRAM/HZG SK7 ....58 A2
  DID/WITH M20 ....40 D7
  HALE/TIMP WA15 ....54 B8
  MCFLDN SK10 ....72 C8
  WILM/AE SK9 ....93 J3
Wilmslow Wk MCFLDS SK11 ....9 H6
Wilpshire Av WGTN/LGST M12 ....28 B6
Wilsbury Gra NWCHW CW8 ....109 J7
Wilsden Rd WDN WA8 ....45 M6
Wilson Av WARRS WA4 ....49 M4
Wilson Crs NWCHE CW9 ....111 H1
Wilson Dr NWCHE CW9 ....128 C4
Wilson La GOL/RIS/CU WA3 ....24 G8
Wilson Patten St WARR WA1 ....18 B7
Wilson Rd HTNM SK4 ....41 H5
Wilson St OP/CLY M11 ....28 A1
  WARRW/BUR WA5 ....47 L8
Wilsthorpe Cl BRKG/LEV M19 ....41 K2
Wilton Av CHD/CHDH SK8 ....55 J5
Wilton Ct DTN/ASHW M34 ....28 G5
Wilton Dr HALE/TIMP WA15 ....53 H7
Wilton Gv DTN/ASHW M34 ....28 G5
Wilton Paddock
  DTN/ASHW M34 ....28 G5
Wiltshire Av RDSH SK5 ....42 B4
Wiltshire Cl MCFLDN SK10 ....116 E2
Wiltshire Rd PART M31 ....36 D6
  WARRW/BUR WA5 ....47 N1
Wilwick La MCFLDS SK11 ....115 M8
Wimberry Dr NEWUL ST5 ....201 N6
  RUNC WA7 ....10 E3
Wimbledon Dr EDGY/DAV SK3 ....56 C3
Wimborne Cl CHD/CHDH SK8 ....56 C3
Wimpory St OP/CLY M11 ....28 C1
Wimbolt St OFTN SK2 ....57 J3
Wincanton Av NTHM/RTH M23 ....54 B1
Wincham Av NWCHE CW9 ....110 D1
Wincham La NWCHE CW9 ....110 D1
Wincanton Av DTN/ASHW M34 ....29 M8
  EP CH65 ....7 H7
  WARRW/BUR WA5 ....47 N2
Winchester Cl CW/SHV CW2 ....198 A4

WILM/AE SK9 ....70 G9
Winchester Dr HTNM SK4 ....41 J6
  MCFLDN SK10 ....116 F4
  SALE M33 ....38 A4
Winchester Pk DID/WITH M20 ....40 A8
Winchester Pl WDN WA8 ....45 J7
Winchester Rd
  HALE/TIMP WA15 ....53 M7
Winchester Sq CHSW/BR CH4 ....142 B6
Wincle Av POY/DIS SK12 ....73 M4
Windermere Av CHNE CH2 ....122 B5
  MCFLDN SK10 ....28 C7
  SALE M33 ....33 M5
  WARRN/WOL WA2 ....33 M5
  WDN WA8 ....21 L2
Windermere Cl NSTN CH64 ....77 M6
  OP/CLY M11 ....28 A1
Windermere Dr CONG CW12 ....155 J8
  WILM/AE SK9 ....93 H4
Windermere Rd CW/SHV CW2 ....184 E6
  EP CH65 ....102 E2
  MPL/ROM SK6 ....58 B6
  RNFD/HAY WA11 ....22 F3
  STKP SK1 ....42 A9
  WILM/AE SK9 ....93 H4
  WSFD CW7 ....128 D9
Windermere St WDN WA8 ....45 J3
Windfield Gdns GTS/LS CH66 ....79 P6
Windfields Cl CHD/CHDH SK8 ....56 B6
The Windings MWCH CW10 ....130 K9
Windle Ct CHD/CHDH SK8 ....34 D4
  NSTN CH64 ....77 L2
  OFTN SK2 ....57 L2
Windlehurst Old Rd
  MPL/ROM SK6 ....58 D5
Windlehurst Rd MCFLDN SK10 ....58 D5
  MPL/ROM SK6 ....58 D5
Windmill Av ALS/KID ST7 ....189 J8
  DTN/ASHW M34 ....29 H7
  WARRS WA4 ....48 E3
Windmill Dr
  AUD/MAD/W CW3 ....216 G2
Windmill Gdns STHEL WA9 ....22 B5
Windmill Hill Av RNFD/HAY WA7 ....63 H4
Windmill Hill Av East
  RUNC WA7 ....63 H6
Windmill Hill Av North
  RUNC WA7 ....62 G3
Windmill Hill Av South
  RUNC WA7 ....63 H5
Windmill Hill Av West
  RUNC WA7 ....62 G4
Windmill La AUD/MAD/W CW3 ....209 M9
  DTN/ASHW M34 ....28 C7
  MCFLDN SK10 ....95 P7
  RDSH SK5 ....28 C7
  WARRS WA4 ....48 E9
  WARRS WA4 ....63 L7
  WARRW/BUR WA5 ....47 J2
Windmill Ri CHNE CH2 ....121 N4
Windmill Rd SALE M33 * 39 J5
Windmill St RUNC WA7 ....15 H2
Windscale Rd
  WARRN/WOL WA2 ....34 B6
Windsor Av CHD/CHDH SK8 ....55 H2
  CW/HAS CW1 ....184 C1
  HTNM SK4 ....27 P6
  IRL M44 ....36 C4
  NANT CW5 ....196 G4
  NEWLW WA12 ....23 P7
  SALE M33 ....38 F4
  TPLY/KEL CW6 ....147 H9
  WILM/AE SK9 ....71 H8
Windsor Dr MCFLDN SK10 ....95 L7
  NWCHW CW8 ....108 B8
  POY/DIS SK12 ....73 K2
Windsor Ct WARRS WA4 * 48 G3
Windsor Gv ALS/KID ST7 ....187 K4
  ALT WA14 ....52 D6
  CHSW/BR CH4 ....140 E7
  EP CH65 ....102 C1
  MPL/ROM SK6 ....58 A2
  RNFD/HAY WA11 ....23 L2
  WARRS WA4 ....49 K4
  WSFD CW7 ....149 L5
Windsor Gv CHD/CHDH SK8 ....55 P7
  MPL/ROM SK6 ....43 K6
Windsor Pl CONG CW12 ....155 P9
Windsor Rd BRAM/HZG SK7 ....57 M5
  CHSW/BR CH4 ....142 B4
  CW/SHV CW2 ....184 E6
  DTN/ASHW M34 ....28 C6
  GOL/RIS/CU WA3 ....24 E1
  HYDE SK14 ....43 J1
  MPL/ROM SK6 ....42 B5
  WDN WA8 ....45 N3
Windsor Sq MCFLDS SK11 ....117 K8
Windsor St GTN M18 ....28 C5
  STKP SK1 ....56 C1
  WARRW/BUR WA5 ....47 L8
Windsor Wy KNUT WA16 ....90 D5
Windways GTS/LS CH66 ....79 P6
Windy Bank Av
  GOL/RIS/CU WA3 ....24 G1
Winfield Av DID/WITH M20 ....40 C5
Winfield St RUNC WA7 ....63 L6
Winfrith Av WARRN/WOL WA2 ....34 B7
Winfrith Rd WDN WA8 ....21 K2
Wingate Av STHEL WA9 ....30 C2
Wingate Dr DID/WITH M20 ....40 D6
  HALE/TIMP WA15 ....53 P6
Wingate Rd HTNM SK4 ....41 K4
  WDN WA8 ....21 L3
Wingfield Cl MCFLDN SK10 ....8 C1
Wingfield Dr WILM/AE SK9 ....71 G8
Winghay Rd ALS/KID ST7 ....189 K6
Winhill Rd NM/HAY SK22 ....59 N6
Winifred Rd DID/WITH M20 ....40 C5
  OFTN SK2 ....56 G2

Winifred St HYDE SK14.....43 K1
  WARRN/WOL WA2 ....19 F2
Winkwell St CHSW/BR CH4 ....142 C5
Winmarith Dr HALE/TIMP WA15 ..53 P8
Winmarleigh St WARR WA1 ....18 B6
Winning Hill Cl GTN CW8 ...28 D5
Winnington Av NWCHW CW8 ...109 L4
Winnington Gn OFTN SK2 ......57 K2
Winnington Hl NWCHW CW8 ....12 D1
  NWCHW CW8 ....12 D1
Winnington Rd MPL/ROM SK6 ...43 L8
Winnington St NWCHW CW8 ....12 D1
  WSFD CW7 ....149 N1
The Winnows DTN/ASHW M34 ...29 K6
  RUNC WA7 ....62 B5
Winscombe Dr CHSE CH3........122 D9
Winsfield Rd SALE M33 ....57 K7
Winsford Cl RNFD/HAY WA11 ...23 K2
Winsford Dr WARRW/BUR WA5 ..32 B1
Winsford Gv GTS/LS CH66 ....110 E1
Winsford Rd WSFD CW7 ....168 A5
Winsford Wy CH/BCN CH1 .....121 J9
Winskill Rd IRL M44 ....27 N9
Winslade Cl BRAM/HZG SK7 ....56 C5
Winsley Rd NTHM/RTH M23....39 J6
Winslow Av RDSH SK5.........55 L6
Winslow Cl RUNC WA7........63 H6
Winslow Pl EDGY/DAV SK3 ......40 C2
Winslow St OP/CLY M11......39 L3
Winstanley Cl
  WARRW/BUR WA5 ....47 N2
Winstanley Rd NSTN CH64 .....77 L8
  SALE M33 ....38 D6
Winster Av DID/WITH M20 ....39 P4
Winster Dr NTHLY L27.........44 A4
Winster Gv OFTN SK2 ....56 C1
Winston Av ALS/KID ST7 ......187 N4
  NEWLW WA12 ....23 J6
  STHEL WA9 ....57 F3
Winston Cl MPL/ROM SK6 .....43 J9
Winston Rd SALE M33.........38 C5
Winterbottom La KNUT WA16...67 K7
Winterburn Av CCHDY M21....39 M4
Winterburn Gn OFTN SK2 .....57 L2
Winterford La TPLY/KEL CW6 ..147 M7
Winter Gv STHEL WA9.........22 F6
Wintertea Dr HLWD L26 ......44 A9
Wintermans Rd CCHDY M21 ...39 N2
Winterside Cl NEWLU ST5......201 N6
Winterslow Av NTHM/RTH M23 ..38 C7
Winterton Rd RDSH SK5......28 D8
Winterton Wy MCFLDS SK11 ...117 J9
Winton Av DTN/ASHW M34 ....29 K2
Winton Cl BRAM/HZG SK7 ....56 C6
Winton Gv RUNC WA7 * 63 H5
Winton Rd ALT WA14 ....52 C5
  GOL/RIS/CU WA3 ....24 C4
Winwick Link Rd
  WARRN/WOL WA2 ....33 L2
Winwick Park Av
  WARRN/WOL WA2 ....33 K3
Winwick Rd NEWLW WA12......24 B8
  WARRN/WOL WA2 ....18 D5
Winwick St WARR WA1 ....18 D5
Winwick Vw
  WARRW/BUR WA5 ....23 H8
Winwood Rd DID/WITH M20 ...40 D8
Wirksmoor Rd NM/HAY SK22 ..59 M8
Wirral Cl GOL/RIS/CU WA3 .....41 H8
Wirral Crs EDGY/DAV SK3 ......41 H8
  NSTN CH64 ....77 M8
  NSTN CH64 ....76 C2
Wirswall Rd WHITCH SY13 ....205 P6
Wisbech Dr NTHM/RTH M23 ...39 J7
Wisenholme Cl RUNC WA7....64 C7
Wishaw Sq CCHDY M21 ......39 P2
Wisley Cl RDSH SK5 ....28 F9
Wistaria Rd GTN M18 ....28 D4
Wistaston Av CW/SHV CW2 ...184 F6
Wistaston Green Cl
  CW/SHV CW2 ....184 D6
Wistaston Green Rd
  CW/SHV CW2 ....184 D6
Wistaston Pk CW/SHV CW2 ...184 F7
Wistaston Rd CW/SHV CW2 ....4 C4
  NANT CW5 ....197 M2
Wisterdale Cl CW/SHV CW2 ...184 C9
Witham Av WYTH/NTH M22 ...54 G2
Witham Cl CW/SHV CW2 ......184 C8
Witham Wy BIDD ST8.........175 M8
Withenfield Rd
  NTHM M23 ....39 J8
Withens Cl NWCHW CW8 ......108 F4
Withens Gn OFTN SK2 ....57 L2
Withenshaw La MCFLDS SK11 ..137 J6
Withens La NWCHW CW8 ......108 F4
Withers Av WARRN/WOL WA2 ..33 N8
Wither's La KNUT WA16 ......66 C1
Witherwin Av WARRS WA4 ....49 J8
Withington Av
  GOL/RIS/CU WA3 ....26 A5
Withington Cl NWCHW CW8 ...13 G7
  SBCH CW11 ....171 P2
Withinlee Rd MCFLDS SK11 ....94 C7
Withins Rd GOL/RIS/CU WA3 ...25 J1
  RNFD/HAY WA11 ....25 J1
Within Wy SPK/HALE L24 ......60 E5
Withnall Dr CW/SHV CW2 .....198 A3
Withnell Rd DID/WITH M20....40 E5
Withy Cl FROD/HEL WA6......84 A5
withycombe Rd
  WARRW/BUR WA5 ....47 J5
Withy Cft CHSE CH3 ....143 K3
Withyfold Dr MCFLDN SK10 ....9 G1
Withypool Dr OFTN SK2 ......57 H2
Withy Tree Gv
  DTN/ASHW M34 * 29 N7
Witley Dr SALE M33 ....38 A2
Witney Gdns WARRS WA4 ....49 H9
Witney La MALPAS SY14 ......192 C8
Wittenbury Rd HTNM SK4 ....41 J6
Witton St NWCHE CW9 ....13 G1
Witton Wk NWCHE CW9 ......13 F2
Witt Rd WDN WA8 ....21 G5

Wivern Pl RUNC WA7........15 H1
Woburn Av NEWLW WA12 ....23 P7
Woburn Cl MCFLDN SK10 .....117 J2
  NWCHE CW9 ....109 N7
  RNFD/HAY WA11 ....23 K2
Woburn Dr CHNE CH2.........122 A4
  CONG CW12 ....175 J1
  HALE/TIMP WA15 ....53 M5
  WDN WA8 ....45 K2
Woburn Rd WARRN/WOL WA2 ..33 K4
Woking Rd CHD/CHDH SK8 ....56 A9
Wold Ct CO CH5 ....140 A2
Wolfe Cl KNUT WA16.........90 C1
  WARRS WA4 ....49 J7
Wolseley Pl DID/WITH M20 ....40 C3
Wolseley Rd SALE M33 ....38 E2
Wolsey Dr ALT WA14 ....52 D4
Wolstanholme Cl CONG CW12 ..155 P9
Wolverham Rd EP CH65......102 E1
Wolverton Dr RUNC WA7......63 H5
  WILM/AE SK9 ....71 L5
Wolvesey Rd WSFD CW7 * 149 K4
Woodacre Gv GTS/LS CH66 ...80 B5
Woodacre Rd GTS/LS CH66 ...80 A5
Woodacres Ct WILM/AE SK9 ...71 H8
Woodale Cl WARRW/BUR WA5 ..32 B9
Woodall Cl SALE M33 ....38 C4
Woodall Dr RUNC WA7........15 C5
Woodavens Gv
  AUD/MAD/W CW3 ....216 B3
Woodbank Av MPL/ROM SK6 ...42 D5
Woodbank Av STKP SK1.......42 A8
Woodbank Cl CW/SHV CW2 ...184 G9
Woodbank La CH/BCN CH1 ...101 H7
Woodbank Rd EP CH65......102 D3
  WARRW/BUR WA5 ....47 L3
Woodbine Av IRL M44........56 C4
Woodbine Crs OFTN SK2.......41 N9
Woodbine Rd LYMM WA13.....51 H3
Woodbourne Rd HTNM SK4 ...41 K2
  NM/HAY SK22 ....75 L1
  SALE M33 ....38 D6
Woodbray Av BNG/LEV M19 ...40 F3
Woodbridge Av
  DTN/ASHW M34 ....29 K2
Woodbridge Cl WARRS WA4 ...65 H2
Woodbridge Gv
  NTHM/RTH M23 ....39 K7
Woodbrook Rd WILM/AE SK9 ..93 K4
Woodburn Rd WYTH/NTH M22 ..39 N8
Woodbury Crs DUR SK16 * 29 P2
Woodbury Rd EDGY/DAV SK3 ...41 J9
Woodchurch La GTS/LS CH66 ...80 A8
Woodclose GTS/LS CH66......79 L4
Woodcock La ALS/KID ST7 ....189 L2
Woodcote Av BRAM/HZG SK7 ..56 C6
  EP CH65 ....102 D2
Woodcote Cl
  WARRN/WOL WA2 ....33 N7
Woodcote Pl SBCH CW11 .....171 L9
Woodcote Rd ALT WA14 ......38 A7
Woodcote Vw WILM/AE SK9 ...71 P5
Woodcott Av WSFD CW7 .....149 K1
Woodcott Cl OFTN SK2 ....57 K1
Woodcroft Av BNG/LEV M19 ...40 F4
Woodcroft Cl CHD/CHDH SK8 ..68 B8
Woodcroft Wy STHEL WA9 * ...31 H4
Woodcut Cl ALS/KID ST7 ......187 L5
Wood End BRAM/HZG SK7 .....56 D5
Woodend Cl MWCH CW10 ....151 J4
Woodend La GOL/RIS/CU WA3 ..35 L6
  KNUT WA16 ....70 A6
Wood End La NSTN CH64......78 C9
Woodend Rd EDGY/DAV SK3 ...56 F5
  EP CH65 ....102 D3
  WYTH/NTH M22 ....54 F3
Woodfall Cl NSTN CH64.......77 N7
Woodfall Gv NSTN CH64......77 M7
Woodfall La NSTN CH64.......77 M7
Woodfield WYTH/NTH M22 ....54 F4
Woodfield Av FLINT CH6......98 B7
  MPL/ROM SK6 ....42 F4
Woodfield Cl CHSW/BR CH4 ...140 E7
Woodfield Ct OFTN SK2 * 56 C3
Woodfield Crs MPL/ROM SK6 ...42 E6
Woodfield Gv CHNE CH2 .....122 C6
  SALE M33 ....38 D2
Woodfield Rd ALT WA14 ......52 D5
  CHD/CHDH SK8 ....68 B8
Woodfield Rd North EP CH65 ...6 C4
Woodfin Cft MCFLDS SK11 ....114 C1
Woodfold Av BNG/LEV M19 ....28 A7
Woodford Av DTN/ASHW M34 ..29 N5
  GOL/RIS/CU WA3 ....24 F2
Woodford Cl CW/SHV CW2 ....184 F6
  FROD/HEL WA6 ....105 H2
  RUNC WA7 ....61 P8
  WARRS WA4 ....49 L4
Woodford Gdns
  DID/WITH M20 ....40 B6
Woodford La MCFLDN SK10 ....72 C8
  WSFD CW7 ....149 K2
Woodford La West WSFD CW7 .149 J5
Woodford Rd BRAM/HZG SK7 ..72 E1
  POY/DIS SK12 ....73 H1
  WILM/AE SK9 ....71 N3
Woodgate Av ALS/KID ST7 ....188 B5
Woodgate Cl MPL/ROM SK6 ...42 E5
Woodgreen La NANT CW5 ....168 D4
Wood Gv DTN/ASHW M34 ....29 M5
  MPL/ROM SK6 ....42 F3
Woodhall Av DID/WITH M20 ...40 B7
Woodhall Cl BRAM/HZG SK7 ...72 D3
  WARRW/BUR WA5 ....32 D8
Woodhall Crs RDSH SK5.......41 P4
Woodhall Rd ALS/KID ST7.....189 L5
  RDSH SK5 ....41 P4
Woodham Cl NWCHW CW8 ...109 L7
Woodham Gv NSTN CH64.....77 M8
Woodham Rd NTHM/RTH M23 ..39 J7

Woodhatch Rd RUNC WA7....62 E9
Woodhead Dr
  HALE/TIMP WA15 ....53 K6
Woodhead Rd
  HALE/TIMP WA15 ....53 K6
Wood Hey Gv
  DTN/ASHW M34 * 29 N7
Woodhey Hall La NANT CW5 ..194 E1
Woodhey La NANT CW5 .....194 E0
Woodheys HTNM SK4.........40 G5
Woodheys Dr SALE M33......38 A7
Woodhey Rd WGTN/LGST M12 ..28 B5
Woodhill Cl
  GOL/RIS/CU WA3 ....34 C5
  MCFLDS SK11 ....135 M2
Woodhouse La
  AUD/MAD/W CW3 ....217 K4
  BIDD ST8 ....175 M7
  MCFLDS SK11 ....135 L2
Woodhouse La SALE M33......37 N7
  SALE M33 ....38 A6
Woodhouse La East
  HALE/TIMP WA15 ....38 E7
Woodhouse Rd
  WYTH/NTH M22 ....54 F2
  WYTH/NTH M22 ....54 F8
Woodhouse St GTN M18 ......28 D4
Woodhouse St PART M31......36 F4
Woodlake Av CCHDY M21 ....39 M4
Woodland Av BRAM/HZG SK7 ...57 L6
  CW/HAS CW1 ....185 M5
  GTN M18 ....28 E5
  LYMM WA13 ....51 F5
  NANT CW5 ....11 F5
  NEWLW WA12 * 24 B6
  WDN WA8 ....45 M6
Woodland Bnk CHNE CH2 ....122 G2
Woodland Cl MCFLDS SK11 ...114 C1
Woodland Ct ALS/KID ST7 ....187 P4
Woodland Dr LYMM WA13....50 F5
Woodland End
  MCFLDS SK11 ....114 C1
Woodland Gdns
  CW/HAS CW1 ....185 L2
Woodland Rd ALS/KID ST7 ....173 H9
  BNG/LEV M19 ....28 B5
  EP CH65 ....102 D2
  GTN M18 ....28 E5
Woodlands Av ALS/KID ST7 ..188 F6
  CHD/CHDH SK8 ....56 A5
  CONG CW12 ....155 M6
  IRL M44 ....56 A3
  MPL/ROM SK6 ....42 F5
Woodlands Av CHD/CHDH SK8 ..56 A7
  NSTN CH64 ....77 K5
  TPLY/KEL CW6 ....147 L2
Woodlands Ct CO CH5 ....140 A2
Woodlands Crs KNUT WA16 ...67 J2
Woodlands Dr CHNE CH2 .....121 P7
  HOLMCH CW4 ....132 B2
  KNUT WA16 ....90 F3
  MPL/ROM SK6 ....42 G5
  OFTN SK2 ....42 B8
  WARRS WA4 ....49 M4
Woodlands Gv NWCHW CW8 ..109 H1
Woodlands La CHSE CH3 .....143 J1
  HALE/TIMP WA15 ....53 J2
Woodlands Pk KNUT WA16 * ..131 K1
Woodlands Rd ALS/KID ST7 ...188 D7
  BNG/LEV M19 ....40 C3
  CW/SHV CW2 * 5 F7
  DTN/ASHW M34 ....29 M5
  EDGY/DAV SK3 ....16 C6
  GOL/RIS/CU WA3 ....24 D1
  MCFLDS SK11 ....95 K1
  NM/HAY SK22 ....59 M8
  OP/CLY M11 ....28 B2
  STHEL WA9 ....22 A5
  WARR WA1 ....19 J4
  WILM/AE SK9 ....48 M6
Woodlands Rd East
  NWCHW CW8 ....109 L7
The Woodlands NWCHE CW9 ..88 G7
Woodlands St WGTN/LGST M12 ..28 B5
Woodlands Wy
  TPLY/KEL CW6 ....147 H7
Wood La CHSE CH3 ....164 F7
  CHSW/BR CH4 ....140 F6
  HALE/TIMP WA15 ....53 L2
  HOLMCH CW4 ....131 P2
  KNUT WA16 ....69 M5
  MPL/ROM SK6 ....58 B2
  MWCH CW10 ....152 B6
  NSTN CH64 ....77 J3
  NSTN CH64 ....100 A2
  NWCHW CW8 ....108 G4
  PART M31 ....36 F4
  RUNC WA7 ....62 G0
  RUNC WA7 ....84 D2
  TPLY/KEL CW6 ....146 B3
  WARRS WA4 ....48 G7
Wood La East MCFLDN SK10 ...73 P6
Wood La North MCFLDN SK10 ..73 P6
Wood La South MCFLDN SK10 ..73 N7
Woodlark Cl WSFD CW7......150 A2
Woodlea Av BNG/LEV M19 ....40 F2
Woodlea Cl NSTN CH64 ......77 K4
Woodlea Dr MCFLDN SK10 ....95 L5
Woodley Cl OFTN SK2 ....56 C3
Woodley Fold
  WARRW/BUR WA5 ....47 K3
Woodman Dr STKP SK1.......17 F3
Wood Mt HALE/TIMP WA15 ...53 M2

Woodmount Cl MPL/ROM SK6 ..43 K6
Woodnewton Cl GTN M18 ....28 C5
Woodnoth Dr CW/SHV CW2 ..198 B2
Wood Orchard La
  AUD/MAD/W CW3 ....217 J3
Woodpecker Cl
  GOL/RIS/CU WA3 ....34 G4
Woodpecker Dr ALS/KID ST7 ..184 F7
  NWCHE CW9 ....109 P8
Woodridge RUNC WA7 ....62 G5
Woodridge HALE/TIMP WA15 ..38 D7
Woodrow Wy IRL M44 ....27 H9
Woodroyd Cl BRAM/HZG SK7 ..56 D6
Woodruff St WGTN/LGST M12 ..28 B5
Woodruffe Gdns
  MPL/ROM SK6 ....42 F8
Woods Cl ALS/KID ST7 ....91 K7
Woodsfin La CHSE CH5 ......179 L1
Woods Gv CHD/CHDH SK8 ....56 B8
Woodshutt's St ALS/KID ST7 ..188 F7
Woodside ALS/KID ST7 ......188 G4
  KNUT WA16 ....90 F3
  MCFLDS SK11 ....115 J9
Woodside Av ALS/KID ST7 ....189 H7
  BNG/LEV M19 ....40 C3
  CW/SHV CW2 ....184 F6
  FROD/HEL WA6 ....84 B6
Woodside Dr MPL/ROM SK6 ...58 E2
  LYMM WA13 ....51 H6
  POY/DIS SK12 ....73 L2
Woodside Rd CH/BCN CH1 ...120 F6
  LYMM WA13 ....51 J6
  RNFD/HAY WA11 ....25 J5
  WARRS WA4 ....47 K1
Woodside St NM/HAY SK22 ...59 M9
Woods La CHD/CHDH SK8 ....56 B8
  NWCHW CW8 ....107 N7
Woods Moor La
  EDGY/DAV SK3 ....56 G3
Woodsome Cl EP CH65......102 D5
Woodsome Dr EP CH65......102 D3
Wood Sorrel Wy
  GOL/RIS/CU WA3 ....24 G1
Wood Sq DROY M43.........27 M9
The Woods ALT WA14.........53 J1
Woodstock Av CHD/CHDH SK8 ..56 A8
  NEWLW WA12 ....23 P7
  RDSH SK5 ....41 N3
Woodstock Cl MCFLDN SK10 ..116 C2
Woodstock Crs MPL/ROM SK6 ..42 F5
Woodstock Dr MWCH CW10 ..151 L5
Woodstock Gdns WARRS WA4 ..49 H9
Woodstock Gn RDSH SK5.....41 P3
Woodstock Gv WDN WA8.....45 K5
Woodstock Rd ALT WA14.....37 P8
  BURS/TUN ST6 ....189 J9
Woodstock St
  BURS/TUN ST6 ....189 K8
  ALS/KID ST7 ....189 L1
Wood St ALS/KID ST7 ....201 H4
  ALT WA14 ....53 H5
  CHD/CHDH SK8 ....55 M1
  CONG CW12 * 184 D2
  CW/SHV CW2 * 5 F7
  DTN/ASHW M54 ....29 M5
  EDGY/DAV SK3 ....16 C6
  GOL/RIS/CU WA3 ....24 D1
  MCFLDS SK11 * 5 F1
  NM/HAY SK22 ....59 M8
  OP/CLY M11 ....28 B2
  STHEL WA9 ....22 A5
  WARR WA1 ....19 J4
  WARR WA6 ....46 M6
Woodthorn Cl RUNC WA7 ....63 K2
Woodthorpe Dr
  CHD/CHDH SK8 ....56 A5
Wood Top Cl OFTN SK2 ......42 D9
Woodvale Av ALS/KID ST7 ....52 C5
Wood V STHEL WA9 ....30 D2
Woodvale Cl
  WARRN/WOL WA2 ....33 P8
Woodvale Gv GTS/LS CH66 ....79 P7
  KNUT WA16 ....90 E5
Wood Vw ALS/KID ST7 ......201 K6
  WYTH/NTH M22 ....39 N7
Woodview Av BNG/LEV M19 ...40 C3
Woodview Crs WDN WA8.....44 G0
Woodview Rd WDN WA8.....44 G7
Woodville Dr MPL/ROM SK6 ...58 C3
  SALE M33 ....38 D3
Woodville Gv RDSH SK5......41 N2
Woodville Pl WDN WA8.......45 K6
Woodville Rd ALT WA14......52 C5
  SALE M33 ....38 D5
Woodward St NWCHW CW8 ..108 F3
Woodward Wk CHSE CH3 ....124 B8
Woodwise La NTHM/RTH M23 ..39 H8
Woolacombe Av STHEL WA9 ...31 H5
Woolaston Dr ALS/KID ST7 ...187 P5
Woollen Rd IRL M44.........35 P1
Woolley Cl FROD/HEL WA6....84 B5
Woolmer Cl GOL/RIS/CU WA3 ...35 J4
Woolston Av CONG CW12 ....155 P9
Woolston Dr CW/SHV CW2 ...198 D5
Woolston Grange Av
  WARRN/WOL WA2 ....34 D6
Woolston La NANT CW5 ......22 C2
Woolton Ct GTS/LS CH66 .....80 A5
Wootton Cl CW/SHV CW2.....184 H8
Worcester Av DTN/ASHW M34 ..29 N8
  GOL/RIS/CU WA3 ....24 D1
  RDSH SK5 ....41 N3
Worcester Cl ALS/KID ST7 ....188 F9
  MPL/ROM SK6 ....42 F6
  WARRW/BUR WA5 ....47 F2
Worcester Pl CH/BCN CH1 ....121 K6
Worcester Rd CHD/CHDH SK8 ..56 A3
  SALE M33 ....38 A5

Worcester St EP CH65.........7 F2
Worcester Wk EP CH65 * 7 F2
Wordsworth Av CW STHEL WA9 ..20 F5
  WARRS WA4 ....48 A3
Wordsworth Cl CW/SHV CW2 ..184 F7
  SBCH CW11 ....171 J3
Wordsworth Crs CH/BCN CH1 ..121 K6
Wordsworth Dr CW/HAS CW1 ..5 K2
Wordsworth Ms CH/BCN CH1 ..121 K6
Wordsworth Rd
  DTN/ASHW M34 ....42 F1
  RDSH SK5 ....28 D8
Wordsworth Sq
  CH/BCN CH1 ....121 J6
Wordsworth Wy
  ALS/KID ST7 ....187 P4
  GTS/LS CH66 ....102 A3
Works La NWCHE CW9 ......110 E3
World Wy MANAIR M90 ......54 D7
Worleston St CONG CW12 ....155 N7
Worrall St CONG CW12 ......155 N7
  EDGY/DAV SK3 ....41 M9
Worsborough Av
  WARRW/BUR WA5 ....47 M2
Worsley Av CH/BCN CH1 .....120 D5
  WARRS WA4 ....49 H5
Worsley Brow STHEL WA9 .....29 K8
Worsley Ct WARRS WA4 ......42 A9
Worsley Dr CONG CW12 .....156 B9
Worsley Gv BNG/LEV M19 ....28 A8
Worsley Rd WARRS WA4 .....48 A1
  RNFD/HAY WA11 ....22 D3
  WARRW/BUR WA5 ....18 A1
Worthing Cl OFTN SK2 ....57 K1
Worthing St MDTN M24.......26 D2
Worthington Av PART M31 ....36 E5
Worthington Cl
  MCFLDS SK11 ....116 B4
  CHNE CH2 ....121 J6
  RUNC WA7 ....62 E7
Worthington Rd
  DTN/ASHW M54 ....29 P7
  SALE M33 ....39 H4
Worthington St WHITCH SY13 ..213 N5
Worth's La DTN/ASHW M34 ...31 J4
Wray Av STHEL WA9.........31 H1
Wrekin Av NTHM/RTH M23 ...38 B4
Wrekin Wy CHSW/BR CH4 ...142 B4
Wrenbury Cl NEWLU ST5.....201 N6
Wrenbury Av DID/WITH M20 ..40 A1
Wrenbury Crs EDGY/DAV SK3 ..56 C1
Wrenbury Dr CHD/CHDH SK8 ..55 N1
Wrenbury Hall Dr NANT CW5 ..207 P1
Wrenbury Heath Rd
  NANT CW5 ....207 P1
Wrenbury Rd MALPAS SY14 ..199 P6
  NANT CW5 ....207 K3
Wren Cl BIDD ST8 ....175 M9
  CW/HAS CW1 * 5 H1
  GOL/RIS/CU WA3 ....34 G4
  MCFLDN SK10 ....116 C5
  OFTN SK2 ....57 M2
  WARRW/BUR WA5 ....62 E8
Wren Dr IRL M44 ....27 N5
Wrenmere Cl SBCH CW11 ....171 K1
Wrenshot La KNUT WA16 .....67 J1
Wrexham Cl BIDD ST8.......175 L8
  WARRW/BUR WA5 ....33 H7
Wrexham Rd CHSW/BR CH4 ..160 C6
  CHSW/BR CH4 ....160 C6
  MALPAS SY14 ....203 M4
  NANT CW5 ....182 C9
  TPLY/KEL CW6 ....180 E7
  WHITCH SY13 ....213 K6
  WRXS/E LL13 ....176 F9
Wright Av NEWLU ST5.......201 N6
  NWCHE CW9 ....110 C6
Wright Ct NANT CW5.........10 E6
Wrights Bank North OFTN SK2 ..57 K2
Wrights Bank South OFTN SK2 ..57 K1
Wrights Gn WARRS WA4 * 49 J9
Wright's La SBCH CW11 ......172 A3
  WARRW/BUR WA5 ....32 B5
  WDN WA8 ....42 A4
Wright St ALS/KID ST7 ....188 F7
  DTN/ASHW M34 ....29 L1
Wrigley Av MPL/ROM SK6 ....26 M8
Wrigley Rd RNFD/HAY WA11 ...23 J5
Wrinehill Rd NANT CW5 .....198 C8
Wroxham Av DTN/ASHW M34 ..28 G6
Wroxham Cl CHNE CH2.........85 H9
Wroxham Rd
  WARRW/BUR WA5 ....47 J1
Wryneck Cl ECCL WA10......30 A1
Wyatt St BURS/TUN ST6 .....189 L9
  HTNM SK4 ....16 E3
Wybersley Rd MPL/ROM SK6 ..58 E8
  NANT CW5 ....197 J4
Wybunbury La NANT CW5....198 A9
Wybunbury Rd NANT CW5 ...197 L2
Wyche La NWCHE CW9 ......109 M4
Wyche La TPLY/KEL CW6 .....166 C9
Wychelm Rd PART M31......36 F4
Wyche Rd TPLY/KEL CW6 .....166 C9
Wych Fold HYDE SK14........43 K1
Wych-house La MWCH CW10 ..151 J1
Wych La MCFLDN SK10 ......75 J9
Wychwood ALT WA14 ....52 D4
Wychwood Av LYMM WA13 ...50 C4
Wychwood Dr CW/SHV CW2 ..199 K5
Wycliffe Av WILM/AE SK9 ....71 H3
Wycliffe Ct CHNE CH2.......122 B9
Wycliffe Rd GTS/LS CH66 ....102 B1
  RNFD/HAY WA11 ....23 J2
Wycliffe St HTNM SK4.......16 B5
Wycombe Av GTN M18......28 C5
Wyecroft Cl MPL/ROM SK6 ...42 C5
Wyedale EP CH65 ....102 D1
Wyedale Rd RNFD/HAY WA11 ..22 C5

Wyken Gv RNFD/HAY WA11 ....22 A4
Wylam Wk WGTN/LGST M12 ......28 B6
Wynbank Cl ALS/KID ST7 ....201 H7
Wynchgate Rd BRAM/HZG SK7 ...57 N4
Wyncroft Cl EP CH65 ....102 C1
WDN WA8 ....45 J8
Wyncroft Rd WDN WA8 ....J8 J8
Wyndham Cl BRAM/HZG SK7 ......56 E8
NWCHE CW9 ....109 P7
Wyndham Crs GTS/LS CH66 ....102 A2
Wyndham Rd CHI/BCN CH1 ....120 F7
The Wynd TPLY/KEL CW6 ....125 H7
Wyne Cl BRAM/HZG SK7 ....57 N4
Wynfield Av WYTH/NTH M22 ....55 H8
Wyngate Rd CHD/CHDH SK8 ....55 P6
HALE/TIMP WA15 ....53 K7
Wynne Cl DTN/ASHW M34 ....29 M8
Wynne Av DTN/ASHW M34 ....21 L8
Wynnstay Rd CHSW/BR CH4 ....140 C6
SALE M33 ....38 E3
Wynter La MALPAS SY14 ....191 J4
Wynyard Cl SALE M33 ....38 C6
Wynyard Rd WYTH/NTH M22 ....54 E4
Wysall Cl RNFD/HAY WA11 ....12 C1
Wythburn Gv RUNC WA7 ....62 C9
Wythburn Rd STKP SK1 ....42 A9
Wythenshawe Pk
NTHM/RTH M23 * 39 K8
Wythenshawe Rd
NTHM/RTH M23 ....39 K7
SALE M33 ....39 H4
Wythens Rd CHD/CHDH SK8 ....55 K7
Wythin St TPLY/KEL CW6 ....166 M8
Wyvern Av HTNM SK4 ....41 M3
Wyville Cl BRAM/HZG SK7 ....57 N5

Y

Yardington WHITCH SY13 ....213 L5
Yardley Av WARRW/BUR WA5 ....33 J8
Yarmouth Dr NTHM/RTH M23 ....39 L7
Yarmouth Rd
WARRW/BUR WA5 ....47 J1
Yarrow Cl CHSW/BR CH4 ....140 C7
Yarwood Av NTHM/RTH M23 ....39 J9
Yarwood CI NWCHW CW8 ....12 E5
Yarwoodheath La ALT WA14 ....52 C7
Yarwood St ALT WA14 ....53 H4
Yatehouse La MWCH CW10 ....130 B6
Yates Cl WARRW/BUR WA5 ....47 N2
Yates Rd CHNE CH2 ....103 N3
NM/HAY SK22 ....59 N8
Yates St CW/SHV CW2 * 4 D6
STKP SK1 ....42 A5
Yattendon Av NTHM/RTH M23 ......38 G8
Yealand Av HTNM SK4 ....16 C1
Yeald Brow LYMM WA13 ....50 B4
Yeardsley Av CHF/WBR SK23 ....75 P3
Yeardsley Cl BRAM/HZG SK7 ....56 E4
Yeardsley Gn CHF/WBR SK23 ....75 P6
Yeardsley La CHF/WBR SK23 ....75 P5
Yeardsleys La FROD/HEL WA6 .....107 L7
Yeld La TPLY/KEL CW6 ....125 K5
Yeoford Dr ALT WA14 ....52 F1
Yeoman Cl BRAM/HZG SK7 * 57 K4
Yeoman Wy GTS/LS CH66 ....102 A3
Yeovil Cl WARR WA1 ....34 D8
Yerburgh St CHNE CH2 ....121 N7
Yewdale Dr GTS/LS CH66 ....102 B3

Yewdale Rd OFTN SK2 ....57 H1
Yewlands NWCHW CW8 ....107 P7
Yew St DTN/ASHW M34 ....29 M3
HTNM SK4 ....41 J7
Yew Tree Rd BNG/LEV M19 ....28 A8
BRAM/HZG SK7 ....57 M7
NEWLM WA12 ....23 L5
STHEL WA9 ....31 H2
WYTH/NTH M22 ....39 N7
Yew Tree Cl CHNE CH2 ....103 N3
CHSW/BR CH4 ....140 C7
LYMM WA13 ....50 E3
MADHL SY14 ....180 B6
MCFLDN SK10 ....99 M5
MCFLDS SK11 ....116 C6
MPL/ROM SK6 ....58 C2
NANT CW5 ....130 A9
Yewtree Cl NSTN CH64 ....77 M6
Yew Tree Ci TPLY/KEL CW6 ....148 B3
York Av ALT WA14 ....71 M7
BRAM/HZG SK7 ....57 L8
CHNE CH2 ....122 C3
MANAIR M90 ....54 B8
WARRS WA4 ....47 J4
WSFD WA7 ....149 M4
York Pl RUNC WA7 ....15 F3
York Rd ALT WA14 ....53 H6
DTN/ASHW M34 ....29 M5
EP CH65 ....2 C4
HTNM SK4 ....41 J3
IRL M44 ....38 D3
SALE M33 ....38 D3
WDN WA8 ....49 J5
WARRS WA4 ....45 J7
Yorkshire Rd PART M31 ....36 D6

Yew Tree Park Rd
CHD/CHDH SK8 ....56 B9
Yew Tree Rd CW/SHV CW2 ....184 C8
DTN/ASHW M34 ....29 L8
EDGY/DAV SK3 ....56 F4
MCFLDN SK10 ....73 P5
Yewtree Rd KNUT WA16 ....111 M1
Yew Tree Ter ALS/KID ST7 ....189 J8
Yew Tree Wy GOL/RIS/CU WA3 .....24 D2
MCFLDN SK10 ....95 H7
The Yonne CH/BCN CH1 ....2 C4
York Av GOL/RIS/CU WA3 ....25 P7
SALE M33 ....38 E5
WARRW/BUR WA5 ....32 B9
York Cl ALS/KID ST7 ....188 F9
BIDD ST8 ....175 L7
CHD/CHDH SK8 ....56 A2
York Ct WARRS WA4 * 48 C6
York Crs WILM/AE SK9 ....71 H7
York Dr ALT WA14 ....53 H6
BRAM/HZG SK7 ....56 A7
CHNE CH2 ....122 C3
MANAIR M90 ....54 B8
WARRS WA4 ....45 J7
WSFD WA7 ....149 M4
York Pl RUNC WA7 ....15 F3
York Rd ALT WA14 ....53 H6
DTN/ASHW M34 ....29 M5
EP CH65 ....2 C4
HTNM SK4 ....41 J3
IRL M44 ....38 D3
SALE M33 ....38 D3
WDN WA8 ....49 J5
WARRS WA4 ....45 J7
Yorkshire Rd PART M31 ....36 D6

York St BNG/LEV M19 ....28 A9
CH/BCN CH1 ....3 F5
DID/WITH M20 ....40 C5
DTN/ASHW M34 ....29 L1
EDGY/DAV SK3 ....16 E6
HALE/TIMP WA15 ....53 J4
MCFLDN SK10 ....16 E6
RUNC WA7 ....14 E3
WARRS WA4 ....48 E5
York Ter SALE M33 * 38 D2
Yulan Dr SALE M33 ....57 P4
Yule St EDGY/DAV SK3 ....16 C6

Z

Zan Dr SBCH CW11 ....171 M6
Zara Ct RNFD/HAY WA11 ....22 G2
Zinnia Dr IRL M44 ....27 J9
Zion St NWCHW CW8 ....12 C4
Zodiac Dr BURS/TUN ST6 ....189 N9
Zurich Gdns BRAM/HZG SK7 ....56 E4

Index – featured places

AA Office
CHD/CHDH SK8 ....55 N1
Abbey Gate College
CHSE CH3 ....162 A6
CHSE CH3 ....162 F1
Abbey Gate School
CHNE CH2 ....2 D1
Abbey Hey Primary School
GTN M18 ....28 E4
Abbotsfield Road
Industrial Park
STHEL WA9 ....31 K3
Abingdon Primary School
RDSH SK5 ....41 N1
Acacias CP School
BNG/LEV M19 ....40 G1
The Accord Clinic
MWCH CW10 ....151 J1
Ackers Crossing
CONG CW12 ....174 C7
Acorn Business Park
EDGY/DAV SK3 ....16 D5
Acorns Caravan Park
WSFD WA7 ....127 L6
Acresfield Primary School
CHNE CH2 ....122 A3
Acton CE Primary School
NANT CW5 ....183 J9
Adderley CE Primary School
MKTDR TF9 ....216 G8
Adelaide School
CW/HAS CW1 ....4 D1
Adlington Industrial Estate
MCFLDN SK10 ....73 J5
Adlington Primary School
MCFLDN SK10 ....73 L9
Adlington Road Business Park
MCFLDN SK10 ....95 M4
Adswood Clinic
EDGY/DAV SK3 ....56 E2
Adswood Industrial Estate
EDGY/DAV SK3 ....56 D1
Adswood Primary School
EDGY/DAV SK3 ....56 D2
Aircraft Factory
CHSW/BR CH4 ....141 H4
Alban Retail Park
WARRN/WOL WA2 ....33 K6
Albert Road Medical Centre
WDN WA8 ....45 P6
Alderley Edge Cricket Club
WILM/AE SK9 ....93 K4
Alderley Edge Golf Club
WILM/AE SK9 ....92 G2
Alderley Edge Hotel
WILM/AE SK9 ....93 K5
Alderley Edge Primary School
WILM/AE SK9 ....93 H3
Alderley Edge School for Girls
WILM/AE SK9 ....93 J3
Alderman Bolton
Community School
WARRS WA4 ....48 G4
Alder Root Golf Club
WARRW/BUR WA5 ....32 G1
Aldersey Green Golf Club
CHSE CH3 ....178 D2
The Alexandra Hospital
CHD/CHDH SK8 ....55 M1
Alexandra Industrial Estate
DTN/ASHW M34 ....29 N5
WDN WA8 ....21 F5
Alexandra Park Primary School
EDGY/DAV SK3 ....41 K9
Allanson Street CP School
STHEL WA9 ....22 B3
All Hallows Catholic High School
MCFLDS SK11 ....8 A5

All Saints CE Primary School
HTNM SK4 ....41 L4
MPL/ROM SK6 ....58 E2
All Saints CE Primary School
RUNC WA7 ....14 E1
All Saints Primary School
GTN M18 ....28 B3
All Saints RC Primary School
GOL/RIS/CU WA3 ....24 D1
All Saints Upton Primary School
WDN WA8 ....45 H4
Alma Lodge Hotel
OFTN SK2 ....56 G1
Alma Park Primary School
BNG/LEV M19 ....28 A9
Alpha Court Industrial Estate
DTN/ASHW M34 ....29 J6
Alsager Cricket Club
ALS/KID ST7 ....187 P4
Alsager Golf & Country Club
ALS/KID ST7 ....188 E7
Alsager Highfields
Primary School
ALS/KID ST7 ....187 P4
Alsager Leisure Centre
ALS/KID ST7 ....187 M4
Altrincham CE Primary School
ALT WA14 ....52 C2
Altrincham College of Arts
HALE/TIMP WA15 ....53 L3
Altrincham Crematorium
ALT WA14 ....37 J8
Altrincham FC
HALE/TIMP WA15 ....53 K4
Altrincham General Hospital
ALT WA14 ....52 C3
Altrincham Golf Club
HALE/TIMP WA15 ....53 K2
Altrincham Grammar
School for Boys
ALT WA14 ....53 H5
Altrincham Grammar
School for Girls
ALT WA14 ....52 G4
Altrincham Ice Rink
ALT WA14 ....53 H1
Altrincham Industrial Centre
ALT WA14 ....52 E1
Altrincham (Kersal) RFC
HALE/TIMP WA15 ....38 F9
Altrincham Leisure Centre
HALE/TIMP WA15 ....53 J2
Altrincham
Preparatory School
ALT WA14 ....52 G5
Altrincham Priory Hospital
HALE/TIMP WA15 ....53 L7
Altrincham Retail Park
ALT WA14 ....37 P9
Alvanley Industrial Estate
MPL/ROM SK6 ....42 E4
Alvanley Primary School
FROD/HEL WA6 ....105 K3
Alvaston Business Park
NANT CW5 ....183 P9
Amalgamated Sports Club
POY/DIS SK12 ....58 F9
Andersons Industrial Estate
WDN WA8 ....21 H6
Anderton Boat Lift
NWCHW CW9 ....109 M1
Annandale Medical Centre
KNUT WA16 ....90 G2
KNUT WA16 ....91 L1
Ann Street Health Centre
DTN/ASHW M34 ....29 L6

Antrobus St Marks School
NWCHE CW9 ....87 L1
Apedale Business Park
NEWLM ST5 ....201 M8
Apollo Cinema
Bingo & Social Club
CW/HAS CW1 ....5 F3
Appleton Thorn Primary School
WARRS WA4 ....65 L2
Appleton Thorn Trading Estate
WARRS WA4 ....65 M1
Aquinas College
OFTN SK2 ....57 H1
Arcadia Sports Centre
BNG/LEV M19 ....28 A8
Arclid Industrial Estate
SBCH CW11 ....172 D1
Arden Business Centre
MPL/ROM SK6 ....42 D2
Arden Primary School
MPL/ROM SK6 ....42 C5
Arley Hall & Gardens
NWCHE CW9 ....66 D8
Arrow Trading Estate
DTN/ASHW M34 ....29 K4
Art Theatre
NM/HAY SK22 ....59 M8
Ashdene Primary School
WILM/AE SK9 ....71 H9
Ash Grove Primary School
MCFLDS SK11 ....117 J8
Ashley CE (Controlled)
Primary School
HALE/TIMP WA15 ....69 K1
Ashley Retail Park
WDN WA8 ....21 K4
Ashley School
WDN WA8 ....20 B1
Ashmount Industrial Centre
FLINT CH6 ....98 A5
Ashton Hayes Primary School
CHSE CH3 ....124 D3
Ashton on Mersey School
SALE M33 ....38 C4
Ashton upon Mersey
Cricket & Tennis Club
SALE M33 ....38 B1
Ashton upon Mersey Golf Club
SALE M33 ....38 B1
Ashurst Primary School
RNFD/HAY WA11 ....22 B3
Aspinal Primary School
NWCHW CW8 ....109 K6
Astbury Golf Club
CONG CW12 ....174 F2
Astbury Mere Country Park
CONG CW12 ....155 K8
Astbury St Marys CE
Primary School
CONG CW12 ....174 C1
Astmoor Industrial Estate
RUNC WA7 ....62 B3
RUNC WA7 ....62 D3
Astmoor Primary School
RUNC WA7 ....62 B3
Aston Primary School
RUNC WA7 ....84 G4
Atherton Infant School
EP CH65 ....80 B8
Atlantic Business Centre
ALT WA14 ....37 P9
Atlas Trading Estate
RDSH SK5 ....41 M1
Audenshaw High School
DTN/ASHW M34 ....29 L3
Audenshaw Primary School
DTN/ASHW M34 ....29 J2
Audley Cricket Club
ALS/KID ST7 ....200 F5

Aviation Viewing Park
MANAIR M90 ....70 C1
Avicenna Grammar School
DID/WITH M20 ....40 A4
Avondale High School
EDGY/DAV SK3 ....41 K9
Avondale Industrial Estate
EDGY/DAV SK3 ....41 J8
Avondale Recreation Centre
EDGY/DAV SK3 ....41 J9
Avro Golf Club
BRAM/HZG SK7 ....72 E6
Baguley Hall Primary School
NTHM/RTH M23 ....54 C1
Baileys Business Park
MCFLDN SK10 ....95 M6
Bamford Business Park
MCFLDN SK10 ....41 M3
Banbury Nursery School
ALS/KID ST7 ....188 F7
Bankfield School
WDN WA8 ....45 K6
Bankfield Trading Estate
RDSH SK5 ....41 M4
Bank Quay Trading Estate
WARRS WA4 ....48 B3
Banks Lane Primary School
STKP SK1 ....42 A8
Barbridge Junction
NANT CW5 ....182 E1
Barleycastle Trading Estate
WARRS WA4 ....65 L2
Barlow Hall Primary School
CCHDY M21 ....39 M3
Barlow Medical Centre
DID/WITH M20 ....40 B5
The Barlow RC High School
DID/WITH M20 ....40 B6
Barnton Primary School
NWCHW CW8 ....87 J9
Barony Hospital
NANT CW5 ....10 C1
Barrack Hill Primary School
MPL/ROM SK6 ....42 F6
Barrington Medical Centre
ALT WA14 ....53 H1
Barrow CE Primary School
CHSE CH3 ....123 L5
Barrow Hall County
Primary School
WARRW/BUR WA5 ....32 B9
Beach Tennis Club
NWCHW CW8 ....109 K6
Beamont Infant School
WARRN/WOL WA2 ....19 G1
Beaver Road Primary School
DID/WITH M20 ....40 C5
Beech Hall School
MCFLDN SK10 ....117 J2
Beechwood Primary School
CW/HAS CW1 ....4 D1
RUNC WA7 ....4 D1
Beeston Castle
TPLY/KEL CW6 ....165 L6
Belfry House Hotel
WILM/AE SK9 ....55 M9
Belgrave Primary School
ALT WA14 ....53 H1
Belle Vue Regional
Hockey Centre
WGTN/LGST M12 ....28 A5
Bell Meadow Business Park
CHSW/BR CH4 ....161 H4
Bell Tower
CH/BCN CH1 ....2 E4
Belmore Hotel
SALE M33 ....38 E6
Benchill Primary School
WYTH/NTH M22 ....54 E1

The Berkeley Primary School
CW/SHV CW2 ....185 H9
Best Western Hollin Hall Hotel
MCFLDN SK10 ....95 P6
Bethesda School
CHD/CHDH SK8 ....55 M4
Betley Primary School
AUD/MAD/W CW5 ....199 N9
Bewsey Business Centre
WARRW/BUR WA5 ....18 A3
Bewsey Industrial Estate
WARRN/WOL WA2 ....18 B2
WARRW/BUR WA5 ....18 A2
Bewsey Lodge Primary School
WARRW/BUR WA5 ....33 H9
Bexton CP School
KNUT WA16 ....90 D6
Bickerton Hill
MALPAS SY14 ....179 L9
Bickerton Holy Trinity CE
Primary School
MALPAS SY14 ....179 N9
Biddulph Grange Country Park
BIDD ST8 ....175 M6
Biddulph Grange Gardens NT
BIDD ST8 ....175 M6
Biddulph Valley
Leisure Centre
BIDD ST8 ....175 L8
Bingswood Industrial Estate
CHF/WBR SK23 ....75 P6
The Birches School
DID/WITH M20 ....39 P3
Birchwood CE Primary School
GOL/RIS/CU WA3 ....34 G4
Birchwood Community
High School
GOL/RIS/CU WA3 ....34 E5
Birchwood Golf Club
GOL/RIS/CU WA3 ....34 E2
Birchwood Medical Centre
GOL/RIS/CU WA3 ....34 F5
Birchwood Nursery School
ALS/KID ST7 ....189 J6
Birchwood One Business Park
GOL/RIS/CU WA3 ....34 F5
Bishop (Bluecoat) CE
High School
CHSE CH3 ....143 J2
Bishop Heber County
High School
MALPAS SY14 ....204 B1
Bishop Wilson CE
Primary School
NSTN CH64 ....100 B3
B&J Leisure Centre
WILM/AE SK9 ....71 J7
Blackbrook St Marys Catholic
Primary School
RNFD/HAY WA11 ....22 C3
Blackbrook Trading Estate
BNG/LEV M19 ....28 B9
Black Cat Industrial Estate
WDN WA8 ....21 H6
Blackfirs Primary School
CONG CW12 ....155 H6
Blacon Clinic
CH/BCN CH1 ....121 H6
Blacon County High School
CH/BCN CH1 ....120 G7
Blacon Hall Junior School
CH/BCN CH1 ....121 H6
Blacon Infant School
CH/BCN CH1 ....121 H6
Blessed Thomas Holford
Secondary School
HALE/TIMP WA15 ....53 J3
Blossoms Hotel
CH/BCN CH1 ....3 F4

Blue Chip Business Park
ALT WA14 ....**37** N9
Blue Planet Aquarium
EP CH65 ....**102** F3
Blundells Hill Golf Club
RAIN/WH L35 ....**30** A7
Boat Museum
EP CH65 ....**7** G1
Bodmin Road Clinic
SALE M33 ....**38** A3
Bold Business Centre
STHEL WA9 ....**31** N1
Bold Industrial Estate
WDN WA8 ....**46** A2
Bold Industrial Park
STHEL WA9 ....**31** N2
Bold Street Medical Centre
WARR WA1 ....**18** C7
Bollinbrook CE Primary School
MCFLDN SK10 ....**117** J2
Bollin CP School
ALT WA14 ....**52** F6
Bollington Cross CE
Primary School
MCFLDN SK10 ....**95** K6
Bollington Leisure Centre
MCFLDN SK10 ....**95** L7
Bollington Medical Centre
MCFLDN SK10 ....**95** M5
Bolshaw Primary School
CHD/CHDH SK8 ....**55** K8
The Borchardt Medical Centre
DID/WITH M20 ....**40** A2
The Borders Industrial Park
CHSW/BR CH4 ....**141** N3
Borough Cemetery
WDN WA8 ....**45** N4
Borron Road Industrial Estate
NEWLW WA12 ....**23** N5
Bosley Locks
CONG CW12 ....**156** G1
Boughton Health Centre
CHSE CH3 ....**3** J5
Boughton Heath
Primary School
CHSE CH3 ....**143** K2
Boughton St Pauls
Nursery & Infants
CHSE CH3 ....**3** H3
Bowdon CE Primary School
ALT WA14 ....**52** G6
Bowdon Cricket Club
ALT WA14 ....**52** G6
Bowdon Preparatory
School for Girls
ALT WA14 ....**52** G5
Bowdon RUFC
HALE/TIMP WA15 ....**53** N3
Bowdon Vale Cricket Club
ALT WA14 ....**52** G7
Bowers Business Park
WDN WA8 ....**46** A8
Bowling Alley
CH/BCN CH1 ....**121** J8
EDGY/DAV SK3 ....**17** F6
Brabyns Recreation Centre
MPL/ROM SK6 ....**43** M9
Brabyns School
MPL/ROM SK6 ....**43** M9
Bradshaw Hall J&I School
CHD/CHDH SK8 ....**55** N6
Bradshaw Primary School
WARRS WA4 ....**49** K5
Bramall Hall
BRAM/HZG SK7 ....**56** D6
Bramall Park Golf Club
CHD/CHDH SK8 ....**56** C6
Bramall Park Lawn Tennis Club
BRAM/HZG SK7 ....**56** D5
Bramall Park Tennis Club
BRAM/HZG SK7 ....**56** D7
Bramhall Golf Club
BRAM/HZG SK7 ....**56** F9
Bramhall Health Centre
BRAM/HZG SK7 ....**56** E9
Bramhall High School
BRAM/HZG SK7 ....**56** F7
Bramhall Moor Industrial Estate
BRAM/HZG SK7 ....**57** H5
Bramhall Park Medical Centre
BRAM/HZG SK7 ....**56** E5
Bramhall Village
Shopping Centre
BRAM/HZG SK7 ....**56** D9
Bredbury Clinic
MPL/ROM SK6 ....**42** E4
Bredbury Green Primary School
MPL/ROM SK6 ....**42** E7
Bredbury Hall
Hotel & Country Club
MPL/ROM SK6 ....**42** C6
Brentwood Special School
ALT WA14 ....**38** B9
Brereton CE Primary School
SBCH CW11 ....**153** K5
Brickfield Business Centre
NWCHE CW9 ....**110** D3
Bridestone Shopping Centre
CONG CW12 ....**155** M7
Bridge College
OFTN SK2 ....**42** C8
Bridgegate
CH/BCN CH1 ....**2** E6
Bridge Hall Primary School
EDGY/DAV SK3 ....**56** D1
Bridge Hotel
MCFLDN SK10 ....**94** G7
Bridge House Medical Centre
CHD/CHDH SK8 ....**56** B4
Bridgemere CE Primary School
NANT CW5 ....**210** D6

Bridgeside Business Centre
NTHM/RTH M23 ....**42** C2
Bridgewater Community
High School (Lower)
WARRS WA4 ....**48** F9
Bridgewater Upper School
WARRS WA4 ....**48** F9
Brierley Business Centre
CW/HAS CW1 ....**5** G2
Brierley Primary School
CW/HAS CW1 ....**5** G2
Brighton Road Industrial Estate
HTNM WA3 ....**41** J7
Brindale Primary School
RDSH SK5 ....**42** B4
Brindley Arts Centre
RUNC WA7 ....**15** F2
Brine Leas County High School
NANT CW5 ....**196** G4
Brinksway Trading Estate
HTNM SK4 ....**16** B6
Brinnington Health Centre
RDSH SK5 ....**42** B3
Broadheath Primary School
ALT WA14 ....**37** P8
Broad Oak Community
Primary School
STHEL WA9 ....**22** E6
Broadoak High School
PART M31 ....**36** D6
Broad Oak Primary School
DID/WITH M20 ....**40** C8
Broadstone Hall Primary School
HTNM SK4 ....**41** L2
Broad Street Infant School
CW/HAS CW1 ....**185** J2
Broadway Industrial Estate
HYDE SK14 ....**29** P4
Broken Cross Primary School
MCFLDS SK11 ....**116** E5
Bromilston Primary School
WHITCH SY13 ....**212** A9
Brook Acre Primary School
WARRN/WOL WA2 ....**33** P7
Brookburn Primary School
CCHDY M21 ....**39** K1
Brooke Dean Community School
WILM/AE SK9 ....**71** M2
Brookfield Business Park
CHD/CHDH SK8 ....**55** P2
Brookfield School
WDN WA8 ....**46** B5
Brookhead Junior School
CHD/CHDH SK8 ....**55** P2
Brooklands Primary School
SALE M33 ....**38** D6
Brookside Hotel
CHNE CW2 ....**121** N7
Brookside Primary School
GTS/LS CH66 ....**80** A9
MPL/ROM SK6 ....**58** C9
Brooks Lane Industrial Estate
MWCH CW10 ....**151** K2
Brookvale Primary School
RUNC WA7 ....**62** F9
Brookvale Recreation Centre
RUNC WA7 ....**62** F9
Brookway High School
NTHM/RTH M23 ....**39** H8
Broomfield County
Junior School
WARRS WA4 ....**48** G8
Broomwood CP School
HALE/TIMP WA15 ....**53** P2
Broughton Industrial Estate
CHSW/BR CH4 ....**141** K4
Broughton J&I School
CHSW/BR CH4 ....**140** C6
Broughton Shopping Park
CHSW/BR CH4 ....**141** J6
The Brow Primary School
RUNC WA7 ....**62** D5
Broxton Hall Hotel
CHSE CH3 ....**178** G7
Bruche Community
Primary School
WARR WA1 ....**34** B9
Brunner Business Centre
NWCHW CW9 ....**109** M3
Bruntwood Primary School
CHD/CHDH SK8 ....**55** N5
Brymau Four Trading Estate
CHSW/BR CH4 ....**141** P3
Brymau One Trading Estate
CHSW/BR CH4 ....**142** A3
Brymau Three Trading Estate
CHSW/BR CH4 ....**142** A3
Brymau Two Trading Estate
CHSW/BR CH4 ....**142** A3
Budworth Sailing Club
NWCHE CW9 ....**88** A6
Buerton Primary School
AUD/MAD/W CW3 ....**217** N2
Buglawton Hall School
CONG CW12 ....**156** C5
Buglawton Industrial Estate
CONG CW12 ....**155** P5
Buglawton Primary School
CONG CW12 ....**156** A6
Bunbury Aldersey CE
Primary School
TPLY/KEL CW6 ....**166** A9
Burnage High School for Boys
BNG/LEV M19 ....**40** G3
Burnage RC
HTNM SK4 ....**40** F7
Burtonwood
Industrial Estate
WARRW/BUR WA5 ....**32** C1
Burtonwood Primary School
WARRW/BUR WA5 ....**32** B1
Button Lane School
NTHM/RTH M23 ....**39** J6

Byley Primary School
MWCH CW10 ....**130** F4
Cadishead Junior School
IRL M44 ....**36** C2
Cadishead Recreation Centre
IRL M44 ....**36** C3
Cale Green Primary School
EDGY/DAV SK3 ....**41** M9
Calveley CP School
TPLY/KEL CW6 ....**167** L7
Calveley Mill Industrial Estate
TPLY/KEL CW6 ....**167** H7
Cambridge Road
Primary School
EP CH65 ....**7** F5
Campanile Hotel
RUNC WA7 ....**14** E2
Canalside Industrial Estate
EP CH65 ....**7** H2
Capenhurst CE Primary School
EP CH65 ....**101** M4
Capenhurst Grange
School
GTS/LS CH66 ....**101** P2
Capenhurst Learning Centre
EP CH65 ....**101** N3
Capesthorne Hall
MCFLDS SK11 ....**115** J6
Capital Business Centre
BRAM/HZG SK7 ....**56** D9
Cardinal Newman RC
High School
WARRS WA4 ....**49** H2
Carrington Business Park
PART M31 ....**37** H2
Castlefields Health Centre
RUNC WA7 ....**62** E4
Castle Hill School
RUNC WA7 ....**62** B2
Castle Park Industrial Estate
FLINT CH6 ....**98** A4
Castle Primary School
ALS/KID ST7 ....**189** M2
Castle Tennis & Bowling Club
NWCHW CW8 ....**12** C5
The Castle
CH/BCN CH1 ....**2** D7
Castleview Primary School
RUNC WA7 ....**62** B6
Catalyst Science
Discovery Centre
WDN WA8 ....**61** N1
The Catholic High School
CHSW/BR CH4 ....**142** F4
Causeway Medical Centre
WARRS WA4 ....**48** D4
Cavendish Road
Primary School
DID/WITH M20 ....**40** B3
Cavendish Special School
RUNC WA7 ....**61** P9
Cedars Medical Centre
ALS/KID ST7 ....**187** P5
Central Primary School
DTN/ASHW M34 ....**29** L6
Chadkirk Industrial Estate
MPL/ROM SK6 ....**42** G8
Chaigley School
WARRS WA4 ....**49** N3
Chantry Court
CH/BCN CH1 ....**121** H9
Chapelfield Clinic
WDN WA8 ....**45** H6
Chapel Medical Centre
IRL M44 ....**27** N7
Chapel Museum
ALS/KID ST7 ....**189** M2
Chapel Street Clinic
WDN WA8 ....**21** H5
Chapel Street Primary School
BNG/LEV M19 ....**28** B8
Cheadle Catholic
Primary School
CHD/CHDH SK8 ....**55** N5
Cheadle Cricket Club
CHD/CHDH SK8 ....**55** L2
Cheadle Golf Club
CHD/CHDH SK8 ....**55** N3
Cheadle Heath Clinic
EDGY/DAV SK3 ....**41** M8
Cheadle Heath Primary School
EDGY/DAV SK3 ....**41** H9
Cheadle Heath Sports Centre
CHD/CHDH SK8 ....**56** A1
Cheadle Hulme College
CHD/CHDH SK8 ....**56** B8
Cheadle Hulme Medical Centre
CHD/CHDH SK8 ....**56** A7
Cheadle Hulme
Recreation Centre
CHD/CHDH SK8 ....**56** B8
Cheadle Hulme School
CHD/CHDH SK8 ....**56** A8
Cheadle Primary School
CHD/CHDH SK8 ....**55** M1
Cheadle Royal Hospital
CHD/CHDH SK8 ....**55** L5
Cheadle Royal Business Park
CHD/CHDH SK8 ....**55** L4
Cheadle Royal
Shopping Centre
CHD/CHDH SK8 ....**55** M5
Cheadle Swimming &
Recreation Centre
CHD/CHDH SK8 ....**55** N3
Cheadle Town FC
CHD/CHDH SK8 ....**55** N2
Chelford Primary School
MCFLDS SK11 ....**114** B1
Cherry Grove Primary School
CHSE CH3 ....**143** J1
Cherry Manor Primary School
SALE M33 ....**37** P6

Cherry Tree Community School
LYMM WA13 ....**50** C5
Cherry Tree Hospital
OFTN SK2 ....**57** J2
Cheshire College of
Agriculture
NANT CW5 ....**183** M7
Cheshire County
Officers Sports Club
CHNE CH2 ....**122** B5
Cheshire Health Clinic
SBCH CW11 ....**171** N2
Cheshire Magistrates Court
MCFLDN SK10 ....**8** E2
The Cheshire Military Museum
CH/BCN CH1 ....**2** D6
Cheshire Oaks Retail Outlet
EP CH65 ....**102** G2
Chester Boughton Hall
Cricket Club
CHSE CH3 ....**143** K1
Chester Business Centre
CH/BCN CH1 ....**3** F4
Chester Business Park
CHSW/BR CH4 ....**142** E7
Chester Cathedral
CH/BCN CH1 ....**2** E4
Chester City FC (Deva Stadium)
CH/BCN CH1 ....**142** A1
Chester College of
Higher Education
CH/BCN CH1 ....**121** M8
Chester County Court
CH/BCN CH1 ....**2** D4
Chester Court Hotel
CHNE CH2 ....**122** A7
The Chester Crabwall
Manor Hotel
CH/BCN CH1 ....**121** H4
Chester Crematorium
CH/BCN CH1 ....**121** K7
Chester Figure Clinic
CH/BCN CH1 ....**2** E4
Chester & Ellesmere Port
Police HQ
CH/BCN CH1 ....**121** K6
The Chestergate Clinic
MCFLDN SK10 ....**8** D3
Chester Golf Club
CHSW/BR CH4 ....**2** A6
The Chester Grosvenor &
Grosvenor Spa Hotel
CH/BCN CH1 ....**2** E4
Chester Racecourse
CH/BCN CH1 ....**2** B6
Chester Retail Park
CH/BCN CH1 ....**121** K9
Chester RUFC
CHSE CH3 ....**122** E9
Chester Southerly
Caravan Park
CHSW/BR CH4 ....**141** N9
Chesterton Clinic
NEWUL ST5 ....**201** P9
Chesterton High School
NEWUL ST5 ....**201** P8
Chester Toy Museum
CH/BCN CH1 ....**2** E5
Chester Visitors Centre
CH/BCN CH1 ....**3** F4
Chester Zoo
CHNE CH2 ....**121** P2
Chestnut Lodge Special School
WDN WA8 ....**20** C1
Childer Thornton
Primary School
GTS/LS CH66 ....**79** M5
The Chimney House Hotel
SBCH CW11 ....**172** C1
Cholmondeley Castle Gardens
MALPAS SY14 ....**193** L4
Chorlton-cum-Hardy
Cricket Club
CCHDY M21 ....**39** L2
Chorlton-cum-Hardy Golf Club
CCHDY M21 ....**39** M3
Chorlton Park Primary School
CCHDY M21 ....**39** M1
Chorlton Water Park
CCHDY M21 ....**39** M4
Christ Church CE
Primary School
EP CH65 ....**102** D2
NWCHW CW8 ....**107** M3
Christie Hospital &
Holt Radium Institute
DID/WITH M20 ....**40** C2
Christie Street Industrial Estate
STKP SK1 ....**41** P9
Christleton County
High School
CHSE CH3 ....**143** N3
Christleton Primary School
CHSE CH3 ....**143** M2
Christleton Sports Centre
CHSE CH3 ....**143** P5
Christleton Sports Club
CHSE CH3 ....**143** P1
Church Coppenhall
Junior School
CW/HAS CW1 ....**185** N1
Church Lawton Gate CP School
ALS/KID ST7 ....**188** C3
Church Lawton Primary School
ALS/KID ST7 ....**188** C3
Church Street Industrial Estate
WARR WA1 ....**19** F6
Cineworld
RUNC WA7 ....**62** D7
Cinnamon Brow CE
Primary School
WARRN/WOL WA2 ....**34** A5

City College Manchester
DID/WITH M20 ....**40** A4
NTHM/RTH M23 ....**38** G8
NTHM/RTH M23 ....**39** J8
NTHM/RTH M23 ....**39** M7
City Course Trading Estate
OP/CLY M11 ....**28** A2
City Walls Medical Centre
CH/BCN CH1 ....**2** C4
Civic Hall
..................................**6** D6
The Civic Hall
MCFLDN SK10 ....**95** N5
Clarendon Fields Primary
School *DUK* SK16 ....**29** P1
Clayton Industrial Estate
MWCH CW10 ....**28** D2
Cledford Infant School
MWCH CW10 ....**151** J3
Cledford Junior School
MWCH CW10 ....**151** J4
The Clinic Centre
MCFLDN SK10 ....**117** K7
Clinic for the Handicapped
WARRN/WOL WA2 ....**18** C4
Clock Face Country Park
STHEL ST7 ....**31** L5
Clough Hall School
MCFLDN ST7 ....**189** H7
Cloughwood Special School
NWCHW CW8 ....**109** M7
The Club Theatre
ALT WA14 ....**53** H4
Clutton CE Primary School
MALPAS SY14 ....**178** C7
The Cobbs Infant School
WARRS WA4 ....**48** C7
Cockhedge Centre
WARR WA1 ....**18** E5
Collins Industrial Estate
WARR WA1 ....**22** A4
Comberbach Primary School
NWCHE CW9 ....**87** L5
Comfort Inn
WGTN/LGST M12 ....**28** A3
Commercial Business Centre
RAIN/WH L35 ....**30** B5
Commonwealth House
MANAIR M90 ....**54** D7
Concord Business Park
WYTH/NTH M22 ....**54** E6
WYTH/NTH M22 ....**54** G6
Congleton Business Centre
CONG CW12 ....**155** N7
Congleton Business Park
CONG CW12 ....**155** L6
Congleton Golf Club
CONG CW12 ....**175** J1
Congleton High School
CONG CW12 ....**154** G7
Congleton Leisure Centre
CONG CW12 ....**155** N7
Constance Industrial Estate
WDN WA8 ....**21** M3
Coppenhall Cemetery
CW/HAS CW1 ....**185** J2
Coppenhall County
High School
CW/HAS CW1 ....**185** L2
Coppenhall Leisure Centre
CW/HAS CW1 ....**185** L3
Copper Beeches School
SALE M33 ....**38** C4
Cornishway Industrial Estate
WYTH/NTH M22 ....**54** F7
Cornwall Street
Industrial Estate
OP/CLY M11 ....**28** D2
Corrie Primary School
DTN/ASHW M34 ....**29** M8
Cottons Hotel
KNUT WA16 ....**68** B9
Countess of Chester Hospital
CHNE CH2 ....**121** M5
County Hotel
BRAM/HZG SK7 ....**56** E8
The Courts
STKP SK1 ....**17** G3
Crackley Bank Primary School
NEWUL ST5 ....**201** P7
Cranberry Infant School
ALS/KID ST7 ....**187** L5
Cranford Lodge Hospital
KNUT WA16 ....**90** D4
Cransley School
NWCHE CW9 ....**87** N4
Craxton Wood Hotel
GTS/LS CH66 ....**100** G3
Cresta Court Hotel
ALT WA14 ....**53** H2
Crewe AFC
(Alexandra Stadium)
CW/SHV CW2 ....**5** G7
Crewe Business Park
CW/HAS CW1 ....**185** M5
Crewe Cemetery
CW/HAS CW1 ....**185** J2
Crewe Crematorium
CW/HAS CW1 ....**185** J3
Crewe Gates Industrial Estate
CW/HAS CW1 ....**185** N6
Crewe Golf Club
CW/HAS CW1 ....**186** C5
Crewe Hall Hotel
CW/HAS CW1 ....**186** A7
Crewe Squash Club
CW/SHV CW2 ....**184** E4
Crewe Vagrants Cricket &
Hockey Club
NANT CW5 ....**197** M3
Croft County Primary School
GOL/RIS/CU WA3 ....**25** K9

Cromdale Way Community Hall
& Health Centre
WARRW/BUR WA5 ....47 J1
Cromwell Special School
DTN/ASHW M34 ....28 F7
Cronton CE Primary School
ALT WA8 ....45 J1
Crosland Industrial Estate
MPL/ROM SK6 ....42 D4
Crossacres J&I School
WYTH/NTH M22 ....55 H3
Cross Clinic
LYMM WA13 ....50 E4
Crowcroft Park Primary School
WGTN/LGST M12 ....28 A6
Crown Courts
CH/BCN CH1 ....2 D6
Crown Hotel
NANT CW5 ....10 B5
Crown Industrial Estate
ALT WA14 ....38 B9
Crown Royal Industrial Park
STKP SK1 ....17 H6
Cuddington Primary School
NWCHW CW8 ....127 J1
Culcheth Clinic
GOL/RIS/CU WA3 ....25 N6
Culcheth Hall School
ALT WA14 ....52 C4
Culcheth Primary &
High School
GOL/RIS/CU WA3 ....26 A6
Culcheth Sports Club
GOL/RIS/CU WA3 ....25 P6
Cumberland Athletics Track
CW/HAS CW1 ....5 G1
The Curzon Hotel
CHSE/BR CH4 ....142 D3
The Dale Primary School
MPL/ROM SK6 ....43 J9
Dallam Community
Primary School
WARRW/BUR WA5 ....33 J7
Dane Bank Primary School
DTN/ASHW M34 ....28 G7
Danebridge Medical Centre
NWCHE CW9 ....13 F3
Dane Mill Business Centre
CONG CW12 ....155 L7
Dane Road Industrial Estate
SALE M33 ....38 F3
Daneside Business Park
CONG CW12 ....155 N6
Daneside Theatre
CONG CW12 ....155 M7
Daresbury Park Business Park
WARRS WA4 ....63 K6
Daresbury Park Hotel
WARRS WA4 ....63 L6
Daresbury Primary School
WARRS WA4 ....63 M4
Darland High School
WRX/CR/LL LL12 ....160 F9
Darnhall Primary School
WSFD CW7 ....149 M4
Darwin Street Primary School
NWCHW CW8 ....12 C5
Davenham CE Primary School
NWCHE CW9 ....128 G1
Davenham Cricket Club
NWCHE CW9 ....128 G1
Davenport Golf Club
POY/DIS SK12 ....73 P2
Daven Primary School
CONG CW12 ....155 N8
David Cuthbert
Business Centre
OP/CLY M11 ....28 C2
The David Lewis School
WILM/AE SK9 ....92 C7
David Medical Centre
CCHDY M21 ....39 M2
Deacon Trading Estate
NEWLW WA12 ....23 L7
Dean Lane Medical Centre
BRAM/HZG SK7 ....57 K7
Dean Row Community
Junior School
WILM/AE SK9 ....71 N5
Deanway Trading Estate
MCFLDN SK10 ....95 L5
Deanway Trading Estate
WILM/AE SK9 ....71 M3
Dee Banks Special School
CHSE CH3 ....143 J3
Dee Point County
Primary School
CH/BCN CH1 ....120 G8
Delacre CE Primary School
NWCHW CW8 ....125 P6
Delamere Forest Golf Club
NWCHW CW8 ....126 B2
Delamere Forest School
FROD/HEL WA6 ....106 G8
Delta Business Park
DTN/ASHW M34 ....29 L2
Delves CE Primary School
NANT CW5 ....198 A8
Demmings Infant School
CHD/CHDH SK8 ....55 L7
Dene Hotel
CHNE CH2 ....122 A7
Denton Cemetery
DTN/ASHW M34 ....29 M9
Denton Cricket & Sports Club
DTN/ASHW M34 ....29 L4
Denton Drive Industrial Estate
NWCHE CW9 ....110 C2
Denton Golf Club
DTN/ASHW M34 ....29 H5
Denton St Lawrence
Cricket Club
DTN/ASHW M34 ....29 M7

Deva Roman Experience
CH/BCN CH1 ....2 D5
De Vere Carden Park Hotel
MALPAS SY14 ....178 B9
De Vere Mottram Hall Hotel
MCFLDN SK10 ....94 D2
Dial Park Primary School
OFTN SK2 ....57 K3
Didsbury CE Primary School
DID/WITH M20 ....40 C5
Didsbury Cricket Club
DID/WITH M20 ....40 D7
Didsbury Golf Club
WYTH/NTH M22 ....40 A7
Didsbury Medical Centre
DID/WITH M20 ....40 B4
Didsbury Road Primary School
HTNM SK4 ....40 A4
The Dingle Primary School
CW/HAS CW1 ....186 B2
Disley Golf Club
POY/DIS SK12 ....58 G8
Disley Primary School
POY/DIS SK12 ....59 H9
The District CE Primary School
NEWLW WA12 ....23 L6
Ditton CE Primary School
WDN WA8 ....44 C6
Ditton CP School
WDN WA8 ....20 A1
Ditton Hall St Michaels RC
Primary School
WDN WA8 ....45 H8
Ditton Medical Centre
WDN WA8 ....20 A2
The Dodington Lodge Hotel
WHITCH SY13 ....213 M7
Dodleston CE Primary School
CHSW/BR CH4 ....160 D2
Dorin Park Special School
CHNE CH2 ....121 N5
Dorothy Clive
MKTDR TF9 ....219 N9
Dove Bank Primary School
ALS/KID ST7 ....189 J6
Droylsden Swimming Pool
DROY M43 ....28 G1
Drug Dependency Clinic
WDN WA8 ....21 H5
Ducie Athletics Ground
Running Track
GTN M18 ....28 B5
Dunge Valley (Gardens)
CHF/WBR SK23 ....97 J2
Dunham Forest Golf &
Country Club
ALT WA14 ....52 D3
Dunham Hill Primary School
FROD/HEL WA6 ....104 E6
Dunkirk Trading Estate
CH/BCN CH1 ....101 P6
Duttons Business Centre
CHNE CH2 ....12 E4
Dutton Viaduct
NWCHW CW8 ....85 N8
Eagle Sports Club
WARRW/BUR WA5 ....47 L3
Earnswood Medical Centre
CW/HAS CW1 ....4 D2
Eastside Industrial Estate
STHEL WA9 ....22 A7
Eaton Bank Industrial Estate
CONG CW12 ....155 P6
Eaton Bank School
CONG CW12 ....155 P5
Eaton Golf Club
CHSE CH3 ....144 C5
Eaton Hotel
CH/BCN CH1 ....3 G5
Eaton Place Business Centre
SALE M33 ....38 D4
Eaton Primary School
TPLY/KEL CW6 ....147 M7
Eaves Primary School
STHEL WA9 ....31 H2
Eccleston CE Primary School
CHSW/BR CH4 ....142 F8
Eccleston Park Golf Club
STHEL WA9 ....30 A2
Edleston Primary School
CW/SHV CW2 ....5 F5
Edwardian Pumping Station
NWCHW CW8 ....12 E5
Egerton Park Arts College
DTN/ASHW M34 ....29 L4
Egerton Park Community
High School
DTN/ASHW M34 ....29 K5
Egerton Primary School
KNUT WA16 ....90 D3
Ellesmere Port
Business Centre
EP CH65 ....6 D5
Ellesmere Port Catholic
High School
EP CH65 ....102 B1
Ellesmere Port Clinic
EP CH65 ....6 D7
Ellesmere Port Golf Centre
GTS/LS CH66 ....79 M5
Ellesmere Port Hospital
EP CH65 ....102 C2
Ellesmere Port Stadium
EP CH65 ....102 G1
Elmridge Primary School
HALE/TIMP WA15 ....53 N7
Elms Medical Centre
CHNE CH2 ....121 P8
Elton Primary School
CHNE CH2 ....82 A9
Elworth CE Primary School
SBCH CW11 ....171 K2
Elworth Hall Primary School
SBCH CW11 ....171 K2

Elworth Mount Pleasant
Cricket Club
SBCH CW11 ....171 J1
English Martyrs RC
Primary School
RNFD/HAY WA11 ....23 H2
Ensor Trading Estate
NM/HAY SK22 ....59 N9
Enterprise Trading Estate
GTN M18 ....28 E3
Epic Leisure Centre
EP CH65 ....6 E7
Eric Moore Health Centre
WARRN/WOL WA2 ....18 C4
Etchells Primary School
CHD/CHDH SK8 ....55 L6
Etrop Grange Hotel &
Restaurant
MANAIR M90 ....54 D6
Europa Business Park
CW/HAS CW1 ....56 B1
Evelyn Street Primary School
WARRW/BUR WA5 ....48 A3
Everite Road Industrial Estate
WDN WA8 ....45 H8
Ewing School
DID/WITH M20 ....40 B3
Excalibur Industrial Estate
ALS/KID ST7 ....188 A5
Excalibur Primary School
ALS/KID ST7 ....188 A6
Express by Holiday Inn
GTN M18 ....28 E4
Express Industrial Estate
WDN WA8 ....44 G8
Fairfield Golf & Sailing Club
DTN/ASHW M34 ....29 H2
Fairfield High School
WDN WA8 ....45 H4
Fairfield High School for Girls
DROY M43 ....28 F1
Fairfield J&I School
WDN WA8 ....45 P5
Fairfield Primary School
WARR WA1 ....19 G3
Fairfield Road Primary School
DROY M43 ....28 F1
Fairhill Industrial Estate
IRL M44 ....36 E1
Fairway Primary School
OFTN SK2 ....57 M4
Fairway Trading Estate
WDN WA8 ....20 D6
Fallibroome High School
MCFLDN SK10 ....116 E2
Farndon Health Centre
CHSE CH3 ....176 C7
Farndon Primary School
CHSE CH3 ....176 C6
Farnworth CE Primary School
WDN WA8 ....45 N3
Fearnhead Cross Medical Centre
WARRN/WOL WA2 ....32 A4
Fence Avenue Industrial Estate
MCFLDN SK10 ....9 G2
Fiddlers Lane Primary School
IRL M44 ....27 P6
Fir Grove Hotel
WARRS WA4 ....49 J4
Firs CP School
SALE M33 ....38 A4
The Firs School
CHNE CH2 ....121 P6
Fir Tree Primary School
RDSH SK5 ....28 E7
Fishwicks Industrial Estate
RNFD/HAY WA11 ....23 K1
STHEL WA9 ....22 B9
Flash CE Primary School
BUX SK17 ....139 L8
Fleet Lane Industrial Estate
STHEL WA9 ....31 J6
Fleming Industrial Estate
WARR WA1 ....19 F5
Flint Castle
FLINT CH6 ....98 B4
Flint Child Health Clinic
FLINT CH6 ....98 B6
Flint FC
FLINT CH6 ....98 B5
Flint High School
FLINT CH6 ....98 A3
Flint Leisure Centre
FLINT CH6 ....98 A5
Flowcrete Business Park
SBCH CW11 ....152 A9
Fordton Leisure Centre
WARRN/WOL WA2 ....33 K5
Forest Gate Community
Primary School
PART M31 ....36 C5
Forest Hills Hotel &
Leisure Complex
FROD/HEL WA6 ....83 P7
Forest Park School
SALE M33 ....38 D4
Forest Primary School
NWCHW CW8 ....108 E3
Forest School
HALE/TIMP WA15 ....53 K1
The Forge Shopping Centre
WARRS WA4 ....48 E6
Forum Leisure Centre
WYTH/NTH M22 ....54 E4
The Forum Shopping Centre
CH/BCN CH1 ....2 D4
Four Acre Lane
Shopping Centre
STHEL WA9 ....30 G4
Freeport Take Outlet Mall
ALS/KID ST7 ....201 M1
Frodsham CE Primary School
FROD/HEL WA6 ....84 A6

Frodsham Golf Club
FROD/HEL WA6 ....83 P8
Frodsham Science &
Technology College
FROD/HEL WA6 ....83 P5
Fulshaw CE Primary School
WILM/AE SK9 ....71 H8
Furness Vale Business Centre
CHF/WBR SK23 ....75 P2
Furness Vale Primary School
CHF/WBR SK23 ....75 P5
Gadbrook Business Centre
NWCHE CW9 ....110 D7
Gainsborough County
Junior School
CW/SHV CW2 ....4 B6
Gainsborough Infants School
CW/SHV CW2 ....4 C5
Galleon Leisure Centre
DID/WITH M20 ....40 D8
Garden Lane Medical Centre
CH/BCN CH1 ....2 A2
Garrick Playhouse
ALT WA14 ....53 H1
Garrick Theatre
EDGY/DAV SK3 ....17 F5
Garven Place Clinic
WARR WA1 ....18 B6
Gas Works Industrial Estate
ALS/KID ST7 ....188 G6
Gateway Theatre
CH/BCN CH1 ....2 C4
Gateworth Industrial Estate
WARRW/BUR WA5 ....47 P4
Gatley Golf Club
CHD/CHDH SK8 ....55 K4
Gatley Health Centre
CHD/CHDH SK8 ....55 J1
Gatley Primary School
CHD/CHDH SK8 ....55 J2
Gawsworth Hall
MCFLDS SK11 ....135 M3
Gawsworth Primary School
MCFLDS SK11 ....135 L1
Gemini Business Park
WARRW/BUR WA5 ....33 H5
General Cemetery
CHSW/BR CH4 ....142 E3
Glazebury CE Primary School
GOL/RIS/CU WA3 ....26 C2
Globe Lane Industrial Estate
DUK SK16 ....29 P2
Globe Lane Primary School
DUK SK16 ....29 P3
Golborne CP School
GOL/RIS/CU WA3 ....24 C1
Goldenhill Golf Club
BURS/TUN ST6 ....189 M9
Goldenhill St Josephs Catholic
Primary School
BURS/TUN ST6 ....189 K9
Golden Square Shopping Centre
WARR WA1 ....18 C6
Golden Triangle Industrial Estate
WDN WA8 ....45 J9
Goostrey Business Park
HOLMCW CW4 ....131 L2
Goostrey Primary School
HOLMCW CW4 ....132 D3
Gorse Covert Primary School
GOL/RIS/CU WA3 ....35 J2
Gorsewood Primary School
RUNC WA7 ....63 J7
Gorsey Bank Primary School
WILM/AE SK9 ....71 H7
Gorsthills Primary School
GTS/LS CH66 ....101 N1
Gorton Brook First School
WGTN/LGST M12 ....28 A3
Gorton Industrial Estate
GTN M18 ....28 C3
Gorton Medical Centre
GTN M18 ....28 D4
Gorton Mount Primary School
GTN M18 ....28 B6
Gorton Retail Market
GTN M18 ....28 D4
Goyt Valley Industrial Estate
CHF/WBR SK23 ....75 P2
Graham CE Primary School
NWCHE CW9 ....110 G2
Grand Junction Retail Park
CW/HAS CW1 ....5 G3
The Grange
Comprehensive School
RUNC WA7 ....15 K5
The Grange Country Club
NSTN CH64 ....77 M1
The Grange Infant School
RUNC WA7 ....15 K4
The Grange Junior School
NWCHW CW8 ....109 J6
RUNC WA7 ....15 K4
Grange Primary School
WILM/AE SK9 ....71 L2
WSFD CW7 ....149 K1
The Grange School
NWCHW CW8 ....109 K7
Grange Valley Primary School
RNFD/HAY WA11 ....23 H4
Grappenhall Clinic
WARRS WA4 ....49 K5
Grappenhall Cricket Club
WARRS WA4 ....49 J6
Grappenhall Hall School
WARRS WA4 ....49 K6
Grappenhall Heys
Primary School
WARRS WA4 ....49 J3
Grappenhall Sports Club
WARRS WA4 ....49 J6
Great Budworth CE
Primary School
NWCHE CW9 ....88 B5

Greater Grace School
CHNE CH2 ....102 D8
Great Moor Clinic
OFTN SK2 ....57 J2
Great Moor Primary School
OFTN SK2 ....57 H3
Great Sankey County
High School
WARRW/BUR WA5 ....32 B9
Great Sankey Primary School
WARRW/BUR WA5 ....47 L2
Great Sutton Health Centre
GTS/LS CH66 ....79 P9
Greave Primary School
MPL/ROM SK6 ....43 H4
Greenbank Residential School
NWCHW CW8 ....12 B7
Greenbank School
CHD/CHDH SK8 ....56 A6
Greenbrow Infant School
NTHM/RTH M23 ....54 B4
Greencourts Business Park
WYTH/NTH M22 ....55 J8
Green End Junior School
BNC/LEV M19 ....40 F3
Greenfield Farm
Industrial Estate
CONG CW12 ....155 K6
Greenfields Primary School
WSFD CW7 ....149 J1
Green Lane Industrial Estate
HTNM SK4 ....16 B3
Green Lane Special School
WARR WA1 ....34 C8
Greenoaks Farm
Industrial Estate
WDN WA8 ....46 B7
Green Oaks Shopping Centre
WDN WA8 ....21 K2
Gresty Brook Medical Centre
CW/SHV CW2 ....185 J8
Greswell Primary School
DTN/ASHW M34 ....29 L7
Greyhound Retail Park
CH/BCN CH1 ....121 J8
Greyhound &
Speedway Stadium
GTN M18 ....28 B4
Grosvenor Business Park
MPL/ROM SK6 ....42 E2
Grosvenor Medical Centre
CW/HAS CW1 ....4 B1
Grosvenor Museum
CH/BCN CH1 ....2 E6
Grosvenor Nuffield Hospital
CHSW/BR CH4 ....142 E4
Grosvenor Pulford Hotel
CHSW/BR CH4 ....160 F7
Grosvenor Shopping Centre
CH/BCN CH1 ....2 E5
MCFLDS SK11 ....8 E4
Guardian Medical Centre
WARRW/BUR WA5 ....48 B1
Guardian Street
Industrial Estate
WARRW/BUR WA5 ....18 A4
Guide Bridge Industrial Estate
DTN/ASHW M34 ....29 L1
Guide Bridge Theatre
DTN/ASHW M34 ....29 L1
Guide Bridge Trading Estate
DTN/ASHW M34 ....29 L1
Guilden Sutton
Primary School
CHSE CH3 ....122 F6
Guild Hall
CH/BCN CH1 ....2 C4
Gulliver's World Theme Park
WARRW/BUR WA5 ....33 H7
Gwynedd Primary School
FLINT CH6 ....98 A7
Hague Bar Primary School
NM/HAY SK22 ....59 J7
Halebanks Cricket Club
HALE/TIMP WA15 ....53 P9
Hale Barns Cricket Club
HALE/TIMP WA15 ....54 A7
Hale CE Primary School
SPK/HALE L24 ....60 E5
Hale Golf Club
HALE/TIMP WA15 ....53 L8
Hale Preparatory School
HALE/TIMP WA15 ....53 J4
Hale Road Industrial Estate
WDN WA8 ....61 J1
Halewood CE Primary School
HLWD L26 ....44 A6
Halewood Sports Centre
HLWD L26 ....44 A8
Halewood St Marks Catholic
Primary School
HLWD L26 ....44 A7
Halewood Park Primary School
RUNC WA7 ....62 C8
Halton College
WDN WA8 ....21 H4
Halton College of
Further Education
WDN WA8 ....21 G3
Halton General Hospital
RUNC WA7 ....62 D8
Halton High School
RUNC WA7 ....62 D6
Halton House School
RUNC WA7 ....62 D7
Halton Lodge Primary School
RUNC WA7 ....62 B6
Halton Magistrates Court
RUNC WA7 ....62 D6
Hammond School
CHNE CH2 ....122 D4
Hampton Heath
Industrial Estate
MALPAS SY14 ....192 C3

Handbridge Medical Centre *CHSW/BR CH4* ...2 E7
Handforth Health Centre *WILM/AE SK9* ...71 M3
Hanover Business Park *ALT WA14* ...37 N9
Hanover International Hotel & Club *WARRS WA4* ...64 G4
Happy Feet Health Centre *FLINT CH6* ...98 A5
Hare Hill (NT) *MCFLDN SK10* ...94 A7
The Harlequin Theatre *NWCHE CW9* ...12 E3
Harrytown Catholic High School *MPL/ROM SK6* ...42 F6
Hartford Business Centre *NWCHW CW8* ...109 H8
Hartford Hall Hotel *NWCHW CW8* ...109 L8
Hartford High School *NWCHW CW8* ...109 L7
Hartford Manor *NWCHW CW8* ...109 M7
Hartford Manor Primary School *NWCHW CW8* ...109 L7
Hartford Primary School *NWCHW CW8* ...109 K8
Harthill Primary School *CHSE CH3* ...179 L5
Haslington Cricket Club *CW/HAS CW1* ...186 B2
Haslington Primary School *CW/HAS CW1* ...186 B4
Hat Works *EDGY/DAV SK3* ...17 F5
Havannah Business Centre *CONG CW12* ...155 P7
Havannah Primary School *CONG CW12* ...155 P4
Hawarden Airport *CHSW/BR CH4* ...141 H5
Hawarden Castle *CQ CH5* ...140 C3
Hawarden Health Centre *CQ CH5* ...140 B2
Hawarden Industrial Park *CHSW/BR CH4* ...140 F3
Hawarden Infant School *CQ CH5* ...140 B2
Hawthorne Business Park *WARRW/BUR WA5* ...33 J8
Hawthorns Special School *DTN/ASHW M34* ...29 K4
Haydock Cricket Club *RNFD/HAY WA11* ...22 G3
Haydock High School *RNFD/HAY WA11* ...22 G3
Haydock Lane Industrial Estate *RNFD/HAY WA11* ...23 J1
Haydock Medical Centre *RNFD/HAY WA11* ...23 H3
Haydock Park Golf Club *NEWLW WA12* ...24 B4
Hazel Grove Clinic *BRAM/HZG SK7* ...57 L4
Hazel Grove Golf Club *BRAM/HZG SK7* ...57 P6
Hazel Grove High School *BRAM/HZG SK7* ...57 J6
Hazel Grove Pools & Fitness Centre *BRAM/HZG SK7* ...56 G6
Hazel Grove Primary School *BRAM/HZG SK7* ...57 L4
Hazel Grove Recreation Centre *BRAM/HZG SK7* ...57 J7
Heald Green Medical Centre *CHD/CHDH SK8* ...55 K7
The Heath Comprehensive School *RUNC WA7* ...61 P7
Heath Lane Medical Centre *CHSE CH3* ...143 J1
Heath Road Medical Centre *RUNC WA7* ...15 G6
Heaton Moor Golf Club *HTNM SK4* ...41 H3
Heaton Moor Medical Centre *HTNM SK4* ...41 K3
Heaton Moor RUFC *HTNM SK4* ...41 J5
Heaton Norris Health Centre *HTNM SK4* ...16 D1
Heaton Special School *HTNM SK4* ...41 J3
Hebden Green Community School *WSFD CW7* ...149 J3
Helsby Golf Club *FROD/HEL WA6* ...105 H5
Helsby Health Centre *FROD/HEL WA6* ...105 H1
Helsby High School *FROD/HEL WA6* ...83 K8
Hempshaw Business Centre *STKP SK1* ...42 A9
Henbury High School *MCFLDN SK10* ...116 E4
Heritage Centre *CH/BCN CH1* ...2 E5
Hermitage Primary School *HOLMCH CW4* ...132 A8
Heyes Lane J&I School *HALE/TIMP WA15* ...38 E8
Heyrose Golf Club *KNUT WA16* ...89 J2
Highbank Trading Estate *OP/CLY M11* ...28 D2
Higher Openshaw Community School *OP/CLY M11* ...28 D1

Highfield Cemetery *MPL/ROM SK6* ...42 E6
Highfield Primary School *CH/BCN CH1* ...121 J7
Highfields County Primary School *NANT CW5* ...10 E2
Highfield Special School *HLWD L26* ...44 A8
High Lane Medical Centre *MPL/ROM SK6* ...58 C8
High Lane Primary School *MPL/ROM SK6* ...58 C7
High Legh CP School *KNUT WA16* ...67 J1
High Street Primary School *WSFD CW7* ...149 M1
Hillcrest Grammar School *EDGY/DAV SK3* ...56 F1
Hillcrest Hotel *WDN WA8* ...45 M2
Hillgate Business Centre *STKP SK1* ...17 H7
Hillside Primary School *FROD/HEL WA6* ...83 K8
Hill Top Primary School *WHITCH SY13* ...188 F9
Hill Valley Golf & Country Club *WHITCH SY13* ...213 N3
Hillview Primary School *RUNC WA7* ...84 C1
Hinderton School *CQ CH5* ...102 C1
HM Remand Centre *GOL/RIS/CU WA3* ...25 N9
HM Young Offenders Institute *WARRS WA4* ...65 L2
Holcroft Clinic *GOL/RIS/CU WA3* ...25 N6
Holiday Inn *CHSW/BR CH4* ...142 C8
RNFD/HAY WA11 ...23 M1
RUNC WA7 ...84 D1
WARR WA1 ...34 G9
Hollinhey Primary School *MCFLDS SK11* ...117 M9
Holly Bank Caravan Park *GOL/RIS/CU WA3* ...35 P7
Holly House Estate *MWCH CW10* ...131 H4
Holly Lodge Hotel *HOLMCH CW4* ...131 P8
Holmes Chapel Business Centre *HOLMCH CW4* ...132 A8
Holmes Chapel Comprehensive School *HOLMCH CW4* ...131 M9
Holmes Chapel Health Centre *HOLMCH CW4* ...131 P8
Holmes Chapel Primary School *HOLMCH CW4* ...131 N8
Holt Primary School *WRXS/E L13* ...176 F8
Holy Family Catholic Primary School *SALE M33* ...39 H4
Holy Family RC Primary School *WDN WA8* ...45 K1
Holy Spirit Catholic Primary School *STHEL WA9* ...22 E6
The Holy Spirit RC Aided Primary School *BRAM/HZG SK7* ...62 B6
Hong Sing Chinese Medical Centre *BRAM/HZG SK7* ...57 L4
Hood Manor Medical Centre *WARRW/BUR WA5* ...47 N2
Hoole CE Primary School *CHNE CH2* ...122 B8
Hoole Hall Hotel *CHNE CH2* ...122 D6
Horns Mill Primary School *FROD/HEL WA6* ...104 C3
Houldsworth Golf Club *RDSH SK5* ...28 E9
Houldsworth Medical Centre *RDSH SK5* ...41 N1
Howley Quay Industrial Estate *WARR WA1* ...19 H5
Hulme Hall Grammar School *CHD/CHDH SK8* ...56 A6
Hungerford Medical Centre *CW/HAS CW1* ...5 J2
Hungerford Primary School *CW/HAS CW1* ...5 J2
Hunters Lodge Hotel *CW/HAS CW1* ...185 N3
Huntington Primary School *CHSE CH3* ...143 J5
Huntsbank Business Park *CW/SHV CW2* ...184 E9
Hurdsfield Community Primary School *MCFLDN SK10* ...117 M2
Hurdsfield Industrial Estate *MCFLDN SK10* ...117 K2
Hurdsfield Junior School *MCFLDN SK10* ...117 M3
Hurleston Junction *NANT CW5* ...183 H5
Hurstfield Industrial Estate *HTNM SK4* ...41 M2
Hursthead Primary School *CHD/CHDH SK8* ...56 C9
Huxley CE Primary School *CHSE CH3* ...164 F2
Hyde Cricket Club *HYDE SK14* ...43 L4

Industrial Hygiene Research Laboratories *MCFLDN SK10* ...93 K9
Innkeeper's Lodge *CHNE CH2* ...122 D5
CHSE CH3 ...143 M2
Innkeeper's Lodge Hotel *SBCH CW11* ...155 J5
WILM/AE SK9 ...93 J1
Innkeeper's Lodge Warrington *GOL/RIS/CU WA3* ...24 C3
The Instructor College *STKP SK1* ...17 G5
International Business Centre *WARRW/BUR WA5* ...32 F6
Irlam & Cadishead Community High School *IRL M44* ...36 D1
Irlam County Primary School *IRL M44* ...27 M8
Irlam Endowed Primary School *IRL M44* ...27 N7
Irlam Industrial Estate *IRL M44* ...36 D1
Irlam Swimming Pool *IRL M44* ...27 N8
Iron Bridge *CHSW/BR CH4* ...162 A4
Irwin Road Health Centre *STHEL WA9* ...31 J1
Ivy Bank Primary School *WARRS WA4* ...116 C7
Ivy Bank Trading Estate *KNUT WA16* ...91 L1
Jamage Industrial Estate *ALS/KID ST7* ...201 M1
Jeff Joseph Sale Moor Technology College *SALE M33* ...38 G6
JH Godwin Primary School *CH/BCN CH1* ...120 G7
Jodrell Bank Telescope *MCFLDS SK11* ...113 N9
Jodrell Bank Visitor Centre & Arboretum *MCFLDS SK11* ...132 C1
John Street Medical Centre *GOL/RIS/CU WA3* ...24 C1
John Street Primary School *EP CH65* ...6 E2
Kelsall Medical Centre *TPLY/KEL CW6* ...125 J6
Kelsall Primary School *TPLY/KEL CW6* ...125 H7
Kelsborrow Castle *TPLY/KEL CW6* ...125 K7
Kenmore Medical Centre *WILM/AE SK9* ...71 J8
Kerfoot Business Park *WARRN/WOL WA2* ...33 K8
Kidsgrove Medical Centre *ALS/KID ST7* ...189 L6
Kidsgrove Ski Centre *ALS/KID ST7* ...189 H9
Kidsgrove Sports Club *ALS/KID ST7* ...189 H7
Kiltearn Medical Centre *NANT CW5* ...10 B5
King Charles Tower *CH/BCN CH1* ...2 E3
Kingsfield First School *BIDD ST8* ...175 L9
Kings Grove High School *CW/SHV CW2* ...4 A6
Kingsley Community Primary School *FROD/HEL WA6* ...106 D2
King's School *MCFLDN SK10* ...9 H3
The Kings School *CHSW/BR CH4* ...142 D6
The King's School *CHSW/BR CH4* ...8 D3
King Street Trading Estate *MWCH CW10* ...130 B9
Kingsway High School *CHNE CH2* ...122 A6
Kingsway Secondary School *CHD/CHDH SK8* ...55 L3
Kingsway Secondary School *CHD/CHDH SK8* ...55 L2
Kirkfield Hotel *NEWLW WA12* ...24 A5
Knights Grange Golf Course & Sports Complex *WSFD CW7* ...128 C8
Knowles Industrial Estate *CHF/WBR SK23* ...75 P3
Knutsford Civic Hall & Cinema *KNUT WA16* ...90 E4
Knutsford Crown Courts *KNUT WA16* ...90 E4
Knutsford FC *KNUT WA16* ...90 D2
Knutsford Golf Club *KNUT WA16* ...90 E2
Knutsford High School (Upper School) *KNUT WA16* ...90 D4
Knutsford High School (Lower School) *KNUT WA16* ...90 B4
Knutsford Leisure Centre *KNUT WA16* ...90 D4
Knutsford Sports Club *KNUT WA16* ...90 D2
Knutsford Squash Racquets Club *KNUT WA16* ...90 F4
Kus Industrial Estate *CQ CH5* ...140 E4
Lacey Green Primary School *WILM/AE SK9* ...71 J5

Lache Health Centre *CHSW/BR CH4* ...142 C5
Lache Primary School *CHSW/BR CH4* ...142 C5
Lady Barn House School *CHD/CHDH SK8* ...55 M4
Ladybarn Primary School *DID/WITH M20* ...40 E2
Ladybridge Primary School *CHD/CHDH SK8* ...56 B5
Ladybrook Primary School *BRAM/HZG SK7* ...56 F8
Lakemore Country Park *SBCH CW11* ...171 J8
Lamb Cottage Caravan Park *NWCHW CW8* ...127 M4
Lambs Grange School *NWCHW CW8* ...108 B9
Lambs House School *CONG CW12* ...155 P6
Lancasterian School *DID/WITH M20* ...39 P3
Lane End Primary School *CHD/CHDH SK8* ...56 C5
Langley Road Industrial Estate *IRL M44* ...65 M4
Lark Hill Primary School *EDGY/DAV SK3* ...16 B6
Latchford CE Primary School *WARRS WA4* ...48 D3
Latchford Medical Centre *WARRS WA4* ...48 G4
Lawn Cemetery *ALT WA14* ...37 J8
Lawnhurst Trading Estate *CHD/CHDH SK8* ...56 B2
Leaf Lane School *WSFD CW7* ...129 H9
Lea Green Business Park *STHEL WA9* ...30 E4
Leftwich Community Primary School *NWCHE CW9* ...110 A8
Legh Vale Primary School *RNFD/HAY WA11* ...22 F3
Leigh Golf Club *GOL/RIS/CU WA3* ...25 M5
Leighton Hospital *CW/HAS CW1* ...169 M8
Leighton Primary School *CW/HAS CW1* ...169 N9
Levenshulme Baths *BNG/LEV M19* ...28 B8
Levenshulme Health Centre *BNG/LEV M19* ...28 B8
Levenshulme High School For Girls *BNG/LEV M19* ...41 H1
Levenshulme Trading Estate *BNG/LEV M19* ...28 C7
Lime Tree Primary School *SALE M33* ...39 H5
Linden Road Primary School *DTN/ASHW M34* ...29 N6
Lindow Primary School *WILM/AE SK9* ...92 F2
Lingley Mere Business Park *WARRW/BUR WA5* ...32 B8
Linley Trading Estate *ALS/KID ST7* ...188 E7
Lisburne School *OFTN SK2* ...57 L1
Little Bollington CE Primary School *ALT WA14* ...51 P6
Little Budworth Country Park *TPLY/KEL CW6* ...147 P2
Little Leigh Primary School *NWCHW CW8* ...86 F8
Little Moreton Hall (NT) *CONG CW12* ...173 P7
Little Sutton CE Primary School *GTS/LS CH66* ...79 L7
Little Theatre *KNUT WA16* ...90 D3
The Little Theatre *CH/BCN CH1* ...2 E2
Liverpool University Botanic Gardens (Ness Gardens) *NSTN CH64* ...77 N9
Llyndir Hall Hotel *WRX/GR/LL L12* ...160 F8
L & M Business Park *ALT WA14* ...52 F1
Locking Stumps Primary School *GOL/RIS/CU WA3* ...34 D3
Lodgefield Community Primary School *CW/SHV CW2* ...184 E4
Longbarn County Primary School *WARRN/WOL WA2* ...34 C7
Long Lane County Primary School *WARRN/WOL WA2* ...33 L7
Longridge Trading Estate *KNUT WA16* ...91 H2
Longsight Cricket Club *WGTN/LGST M12* ...28 A6
Longton Lane Community Primary School *RAIN/WH L35* ...30 A3
Longton Medical Centre *RAIN/WH L35* ...30 A5
The Longview Hotel *KNUT WA16* ...90 D3
Loomer Road Industrial Estate *NEWLU ST5* ...201 P9
Loreto Convent Grammar School *ALT WA14* ...52 G2

Loreto Preparatory School *ALT WA14* ...52 F2
Lostock Gralam FC *NWCHE CW9* ...110 F2
Lostock Hall Primary School *POY/DIS SK12* ...73 H3
Lostock Social & Sports Club *NWCHE CW9* ...110 E3
Loushers Lane Special School *GOL/RIS/CU WA3* ...34 F5
Loushers Lane Special School *WARRS WA4* ...48 F5
Lower Park Primary School *POY/DIS SK12* ...73 J2
Lower Peover CE VA Primary School *KNUT WA16* ...112 C3
Lowerworks Mill *MCFLDS SK11* ...157 J5
Lowfield Industrial Estate *STHEL WA9* ...30 C3
Lowton Business Park *GOL/RIS/CU WA3* ...25 J1
Lowton High School *GOL/RIS/CU WA3* ...25 K1
Lowton J&I School *GOL/RIS/CU WA3* ...25 J2
Lowton St Marys CE Primary School *GOL/RIS/CU WA3* ...25 J1
Lowton West Primary School *GOL/RIS/CU WA3* ...24 F1
Lud's Church (Cave) *MCFLDS SK11* ...159 K2
Ludworth Primary School *MPL/ROM SK6* ...43 M8
Lum Head School *CHD/CHDH SK8* ...55 K4
Lunts Heath Primary School *WDN WA8* ...45 P2
The Lyceum *CW/HAS CW1* ...5 F2
Lyme Community Primary School *NEWLW WA12* ...23 K5
Lyme Green Business Park *MCFLDS SK11* ...117 J9
Lyme Park Country Park *POY/DIS SK12* ...74 F4
Lyme Park (NT) *POY/DIS SK12* ...74 F5
Lymm Golf Club *LYMM WA13* ...50 D2
Lymm High School *LYMM WA13* ...51 H4
Lymm Hotel *LYMM WA13* ...50 D4
Lymm RFC *LYMM WA13* ...50 E6
Lyon Industrial Estate *ALT WA14* ...37 N9
STHEL WA9 ...31 J4
Mablins Lane Community Primary School *CW/HAS CW1* ...170 A4
Macclesfield Athletics Track *MCFLDN SK10* ...116 C2
Macclesfield College of FE *MCFLDS SK11* ...117 H6
Macclesfield Crematorium *MCFLDN SK10* ...8 B1
Macclesfield District General Hospital *MCFLDN SK10* ...8 A3
Macclesfield Golf Club *MCFLDS SK11* ...117 M6
Macclesfield Leisure Centre *MCFLDN SK10* ...116 C2
Macclesfield Preparatory School *MCFLDS SK11* ...8 A4
Macclesfield Silk Museum *MCFLDS SK11* ...8 E5
Macclesfield Town FC (Moss Rose Ground) *MCFLDS SK11* ...117 K8
Macclesfield West Park Museum *MCFLDN SK10* ...8 C2
Macdonald Road Medical Centre *IRL M44* ...27 M8
Mackenzie Industrial Estate *CHD/CHDH SK8* ...56 B1
Macon Business Park *CW/HAS CW1* ...5 H5
Mads Little Theatre *CW/HAS CW1* ...9 F6
Magda House Medical Centre *OFTN SK2* ...57 K3
Maiden Castle Hillfort *MALPAS SY14* ...192 C1
Malbank School & 6th Form College *NANT CW5* ...196 D1
Malbern Industrial Estate *DTN/ASHW M34* ...29 J5
Malkins Bank Golf Club *SBCH CW11* ...172 A7
Malpas Alport Endowed Primary School *MALPAS SY14* ...204 A2
Manchester Airport World Freight Terminal *MANAIR M90* ...54 C8
Manchester Business Park *MANAIR M90* ...54 E7
Manchester College of Arts & Technology *OP/CLY M11* ...28 B2
The Manchester Crematorium *CCHDY M21* ...39 M2

Manchester
International Airport
MANAIR M90 ....**70** D1
Manchester Medical Centre
KNUT WA16 ....**90** D3
Manchester
Metropolitan University
ALS/KID ST7 ....**187**M4
DID/WITH M20 ....**40** A5
DID/WITH M20 ....**40** C6
Manchester
Metropolitan University
Institute of Education
(Crewe)
CW/HAS CW1 ....**185**M5
Manchester
Metropolitan University
Institute of Education
(Didsbury)
DID/WITH M20 ....**40** B6
Manchester Preparatory School
DID/WITH M20 ....**40** C4
Manchester RUFC
CHD/CHDH SK8 ....**56** A9
Manchester
Southern Cemetery
CCHDY M21 ....**39** N2
Manley County
Primary School
FROD/HEL WA6 ....**105** N6
Manor Green Primary School
DTN/ASHW M34 ....**29** N9
Manor High School
SALE M33 ....**37** P3
Manor House Hotel
ALS/KID ST7 ....**188** A6
The Manor House
Primary School
FROD/HEL WA6 ....**84** A4
Manor Industrial Estate
WARRS WA4 ....**48** G3
Manor Lane Industrial Estate
CSH/BR CH4 ....**140** F4
Manor Park County
Primary School
KNUT WA16 ....**90** G3
Mansfield Primary School
EP CH65 ....**102** B1
Manway Business Park
ALT WA14 ....**38** B9
The Maples Medical Centre
NTHM/RTH M23 ....**54** B3
Marbury
NWCHE CW9 ....**87** N8
Marcliffe Industrial Estate
BRAM/HZG SK7 ....**57** M6
The Margaret Thompson
Medical Centre
SPK/HALE L24 ....**60** A2
The Market Centre
CW/HAS CW1 ....**5** F2
The Marlborough
Primary School
MCFLDN SK10 ....**95** K9
Marlfield Primary School
CONG CW12 ....**155** L8
Marple Clinic
MPL/ROM SK6 ....**58** D1
Marple Golf Club
MPL/ROM SK6 ....**58** C4
Marple Hall School
MPL/ROM SK6 ....**43** H9
Marriott Hotel
HALE/TIMP WA15 ....**54** A8
Marsh Lane Trading Estate
NM/HAY SK22 ....**59** P8
Marsland Street
Industrial Centre
BRAM/HZG SK7 ....**57** K5
Martlew Day Hospital
STHEL WA9 ....**30** B3
Marton & District CE
Primary School
MCFLDS SK11 ....**134** D6
Marton Meadows Golf Club
MCFLDS SK11 ....**134** D6
Maryhill High School
ALS/KID ST7 ....**189** J5
Maryhill Primary School
ALS/KID ST7 ....**189** K5
Massey Hall School
WARRS WA4 ....**49** P5
Maternity &
Child Welfare Clinic
STHEL WA9 ....**22** D6
Mauldeth Medical Centre
DID/WITH M20 ....**40** E1
Mauldeth Road Primary School
DID/WITH M20 ....**40** C1
Maypole Farm Estate
PART M31 ....**37** J2
Meadow Industrial Estate
RDSH SK5 ....**41** N5
Meadow Lane Industrial Park
EP CH65 ....**7** G3
Meadway Health Centre
GTS/LS CH66 ....**102** A2
Melland High School
RDSH SK5 ....**28** D7
Mellor Primary School
MPL/ROM SK6 ....**59** J1
Mellor Sports Club
MPL/ROM SK6 ....**59** H1
Mellor & Towncliffe Golf Club
MPL/ROM SK6 ....**59** H2
Menorah Synagogue
WYTH/NTH M22 ....**54** C1
Mere Court Hotel &
Conference Centre
KNUT WA16 ....**67** L3

Mere Golf & Country Club
KNUT WA16 ....**68** A6
Mersey Trading Estate
HTNM SK4 ....**40** C7
Mersey Vale Primary School
HTNM SK4 ....**41** H7
Mersey View
FROD/HEL WA6 ....**83** P6
Merseyway Centre
STKP SK1 ....**17** F3
Merton Bank Primary School
STHEL WA9 ....**22** A5
Merton House School
CH/BCN CH1 ....**121**M7
Mickle Trafford Village School
CHNE CH2 ....**122** F3
Mid Cheshire College
NWCHE CW9 ....**13** F6
NWCHE CW8 ....**109** L6
WSFD CW7 ....**149**M1
Middlehurst Special School
ALS/KID ST7 ....**189** P9
Middlewich Athletic FC
MWCH CW10 ....**130** A9
Middlewich County
High School
MWCH CW10 ....**151** J2
Middlewich Cricket Club
MWCH CW10 ....**130** A9
Middlewich Leisure Centre
MWCH CW10 ....**151** J2
Middlewich Medical Centre
MWCH CW10 ....**151** J2
Middlewich Primary School
MWCH CW10 ....**151** H1
Middlewich Road
Industrial Estate
MWCH CW10 ....**130** E5
Millbank Business Centre
NWCHE CW9 ....**13** J2
Millbrook Business Centre
NTHM/RTH M23 ....**54** A1
Millbrook Industrial Estate
NTHM/RTH M23 ....**54** A1
Millfields Primary School
NANT CW5 ....**196** D2
PS/BROM CH62 ....**79** J1
Mill Green Special School
NEWLW WA12 ....**24** A6
Mill Hotel
CH/BCN CH1 ....**3** G3
Millingford Industrial Estate
GOL/RIS/CU WA3 ....**24** D1
Mill Lane Industrial Estate
EP CH65 ....**103** H1
Mill Street Medical Centre
CW/SHV CW2 ....**5** F6
Mill View Primary School
CHNE CH2 ....**121** P5
Moat House School
HTNM SK4 ....**41** M5
Mobberley CE Primary School
KNUT WA16 ....**69** N9
Mollington Banastre Hotel
CH/BCN CH1 ....**121** J4
Monks Coppenhall
Primary School
CONG CW12 ....**185** L1
Moody Street Medical Centre
CONG CW12 ....**155**M8
Moor Allerton School
DID/WITH M20 ....**40** A4
Moore Primary School
WARRS WA4 ....**63** L1
Moore RUFC
WARRS WA4 ....**47**M9
Moorfield Community
Primary School
IRL M44 ....**27** N6
Moorfield Primary School
BRAM/HZG SK7 ....**57** J6
WDN WA8 ....**46** B4
Moorfoot Road Industrial Estate
STHEL WA9 ....**22** D5
Moorlands Junior School
SALE M33 ....**39** H3
Moor Lane Business Centre
WDN WA8 ....**21** G5
Moravian College
DROY M43 ....**28** G1
Moss Hey Primary School
BRAM/HZG SK7 ....**57** J2
Moss Lane Business Centre
SBCH CW11 ....**171** J2
Moss Lane Industrial Estate
SBCH CW11 ....**171** N1
Mossley CE Primary School
CONG CW12 ....**175** J1
Moss View Primary School
PART M31 ....**36** F5
Mottram Hall Golf Club
MCFLDN SK10 ....**94** D1
Mottram St Andrew
Primary School
MCFLDN SK10 ....**94** B3
Mouldsworth
Motor Museum
CHSE CH3 ....**124** D2
Moulton Primary School
NWCHE CW9 ....**128** G3
Mow Cop Castle (NT)
ALS/KID ST7 ....**189**M1
Murdishaw Health Centre
RUNC WA7 ....**43** H7
Nantwich & Border Counties
Yacht Club
NANT CW5 ....**196** C1
Nantwich CC & RUFC
NANT CW5 ....**10** E1
Nantwich Civic Hall
NANT CW5 ....**10** C5
Nantwich Museum
NANT CW5 ....**10** B6

Nantwich Players Theatre
NANT CW5 ....**10** B6
Nantwich Swimming Pool
NANT CW5 ....**10** A4
Nantwich Town FC
NANT CW5 ....**10** E6
National Trading Estate
BRAM/HZG SK7 ....**57** J4
Nat Lane Retail Park
WSFD CW7 ....**128** G9
WSFD CW7 ....**150** B2
Navigation Primary School
HALE/TIMP WA15 ....**53** H1
Nelson Business Centre
DTN/ASHW M34 ....**29**M5
Nelson Industrial Estate
ALS/KID ST7 ....**188** E7
Neston CC
NSTN CH64 ....**77** J5
Neston High School
NSTN CH64 ....**77**M4
Neston Medical Centre
NSTN CH64 ....**77** L5
Neston Primary School
NSTN CH64 ....**77**M4
Neston Recreation Centre
NSTN CH64 ....**77**M4
Nether Alderley
Primary School
MCFLDN SK10 ....**93** J7
Network Clinic
MCFLDN SK10 ....**95**M6
Nevill Road J&I School
BRAM/HZG SK7 ....**56** E5
Newall Green High School
NTHM/RTH M23 ....**54** B3
Newall Green Primary School
NTHM/RTH M23 ....**54** D3
Newby Road Industrial Estate
BRAM/HZG SK7 ....**57** K5
Newdigate Centre (VCTS)
CW/HAS CW1 ....**4** E1
New Gate
CH/BCN CH1 ....**3** F5
New Kingsway Health Centre
DID/WITH M20 ....**40** E4
New Market Hall
RUNC WA7 ....**15** F1
New Mills CP School
NM/HAY SK22 ....**59**M7
New Mills FC
NM/HAY SK22 ....**59** P7
New Mills Golf Club
NM/HAY SK22 ....**59** L6
New Mills Leisure Centre &
Swimming Pool
NM/HAY SK22 ....**59** N7
New Mills School
NM/HAY SK22 ....**59** N7
New Road Business Centre
WSFD CW7 ....**128** F9
Newton Bank
Preparatory School
NEWLW WA12 ....**24** A5
Newton Community Hospital
NEWLW WA12 ....**23**M8
Newton Health Clinic
NEWLW WA12 ....**23**M5
Newton-le-Willows Cemetery
NEWLW WA12 ....**23** P7
Newton-le-Willows
Community High School
NEWLW WA12 ....**23** P4
Newton Le Willows
Primary School
NEWLW WA12 ....**23** N6
Newton-le-Willows Sports Club
NEWLW WA12 ....**23** N5
Newton Primary School
CHNE CH2 ....**121** P7
Newtown Primary School
NM/HAY SK22 ....**59**M9
Norbury Hall Primary School
BRAM/HZG SK7 ....**57** L6
Norfolk House School
SBCH CW11 ....**171** N2
Norley CE Primary School
FROD/HEL WA6 ....**107** L7
Norris Bank Medical Centre
HTNM SK4 ....**16** A4
Norris Bank Primary School
HTNM SK4 ....**41** J5
North Area Sixth
Form College
HTNM SK4 ....**41** J2
Northbank Industrial Park
IRL M44 ....**27** N9
IRL M44 ....**36** D2
North Cestrian
Grammar School
ALT WA14 ....**52** C2
North Cheshire Jewish
Primary School
CHD/CHDH SK8 ....**55** K5
Northenden Golf Club
WYTH/NTH M22 ....**39** P6
Northenden Primary School
WYTH/NTH M22 ....**39** N7
Northern Moor Clinic
NTHM/RTH M23 ....**39** J7
Northgate
CH/BCN CH1 ....**2** D3
Northgate Arena
Leisure Centre
CHNE CH2 ....**2** D2
Northgate Medical Centre
CH/BCN CH1 ....**2** D2
North Heaton Primary School
HTNM SK4 ....**41** K2
North Quays Business Park
ALT WA14 ....**38** B7
North Reddish Health Centre
RDSH SK5 ....**28** E8

North Reddish Infant School
RDSH SK5 ....**28** F8
Northwich Retail Park
NWCHE CW9 ....**110** C3
Northwich Rowing Club
NWCHE CW9 ....**12** E6
Northwich Sailing Club
WSFD CW7 ....**149** P4
Northwich Victoria FC
NWCHE CW9 ....**13** G3
Northwich Victoria Infirmary
NWCHW CW8 ....**12** D2
Norton Priory
Museum & Gardens
RUNC WA7 ....**62** F3
Norton Priory
Recreation Centre
RUNC WA7 ....**62** F4
Nutgrove Methodist
Primary School
STHEL WA9 ....**30** C1
Oakdene Primary School
RAIN/WH L35 ....**30** B6
Oakenclough Primary School
WILM/AE SK9 ....**71**M5
Oakfield Junior School
WDN WA8 ....**45** H7
Oakfield Trading Estate
HALE/TIMP WA15 ....**53** J2
Oakgrove School
CHD/CHDH SK8 ....**55** L8
Oaklands Golf & Country Club
TPLY/KEL CW6 ....**147** H6
Oaklands Infant School
WILM/AE SK9 ....**71** N5
Oaklands Special School
WSFD CW7 ....**149** K3
Oakley Centre
CW/HAS CW1 ....**4** E1
The Oaks Business Park
NTHM/RTH M23 ....**38** G9
The Oaks Community
Primary School
EP CH65 ....**102** F1
Oakwood Avenue
Primary School
WARR WA1 ....**19** J1
Oakwood High School
CCHDY M21 ....**39** L3
CCHDY M21 ....**39**M1
Oakwood Medical Centre
NWCHW CW8 ....**109** J2
Odeon Theatre
CH/BCN CH1 ....**2** D3
Offerton Green Clinic
OFTN SK2 ....**57**M2
Offerton Hall Primary School
OFTN SK2 ....**57** L1
Offerton Health Centre
STKP SK1 ....**42** A3
Offerton High School
OFTN SK2 ....**42** D9
Offerton Industrial Estate
OFTN SK2 ....**42** B8
Offley Infant School
SBCH CW11 ....**171** N1
Offley Junior School
SBCH CW11 ....**171** N1
Old Boston Trading Estate
RNFD/HAY WA11 ....**23** L1
Oldfield County
Primary School
CHSE CH3 ....**122** D8
Old Foundry Estate
WDN WA8 ....**21** K5
Old Hall Clinic
CHD/CHDH SK8 ....**55** K1
Old Hall Drive Primary School
GTN M18 ....**28** D5
Old Hall Primary School
WARRW/BUR WA5 ....**32** G8
Old Man of Mow
ALS/KID ST7 ....**174** E9
Old Moat J&I School
DID/WITH M20 ....**40** B1
Old Rectory Hotel
DTN/ASHW M34 ....**42** F1
Oldwood Primary School
WYTH/NTH M22 ....**54** D5
Olympic House
MANAIR M90 ....**54** E8
Onneley Golf Club
AUD/MAD/W CW3 ....**219**M2
Oriel Bank High School
EDGY/DAV SK3 ....**56** F2
Orion Business Park
CHD/CHDH SK8 ....**56** C2
Orrishmere Primary School
CHD/CHDH SK8 ....**56** A4
Ortenbrook School
MCFLDN SK10 ....**36** D6
The Osteopathic
Health Centre
CH/BCN CH1 ....**121** L8
Oughtrington Primary School
LYMM WA13 ....**51** H3
Oulton Park
Motor Racing Circuit
TPLY/KEL CW6 ....**147** H4
Our Lady Mother of the
Saviour Catholic Primary
RUNC WA7 ....**62** G8
Our Lady of Lourdes RC
Primary School
PART M31 ....**36** D5
Our Lady of Perpetual Succour
RC Primary School
WDN WA8 ....**44** F7
Our Lady RC Primary School
WARRS WA4 ....**48** G4

Our Ladys Catholic Infant School
EP CH65 ....**102** C1
Our Ladys Catholic
Primary School
EDGY/DAV SK3 ....**16** E7
Our Ladys RC Junior School
EP CH65 ....**102** C1
Overdale School
MPL/ROM SK6 ....**42** E7
Over Hall Community School
WSFD CW7 ....**149** K3
Oxhey First School
BIDD ST8 ....**175**M8
Packmoor Primary School
ALS/KID ST7 ....**189** P7
Paddington House Hotel
WARR WA1 ....**34** B9
Padgate Business Centre
WARR WA1 ....**34** B8
Padgate Community
High School
WARRN/WOL WA2 ....**34** B7
Padgate Community
High School
WARRN/WOL WA2 ....**34** A4
Padgate Medical Centre
WARRN/WOL WA2 ....**34** B7
Paerr Hall
WARR WA1 ....**18** C7
Palacefields Primary School
RUNC WA7 ....**62** E8
Palace Theatre
WARR WA1 ....**18** D6
Palatine Industrial Estate
WARRS WA4 ....**48** E4
Paradise Mill
MCFLDS SK11 ....**9** F6
Parkdale Industrial Estate
WARR WA1 ....**19** C7
Parker International Estate
DUK SK16 ....**29** P2
Parkgate Industrial Estate
KNUT WA16 ....**90** C1
Parkgate Primary School
NSTN CH64 ....**77** J4
Parklands High School
WYTH/NTH M22 ....**54** E4
Parklands Primary School
GTS/LS CH66 ....**79** P7
Park Lane Special School
MCFLDS SK11 ....**117** H6
Park Medical Centre
CHNE CH2 ....**122** A7
The Park Primary School
GTN M18 ....**62** E7
Park Road CP School
ALT WA14 ....**38** B8
SALE M33 ....**38** D2
Park Road Primary School
WARRW/BUR WA5 ....**47** J1
Park Royal Community School
MCFLDS SK11 ....**9** G8
Parr Industrial Estate
STHEL WA9 ....**22** C7
Parr Swimming Baths
STHEL WA9 ....**22** A6
Parrs Wood High School
DID/WITH M20 ....**40** E7
Partington CP School
PART M31 ....**36** E5
Partington Health Centre
PART M31 ....**36** E5
Partington Shopping Centre
PART M31 ....**36** E5
Partington Sports Centre
PART M31 ....**36** E6
Patterdale Lodge
Medical Centre
NEWLW WA12 ....**23** L6
Peacefield Primary School
MPL/ROM SK6 ....**58** C2
Peacock County Primary School
GTN M18 ....**28** C3
Pear New Mill Industrial Estate
MPL/ROM SK6 ....**42** B6
Pear Tree Primary School
NANT CW5 ....**11** G7
Pebble Brook
CW/SHV CW2 ....**185** J7
Peckforton Castle
TPLY/KEL CW6 ....**165** K8
The Peel Centre
STKP SK1 ....**17** J3
Peel Moat Recreation Centre
HTNM SK4 ....**41** J3
Peerglow Industrial Estate
ALT WA14 ....**38** B8
Penketh Business Park
WARRW/BUR WA5 ....**47**M1
Penketh County High School
WARRW/BUR WA5 ....**47** K2
Penketh Health Clinic
WARRW/BUR WA5 ....**47** J3
Penketh Primary School
WARRW/BUR WA5 ....**47** H3
Penketh South Community
Primary School
WARRW/BUR WA5 ....**47** K4
Penketh Swimming Baths
WARRW/BUR WA5 ....**47** J2
Penkford School
NEWLW WA12 ....**23** J7
Penlake Industrial Estate
STHEL WA9 ....**31** K2
Peover Golf Club
KNUT WA16 ....**112** A3
Peover Hall
KNUT WA16 ....**113** J5
Peover Superior Endowed
Primary School
KNUT WA16 ....**113**M4

Percyvale Science Building
 MCFLDN SK10 ....8 E2
Pewithall Primary School
 RUNC WA7 ....61 P7
The Pheasant Inn
 CHSE CH5 ....180 A2
Phoenix Medical Centre
 STKP SK1 ....17 H7
Pictor Special School
 SALE M33 ....38 C4
Pikemere Primary School
 ALS/KID ST7 ....187 M3
Pinnacle Business Centre
 HTNM SK4 ....17 F1
Pinners Brow Retail Park
 WARRN/WOL WA2 ....18 E4
Piper Hill School
 NTHM/RTH M23 ....39 L6
Pius XII RC Primary School
 GTS/LS CH66 ....79 P7
Plasman Industrial Centre
 BNG/LEV M19 ....28 A8
 BNG/LEV M19 ....28 D8
Pool Bank Business Park
 CHSE CH5 ....124 B8
Poole Hall Industrial Estate
 EP CH65 ....80 B4
Pooltown Junior School
 EP CH65 ....80 B8
Port Arcades
 EP CH65 ....6 E5
Portal Golf & Country Club
 TPLY/KEL CW6 ....147 J8
Portwood Trading Estate
 STKP SK1 ....17 K2
Pott Shrigley CE
 Primary School
 MCFLDN SK10 ....96 B2
Poulton Park Golf Club
 WARRN/WOL WA2 ....34 B4
Pownall Green Primary School
 BRAM/HZG SK7 ....56 E8
Pownall Hall School
 WILM/AE SK9 ....71 H6
Poynton Clinic
 POY/DIS SK12 ....73 L2
Poynton High School
 POY/DIS SK12 ....73 M3
Poynton Leisure Centre
 POY/DIS SK12 ....73 M4
Poynton Sports Club
 POY/DIS SK12 ....73 L2
Premier Lodge
 ALT WA14 ....38 B7
 CHNE CH2 ....121 M6
 KNUT WA16 ....67 M4
 KNUT WA16 ....68 A5
 MCFLDS SK11 ....116 F8
 NANT CW5 ....11 J4
 NWCHW CW8 ....109 P8
 NWCHW CW8 ....127 L1
 RAIN/WH L35 ....30 D7
 STKP SK1 ....17 H4
 WARR WA1 ....49 P1
 WARRN/WOL WA2 ....54 F4
 WARRS WA4 ....54 F4
 WILM/AE SK9 ....70 C7
 WILM/AE SK9 ....71 M5
 WILM/AE SK9 ....93 J5
Premier Lodge (Wirral South)
 GTS/LS CH66 ....101 H3
Prestbury CE Primary School
 MCFLDN SK10 ....94 F6
Prestbury Golf Club
 MCFLDN SK10 ....94 F9
Prestbury Village
 Lawn Tennis Club
 MCFLDN SK10 ....94 F6
Priestley Business Centre
 WARRW/BUR WA5 ....48 B2
Priestley Sixth Form College
 WARRS WA4 ....48 E4
Priestnall School
 HTNM SK4 ....40 G5
Priorsleigh Medical Centre
 POY/DIS SK12 ....73 L2
Prospect Vale Primary School
 CHD/CHDH SK8 ....55 K6
Pryors Bank School
 MCFLDN SK10 ....9 J4
Puss Bank School
 MCFLDN SK10 ....94 E2
Pyramid
 WARR WA1 ....18 C7
Quality Hotel
 ALT WA14 ....53 H5
 GTS/LS CH66 ....79 K7
 NWCHW CW8 ....12 E5
Quarry Bank Mill &
 Styal Estate (NT)
 WILM/AE SK9 ....70 G4
Quay Business Centre
 WARRN/WOL WA2 ....33 K5
The Queen Hotel
 CH/BCN CH1 ....3 H2
Queensgate CE Primary School
 BRAM/HZG SK7 ....72 E2
Queen's Park Golf Club
 CHSV/SHV CW2 ....184 E4
Queens Park High School
 CHSW/BR CH4 ....3 F7
Queens Road Primary School
 CHD/CHDH SK8 ....56 A4
The Queens School
 CH/BCN CH1 ....2 C4
 CH/BCN CH1 ....121 M7
Queensway Business Centre
 WDN WA8 ....61 M1
The Quinta Primary School
 CONG CW12 ....155 J8
Rack House Primary School
 NTHM/RTH M23 ....39 K7
Radisson SAS Hotel
 MANAIR M90 ....54 D8

Radnor Park Trading Estate
 CONG CW12 ....155 H5
RAF Burtonwood
 WARRW/BUR WA5 ....32 D9
The Railway Age Museum
 CW/SHV CW2 ....5 G5
Railway Street Industrial Estate
 GTN M18 ....28 C3
Rainbow Medical Centre
 STHEL WA9 ....31 K1
Rainhill Clinic
 RAIN/WH L35 ....30 B5
Rainhill High School
 RAIN/WH L35 ....30 C6
Rainow Primary School
 MCFLDN SK10 ....96 B9
Ramillies Hall School
 CHD/CHDH SK8 ....56 C5
Ravenbank Primary School
 LYMM WA13 ....50 F4
Ravensmead Primary School
 ALS/KID ST7 ....201 H4
Reaseheath College
 NANT CW5 ....183 M7
Reaseheath Golf Club
 NANT CW5 ....183 M7
Record Business Park
 NANT CW5 ....33 K8
Rector Drew Junior
 Aided School
 CO CH5 ....140 B2
Reddish Vale Golf Club
 NWCHE CW9 ....41 P2
Reddish Vale School
 RDSH SK5 ....41 N1
Regal Cinema
 NWCHE CW9 ....12 E5
Regency Hospital
 MCFLDS SK11 ....8 B3
Regent Cinema
 MPL/ROM SK6 ....58 D1
Regents Theological College
 NANT CW5 ....11 F6
Reginald Mitchell
 Primary School
 ALS/KID ST7 ....188 F7
Reginald Road Industrial Park
 STHEL WA9 ....31 L2
Richard Evans Community
 Primary School
 RNFD/HAY WA11 ....22 D5
Richard Evans Infant School
 RNFD/HAY WA11 ....22 E5
Richard Heathcote Community
 Primary School
 ALS/KID ST7 ....201 H9
The Ridge College
 MPL/ROM SK6 ....58 C2
Ridge Danyers College
 CHD/CHDH SK8 ....55 N4
The Ridings Infant School
 CH/BCN CH1 ....120 E2
Ringstones Industrial Estate
 CHF/WBR SK23 ....75 P4
Ringway Golf Club
 HALE/TIMP WA15 ....53 N6
Ringway Primary School
 WYTH/NTH M22 ....54 F7
Ringway Trading Estate
 WYTH/NTH M22 ....54 G7
Risley Moss Nature Park
 GOL/RIS/CU WA3 ....35 J4
Rivacre Business Centre
 GTS/LS CH66 ....80 A8
Rivacre Valley Country Park
 GTS/LS CH66 ....80 A5
Rivacre Valley CP School
 GTS/LS CH66 ....80 A6
Riverside Business Park
 WILM/AE SK9 ....71 K7
Riverside Retail Park
 ALT WA14 ....19 F7
Riverside Trading Estate
 NWCHW CW8 ....12 E4
 WARRW/BUR WA5 ....47 H6
The Roaches Lower School
 LEEK ST13 ....159 M5
Robins Lane Primary School
 STHEL WA9 ....22 A9
Robson Street Clinic
 WARR WA1 ....19 H4
Rode Heath Primary School
 ALS/KID ST7 ....188 B1
Romiley Golf Club
 MPL/ROM SK6 ....43 J5
Romiley Health Centre
 MPL/ROM SK6 ....43 H6
Romiley Primary School
 MPL/ROM SK6 ....43 J6
The Roodee Racecourse
 CH/BCN CH1 ....2 B6
Rookery Hall
 NANT CW5 ....183 P4
Rosebank School
 NWCHW CW8 ....87 J9
Rose Hill Primary School
 MPL/ROM SK6 ....58 C1
Rossett Clinic
 WRX/GR/LL LL12 ....160 F9
Rossmore Primary School
 GTS/LS CH66 ....79 N6
Rossmore Trading Estate
 EP CH65 ....6 A1
Rother Drive Business Park
 EP CH65 ....80 C6
Roundthorn Industrial Estate
 NTHM/RTH M23 ....39 H9
 NTHM/RTH M23 ....54 A2
Roundwood School
 WYTH/NTH M22 ....39 M9
Rowhurst Industrial Estate
 NEWLW WA12 ....201 M8
Rowing Club
 CH/BCN CH1 ....3 G5

Rowton Hall
 Country House Hotel
 CHSE CH5 ....143 N5
Royal Oak Industrial Estate
 STKP SK1 ....17 H7
Royal Oak Primary School
 NTHM/RTH M25 ....39 K9
Rubicon School
 WHTCH SY13 ....213 K5
Rudheath Cemetery
 NWCHE CW9 ....110 C7
Rudheath County
 High School
 NWCHE CW9 ....110 D5
Rudheath Leisure Centre
 NWCHE CW9 ....110 D5
Rudheath Primary School
 NWCHE CW9 ....110 E6
Runcorn AFC
 RUNC WA7 ....15 H1
Runcorn County Court
 RUNC WA7 ....62 D6
Runcorn Golf Club
 RUNC WA7 ....61 N7
Runcorn Rowing Club
 RUNC WA7 ....84 B1
Runcorn Ski Slope
 RUNC WA7 ....62 F7
Rushton CE Primary School
 MCFLDS SK11 ....157 P8
The Ruskin High School
 CW/SHV CW2 ....4 D6
Russell Scott Primary School
 DTN/ASHW M34 ....29 L5
The Russett Special School
 NWCHW CW8 ....108 G4
Rycroft Park Sports Club
 CHD/CHDH SK8 ....55 P6
Ryles Park County High School
 MCFLDS SK11 ....117 J6
The Ryleys School
 WILM/AE SK9 ....93 H4
Sacred Heart RC Infant School
 GTN M18 ....28 C5
Sacred Heart RC
 Primary School
 NTHM/RTH M23 ....54 B1
 WARRW/BUR WA5 ....48 A2
Saighton CE Primary School
 CHSE CH3 ....143 N9
St Aelreds RC
 Technology College
 NEWLW WA12 ....23 P5
St Aidans Catholic
 Primary School
 NTHM/RTH M23 ....39 L7
St Albans Catholic
 Primary School
 MCFLDN SK10 ....116 F3
St Albans RC Primary School
 WARRW/BUR WA5 ....18 A3
St Ambrose College
 HALE/TIMP WA15 ....53 M6
St Ambrose
 Preparatory School
 HALE/TIMP WA15 ....53 M7
St Ambrose RC Primary School
 CCHDY M21 ....39 N4
 EDGY/DAV SK3 ....56 D2
 SPK/HALE L24 ....60 A4
St Andrews CE Primary School
 BNG/LEV M19 ....28 B9
 WARRN/WOL WA2 ....33 M5
St Annes Catholic
 Primary School
 NANT CW5 ....196 F4
St Annes CE (aided)
 Primary School
 SALE M33 ....38 F4
St Annes Ear Nose &
 Throat Hospital
 ALT WA14 ....52 G4
St Annes Primary School
 DTN/ASHW M34 ....29 N5
St Annes RC High School
 HTNM SK4 ....41 L4
St Annes RC Primary School
 DTN/ASHW M34 ....28 G2
 STHEL WA9 ....31 J1
St Anns CE Primary School
 RAIN/WH L35 ....30 B5
 WARRN/WOL WA2 ....33 M8
St Anthonys RC Primary School
 CHSW/BR CH4 ....142 A4
 WYTH/NTH M22 ....54 F6
St Augustine of Canterbury RC
 High School
 RNFD/HAY WA11 ....22 C4
St Augustines Catholic
 Primary School
 WARRS WA4 ....49 H3
St Augustines RC Primary School
 RUNC WA7 ....62 E4
St Austins RC Primary School
 STHEL WA9 ....30 B1
St Barnabas CE Primary School
 MCFLDS SK11 ....117 K6
 WARRW/BUR WA5 ....48 B2
St Barnabas Primary School
 OP/CLY M11 ....28 B1
St Bartholomews RC
 Primary School
 RAIN/WH L35 ....30 D7
St Basil RC Primary School
 RAIN/WH L35 ....44 C4
St Bedes Catholic
 Primary School
 NWCHW CW8 ....109 H5
St Bedes RC J&I School
 WDN WA8 ....45 N6
St Benedict's Catholic
 Primary School
 WILM/AE SK9 ....71 N3

St Benedicts RC Primary School
 WARRN/WOL WA2 ....19 H1
 WILM/AE SK9 ....71 N2
St Bernadettes RC
 Primary School
 RDSH SK5 ....28 A4
St Bernards RC Primary School
 BNG/LEV M19 ....40 G2
 EP CH65 ....102 F1
St Berteline CE Primary School
 RUNC WA7 ....62 G6
St Brides School
 MCFLDN SK10 ....8 C3
St Bridgets Catholic
 Primary School
 WARRN/WOL WA2 ....34 A5
St Catherines Centre for Girls
 RNFD/HAY WA11 ....22 C3
St Catherines
 Preparatory School
 MPL/ROM SK6 ....43 N9
St Catherines RC
 Primary School
 DID/WITH M20 ....40 D5
 GOL/RIS/CU WA3 ....24 C1
St Chads Catholic High School
 RUNC WA7 ....62 B7
St Chads CE Primary School
 NEWLW ST5 ....201 N5
 WSFD CW7 ....149 N2
St Christophers RC
 Primary School
 MPL/ROM SK6 ....42 F6
St Clares RC Primary School
 CHSW/BR CH4 ....142 C5
St Clements CE Primary School
 OP/CLY M11 ....28 E2
St Clements RC Primary School
 RUNC WA7 ....14 E5
St Cuthberts Catholic
 High School
 STHEL WA9 ....22 D8
St Cuthberts RC Primary School
 DID/WITH M20 ....40 D3
St Davids High School
 CHSW/BR CH4 ....141 N3
St Davids RC Primary School
 CHSW/BR CH4 ....141 P5
St Edwards C Primary School
 RUNC WA7 ....15 H1
St Edwards RC Primary School
 MCFLDS SK11 ....117 J7
St Elisabeths CE
 Primary School
 RDSH SK5 ....28 D9
St Elizabeth RC Primary School
 WYTH/NTH M22 ....54 C5
St Gabriel's RC Primary School
 ALS/KID ST7 ....187 N5
St Georges CE Primary School
 NM/HAY SK22 ....59 N7
 OFTN SK2 ....56 F1
St Gregorys RC High School
 WARRW/BUR WA5 ....47 P2
St Gregorys RC Primary School
 MCFLDN SK10 ....95 M5
St Helens AFC
 STHEL WA9 ....31 L1
St Helens CE Primary School
 GOL/RIS/CU WA3 ....36 A6
St Helens Hospital
 STHEL WA9 ....22 A8
St Hilarys School
 WILM/AE SK9 ....93 J4
St Hughs RC Primary School
 HALE/TIMP WA15 ....38 C9
St James CE Primary School
 AUD/MAD/W CW3 ....209 H9
 GTN M18 ....28 D3
St James Primary School
 RNFD/HAY WA11 ....23 J3
St James RC High School
 CHD/CHDH SK8 ....55 P8
St John Fisher RC
 Primary School
 DTN/ASHW M34 ....29 P8
 WDN WA8 ....48 B6
St John Fisher & St Thomas More
 RC Primary School
 WYTH/NTH M22 ....54 F3
St Johns CE Primary School
 FROD/HEL WA6 ....106 G2
 HTNM SK4 ....40 F6
 MCFLDN SK10 ....95 N6
 MCFLDS SK11 ....116 C5
 SBCH CW11 ....172 B3
 WSFD CW7 ....149 K1
St Johns Medical Centre
 ALT WA14 ....52 G4
St Johns Primary School
 IRL M44 ....27 N6
St Johns Wood
 Community School
 KNUT WA16 ....91 H3
St John Vianney RC
 Primary School
 STHEL WA9 ....30 D2
St John Vianney School
 WYTH/NTH M22 ....41 J4
St Josephs Catholic
 Primary School
 WARRW/BUR WA5 ....47 J2
St Josephs RC CP School
 BURS/TUN ST6 ....189 M9
St Josephs RC Primary &
 Nursery School
 RDSH SK5 ....28 E9
St Lewis's Catholic
 Primary School
 GOL/RIS/CU WA5 ....25 K8

St Lukes CE Primary School
 GOL/RIS/CU WA3 ....24 C2
St Lukes RC Primary School
 FROD/HEL WA6 ....84 A5
St Margarets CE Controlled
 Infant School
 WARRN/WOL WA2 ....33 M6
St Margarets CE Primary School
 WARRN/WOL WA2 ....33 M7
St Margarets Ward RC
 Primary School
 SALE M33 ....37 P6
St Marks CE Primary School
 MPL/ROM SK6 ....42 F4
St Martins Catholic
 Primary School
 RUNC WA7 ....63 J7
St Martins Clinic
 CH/BCN CH1 ....2 D4
St Martins Gate
 CH/BCN CH1 ....2 C3
St Martins School
 SALE M33 ....38 B3
St Marys Catholic Junior School
 NEWLW WA12 ....201 K4
St Marys Catholic
 Primary School
 CONG CW12 ....155 M7
 CW/SHV CW2 ....184 C6
 MWCH CW10 ....151 J2
St Marys Catholic School
 NEWLW WA12 ....23 N5
St Mary's Centre
 CH/BCN CH1 ....2 E6
St Mary's CE Primary School
 IRL M44 ....36 B2
 MCFLDS SK11 ....157 K2
 MPL/ROM SK6 ....41 P2
 RUNC WA7 ....62 B5
St Marys RC Primary School
 BNG/LEV M19 ....28 A9
 DTN/ASHW M34 ....29 L6
 FLINT CH6 ....98 B7
 HTNM SK4 ....16 E2
 MPL/ROM SK6 ....43 M9
 NM/HAY SK22 ....59 M7
St Matthews CE Primary School
 EDGY/DAV SK3 ....16 D7
 STHEL WA9 ....30 B1
 WARRS WA4 ....64 C4
St Michael Jubilee Golf Club
 WDN WA8 ....20 D4
St Michaels Catholic
 Primary School
 WDN WA8 ....45 J8
St Monicas RC Primary School
 WARRS WA4 ....48 F8
St Nicholas Catholic
 High School
 NWCHW CW8 ....12 B7
St Oswalds CE Aided
 Primary School
 CHSE CH3 ....121 H1
St Oswalds RC Primary School
 WARR WA1 ....33 P8
St Oswalds Worleston CE
 Primary School
 NANT CW5 ....183 N2
St Paul of the Cross Catholic
 Primary School
 WARRW/BUR WA5 ....32 B2
St Pauls Catholic High School
 NTHM/RTH M23 ....54 D3
St Pauls Catholic
 Primary School
 POY/DIS SK12 ....73 L4
St Pauls CE Primary School
 DID/WITH M20 ....40 C2
 RDSH SK5 ....42 A4
St Peter & St Paul RC
 High School
 WDN WA8 ....45 M5
St Peters Catholic
 Primary School
 BRAM/HZG SK7 ....57 K6
 WARR WA1 ....34 D9
St Peters CE Primary School
 AULW CL7 ....29 N1
 NEWLW WA12 ....23 P5
St Peters Nursery School
 CONG CW12 ....155 M8
St Peters Primary School
 NTHM/RTH M23 ....54 C4
 TPLY/KEL CW6 ....145 P4
 WRX/GR/LL LL12 ....160 F9
St Peters RC High &
 Lower School
 GTN M18 ....28 D7
St Peters RC High School
 Upper School
 DROY M43 ....28 E1
St Philips Church
 Community School
 WARRW/BUR WA5 ....32 E7
St Philips RC Primary School
 OFTN SK2 ....57 L1
St Richard Gwyn RC
 High School
 FLINT CH6 ....98 B7
St Saviours Primary School
 ALS/KID ST7 ....188 E7
St Saviour's RC J&I School
 GTS/LS CH66 ....102 A1
St Simons Catholic
 Primary School
 BRAM/HZG SK7 ....57 L4
St Stephens Catholic
 Primary School
 WARRN/WOL WA2 ....33 L5
St Stephens CE Primary School
 BRAM/HZG SK7 ....57 M3
 DTN/ASHW M34 ....29 L1
St Teresas RC Primary School
 IRL M44 ....27 L9

St Theresas Primary School
  CH/BCN CH1 ....121 J6
  STHEL WA9 ....31 H5
St Thomas Aquinas RC
  High School
  CCHDY M21 ....39 M1
St Thomas CE (A)
  Primary School
  ALS/KID ST7 ....189 J7
St Thomas CE Primary School
  HTNM SK4 ....41 K2
  STKP SK1 ....17 H6
  WARRS WA4 ....48 F6
St Thomas Hospital
  EDCY/DAV SK3 ....41 M9
St Thomas More RC High School
  CW/SHV CW2 ....4 A7
  DTN/ASHW M34 ....29 M7
St Thomas of Canterbury CE
  Junior School
  CH/BCN CH1 ....2 C1
St Vincent RC Infant School
  HALE/TIMP WA15 ....53 J2
St Vincents Catholic
  Primary School
  WARRW/BUR WA5 ....47 J4
St Vincents RC Primary School
  KNUT WA16 ....90 G4
St Weburgh CE Primary School
  WARRS WA4 ....48 D5
St Werburghs & Columbas RC
  Primary School
  CHNE CH2 ....3 K1
St Wilfrids Catholic
  Primary School
  NWCHW CW8 ....109 M7
St Wilfrids CE Aided
  Primary School
  WARRS WA4 ....49 K6
St Wilfrids CE Primary School
  WYTH/NTH M22 ....39 P8
St Winefrides RC
  Primary School
  NSTN CH64 ....77 M6
St Winifreds RC Primary School
  HTNM SK4 ....41 H6
Sale Cricket Club
  SALE M33 ....38 G3
Sale Golf Club
  SALE M33 ....39 J3
Sale Grammar School
  SALE M33 ....38 F5
Sale Leisure Centre
  SALE M33 ....38 F3
Sale Water Park
  SALE M33 ....39 H2
Salt Museum
  NWCHW CW9 ....13 F5
Saltney Clinic
  CHSW/BR CH4 ....141 N4
Saltney Ferry Primary School
  CHSW/BR CH4 ....141 M4
Salt Works Wharf
  RUNC WA7 ....61 J6
Sandbach High School
  SBCH CW11 ....171 M2
Sandbach Primary School
  SBCH CW11 ....171 M3
Sandbach RUFC
  SBCH CW11 ....171 N1
Sandbach School
  SBCH CW11 ....171 M3
Sandbach Town Hall
  SBCH CW11 ....171 N3
Sandilands Primary School
  NTHM/RTH M23 ....38 F8
Sandiway Golf Club
  NWCHW CW8 ....127 N1
Sandiway Primary School
  NWCHW CW8 ....108 C9
Sankey Bridge Industrial Estate
  WARRW/BUR WA5 ....47 N3
Sankey Medical Centre
  WARRW/BUR WA5 ....32 B9
Sankey Valley
  WARRW/BUR WA5 ....32 G7
Sankey Valley Industrial Estate
  NEWLW WA12 ....23 M7
  NEWLW WA12 ....24 A8
Sankey Valley St James CE
  Primary School
  WARRW/BUR WA5 ....47 N1
Sarah Bartholomew School
  TPLY/KEL CW6 ....147 L2
Savoy Cinema
  HTNM SK4 ....41 H5
Saxon Holme Hotel
  HTNM SK4 ....41 L4
Scholar Green Primary School
  ALS/KID ST7 ....188 G2
School Street Industrial Estate
  BRAM/HZG SK7 ....57 L5
Sealand Industrial Estate
  CH/BCN CH1 ....121 J9
  CH/BCN CH1 ....142 A1
Sett Valley Medical Centre
  NM/HAY SK22 ....59 N7
Shaare Sedek Synagogue
  DID/WITH M20 ....40 A4
Shavington County
  High School
  CW/SHV CW2 ....197 P2
Shavington Primary School
  CW/SHV CW2 ....198 B2
Shavington Sports Centre
  CW/SHV CW2 ....197 P2
Shawgrove School
  DID/WITH M20 ....40 A2
Shaw Heath Health Centre
  EDCY/DAV SK3 ....41 M9
Shay Lane Medical Centre
  HALE/TIMP WA15 ....53 N6
Shepley North Industrial Estate
  DTN/ASHW M34 ....29 N2

Shepley South Industrial Estate
  DTN/ASHW M34 ....29 N3
Sherdley Park Golf Club
  STHEL WA9 ....30 F1
Sherdley Primary School
  STHEL WA9 ....31 H2
Shocklach Oviatt CE
  MALPAS SY14 ....190 E8
The Shopping Centre
  CHD/CHDH SK8 ....56 A5
Showcase Cinemas Belle Vue
  WGTN/LGST M12 ....28 B4
Shrigley Hall Hotel Golf &
  Country Club
  MCFLDN SK10 ....96 A1
Silk Road Business Park
  MCFLDN SK10 ....9 F5
Simms Cross County
  Primary School
  WDN WA8 ....21 G3
Sir John Deanes College
  NWCHW CW8 ....13 F6
Sir John Talbot's School
  WHITCH SY13 ....213 N4
Sir Thomas Boteler
  High School
  WARRS WA4 ....48 C4
Sir Thomas Boughey
  High School
  ALS/KID ST7 ....200 C8
Slicks Business Centre
  NWCHW CW8 ....109 L2
Smallwood CE Primary School
  SBCH CW11 ....173 H4
Snipe Retail Park
  DTN/ASHW M34 ....29 K1
Sound & District
  Primary School
  NANT CW5 ....208 A1
South Cheshire College
  CW/SHV CW2 ....4 B7
Southern Cross School
  CCHDY M21 ....39 M3
Southfields School
  SALE M33 ....38 C5
South Manchester High School
  WYTH/NTH M22 ....54 F4
Southmoor Business Park
  NTHM/RTH M23 ....39 H9
Southmoor Industrial Estate
  NTHM/RTH M23 ....54 A1
South Park Court
  Business Centre
  MCFLDS SK11 ....8 E7
South Reddish Medical Centre
  RDSH SK5 ....41 N4
South Trafford College
  ALT WA14 ....38 A8
South Wirral High School
  PS/BROM CH62 ....79 H1
Springfield Hotel
  MPL/ROM SK6 ....43 L9
Springfield Primary School
  SALE M33 ....38 E4
Springfield School
  CW/HAS CW1 ....185 M5
Springhead Primary School
  ALS/KID ST7 ....201 N1
Springvale Business Centre
  SBCH CW11 ....171 J3
Springvale Industrial Estate
  SBCH CW11 ....171 J3
Springwood Primary School
  MPL/ROM SK6 ....43 K5
Spurley Hey High School
  GTN M18 ....28 B7
Staffordshire County Council
  BURS/TUN ST6 ....189 L9
Stag Industrial Estate
  ALT WA14 ....52 F1
Stamford Park J&I School
  HALE/TIMP WA15 ....53 J4
Stanley Green Industrial Estate
  CHD/CHDH SK8 ....55 N9
  CHD/CHDH SK8 ....71 N2
Stanley Green Retail Park
  CHD/CHDH SK8 ....55 P9
Stanley Road Industrial Estate
  KNUT WA16 ....90 E4
Stanney High School
  EP CH65 ....102 E2
Stanneylands Hotel
  WILM/AE SK9 ....71 K4
Stanney Mill Industrial Estate
  CHNE CH2 ....103 H3
Stanney Mill Industrial Park
  EP CH65 ....103 H1
Stanney Ten Industrial Estate
  EP CH65 ....103 H2
Stanney Woods Country Park
  EP CH65 ....102 D3
Stapeley Broad Lane
  Primary School
  NANT CW5 ....197 M4
Stapeley Water Gardens
  NANT CW5 ....197 N4
Statham Primary School
  LYMM WA13 ....50 C3
Station Road Industrial Estate
  WARRS WA4 ....49 N5
Stella Maris School
  HTNM SK4 ....40 F6
Stepping Hill Hospital
  OFTN SK2 ....57 H1
Stepping Stones
  Montessori School
  MCFLDN SK10 ....8 C3
Stewards Cottage
  Club House
  MALPAS SY14 ....193 L8
Stockport Air Raid Shelter
  STKP SK1 ....17 F4

Stockport CC
  EDGY/DAV SK3 ....56 F1
Stockport College of FE & HE
  EDGY/DAV SK3 ....17 F7
Stockport County Court
  STKP SK1 ....17 F5
Stockport County FC &
  Sale Sharks RUFC
  (Edgeley Park)
  EDGY/DAV SK3 ....41 L9
Stockport Crematorium
  OFTN SK2 ....41 P9
Stockport Golf Club
  OFTN SK2 ....57 P2
Stockport Grammar School
  OFTN SK2 ....56 G2
Stockport RUFC
  BRAM/HZG SK7 ....56 F7
Stockport School
  OFTN SK2 ....57 H2
Stockport Trading Estate
  HTNM SK4 ....41 J8
Stockton Heath Community
  Primary School
  WARRS WA4 ....48 E6
Stockton Heath Medical Centre
  WARRS WA4 ....48 E6
Stone Cross Business Park
  GOL/RIS/CU WA3 ....24 D2
St Richards RC Primary School
  WGTN/LGST M12 ....28 B6
Stud Green Industrial Park
  SALE M33 ....152 A9
Styal Golf Club
  WILM/AE SK9 ....71 J1
Styal Primary School
  WILM/AE SK9 ....70 G2
Sutton Community
  Leisure Centre Track
  STHEL WA9 ....30 F2
Sutton Cricket Club
  STHEL WA9 ....31 H2
Sutton Green Primary School
  GTS/LS CH66 ....79 M8
Sutton Hall Golf Club
  RUNC WA7 ....84 E2
Sutton High School
  GTS/LS CH66 ....80 A8
Sutton High Sports College
  STHEL WA9 ....30 G2
Sutton Manor Community
  Primary School
  STHEL WA9 ....30 F6
Sutton Oak CE Primary School
  STHEL WA9 ....22 C9
The Swan Hotel
  TPLY/KEL CW6 ....146 G8
Swanlow Medical Centre
  WSFD CW7 ....149 L2
Sycamore Lane Community
  Primary School
  WARRW/BUR WA5 ....47 M2
Tabley House
  KNUT WA16 ....89 P5
Talke Clinic
  ALS/KID ST7 ....201 N1
Tameside Business
  Development Centre
  DTN/ASHW M34 ....29 J6
Tameside Business Park
  DUK SK16 ....29 P2
Tameside College of Technology
  HYDE SK14 ....43 J1
Tame Valley Primary School
  WARR WA1 ....18 E7
Tanning Court Industrial Estate
  WARR WA1 ....17 G6
Tarporley Business Centre
  TPLY/KEL CW6 ....146 G9
Tarporley CE Primary School
  TPLY/KEL CW6 ....147 H9
Tarporley County High School
  TPLY/KEL CW6 ....166 A1
Tarporley War Memorial
  Hospital
  TPLY/KEL CW6 ....147 H8
Tarvin Primary School
  CHSE CH3 ....145 H1
Tarvin Road Medical Centre
  CHSE CH3 ....3 K4
Tattenhall Park Primary School
  CHSE CH3 ....164 A7
Tatton Park (NT)
  KNUT WA16 ....68 C6
Tavistock Industrial Estate
  OP/CLY M11 ....28 D3
Taxal & Fernilee Primary School
  CHF/WBR SK23 ....75 P8
Tegg's Nose Country Park
  MCFLDS SK11 ....118 B7
Terminal 1
  MANAIR M90 ....54 D9
Terminal 2
  MANAIR M90 ....54 C7
Terminal 3
  MANAIR M90 ....54 E9
Terra Nova School
  HOLMCH WA14 ....132 C2
Thames Trading Centre
  IRL M44 ....36 E1
Thelwall Infant School
  WARRS WA4 ....49 L4
Thelwall Junior School
  WARRS WA4 ....49 M4
Thelwall New Road
  Industrial Estate
  WARRS WA4 ....49 L3
Thelwall New Road Surgery
  WARRS WA4 ....49 K4
Thomas Wedge Junior School
  CH/BCN CH1 ....120 D2
Thorn Grove Primary School
  CHD/CHDH SK8 ....56 A9

Thursfield Primary School
  ALS/KID ST7 ....189 M5
Tilston Parochial CE
  Primary School
  MALPAS SY14 ....191 J4
Timperley Health Centre
  HALE/TIMP WA15 ....38 D9
Tithe Barn Primary School
  HTNM SK4 ....41 H5
Torkington Primary School
  BRAM/HZG SK7 ....57 N5
Tower College
  RAIN/WH L35 ....30 C7
Towers Business Park
  DID/WITH M20 ....39 P4
  DID/WITH M20 ....40 C7
Trafford Healthcare
  SALE M33 ....38 G5
Trafford Water Sports Centre
  SALE M33 ....39 H2
Travel Inn
  CHD/CHDH SK8 ....55 L5
  CHNE CH2 ....104 C2
  CW/SHV CW2 ....184 C4
  DTN/ASHW M34 ....29 J6
  GOL/RIS/CU WA3 ....30 B6
  MCFLDN SK10 ....95 K8
  NEWLW WA12 ....23 M7
  OFTN SK2 ....56 G1
  RUNC WA7 ....85 H1
  SALE M33 ....38 A2
  STHEL WA9 ....30 E5
  WARR WA1 ....48 C5
Travelodge
  ALS/KID ST7 ....201 N3
  CW/SHV CW2 ....200 B1
  DID/WITH M20 ....40 E7
  KNUT WA16 ....50 B9
  KNUT WA16 ....89 N1
  KNUT WA16 ....90 A6
  MCFLDN SK10 ....73 J6
  MWCH CW7 ....130 D9
  PS/BROM CH62 ....79 K2
  RNFD/HAY WA11 ....25 J3
  WARR WA1 ....18 C5
  WDN WA8 ....46 A7
Trident Industrial Estate
  GOL/RIS/CU WA3 ....34 F2
Trident Retail Park
  RUNC WA7 ....62 C7
Tudor Industrial Estate
  DUK SK16 ....29 N3
Tushingham with Grindley CE
  Primary School
  MALPAS SY14 ....205 H5
Twiss Green Primary School
  GOL/RIS/CU WA3 ....25 N5
Two Trees High School
  DTN/ASHW M34 ....29 P8
Tyntesfield CP School
  SALE M33 ....38 B7
Tytherington Business Park
  MCFLDN SK10 ....95 L8
Tytherington County
  High School
  MCFLDN SK10 ....117 K2
The Tytherington Golf Club
  MCFLDN SK10 ....95 J8
Tytherington Shopping Centre
  MCFLDN SK10 ....117 K1
UCG Cinema
  DID/WITH M20 ....40 E7
  EDGY/DAV SK3 ....17 F6
Underwood Industrial Estate
  CW/HAS CW1 ....184 C2
Underwood West Junior &
  Infants School
  CW/HAS CW1 ....184 C2
Union Industrial Estate
  MCFLDS SK11 ....9 H5
University of Manchester
  MCFLDS SK11 ....132 C1
Upton-by-Chester Golf Club
  CHNE CH2 ....121 N4
Upton by Chester High School
  CHNE CH2 ....122 A5
Upton Heath CE
  Primary School
  CHNE CH2 ....121 P4
Upton Medical Centre
  WDN WA8 ....45 H4
Upton Priory Junior School
  MCFLDN SK10 ....116 F2
Upton Westlea
  Primary School
  CHNE CH2 ....121 P5
Utkinton St Pauls
  Primary School
  TPLY/KEL CW6 ....146 F2
Vale Royal Abbey Golf Club
  NWCHW CW8 ....128 C3
Valley Brook Business Centre
  CW/SHV CW2 ....5 F5
Valley Special School
  BRAM/HZG SK7 ....72 C1
Vauxhall Industrial Estate
  RDSH SK5 ....41 M2
  RDSH SK5 ....41 N4
Verdin High School
  WSFD CW7 ....128 D9
Vernon Industrial Estate
  STKP SK1 ....17 H5
  STKP SK1 ....17 K2
The Vernon Infant School
  POY/DIS SK12 ....73 L3
The Vernon Junior School
  POY/DIS SK12 ....73 L3
Vernon Park Museum
  STKP SK1 ....42 A6
Vernon Park Primary School
  STKP SK1 ....17 J4

Vicars Cross Golf Club
  CHSE CH3 ....123 H8
Victoria Community
  Technology School
  CW/HAS CW1 ....185 J3
Victoria Infant School
  CH/BCN CH1 ....2 C1
Victoria Park Arena
  WARRS WA4 ....19 J7
Victoria Road Primary School
  NWCHW CW9 ....13 J2
  RUNC WA7 ....14 E4
Victoria Trading Estate
  NWCHW CW8 ....30 B5
Vine Tree Primary School
  CW/SHV CW2 ....4 A7
Virgin Cinemas
  CH/BCN CH1 ....121 J8
VUE Cinema
  CH65 ....102 G3
Vulcan Industrial Estate
  NEWLW WA12 ....23 P8
Wadebrook Trading Estate
  NWCHW CW9 ....110 G6
Wade Deacon County
  High School
  WDN WA8 ....45 N5
Wallerscote Primary School
  NWCHW CW8 ....108 G4
Walton Hall
  WARRS WA4 ....48 C9
Walton Hall Golf Club
  WARRS WA4 ....48 B8
Walton Lea Crematorium
  WARRS WA4 ....48 B8
Walton Park Leisure Centre
  SALE M33 ....38 D6
Wardle Industrial Estate
  NANT CW5 ....182 C1
Warford Hall Hospital
  MCFLDN SK10 ....92 F3
  WILM/AE SK9 ....92 D7
Wargrave House School
  NEWLW WA12 ....23 N7
Wargrave Primary School
  NEWLW WA12 ....23 N8
War Memorial Hospital
  CONG CW12 ....155 P9
Warmingham CE
  Primary School
  SBCH CW11 ....170 D1
Warren Wood Primary School
  OFTN SK2 ....57 N2
Warrington Business Centre
  WARR WA1 ....18 D5
Warrington Business Park
  WARRW/WOL WA2 ....33 M7
Warrington Central
  Trading Estate
  WARRN/WOL WA2 ....18 B3
Warrington Collegiate Institute
  WARRN/WOL WA2 ....33 L7
Warrington Community
  Health Care
  WARRN/WOL WA2 ....33 J2
Warrington Golf Club
  WARRS WA4 ....64 E1
Warrington Hospital
  WARRS WA4 ....48 A1
Warrington Museum & Library
  WARR WA1 ....18 C7
Warrington New Town
  Cricket Club
  WARRW/BUR WA5 ....47 N1
Warrington Sports Club
  WARRS WA4 ....48 C8
Warrington Town AFC
  WARRS WA4 ....48 G5
Warrington Wolves RLFC
  (Halliwell Jones Stadium)
  WARRW/WOL WA2 ....18 C3
Washway Road
  Medical Centre
  SALE M33 ....38 D4
Watch Lane Flash
  Nature Reserve
  SBCH CW11 ....170 C4
Watergate
  CH/BCN CH1 ....2 C5
Waterloo Industrial Park
  STKP SK1 ....17 H5
Water Mill
  MALPAS SY14 ....178 B9
Waters Green Clinic
  MCFLDS SK11 ....9 F4
The Waterside Hotel
  CHD/CHDH SK8 ....55 M3
The Waterside Hotel
  MCFLDN SK10 ....40 D8
Water Street School
  MCFLDN SK10 ....95 N5
Watford Bridge
  Industrial Estate
  NM/HAY SK22 ....59 N6
Waverton Community
  Primary School
  CHSE CH3 ....144 A5
Waymills Industrial Estate
  WHITCH SY13 ....213 N6
Weatherstone Business Centre
  NSTN CH64 ....78 A5
Weaverham High School
  NWCHW CW8 ....108 A4
Weaver Park Industrial Estate
  FROD/HEL WA6 ....84 B3
The Weaver Primary School
  NANT CW5 ....196 F5
Wedgwood's Monument
  ALS/KID ST7 ....201 L4
Welcome Lodge
  WARRW/BUR WA5 ....32 E5

Welkin Road Industrial Estate
STKP SK1 ....**42** A5
Wellfield Junior School
SALE M33 ....**38** C2
Well Green Primary School
HALE/TIMP WA15 ....**53** M5
Wellington School
HALE/TIMP WA15 ....**53** K1
Wellington Street
Industrial Estate
WDN WA8 ....**21** G6
Werneth Low Golf Club
HYDE SK14 ....**43** N2
Werneth School
MPL/ROM SK6 ....**42** E6
West Bank Medical Centre
WDN WA8 ....**61** N1
West Bank Primary School
WDN WA8 ....**61** M2
Westbrook Medical Centre
WARRW/BUR WA5 ....**32** F7
West Cheshire College
CHSW/BAR CH4 ....**142** F3
Westcliffe Hospital
BURS/TUN ST6 ....**189** P9
West End Primary School
DTN/ASHW M34 ....**28** G6
Western Avenue
Medical Centre
CH/BCN CH1 ....**120** G7
Westernlea Clinic
DTN/ASHW M34 ....**29** L4
Westfield Primary School
RUNC WA7 ....**14** C4
West Heath Shopping Centre
CONG CW12 ....**155** J7
Westminster Hotel
CH/BCN CH1 ....**3** G2
Westminster Industrial Park
EP CH65 ....**80** B7
Westminster Retail Park
EP CH65 ....**7** G2
Westmorland Primary School
RDSH SK5 ....**42** B2
Weston Point Primary School
RUNC WA7 ....**61** L7
Weston Primary School
RUNC WA7 ....**61** N8
Weston Village
Primary School
CW/SHV CW2 ....**199** H1
Westside Industrial Estate
STHEL WA9 ....**22** A7
Westwood Trading Estate
MPL/ROM SK6 ....**58** B2
Whaley Bridge Primary School
CHF/WBR SK23 ....**75** P7
Wharton CE Controlled
Junior School
WSFD CW7 ....**149** P1
Wharton (Donefields)
Industrial Estate
WSFD CW7 ....**128** G9
Wharton Retail Park
WSFD CW7 ....**128** F8
Wharton's Lock
TPLY/KEL CW6 ....**165** L4

Wheelock Primary School
SBCH CW11 ....**171** M5
Whirley Primary School
MCFLDN SK10 ....**116** D3
Whitby Heath
Primary School
EP CH65 ....**102** D1
The Whitby High School
GTS/LS CH66 ....**102** C3
Whitchurch Business Park
WHITCH SY13 ....**214** A6
Whitchurch CE Infant School
WHITCH SY13 ....**213** N6
Whitchurch CE Junior School
WHITCH SY13 ....**213** N5
Whitchurch Hospital
WHITCH SY13 ....**213** M5
Whitegate CE Primary School
NWCHW CW8 ....**128** A4
Whitehill Industrial Estate
HTNM SK4 ....**41** M3
Whitehill Primary School
HTNM SK4 ....**41** M4
The White House Manor
Townhouse Hotel
MCFLDN SK10 ....**94** G6
White House School
WHITCH SY13 ....**213** N8
White Lion Hotel
CW/SHV CW2 ....**199** H2
Whitley Primary School
WARRS WA4 ....**86** F1
Widnes Community
Midwifery & Ante-natal
WDN WA8 ....**45** M5
Widnes Crematorium
WDN WA8 ....**45** M4
Widnes Cricket Club
WDN WA8 ....**45** P3
Widnes Golf Club
WDN WA8 ....**45** M6
Widnes Public Baths
WDN WA8 ....**21** H3
Widnes & Runcorn
6th Form College
WDN WA8 ....**45** L2
Widnes Vikings RLFC
(Halton Stadium)
WDN WA8 ....**21** F3
The Wild Boar Hotel
TPLY/KEL CW6 ....**166** A6
Wildlife Sanctuary
WHITCH SY13 ....**205** L7
Willaston Primary School
NANT CW5 ....**197** K1
NSTN CH64 ....**78** D5
William Beamont
Community School
WARRN/WOL WA2 ....**33** L7
William Stockton
Primary School
EP CH65 ....**6** C4
Willington Hall Hotel
TPLY/KEL CW6 ....**146** C2
Willow Grove Cemetery
RDSH SK5 ....**41** P3

The Willows Primary School
HALE/TIMP WA15 ....**53** K1
WYTH/NTH M22 ....**54** E5
Willow Tree Primary School
STHEL WA9 ....**31** J4
Willow Wood Infant School
WSFD CW7 ....**129** H9
Willow Wood Junior School
WSFD CW7 ....**129** H9
Wilmslow Albion FC
WILM/AE SK9 ....**71** J3
Wilmslow Golf Club
KNUT WA16 ....**92** D4
Wilmslow Health Centre
WILM/AE SK9 ....**71** J8
Wilmslow High School
WILM/AE SK9 ....**71** K8
Wilmslow Leisure Centre
WILM/AE SK9 ....**71** K8
Wilmslow
Preparatory School
WILM/AE SK9 ....**71** K7
Wilmslow RFC
WILM/AE SK9 ....**71** H5
Wilmslow Road
Medical Centre
WILM/AE SK9 ....**71** M2
Wimboldsley Primary School
MWCH CW10 ....**150** F6
Wincham Business Park
NWCHE CW9 ....**110** D1
Wincham CP School
NWCHE CW9 ....**88** F8
Wincle CE Primary School
MCFLDS SK11 ....**158** D1
Windlehurst School
MPL/ROM SK6 ....**58** D5
Windmill Hill Primary School
RUNC WA7 ....**62** G4
Windmill Lane
Industrial Estate
DTN/ASHW M34 ....**29** J7
Windmill Shopping Centre
WDN WA8 ....**21** K2
Winnington Park
Primary School
NWCHW CW8 ....**12** A4
Winnington Park RFC
NWCHW CW8 ....**109** L5
Winsford Handley Hill
CP School
WSFD CW7 ....**149** L2
Winsford Industrial Estate
WSFD CW7 ....**129** J8
WSFD CW7 ....**150** D1
Winstanley Industrial Estate
WARRN/WOL WA2 ....**33** L2
Winwick CE Primary School
WARRN/WOL WA2 ....**33** L2
Winwick Parish
Leisure Centre
WARRN/WOL WA2 ....**33** L2
Wirral Country Park
NSTN CH64 ....**78** C6
Wistaston Green J&I School
CW/SHV CW2 ....**184** F6

Wistaston Junior School
CW/SHV CW2 ....**184** E8
Wistaston Road
Business Centre
CW/SHV CW2 ....**4** C3
Wistaston Westfield
Infant School
CW/SHV CW2 ....**184** D8
Withington Bowling Club
RUSH/FAL M14 ....**40** D1
Withington Golf Club
DID/WITH M20 ....**40** A6
Withington Hospital
DID/WITH M20 ....**40** A2
Withington Swimming Baths
DID/WITH M20 ....**40** C2
Witton Albion FC
NWCHE CW9 ....**110** D2
Witton Churchwalk CE
Primary School
NWCHE CW9 ....**13** H2
Wolverham Primary School
EP CH65 ....**7** G6
Woodbank Park
Athletics Track
STKP SK1 ....**42** B7
Woodcocks Well CE
Primary School
WILM/AE SK9 ....**189** L2
Woodcote Hotel
GTS/LS CH66 ....**79** K4
Woodfall Infant School
NSTN CH64 ....**77** N7
Woodfall Junior School
NSTN CH64 ....**77** N7
Woodfield Primary School
CHNE CH2 ....**122** B6
Woodford Aerodrome
BRAM/HZG SK7 ....**72** F5
Woodford Court
Industrial Estate
WSFD CW7 ....**149** J2
Woodford Cricket Club
BRAM/HZG SK7 ....**72** D4
Woodford Lodge County
High School
WSFD CW7 ....**149** J3
Woodford Park
Industrial Estate
WSFD CW7 ....**149** H3
Woodheys Primary School
SALE M33 ....**38** B6
Woodhouse Middle School
BIDD ST8 ....**175** M7
Woodlands Industrial Estate
NEWLW WA12 ....**23** N3
Woodlands
Infant School
GTS/LS CH66 ....**102** B2
Woodlands Junior School
GTS/LS CH66 ....**102** B3
Woodlands Park
KNUT WA16 ....**131** K1
Wood Lane Primary School
ALS/KID ST7 ....**201** J6
Woodley Health Centre
MPL/ROM SK6 ....**42** F3

Woodley Primary School
MPL/ROM SK6 ....**42** G3
Woodley Sports Centre
MPL/ROM SK6 ....**42** F7
Wood Memorial CP School
CHSW/BAR CH4 ....**142** M1
Woodside County
Primary School
RUNC WA7 ....**62** C7
Woodside School
WYTH/NTH M22 ....**55** H3
Woolston CE Primary School
WARR WA1 ....**34** D8
Woolston Community
High School
WARR WA1 ....**34** C9
Woolston Community
Primary School
WARR WA1 ....**34** D9
Woore Primary School
AUD/MAD/W CW3 ....**218** G4
Worthington Primary School
SALE M33 ....**39** J4
Worth Primary School
POY/DIS SK12 ....**73** M3
Wrenbury Industrial Estate
NANT CW5 ....**207** K3
Wrenbury Primary School
NANT CW5 ....**207** J2
Wright Robinson
Sports College
GTN M18 ....**28** F3
The Wyche Primary School
NANT CW5 ....**10** B4
The Wycliffe Hotel
EDGY/DAV SK3 ....**41** K9
Wythenshawe Hall
Country Park
NTHM/RTH M23 ....**39** L8
Wythenshawe Hospital
NTHM/RTH M23 ....**54** B3
Wythenshawe Park Track
NTHM/RTH M23 ....**39** K7
Yew Tree Trading Estate
RNFD/HAY WA11 ....**23** L7
Yorston Lodge School
KNUT WA16 ....**90** D4
Ysgol Croes Atti
Primary School
FLINT CH6 ....**98** C6
Zan Industrial Park
SBCH CW11 ....**171** M6

Acknowledgements

The Post Office is a registered trademark of Post Office Ltd. in the UK and other countries.

Schools address data provided by Education Direct.

Petrol station information supplied by Johnsons

One-way street data provided by © Tele Atlas N.V. Tele Atlas ◄

Garden centre information provided by

Garden Centre Association  Britains best garden centres

Wyevale Garden Centres 🌳

The statement on the front cover of this atlas is sourced, selected and quoted from a reader comment and feedback form received in 2004.